HOT & SPICY
RECIPES 500

HOT & SPICY RECIPES 500

Bring the pungent tastes and aromas of spices into your kitchen with heart-warming, piquant recipes from the spice-loving cuisines of the world, shown in more than 500 mouthwatering photographs

EDITED BY BEVERLEY JOLLANDS

HERMES
HOUSE

This edition is published by Hermes House, an imprint of Anness Publishing Ltd,
108 Great Russell Street, London WC1B 3NA; info@anness.com

www.hermeshouse.com; www.annesspublishing.com; twitter: @Anness_Books

If you like the images in this book and would like to investigate using them for publishing,
promotions or advertising, please visit our website www.practicalpictures.com for more information.

Publisher: Joanna Lorenz
Editorial Director: Helen Sudell
Executive Editor: Joanne Rippin
Jacket Design: Adelle Morris
Production Controller: Rosanna Anness

© Anness Publishing Ltd 2015

NOTES
Bracketed terms are intended for American readers. For all recipes, quantities are given in both metric and
imperial measures and, where appropriate, in standard cups and spoons. Follow one set of measures, but not a mixture, because
they are not interchangeable. Standard spoon and cup measures are level. 1 tsp = 5ml, 1 tbsp = 15ml, 1 cup = 250ml/8fl oz.
Australian standard tablespoons are 20ml. Australian readers should use 3 tsp in place of 1 tbsp for measuring small quantities.
American pints are 16fl oz/2 cups. American readers should use 20fl oz/2.5 cups in place of 1 pint when measuring liquids.
Electric oven temperatures in this book are for conventional ovens. When using a fan oven, the
temperature will probably need to be reduced by about 10–20°C/20–40°F. Since ovens vary, you should
check with your manufacturer's instruction book for guidance. The nutritional analysis given for each recipe is calculated
per portion (i.e. serving or item), unless otherwise stated. If the recipe gives a range, such as Serves 4–6, then the nutritional analysis
will be for the smaller portion size, i.e. 6 servings. The analysis does not include optional ingredients, such as salt added to taste.
Medium (US large) eggs are used unless otherwise stated.

Main front cover image shows Sweet and Spicy Chicken, for recipe, see page 99

PUBLISHER'S NOTE
Although the advice and information in this book are believed to be accurate and true at the time of going to press, neither the authors nor the
publisher can accept any legal responsibility or liability for any errors or omissions that may have been made nor for any inaccuracies nor for any
loss, harm or injury that comes about from following instructions or advice in this book.

CONTENTS

Introduction

Even before we taste spiced food, the evocative aroma of spices stimulates the appetite and heightens our gastronomic anticipation. This book offers a wonderful collection of over 500 spiced recipes that will fill your home with evocative smells as you cook, and bring delightful taste sensations as you eat.

Spices have played a major part in the history and economic development of many countries for centuries, and at points have been so highly prized that their worth was above gold itself. Exotic and aromatic spices give us pleasure in our enjoyment of food and they are invaluable in folk medicines and modern medications. They have even entered our language, in phrases such as "the spice of life" and "spicing things up". Today we take the commonplace availability of exotic ingredients for granted. It is difficult for us to imagine that a handful of cardamoms was the equivalent of a man's annual wage, that slaves were sold for a few handfuls of peppercorns and that dockworkers in London were made to sew up their pockets to avoid the theft of even a single nutmeg.

Market stalls in the Middle East display the delightful colours and aromas of our favourite spices.

Making your own spice mixtures from freshly bought ingredients adds depth to your cooking.

The rarity and expense of spices has diminished, as has their exotic mystery, and as we explore exotic locations, and eat food from all corners of the globe in our own cities, we are becoming more familiar with the wide variety of ways in which spices and aromatic flavourings can enhance all types of dishes.

Indian cooking is distinctively spicy and is characterized by the use of a greater range of dried spices than any other cuisine in the world. Up to 15 spices may be blended to flavour one dish, and the way they are toasted, ground, and added at particular stages adds to the complex tastes of the food. The spices most often used in Indian cuisine include coriander, cumin, turmeric, black pepper, mustard seeds, fennel seeds, cardamom, cloves, garlic and ginger, while chillies are valued for both fire and flavour. When using a range of spices, remember that they quickly lose their flavour, so buy small quantities and store in airtight containers.

Cooks from the countries of the Far East use liberal quantities of fresh ginger and garlic and favour such spices as sesame seeds and star anise. Thai food tends to be very hot, with tiny fiery Thai chillies appearing in many dishes. The heat is tempered by the fresh, light flavours of lemon grass and lime leaves, and the soothing effect of coconut milk.

South American food is also characterized by the liberal use of chillies. Several different types are often combined in the same dish, each chilli contributing its own distinctive flavour as well as the fire for which they are famous. Mexican chillies had already travelled to the Caribbean islands by the time Columbus arrived, and their use characterizes all island cooking. Allspice and cayenne are also widely used in the Caribbean, with traditional recipes typically combining them with pungent herbs. Around the Mediterranean and the Middle East it is the warm spices, such as cinnamon, coriander, saffron and cumin, that create the typical flavours of the food. In North Africa harissa – an explosive chilli sauce – is added to many dishes or as a condiment, to add fire to fragrant spice combinations. Many central European dishes are flavoured with spices such as caraway, dill, cardamom and fennel, which are equally at home in sweet or savoury dishes, while in northern Europe nutmeg, cinnamon and cloves are a traditional part of celebration dishes such as Christmas pudding and Easter biscuits.

Frying spices before adding any liquid helps to brings out their complex flavours.

While many of the recipes in this book are delightfully familiar, others challenge you to use new and exciting spice blends. Quantities given in recipes are a guide: experiment to discover the combinations you prefer, and if you have a particular fondness for a spice, add a little more, and prove that spices can make a world of difference. With over 500 photographs and step-by-step instructions this recipe book is the essential resource for lovers of spicy food.

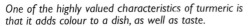

One of the highly valued characteristics of turmeric is that it adds colour to a dish, as well as taste.

Juniper berries, cardamom pods, allspice berries and cinnamon sticks tied in a piece of muslin (cheesecloth) will add a spicy flavour to stocks and soups.

Malaysian Spicy Prawn Soup

Introduced to Malaysia and Singapore from China, this popular dish, known as Hokkien prawn noodle soup, is full of hot spicy flavours, plus the citrus tang of lemon grass, which is ideally suited to fish recipes. In South-east Asia the soup is traditionally served topped with crisp-fried cubes of pork fat, but in this recipe, crispy bacon is used instead.

Serves 4–6
For the stock
45ml/3 tbsp dried prawns (shrimp)
1 dried red chilli
50g/2oz fresh root ginger, peeled and sliced
2 onions, quartered
4 cloves garlic, bruised
2 lemon grass stalks, bruised
2.5ml/¹⁄₂ tsp black peppercorns
30–45ml/2–3 tbsp dark soy sauce
700g/1lb 10oz pork and chicken bones

For the soup
15ml/1 tbsp sugar
6 rashers (strips) streaky (fatty) bacon, sliced
150g/5oz fresh egg noodles
20 large prawns (shrimp), peeled (add the shells to the stock)
90g/3¹⁄₂oz beansprouts
2 spring onions (scallions), trimmed and finely sliced
salt and ground black pepper

1 Put all the stock ingredients into a deep pan along with the prawn shells. Pour in 2 litres/3¹⁄₂ pints/8 cups water and bring to the boil. Reduce the heat and simmer gently, uncovered, for about 2 hours, until the stock has reduced by half. Strain the stock into a clean pan and put it over a low heat to keep hot. Season with salt and pepper to taste.

2 In a small pan heat the sugar with 15ml/1 tbsp water, until it turns a rich brown. Add it to the stock and mix well. In a heavy pan, dry-fry the bacon until it turns crispy and golden. Drain on paper towels and set aside.

3 Plunge the noodles into the hot stock for 1 minute to heat through, then divide them among four bowls. Add the prawns to the stock, heat for 1 minute, remove with a slotted spoon and add to the bowls, top with beansprouts and pour on the hot stock. Sprinkle bacon and spring onions on the top to serve.

Noodles in Spicy Tangy Soup

This lovely tangy dish is influenced by the characteristic flavourings of Thailand: the soup has interesting sour notes that come from tamarind and salted soya beans.

Serves 4
vegetable oil, for deep-frying
225g/8oz firm tofu, rinsed, drained and cut into cubes
60ml/4 tbsp dried prawns (shrimp), soaked until rehydrated
5ml/1 tsp shrimp paste
4 garlic cloves, chopped
4–6 dried red chillies, soaked to soften, drained, seeded and the pulp scraped out
90g/3¹⁄₂oz/³⁄₄ cup roasted peanuts, ground
50g/2oz salted soya beans
2 lemon grass stalks, trimmed, halved and bruised
30ml/2 tbsp sugar
15–30ml/1–2 tbsp tamarind paste
150g/5oz dried rice vermicelli, soaked in hot water until pliable
a handful of beansprouts, rinsed and drained
4 quails' eggs, hard-boiled, shelled and halved
2 spring onions (scallions), finely sliced
salt and ground black pepper
fresh coriander (cilantro) leaves, finely chopped, to garnish

1 In a wok, heat enough vegetable oil for deep-frying. Drop in the tofu and deep-fry until golden. Drain and set aside.

2 Using a mortar and pestle or food processor, grind the dried prawns, shrimp paste, garlic and chilli pulp together to a paste.

3 Heat 30ml/2 tbsp of vegetable oil in a wok and stir in the paste. Fry for 1 minute until fragrant, then add the peanuts, salted soya beans and lemon grass. Fry for another minute. Stir in the sugar and tamarind paste, followed by 900ml/1¹⁄₂ pints/3³⁄₄ cups water. Mix and bring to the boil. Reduce the heat and simmer gently for 10 minutes. Season with salt and pepper.

4 Drain the noodles and plunge into the broth to heat through. Divide the noodles among serving bowls, sprinkle over the beansprouts and add the deep-fried tofu, halved quails' eggs and spring onions. Ladle the spicy broth over the top, garnish with the coriander and serve immediately.

Coconut and Seafood Soup with Thai Spices

The long list of ingredients makes this Thai-inspired recipe look complex, but, in fact, it is very easy to put together.

Serves 4
600ml/1 pint/2½ cups fish stock
5 thin slices fresh galangal or fresh root ginger
2 lemon grass stalks, chopped
3 kaffir lime leaves, shredded
25g/1oz garlic chives
15g/½oz fresh coriander (cilantro)

15ml/1 tbsp vegetable oil
4 shallots, chopped
400ml/14fl oz can coconut milk
30–45ml/2–3 tbsp nam pla
45–60ml/3–4 tbsp Thai green curry paste
450g/1lb large raw prawns (shrimp), peeled and deveined
450g/1lb prepared squid
a little lime juice (optional)
salt and ground black pepper
60ml/4 tbsp crisp fried shallot slices, to serve

1 Pour the fish stock into a pan and add the slices of galangal or ginger, lemon grass and half the kaffir lime leaves.

2 Reserving a few garlic chives for the garnish, snip the remainder and add half to the pan with the coriander stalks. Bring to the boil, reduce the heat and cover the pan, then simmer gently for 20 minutes. Strain the stock.

3 Rinse out the pan. Add the oil and cook the chopped shallots over a medium heat for 5–10 minutes, until the shallots are beginning to brown.

4 Stir in the strained stock, coconut milk, the remaining kaffir lime leaves and 30ml/2 tbsp of the nam pla. Heat gently until simmering and cook over a low heat for 5–10 minutes.

5 Stir in the curry paste and prawns, then cook for 3 minutes. Add the squid and cook for a further 2 minutes. Add the lime juice, if using, and season, adding more nam pla to taste.

6 Stir in the remaining chives and the coriander. Serve in bowls sprinkled with fried shallots and whole garlic chives.

Butternut, Prawn and Chilli Soup

This satisfying recipe is quite hearty, and is something of a cross between a soup and a casserole. The banana flower isn't essential, but it does add a unique and interesting flavour.

Serves 4
1 butternut squash, about 300g/11oz
1 litre/1¾ pints/4 cups vegetable stock
90g/3½oz/scant 1 cup green beans, cut into 2.5cm/1in pieces

45g/1¾oz dried banana flower (optional)
15ml/1 tbsp nam pla
225g/8oz raw prawns (shrimp), peeled
small bunch fresh basil
cooked rice, to serve

For the chilli paste
115g/4oz shallots, sliced
10 drained bottled green peppercorns
1 small fresh green chilli, seeded and finely chopped
2.5ml/½ tsp shrimp paste

1 Peel the butternut squash and cut it in half. Scoop out the seeds with a spoon and discard, then cut the flesh into neat cubes. Set aside.

2 To make the chilli paste, pound the shallots, peppercorns, chilli and shrimp paste together using a mortar and pestle or purée them in a blender.

3 Heat the stock gently in a large pan, then stir in the chilli paste. Add the squash, beans and banana flower, if using. Bring to the boil and cook for 15 minutes.

4 Add the nam pla, prawns and basil to the pan. Bring to simmering point, then simmer for 3 minutes. Serve in warmed bowls, accompanied by rice.

> **Cook's Tip**
> Purplish-crimson banana flowers, which grow at the end of bunches of plantains, are eaten as a vegetable in South-east Asia. They have an astringent, slightly bitter flavour.

Coconut and Seafood Soup: Energy 205kcal/871kJ; Protein 37.7g; Carbohydrate 7.5g, of which sugars 5.8g; Fat 3g, of which saturates 0.8g; Cholesterol 473mg; Calcium 144mg; Fibre 0.4g; Sodium 449mg.
Butternut, Prawn and Chilli Soup: Energy 73kcal/307kJ; Protein 11.8g; Carbohydrate 5.3g, of which sugars 4g; Fat 0.7g, of which saturates 0.2g; Cholesterol 113mg; Calcium 90mg; Fibre 1.7g; Sodium 669mg.

Aromatic Mediterranean Fish Soup

This spicy chunky soup, which is almost a stew, makes a robust and wonderfully spicy meal in a bowl. Serve it with crisp-baked croûtes spread with piquant garlic mayonnaise.

Serves 4

30ml/2 tbsp olive oil
2 large thick leeks, white and green parts separated, both thinly sliced
5ml/1 tsp crushed coriander seeds
good pinch of dried red chilli flakes
300g/11oz small salad potatoes, thickly sliced
200g/7oz can Italian peeled chopped plum tomatoes

600ml/1 pint/2½ cups fish stock
150ml/¼ pint/⅔ cup fruity white wine
1 fresh bay leaf
1 star anise
strip of pared orange rind
good pinch of saffron strands
450g/1lb white fish fillets, such as monkfish, sea bass, cod or haddock
450g/1lb small squid, cleaned
250g/9oz raw prawns (shrimp), peeled
30–45ml/2–3 tbsp chopped parsley
salt and ground black pepper

To serve

1 short French loaf, sliced and toasted
garlic mayonnaise

1 Gently heat the oil in a pan, then add the green part of the leeks, the coriander and the chilli, and cook for 5 minutes. Add the potatoes and tomatoes and pour in the stock and wine. Add the bay leaf, star anise, orange rind and saffron.

2 Bring to the boil, reduce the heat and part-cover the pan. Simmer for 20 minutes or until the potatoes are tender. Taste and adjust the seasoning.

3 Cut the fish into chunks. Cut the squid sacs into rectangles and score a criss-cross pattern into them. Add the fish to the stew and cook gently for 4 minutes. Add the prawns and cook for 1 minute. Add the squid and the shredded white part of the leek and cook, stirring occasionally, for 2 minutes.

4 Stir in the chopped parsley and serve with toasted French bread and spicy garlic mayonnaise.

Paprika Fish Soup with Dumplings

This fish soup takes much less time to make compared with a meat-based one. Use a variety of whatever fish is available, such as perch, catfish, cod, snapper or carp. The method for making the dumplings is the same whether you use semolina or flour.

Serves 4–8

3 rindless bacon rashers (strips), diced
675g/1½lb assorted fresh fish, skinned, boned and diced
15ml/1 tbsp paprika, plus extra to garnish

1.5 litres/2½ pints/6¼ cups fish stock or water
3 firm tomatoes, peeled and chopped
4 waxy potatoes, peeled and grated
5–10ml/1–2 tsp chopped fresh marjoram, plus extra leaves to garnish

For the dumplings

75g/3oz/½ cup semolina or plain (all-purpose) flour
1 egg, beaten
45ml/3 tbsp milk or water
generous pinch of salt
15ml/1 tbsp chopped fresh parsley

1 Dry-fry the diced bacon in a large pan until the fat runs out and the bacon is pale golden brown, then add the pieces of assorted fish. Fry for 1–2 minutes, taking care not to break up the pieces of fish.

2 Sprinkle in the paprika, pour in the fish stock or water, bring to the boil and simmer for 10 minutes.

3 Stir the chopped tomatoes, grated potato and chopped marjoram into the pan. Bring back to a simmer and cook gently for 10 minutes, stirring occasionally.

4 Meanwhile, make the dumplings by mixing all the ingredients together to a smooth batter, then leave to stand, covered with clear film (plastic wrap), for 5–10 minutes.

5 Drop spoonfuls of the dumpling batter into the soup and cook for 10 minutes, turning the dumplings in the liquid occasionally to make sure they are covered. Serve hot, with a little marjoram and paprika.

Mediterranean Fish Soup: Energy 326kcal/1379kJ; Protein 49.7g; Carbohydrate 17.5g, of which sugars 4.4g; Fat 4.2g, of which saturates 0.9g; Cholesterol 421mg; Calcium 106mg; Fibre 2.9g; Sodium 333mg.
Paprika Fish Soup with Dumplings: Energy 154kcal/649kJ; Protein 18g; Carbohydrate 14.5g, of which sugars 1.8g; Fat 3g, of which saturates 0.5g; Cholesterol 63mg; Calcium 29mg; Fibre 1g; Sodium 67mg.

Provençal Fish Soup with Chilli-spiced Rouille

This delicious soup is full of Provençal flavours and is served with an authentic chilli-spiked rouille.

Serves 4–6
30ml/2 tbsp olive oil
1 leek, sliced
2 celery sticks, chopped
1 onion, chopped
2 garlic cloves, chopped
4 ripe tomatoes, chopped
15ml/1 tbsp tomato purée (paste)
150ml/¼ pint/⅔ cup white wine
1 bay leaf

5ml/1 tsp saffron strands
1kg/2¼lb mixed fish fillets and prepared shellfish
fish trimmings, bones and heads
salt and ground black pepper
croûtons and grated Gruyère cheese, to serve

For the rouille
1 slice of white bread, crusts removed
1 red (bell) pepper, cored, seeded and quartered
1–2 fresh red chillies, seeded and chopped
2 garlic cloves, crushed

1 To make the rouille, soak the bread in 30–45ml/2–3 tbsp cold water for 10 minutes. Grill the pepper quarters, skin side up, until the skin is charred and blistered. Drain the bread and squeeze out the excess moisture. When the pepper is cool enough to handle, peel off the skin. Roughly chop the flesh and place in a food processor with the bread, chillies and garlic. Process to a coarse paste, adding a little olive oil. Set aside.

2 Heat the olive oil in a large pan. Add the leek, celery, onion and garlic. Cook gently for 10 minutes. Add the tomatoes, tomato purée, wine, bay leaf, saffron, shellfish and fish trimmings. Bring to the boil, cover and simmer for 30 minutes. Strain through a colander pressing out the liquid. Cut the fish fillets into chunks and add to the strained soup. Cover and simmer for 5–10 minutes until the fish is cooked.

3 Put half the cooked fish into a food processor with about 300ml/½ pint/1¼ cups of the soup. Process until just blended then stir back into the remaining soup. Season to taste, reheat gently and serve with the rouille, croûtons and cheese.

Red Curry Monkfish Soup

This light and creamy coconut soup provides a base for a colourful fusion of red-curried monkfish and pad Thai, the classic stir-fried noodle dish of Thailand.

Serves 4
175g/6oz flat rice noodles
30ml/2 tbsp vegetable oil
2 garlic cloves, chopped
15ml/1 tbsp red curry paste
450g/1lb monkfish tail, cut into bitesize pieces
300ml/½ pint/1¼ cups coconut cream

750ml/1¼ pints/3 cups hot chicken stock
45ml/3 tbsp nam pla
15ml/1 tbsp palm sugar
60ml/4 tbsp roughly chopped roasted peanuts
4 spring onions (scallions), shredded lengthways
50g/2oz beansprouts
large handful of fresh Thai basil leaves
salt and ground black pepper
1 red chilli, seeded and cut lengthways into slivers, to garnish

1 Soak the noodles in boiling water for 10 minutes, or according to the packet instructions. Drain.

2 Heat the oil in a wok or pan over a high heat. Add the garlic and cook for 2 minutes. Stir in the curry paste and cook for 1 minute.

3 Add the monkfish and stir-fry over a high heat for 4–5 minutes, until just tender. Pour in the coconut cream and stock. Stir in the nam pla and sugar, and bring just to the boil. Add the noodles and cook for 1–2 minutes, until tender.

4 Stir in half the peanuts, half the spring onions, half the beansprouts, the basil and seasoning. Ladle the soup into deep bowls and sprinkle over the remaining peanuts. Garnish with the remaining spring onions, beansprouts and the red chilli.

Variation
Another firm-fleshed white fish, such as cod or pollack, could be substituted for the monkfish.

Spicy Vietnamese Beef Noodle Soup

This classic noodle soup is Vietnamese street food and a family favourite. It makes a satisfying meal.

Serves 6
500g/1¼lb dried rice noodles, soaked for 20 minutes
250g/9oz beef sirloin, thinly sliced across the grain
1 onion, halved and finely sliced
6–8 spring onions (scallions), cut into long pieces
2–3 red Thai chillies, seeded and finely sliced
115g/4oz/½ cup beansprouts
1 large bunch each fresh coriander (cilantro) and mint, stalks removed, leaves chopped
2 limes, cut in wedges, and hoisin sauce, nuoc mam or nuoc cham to serve

For the stock
1.5kg/3lb 5oz oxtail, trimmed of fat and cut into thick pieces
1kg/2¼lb beef shank or brisket
2 large onions, quartered
2 carrots, cut into chunks
7.5cm/3in fresh root ginger, cut into chunks
6 cloves
2 cinnamon sticks
6 star anise
5ml/1 tsp black peppercorns
30ml/2 tbsp soy sauce
45–60ml/3–4 tbsp nuoc mam
salt

1 To make the stock, cover the oxtail with water in a large, deep pan, bring to the boil and blanch for about 10 minutes. Drain and clean out the pan then return the oxtail to the pan with the other ingredients, apart from the *nuoc mam* and salt, and cover with about 3 litres/5¼ pints/12 cups water. Bring to the boil and simmer, covered, for 2–3 hours.

2 Simmer uncovered for an hour, until reduced to about 2 litres/3½ pints/8 cups. Skim, then strain the stock into another pan. Bring to the boil, stir in the *nuoc mam*, season to taste, then reduce the heat and leave to simmer until ready to use.

3 Bring a pan of water to the boil, and add the drained noodles. Cook for about 4 minutes or until tender. Drain and divide equally among six wide soup bowls. Top each serving with the slices of beef, onion, spring onions, chillies and beansprouts. Ladle the hot stock over, top with the fresh herbs and serve with the lime wedges. Pass around the hoisin sauce, *nuoc mam* or *nuoc cham*.

Beef, Chilli and Soy-bean Broth

This rich stew from Korea is called *doenjang chige*. Although it has the same fermented soy-bean paste foundation as many other Korean soups, it is an altogether thicker and heartier casserole. The comparatively slow cooking imparts a deep, complex flavour, full of spiciness. This is a satisfyingly warm dish, ideal for cold winter evenings, and particularly suits the flavour of flame-grilled meat if served as an accompaniment.

Serves 2
½ courgette (zucchini)
25g/1oz enoki mushrooms
15ml/1 tbsp sesame oil, plus extra for drizzling
50g/2oz beef, finely chopped
30ml/2 tbsp doenjang (soy-bean paste)
¼ onion, finely chopped
10ml/2 tsp finely chopped garlic
550ml/18fl oz/2½ cups fish stock
1 red chilli, seeded and sliced diagonally
¼ block firm tofu, diced
1 spring onion (scallion), sliced, to garnish

1 Thickly slice the courgette, and then cut the slices into quarters. Discard the caps from the enoki mushrooms.

2 In a casserole dish or heavy pan, heat the sesame oil over high heat. Add the beef and *doenjang* to the pan, and cook until golden brown. Then add the onion and garlic to the pan and sauté gently. Add the fish stock and bring to the boil.

3 Then add the sliced chillies and courgette slices to the pan, and boil for 5 minutes. Add the tofu and mushrooms, and boil for a further 2 minutes. Reduce the heat and simmer the stew gently for 15 minutes.

4 Garnish with sliced spring onion and a drizzle of sesame oil, and serve.

> **Cook's Tip**
> Enoki mushrooms, sometimes called snow puff mushrooms, are available at most Asian stores and in some supermarkets.

Fiery Beef and Aubergine Soup

This wonderful Cambodian soup is sweet, spicy and tangy, flavoured with the herbal condiment *kroeung* and the fish sauce, *tuk trey*.

Serves 6
4 dried chillies
15ml/1 tbsp vegetable oil
75ml/5 tbsp kroeung
2–3 fresh red chillies
75ml/5 tbsp tamarind extract
15–30ml/1–2 tbsp tuk trey
30ml/2 tbsp palm sugar (jaggery)
12 Thai aubergines (eggplants),
   stems removed, cut into chunks

1 bunch watercress or rocket
   (arugula), trimmed and
   chopped
1 handful fresh curry leaves
sea salt and ground black pepper

For the stock
1kg/2¼lb beef shanks or brisket
2 large onions, quartered
2–3 carrots, cut into chunks
90g/3½oz fresh root ginger, sliced
2 cinnamon sticks
4 star anise
5ml/1 tsp black peppercorns
30ml/2 tbsp soy sauce
45–60ml/3–4 tbsp tuk trey

1 To make the stock, put the beef shanks into a deep pan with all the other stock ingredients except the soy sauce and *tuk trey*. Cover with 3 litres/5 pints/12 cups water and bring to the boil. Reduce the heat and simmer, covered, for 2–3 hours.

2 Soak the dried chillies in water for 30 minutes. Split them open, remove the seeds and scrape out the pulp. Stir the soy sauce and *tuk trey* into the stock. Simmer, uncovered, for another hour, to reduce to about 2 litres/3½ pints/7¾ cups. Skim and strain. Tear half the meat into thin strips and reserve.

3 Heat the oil in a wok and stir in the *kroeung*, the pulp from the dried chillies and the whole fresh chillies. Stir the paste until it begins to darken. Add the tamarind extract, *tuk trey*, sugar and stock. Stir well and bring to the boil. Reduce the heat and add the beef, aubergines and watercress or rocket. Cook for about 20 minutes to allow the flavours to mingle.

4 Meanwhile, heat a heavy pan over a high heat, add the curry leaves and dry-fry them until they begin to crackle. Season the soup to taste, stir in half the curry leaves and ladle into bowls. Sprinkle the remaining curry leaves over the top and serve

Castilian Garlic and Paprika Soup

This rich, dark garlic soup, from central Spain, divides people into two groups: you either love it or hate it. The pitiless sun beats down on La Mancha, one of the poorest regions of Spain, and the local soup has harsh, strong tastes to match the climate. Poaching a whole egg in each bowl just before serving transforms the soup into a complete meal.

Serves 4
30ml/2 tbsp olive oil
4 large garlic cloves, peeled
4 slices stale country bread
20ml/4 tsp paprika
1 litre/1¾ pints/4 cups
   beef stock
1.5ml/¼ tsp ground cumin
4 free-range (farm-fresh) eggs
salt and ground black pepper
chopped fresh parsley, to garnish

1 Preheat the oven to 230°C/450°F/Gas 8. Heat the olive oil in a large pan. Add the whole peeled garlic cloves and cook until they are golden, then remove and set aside. Fry the slices of bread in the oil until golden, then set these aside.

2 Add 15ml/1 tbsp of the paprika to the pan, and fry for a few seconds. Stir in the beef stock, cumin and remaining paprika, then add the reserved garlic, crushing the cloves with the back of a wooden spoon. Season to taste, then cook for about 5 minutes.

3 Break up the slices of fried bread into bitesize pieces and stir them into the soup. Ladle the soup into four ovenproof bowls.

4 Carefully break an egg into each bowl of soup and place in the oven for about 3 minutes, until the eggs are set. Sprinkle the soup with chopped fresh parsley and serve immediately.

Variation
If you prefer, you can simply whisk the eggs into the soup while it is very hot, before ladling it into bowls. The heat of the soup will cook them lightly.

Castilian Garlic and Paprika Soup Energy 299kcal/1249kJ; Protein 11.6g; Carbohydrate 24.6g, of which sugars 2.8g; Fat 18g, of which saturates 3.1g; Cholesterol 190mg; Calcium 170mg; Fibre 3g; Sodium 323mg.
Fiery Beef and Aubergine Soup: Energy 303kcal/1276kJ; Protein 37g; Carbohydrate 16.5g, of which sugars 14.5g; Fat 10.6g, of which saturates 4.2g; Cholesterol 90mg; Calcium 35mg; Fibre 2.4g; Sodium 300mg.

Spiced Lamb Broth

This hearty soup is a popular dish at street food stalls in Singaore as well as in the coffee shops. It is a soup that comes into its own late at night, when it is valued for its restorative qualities. It also makes a great supper dish, served with chunks of crusty bread or Indian flatbread.

Serves 4–6

25g/1oz fresh root ginger, peeled and chopped
4–6 garlic cloves, chopped
1 red chilli, seeded and chopped
15ml/1 tbsp ghee or vegetable oil
5ml/1 tsp coriander seeds
5ml/1 tsp cumin seeds
5ml/1 tsp ground fenugreek
5ml/1 tsp sugar
450g/1lb meaty lamb ribs, chopped into bitesize pieces
2 litres/3½ pints/8 cups lamb stock or water
10ml/2 tsp tomato purée (paste)
1 cinnamon stick
4–6 cardamom pods, bruised
2 tomatoes, peeled and quartered
salt and ground black pepper
fresh coriander (cilantro) leaves, roughly chopped, to garnish

1 Using a mortar and pestle or a food processor, grind the ginger, garlic and chilli to a paste. Heat the ghee or oil in a heavy pan and stir in the coriander and cumin seeds. Add the ginger, garlic and chilli paste along with the fenugreek and sugar. Stir until fragrant and beginning to colour. Add the lamb, searing the meat on both sides.

2 Pour in the stock or water and stir in the tomato purée, cinnamon stick and cardamom pods. Bring to the boil, then reduce the heat, cover the pan and simmer gently for about 1½ hours, until the meat is very tender.

3 Season to taste with salt and pepper. Stir in the tomatoes, and garnish with coriander. Serve hot with chunks of fresh crusty bread or Indian flatbread.

Variation
The dish can be made with breast of lamb, chopped into chunks, or with lamb cutlets.

Cinnamon-spiced Turkish Wedding Soup

This soup, served at Turkish weddings, is steeped in tradition and varies little throughout the country, the only difference being the inclusion of cinnamon in some areas to flavour the stock. It contains chunks of cooked lamb, stewed slowly so that it is extremely tender. The soup has a slightly sour flavour, from the classic liaison of lemon, egg and yogurt.

Serves 4–6

500g/1¼lb lamb on the bone – neck, leg or shoulder
2 carrots, roughly chopped
2 potatoes, roughly chopped
1 cinnamon stick
45ml/3 tbsp strained natural (plain) yogurt
45ml/3 tbsp flour
1 egg yolk
juice of ½ lemon
30ml/2 tbsp butter
5ml/1 tsp paprika
salt and ground black pepper

1 Place the lamb in a deep pan with the carrots, potatoes and cinnamon. Pour in 2 litres/3½ pints/8 cups water and bring to the boil, then skim any scum off the surface and lower the heat. Cover and simmer for about 1½ hours, until the meat is so tender that it almost falls off the bone. Lift the lamb out of the pan and place it on a chopping board.

2 Remove the meat from the bone and chop it into small pieces. Strain the stock and discard the carrots and potatoes. Pour the stock back into the pan, season and bring to the boil.

3 In a deep bowl, beat the yogurt with the flour. Add the egg yolk and lemon juice and beat well again, then pour in about 250ml/8fl oz/1 cup of the hot stock, beating all the time.

4 Lower the heat under the pan and pour the yogurt mixture into the stock, beating constantly so that it is well blended. Add the meat and heat through.

5 Melt the butter in a small pan and stir in the paprika. Ladle the soup into bowls and drizzle the pepper butter over the top. Serve immediately.

Spiced Lamb Broth: Energy 166kcal/693kJ; Protein 15.2g; Carbohydrate 2.8g, of which sugars 2.5g; Fat 10.6g, of which saturates 5.2g; Cholesterol 62mg; Calcium 12mg; Fibre 0.5g; Sodium 87mg.
Cinnamon-spiced Soup: Energy 226kcal/943kJ; Protein 15g; Carbohydrate 14.4g, of which sugars 3.6g; Fat 12.4g, of which saturates 6.2g; Cholesterol 88mg; Calcium 54mg; Fibre 1.4g; Sodium 87mg.

Aromatic Tofu Soup with Ginger

This is a refreshing, light clear broth. The soup is reliant on a well-flavoured and aromatic stock so use the freshest ingredients.

Serves 4

115g/4oz/scant 2 cups dried
  shiitake mushrooms, soaked in
  water for 20 minutes
15ml/1 tbsp vegetable oil
2 shallots, halved and sliced
2 Thai chillies, seeded and sliced
4cm/1½in fresh root ginger,
  peeled and finely chopped
15ml/1 tbsp nuoc mam
350g/12oz tofu, rinsed, drained
  and cut into bitesize cubes
4 tomatoes, skinned, seeded and
  cut into thin strips

salt and ground black pepper
1 bunch coriander (cilantro),
  stems removed, finely chopped,
  to garnish

For the stock

1 meaty chicken carcass or
  500g/1½lb pork ribs
25g/1oz dried squid or prawns
  (shrimp), soaked in water for
  15 minutes
2 onions, peeled and quartered
2 garlic cloves, crushed
7.5cm/3in fresh ginger, chopped
15ml/1 tbsp nuoc mam
6 black peppercorns
2 star anise
4 cloves
1 cinnamon stick
sea salt

1 To make the stock, put the chicken carcass or pork ribs in a deep pan. Add the dried squid or prawns, rinsed, with the remaining stock ingredients, except the salt, and pour in 2 litres/3½ pints/8 cups water. Bring to the boil, skim, then reduce the heat and simmer with the lid on for 1½–2 hours.

2 Remove the lid and simmer for a further 30 minutes to reduce. Skim off any fat, season, then strain and measure out 1.5 litres/2½ pints/6¼ cups.

3 Squeeze dry the shiitake mushrooms, discard the stems and slice the caps into thin strips. Heat the oil in a large pan and stir in the shallots, chillies and ginger. Add the *nuoc mam* and stock.

4 Add the tofu, mushrooms and tomatoes and bring to the boil. Reduce the heat and simmer for 5–10 minutes. Season to taste and sprinkle the finely chopped fresh coriander over the top. Serve piping hot.

Chilli Pork and Prawn Soup

This soup is enhanced with the intense sweet and smoky flavour of dried squid. It is a popular dish in Cambodia.

Serves 4

225g/8oz pork tenderloin
225g/8oz dried rice noodles,
  soaked for 20 minutes
20 raw prawns (shrimp), shelled
  and deveined
115g/4oz/½ cup beansprouts
2 spring onions (scallions), sliced
2 fresh green or red chillies,
  seeded and finely sliced

1 garlic clove, finely sliced
1 bunch each coriander (cilantro)
  and basil, stalks removed, leaves
  roughly chopped
1 lime, cut into quarters, and
  nuoc cham, to serve

For the stock

25g/1oz dried squid
675g/1½lb pork ribs
1 onion, quartered
225g/8oz carrots, cut into chunks
15ml/1 tbsp nuoc mam
15ml/1 tbsp soy sauce
6 black peppercorns
salt

1 To make the stock, soak the dried squid in water for 30 minutes, rinse and drain. Put the ribs in a large pan and cover with approximately 2.5 litres/4½ pints/10 cups water. Bring to the boil, skim off any fat, and add the dried squid with the remaining stock ingredients. Cover the pan and simmer for 1 hour, then skim off any foam or fat and continue to simmer, uncovered, for a further 1½ hours. Strain and season.

2 Pour the stock into a clean pan and bring to the boil. Reduce the heat, add the pork tenderloin and simmer for 25 minutes. Lift the tenderloin out of the stock, place it on a board and cut it into thin slices. Meanwhile, keep the stock simmering gently.

3 Bring a pan of water to the boil. Drain the rice noodles and add to the water. Cook for about 5 minutes, separating them if they stick together. Drain and divide among four bowls.

4 Drop the prawns into the simmering stock for 1 minute. Lift out and layer them with the slices of pork on the noodles. Ladle the hot stock over and sprinkle with beansprouts, spring onions, chillies, garlic and herbs. Serve each bowl of soup with a wedge of lime and *nuoc cham* to splash on top.

Aromatic Soup with Ginger: Energy 220kcal/919kJ; Protein 12g; Carbohydrate 26g, of which sugars 4g; Fat 8g, of which saturates 1g; Cholesterol 0mg; Calcium 47.8mg; Fibre 1.1g; Sodium 500mg.
Chilli, Pork and Prawn Soup: Energy 319kcal/1339kJ; Protein 22g; Carbohydrate 50g, of which sugars 1g; Fat 3g, of which saturates 0g; Cholesterol 49mg; Calcium 91mg; Fibre 0.6g; Sodium 500mg.

Spicy Malaysian Chicken Soup

This fragrant soup is nutritious and delicious. It can be served as a complete meal, accompanied by deep-fried potato fritters or rice cakes.

Serves 6

1 small chicken, about 900g/2lb
2 lemon grass stalks, bruised
25g/1oz fresh root ginger, peeled and sliced
2 fresh kaffir lime leaves
1 dried red chilli
30ml/2 tbsp vegetable oil
50g/2oz mung bean thread noodles, soaked until pliable
3 hard-boiled eggs, peeled and halved
115g/4oz beansprouts
1 small bunch of fresh coriander (cilantro), stems removed and leaves roughly chopped, to garnish
2 limes, quartered, chilli oil and soy sauce, to serve

For the curry paste

8 shallots, chopped
8 garlic cloves, chopped
6 candlenuts or macadamia nuts
50g/2oz galangal, chopped
2 lemon grass stalks, chopped
4 fresh kaffir lime leaves
15ml/1 tbsp ground coriander
10ml/2 tsp ground turmeric
15ml/1 tbsp vegetable oil

1 Using a mortar and pestle or a food processor, grind all the ingredients for the curry paste together to make a fairly smooth paste. Set aside.

2 Put the chicken, lemon grass, ginger, lime leaves and chilli into a deep pan and pour in enough water to cover. Bring to the boil, reduce the heat, cover and simmer for about 1 hour, until the chicken is tender. Remove the chicken from the stock, discard the skin and tear the meat into shreds. Strain the stock.

3 In a wok or heavy pan, heat the oil. Stir in the curry paste and cook for 1–2 minutes, until fragrant. Pour in the stock and stir well. Season to taste with salt and pepper.

4 Divide the noodles among six bowls. Add the hard-boiled eggs, beansprouts and shredded chicken. Ladle the steaming broth into each bowl and garnish with coriander. Serve immediately with the lime wedges, chilli oil and soy sauce to squeeze, drizzle and pour over it.

Chicken Soup with Cinnamon and Fennel

This recipe is a delightful fusion of Portuguese and Malaysian influences. It is traditionally cooked in an earthenware pot.

Serves 4–6

1 chicken, about 1kg/2¼lb
2 cinnamon sticks
5ml/1 tsp black peppercorns
5ml/1 tsp fennel seeds
5ml/1 tsp cumin seeds
15ml/1 tbsp ghee or vegetable oil with a little butter
15–30ml/1–2 tbsp brown mustard seeds
a handful of fresh curry leaves
salt and ground black pepper
2 limes, quartered, to serve

For the curry paste

40g/1½oz fresh root ginger, peeled and chopped
4 garlic cloves, chopped
4 shallots, chopped
2 lemon grass stalks, chopped
4 dried red chillies, soaked to soften, drained, seeded and the pulp scraped out
15–30ml/1–2 tbsp curry powder

1 To make the curry paste, grind the ginger with the garlic, shallots and lemon grass, using a mortar and pestle or food processor. Add the chilli pulp and curry powder and set aside.

2 Put the chicken in a deep pan with the cinnamon sticks, peppercorns, fennel and cumin seeds. Add enough water to just cover, and bring it to the boil. Reduce the heat and cook gently for about 1 hour, until the chicken is cooked. Remove the chicken from the broth. Remove the skin, shred the meat and set aside. Strain the broth.

3 In an earthenware pot or wok, heat the ghee or oil. Stir in the mustard seeds and, once they begin to pop and give off a nutty aroma, add the curry paste. Fry the paste until fragrant, then pour in the strained broth. Bring the broth to the boil and season to taste with salt and pepper.

4 Add the curry leaves and shredded chicken to the broth, and ladle the soup into bowls. Serve with wedges of lime to squeeze into the soup.

Chicken Soup: Energy 264kcal/1093kJ; Protein 20.7g; Carbohydrate 1.6g, of which sugars 1g; Fat 19.4g, of which saturates 6.3g; Cholesterol 112mg; Calcium 19mg; Fibre 0.5g; Sodium 104mg.
Spicy Chicken Soup: Energy 493kcal/2050kJ; Protein 36g; Carbohydrate 8.5g, of which sugars 1g; Fat 35.1g, of which saturates 9.1g; Cholesterol 258mg; Calcium 47mg; Fibre 0.8g; Sodium 178mg.

Lime and Ginger-infused Duck Soup

This rich soup originates in southern China. It can be made with chicken stock and leftover meat from a roasted duck, or by roasting a duck and slicing off the breast and thigh meat for the soup.

Serves 4–6
1 lean duck, approximately 1.5kg/3lb 5oz
2 preserved limes
25g/1oz fresh root ginger, thinly sliced
sea salt and ground black pepper

For the garnish
vegetable oil, for frying
25g/1oz fresh root ginger, thinly sliced into strips
2 garlic cloves, thinly sliced
2 spring onions (scallions), finely sliced

1 Place the duck in a large pan with enough water to cover. Season with salt and pepper and bring the water to the boil. Reduce the heat, cover the pot, and simmer for 1½ hours.

2 Add the preserved limes and ginger. Simmer for another hour, skimming off the fat, until the liquid has reduced a little and the duck is so tender that it almost falls off the bone.

3 Meanwhile heat some vegetable oil in a wok. Stir in the ginger and garlic strips and fry until gold and crispy. Drain well on paper towels and set aside for garnishing.

4 Remove the duck from the broth and shred the meat into individual bowls. Check the broth for seasoning, then ladle it over the duck in the bowls. Sprinkle the spring onions with the fried ginger and garlic over the top and serve.

> **Cook's Tips**
> • With the addition of noodles, this soup could be served as a meal in itself.
> • Preserved limes have a distinctive, bitter flavour. Look for them in Asian markets.

Chicken Soup with Lemon Grass and Ginger

This soup has many variations on the recipe all over South-east Asia. It is light and refreshing, and the perfect choice for a hot day, as well as a great pick-me-up. The fresh, citrus aroma of lemon grass and lime, combined with the warmth of the chillies, is invigorating and awakens the senses.

Serves 4
2 lemon grass stalks, trimmed, cut into 3, and lightly bruised
15ml/1 tbsp nam pla
90g/3½oz/½ cup short grain rice, rinsed
1 small bunch coriander (cilantro)
leaves, finely chopped and 1 green or red chilli, seeded and cut into thin strips, to garnish
1 lime, cut in wedges, to serve
sea salt
ground black pepper

For the stock
1 small chicken or 2 meaty chicken legs
1 onion, quartered
2 cloves garlic, crushed
25g/1oz fresh root ginger, sliced
2 lemon grass stalks, cut in half lengthways and bruised
2 dried red chillies
30ml/2 tbsp nuoc mam

1 Put the chicken into a deep pan. Add all the other stock ingredients and pour in 2 litres/3½ pints/8 cups water. Bring to the boil for a few minutes, then reduce the heat and simmer gently with the lid on for 2 hours.

2 Lift the chicken out of the stock. Remove the skin from the chicken and shred the meat. Set aside. Skim off any fat from the stock, strain and reserve.

3 Pour the stock back into the deep pan and bring to the boil. Reduce the heat and stir in the lemon grass stalks and nam pla. Stir in the rice and simmer, uncovered, for about 40 minutes. Add the shredded chicken and season to taste.

4 Ladle the piping hot soup into warmed individual bowls, garnish with chopped coriander and the thin strips of chilli and serve with lime wedges to squeeze over.

Lime and Ginger Soup: Energy 114kcal/479kJ; Protein 13.9g; Carbohydrate 0.4g, of which sugars 0.4g; Fat 6.4g, of which saturates 1.7g; Cholesterol 75mg; Calcium 11mg; Fibre 0.1g; Sodium 78mg.
Chicken Soup with Ginger: Energy 147kcal/615kJ; Protein 12.8g; Carbohydrate 19.8g, of which sugars 1.4g; Fat 1.7g, of which saturates 0.4g; Cholesterol 53mg; Calcium 37mg; Fibre 0.8g; Sodium 320mg.

Aromatic Five-spice Duck Broth

This soup has a lively, spicy flavour, for those who love fiery food. Fresh or marinated chillies may be served with it as a side dish.

Serves 4

15ml/1 tbsp vegetable oil
2 shallots, thinly sliced
4cm/1½in fresh root ginger, peeled and sliced
15ml/1 tbsp soy sauce
5ml/1 tsp five-spice powder
10ml/2 tsp sugar
175g/6oz pak choi (bok choy)
450g/1lb fresh egg noodles
350g/12oz roast duck, sliced
sea salt

For the stock

1 chicken or duck carcass
2 carrots, peeled and quartered
2 onions, peeled and quartered
4cm/1½in fresh root ginger, peeled and cut into chunks
2 lemon grass stalks, chopped
30ml/2 tbsp nuoc mam
15ml/1 tbsp soy sauce
6 black peppercorns

For the garnish

4 spring onions (scallions), sliced
1–2 red Serrano chillies, seeded and finely sliced
1 bunch each coriander (cilantro) and basil, stalks removed, leaves chopped

1 To make the stock, put the chicken or duck carcass into a deep pan. Add all the other stock ingredients and 2.5 litres/4½ pints/10¼ cups water. Bring to the boil, and boil for a few minutes, skim off any foam, then reduce the heat and simmer gently with the lid on for 2–3 hours. Remove the lid and continue to simmer for a further 30 minutes to reduce the stock. Skim off any fat, season with salt, then strain the stock. Measure out 2 litres/3½ pints/8 cups.

2 Heat the oil in a deep pan and stir in the shallots and ginger. Add the soy sauce, five-spice powder, sugar and stock and bring to the boil. Reduce the heat and simmer for 15 minutes.

3 Meanwhile, cut the pak choi into wide strips and blanch in boiling water. Drain and refresh. Bring a large pan of water to the boil, then add the noodles. Cook for 5 minutes, then drain.

4 Divide the noodles among four bowls, lay the pak choi and sliced duck over them, and then ladle over the hot broth. Garnish with the spring onions, chillies and herbs, and serve.

Spicy Turkish Red Lentil Soup with Cumin and Fenugreek

Lentil soups vary widely in Turkey. In Istanbul and Izmir they are light and subtly spiced, and are served as an appetizer or snack. In Anatolia they are made with mutton and flavoured with tomato and spices, and are usually served as a meal on their own.

Serves 4–6

30–45ml/2–3 tbsp olive or sunflower oil
1 large onion, finely chopped
2 garlic cloves, finely chopped
1 fresh red chilli, seeded and finely chopped
5–10ml/1–2 tsp cumin seeds
5–10ml/1–2 tsp coriander seeds
1 carrot, finely chopped
scant 5ml/1 tsp ground fenugreek
5ml/1 tsp sugar
15ml/1 tbsp tomato purée (paste)
250g/9oz/generous 1 cup split red lentils
1.75 litres/3 pints/7½ cups chicken stock
salt and ground black pepper

To serve

1 small red onion, finely chopped
1 large bunch of fresh flat leaf parsley, finely chopped
4–6 lemon wedges

1 Heat the oil in a heavy pan and stir in the onion, garlic, chilli, cumin and coriander seeds. When the onion begins to colour, toss in the carrot and cook for 2–3 minutes. Add the fenugreek, sugar and tomato purée and stir in the lentils.

2 Pour in the stock, stir well and bring to the boil. Lower the heat, partially cover the pan and simmer for 30–40 minutes, until the lentils have broken up.

3 If the soup is too thick, thin it down with a little water. Season with salt and pepper to taste.

4 Serve the soup straight from the pan or, if you prefer a smooth texture, whizz it in a blender, then reheat if necessary.

5 Ladle the soup into bowls and sprinkle liberally with the chopped onion and parsley. Serve with a wedge of lemon to squeeze over the soup.

Aromatic Duck Broth: Energy 673kcal/2836kJ; Protein 37g; Carbohydrate 86g, of which sugars 22g; Fat 6g, of which saturates 1g; Cholesterol 81mg; Calcium 4mg; Fibre 0.7g; Sodium 700mg.
Spicy Lentil Soup: Energy 203kcal/856kJ; Protein 11.1g; Carbohydrate 31.8g, of which sugars 7.3g; Fat 4.4g, of which saturates 0.6g; Cholesterol 0mg; Calcium 45mg; Fibre 3.5g; Sodium 26mg.

Garlic and Butternut Squash Soup with Chilli Salsa

This is a wonderful, richly flavoured soup, given bite by the spicy tomato salsa.

Serves 6

2 garlic bulbs, outer papery
   skin removed
a few fresh thyme sprigs
75ml/5 tbsp olive oil
1 large butternut squash, halved
2 onions, chopped
5ml/1 tsp ground coriander
1.2 litres/2 pints/5 cups vegetable
   or chicken stock

30–45ml/2–3 tbsp fresh oregano
   or marjoram, stems removed,
   leaves chopped
salt and ground black pepper

For the salsa
4 large ripe tomatoes, halved
   and seeded
1 red (bell) pepper
1 large fresh red chilli, seeded
30ml/2 tbsp extra virgin
   olive oil
15ml/1 tbsp balsamic vinegar
pinch of caster (superfine) sugar

1 Preheat the oven to 220°C/425°F/Gas 7. Wrap the garlic bulbs in foil with the thyme and 7.5ml/1½ tsp of the oil. Put the parcel on a baking sheet with the squash and the tomatoes, pepper and fresh chilli for the salsa. Brush the squash with 10ml/2 tsp of the remaining oil. Roast for 25 minutes, then remove the tomatoes, pepper and chilli. Reduce the oven temperature to 190°C/375°F/Gas 5 and roast the squash and garlic for a further 20–25 minutes, or until tender.

2 Heat the remaining oil in a large non-stick pan and cook the onions and ground coriander gently for about 10 minutes.

3 Meanwhile, skin the pepper and chilli, then process them with the tomatoes and the oil for the salsa. Stir in the vinegar and seasoning to taste, adding a pinch of sugar if necessary.

4 Squeeze the roasted garlic out of its skin into the onions and add the squash, scooped out of its skin. Add the stock, season with salt and pepper, and simmer for 10 minutes. Stir in half the chopped fresh herbs then process or strain the soup. Reheat and taste for seasoning. Serve in warmed bowls topped with a spoonful of salsa and sprinkled with the remaining herbs.

Spanish Onion Soup with Saffron and Almonds

The Spanish combination of onions, sherry and saffron gives this pale yellow soup a beguiling flavour that is perfect for the opening course of a meal.

Serves 4
40g/1½oz/3 tbsp butter
2 large yellow onions, thinly sliced
1 small garlic clove, finely
   chopped
pinch of saffron threads

50g/2oz blanched almonds,
   toasted and finely ground
750ml/1¼ pints/3 cups chicken
   or vegetable stock
45ml/3 tbsp fino sherry
2.5ml/½ tsp paprika
salt and ground black pepper

For the garnish
30ml/2 tbsp flaked or slivered
   almonds, toasted
chopped fresh parsley

1 Melt the butter in a heavy pan over a low heat. Add the onions and garlic, stirring to ensure that they are thoroughly coated in the melted butter, then cover the pan and cook very gently, stirring frequently, for about 20 minutes, or until the onions are soft and golden yellow.

2 Add the saffron threads to the pan and cook, uncovered, for 3–4 minutes, then add the finely ground almonds and cook, stirring the ingredients constantly, for a further 2–3 minutes.

3 Pour in the chicken or vegetable stock and sherry into the pan and stir in 5ml/1 tsp salt and the paprika. Season with plenty of black pepper. Bring to the boil, then lower the heat and simmer gently for about 10 minutes.

4 Pour the soup into a food processor and process until smooth, then return it to the rinsed pan. Reheat slowly, without allowing the soup to boil, stirring occasionally. Taste for seasoning, adding more salt and pepper if required.

5 Ladle the soup into heated bowls, garnish with the toasted flaked or slivered almonds and a little chopped fresh parsley and serve immediately.

Garlic and Butternut Soup: Energy 238kcal/986kJ; Protein 2.9g; Carbohydrate 11.9g, of which sugars 10.3g; Fat 20.2g, of which saturates 3.1g; Cholesterol 0mg; Calcium 79mg; Fibre 4.1g; Sodium 11mg.
Spanish Onion Soup: Energy 233kcal/966kJ; Protein 7.2g; Carbohydrate 16.2g, of which sugars 12.3g; Fat 16g, of which saturates 5.2g; Cholesterol 27mg; Calcium 51mg; Fibre 3.3g; Sodium 398mg.

Curried Butternut Squash Soup with Horseradish Cream

The combination of cream, curry powder and horseradish makes a wonderful topping for this beautiful golden soup. The gentle sweetness of the squash and apple are enlivened with curry spices.

Serves 6
1 butternut squash
1 cooking apple
25g/1oz/2 tbsp butter
1 onion, finely chopped
5–10ml/1–2 tsp curry powder
900ml/1 1/2 pints/3 3/4 cups chicken
   or vegetable stock
5ml/1 tsp chopped fresh sage
150ml/1/4 pint/2/3 cup apple juice
salt and ground black pepper
curry powder, to garnish

For the horseradish cream
60ml/4 tbsp double (heavy) cream
10ml/2 tsp horseradish sauce
2.5ml/1/2 tsp curry powder

1 Peel the squash, remove the seeds and chop the flesh. Peel, core and chop the apple.

2 Heat the butter in a large pan. Add the onion and cook, stirring occasionally, for 5 minutes until soft. Stir in the curry powder. Cook to bring out the flavour, stirring constantly, for 2 minutes.

3 Add the stock, squash, apple and sage. Bring to the boil, lower the heat, cover and simmer for 20 minutes until the squash and apple are soft.

4 Meanwhile, make the horseradish cream. Whip the cream in a bowl until stiff, then stir in the horseradish sauce and curry powder. Cover and chill until required.

5 Purée the soup in a blender or food processor. Return to the clean pan and add the apple juice, with salt and pepper to taste. Reheat gently, without allowing the soup to boil.

6 Serve the soup in individual bowls, topping each portion with a spoonful of horseradish cream and a dusting of curry powder. Garnish with a few lime shreds, if you like.

Ginger and Star Anise Miso Broth

The Japanese eat miso broth, a simple but highly nutritious soup, almost every day – it is standard breakfast fare and is also eaten with rice or noodles later in the day.

Serves 4
1 bunch of spring onions
   (scallions) or 5 baby leeks
15g/1/2oz fresh coriander
   (cilantro)
3 thin slices fresh root ginger
2 star anise
1 small dried red chilli
1.2 litres/2 pints/5 cups dashi
   stock or vegetable stock
225g/8oz pak choi (bok choy) or
   other Asian greens, thickly sliced
200g/7oz firm tofu, cut into
   2.5cm/1in cubes
60ml/4 tbsp red miso
30–45ml/2–3 tbsp shoyu
1 fresh red chilli, seeded and
   shredded

1 Cut the green tops off the spring onions or baby leeks and slice the rest of the spring onions or leeks finely. Place the green tops in a large saucepan with the coriander stalks, fresh root ginger, star anise, dried chilli and dashi or vegetable stock.

2 Heat the mixture gently until boiling, then lower the heat and simmer for 10 minutes. Strain, return to the pan and reheat until simmering. Add the green portion of the sliced spring onions or leeks to the soup with the pak choi or greens and tofu. Cook for 2 minutes.

3 Mix 45ml/3 tbsp of the miso with a little of the hot soup in a bowl, then stir it into the soup. Taste the soup and add more miso with soy sauce to taste.

4 Chop the coriander leaves and stir most of them into the soup with the white part of the spring onions or leeks. Cook for 1 minute, then ladle the soup into warmed bowls. Sprinkle with the remaining coriander and the red chilli. Serve at once.

> **Cook's Tips**
> Dashi powder and shoyu (Japanese soy sauce) are available in most Asian and Chinese stores.

Curried Butternut Squash Soup: Energy 120kcal/502kJ; Protein 11.4g; Carbohydrate 5.1g, of which sugars 3.8g; Fat 6.2g, of which saturates 3.5g; Cholesterol 124mg; Calcium 87mg; Fibre 1.7g; Sodium 125mg.
Ginger and Star Anise Miso Broth: Energy 64kcal/267kJ; Protein 6.9g; Carbohydrate 2.7g, of which sugars 2.3g; Fat 3g, of which saturates 0.4g; Cholesterol 0mg; Calcium 394mg; Fibre 1.6g; Sodium 617mg.

Velvety Pumpkin Soup with Rice and Cinnamon

Modern Moroccan streets and markets are full of colourful seasonal produce that inspire you to buy, go home and start cooking. The pumpkin season is particularly delightful, with the huge orange vegetables piled up on stalls and wooden carts. The sellers patiently peel and slice the pumpkins ready for making this delicious winter soup.

Serves 4
1kg/2¼lb pumpkin
750ml/1¼ pints/3 cups
  chicken stock
750ml/1¼ pints/3 cups milk
10–15ml/2–3 tsp sugar
75g/3oz/½ cup cooked
  white rice
salt and ground black pepper
5ml/1 tsp ground cinnamon,
  to serve

1 Remove any seeds or fibre from the pumpkin, cut off the peel and chop the flesh. Put the prepared pumpkin in a pan and add the stock, milk, sugar and seasoning. Bring to the boil, then reduce the heat and simmer for about 20 minutes, or until the pumpkin is tender.

2 Drain the pumpkin, reserving the liquid, and purée it in a food processor, then return it to the pan.

3 Bring the soup back to the boil again, throw in the rice and simmer for a few minutes, until the grains are heated through. Check the seasoning, pour into bowls and dust with cinnamon. Serve piping hot, with chunks of bread.

> **Variations**
> • Pumpkin makes a delicious soup, but you could also use butternut squash in this recipe.
> • For a nutty flavour and a chewier texture, substitute cooked brown rice for the white rice.
> • Sprinkle a handful of toasted pumpkin seeds over the top of each bowl before serving the soup.

Cinnamon-scented Moroccan Chickpea and Lentil Soup

This soup is believed to have originated from a semolina gruel that the Berbers prepared to warm themselves during the cold winters in the Atlas Mountains. It is served to break the fast during the Muslim month of Ramadan.

Serves 8
30–45ml/2–3 tbsp olive oil
2 onions, halved and sliced
2.5ml/½ tsp ground ginger
2.5ml/½ tsp ground turmeric
5ml/1 tsp ground cinnamon
pinch of saffron threads
2 × 400g/14oz cans chopped
  tomatoes
5–10ml/1–2 tsp sugar
175g/6oz/¾ cup brown or green
  lentils, picked over and rinsed
about 1.75 litres/3 pints/7½ cups
  meat or vegetable stock, or
  water
200g/7oz/1 generous cup dried
  chickpeas, soaked overnight,
  drained and boiled in plenty of
  water until tender
200g/7oz/1 generous cup dried
  broad (fava) beans, soaked
  overnight, drained and boiled
  until tender
small bunch of fresh coriander
  (cilantro), chopped
small bunch of flat leaf parsley,
  chopped
salt and ground black pepper

1 Heat the olive oil in a stockpot or large pan. Add the onions and cook gently, stirring, for about 15 minutes, or until they are soft but not browned.

2 Add the ground ginger, turmeric, cinnamon and saffron to the cooked onions in the pan, followed by the chopped tomatoes and a little sugar. Stir in the rinsed lentils and pour in the stock or water.

3 Bring to the boil, then reduce the heat, cover and simmer for about 25 minutes, or until the lentils are tender.

4 Stir in the cooked chickpeas and beans, bring back to the boil, cover and simmer for a further 10–15 minutes.

5 Stir in the fresh herbs and season to taste. Serve piping hot with warm crusty bread or rolls.

Garlic and Tomato Soup with Couscous

Israeli couscous is a toasted, round pasta, which is much larger than regular couscous. It makes a wonderful addition to this warm and comforting soup, which is easy to make and uses largely store-cupboard ingredients. For a really garlicky flavour, an extra clove of chopped raw garlic is added just before serving.

Serves 4–6

30ml/2 tbsp olive oil
1 onion, chopped
1–2 carrots, diced
400g/14oz can chopped
   tomatoes
6 garlic cloves, roughly chopped,
   plus 1 extra garlic clove
   to serve
1.5 litres/2½ pints/6¼ cups
   vegetable or chicken stock
200–250g/7–9oz/1–1½ cups
   Israeli couscous
2–3 mint sprigs, chopped, or
   several pinches of dried mint
1.5ml/¼ tsp ground cumin
¼ bunch fresh coriander
   (cilantro), or about 5 sprigs,
   chopped
cayenne pepper, to taste
salt and ground black pepper

1 Heat the oil in a large pan, add the onion and carrots and cook gently for about 10 minutes until softened.

2 Add the tomatoes to the onion and carrot mixture. Stir in half the roughly chopped garlic, the stock, couscous, mint, ground cumin, coriander, and cayenne pepper, and season with salt and pepper to taste.

3 Bring the soup to the boil, add the remaining chopped garlic, then reduce the heat slightly and simmer gently for 7–10 minutes, stirring occassionally, or until the couscous is just tender. Chop the extra clove of garlic finely and stir it into the soup. Serve piping hot, ladled into individual serving bowls.

Variation
If you can't get Israeli couscous, also known as pearl couscous, substitute small soup pasta shapes, such as stellete or risi.

Moroccan Tomato and Ras el Hanout Soup

Ras el hanout, a subtle Moroccan mixture of dozens of different spices, gives it a lovely, warming kick. Garlic lovers may like to add a crushed garlic clove and a little salt to the yogurt that is swirled into the soup before serving. This is the daily soup in many Moroccan households.

Serves 4

45–60ml/3–4 tbsp olive oil
3–4 cloves
2 onions, chopped
1 butternut squash, peeled,
   seeded and cut into chunks
4 celery stalks, chopped
2 carrots, peeled and chopped
8 large, ripe tomatoes, skinned
   and roughly chopped
5–10ml/1–2 tsp sugar
15ml/1 tbsp tomato purée (paste)
5–10ml/1–2 tsp ras el hanout
2.5ml/½ tsp ground turmeric
large bunch of fresh coriander
   (cilantro), chopped (reserve
   a few sprigs for garnish)
1.75 litres/3 pints/7½ cups
   vegetable stock
a handful dried egg noodles or
   capellini, broken into pieces
salt and ground black pepper
60–75ml/4–5 tbsp creamy natural
   (plain) yogurt, to serve

1 In a deep, heavy pan, heat the oil and add the cloves, onions, squash, celery and carrots. Fry until they begin to colour, then stir in the tomatoes and sugar. Cook the tomatoes until the water reduces and they begin to pulp.

2 Stir in the tomato purée, ras el hanout, turmeric and chopped coriander. Pour in the stock and bring the liquid to the boil. Reduce the heat and simmer for 30–40 minutes until the vegetables are very tender and the liquid has reduced a little.

3 Leave the liquid to cool slightly before processing in a food processor or blender, then return to the pan and add the pasta. Alternatively, simply add the pasta to the unblended soup and cook for a further 8–10 minutes, or until the pasta is soft.

4 Season the soup to taste and ladle it into bowls. Spoon a swirl of yogurt into each one, garnish with the extra coriander and serve with freshly baked bread.

Spiced Bean Soup

This delicious soup, of black-eyed beans and turmeric-tinted tomato broth, is flavoured with tangy lemon and speckled with chopped fresh coriander. It is a Sephardi Jewish recipe, and shows the influence of western Mediterranean cuisines – those of North Africa and the Iberian Peninsula – in its use of tomatoes, garlic and spices.

Serves 4

175g/6oz/1 cup black-eyed
  beans (peas)
15ml/1 tbsp olive oil
2 onions, chopped
4 garlic cloves, chopped
1 medium-hot or 2–3 mild fresh
  chillies, chopped
5ml/1 tsp ground cumin
5ml/1 tsp ground turmeric
250g/9oz fresh or canned
  tomatoes, diced
600ml/1 pint/2½ cups chicken,
  beef or vegetable stock
1 small bunch fresh coriander
  (cilantro), stalks removed, leaves
  roughly chopped
juice of ½ lemon
pitta bread, to serve

1 Put the beans in a pan, cover with cold water, bring to the boil, then cook for 5 minutes. Remove from the heat, cover and leave to stand for 2 hours.

2 Heat the olive oil in a large pan, add the onions, garlic and chilli and cook for 5 minutes, stirring occasionally, until the onion is soft but not browned.

3 Stir in the cumin, turmeric, tomatoes, stock, half the chopped coriander and the beans and simmer for 20–30 minutes.

4 Stir in the lemon juice and remaining coriander and serve at once accompanied by pitta bread.

Cook's Tip
Black-eyed beans are small and cream-coloured with a nutty, earthy flavour. To save preparation time, make this soup using canned beans, draining and rinsing them well before adding them to the pan.

Hot Red Lentil Soup

Red lentils and vegetables are cooked and puréed, then sharpened with lots of lemon juice. In hot weather, it is also good served cold, adding even more lemon. This soup is also known as Esau's soup and is sometimes served as part of a sabbath meal in Jewish households.

Serves 4

45ml/3 tbsp olive oil
1 onion, chopped
2 celery sticks, chopped
1–2 carrots, sliced
8 garlic cloves, chopped
1 potato, peeled and diced
250g/9oz/generous 1 cup
  red lentils
1 litre/1¾ pints/4 cups
  vegetable stock
2 bay leaves
1–2 lemons, halved
2.5ml/½ tsp ground cumin, or
  to taste
cayenne pepper or Tabasco sauce,
  to taste
salt and ground black pepper
lemon slices and chopped
  fresh flat leaf parsley leaves,
  to serve

1 Heat the oil in a large pan. Add the onion and cook for about 5 minutes, or until softened. Stir in the celery, carrots, half the garlic and all the potato. Cook for a few minutes until beginning to soften.

2 Add the lentils and stock to the pan and bring to the boil. Reduce the heat, cover and simmer for about 30 minutes, until the potato and lentils are tender.

3 Add the bay leaves, remaining garlic and half the lemons to the pan and cook the soup for a further 10 minutes. Remove the bay leaves. Squeeze the juice from the remaining lemons, then stir into the soup, to taste.

4 Pour the soup into a food processor or blender and process until smooth. (You may need to do this in batches.) Tip the soup back into the pan, stir in the cumin, cayenne pepper or Tabasco sauce, and season with salt and pepper.

5 Ladle the soup into bowls and top each portion with lemon slices and a sprinkling of chopped fresh flat leaf parsley.

Spiced Bean Soup: Energy 161kcal/682kJ; Protein 9.9g; Carbohydrate 23g, of which sugars 3g; Fat 3.5g, of which saturates 0.6g; Cholesterol 0mg; Calcium 47mg; Fibre 5.6g; Sodium 507mg.
Hot Red Lentil Soup: Energy 235kcal/991kJ; Protein 13g; Carbohydrate 28.4g, of which sugars 3.7g; Fat 8.9g, of which saturates 2.2g; Cholesterol 0mg; Calcium 66mg; Fibre 2.9g; Sodium 40mg.

Spiced North African Soup

Known as *harira*, this traditional Moroccan soup is often served in the evening as a starter, but it also makes a hearty and satisfying lunch.

Serves 6
1 large onion, chopped
1.2 litres/2 pints/5 cups
   vegetable stock
5ml/1 tsp ground cinnamon
5ml/1 tsp turmeric
15ml/1 tbsp grated fresh root
   ginger
pinch cayenne pepper
2 carrots, diced
2 celery sticks, diced
400g/14oz can chopped
   tomatoes
450g/1lb floury potatoes, diced
5 strands saffron
400g/14oz can chickpeas,
   drained
30ml/2 tbsp chopped fresh
   coriander (cilantro)
15ml/1 tbsp lemon juice
salt and ground black pepper
fried wedges of lemon, to serve

1 Place the onion in a large pot with 300ml/½ pint/1¼ cups of the vegetable stock. Simmer gently for about 10 minutes.

2 Meanwhile, mix together the cinnamon, turmeric, ginger, cayenne pepper and 30ml/2 tbsp of stock to form a paste. Stir into the onion mixture with the carrots, celery and the remaining stock.

3 Bring the mixture to a boil, reduce the heat, then cover and gently simmer for 5 minutes.

4 Add the tomatoes and potatoes and simmer gently, covered, for 20 minutes. Add the saffron, chickpeas, coriander and lemon juice. Season to taste and when piping hot serve with fried wedges of lemon.

> **Cook's Tip**
> This recipe is a vegetarian version of the soup, but in Morocco it is often made with cubed lean lamb, and enriched with eggs beaten into the hot soup just before serving, turning it into a substantial meal. It is traditionally served with hard-boiled eggs sprinkled with cumin, dried fruits and sweetmeats.

Curried Parsnip Soup with Sesame Naan Croûtons

The mild sweetness of parsnips is given an exciting lift with a blend of spices in this simple soup.

Serves 4
30ml/2 tbsp olive oil
1 onion, chopped
1 garlic clove, crushed
1 small green chilli, seeded and
   finely chopped
15ml/1 tbsp grated fresh root
   ginger
5 large parsnips, diced
5ml/1 tsp cumin seeds
5ml/1 tsp ground coriander
2.5ml/½ tsp ground turmeric
30ml/2 tbsp mango chutney
1.2 litres/2 pints/5 cups water
juice of 1 lime
salt and ground black pepper
chopped fresh coriander (cilantro),
   to garnish (optional)
60ml/4 tbsp natural (plain) yogurt
   and mango chutney, to serve

**For the sesame naan
croûtons**
45ml/3 tbsp olive oil
1 large naan, cut into
   small dice
15ml/1 tbsp sesame seeds

1 Heat the oil in a large pan and add the onion, garlic, chilli and ginger. Cook for 4–5 minutes, until the onion has softened. Add the parsnips and cook for 2–3 minutes. Sprinkle in the cumin seeds, coriander and turmeric, and cook for 1 minute, stirring.

2 Add the chutney and the water. Season well and bring to the boil. Reduce the heat and simmer for 15 minutes, until the parsnips are soft. Cool the soup slightly, then process it in a food processor or blender until smooth, and return it to the pan. Stir in the lime juice.

3 To make the croûtons, heat the oil in a large frying pan and cook the diced naan for 3–4 minutes, stirring, until golden all over. Remove from the heat and drain off any excess oil. Add the sesame seeds to the croûtons and return to the heat for 30 seconds, until the seeds are pale golden.

4 Ladle the soup into bowls. Spoon a little yogurt into each bowl, then top with mango chutney and some of the croûtons. Garnish with chopped fresh coriander, if you like.

Spiced Mango Soup with Yogurt

This delicious, light soup is an unusual combination of fruit and spices. It is best served lightly chilled and makes a refreshing, fruity start to a spicy meal.

Serves 4

2 ripe mangoes
15ml/1 tbsp gram flour
120ml/4fl oz/½ cup natural
  (plain) yogurt
900ml/1½ pints/3¾ cups
  cold water

2.5ml/½ tsp grated fresh root
  ginger
2 fresh red chillies, seeded and
  finely chopped
30ml/2 tbsp olive oil
2.5ml/½ tsp mustard seeds
2.5ml/½ tsp cumin seeds
8 curry leaves
salt and ground black pepper
fresh mint leaves, shredded
  and natural (plain) yogurt,
  to garnish

1 Peel the mangoes, remove the stones and cut the flesh roughly into chunks. Put into a food processor or blender and purée until smooth.

2 Pour into a pan and stir in the gram flour, yogurt, water, ginger and chillies. Bring the mixture slowly to the boil, stirring occasionally. Simmer for 4–5 minutes until thickened slightly, then remove from the heat and set aside.

3 Heat the oil in a frying pan. Add the mustard seeds and cook for a few seconds until they begin to pop, then add the cumin seeds.

4 Add the curry leaves and continue to cook for 5 minutes. Stir the spice mixture into the soup, return it to the heat and cook for 10 minutes.

5 Press the soup through a sieve (strainer), if you wish to remove the spices, then season to taste. Leave the soup to cool completely, then chill for at least 1 hour.

6 Ladle the soup into bowls, and top each bowl with a dollop of plain yogurt. Garnish the soup with shredded mint leaves and serve.

Andalusian Avocado Soup with Cumin and Paprika

Andalusia is home to both avocados and gazpacho, so it is not surprising that this soup, which is also known as green gazpacho, was invented there. In southern Spain, this deliciously mild, creamy soup is the perfect chilled summer appetizer.

Serves 4

3 ripe avocados
1 bunch spring onions (scallions),
  white parts only, trimmed and
  roughly chopped

2 garlic cloves, chopped
juice of 1 lemon
1.5ml/¼ tsp ground cumin
1.5ml/¼ tsp paprika
450ml/¾ pint/scant 2 cups fresh
  chicken stock, cooled, and all
  fat skimmed off
300ml/½ pint/1¼ cups
  iced water
salt and ground black pepper
roughly chopped fresh flat leaf
  parsley, to garnish

1 Starting half a day ahead, put the flesh of one avocado in a food processor or blender. Add the spring onions, garlic and lemon juice and purée until smooth. Add the second avocado and purée, then the third, with the spices and seasoning. Purée until smooth.

2 Gradually add the chicken stock. Pour the soup into a metal bowl and chill.

3 To serve, stir in the iced water, then season to taste with plenty of salt and black pepper. Garnish with chopped parsley and serve immediately.

> **Cook's Tips**
> • Hass avocados, with bumpy skin that turns purplish black when ripe, generally have the best flavour. They should be perfectly ripe for this recipe.
> • Avocado flesh blackens when exposed to air, but the lemon juice in this recipe preserves the colour of the soup.

Saffron Fish Cakes with Cucumber and Cinnamon Salad

A scented cucumber salad makes a superbly refreshing accompaniment for these Moroccan-inspired fish cakes. Canned tuna can be substituted for fresh fish.

Serves 4
450g/1lb white fish fillets, such as
   sea bass, ling or haddock,
   skinned and cut into chunks
10ml/2 tsp harissa
rind of ½ preserved lemon,
   finely chopped
small bunch of fresh coriander
   (cilantro), finely chopped

1 egg
5ml/1 tsp honey
pinch of saffron threads, soaked
   in 5ml/1 tsp water
sunflower oil, for frying
salt and ground black pepper

For the salad
2 cucumbers, peeled and grated
juice of 1 orange
juice of ½ lemon
15–30ml/1–2 tbsp orange
   flower water
15–20ml/3–4 tsp sugar
2.5ml/½ tsp ground cinnamon

1 Make the salad in advance to allow time for chilling before serving. Place the cucumber in a sieve (strainer) over a bowl. Sprinkle with salt and leave to drain for about 10 minutes. Using your hands, squeeze out the excess liquid and place the cucumber in a bowl.

2 Combine the orange and lemon juice, orange flower water and sugar and pour over the cucumber. Toss well, sprinkle with cinnamon and chill for at least 1 hour.

3 To make the fish cakes, put the fish, harissa, preserved lemon, coriander, egg, honey and saffron, with its soaking water, in a food processor. Add seasoning and process until smooth. Divide the mixture into 16 portions. Roll each one into a ball and flatten in the palm of your hand.

4 Heat the oil in a large frying pan and fry the fish cakes in batches, until golden brown on each side. Drain them on kitchen paper and keep hot until all the fish cakes are cooked. Serve immediately with the chilled cucumber salad.

Cinnamon Fish Cakes with Currants, Pine Nuts and Herbs

Whether eaten as an appetizer or served as a main course accompanied by a salad, these fresh, tasty Middle Eastern fish cakes are delicious. They are flavoured with cinnamon and a classic trio of herbs – parsley, mint and dill.

Serves 4
450g/1lb skinless fresh white fish
   fillets, such as haddock or
   sea bass
2 slices of day-old bread, sprinkled
   with water and left for a few
   minutes, then squeezed dry
1 red onion, finely chopped
30ml/2 tbsp currants, soaked in
   warm water for 5–10 minutes
   and drained

30ml/2 tbsp pine nuts
1 small bunch each of fresh
   flat leaf parsley, mint and dill,
   stems removed, leaves finely
   chopped
1 egg
5–10ml/1–2 tsp tomato purée
   (paste) or ketchup
15ml/1 tbsp ground cinnamon
45–60ml/3–4 tbsp plain (all-
   purpose) flour
45–60ml/3–4 tbsp sunflower oil
salt and ground black pepper

To serve
1 small bunch of fresh flat leaf
   parsley
1–2 lemons or limes, cut into
   wedges

1 In a bowl, break up the fish with a fork. Add the bread, onion, currants and pine nuts, toss in the herbs and mix well.

2 In another small bowl, beat the egg with the tomato purée and 10ml/2 tsp of the cinnamon. Pour the mixture over the fish and season with salt and pepper, then mix with your hands and mould into small balls.

3 Mix the flour on a plate with the remaining cinnamon. Press each ball into a flat cake and coat in the flour.

4 Heat the oil in a wide, shallow pan and fry the fish cakes in batches for 8–10 minutes, until golden brown. Lift out and drain on kitchen paper. Serve hot on a bed of parsley, with lemon or lime wedges for squeezing.

Saffron Fish Cakes: Energy 115kcal/481kJ; Protein 15.5g; Carbohydrate 5.6g, of which sugars 5.5g; Fat 3.5g, of which saturates 0.6g; Cholesterol 66mg; Calcium 42mg; Fibre 0.8g; Sodium 63mg.
Cinnamon Fish Cakes: Energy 317kcal/1324kJ; Protein 26.1g; Carbohydrate 17.8g, of which sugars 2.5g; Fat 16.2g, of which saturates 1.9g; Cholesterol 99mg; Calcium 79mg; Fibre 1.6g; Sodium 169mg.

Salmon, Sesame and Ginger Fish Cakes

These light fish cakes are scented with the exotic flavours of sesame, lime and ginger. They make a tempting appetizer served simply with a wedge of lime for squeezing over, but are also perfect for a light lunch or supper, served with a crunchy, refreshing salad. In this case you may want to use the mixture to make a smaller number of larger fish cakes, which will take a few more minutes each side to cook through.

Makes 25
500g/1¼lb salmon fillet, skinned and boned
45ml/3 tbsp dried breadcrumbs
30ml/2 tbsp mayonnaise
30ml/2 tbsp sesame seeds
30ml/2 tbsp light soy sauce
finely grated zest of 2 limes
10ml/2 tsp finely grated fresh root ginger
4 spring onions (scallions), finely sliced
vegetable oil, for frying
salt and ground black pepper
spring onion slivers, to garnish
lime wedges, to serve

1 Finely chop the salmon and place in a bowl. Add the breadcrumbs, mayonnaise, sesame seeds, soy sauce, lime zest, ginger and spring onions and use your fingers to mix well, distributing all the ingredients evenly.

2 With wet hands, divide the mixture into 25 portions and shape each one into a small round cake.

3 Place the cakes on a baking sheet, lined with baking parchment, cover and chill for several hours or overnight.

4 When you are ready to cook the fish cakes heat about 5cm/2in vegetable oil in a wok.

5 Working in batches, shallow fry the fish cakes over a medium heat for 2–3 minutes on each side.

6 Drain the fish cakes well on kitchen paper and serve warm or at room temperature, garnished with spring onion slivers and plenty of lime wedges for squeezing over.

Ginger and Chilli Steamed Fish Custards

These pretty little custards make an unusual and exotic appetizer for a dinner party. The pandanus leaves impart a distinctive flavour – but don't be tempted to eat them once the custards are cooked: they are inedible.

Serves 4
2 eggs
200ml/7fl oz/scant 1 cup coconut cream
60ml/4 tbsp chopped fresh coriander (cilantro)
1 red chilli, seeded and sliced
15ml/1 tbsp finely chopped lemon grass
2 kaffir lime leaves, finely shredded
30ml/2 tbsp red Thai curry paste
1 garlic clove, crushed
5ml/1 tsp finely grated fresh root ginger
2 spring onions (scallions), finely sliced
300g/11oz mixed firm white fish fillets (cod, halibut or haddock), skinned
200g/7oz raw tiger prawns (shrimp), peeled and deveined
4–6 pandanus (screwpine) leaves
salt and ground black pepper
shredded cucumber, steamed rice and soy sauce, to serve

1 Beat the eggs in a bowl, then stir in the coconut cream, coriander, chilli, lemon grass, lime leaves, curry paste, garlic, ginger and spring onions. Finely chop the fish and roughly chop the prawns and add to the egg mixture. Stir well and season.

2 Grease four ramekins and line them with the pandanus leaves. Divide the fish mixture between them, then arrange in a bamboo steamer.

3 Pour 5cm/2in water into a wok and bring to the boil. Suspend the steamer over the water, cover, reduce the heat to low and steam for 25–30 minutes, or until cooked through. Serve with shredded cucumber, steamed rice and soy sauce.

> **Cook's Tip**
> Pandanus leaves are available from Asian markets.

Chargrilled Sardines with Chilli and Dill Dressing

Tangy, charred vine leaves and tomatoes make perfect partners for the oily flesh of the sardines.

Serves 3–4

12 sardines, scaled, gutted and thoroughly washed
juice of ½ lemon
30ml/2 tbsp olive oil, plus extra for brushing
12 fresh or preserved vine leaves
4–6 vine tomatoes, halved or quartered

salt and ground black pepper
lemon wedges, to serve

For the dressing
60ml/4 tbsp olive oil
juice of 1 lemon
15ml/1 tbsp balsamic or white wine vinegar
5–10ml/1–2 tsp clear honey
5ml/1 tsp hot paprika, or 1 fresh red chilli, finely chopped
a few fresh dill fronds and flat leaf parsley sprigs, finely chopped

1 Put all the dressing ingredients in a bowl, season with salt and pepper and mix well.

2 Pat the sardines dry and lay them in a flat dish. Mix the lemon juice with 30ml/2 tbsp oil and brush over the sardines.

3 Get the barbecue ready for cooking. Meanwhile, spread the vine leaves out on a flat surface and place a sardine on each leaf. Sprinkle each one with a little salt and wrap loosely in the leaf like a cigar, with the tail and head poking out.

4 Brush each leaf with a little oil and place seam side down to keep them from unravelling. Thread the tomatoes on skewers and sprinkle with a little salt.

5 Cook the sardines and tomatoes on the barbecue for 2–3 minutes on each side, until the vine leaves are charred and the tomatoes are soft.

6 Transfer the sardines and tomatoes to a serving dish and drizzle with the dressing. Serve immediately, with lemon wedges for squeezing.

Spiced Sardines with Grapefruit and Fennel Salad

Sardines spiced with cumin and coriander are popular in the coastal regions of Morocco, in restaurants and as street food.

12 fresh sardines, gutted, rinsed and dried
small bunch of fresh coriander (cilantro), chopped
coarse salt
2 lemons, cut into wedges, to serve

Serves 4–6

1 onion, grated
60–90ml/4–6 tbsp olive oil
5ml/1 tsp ground cinnamon
10ml/2 tsp cumin seeds, roasted and ground
10ml/2 tsp coriander seeds, roasted and ground
5ml/1 tsp paprika
5ml/1 tsp ground black pepper

For the salad
2 ruby grapefruits, peeled
5ml/1 tsp sea salt
1 fennel bulb, trimmed and sliced
2–3 spring onions (scallions), finely sliced
2.5ml/½ tsp ground roasted cumin
30–45ml/2–3 tbsp olive oil
handful of black olives

1 In a bowl, mix the grated onion with the olive oil, cinnamon, ground roasted cumin and coriander seeds, paprika and black pepper. Make several slashes into the flesh of the sardines and smear the onion and spice mixture all over the fish, inside and out and into the gashes. Leave for about 1 hour.

2 Meanwhile, prepare the salad. Remove the pith from the grapefruit. Cut between the membranes to remove the segments intact. Cut each grapefruit segment in half, place in a bowl and sprinkle with salt. Add the fennel slices to the grapefruit with the spring onions, cumin and olive oil. Toss lightly, then garnish with the olives.

3 Preheat the grill (broiler) or barbecue. Cook the cleaned sardines for 3–4 minutes on each side, basting with any of the leftover marinade.

4 Sprinkle with fresh coriander and serve immediately, with lemon wedges for squeezing over and accompanied by the grapefruit and fennel salad.

Sardines with Grapefruit Salad: Energy 274kcal/1142kJ; Protein 18.7g; Carbohydrate 7.3g, of which sugars 6.1g; Fat 19.2g, of which saturates 3.9g; Cholesterol 0mg; Calcium 106mg; Fibre 2.3g; Sodium 109mg.
Sardines with Chilli Dressing: Energy 300kcal/1245kJ; Protein 16.5g; Carbohydrate 5.3g, of which sugars 5.3g; Fat 23.7g, of which saturates 4.5g; Cholesterol 0mg; Calcium 82mg; Fibre 1.5g; Sodium 101mg.

Chilli-spiced Fried Plaice

In this beautifully presented Japanese dish the flesh of the fish and also the skeleton is deep-fried to such crispness that you can eat it all.

Serves 4

4 small plaice or flounder, about
 500–675g/1¼–1½lb total
 weight, gutted
60ml/4 tbsp cornflour
 (cornstarch)
vegetable oil, for deep-frying
salt

For the condiment

130g/4½oz mooli (daikon), peeled
4 dried chillies, seeded
1 bunch of chives, finely chopped
 (to make 50ml/2fl oz/½ cup)

For the sauce

20ml/4 tsp rice vinegar
20ml/4 tsp shoyu

1 Use a very sharp knife to make deep cuts around the gills and across the tail of the fish. Cut through the skin from the head down to the tail along the centre. Slide the tip of the knife under the flesh near the head and gently cut the fillet from the bone. Fold the fillet with your hand as you cut, as if peeling it from the bone. Keep the knife horizontal.

2 Repeat for the other half, then turn the fish over and do the same to get four fillets from each fish. Place in a dish and sprinkle with a little salt on both sides. Keep the bony skeletons.

3 Pierce the mooli with a skewer or chopstick in four places to make holes, then insert the chillies. Leave for 15 minutes then grate finely. Squeeze out the moisture with your hand. Press a quarter of the grated mooli and chilli into an egg cup, then turn out on to a plate. Make three more mounds.

4 Cut the fish fillets into four slices crossways and coat in cornflour. Heat the oil in a wok or pan to 175°C/345°F. Deep-fry the fillets, two to three at a time, until light golden brown. Raise the temperature to 180°C/350°F. Dust the skeletons with cornflour and cook until crisp. Drain and sprinkle with salt.

5 Mix the rice vinegar and shoyu in a bowl. Arrange the fish on the plates, with the mooli moulds and chives. To eat, mix the condiment and fish with the sauce.

Fish Parcels with Spicy Dipping Sauce

The piquant dipping sauce complements these crisp fish parcels perfectly.

Serves 4

about 30 preserved vine leaves
4–5 large white fish fillets,
 skinned, such as haddock, ling
 or monkfish

For the marinade

small bunch of fresh coriander
 (cilantro), finely chopped
2–3 garlic cloves, chopped
5–10ml/1–2 tsp ground cumin
60ml/4 tbsp olive oil
juice of 1 lemon
salt

For the dipping sauce

50ml/2fl oz/¼ cup white wine
 vinegar or lemon juice
115g/4oz/½ cup caster
 (superfine) sugar
15–30ml/1–2 tbsp water
pinch of saffron threads
1 onion, finely chopped
2 garlic cloves, finely chopped
2–3 spring onions (scallions),
 finely sliced
25g/1oz fresh root ginger, peeled
 and grated
2 hot red or green chillies, seeded
 and finely sliced
small bunch fresh coriander
 (cilantro), chopped
small bunch of mint, chopped

1 To make the marinade, pound the ingredients in a mortar with a pestle or process them in a food processor. Set aside. Rinse the vine leaves then soak in cold water. Remove any bones from the fish and cut each fillet into about eight pieces. Coat the fish in the marinade, cover and chill for 1 hour.

2 Meanwhile, prepare the dipping sauce. Heat the vinegar or lemon juice with the sugar and water until the sugar has dissolved. Boil for about 1 minute, then leave to cool. Add the remaining ingredients. Spoon the sauce into dipping bowls.

3 Drain the vine leaves and pat dry. Place a piece of marinated fish in the centre of a leaf. Fold the edges over, then wrap into a small parcel. Repeat with the other pieces of fish and leaves. Thread the parcels on to skewers and brush with marinade.

4 Preheat the grill (broiler) or barbecue and cook the kebabs for 2–3 minutes each side. Serve with chilli sauce for dipping.

Deep-fried Marinated Small Fish

This delicious selection of crispy fried fish has a Japanese-inspired marinade that is spiced with chillies to give a tongue-tingling effect.

Serves 4
450g/1lb sprats (small whitebait)
plain (all-purpose) flour, for
   dusting
1 small carrot
⅓ cucumber
2 spring onions (scallions)
4cm/1½in piece fresh root
   ginger, peeled
1 dried red chilli
75ml/5 tbsp rice vinegar
60ml/4 tbsp shoyu
15ml/1 tbsp mirin
30ml/2 tbsp sake
vegetable oil, for deep-frying

1 Wipe the fish dry with paper, then put them in a plastic bag with a handful of flour. Seal and shake to coat.

2 Cut the carrot and cucumber into thin strips. Cut the spring onions into three, then slice into thin, lengthways strips. Slice the ginger into thin, lengthways strips and rinse in cold water. Drain. Seed and chop the chilli into thin rings.

3 In a mixing bowl, mix the rice vinegar, shoyu, mirin and sake together to make a marinade. Add the chilli and all the sliced vegetables. Stir well.

4 Pour plenty of oil into a deep pan and heat to 180°C/350°F. Deep-fry the fish five or six at a time until golden brown. Drain on layered kitchen paper, then plunge the hot fish into the marinade. Leave to marinate for at least an hour. Serve the fish cold in a shallow bowl topped with the marinated vegetables.

> **Variation**
> *You can prepare small sardines in this way, too. They have tougher bones and need to be deep-fried twice. Heat the oil and deep-fry until the outside of the fish is just crisp but still pale. Drain and wait for 5 minutes, then put them back into the hot oil again and cook until golden brown.*

Turbot Sashimi Salad with Wasabi

This salad is dressed with wasabi, sometimes known as Japanese horseradish because of its similar flavour. For sashimi, or raw fish, you need an ultra-sharp knife and ultra-fresh fish, which must be kept cool during preparation.

Serves 4
ice cubes
400g/14oz very fresh thick
   turbot, skinned and filleted
300g/11oz mixed salad leaves
8 radishes, thinly sliced

For the wasabi dressing
25g/1oz rocket (arugula) leaves
50g/2oz cucumber, chopped
90ml/6 tbsp rice vinegar
   (use brown if available)
75ml/5 tbsp olive oil
5ml/1 tsp salt
15ml/1 tbsp wasabi paste from a
   tube, or the same amount of
   wasabi powder mixed with
   7.5ml/1½ tsp water

1 First make the dressing. Roughly tear the rocket leaves and process with the cucumber and rice vinegar in a food processor or blender. Pour into a small bowl and add the rest of the dressing ingredients, except for the wasabi. Check the seasoning and add more salt, if required. Chill until needed.

2 Chill the serving plates while you prepare the fish, if you like.

3 Prepare a bowl of cold water with a few ice cubes. Cut the turbot fillet in half lengthways, then cut into 5mm/¼in thick slices crossways. Plunge these into the ice-cold water as you slice. After 2 minutes or so, they will start to curl and become firm. Take out and drain on kitchen paper.

4 In a large bowl, mix the fish, salad leaves and radishes. Mix the wasabi into the dressing and toss well with the salad. Serve immediately.

> **Cook's Tip**
> *Wasabi is an important flavouring in Japanese cuisine. The roots are processed into a paste which is available in supermarkets. It has a pungent flavour and needs to be used sparingly.*

Chargrilled Tuna with Sesame Seeds and Pink Peppercorns

Shiso leaves, also known as parilla, are related to basil and mint. They have a pungent flavour, a little like anise, and taste wonderful when wrapped around the tuna. The vegetables, chewy arame and crunchy mooli, offer a contrast of flavour, texture and colour. Use sashimi-quality tuna from a Japanese food store or first-rate fishmonger, and ask for the piece of fish to be trimmed to a neat rectangular shape.

Serves 4
15g/½oz dried arame seaweed, rinsed in water
60ml/4 tbsp tamari
30ml/2 tbsp mirin
120ml/4fl oz/½ cup water
5ml/1 tsp white sesame seeds
250g/9oz sashimi tuna
15ml/1 tbsp black sesame seeds
10ml/2 tsp dried pink peppercorns
2.5ml/½ tsp sunflower oil
16 fresh shiso leaves
7.5ml/1½ tsp wasabi paste
50g/2oz finely grated mooli (daikon)

1 Drain the arame, then soak it in the tamari, mirin and water for 1 hour. Pour the liquid from the arame into a small pan and put the arame in a serving bowl. Bring the liquid to a simmer.

2 Cook for 3–5 minutes, or until syrupy, cool for 2 minutes and pour over the arame. Sprinkle with the white sesame seeds and cover until needed.

3 Place the tuna in a flat freezerproof container. Lightly grind the black sesame seeds and pink peppercorns in a spice mill. Brush the oil over the tuna, then roll the tuna into the spice mixture to coat it evenly.

4 Heat a griddle until it is fiercely hot and smoking slightly. Sear the tuna for 30 seconds on each of the four sides. Put it back in its container and freeze for 5 minutes to stop it cooking further.

5 Slice it into 5mm/¼in wide pieces and arrange on plates with the shiso leaves, a blob of wasabi and a mound each of arame and mooli.

Tuna and Wasabi Sashimi

This dish is called *maguro butsu*. When preparing big fish like tuna or swordfish for sashimi, Japanese fishmongers cut the filleted flesh lengthways to make long rectangular shapes, and the trimmings are then sold cheaply. *Butsu* is a chopped trimming, which has all the quality of the best tuna sashimi. It is simply dressed with a piquant marinade of wasabi and shoyu.

Serves 4
400g/14oz very fresh tuna, skinned
1 carton mustard and cress (optional)
20ml/4 tsp wasabi paste from a tube, or the same amount of wasabi powder mixed with 10ml/2 tsp water
60ml/4 tbsp shoyu
8 spring onions (scallions), green part only, finely chopped
4 shiso leaves, cut into thin slivers lengthways

1 Cut the tuna into 2cm/¾in cubes. If using mustard and cress, tie into pretty bunches or arrange as a bed in four small serving bowls or plates.

2 Just 5–10 minutes before serving, blend the wasabi paste with the shoyu in a bowl, then add the tuna and spring onions. Mix well and leave to marinate for 5 minutes.

3 Divide the tuna cubes among the bowls and add a few slivers of shiso leaves on top. Serve immediately.

Cook's Tip
Japanese sashimi, a dish of very fresh raw seafood thinly sliced and served with a dipping sauce and simple garnishes, is usually served as the first course of a meal. As it is considered the greatest delicacy in Japanese cuisine, it is served first so that the palate is unaffected by other foods. Shoyu, or Japanese soy sauce, and fiery wasabi are traditional accompaniments, often mixed together in a dipping sauce. The slices of fish are often presented on shiso leaves, which have an aroma rather like apple mint and are also used as a flavouring in Japanese salads and meat and fish dishes.

Bruschetta with Anchovies, Quail's Eggs and Roasted Cumin

All over the Middle East and North Africa, hard-boiled eggs are enjoyed as a snack or appetizer: they may be dipped in salt and paprika, in the thyme and sumac mixture, *zahtar*, or in roasted cumin. Bitesize quail's eggs dipped in warm, aromatic, freshly roasted cumin make great picnic food. They also marry well with anchovies to make this tasty bruschetta.

Serves 4–6
1 ciabatta loaf
2–3 garlic cloves
30–45ml/2–3 tbsp olive oil
1 red onion, halved and finely sliced
12 quail's eggs, boiled for about 4 minutes, shelled and halved
50g/2oz anchovy fillets
10–15ml/2–3 tsp cumin seeds, roasted and ground
small bunch of flat leaf parsley, roughly chopped
coarse salt

1 Preheat the grill (broiler) on the hottest setting. Slice the loaf of bread horizontally in half and toast the cut side until golden.

2 Smash the garlic cloves with the flat blade of a knife to remove their skins and crush the flesh slightly. Rub the garlic over the toasted bread. Drizzle the olive oil over the bread and sprinkle with a little salt (not too much as the anchovies will be salty).

3 Cut each length of bread into four to six equal pieces. Pile the onion slices, quail's egg halves and anchovy fillets on the pieces of bread. Sprinkle liberally with the ground roasted cumin and chopped parsley and serve immediately while the bread is still warm.

Cook's Tip
Select anchovy fillets preserved in salt or oil. Soak anchovy fillets preserved in salt in a little milk for about 15 minutes to reduce the salty flavour, then drain (discarding the milk) and pat dry on kitchen paper. Drain fillets preserved in oil.

Grilled Eel Wrapped in Bacon with Lemon Grass and Ginger

Rich in flavour, eel is delicious grilled, braised, or stir-fried. Serve this spicy dish with a dipping sauce, a crunchy salad, and jasmine rice.

Serves 4–6
2 lemon grass stalks, trimmed and chopped
25g/1oz fresh root ginger, peeled and chopped
2 garlic cloves, chopped
2 shallots, chopped
15ml/1 tbsp palm sugar (jaggery)
15ml/1 tbsp vegetable or groundnut (peanut) oil
30ml/2 tbsp nuoc mam or tuk trey
1.2kg/2¹⁄₂lb fresh eel, skinned and cut into 2.5cm/1in pieces
12 rashers (slices) streaky (fatty) bacon
ground black pepper
a small bunch of fresh coriander (cilantro) leaves, to garnish
nuoc cham, for dipping

1 Using a mortar and pestle, pound the lemon grass, ginger, garlic and shallots with the sugar to form a paste. Add the oil and *nuoc mam* or *tuk trey*, mix well and season with black pepper. Put the eel pieces in a dish and smear them thoroughly with the paste. Cover and place in the refrigerator for 2–3 hours to marinate.

2 Wrap each piece of marinated eel in a strip of bacon, gathering up as much of the marinade as possible.

3 To cook the eel parcels, you can use a conventional grill (broiler), a well-oiled griddle pan, or a barbecue. If grilling over charcoal, skewer the eel parcels; otherwise, spread them over the grill or griddle pan. Cook the eel parcels until browned and crispy, roughly 2–3 minutes on each side. Serve with fresh coriander leaves and *nuoc cham* for dipping.

Cook's Tip
When buying fresh eel, ask the fishmonger to gut it, cut off the head, bone it, skin it and slice it for you.

Spicy Fried Mackerel

This ginger-spiced dish goes down very well with chilled light beer. Try it served hot but it is also excellent cold and is very good served with salad.

Serves 4
675g/1½lb mackerel, filleted
60ml/4 tbsp shoyu
60ml/4 tbsp sake
60ml/4 tbsp caster (superfine) sugar
1 garlic clove, crushed
2cm/¾in piece fresh root ginger, peeled and finely grated
2–3 shiso leaves, chopped into thin strips (optional)
cornflour (cornstarch), for dusting
vegetable oil, for deep-frying
1 lime, cut into thick wedges

1 Using a pair of tweezers, remove any remaining bones from the mackerel. Cut the fillets in half lengthways, then slice diagonally crossways into bitesize pieces.

2 Mix the shoyu, sake, sugar, garlic, grated ginger and shiso in a mixing bowl to make the marinade. Add the mackerel pieces and leave to marinate for 20 minutes.

3 Drain and pat dry gently with kitchen paper. Dust the fillets with cornflour.

4 Heat plenty of vegetable oil in a wok or a deep-fryer. The temperature of the oil must be kept around 180°C/350°F. Deep-fry the mackerel fillets, a few pieces at a time, until they turn a shiny brown colour.

5 Remove the fish pieces as soon as they are done and drain on kitchen paper. Keep them warm while you cook the rest, then serve at once with wedges of lime.

> **Cook's Tips**
> • Shiso leaves are only sold in Japanese food stores. If you can't find them, use 5–6 chopped basil leaves instead.
> • Fresh mackerel should be firm and glistening, with shiny eyes. Get the fishmonger to fillet the fish for you.

Braised Squid with Cinnamon

Some good wines are made in Turkey, and restaurants along the Mediterranean and Aegean coasts incorporate wine in dishes such as this robust, dark squid stew, in which the sauce, made with red wine, is subtly enriched with the sweetness and fragrance of cinnamon.

Serves 4
30–45ml/2–3 tbsp olive oil
2 red onions, cut in half lengthways and sliced along the grain
3–4 garlic cloves, chopped
about 750g/1lb 10oz fresh squid (for preparation see Cook's Tip), cut into thick rings
45–60ml/3–4 tbsp black olives, pitted
5–10ml/1–2 tsp ground cinnamon
5–10ml/1–2 tsp sugar
about 300ml/½ pint/1¼ cups red wine
2 bay leaves
1 small bunch each of fresh flat leaf parsley and dill, finely chopped
salt and ground black pepper
lemon wedges, to serve

1 Heat the oil in a heavy pan and cook the onions and garlic until golden. Add the squid heads and rings and stir-fry them for 2–3 minutes, until they begin to colour. Toss in the olives, cinnamon and sugar; pour in the wine and add the bay leaves. Stir well.

2 Bubble up the liquid, then lower the heat and cover the pan. Cook gently for 35–40 minutes, until the liquid has reduced to a small amount of sauce and the squid is tender.

3 Season the squid with salt and pepper and toss in the herbs. Serve immediately, with lemon wedges.

> **Cook's Tip**
> To prepare squid, rinse it and peel off the thin film of skin, sever the head and trim the tentacles. With your finger, pull out the backbone and reach down into the body pouch to remove the ink sac and any mushy bits. Rinse the pouch inside and out and pat dry. Use the pouch and head, discard the rest.

Pan-fried Baby Squid with Moroccan Spices

You need to work quickly to cook this dish, then serve it immediately, so that the squid is just cooked and tender. Baby squid are widely available ready prepared. The flavours of turmeric, ginger and harissa are fabulous with the contrasting sweetness of the squid, which is reinforced by the addition of a spoonful of honey, and the whole dish is sharpened up by the zesty lemon juice.

Serves 4

8 baby squid, prepared,
   with tentacles
5ml/1 tsp ground turmeric
15ml/1 tbsp olive oil
2 garlic cloves, finely chopped
15g/½oz fresh root ginger, peeled
   and finely chopped
5–10ml/1–2 tsp honey
juice of 1 lemon
10ml/2 tsp harissa
salt
small bunch of fresh coriander
   (cilantro), roughly chopped,
   to serve

1 Pat dry the squid bodies, inside and out, and dry the tentacles. Sprinkle the squid and tentacles with the ground turmeric.

2 Heat the olive oil in a large heavy frying pan and stir in the garlic and ginger. Just as the ginger and garlic begin to colour, add the squid and tentacles and fry quickly on both sides over a high heat. (Don't overcook the squid, otherwise it will become rubbery.)

3 Add the honey, lemon juice and harissa and stir to form a thick, spicy, caramelized sauce. Season with salt, sprinkle with the chopped coriander and serve immediately.

> **Cook's Tip**
> Harissa, the fiery red paste used in the cuisines of Tunisia, Algeria and Morocco, is made from chillies, olive oil and garlic. The chillies are often smoked, and other flavourings include coriander and cumin.

Squid with Paprika and Garlic

Squid are part of every Spanish tapas bar selection, and are usually deep-fried. Here is a modern recipe, which is unusual in that it uses fresh chillies. Serve it as a tapas dish.

Serves 6–8

500g/1¼lb very small squid,
   cleaned
90ml/6 tbsp olive oil, plus extra
1 fresh red chilli, seeded and
   finely chopped
10ml/2 tsp Spanish mild
   smoked paprika
30ml/2 tbsp cornflour
   (cornstarch)
2 garlic cloves, finely chopped
15ml/1 tbsp sherry vinegar
5ml/1 tsp grated lemon rind
30–45ml/2–3 tbsp finely chopped
   fresh parsley
salt and ground black pepper

1 Using a sharp knife, cut the squid body sacs into rings and cut the tentacles into bitesize pieces.

2 Place the squid in a bowl and pour over 30ml/2 tbsp of the olive oil, half the chilli and the paprika. Season with a little salt and some pepper, cover with clear film (plastic wrap), place in the refrigerator and leave to marinate for 2–4 hours.

3 Toss the squid in the cornflour and divide it into two batches. Heat the remaining oil in a wok or deep frying pan over a high heat until very hot. Add the first batch of squid and quickly stir-fry for 1–2 minutes, or until it becomes opaque and the tentacles curl.

4 Add half the garlic. Stir, then turn out into a bowl. Repeat with the second batch, adding more oil if needed.

5 Sprinkle with the sherry vinegar, lemon rind, remaining chilli and parsley. Season and serve hot or cool.

> **Cook's Tip**
> Smoked paprika, known as pimenton, has a wonderful, subtle flavour. If you cannot find it, you can use mild paprika instead.

Pan-fried Baby Squid with Spices: Energy 154kcal/647kJ; Protein 19.8g; Carbohydrate 5.8g, of which sugars 4.3g; Fat 5.9g, of which saturates 1g; Cholesterol 281mg; Calcium 54mg; Fibre 1g; Sodium 144mg.
Squid with Paprika: Energy 1406kcal/5868kJ; Protein 102.2g; Carbohydrate 38.1g, of which sugars 1.4g; Fat 95.2g, of which saturates 14.6g; Cholesterol 1424mg; Calcium 211mg; Fibre 3.1g; Sodium 710mg.

Black-pepper-spiced Fried Squid

Cooking squid this way couldn't be simpler. Salt and pepper are used to season the fish, and that's it. A Chinese tradition for all sorts of fish and shellfish, this is a Vietnamese and Cambodian favourite too. It makes ideal snack and finger food. The tender squid can be served on its own, with noodles or – as it is in the streets of Saigon – with chunks of baguette and chillies. Those who like chilli a lot can replace the black pepper with chopped dried chilli or chilli powder. Butterflied prawns are also delicious cooked in this way.

Serves 4
450g/1lb baby or medium squid
30ml/2 tbsp coarse salt
15ml/1 tbsp ground black pepper
50g/2oz/½ cup rice flour or cornflour (cornstarch)
vegetable oil, for deep-frying
2 limes, cut into wedges

1 Prepare the squid by pulling the head away from the body. Sever the tentacles from the rest and trim them. Reach inside the body sac and pull out the backbone, then clean the squid inside and out, removing any skin. Rinse well in cold water.

2 Using a sharp knife, slice the squid into rings and pat them dry with kitchen paper. Put them in a dish with the tentacles. Combine the salt and pepper with the rice flour or cornflour, add it to the squid and toss well to coat evenly.

3 Heat the oil for deep-frying in a wok or heavy pan. Cook the squid in batches, until the rings turn crisp and golden.

4 Drain on kitchen paper and serve with lime wedges to squeeze over. This dish can also be served with noodles, or with chunks of baguette and fresh chillies.

Cook's Tip
Make sure the oil in the pan is very hot before adding the squid. The squid should cook for only 1–2 minutes; any longer and it will begin to toughen.

Squid Stuffed with Garlic Pork

This Vietnamese recipe calls for tender baby squid to be stuffed with a dill-flavoured pork mixture. The squid can be grilled or fried.

Serves 4
3 dried cloud ear (wood ear) mushrooms
10 dried tiger lily buds
25g/1oz bean thread (cellophane) noodles
8 baby squid, cleaned
350g/12oz minced (ground) pork
3–4 shallots, finely chopped
4 garlic cloves, finely chopped
1 bunch dill fronds, finely chopped
30ml/2 tbsp nuoc mam
5ml/1 tsp palm sugar (jaggery)
ground black pepper
vegetable or groundnut (peanut) oil, for frying
coriander (cilantro) leaves, to garnish
nuoc cham, for drizzling

1 Soak the mushrooms, tiger lily buds and bean thread noodles in lukewarm water for about 15 minutes, until softened. Rinse the squid and pat dry with kitchen paper. Chop the tentacles.

2 Drain the mushrooms, tiger lily buds and bean thread noodles. Squeeze them in kitchen paper to get rid of any excess water, then chop them finely and put them in a bowl. Add the chopped tentacles, minced pork, shallots, garlic and three quarters of the dill. In a small bowl, stir the nuoc mam with the sugar, until it dissolves completely. Add it to the mixture in the bowl and mix well. Season with ground black pepper.

3 Using your fingers, stuff the pork mixture into each squid, packing it in firmly. Leave a little gap at the end to sew together with a needle and cotton thread or to skewer with a cocktail stick (toothpick) so that the filling doesn't spill out on cooking.

4 Heat some oil in a large wok or heavy pan, and fry the squid for about 5 minutes, turning them from time to time. Pierce each one several times to release any excess water – this will cause the oil to spit, so take care when doing this; you may wish to use a spatterproof lid. Continue cooking for a further 10 minutes, until the squid are nicely browned. Serve whole or thinly sliced, garnished with the remaining dill and coriander, and drizzled with nuoc cham.

Black-pepper-spiced Squid: Energy 339kcal/1405kJ; Protein 14g; Carbohydrate 5g, of which sugars 0g; Fat 29g, of which saturates 4g; Cholesterol 146mg; Calcium 70mg; Fibre 0g; Sodium 140mg.
Squid Stuffed with Pork: Energy 315kcal/1311kJ; Protein 25g; Carbohydrate 7.9g, of which sugars 1.9g; Fat 20.4g, of which saturates 4.6g; Cholesterol 170mg; Calcium 18mg; Fibre 0.2g; Sodium 110mg.

Stir-fried Five-spice Squid

Squid is perfect for stir-frying as it needs to be cooked quickly. The five-spice sauce makes the ideal accompaniment to the squid. Scoring the squid makes the strips curl up as they fry.

Serves 6

450g/1lb small squid, cleaned
45ml/3 tbsp oil
2.5cm/1in piece fresh root
  ginger, grated
1 garlic clove, crushed
8 spring onions (scallions), cut
  diagonally into 2.5cm/1in
  lengths
1 red (bell) pepper, cut into strips
1 fresh green chilli, seeded and
  thinly sliced
6 mushrooms, sliced
5ml/1 tsp five-spice powder
30ml/2 tbsp black bean sauce
30ml/2 tbsp soy sauce
5ml/1 tsp sugar
15ml/1 tbsp rice wine or
  dry sherry

1 Pull away the outer skin of the squid and remove the tentacles. Rinse the body sacs inside and out and dry on kitchen paper. Slit the squid bodies open down one side and score the outside of each sac into diamonds with a sharp knife. Cut the flesh into strips.

2 Heat a wok briefly and add the oil. When it is hot, stir-fry the squid quickly. Remove the squid strips from the wok with a slotted spoon as soon as they are done and set aside.

3 Add the ginger, garlic, spring onions, red pepper, chilli and mushrooms to the oil remaining in the wok and stir-fry quickly for 2 minutes.

4 Return the squid to the wok and stir in the five-spice powder. Stir in the black bean sauce, soy sauce, sugar and rice wine or sherry. Bring to the boil and cook, stirring, for 1 minute so that the sauce coats the squid. Serve immediately.

Cook's Tip
As with all stir-fried dishes it is important to have all the ingredients ready before you start to cook.

Chilli-stuffed Grilled Squid

These stuffed squid are quickly cooked on a barbecue. The tentacles are a wonderfully tasty part of the squid so thread them on to the skewers as well.

Serves 6

12 whole squid, total weight about
  675g/1½lb, cleaned
45ml/3 tbsp extra virgin olive oil,
  plus extra for coating
2 onions, finely chopped
3 garlic cloves, crushed
25g/1oz/2 tbsp walnuts, finely
  chopped
7.5ml/1½ tsp ground sumac or
  squeeze of lemon juice
1.5ml/¼ tsp finely chopped fresh
  chilli or dried chilli flakes
75–90g/3–3½oz rocket
  (arugula), any tough stalks
  removed
115g/4oz/1 cup cooked rice
salt and ground black pepper
lemon and lime wedges, to serve

1 Prepare the squid, washing the clumps of tentacles and body well, inside and out, under cold running water. Put the tentacles on a plate, cover and chill. Pull the side flaps or wings away from the body, chop them finely and set aside. Reserve the squid body with the tentacles.

2 Heat a frying pan. Add the oil, onions and garlic and fry for 5 minutes, or until the onions are soft and golden. Add the chopped squid wings and fry for about 1 minute, then stir in the walnuts, sumac and chilli. Add the rocket and continue to stir-fry until it has wilted. Stir in the rice, season well and tip into a bowl to cool.

3 Stuff each squid with the cold mixture and thread two on to each of six skewers, with two clumps of tentacles. Toss in oil and salt. Barbecue on medium-hot coals for about 1½ minutes on each side. When golden, move to a cooler part of the grill to cook for 1½ minutes more on each side. Baste with any remaining oil and salt. Serve with lemon and lime wedges.

Cook's Tip
If you prepare these squid ahead of time, they can be chilled until needed. Bring them to room temperature before grilling.

Japanese-style Crab Cakes with Ginger and Wasabi

Wasabi – a traditional Japanese flavouring – is available as a powder or a paste. It is very hot so should be used sparingly.

Serves 6
450g/1lb fresh dressed crab meat (brown and white meat)
30ml/2 tbsp mayonnaise
4 spring onions (scallions), finely chopped, plus extra to garnish
2.5cm/1in piece of fresh root ginger, grated
30ml/2 tbsp chopped fresh coriander (cilantro)
2.5–5ml/1/2–1 tsp wasabi paste
1 tbsp sesame oil
salt and ground black pepper
50–115g/2–4oz/1–2 cups fresh breadcrumbs
oil, for frying
lettuce leaves, fresh chilli and lime slices, to serve

For the dipping sauce
5ml/1 tsp wasabi paste
90ml/6 tbsp shoyu

1 Make the dipping sauce by mixing the wasabi and the shoyu in a small bowl. Set aside.

2 Mix the crab meat, mayonnaise, spring onions, ginger, coriander, wasabi paste and sesame oil in a bowl. Stir in a little salt and pepper and add enough fresh breadcrumbs to make a mixture that is firm enough to form patties, but is not too stiff.

3 Chill the crab mixture for 30 minutes then use your hands to form it into 12 cakes. Heat a shallow layer of oil in a frying pan and fry the crab cakes for about 3–4 minutes on each side, until browned.

4 Serve the crab cakes with lettuce leaves and lime slices, accompanied by the dipping sauce, garnished with chilli and spring onion slices.

Cook's Tip
Fresh crab meat will have the best flavour, but if it is not available, use frozen or canned crab meat.

Caribbean Chilli Crab Cakes

Crab meat makes wonderful fish cakes, as shown by these gutsy morsels. Served with a rich tomato dip, they make great party food.

Makes about 15
225g/8oz white crab meat (fresh, frozen or canned)
115g/4oz cooked floury potatoes, mashed
30ml/2 tbsp fresh herb seasoning
2.5ml/1/2 tsp mild mustard
2.5ml/1/2 tsp ground black pepper
1/2 fresh hot chilli, finely chopped
5ml/1 tsp fresh oregano
1 egg, beaten
plain (all-purpose) flour, for dredging

vegetable oil, for frying
lime wedges and coriander (cilantro) sprigs, to garnish
fresh whole chilli peppers, to garnish

For the tomato dip
15g/1/2oz/1 tbsp butter or margarine
1/2 onion, finely chopped
2 canned plum tomatoes, chopped
1 garlic clove, crushed
150ml/1/4 pint/2/3 cup water
5–10ml/1–2 tsp malt vinegar
15ml/1 tbsp chopped fresh coriander (cilantro)
1/2 hot fresh chilli, chopped

1 Mix together the crab meat, potatoes, herb seasoning, mustard, pepper and chilli, oregano and egg in a large bowl. Chill the mixture for at least 30 minutes.

2 Meanwhile, make the tomato dip. Melt the butter or margarine in a small pan over a medium heat. Add the onion, tomatoes and garlic and sauté for about 5 minutes until the onion is tender. Add the water, vinegar, coriander and fresh chilli.

3 Bring to the boil, reduce the heat and simmer for about 10 minutes. Transfer the mixture to a food processor or blender and blend to a smooth purée.

4 Shape the chilled crab mixture into rounds and dredge with flour, shaking off the excess. Heat a little oil in a frying pan and fry, a few cakes at a time, for 2–3 minutes on each side. Drain on kitchen paper and keep warm in a low oven while cooking the remainder. Garnish with lime wedges, coriander sprigs and whole chillies and serve with the tomato dip.

Crab Cakes with Ginger: Energy 190kcal/795kJ; Protein 16.2g; Carbohydrate 7.1g, of which sugars 0.6g; Fat 11g, of which saturates 1.4g; Cholesterol 55mg; Calcium 35mg; Fibre 0.3g; Sodium 388mg.
Caribbean Chilli Crab Cakes: Energy 70kcal/290kJ; Protein 3.5g; Carbohydrate 2.9g, of which sugars 0.7g; Fat 5g, of which saturates 1.1g; Cholesterol 26mg; Calcium 24mg; Fibre 0.3g; Sodium 95mg.

Spiced Clams

Spanish clams, especially in the North, are much larger than clams found elsewhere, and have more succulent bodies. This modern recipe uses Arab spicing to make a hot dip or sauce. Serve with plenty of fresh bread to mop up the delicious juices.

Serves 3–4

500g/1¼lb small clams
1 small onion, finely chopped
1 celery stick, sliced
2 garlic cloves, finely chopped
2.5cm/1in piece fresh root ginger, grated
30ml/2 tbsp olive oil
1.5ml/¼ tsp chilli powder
5ml/1 tsp ground turmeric
30ml/2 tbsp chopped fresh parsley
30ml/2 tbsp dry white wine
salt and ground black pepper
celery leaves, to garnish
fresh bread, to serve

1 Scrub the clams under cold running water, discarding any shells that are broken or open.

2 Place the onion, celery, garlic and ginger in a large pan, add the olive oil, spices and chopped parsley and stir-fry gently for about 5 minutes. Add the clams to the pan and cook for 2 minutes.

3 Add the wine, then cover and cook gently for 2–3 minutes, shaking the pan occasionally, until all the shells have opened.

4 Season with salt and pepper. Discard any clams whose shells remain closed, then serve, garnished with the celery leaves.

> **Cook's Tips**
> • One of the best and most succulent varieties of clam is the carpet shell, which is perfect used in this dish. They have grooved brown shells with a yellow lattice pattern, from which they get their common name.
> • Before cooking the clams, check that all the shells are closed and discard any that are not. Any clams that do not open after cooking should also be discarded.

Fragrant Scallops with Ginger

Serve these juicy, fragrant scallops with their subtly spiced flavour as an indulgent main course for a special occasion. For the best results, use the freshest scallops you can find, and if you're worried about shucking them yourself, ask your fishmonger to do it for you.

Serves 4

24 king scallops in their shells, cleaned
15ml/1 tbsp very finely shredded fresh root ginger
5ml/1 tsp very finely chopped garlic
1 large red chilli, seeded and very finely chopped
15ml/1 tbsp light soy sauce
15ml/1 tbsp Chinese rice wine
a few drops of sesame oil
2–3 spring onions (scallions), very finely shredded
15ml/1 tbsp very finely chopped fresh chives
noodles or rice, to serve

1 Remove the scallops from their shells, then remove the membrane and hard white muscle from each one. Arrrange the scallops on two plates. Rinse the shells, dry and set aside.

2 Fill two woks with 5cm/2in water and place a trivet in the base of each one. Bring to the boil.

3 Meanwhile, mix together the ginger, garlic, chilli, soy sauce, rice wine, sesame oil, spring onions and chives and spoon over the scallops.

4 Lower a plate of scallops into each of the woks. Turn the heat to low, cover and steam for 10–12 minutes, or until just cooked through.

5 Divide the scallops among four, or eight, of the reserved shells and serve immediately with noodles or rice.

> **Cook's Tip**
> If scallops are not available in their shells serve the scallops in shallow, warmed dishes.

Spiced Clams: Energy 126kcal/526kJ; Protein 12.5g; Carbohydrate 4.5g, of which sugars 2.2g; Fat 6g, of which saturates 0.9g; Cholesterol 50mg; Calcium 69mg; Fibre 0.6g; Sodium 906mg.
Scallops with Ginger: Energy 392kcal/1621kJ; Protein 13.6g; Carbohydrate 4.5g, of which sugars 2.5g; Fat 34.1g, of which saturates 22.4g; Cholesterol 115mg; Calcium 63mg; Fibre 0.4g; Sodium 168mg.

Thai Seafood with Lemon Grass

Lemon grass has an incomparable flavour and is widely used in Thai cookery, especially with seafood. If clams are not available, use a few extra mussels instead.

Serves 6
1.75kg/4–4½lb mussels
450g/1lb baby clams
120ml/4fl oz/½ cup dry white wine
1 bunch spring onions (scallions), chopped
2 lemon grass stalks, chopped
6 kaffir lime leaves, chopped
10ml/2 tsp Thai green curry paste
200ml/7fl oz/scant 1 cup coconut cream
30ml/2 tbsp chopped fresh coriander (cilantro)
salt and ground black pepper
garlic chives, to garnish

1 Clean the mussels by pulling off the beards, scrubbing the shells well and removing any barnacles. Discard any mussels that are broken or do not close when tapped. Wash the clams.

2 Put the wine in a large pan with the spring onions, lemon grass, kaffir lime leaves and curry paste. Simmer until the wine has almost evaporated.

3 Add the mussels and clams to the pan, cover tightly and steam the shellfish over a high heat for 5–6 minutes, until the shells have opened.

4 Using a slotted spoon, transfer the mussels and clams to a heated serving bowl and keep hot. Discard any shellfish that remain closed. Strain the cooking liquid into a clean pan and simmer to reduce to about 250ml/8fl oz/1 cup.

5 Stir in the coconut cream and coriander, with salt and pepper to taste. Heat through. Pour the sauce over the mussels and clams and serve, garnished with garlic chives.

> **Cook's Tip**
> It's wise to buy a few extra mussels in case there are any that have to be discarded.

Mussels Stuffed with Cinnamon-spiced Pilaff

These Turkish stuffed mussels are sold by street vendors around the Golden Horn, at the boat crossings over the Bosphorus, and in the main bazaars.

Serves 4
16 large fresh mussels, cleaned
45–60ml/3–4 tbsp olive oil
2–3 shallots, finely chopped
30ml/2 tbsp pine nuts
30ml/2 tbsp currants, soaked in warm water for 5–10 minutes and drained
10ml/2 tsp ground cinnamon
5ml/1 tsp ground allspice
5–10ml/1–2 tsp sugar
5–10ml/1–2 tsp tomato purée (paste)
115g/4oz/generous ½ cup short grain or pudding rice, well rinsed and drained
1 small bunch each of fresh flat leaf parsley, mint and dill, finely chopped
salt and ground black pepper
lemon wedges and fresh flat leaf parsley sprigs, to serve

1 Keep the mussels in a bowl of cold water while you prepare the stuffing. Heat the oil in a heavy pan, stir in the shallots and cook until they soften. Add the pine nuts and currants, stir for 1–2 minutes until the pine nuts turn golden and the currants plump up, then stir in the cinnamon, allspice, sugar and tomato purée. Now add the rice, and stir until it is well coated.

2 Pour in enough water to just cover the rice. Season with salt and pepper and bring to the boil. Lower the heat, partially cover the pan and simmer for 10–12 minutes, until all the water has been absorbed. Tip the rice on to a plate, leave to cool, then toss in the herbs.

3 Prise open each mussel shell, stuff a spoonful of rice into each shell, then close the shells and pack tightly into a steamer filled with water. Cover with a sheet of baking parchment, put a plate on top and weigh it down to prevent the mussels from opening. Place the lid on the steamer and bring the water to the boil. Lower the heat and steam the mussels for 15–20 minutes. Serve warm on a bed of parsley, with lemon wedges.

Thai Seafood with Lemon Grass: Energy 205kcal/871kJ; Protein 37.7g; Carbohydrate 7.5g, of which sugars 5.8g; Fat 3g, of which saturates 0.8g; Cholesterol 473mg; Calcium 144mg; Fibre 0.4g; Sodium 449mg.
Mussels Stuffed with Pilaff: Energy 319kcal/1328kJ; Protein 13.3g; Carbohydrate 32.7g, of which sugars 7.5g; Fat 15g, of which saturates 1.9g; Cholesterol 33mg; Calcium 49mg; Fibre 0.5g; Sodium 237mg.

Piri-Piri Prawns with Aïoli

The word *piri-piri* comes from Portugal and is the name of a small chilli, but it is also used to describe a hot pepper sauce. If you like your chilli dishes seriously hot, you can also add a crumbled dried red chilli to the dish at step 2.

Serves 4
1 fresh red chilli, seeded and
   finely chopped
2.5ml/½ tsp paprika
2.5ml/½ tsp ground coriander
1 garlic clove, crushed
juice of ½ lime
30ml/2 tbsp olive oil
20 large raw prawns (shrimp) in
   shells, heads removed and
   deveined
salt and ground black pepper

For the aïoli
150ml/¼ pint/⅔ cup
   mayonnaise
2 garlic cloves, crushed
5ml/1 tsp Dijon mustard

1 Make the aïoli. Mix the mayonnaise, garlic and mustard in a small bowl and set aside.

2 Mix the chilli, paprika, coriander, garlic, lime juice and olive oil in a bowl. Add salt and pepper to taste. Place the prawns in a dish. Add the spice mixture and mix well. Cover and leave in a cool place for 30 minutes.

3 Thread the prawns on to metal skewers and grill (broil) or barbecue, basting and turning frequently, for 6–8 minutes until they are pink. Serve with the aïoli, garnished with two or three extra chillies.

Cook's Tip
Turn the prawns in the spices while they are marinating.

Variation
The piri-piri marinade can be used for all types of fish. It is also very good with chicken, although this will need to be marinated and cooked for longer.

Prawn Parcels with Lemon Grass and Galangal

These succulent pink prawns coated in a fragrant spice paste make the perfect dish for informal entertaining. Serve the prawns in their paper parcels and allow your guests to unwrap them at the table and enjoy the heady aroma of Thai spices as each packet is opened.

Serves 4
2 lemon grass stalks, very
   finely chopped
5ml/1 tsp very finely chopped
   galangal
4 garlic cloves, finely chopped
finely grated rind and juice
   of 1 lime
4 spring onions (scallions),
   chopped
10ml/2 tsp palm sugar (jaggery)
15ml/1 tbsp soy sauce
5ml/1 tsp nam pla
5ml/1 tsp chilli oil
45ml/3 tbsp chopped fresh
   coriander (cilantro) leaves
30ml/2 tbsp chopped fresh Thai
   basil leaves
1kg/2¼lb raw tiger prawns
   (shrimp), peeled and deveined
   with tails left on
basil leaves and lime wedges,
   to garnish

1 Place the lemon grass, galangal, garlic, lime rind and juice and spring onions in a food processor. Blend in short bursts until the mixture forms a coarse paste. Transfer the paste to a large bowl and stir in the palm sugar, soy sauce, *nam pla*, chilli oil and chopped herbs.

2 Add the prawns to the paste and toss to coat evenly. Cover and marinate in the refrigerator for 30 minutes–1 hour.

3 Cut out eight 20cm/8in squares of baking parchment. Place one-eighth of the prawn mixture in the centre of each, then fold over the edges and twist together to make a sealed parcel.

4 Place the parcels in a large bamboo steamer, cover and steam over a wok of simmering water for 10 minutes, or until the prawns are just cooked through. Serve immediately, garnished with basil leaves and lime wedges.

Turkish Chilli Prawns

This popular prawn dish is often served as a hot meze in the fish restaurants of Izmir and Istanbul. The Mediterranean version, found in the coastal regions of south-west Turkey, is flavoured with a dose of garlic, red pepper and coriander seeds. It is delicious served with a green salad.

Serves 4

30–45ml/2–3 tbsp olive oil
1 onion, cut in half lengthways and finely sliced along the grain
1 green (bell) pepper, finely sliced
2–3 garlic cloves, chopped
5–10ml/1–2 tsp coriander seeds
5–10ml/1–2 tsp Turkish red pepper, or 1 fresh red chilli, seeded and chopped
5–10ml/1–2 tsp sugar
splash of white wine vinegar
2 x 400g/14oz cans chopped tomatoes
1 small bunch of fresh flat leaf parsley, chopped
500g/1¼lb fresh raw prawns (shrimp), shelled, thoroughly cleaned and drained
about 120g/4oz kasar peyniri, Parmesan or strong dry Cheddar cheese, grated
salt and ground black pepper

1 Heat the oil in a heavy pan, stir in the onion, green pepper, garlic, coriander seeds and red pepper or chilli and cook until they begin to colour.

2 Stir in the sugar, vinegar, tomatoes and parsley, then cook gently for about 25 minutes, until you have a chunky sauce. While the sauce is cooking, preheat the oven to 200°C/400°F/Gas 6.

3 Season the sauce with salt and pepper and stir in the prawns. Spoon the mixture into individual earthenware pots and sprinkle the top with the grated cheese. Bake for 25 minutes, or until the cheese is nicely browned on top.

Cook's Tip
Kasar peyniri is a tangy, hard Turkish cheese made from sheep's milk.

Grilled Prawns with Lemon Grass

Next to every fish stall in every market in Vietnam and Cambodia, there is bound to be someone cooking up fragrant, citrus-scented snacks for customers to eat as they wander around the market. The aromatic scent of lemon grass is hard to resist.

Serves 4

16 king prawns (jumbo shrimp), cleaned, with shells intact
120ml/4fl oz/½ cup nuoc mam
30ml/2 tbsp sugar
15ml/1 tbsp vegetable or sesame oil
3 lemon grass stalks, trimmed and finely chopped

1 Using a small sharp knife, carefully slice open each king prawn shell along the back and pull out the black vein, using the point of the knife. Try to keep the rest of the shell intact. Place the deveined prawns in a shallow dish and set aside.

2 Put the nuoc mam in a small bowl with the sugar, and beat together until the sugar has dissolved completely. Add the oil and lemon grass and mix well.

3 Pour the marinade over the prawns, using your fingers to rub it all over the prawns and inside the shells too. Cover the dish with clear film (plastic wrap) and chill for at least 4 hours.

4 Cook the prawns on a barbecue or under a grill (broiler) for 2–3 minutes each side. Serve with little bowls of water for rinsing sticky fingers.

Cook's Tips
• Big, juicy king prawns (jumbo shrimp) are best for this recipe, but you can use smaller ones if the large king prawns are not available.
• Leaving the shells on the prawns protects the flesh from the heat of the barbecue and stops them drying out.
• The top of the lemon grass stem is very woody and should not be chopped: having trimmed away the root, use the bottom 7.5–10cm/3–4in for this marinade.

Turkish Chilli Prawns: Energy 338kcal/1413kJ; Protein 35.9g; Carbohydrate 11.2g, of which sugars 10.8g; Fat 16.9g, of which saturates 7.3g; Cholesterol 274mg; Calcium 481mg; Fibre 2.9g; Sodium 585mg.
Grilled Prawns with Lemon Grass: Energy 174kcal/726kJ; Protein 13g; Carbohydrate 11g, of which sugars 3g; Fat 9g, of which saturates 1g; Cholesterol 169mg; Calcium 30mg; Fibre 0.3g; Sodium 30mg.

Israeli Sweet and Sour Tongue with Ginger

Tongue is a favourite ingredient in the Ashkenazi Jewish kitchen. It is a cheap but very nutritious meat and although in recent years it has rather gone out of fashion in the West it is now reappearing on the menus of smart restaurants. It is wonderful served hot with the sweet and sour sauce in this recipe, and the leftovers are also very good cold, without the sauce, thinly sliced for sandwiches or a salad.

Serves 8
1kg/2¼lb fresh ox tongue
2–3 onions, 1 sliced and 1–2 chopped
3 bay leaves
½–1 stock (bouillon) cube or a small amount of stock powder or bouillon
45ml/3 tbsp vegetable oil
60ml/4 tbsp potato flour
120ml/4fl oz/½ cup honey
150g/5oz/1 cup raisins
2.5ml/½ tsp salt
2.5ml/½ tsp ground ginger
1 lemon, sliced
fresh rosemary sprigs, to garnish

1 Put the tongue, sliced onion and bay leaves in a large pan. Pour over cold water to cover and add the stock cube, powder or bouillon. Bring to the boil, reduce the heat, cover and simmer gently for 2–3 hours. Lift the tongue out of the stock, remove the skin and bones and keep warm. Strain the stock and set aside.

2 In a small frying pan, heat the oil, add the chopped onion and cook for about 5 minutes, until softened.

3 Stir the potato flour into the onions and gradually add about 500ml/17fl oz/2¼ cups of the stock, stirring constantly to prevent lumps forming.

4 Stir the honey, raisins, salt and ginger into the sauce and continue to cook until it has thickened and is smooth. Add the lemon slices and set the sauce aside.

5 Slice the tongue thinly and serve generously coated with the sweet-and-sour sauce. Garnish with rosemary.

Garlic and Chilli-cured Dried Beef

Although drying meat may be a technique that is unfamiliar to many cooks, it can result in a deliciously different dish, which is tasty and versatile. This dried beef recipe uses very thin slices of sirloin, which are coated in a spicy paste that has plenty of time to penetrate the meat while it is drying out before cooking.

Serves 4
450g/1lb beef sirloin
2 lemon grass stalks, trimmed and chopped
2 garlic cloves, chopped
2 dried Serrano chillies, seeded and chopped
30–45ml/2–3 tbsp honey
15ml/1 tbsp nuoc mam
30ml/2 tbsp soy sauce
rice wrappers, fresh herbs and dipping sauce, to serve

1 Trim the beef and cut it across the grain into thin, rectangular slices, then set aside.

2 Using a mortar and pestle, grind the chopped lemon grass, garlic and chillies to a paste. Stir in the honey, *nuoc mam* and soy sauce. Put the beef into a bowl, add the paste and rub it into the meat. Spread out the meat on a wire rack and place it in the refrigerator, uncovered, for 2 days, or until dry and hard.

3 Cook the dried beef on the barbecue or under a grill (broiler), and serve on its own, or with rice wrappers, herbs and dipping sauce.

Variation
This recipe also works well with venison. Cut the meat into thin strips to make a South-east Asian version of biltong.

Cook's Tip
Drying is an ancient method of preserving food, which also intensifies flavour. In hot countries beef can be dried quickly in the sun, but in cooler areas it dries more slowly, so needs to be put in the refrigerator to prevent it going off.

Sweet and Sour Tongue: Energy 446kcal/1864kJ; Protein 21g; Carbohydrate 30.6g, of which sugars 28.1g; Fat 27.6g, of which saturates 0.7g; Cholesterol 98mg; Calcium 34mg; Fibre 1.3g; Sodium 1528mg.
Garlic and Chilli-cured Beef: Energy 138kcal/581kJ; Protein 18g; Carbohydrate 9g, of which sugars 8g; Fat 3g, of which saturates 2g; Cholesterol 38mg; Calcium 7mg; Fibre 0.1g; Sodium 40mg

Spiced Beef and Potato Puffs

These crisp, golden pillows of pastry filled with spiced beef and potatoes are delicious served straight from the wok. The light pastry puffs up in the hot oil and contrasts enticingly with the fragrant spiced beef.

Serves 4

15ml/1 tbsp sunflower oil
1/2 small onion, finely chopped
3 garlic cloves, crushed
5ml/1 tsp fresh root ginger, grated
1 red chilli, seeded and chopped
30ml/2 tbsp hot curry powder
75g/3oz minced (ground) beef
115g/4oz mashed potato
60ml/4 tbsp chopped fresh
    coriander (cilantro)
2 sheets ready-rolled, fresh puff
    pastry
1 egg, lightly beaten
vegetable oil, for frying
salt and ground black pepper
fresh coriander (cilantro) leaves, to
    garnish
tomato ketchup, to serve

1 Heat the oil in a wok, then add the onion, garlic, ginger and chilli. Stir-fry over a medium heat for 2–3 minutes. Add the curry powder and beef and stir-fry over a high heat for a further 4–5 minutes, or until the beef is browned and just cooked through, then remove from the heat.

2 Transfer the beef mixture to a large bowl and add the mashed potato and chopped fresh coriander. Stir well, then season and set aside.

3 Lay the pastry sheets on a clean, dry surface and cut out 8 rounds, using a 7.5cm/3in pastry (cookie) cutter. Place a large spoonful of the beef mixture in the centre of each pastry round. Brush the edges of the pastry with the beaten egg and fold each round in half to enclose the filling. Press and crimp the edges with the tines of a fork to seal.

4 Fill a wok one-third full of oil and heat to 180°C/350°F (or until a cube of bread, dropped into the oil, browns in 15 seconds).

5 Deep-fry the puffs, in batches, for 2–3 minutes until golden brown. Drain on kitchen paper and serve garnished with fresh coriander leaves. Offer tomato ketchup for dipping.

Indonesian Spicy Burgers

The coconut used in these burgers, which may seem an unusual ingredient, gives them a rich and succulent flavour. They taste wonderful accompanied by a sharp yet sweet mango chutney and can be eaten in mini naan or pitta breads.

Serves 8

500g/1 1/4lb/2 1/2 cups minced
    (ground) beef
5ml/1 tsp anchovy paste
10ml/2 tsp tomato purée (paste)
10ml/2 tsp ground coriander
5ml/1 tsp ground cumin
7.5ml/1 1/2 tsp finely grated fresh
    root ginger
2 garlic cloves, crushed
1 egg white
75g/3oz solid creamed coconut or
    40g/1 1/2oz desiccated (dry
    unsweetened shredded)
    coconut
45ml/3 tbsp chopped fresh
    coriander (cilantro)
salt and ground black pepper
8 fresh vine leaves (optional), to
    serve
mango chutney and mini naan or
    pitta breads, to serve

1 Mix the minced beef, anchovy paste, tomato purée, coriander, cumin, ginger and garlic in a bowl. Add the egg white, with salt and pepper to taste. Using your hands, mix well.

2 Grate the block of coconut and work it gently into the meat mixture so that it doesn't melt, with the fresh coriander. Form the mixture into eight burgers, about 7.5cm/3in in diameter. Chill for 30 minutes.

3 Prepare the barbecue. Once the flames have died down, rake the hot coals to one side and insert a drip tray flat beside them. Position a lightly oiled grill rack over the coals to heat.

4 When the coals are medium-hot, or with a moderate coating of ash, place the chilled burgers on the rack over the drip tray. Cook for 10–15 minutes, turning them over once or twice. Check that they are cooked by breaking off a piece of one of the burgers.

5 If you are using vine leaves, wash them and pat dry with kitchen paper. Wrap one around each burger. Serve with mango chutney and mini naan or pitta breads.

Indonesian Spicy Burgers: Energy 177kcal/734kJ; Protein 13.4g; Carbohydrate 0.8g, of which sugars 0.7g; Fat 13.4g, of which saturates 7g; Cholesterol 38mg; Calcium 22mg; Fibre 1.1g; Sodium 90mg.
Spiced Beef and Potato Puffs: Energy 408kcal/1695kJ; Protein 9g; Carbohydrate 24.2g, of which sugars 1.8g; Fat 31.8g, of which saturates 4.2g; Cholesterol 67mg; Calcium 46mg; Fibre 0.5g; Sodium 202mg.

Lettuce-wrapped Lamb with Cumin

In this tasty appetizer, lamb is stir-fried with garlic, ginger and spices, then served in crisp lettuce leaves with yogurt, a dab of lime pickle and mint leaves – the contrast of hot and spicy with cool and crisp is excellent and appetizing.

Serves 4

450g/1lb lamb neck fillet
2.5ml/½ tsp chilli powder
10ml/2 tsp ground coriander
5ml/1 tsp ground cumin
2.5ml/½ tsp ground turmeric
30ml/2 tbsp groundnut oil
3–4 garlic cloves, chopped
15ml/1 tbsp grated fresh root ginger
150ml/¼ pint/⅔ cup lamb stock or water
4–6 spring onions (scallions), sliced
30ml/2 tbsp chopped fresh coriander (cilantro)
15ml/1 tbsp lemon juice
lettuce leaves, yogurt, lime pickle and mint leaves, to serve

1 Trim the lamb fillet of any fat and cut into small pieces, then mince (grind) in a blender or food processor, taking care not to over-process.

2 In a bowl mix together the chilli powder, ground coriander, cumin and turmeric. Add the lamb and rub the spice mixture into the meat. Cover and leave to marinate for about 1 hour.

3 Heat a wok until hot. Add the oil and swirl it around. When hot, add the garlic and ginger and allow to sizzle for a few seconds.

4 Add the lamb and continue to stir-fry for 2–3 minutes. Pour in the stock and cook until all the stock has been absorbed and the lamb is tender, adding more stock if necessary.

5 Add the spring onions, fresh coriander and lemon juice, then stir-fry for a further 30–45 seconds. Serve at once with the lettuce leaves, yogurt, pickle and mint leaves.

> **Variation**
> Vegetables, such as cooked diced potatoes or peas, can be added to the mince.

Cardamom and Cinnamon-spiced Lamb Kebabs

Lean pieces of turkey, chicken, beef and veal can all be cooked in this way. As well as flavouring the meat, the spiced marinade will help to tenderize it and keep it deliciously moist during cooking.

Serves 4–6

800g/1¾lb tender lean lamb, cubed
1.5ml/¼ tsp ground allspice
1.5ml/¼ tsp ground cinnamon
1.5ml/¼ tsp ground black pepper
1.5ml/¼ tsp ground cardamom
45–60ml/3–4 tbsp chopped fresh parsley
2 onions, chopped
5–8 garlic cloves, chopped
juice of ½ lemon or 45ml/3 tbsp dry white wine
45ml/3 tbsp extra virgin olive oil
sumac, for sprinkling (optional)
30ml/2 tbsp pine nuts
salt
flat breads, such as pitta bread, tortillas or naan bread, tahini, and crunchy vegetable salad, to serve

1 Put the lamb, allspice, cinnamon, black pepper, cardamom, half the parsley, half the onions, the garlic, lemon juice or wine and olive oil in a bowl and mix together. Season with salt now, if you prefer, or sprinkle on after cooking. Set aside and leave to marinate for several hours or overnight in the refrigerator.

2 Meanwhile, light the barbecue and leave for about 40 minutes. When the coals are white and grey, the barbecue is ready for cooking. If using wooden skewers, soak them in water for about 30 minutes to prevent them from burning.

3 Thread the cubes of meat on to wooden or metal skewers, then cook on the barbecue for 2–3 minutes on each side, turning occasionally, until cooked evenly and browned.

4 Transfer the kebabs to a serving dish and sprinkle with the reserved onions, parsley, sumac, if using, pine nuts and salt, if you like. Serve with warmed flat breads to wrap the kebabs in, together with a bowl of tahini for drizzling over and a crunchy vegetable salad.

Lamb with Cumin: Energy 266kcal/1107kJ; Protein 22.9g; Carbohydrate 1.8g, of which sugars 0.5g; Fat 18.7g, of which saturates 6.7g; Cholesterol 86mg; Calcium 23mg; Fibre 0.3g; Sodium 99mg.
Cardamom and Lamb Kebabs: Energy 339kcal/1409kJ; Protein 22.6g; Carbohydrate 2.7g, of which sugars 2.4g; Fat 26.5g, of which saturates 7.9g; Cholesterol 86mg; Calcium 16mg; Fibre 0.7g; Sodium 102mg.

Lamb's Liver with Paprika

This is such a delicious way to eat lamb's liver that it is even possible to convert those who don't usually like it. It is a Turkish dish, which was probably adapted from an Albanian recipe as the Ottoman Empire consumed vast expanses of Eastern Europe. Traditionally served as a hot or cold *meze* dish with sliced red onion and flat leaf parsley, the spiced liver also makes a wonderful dish for supper, served with a salad and a dollop of creamy yogurt if you like.

Serves 4
500g/1¼lb fresh lamb's liver
30ml/2 tbsp plain (all-purpose) flour
5–10ml/1–2 tsp paprika
45–60ml/3–4 tbsp olive oil
2 garlic cloves, finely chopped
5–10ml/1–2 tsp cumin seeds
sea salt
1 large red onion, cut in half lengthways, in half again crossways, and sliced along the grain
a handful of fresh flat leaf parsley, 1 lemon, cut into wedges, to serve

1 Place the liver on a chopping board. Using a sharp knife, remove any skin and ducts, then cut the liver into thin strips or bitesize cubes.

2 Mix the flour with the paprika in a shallow bowl and toss the liver in it until well coated.

3 Heat the oil in a heavy pan. Add the garlic and cumin seeds, season with sea salt and cook until the cumin gives off a nutty aroma. Toss in the liver and stir-fry quickly for 2–3 minutes so that it cooks on all sides. Remove and drain on kitchen paper.

4 Spread the sliced onion on a serving dish, spoon the liver in the middle and garnish with parsley leaves. Serve hot or cold, with the lemon wedges for squeezing.

> **Cook's Tip**
> *Don't overcook the liver or it will become tough: the pieces should still be slightly pink inside.*

Meatballs with Pine Nuts and Cinnamon

Turkish meatballs, known as kofte, are generally made from lamb or beef, although some contain chicken, and they are shaped into round balls or plump ovals. For a great snack, tuck the cooked meatballs into toasted pittas along with sliced red onion, and a spoonful of yogurt.

Serves 4–6
250g/9oz/generous 1 cup lean minced (ground) lamb
1 onion, finely chopped
2 garlic cloves, crushed
10–15ml/2–3 tsp ground cinnamon
30ml/2 tbsp pine nuts
30ml/2 tbsp currants, soaked in warm water for 5–10 minutes and drained
5ml/1 tsp paprika
2 slices of day-old white or brown bread, crusts removed, ground into crumbs
1 egg, lightly beaten
15ml/1 tbsp tomato ketchup
1 bunch each of fresh flat leaf parsley and dill
60ml/4 tbsp plain (all-purpose) flour
sunflower oil, for shallow frying
salt and ground black pepper
lemon wedges, to serve

1 In a bowl, pound the lamb with the onion, garlic and cinnamon. Knead the mixture with your hands in order to knock out the air, then add the pine nuts with the currants, paprika, breadcrumbs, egg and ketchup. Season with salt and black pepper.

2 Finely chop the herbs, reserving 1–2 sprigs of parsley for the garnish, and knead into the mixture, making sure all the ingredients are mixed well together.

3 Take apricot-sized portions of the mixture in your hands and roll into balls. Flatten each ball so that it resembles a thick disc, then coat lightly in the flour.

4 Heat a thin layer of oil in a heavy pan. Add the meatballs and cook for 8–10 minutes, until browned on all sides. Remove with a slotted spoon and drain on kitchen paper. Serve hot with lemon wedges and garnish with parsley.

Lamb's Liver with Paprika: Energy 298kcal/1245kJ; Protein 27g; Carbohydrate 11.8g, of which sugars 4.3g; Fat 16.3g, of which saturates 3.3g; Cholesterol 538mg; Calcium 37mg; Fibre 1.3g; Sodium 94mg.
Meatballs with Pine Nuts: Energy 261kcal/1088kJ; Protein 11.4g; Carbohydrate 15.4g, of which sugars 5.2g; Fat 17.5g, of which saturates 4g; Cholesterol 64mg; Calcium 40mg; Fibre 0.7g; Sodium 129mg.

Fragrant Spiced Lamb on Mini Poppadums

Crisp, melt-in-the-mouth mini poppadums make a great base for these divine little bites. Top them with a drizzle of yogurt and a spoonful of mango chutney, then serve immediately. To make an equally tasty variation, you can use chicken or pork in place of the lamb.

Makes 25

30ml/2 tbsp sunflower oil
4 shallots, finely chopped
30ml/2 tbsp medium curry paste
300g/11oz minced (ground) lamb
90ml/6 tbsp tomato purée (paste)
5ml/1 tsp caster (superfine) sugar
200ml/7fl oz/scant 1 cup coconut cream
juice of 1 lime
60ml/4 tbsp chopped fresh mint leaves
25 mini poppadums
vegetable oil, for frying
salt and ground black pepper
natural (plain) yogurt and mango chutney, to drizzle
red chilli slivers and mint leaves, to garnish

1 Heat the oil in a wok over a medium heat and add the shallots. Stir fry for 4–5 minutes, until softened, then add the curry paste. Stir-fry for 1–2 minutes.

2 Add the lamb and stir-fry over a high heat for 4–5 minutes, then stir in the tomato purée, sugar and coconut cream.

3 Cook the lamb over a gentle heat for 25–30 minutes, or until the meat is tender and all the liquid has been absorbed. Season and stir in the lime juice and mint leaves. Remove from the heat and keep warm.

4 Fill a separate wok one-third full of oil and deep-fry the mini poppadums for 30–40 seconds, until puffed up and crisp. Drain on kitchen paper.

5 Place the poppadums on a serving platter. Put a spoonful of spiced lamb on each one, then top with a little yogurt and mango chutney. Serve immediately, garnished with slivers of red chilli and mint leaves.

Andalusian Mini Kebabs with Spices

The Moors introduced both skewers and the idea of marinating meat to Spain. These little yellow kebabs are a favourite in Andalusia, where many butchers sell the meat ready marinated. The Arab versions used lamb, but pork is used now, because the spicing suits it so perfectly.

Serves 4

2.5ml/½ tsp cumin seeds
2.5ml/½ tsp coriander seeds
2 garlic cloves, finely chopped
5ml/1 tsp paprika
2.5ml/½ tsp dried oregano
15ml/1 tbsp lemon juice
45ml/3 tbsp olive oil
500g/1¼ lb lean cubed pork
salt and ground black pepper

1 Starting a couple of hours in advance, grind the cumin and coriander seeds in a mortar and work in the garlic with a pinch of salt. Add the paprika and oregano and mix in the lemon juice. Stir in the olive oil.

2 Cut the pork into small cubes, then skewer them, three or four at a time, on to cocktail sticks (toothpicks).

3 Put the skewered meat in a shallow dish, and pour over the marinade. Spoon the marinade back over the meat to ensure it is well coated. Leave to marinate in a cool place for 2 hours.

4 Preheat the grill (broiler) to high, and line the grill pan with foil. Spread the kebabs out in a row and place them under the grill, close to the heat. Cook for about 3 minutes on each side, spooning the juices over when you turn them, until the meat is cooked through. Sprinkle with a little salt and pepper, and serve at once.

Cook's Tip
Leaving the meat in a marinade allows the flavours of the spices to penetrate and also results in tender, juicier meat. If it is convenient, you can assemble the kebabs and put them into the marinade earlier in the day, or the day before you need to cook them.

Fragrant Spiced Lamb on Poppadums: Energy 63kcal/260kJ; Protein 2.7g; Carbohydrate 2.7g, of which sugars 1.3g; Fat 4.7g, of which saturates 1.4g; Cholesterol 9mg; Calcium 7mg; Fibre 0.3g; Sodium 45mg.
Mini Kebabs with Spices: Energy 189kcal/793kJ; Protein 30.4g; Carbohydrate 0.8g, of which sugars 0.1g; Fat 7.2g, of which saturates 1.2g; Cholesterol 88mg; Calcium 17mg; Fibre 0.2g; Sodium 77mg.

Five-spice and Ginger Pork Wontons

Fresh ginger and Chinese five-spice powder flavour this version of steamed open dumplings – a favourite snack in many Chinese teahouses.

Makes 36

2 large Chinese cabbage leaves, plus extra for lining the steamer
2 spring onions (scallions), finely chopped
1cm/½in piece fresh root ginger, finely chopped
50g/2oz canned water chestnuts (drained weight), rinsed and finely chopped
225g/8oz minced (ground) pork
2.5ml/½ tsp Chinese five-spice powder
15ml/1 tbsp cornflour (cornstarch)
15ml/1 tbsp light soy sauce
15ml/1 tbsp Chinese rice wine
10ml/2 tsp sesame oil
pinch of caster (superfine) sugar
about 36 wonton wrappers, each 7.5cm/3in square
light soy sauce and hot chilli oil, for dipping

1 Place the Chinese cabbage leaves one on top of another. Cut them lengthways into quarters and then across into thin shreds.

2 Place the shredded Chinese cabbage leaves in a bowl. Mix in the spring onions, ginger, water chestnuts, pork, five-spice powder, cornflour, soy sauce, rice wine, sesame oil and sugar.

3 Set one wonton wrapper on a work surface. Place a heaped teaspoon of the filling in the centre of the wrapper, then lightly dampen the edges with water.

4 Lift the wrapper up around the filling, gathering to form a purse. Squeeze the wrapper firmly around the middle, then tap on the bottom to make a flat base. The top should be open. Place the wonton on a tray and cover with a damp dish towel.

5 Line the steamer with cabbage leaves and steam the dumplings for 12–15 minutes until tender. Remove each batch from the steamer as soon as they are cooked, cover with foil and keep warm. Serve the dumplings hot with soy sauce and chilli oil for dipping.

Spiced Pork Pâté

This pâté has a Vietnamese twist: it is steamed in banana leaves, which are available in African and Asian markets. However, if you cannot find them you can use large spring green (collard) leaves or several Savoy cabbage leaves instead.

Serves 6

45ml/3 tbsp nuoc mam
30ml/2 tbsp sesame oil
15ml/1 tbsp sugar
10ml/2 tsp five-spice powder
2 shallots, peeled and finely chopped
2 garlic cloves, crushed
750g/1lb 10oz/3¼ cups minced (ground) pork
25g/1oz/¼ cup potato starch
7.5ml/1½ tsp baking powder
1 banana leaf, trimmed into a strip 25cm/10in wide
vegetable oil, for brushing
salt and ground black pepper
nuoc cham and a baguette or salad, to serve

1 In a bowl, beat the nuoc mam and oil with the sugar and five-spice powder. Once the sugar has dissolved, stir in the shallots and garlic. Add the pork and seasoning, and knead well until thoroughly combined. Cover and chill for 2–3 hours.

2 Knead the mixture again, thumping it down into the bowl to remove any air. Add the potato starch and baking powder and knead until smooth and pasty. Mould the pork mixture into a fat sausage, about 18cm/7in long, and place it on an oiled dish.

3 Lay the banana leaf on a flat surface, brush it with a little vegetable oil, and place the pork sausage across it. Lift up the edge of the banana leaf nearest to you and fold it over the sausage mixture, tuck in the sides, and roll it up into a firm, tight bundle. Secure the bundle with a piece of string, so that it doesn't unravel during cooking.

4 Fill a wok one-third full with water. Balance a bamboo steamer, with its lid on, above the level of the water. Bring to the boil, lift the lid and place the banana leaf bundle on the rack, being careful not to burn yourself. Re-cover and steam for 45 minutes. Leave the pâté to cool in the leaf, then open it up and cut it into slices. Drizzle with nuoc cham, and serve with a baguette or salad.

Five Spice and Ginger Pork Wontons: Energy 23kcal/96kJ; Protein 1.8g; Carbohydrate 2.9g, of which sugars 0.4g; Fat 0.5g, of which saturates 0.1g; Cholesterol 4mg; Calcium 9mg; Fibre 0.2g; Sodium 35mg.
Spiced Pork Pâté: Energy 234kcal/978kJ; Protein 28g; Carbohydrate 8g, of which sugars 3g; Fat 10g, of which saturates 2g; Cholesterol 79mg; Calcium 46mg; Fibre 0.4g; Sodium 700mg

Chinese Spare Ribs with Spiced Salt

Fragrant with spices, this authentic Chinese dish makes a great starter to an informal meal.

Serves 4

675–900g/1½–2lb meaty pork spare ribs
25ml/1½ tbsp cornflour (cornstarch)
groundnut oil, for deep-frying
coriander (cilantro) sprigs, to garnish

For the spiced salt

5ml/1 tsp Szechuan peppercorns
30ml/2 tbsp coarse sea salt
2.5ml/½ tsp Chinese five-spice powder

For the marinade

30ml/2 tbsp light soy sauce
5ml/1 tsp caster (superfine) sugar
15ml/1 tbsp Chinese rice wine or sherry
ground black pepper

1 Using a heavy sharp cleaver, chop the spare ribs into pieces about 5cm/2in long (or ask your butcher to do this), then place them in a shallow dish.

2 To make the spiced salt, heat a wok to a medium heat. Add the Szechuan peppercorns and salt and dry fry for about 3 minutes, stirring constantly until the mixture colours slightly. Remove from the heat and stir in the five-spice powder. Leave to cool. Using a mortar and pestle grind to a fine powder.

3 Sprinkle 5ml/1 tsp of the spiced salt over the spare ribs and rub in well with your hands. Add the soy sauce, sugar, rice wine or sherry and some ground black pepper, then toss the ribs in the marinade until well coated. Cover and leave to marinate in the refrigerator for about 2 hours, turning occasionally.

4 Pour off any excess marinade. Sprinkle the spare ribs with cornflour and mix well to coat evenly. Half-fill a wok with oil and heat to 180°C/350°F. Deep-fry the spare ribs in batches for 3 minutes until pale golden. Remove and set aside. Reheat the oil to the same temperature. Return the spare ribs to the oil and deep-fry for a second time for 1–2 minutes until crisp and thoroughly cooked. Drain on kitchen paper. Transfer the ribs to a serving plate and sprinkle over 5–7.5ml/1–1½ tsp spiced salt. Garnish with coriander sprigs.

Paprika-spiced Black Pudding Crostini

Spanish morcilla – a version of black pudding – is flavoured with spices and herbs, usually including garlic and oregano, and has a wonderfully rich taste.

Serves 4

15ml/1 tbsp olive oil
1 onion, thinly sliced
2 garlic cloves, thinly sliced

5ml/1 tsp dried oregano
5ml/1 tsp paprika
225g/8oz black pudding (blood sausage), cut into 12 thick slices
1 thin French stick, cut into 12 rounds
30ml/2 tbsp fino sherry
sugar, to taste
salt and ground black pepper
chopped fresh oregano, to garnish

1 Heat the olive oil in a large frying pan and fry the sliced onion, garlic, oregano and paprika for 7–8 minutes until the onion is softened and has turned golden brown.

2 Add the slices of black pudding, then increase the heat and cook them for 3 minutes, without stirring. Turn the slices over carefully with a spatula and cook on the other side for a further 3 minutes until crisp.

3 Arrange the rounds of bread on a large serving plate and top each with a slice of black pudding. Stir the sherry into the onions and add a little sugar to taste. Heat, swirling the mixture around the pan until it is bubbling, then season with salt and black pepper.

4 Spoon a little of the onion mixture on top of each slice of black pudding. Sprinkle the oregano over and serve.

> **Cook's Tip**
> If you are able to find real morcilla, serve it neat to make the most of its subtle flavour: simply fry the slices in olive oil and use to top little rounds of bread. If you cannot find black pudding, you can use red chorizo instead.

Spare Ribs with Spiced Salt: Energy 424kcal/1763kJ; Protein 32.2g; Carbohydrate 2.6g, of which sugars 1.3g; Fat 31.4g, of which saturates 9.8g; Cholesterol 111mg; Calcium 33mg; Fibre 0g; Sodium 345mg.
Black Pudding Crostini: Energy 538kcal/2268kJ; Protein 17.4g; Carbohydrate 81.2g, of which sugars 6.4g; Fat 17.4g, of which saturates 5.6g; Cholesterol 38mg; Calcium 228mg; Fibre 3.7g; Sodium 1271mg.

Moroccan-spiced Sautéed Chicken Livers

Sautéed offal, such as liver and kidney, is quick and easy to cook and its strong, assertive flavour makes it ideal as an appetizer. It can be cooked simply in olive oil and garlic and served with lemon to squeeze over, or given a more elaborate treatment, as in this dish of spiced chicken livers. This makes a delicious, tangy appetizer, whether you serve the pieces of liver scattered over a plate of mixed salad leaves, or spooned on thin slices of toasted bread.

Serves 4
30–45ml/2–3 tbsp olive oil
2–3 garlic cloves, chopped
1 dried red chilli, chopped
5ml/1 tsp cumin seeds
450g/1lb chicken livers, trimmed and cut into bitesize chunks
5ml/1 tsp ground coriander
handful of roasted hazelnuts, roughly chopped
10–15ml/2–3 tsp orange flower water
½ preserved lemon, finely sliced or chopped
salt and ground black pepper
small bunch of fresh coriander (cilantro), finely chopped, to serve

1 Heat the olive oil in a heavy frying pan and stir in the garlic, chilli and cumin seeds. Add the chicken livers and toss over the heat until they are browned on all sides. Reduce the heat a little and continue to cook for 3–5 minutes.

2 When the livers are almost cooked, stir in the ground coriander, hazelnuts, orange flower water and preserved lemon.

3 Season to taste with salt and black pepper and serve immediately, sprinkled with a little fresh coriander.

> **Variation**
> Lamb's liver, trimmed and finely sliced, is also good cooked this way. The trick is to sear the outside so that the middle is almost pink and melts in the mouth. If you don't have orange flower water, try a little balsamic vinegar.

Spring Rolls with Chicken and Sweet Spices

These Moroccan-style spring rolls are delicious dipped in cinnamon-spiced ground almonds and sugar.

Serves 6
30ml/2 tbsp plain (all-purpose) flour
about 30ml/2 tbsp water
12 large spring roll wrappers
sunflower oil, for deep-frying

For the filling
1 small chicken
½ onion, finely chopped
3–4 garlic cloves, finely chopped
25g/1oz/2 tbsp butter
1 cinnamon stick
5ml/1 tsp ground ginger
5ml/1 tsp ras el hanout

pinch of saffron threads
small bunch of flat leaf parsley, chopped
small bunch of fresh coriander (cilantro), chopped
6 eggs, beaten
10ml/2 tsp orange flower water
½ lemon
6–8 spring onions (scallions), thickly sliced
salt and ground black pepper

For the dipping mixture
115g/4oz/1 cup blanched almonds, lightly toasted and coarsely ground
30ml/2 tbsp icing (confectioners') sugar
5–10ml/1–2 tsp ground cinnamon

1 To make the filling, place the chicken in a pan with the onion, garlic, butter, cinnamon, ginger, ras el hanout, saffron and half the herbs. Cover with water and simmer for about 1 hour. Lift out the chicken and set aside. Reduce the liquid to 550ml/18fl oz/2½ cups. Remove from the heat and season. Pour the beaten eggs into the hot stock, stirring until the egg has set, then strain. In a bowl, combine the dipping ingredients.

2 Shred the chicken flesh and mix with the cooked eggs and remaining filling ingredients. Mix the flour with the water to form a paste. Sprinkle some almond mixture over each wrapper. Place a tablespoonful of filling in a line 5cm/2in in from one corner then roll up, folding in the sides to enclose the filling. Seal with a little flour paste. Heat the oil to 180°C/350°F and cook the rolls three or four at a time until crisp and golden. Drain and serve immediately with the dipping mixture.

Stir-fried Giblets with Garlic and Ginger

In Vietnam and Cambodia no food is wasted: almost every part of a chicken is used, and there are specific recipes to which each piece is assigned. Apart from being tossed into the stockpot, chicken giblets are often quickly stir-fried with a spicy seasoning of chilli garlic and ginger and served with rice. If you dislike the idea of eating chicken hearts and neck, this dish will work very well using just livers, which are easily available fresh or frozen from butchers and supermarkets.

Serves 2–4

30ml/2 tbsp groundnut (peanut) oil

2 shallots, halved and finely sliced

2 garlic cloves, finely chopped

I Thai chilli, seeded and finely sliced

25g/1oz fresh root ginger, peeled and shredded

225g/8oz chicken livers, trimmed and finely sliced

115g/4oz mixed giblets, finely sliced

15–30ml/1–2 tbsp nuoc mam

I small bunch coriander (cilantro), finely chopped

ground black pepper

steamed rice, to serve

I Heat the oil in a wok or heavy pan. Stir in the shallots, garlic, chilli and ginger, and stir-fry until golden. Add the chicken livers and mixed giblets and stir-fry for a few minutes more, until browned.

2 Stir in the *nuoc mam*, adjusting the quantity according to taste, and half the chopped coriander. Season with ground black pepper and garnish with the rest of the coriander. Serve hot, with steamed fragrant rice.

Cook's Tip
Nuoc mam *is the Vietnamese version of fish sauce, a salty, pungent liquid made from fermented anchovies or other fish, which is an essential condiment in the cooking of the whole region of South-east Asia. It is used both as a seasoning and as a dipping sauce, normally mixed with other ingredients.*

Turkey, Juniper and Green Peppercorn Terrine

This is an ideal dish for entertaining, as it can be made in advance. If you prefer, arrange some of the pancetta and pistachios as a layer in the middle.

Serves 10–12

225g/8oz chicken livers, trimmed

450g/1lb minced (ground) turkey

450g/1lb minced (ground) pork

225g/8oz pancetta, cubed

50g/2oz/1/2 cup shelled pistachio nuts, roughly chopped

5ml/1 tsp salt

2.5ml/1/2 tsp ground mace

2 garlic cloves, crushed

5ml/1 tsp drained green peppercorns in brine

5ml/1 tsp juniper berries

120ml/4fl oz/1/2 cup dry white wine

30ml/2 tbsp gin

finely grated rind of I orange

8 large vacuum-packed vine leaves in brine

oil, for greasing

spicy chutney, to serve

I Chop the chicken livers finely. Put them in a bowl and mix in the turkey, pork, pancetta, pistachio nuts, salt, mace and garlic.

2 Lightly crush the peppercorns and juniper berries and add them to the mixture. Stir in the white wine, gin and orange rind. Cover and chill overnight to allow the flavours to mingle.

3 Preheat the oven to 160°C/325°F/Gas 3. Rinse the vine leaves under cold running water. Drain and pat dry. Lightly oil a 1.2 litre/2 pint/5 cup loaf tin (pan). Line the tin with the leaves, letting the ends hang over the sides. Pack the mixture into the tin and fold the leaves over to enclose the filling. Brush lightly with oil.

4 Cover the terrine with foil. Place it in a roasting pan and pour in boiling water to come halfway up the sides of the terrine. Bake for 1¾ hours, checking the level of the water occasionally.

5 Leave the terrine to cool, then pour off the surface juices. Cover with clear film (plastic wrap), then with foil and place weights on top. Chill overnight. Serve at room temperature with spicy chutney.

Chicken Satay with Cashew Sambal

Pandanus leaves are frequently used in South-east Asian cooking, in both savoury and sweet dishes. They are very versatile, and in this recipe they give the chicken a delicate flavour.

Serves 6

about 1kg/2¼lb skinless chicken breast fillets
30ml/2 tbsp olive oil
5ml/1 tsp ground coriander
2.5ml/½ tsp ground cumin
2.5cm/1in piece fresh root ginger, finely grated
2 garlic cloves, crushed
5ml/1 tsp caster (superfine) sugar

2.5ml/½ tsp salt
18 long pandanus leaves, each halved to give 20cm/8in lengths
36 long bamboo or wooden skewers

For the hot cashew nut sambal
2 garlic cloves, roughly chopped
4 small fresh hot green chillies (not tiny birdseye chillies), seeded and sliced
50g/2oz/⅓ cup cashew nuts
10ml/2 tsp sugar, preferably palm sugar (jaggery)
75ml/5 tbsp light soy sauce
juice of ½ lime
30ml/2 tbsp coconut cream

1 To make the sambal, place the garlic and chillies in a mortar and grind them quite finely with a pestle. Add the nuts and continue to grind until the mixture is almost smooth, with just a bit of texture. Pound in the remaining ingredients, cover and leave in a cool place until needed.

2 Soak the skewers in water for 30 minutes. Slice the chicken horizontally into thin pieces and then into strips about 2.5cm/1in wide. Toss in the oil. Mix the coriander, cumin, ginger, garlic, sugar and salt together. Rub this mixture into the strips of chicken. Leave to marinate while you prepare the barbecue.

3 Thread a strip of pandanus leaf and a piece of chicken lengthways on to each skewer. Position a lightly oiled grill rack over the coals to heat.

4 Cook over medium-hot coals, meat-side down, covered with a lid or tented heavy-duty foil for 5–7 minutes. Once the meat has seared, move the satays around so that the leaves don't scorch. Serve, hot, with the sambal.

Caramelized Chicken Wings with Fresh Ginger

Cooked in a wok or in the oven, these caramelized wings are drizzled with chilli oil and eaten with the fingers, so that every bit of tender meat can be gnawed off the bone. Variations of this recipe can be found throughout Vietnam and Cambodia, often served with rice and pickles.

Serves 2–4

75ml/5 tbsp sugar
30ml/2 tbsp groundnut (peanut) oil
25g/1oz fresh root ginger, peeled and finely shredded or grated
12 chicken wings, split in two
chilli oil, for drizzling
mixed pickled vegetables, to serve

1 To make the caramel sauce, gently heat the sugar with 60ml/4 tbsp water in a small, heavy pan until it turns golden. Set aside.

2 Heat the oil in a wok or heavy pan. Add the ginger and stir-fry until fragrant. Add the chicken wings and toss them around the wok to brown.

3 Pour in the caramel sauce and make sure the chicken wings are thoroughly coated in it. Reduce the heat, cover the wok or pan, and cook for about 30 minutes, until the chicken is tender, and the sauce has caramelized.

4 Drizzle chilli oil over the wings and serve from the wok or pan with mixed pickled vegetables.

> **Cook's Tip**
> For the pickled vegetables, cut a large carrot and a piece of mooli (daikon) of about the same size into matchsticks. Sprinkle with salt and leave for 30 minutes. Heat 50ml/2fl oz/ ¼ cup rice vinegar with 100ml/3½fl oz/½ cup water and 15ml/1 tbsp sugar until dissolved and leave to cool. Mix in the rinsed vegetables and marinate for up to 24 hours.

Spiced Sweet Potato Turnovers

The subtle sweetness of the potatoes makes a great filling when flavoured with a selection of light spices.

Serves 4

1 sweet potato, about 225g/8oz
30ml/2 tbsp vegetable oil
2 shallots, finely chopped
10ml/2 tsp coriander seeds, crushed
5ml/1 tsp ground cumin
5ml/1 tsp garam masala
115g/4oz/1 cup frozen peas
15ml/1 tbsp chopped fresh mint

salt and ground black pepper
mint sprigs, to garnish

For the pastry

15ml/1 tbsp olive oil
1 small egg
150ml/¼ pint/⅔ cup natural (plain) yogurt
115g/4oz/8 tbsp butter, melted
275g/10oz/2½ cups plain (all-purpose) flour
1.5ml/¼ tsp bicarbonate of soda
10ml/2 tsp paprika
5ml/1 tsp salt
beaten egg, to glaze

1 Cook the sweet potato in boiling salted water for 15–20 minutes, until tender. Drain well and leave to cool. When cool enough to handle, peel the potato and cut into 1cm/½in cubes.

2 Heat the oil in a frying pan, add the shallots and cook until softened. Add the sweet potato and fry until it browns at the edges. Add the spices and fry, for a few seconds. Remove from the heat and add the peas, mint and seasoning. Leave to cool.

3 Preheat the oven to 200°C/400°F/Gas 6. Grease a baking sheet. To make the pastry, whisk together the oil and egg, stir in the yogurt, then add the melted butter. Sift the flour, bicarbonate of soda, paprika and salt into a bowl, then stir into the yogurt mixture to form a soft dough. Turn out the dough, and knead gently. Roll it out, then stamp it out into rounds.

4 Spoon about 10ml/2 tsp of the filling on to one side of each round, then fold over and seal the edges. Re-roll the trimmings and stamp out more rounds until the filling is used up.

5 Arrange the turnovers on the prepared baking sheet and brush the tops with beaten egg. Bake in the oven for about 20 minutes until crisp and golden brown. Serve hot with mint.

Falafel

The secret to making good falafel is to use well-soaked, but not cooked, chickpeas. Do not try to use canned chickpeas for this recipe, as the texture will be mushy and the finished falafel will fall apart.

Serves 6

250g/9oz/generous 1⅓ cups dried chickpeas
1 litre/1¾ pints/4 cups water
45–60ml/3–4 tbsp bulgur wheat
1 large onion, finely chopped
5 garlic cloves, crushed
75ml/5 tbsp chopped fresh parsley

75ml/5 tbsp chopped fresh coriander (cilantro) leaves
45ml/3 tbsp ground cumin
15ml/1 tbsp ground coriander
5ml/1 tsp baking powder
5ml/1 tsp salt
small pinch to 1.5ml/¼ tsp ground black pepper
small pinch to 1.5ml/¼ tsp cayenne pepper
5ml/1 tsp curry powder with a pinch of cardamom seeds
45–60ml/3–4 tbsp gram flour
extra flour, if necessary
vegetable oil, for deep-frying
6 pitta breads, hummus, tahini, chilli sauce, pickles, olives and salads, to serve

1 Place the chickpeas in a large bowl and pour over the water. Leave to soak for 4 hours, drain and grind in a food processor.

2 Put the ground chickpeas in a bowl and stir in the bulgur wheat, onion, garlic, parsley, fresh coriander, ground cumin and coriander, baking powder, salt, black pepper and cayenne pepper, and curry powder, if using. Stir in 45ml/3 tbsp water and leave to stand for about 45 minutes.

3 Stir the gram flour into the falafel batter, adding a little water if it is too thick or a little flour if it is too thin. Using a wet tablespoon and wet hands, shape the mixture into 12–18 balls.

4 In a deep pan or wok, heat the oil for deep-frying to 180°C/350°F. Add the falafel in batches and cook for 3–4 minutes until golden brown.

5 Serve tucked into warmed pitta bread with a spoonful of hummus and a drizzle of tahini. Accompany with chilli sauce, pickles, olives and some salads.

Sweet Potato Turnovers: Energy 660kcal/2760kJ; Protein 13.9g; Carbohydrate 75.8g, of which sugars 9.3g; Fat 35.9g, of which saturates 17g; Cholesterol 105mg; Calcium 216mg; Fibre 5.2g; Sodium 740mg.
Falafel: Energy 303kcal/1282kJ; Protein 18.5g; Carbohydrate 44.7g, of which sugars 5.2g; Fat 6.9g, of which saturates 1.2g; Cholesterol 0mg; Calcium 88mg; Fibre 7.2g; Sodium 16mg.

Deep-fried Sweet Potato and Fresh Ginger Rösti Cakes

This dish is a speciality of Hanoi in Vietnam, where the street sellers are well known for their varied recipes, which are all delicious. Traditionally, the patties are served with herbs and lettuce leaves for wrapping.

Serves 4
50g/2oz/¹/₂ cup plain
   (all-purpose) flour
50g/2oz/¹/₂ cup rice flour
4ml/scant 1 tsp baking powder

10ml/2 tsp sugar
2.5cm/1in fresh root ginger,
   peeled and grated
2 spring onions (scallions), finely
   sliced
1 slim sweet potato, about
   225g/8oz, peeled and cut into
   fine matchsticks
vegetable oil, for deep-frying
salt and ground black pepper
chopped fresh coriander (cilantro),
   to garnish
lettuce leaves and nuoc cham or
   other dipping sauce, to serve

1 Sift the plain and rice flour and baking powder into a bowl. Add the sugar and about 2.5ml/¹/₂ tsp each of salt and pepper. Gradually stir 250ml/8fl oz/1 cup water into the mixture, until thoroughly combined.

2 Add the grated ginger and sliced spring onions to the batter and leave to stand for 30 minutes for the flavours to develop. Add extra ginger if you like a strong flavour.

3 Add the sweet potato matchsticks to the batter and fold them in, making sure they are well coated. Heat enough oil for deep-frying in a wok.

4 Lower a heaped tablespoon of the mixture into the oil, pushing it off the spoon so that it floats in the oil. Fry for 2–3 minutes, turning it over so that it is evenly browned. Drain on kitchen paper. Continue with the rest of the batter.

5 Arrange the patties on lettuce leaves, garnish with coriander, and serve immediately with nuoc cham or another dipping sauce of your choice.

Spiced Chickpea Rissoles Coated with Sesame Seeds

Sesame seeds are used to give a crunchy coating to these spicy patties. Serve with the tahini yogurt dip and warm pitta bread as a light lunch or supper dish.

Serves 4
250g/9oz/1¹/₃ cups dried
   chickpeas
2 garlic cloves, crushed
1 red chilli, seeded and sliced
5ml/1 tsp ground coriander
5ml/1 tsp ground cumin
15ml/1 tbsp chopped fresh mint
15ml/1 tbsp chopped fresh
   parsley

2 spring onions (scallions), finely
   chopped
1 large egg, beaten
sesame seeds, for coating
sunflower oil, for frying
salt and ground black pepper

For the tahini yogurt dip
30ml/2 tbsp light tahini
200g/7oz/scant 1 cup natural
   (plain) yogurt
5ml/1 tsp cayenne pepper, plus
   extra for sprinkling
15ml/1 tbsp chopped fresh mint
1 spring onion (scallion), finely
   sliced

1 Place the chickpeas in a bowl, cover with cold water and leave to soak overnight. Drain and rinse the chickpeas, then place in a pan and cover with cold water. Bring to the boil and boil rapidly for 10 minutes, then reduce the heat and simmer for 1¹/₂–2 hours until tender.

2 Meanwhile, make the tahini yogurt dip. Mix together the tahini, yogurt, cayenne pepper and mint in a small bowl. Sprinkle with the spring onion, extra cayenne pepper and mint and chill.

3 Combine the chickpeas with the garlic, chilli, ground spices, herbs, spring onions and seasoning, then mix in the egg. Place in a food processor and blend until the mixture forms a coarse paste. If the paste seems too soft, chill it for 30 minutes.

4 Form the chilled chickpea paste into 12 patties with your hands, then roll each one in the sesame seeds to coat. Heat enough oil to cover the base of a large frying pan. Fry the rissoles, in batches if necessary, for 6 minutes, turning once.

Chickpea Rissoles: Energy 552kcal/2312kJ; Protein 21.3g; Carbohydrate 63.7g, of which sugars 8.2g; Fat 25.3g, of which saturates 3.6g; Cholesterol 48mg; Calcium 234mg; Fibre 10.8g; Sodium 95mg.
Sweet Potato and Ginger Rösti: Energy 276kcal/1159kJ; Protein 11g; Carbohydrate 35g, of which sugars 6g; Fat 11g, of which saturates 1g; Cholesterol 85mg; Calcium 83mg; Fibre 81g; Sodium 200mg.

Spinach and Nutmeg Spring Rolls

In Morocco, these little savoury pastries may be filled with minced lamb or beef, cheese with herbs, or, as in this recipe, spinach fragrant with freshly grated nutmeg. Easy to make, they are always shaped into cigars or triangles. The filling can be prepared ahead of time but the pastry should not be unwrapped until you are ready to make the pastries, otherwise it will dry out.

Makes 32
8 sheets of ouarka *or*
filo pastry
sunflower oil, for deep-frying

For the spinach filling
50g/2oz/¼ cup butter
1 onion, finely chopped
275g/10oz fresh spinach, cooked,
drained and chopped
small bunch of fresh coriander
(cilantro), finely chopped
pinch of freshly grated
nutmeg
salt and ground black pepper

1 To make the spinach filling, melt the butter in a small heavy pan. Add the chopped onion and cook over a low heat for 15 minutes, stirring occasionally, until softened but not browned. Stir in the spinach and coriander. Season with nutmeg, salt and pepper, then set aside to cool.

2 Lay a sheet of *ouarka* or filo pastry on a work surface, keeping the other sheets covered with a damp cloth or in a plastic bag. Cut the sheet widthways into four strips.

3 Spoon a little of the filling mixture on to the first strip, at the end nearest to you. Fold the corners of the pastry over the mixture to seal it, then roll up the pastry and filling away from you into a tight cigar. As you reach the end of the strip, brush the edges with a little water and continue to roll up the cigar to seal in the filling. Repeat, placing the finished rolls under a damp cloth.

4 Heat the sunflower oil for deep-frying to 180°C/350°F, or until a cube of day-old bread browns in 30 seconds. Add the rolls to the oil in batches and fry over a medium heat until golden brown. Drain on kitchen paper. Serve the rolls while they are still warm.

Cambodian Sweet Potato Cakes

These sweet potato balls from Cambodia are delicious dipped in a fiery sauce, such as *nuoc cham*. Simple to make, they are ideal for serving as nibbles with drinks.

Serves 4
450g/1lb sweet potatoes or taro
root, boiled or baked, and
peeled

30ml/2 tbsp sugar
15ml/1 tbsp Indian curry
powder
25g/1oz fresh root ginger, peeled
and grated
150g/5oz/1¼ cups glutinous
rice flour or plain (all-purpose)
flour
salt
sesame seeds or poppy seeds
vegetable oil, for deep-frying
nuoc cham, to serve

1 In a bowl, mash the cooked sweet potatoes or taro root. Beat in the sugar, curry powder, and ginger. Add the rice flour or plain flour (the latter should be sifted before adding) and salt, and work into a stiff dough – adding more flour if necessary.

2 Pull off lumps of the dough and mould them into small balls using your hands – you should be able to make roughly 24 balls. Roll the balls on a bed of sesame seeds or poppy seeds until they are completely coated.

3 Heat enough oil for deep-frying in a wok. Fry the sweet potato balls in batches, until golden. Drain on kitchen paper. Serve the balls with wooden skewers to make it easier to dip them into the *nuoc cham*.

Cook's Tips
• *Taro root is a staple in South-east Asia. It is used in similar ways to the potato, but has a pronounced nutty taste. The peel can irritate the skin, so it is wise to wear gloves when handling the raw vegetable.*
• *Nuoc cham is a piquant Vietnamese dipping sauce made with chillies, garlic, vinegar and nuoc mam, or Vietnamese fish sauce.*

Spinach and Nutmeg Spring Rolls: Energy 41kcal/171kJ; Protein 0.6g; Carbohydrate 2.8g, of which sugars 0.3g; Fat 3.1g, of which saturates 1g; Cholesterol 3mg; Calcium 23mg; Fibre 0.4g; Sodium 22mg.
Cambodian Sweet Potato Cakes: Energy 354kcal/1495kJ; Protein 5g; Carbohydrate 61g, of which sugars 14.8g; Fat 11.8g, of which saturates 1.5g; Cholesterol 0mg; Calcium 84mg; Fibre 3.9g; Sodium 50mg.

Curry-spiced Pakoras

These delicious bites make a wonderful snack drizzled with the fragrant chutney.

Makes 25
15ml/1 tbsp sunflower oil
20ml/4 tsp cumin seeds
5ml/1 tsp black mustard seeds
1 small onion, finely chopped
10ml/2 tsp grated fresh root
    ginger
2 green chillies, seeded and
    chopped
600g/1lb 5oz potatoes, cooked
200g/7oz fresh peas
juice of 1 lemon
90ml/6 tbsp chopped fresh
    coriander (cilantro) leaves
115g/4oz/1 cup gram flour

25g/1oz/¼ cup self-raising (self-
    rising) flour
40g/1½oz/⅓ cup rice flour
large pinch of turmeric
10ml/2 tsp crushed coriander
    seeds
350ml/12fl oz/1½ cups water
vegetable oil, for frying
salt and ground black pepper

For the chutney
105ml/7 tbsp coconut cream
200ml/7fl oz/scant 1 cup natural
    (plain) yogurt
50g/2oz mint leaves, finely
    chopped
5ml/1 tsp golden caster
    (superfine) sugar
juice of 1 lime

1 Heat a wok over a medium heat and add the sunflower oil. When hot, fry the cumin and mustard seeds for 1–2 minutes. Add the onion, ginger and chillies to the wok and cook for 3–4 minutes. Add the cooked potatoes and peas and stir-fry for a further 5–6 minutes. Season, then stir in the lemon juice and coriander leaves. Leave the mixture to cool slightly, then divide into 25 portions. Shape each portion into a ball and chill.

2 To make the chutney, place all the ingredients in a blender and process until smooth. Season, then chill. To make the batter, put the gram flour, self-raising flour and rice flour in a bowl. Season and add the turmeric and coriander seeds. Gradually whisk in the water to make a smooth batter.

3 Fill a wok one-third full of oil and heat to 180°C/350°F. Working in batches, dip the chilled balls in the batter, then drop into the oil and deep-fry for 1–2 minutes, or until golden. Drain on kitchen paper, and serve immediately with the chutney.

Blanched Spiced Tofu with Soy Dressing

The silky consistency of firm tofu absorbs the dark smoky taste of the soy dressing in this rich and flavourful dish from Korea. Tofu has a nutty quality that blends agreeably with the salty sweetness of soy sauce and the hints of garlic and spring onion in the dressing. Serve it as an appetizer or as an accompaniment to a South-east Asian meal.

Serves 2
2 blocks firm tofu
salt

For the dressing
10ml/2 tsp finely sliced spring
    onion (scallion)
5ml/1 tsp finely chopped garlic
60ml/4 tbsp dark soy sauce
10ml/2 tsp chilli powder
5ml/1 tsp sugar
10ml/2 tsp sesame seeds

1 To make the dressing, mix the spring onion and garlic in a bowl with the soy sauce, chilli powder, sugar and sesame seeds. Leave the dressing to stand for a few minutes, allowing the flavours to mingle.

2 Meanwhile, bring a large pan of water to the boil, and add a pinch of salt. Place the whole blocks of tofu in the water, being careful not to let them break apart.

3 Blanch the tofu for 3 minutes. Remove and place on kitchen paper to remove any excess water.

4 Transfer the blocks of tofu to a serving dish, and cover with the dressing. Leave for 10 minutes to absorb the dressing then serve, slicing the tofu as desired.

> **Cook's Tip**
> Koreans traditionally eat this dish without slicing the tofu, preferring instead to either eat it directly with a spoon or pick it apart with chopsticks. It may be easier, however, to slice it in advance if you are serving it as an accompanying dish.

Indian-spiced Red Lentil and Tomato Dhal

This is Indian comfort food at its best – there's nothing like a bowl of dhal spiced with mustard seeds, cumin and coriander to clear away the blues.

Serves 4

30ml/2 tbsp sunflower oil
1 green chilli, halved
2 red onions, halved and thinly sliced
10ml/2 tsp finely grated garlic
10ml/2 tsp finely grated fresh root ginger
10ml/2 tsp black mustard seeds
15ml/1 tbsp cumin seeds
10ml/2 tsp crushed coriander seeds
10 curry leaves
250g/9oz/generous 1 cup red lentils, rinsed and drained
2.5ml/½ tsp turmeric
2 plum tomatoes, roughly chopped
salt
coriander (cilantro) leaves and crispy fried onion, to garnish (optional)
natural (plain) yogurt, poppadums and griddled flatbread or naans, to serve

1 Heat a wok over a medium heat and add the sunflower oil. When hot add the green chilli and onions, lower the heat and cook gently for 10–12 minutes, until softened. Increase the heat slightly and add the garlic, ginger, mustard seeds, cumin seeds, coriander seeds and curry leaves and stir-fry for 2–3 minutes.

2 Add the lentils to the wok with 700ml/1 pint 2fl oz/scant 3 cups water, the turmeric and tomatoes and season with plenty of salt. Bring the mixture to the boil, cover, reduce the heat and cook very gently for 25–30 minutes, stirring occasionally.

3 Check the seasoning, then garnish with coriander leaves and crispy fried onion, if liked, and serve with yogurt, poppadums and flatbread or naans.

> **Variation**
> Use yellow split peas in place of the lentils. Like red lentils, they do not need to be soaked before cooking.

Green Chilli Stuffed Tofu

These squares of fried tofu have a crispy coating, surrounding a creamy texture with a crunchy filling. They are stuffed with a blend of chilli and chestnut, which gives a piquant contrast with the delicate flavour of the tofu. This Korean-style dish makes an easy accompaniment for a main course, or a great appetizer.

Serves 2

2 blocks firm tofu
30ml/2 tbsp nam pla
5ml/1 tsp sesame oil
2 eggs
7.5ml/1½ tsp cornflour (cornstarch)
vegetable oil, for shallow-frying

For the filling

2 green chillies, finely chopped
2 chestnuts, finely chopped
6 garlic cloves, crushed
10ml/2 tsp sesame seeds

1 Cut the tofu into 2cm/¾in slices, then cut each slice in half. Place the slices on kitchen paper to absorb any excess water.

2 Mix together the nam pla and sesame oil. Transfer the tofu slices to a plate and coat them with the mixture. Leave to marinate for 20 minutes. Meanwhile, put all the filling ingredients into a bowl and combine. Set aside.

3 Beat the eggs in a shallow dish. Add the cornflour and whisk until well combined. Take the slices of tofu and dip them into the beaten egg mixture, coating them evenly on all sides.

4 Place a frying pan over medium heat and add the vegetable oil. Add the tofu slices to the pan and sauté, turning over once, until golden brown.

5 Once cooked, make a slit down the middle of each slice with a sharp knife, without cutting all the way through. Gently stuff a large pinch of the filling into each slice, and serve.

> **Variation**
> Serve the tofu with a light soy dip instead of the spicy filling.

Red Lentil and Tomato Dhal: Energy 295kcal/1242kJ; Protein 16.1g; Carbohydrate 43.7g, of which sugars 8.5g; Fat 7.6g, of which saturates 1g; Cholesterol 0mg; Calcium 71mg; Fibre 4.7g; Sodium 30mg.
Green Chilli Stuffed Tofu: Energy 291kcal/1213kJ; Protein 23g; Carbohydrate 7.8g, of which sugars 1.3g; Fat 19.1g, of which saturates 3.4g; Cholesterol 209mg; Calcium 1014mg; Fibre 0.8g; Sodium 88mg.

Griddled Corn on the Cob with Chipotle Chillies

You can barbecue, grill or oven-bake corn on the cob in this way. Keeping the husks on the corn protects the kernels and encloses the butter, so the flavours are contained. Fresh cobs with husks intact are perfect, but banana leaves or a double layer of foil will also work as a protective layer.

Serves 6
3 dried chipotle chillies
250g/9oz/generous 1 cup butter, softened
7.5ml/1 ½ tsp lemon juice
45ml/3 tbsp chopped fresh flat leaf parsley
6 corn on the cob, with husks intact
salt and ground black pepper

1 Heat a heavy frying pan. Add the dried chillies and roast them by stirring them continuously for 1 minute without letting them scorch. Put them in a bowl with almost boiling water to cover. Use a saucer to keep them submerged, and leave them to rehydrate for up to 1 hour.

2 Drain, remove the seeds and chop the chillies finely. Place the butter in a bowl and add the chillies, lemon juice and parsley. Season to taste and mix well.

3 Peel back the husks from each cob without tearing them. Remove the silk. Smear about 30ml/2 tbsp of the chilli butter over each cob. Pull the husks back over the cobs, ensuring that the butter is well hidden. Put the rest of the butter in a pot, smooth the top and chill to use later. Place the cobs in a bowl of cold water and leave in a cool place for 1–3 hours; longer if that suits your work plan better.

4 Prepare the barbecue. Remove the corn cobs from the water and wrap in pairs in foil. Once the flames have died down, position a lightly oiled grill rack over the coals to heat. When the coals are medium-hot, or have a moderate coating of ash, grill the corn for 15–20 minutes. Remove the foil and cook them for about 5 minutes more, turning them often to char the husks a little. Serve hot, with the rest of the butter.

Roasted Vegetable Quesadillas with Mozzarella and Green Chillies

Barbecuing gives these vegetables a wonderful smoky flavour, enhanced by the bite of green chillies.

Serves 4
8 long baby aubergines (eggplants), total weight about 175g/6oz, halved lengthways
2 red onions, cut into wedges, leaving the roots intact
2 red (bell) peppers, quartered
1 yellow and 1 orange (bell) pepper, quartered
30ml/2 tbsp olive oil
400g/14oz block mozzarella cheese
2 fresh green chillies, seeded and sliced into rounds
15ml/1 tbsp Mexican tomato sauce
8 corn or wheat flour tortillas
handful of fresh basil leaves
salt and ground black pepper

1 Toss the aubergines, onions and peppers in the oil on a large baking tray. Place the peppers, skin side down, on the griddle or directly on the grill rack of a medium hot barbecue and cook until seared and browned underneath. If the food starts to char, remove the rack until the coals cool down.

2 Put the peppers in a bowl, cover with clear film (plastic wrap) and set aside. Grill the onions and aubergines until they have softened slightly and are branded with brown grill marks, then set them aside. Rub the skins off the peppers with your fingers, cut each piece in half and add to the other vegetables.

3 Cut the mozzarella into 20 slices. Place them, together with the roasted vegetables, in a large bowl and add the sliced chillies and the tomato sauce. Stir well to mix, and season with salt and pepper.

4 Place a griddle over the heat. When it is hot, lay a tortilla on the griddle and pile a quarter of the vegetable mixture into the centre. Sprinkle over some basil leaves. When the tortilla has browned underneath, put another tortilla on top, cooked-side down. Turn the quesadilla over and continue to cook until the underside has browned. Keep warm while you cook the remaining quesadillas.

Corn on the Cob with Chillies: Energy 435kcal/1805kJ; Protein 3.4g; Carbohydrate 27.1g, of which sugars 10g; Fat 35.6g, of which saturates 21.9g; Cholesterol 89mg; Calcium 28mg; Fibre 1.8g; Sodium 525mg.
Vegetable Quesadillas: Energy 233kcal/971kJ; Protein 11.8g; Carbohydrate 17.1g, of which sugars 8.5g; Fat 13.6g, of which saturates 7.4g; Cholesterol 29mg; Calcium 214mg; Fibre 2.7g; Sodium 268mg.

Artichoke Hearts with Ginger, Saffron and Preserved Lemons

In this Moroccan dish, tender globe artichoke hearts are poached in a delicious sweet-sour sauce flavoured with honey, garlic, herbs and preserved lemon. The dish can be eaten warm or cold as a first course or as part of a buffet, but it also makes a perfect accompaniment for barbecued meat.

Serves 4
30–45ml/2–3 tbsp olive oil
2 garlic cloves, crushed
scant 5ml/1 tsp ground ginger
pinch of saffron threads
juice of 1/2 lemon
15–30ml/1–2 tbsp honey
peel of 1 preserved lemon, finely sliced
8 artichoke hearts, quartered
150ml/1/4 pint/2/3 cup water
salt

1 Heat the olive oil in a small heavy pan and stir in the garlic. Before the garlic begins to colour, stir in the ginger, saffron, lemon juice, honey and preserved lemon.

2 Add the artichokes to the pan and toss them in the spices and honey. Pour in the water, add a little salt and heat until the liquid is simmering.

3 Cover the pan and simmer for 10–15 minutes until the artichokes are tender, turning them occasionally. If the liquid has not reduced, take the lid off the pan and boil for about 2 minutes until reduced to a coating consistency. Serve warm or at room temperature.

> **Cook's Tip**
> To prepare the artichoke hearts, remove the outer leaves and cut off the stems. Carefully separate the remaining leaves and use a teaspoon to scoop out the choke with all the hairy bits. Trim the hearts and immerse them in water mixed with a squeeze of lemon juice to prevent them from turning black. Frozen prepared hearts are available in some supermarkets and they can be used for this recipe.

Sizzling Spiced Crêpes

These crêpes, filled with mushrooms, prawns and beansprouts, are French in style, Vietnamese in flavour.

Serves 4
115g/4oz/1/2 cup minced (ground) pork
15ml/1 tbsp nuoc mam
2 garlic cloves, crushed
175g/6oz/2/3 cup button (white) mushrooms, finely sliced
about 60ml/4 tbsp vegetable oil
1 onion, finely sliced
1–2 green or red Thai chillies, seeded and finely sliced
115g/4oz prawns (shrimp), shelled and deveined
225g/8oz/1 cup beansprouts
1 small bunch fresh coriander (cilantro), stalks removed, leaves roughly chopped
salt and ground black pepper
nuoc cham, to serve

For the batter
115g/4oz/1 cup rice flour
10ml/2 tsp ground turmeric
10ml/2 tsp curry powder
5ml/1 tsp sugar
2.5ml/1/2 tsp salt
300ml/1/2 pint/1 1/4 cups canned coconut milk
4 spring onions (scallions), trimmed and finely sliced

1 To make the batter, beat the rice flour, spices, sugar and salt with the coconut milk and 300ml/1/2 pint/1 1/4 cups water, until smooth. Stir in the spring onions. Leave to stand for 30 minutes.

2 In a bowl, mix the pork with the nuoc mam, garlic and seasoning and knead well. Lightly sauté the sliced mushrooms in 15ml/1 tbsp of the oil and set aside.

3 Heat 10ml/2 tsp of the oil in a non-stick pan. Stir in a quarter of the onion and the chillies, then add a quarter each of the pork and the prawns. Pour in 150ml/1/4 pint/2/3 cup of the batter, swirling the pan so that it spreads over the pork and prawns right to the edges.

4 Pile a quarter of the filling on one side of the crêpe. Reduce the heat and cover the pan for 2–3 minutes. Remove the lid and cook the crêpe for another 2 minutes until brown underneath. Sprinkle some chopped coriander over the filling and fold the crêpe. Remove and keep warm while you make the remaining crêpes. Serve with nuoc cham, or chilli sauce.

Artichoke Hearts: Energy 142kcal/586kJ; Protein 1.6g; Carbohydrate 4.1g, of which sugars 1.9g; Fat 11.3g, of which saturates 1.6g; Cholesterol 0mg; Calcium 40mg; Fibre 1.6g; Sodium 47mg.
Sizzling Spiced Crêpes: Energy 379kcal/1581kJ; Protein 18g; Carbohydrate 37g, of which sugars 9g; Fat 18g, of which saturates 3g; Cholesterol 77mg; Calcium 119mg; Fibre 3.2g; Sodium 50mg.

Spicy Zahlouk with Courgette and Cauliflower Salad

Zahlouk is a delicious, spicy aubergine and tomato salad from Morocco that can be served as an appetizer, with lots of bread to scoop it up, or use it as one of the dishes in a meze spread.

Serves 4
3 large aubergines (eggplants), peeled and cubed
3–4 large tomatoes, peeled and chopped to a pulp
5ml/1 tsp sugar
3–4 garlic cloves, crushed
60ml/4 tbsp olive oil
juice of 1 lemon
scant 5ml/1 tsp harissa

5ml/1 tsp cumin seeds, roasted and ground
small bunch of flat leaf parsley, chopped
salt

For the courgette and cauliflower salad
1 cauliflower broken into florets
3 small courgettes (zucchini)
60ml/4 tbsp olive oil
juice of 1 lemon
2–3 garlic cloves, crushed
small bunch of parsley, finely chopped
salt and ground black pepper
5ml/1 tsp paprika and flat bread, to serve

1 To make the zahlouk, boil the aubergines in plenty of salted water for about 15 minutes, until they are very soft. Drain and squeeze out the excess water, then chop and mash with a fork.

2 Put the pulped tomatoes in a pan, stir in the sugar, and cook over a gentle heat until they are reduced to a thick sauce. Stir in the mashed aubergines. Add the garlic, olive oil, lemon juice, harissa, cumin and parsley and stir until thoroughly mixed. Season to taste.

3 To make the cauliflower salad, steam the cauliflower until tender. Slice the courgettes and fry in half the olive oil. Drain on kitchen paper.

4 Mash the cauliflower lightly with the remaining olive oil, add the courgette slices, lemon juice and garlic, season to taste then sprinkle the top with paprika. Serve at room temperature with plenty of flat bread and the zahlouk.

Smoky Aubergine and Red Pepper Pâté

Cooking the aubergines whole, over an open flame, gives them a distinctive smoky flavour and aroma, as well as tender, creamy flesh. The subtle flavour of the roasted aubergine contrasts wonderfully with the sweet flavour of the red peppers.

Serves 4–6
2 aubergines (eggplants)
2 red (bell) peppers
3–5 garlic cloves, chopped, or more to taste

2.5ml/½ tsp ground cumin
juice of ½–1 lemon, to taste
2.5ml/½ tsp sherry or wine vinegar
45–60ml/3–4 tbsp extra virgin olive oil
1–2 shakes of cayenne pepper, Tabasco or other hot pepper sauce
coarse sea salt
chopped fresh coriander (cilantro), to garnish
pitta bread wedges or thinly sliced French bread or ciabatta bread, sesame seed crackers and cucumber slices, to serve

1 Place the aubergines and peppers directly over a medium-low gas flame or on the coals of a barbecue. Turn the vegetables frequently until deflated and the skins are charred.

2 Put the aubergines and peppers in a plastic bag or in a bowl and seal tightly. Leave to cool for 30–40 minutes.

3 Peel the vegetables, reserving the juices, and roughly chop the flesh. Put the flesh in a bowl and add the juices, garlic, cumin, lemon juice, vinegar, olive oil, hot pepper seasoning and salt. Mix well to combine. Turn the mixture into a serving bowl and garnish with coriander. Serve with bread, sesame seed crackers and cucumber slices.

> **Cook's Tip**
> Enclosing the hot vegetables in a bag or bowl traps plenty of steam, which helps to loosen the skin from the flesh. It can then be rubbed or peeled off in long pieces.

Aubergine and Red Pepper Pâté: Energy 51kcal/213kJ; Protein 2.2g; Carbohydrate 8.9g, of which sugars 8.3g; Fat 1g, of which saturates 0.2g; Cholesterol 0mg; Calcium 22mg; Fibre 4.4g; Sodium 7mg.
Spicy Zahlouk with Salad: Energy 302kcal/1251kJ; Protein 8.3g; Carbohydrate 12.6g, of which sugars 11.5g; Fat 24.7g, of which saturates 3.7g; Cholesterol 0mg; Calcium 139mg; Fibre 8.6g; Sodium 36mg.

Paprika-spiced Butternut and Aubergine Salad

This delightful salad, served warm, is all the reason you need to get the griddle out in the colder months. Not only do the colour combinations please the eye, but the flavours really work. Look out for slivered pistachios in Middle Eastern shops: they combine brilliantly with the orange butternut squash.

Serves 4

2 aubergines (eggplants)
1 butternut squash, about
    1kg/2¼lb
120ml/4fl oz/½ cup extra virgin
    olive oil
5ml/1 tsp paprika
150g/5oz feta cheese
50g/2oz/⅓ cup pistachio nuts,
    roughly chopped
salt and ground black pepper

1 Slice the aubergines widthways into 5mm/¼in rounds. Spread them out on a tray and sprinkle with a little salt. Leave for 30 minutes.

2 Peel the squash and scoop out the seeds with a spoon, then slice it in the same way. Place the butternut squash slices in a bowl, season lightly with salt and pepper and toss with 30ml/2 tbsp of the oil.

3 Heat the griddle until a few drops of water sprinkled on to the surface evaporate instantly. Lower the heat a little and sear the butternut squash slices in batches. Cook for about 1½ minutes on each side, then put them on a tray. Continue until all the slices have been cooked, then dust them with a little of the paprika.

4 Pat the aubergine slices dry. Toss with the remaining oil and season lightly. Cook in the same way as the squash. When all the slices are cooked, mix the aubergine and squash together in a serving bowl.

5 While the salad is still warm, crumble the feta over the top, sprinkle with the chopped pistachio nuts and dust with the remaining paprika. Serve immediately.

Grilled Aubergine with Harissa and Ginger

Hot, spicy, sweet and fruity are classic flavours of North African cooking and all are abundant in this Moroccan dish. For a spread of tantalizing tastes, serve with artichoke heart and orange salad and the garlicky dip, bissara. Baby aubergines are very effective for this dish as you can slice them in half lengthways and hold them by their stalks.

Serves 4

2 aubergines (eggplants), peeled
    and thickly sliced
olive oil, for frying
2–3 garlic cloves, crushed
5cm/2in piece of fresh root ginger,
    peeled and grated
5ml/1 tsp ground cumin
5ml/1 tsp harissa
75ml/5 tbsp clear honey
juice of 1 lemon
salt
fresh bread, to serve

1 Preheat the grill (broiler) or a griddle. Dip each slice of aubergine in olive oil and cook in a pan under the grill or in a griddle pan. Turn the slices so that they are lightly browned on both sides.

2 In a wide frying pan, fry the garlic in a little olive oil for a few seconds, then stir in the ginger, cumin, harissa, honey and lemon juice. Add enough water to cover the base of the pan and to thin the mixture, then lay the aubergine slices in the pan. Cook the aubergines gently for about 10 minutes, or until they have absorbed all the sauce.

3 Add a little extra water, if necessary, season to taste with salt, and serve at room temperature, with chunks of fresh bread to mop up the juices.

> **Variations**
> Courgettes (zucchini) can also be cooked in this way. If you want to make a feature out of this sumptuous dish, serve it with other grilled (broiled) vegetables and fruit, such as (bell) peppers, chillies, tomatoes, oranges, pineapple and mangoes.

Asian-spiced Courgette Tempura

This is a twist on the classic Japanese tempura, using besan, or chickpea flour, in the batter. Also known as gram flour, golden besan is more commonly used in Indian cooking and gives a wonderfully crisp texture while the courgette inside becomes meltingly tender.

Serves 4

600g/1lb 5oz courgettes (zucchini)

90g/3½oz/¾ cup gram flour
5ml/1 tsp baking powder
2.5ml/½ tsp turmeric
10ml/2 tsp ground coriander
5ml/1 tsp ground cumin
5ml/1 tsp chilli powder
250ml/8fl oz/1 cup beer
sunflower oil, for frying
salt
steamed basmati rice, natural (plain) yogurt and pickles, to serve

1 Cut the courgettes into thick, finger-sized batons and set aside. Sift the gram flour, baking powder, turmeric, ground coriander, cumin and chilli powder into a large bowl.

2 Season the mixture with salt and gradually add the beer, mixing to make a thick batter – do not overmix.

3 Fill a large wok one-third full with sunflower oil and heat to 180°C/350°F (or until a cube of bread, dropped into the oil, browns in 15 seconds).

4 Working in batches, dip the courgette batons in the spiced batter and then deep-fry for 1–2 minutes, or until crisp and golden. Lift out of the wok using a slotted spoon and drain on kitchen paper.

5 Serve the courgettes immediately with steamed basmati rice, yogurt, pickles and chutney.

Cook's Tip
You can cook all kinds of vegetables in this way. Try using onion rings, aubergine (eggplant) slices, or even whole mild chillies.

Light and Crispy Seven-spice Aubergines

Thai seven spice powder is a commercial blend of spices, including coriander, cumin, cinnamon, star anise, chilli, cloves and lemon peel. It gives these aubergines a lovely warm flavour that goes very well with the light, curry batter, which is made with whisked egg whites. If you are unable to find this spice mix, you can use Chinese five-spice powder instead.

Serves 4
500g/1¼lb aubergines (eggplants)
2 egg whites
90ml/6 tbsp cornflour (cornstarch)
5ml/1 tsp salt
15ml/1 tbsp Thai seven-spice powder
15ml/1 tbsp mild chilli powder
sunflower oil, for frying
fresh mint leaves, to garnish
steamed rice or noodles and hot chilli sauce, to serve

1 Slice the aubergines into thin discs and pat them dry with kitchen paper.

2 Whisk the egg whites in a bowl until light and foamy, but not dry. Combine the cornflour, salt, seven-spice powder and chilli powder and spread the mixture evenly on to a large plate.

3 Fill a wok one-third full of sunflower oil and heat to 180°C/350°F (or until a cube of bread, dropped into the oil, browns in 30 seconds).

4 Working in batches, dip the aubergine slices in the egg white and then into the spiced flour mixture to coat. Deep-fry for 3–4 minutes, or until crisp and golden.

5 Remove the aubergine slices from the oil with a wire skimmer or slotted spoon and drain well on kitchen paper. Keep warm while you cook the remaining slices.

6 Serve the aubergines immediately, garnished with mint leaves and accompanied with steamed rice or noodles, and hot chilli sauce for dipping.

Asian-spiced Courgette Tempura: Energy 241kcal/999kJ; Protein 7.3g; Carbohydrate 15.3g, of which sugars 4.6g; Fat 15.6g, of which saturates 1.9g; Cholesterol 0mg; Calcium 83mg; Fibre 3.8g; Sodium 15mg.
Crispy Seven-spice Aubergines: Energy 203kcal/850kJ; Protein 2.7g; Carbohydrate 23.5g, of which sugars 2.5g; Fat 11.7g, of which saturates 1.4g; Cholesterol 0mg; Calcium 17mg; Fibre 2.5g; Sodium 45mg.

Caramelized Mushrooms with Allspice and Herbs

Button mushrooms caramelize beautifully in their own juice, but still keep their moistness and nutty flavour. Turkish cooks usually serve them as a side dish for grilled lamb chops or liver, or as a hot or cold meze dish with chunks of bread to mop up the tasty cooking juices, but they are also good served on toasted crusty bread as a light lunch with a salad. You can use whatever herbs and spices you enjoy and have available to flavour this dish.

Serves 4
45ml/3 tbsp olive oil
15ml/1 tbsp butter
450g/1lb button (white) mushrooms, wiped clean
3–4 garlic cloves, peeled and finely chopped
10ml/2 tsp allspice berries, crushed
10ml/2 tsp coriander seeds
5ml/1 tsp dried mint
1 small bunch each of fresh sage and flat leaf parsley, chopped
salt and ground black pepper
lemon wedges, to serve

1 Heat the oil and butter in a wide, heavy pan, then stir in the mushrooms with the garlic, allspice and coriander. Cover and cook for about 10 minutes, shaking the pan from time to time, until the mushrooms start to caramelize.

2 Remove the lid and toss in the mint with some of the sage and parsley. Cook for a further 5 minutes, until most of the liquid has evaporated, then season with salt and pepper.

3 Tip the mushrooms into a serving dish and sprinkle the rest of the sage and parsley over the top. Serve hot or at room temperature, with lemon wedges for squeezing.

> **Cook's Tip**
> Keep the mushrooms whole, trimming the stalks if necessary. Avoid washing them before cooking as they absorb a lot of water. Instead, wipe the caps with a clean damp cloth.

Turkish Spiced Apples

Vegetables and fruits stuffed with an aromatic pilaff are a great favourite in Turkey. This recipe is for apples, but you can use the same filling for other fruit or vegetables.

Serves 4
4 cooking apples, or any firm, sour apple of your choice
30ml/2 tbsp olive oil
juice of 1/2 lemon
10ml/2 tsp sugar
salt and ground black pepper
1 tomato, 1 lemon and fresh mint or basil leaves, to serve

For the filling
30ml/2 tbsp olive oil
a little butter
1 onion, finely chopped
2 garlic cloves
30ml/2 tbsp pine nuts
30ml/2 tbsp currants, soaked in warm water and drained
5–10ml/1–2 tsp ground cinnamon
5–10ml/1–2 tsp ground allspice
5ml/1 tsp sugar
175g/6oz/scant 1 cup short grain rice, rinsed and drained
1 bunch each of fresh flat leaf parsley and dill, finely chopped

1 To make the filling, heat the oil and butter in a heavy pan, stir in the onion and garlic and cook until they soften. Add the pine nuts and currants and cook until the nuts turn golden.

2 Stir in the spices, sugar and rice, and mix well. Pour in enough water to cover the rice – roughly 1–2cm/1/2–3/4in above the grains – and bring to the boil. Season with salt and pepper and stir, then lower the heat and simmer for about 10–12 minutes, until almost all the water has been absorbed. Toss in the herbs and turn off the heat. Cover and leave to steam for 5 minutes.

3 Preheat the oven to 200°C/400°F/Gas 6. Using a sharp knife, cut the stalk ends off the apples and keep to use as lids. Core each apple, removing some flesh to create a cavity. Take spoonfuls of the rice and pack it into the apples. Replace the lids and stand the apples, tightly packed, in a small baking dish.

4 Mix together 100ml/3½fl oz/scant ½ cup water with the oil, lemon juice and sugar. Pour this mixture around the apples, then bake for 30–40 minutes, until the apples are tender and the cooking juices are slightly caramelized. Serve with a tomato and lemon garnish and a sprinkling of mint or basil leaves.

Cumin-spiced Hummus

This classic Middle Eastern appetizer is made from cooked chickpeas, ground to a paste and flavoured with garlic, lemon juice, tahini, olive oil and cumin. It is delicious served with wedges of toasted pitta bread or crudités. It is traditionally made with dried chickpeas, soaked overnight then simmered in water until tender, but using canned chickpeas gives a satisfactory result and makes it very quick and easy to prepare.

Serves 4–6
400g/14oz can chickpeas,
* drained*
60ml/4 tbsp tahini
2–3 garlic cloves, chopped
juice of ½–1 lemon
cayenne pepper
small pinch to 1.5ml/¼ tsp
* ground cumin, or more to taste*
salt and ground black pepper

1 Put the chickpeas into a bowl and mash them coarsely using a potato masher or a fork. If you prefer a smoother purée, process the chickpeas in a food processor or blender until you have the texture you require.

2 Mix the tahini into the chickpea purée, then stir in the garlic, lemon juice, cayenne, cumin and salt and pepper to taste, adding the ingredients to the processor or blender if you are using one. If the mixture seems too stiff, add a little water. Serve at room temperature.

> **Cook's Tip**
> *Cans of chickpeas usually contain water to which sugar and salt has been added. Drain the chickpeas and rinse them thoroughly under the tap before mashing them.*

> **Variation**
> *Process two roasted red (bell) peppers with the chickpeas, then continue as above. Serve sprinkled with lightly toasted pine nuts and paprika mixed with olive oil.*

Feta and Roast Pepper Dip with Chillies

This is a familiar *meze* in northern Greece, where it is eaten as a dip with pittas, with other dishes, or with toast to accompany a glass of ouzo. The strong, salty feta cheese with the smoky peppers and hot chillies makes a powerful combination to enliven the taste buds. In Greek it is known as *htipiti*, which literally means 'that which is beaten'.

Serves 4
1 yellow or green (bell)
* pepper*
1–2 fresh green chillies
200g/7oz feta cheese
60ml/4 tbsp extra virgin
* olive oil*
juice of 1 lemon
45–60ml/3–4 tbsp milk
ground black pepper
a little finely chopped fresh flat
* leaf parsley, to garnish*
slices of toasted Greek bread or
* pittas, to serve*

1 Thread the pepper and the chillies on metal skewers and turn them over a flame or under the grill (broiler), until the skins are charred all over.

2 Put the pepper and chillies in a plastic bag or in a covered bowl and set them aside until cool enough to handle.

3 Peel off as much of the pepper and chilli skins as possible and wipe the blackened bits off with kitchen paper. Slit the pepper and chillies and discard the seeds and stems.

4 Put the pepper and chilli flesh into a food processor. Add all the other ingredients except the parsley and blend to a fairly smooth paste. Add a little more milk if the mixture seems too stiff. Spread on slices of toast, sprinkle a hint of parsley on top and serve.

> **Variation**
> *Add 75g/3oz sun-dried tomatoes bottled in oil, drained, to the mixture in the food processor.*

Cumin-spiced Hummus: Energy 140kcal/586kJ; Protein 6.9g; Carbohydrate 11.2g, of which sugars 0.4g; Fat 7.8g, of which saturates 1.1g; Cholesterol 0mg; Calcium 97mg; Fibre 3.6g; Sodium 149mg.
Feta and Roast Pepper Dip: Energy 244kcal/1010kJ; Protein 8.8g; Carbohydrate 4.4g, of which sugars 4.3g; Fat 21.4g, of which saturates 8.5g; Cholesterol 35mg; Calcium 205mg; Fibre 0.7g; Sodium 731mg.

Libyan Spicy Pumpkin Dip

This spicy dip is a beautiful warm orange colour and its flavour, spiced with paprika and ginger, is equally warming. It is great to serve at a Thanksgiving feast. It can be stored for at least a week in the refrigerator. Serve chunks of bread or raw vegetables to dip into it.

Serves 6–8
45–60ml/3–4 tbsp olive oil
1 onion, finely chopped
5–8 garlic cloves, roughly chopped
675g/1½lb pumpkin, peeled and diced
5–10ml/1–2 tsp ground cumin
5ml/1 tsp paprika
1.5–2.5ml/¼–½ tsp ground ginger
1.5–2.5ml/¼–½ tsp curry powder
75g/3oz chopped canned tomatoes or diced fresh tomatoes
15–30ml/1–2 tbsp tomato purée (paste)
½–1 red jalapeño or serrano chilli, chopped, or cayenne pepper, to taste
pinch of sugar, if necessary
juice of ½ lemon, or to taste
salt
30ml/2 tbsp chopped fresh coriander (cilantro) leaves, to garnish

1 Heat the oil in a frying pan, add the onion and half the garlic and fry until softened. Add the pieces of pumpkin, then cover the pan and cook for about 10 minutes, or until the pumpkin is half tender.

2 Add the spices to the pan and cook for 1–2 minutes. Stir in the tomatoes, tomato purée, chilli, sugar and salt and cook over a medium-high heat until the liquid has evaporated.

3 When the pumpkin is tender, mash to a coarse purée. Add the remaining garlic and taste for seasoning, then stir in the lemon juice to taste. Serve at room temperature, sprinkled with the chopped fresh coriander.

Variation
Use butternut squash, or any other winter squash, in place of the pumpkin.

Garlic-infused Spicy Bean Dip

Broad (fava) beans are among the oldest vegetables in cultivation, and are a staple ingredient in the cuisines of North Africa, where they are native and are eaten both fresh and dried. This garlicky dip comes from Morocco. Sprinkled with paprika or dried thyme, it makes a tasty appetizer, and is best served with flat bread.

Serves 4
350g/12oz/1¾ cups dried broad (fava) beans, soaked overnight
4 garlic cloves
10ml/2 tsp cumin seeds
60–75ml/4–5 tbsp olive oil
salt
paprika or dried thyme to garnish

1 Drain the beans, remove their wrinkly skins and place them in a large pan with the garlic and cumin seeds. Add enough water to cover the beans and bring to the boil. Boil for 10 minutes, then reduce the heat, cover the pan and simmer gently for about 1 hour, or until the beans are tender.

2 Drain the beans and, while they are still warm, pound or process them with the olive oil until the mixture forms a smooth dip. Season to taste with salt and serve warm or at room temperature, sprinkled with paprika.

Beetroot and Yogurt Relish

Spiked with garlic, this is a smooth, creamy relish that is suitable to eat as part of a selection of meze dishes. It is delicious served with warm pitta bread or slices of fresh baguette.

Serves 4
4 raw beetroot (beets)
500g/1¼ lb/2¼ cups natural (plain) yogurt
2 garlic cloves, crushed
salt and ground black pepper
fresh mint leaves to garnish

1 Boil the beetroot until tender. Drain and refresh. then peel off the skins and grate on to a plate. Pat off excess water. In a bowl, beat the yogurt with garlic, salt and pepper, add the beetroot and mix well. Garnish with mint leaves.

Libyan Spicy Pumpkin Dip: Energy 54kcal/224kJ; Protein 0.9g; Carbohydrate 2.9g, of which sugars 2.3g; Fat 4.4g, of which saturates 0.7g; Cholesterol 0mg; Calcium 37mg; Fibre 1.3g; Sodium 3mg.
Garlic-infused Spicy Bean Dip: Energy 155kcal/650kJ; Protein 7.4g; Carbohydrate 18.4g, of which sugars 3.9g; Fat 6.3g, of which saturates 0.9g; Cholesterol 0mg; Calcium 96mg; Fibre 6.9g; Sodium 394mg.
Beetroot and Yogurt Relish: Energy 95kcal/403kJ; Protein 7.8g; Carbohydrate 14.4g, of which sugars 13g; Fat 1.4g, of which saturates 0.6g; Cholesterol 2mg; Calcium 249mg; Fibre 1.3g; Sodium 137mg.

Baked Chickpea Purée with Paprika and Pine Nuts

This recipe for baked hummus is an eastern Anatolian speciality. Add yogurt to make it light, and serve it hot as an appetizer or light lunch with a tomato and herb salad.

Serves 4
225g/8oz/1¼ cups dried chickpeas, soaked overnight
about 50ml/2fl oz/¼ cup olive oil
juice of 2 lemons
3–4 garlic cloves, crushed
10ml/2 tsp cumin seeds, crushed
30–45ml/2–3 tbsp light tahini
45–60ml/3–4 tbsp thick natural (plain) yogurt
30–45ml/2–3 tbsp pine nuts
40g/1½oz/3 tbsp butter or ghee
5–10ml/1–2 tsp paprika
salt and ground black pepper

1 Drain the chickpeas, tip them into a pan and fill the pan with plenty of cold water. Bring to the boil and boil for 1 minute, then lower the heat and partially cover the pan. Simmer the chickpeas for about 1 hour, until they are soft and easy to mash. Drain, rinse under running water and remove any loose skins.

2 Preheat the oven to 200°C/400°F/Gas 6. Using a large mortar and pestle, pound the chickpeas with the oil, lemon juice, garlic and cumin. Or process the ingredients in a food processor or blender.

3 Beat in the tahini (at this point the mixture will be very stiff), then beat in the yogurt until the purée is light and smooth. Season to taste. Transfer the purée to an ovenproof dish – preferably an earthenware one – and smooth the top with the back of a spoon.

4 Dry-roast the pine nuts in a small heavy pan over a medium heat until golden brown. Lower the heat, add the butter and let it melt, then stir in the paprika.

5 Pour the mixture of pine nuts and spiced butter over the hummus and bake it for about 25 minutes, until it has risen slightly and the butter has been absorbed. Serve straight from the oven.

Artichoke and Cumin Dip

This dip is so easy to make and is unbelievably tasty. Serve it with olives, hummus and wedges of pitta bread to make a summery snack selection. Grilled artichokes bottled in oil have a fabulous flavour and can be used instead of canned artichokes. You can also vary the flavourings – try adding chilli powder in place of the cumin and add a handful of basil leaves to the artichokes before blending the dip.

Serves 4
2 x 400g/14oz cans artichoke hearts, drained
2 garlic cloves, peeled
2.5ml/½ tsp ground cumin
olive oil
salt and ground black pepper
pitta bread, warmed and thickly sliced, to serve

1 Put the artichoke hearts in a food processor or blender, and add the garlic and ground cumin. Pour in a generous drizzle of olive oil.

2 Process to a smooth purée and season with plenty of salt and ground black pepper to taste.

3 Spoon the purée into a serving bowl. Drizzle a little extra olive oil in a swirl over the top and serve with slices of warm pitta bread to scoop up the purée.

Tahini Dip

This is a delightful and very simple dip from Anatolia, often served as an appetizer with toasted pitta bread and a glass of raki.

Serves 2
45ml/3 tbsp tahini
juice of 1 lemon
15–30ml/1–2 tsp dried mint
lemon wedges, to serve

1 Beat the tahini and lemon juice together in a bowl. Add the mint and beat again until thick and creamy. Spoon the dip into a small dish and serve at room temperature with lemon wedges for squeezing.

Artichoke and Cumin Dip: Energy 76kcal/315kJ; Protein 2g; Carbohydrate 3.8g, of which sugars 2g; Fat 6g, of which saturates 0.8g; Cholesterol 0mg; Calcium 84mg; Fibre 2.7g; Sodium 121mg.
Baked Chickpea Purée: Energy 433kcal/1803kJ; Protein 15g; Carbohydrate 29.5g, of which sugars 3g; Fat 29.2g, of which saturates 7.7g; Cholesterol 21mg; Calcium 160mg; Fibre 6.8g; Sodium 91mg.
Tahini Dip: Energy 160kcal/664kJ; Protein 4.3g; Carbohydrate 6.4g, of which sugars 6.2g; Fat 13.3g, of which saturates 1.9g; Cholesterol 0mg; Calcium 155mg; Fibre 1.8g; Sodium 6mg.

Chilli-spiced Turkish Salad

This Turkish *meze* dish is simply a mixture of chopped fresh vegetables. Along with a few simple dishes such as cubes of honey-sweet melon and feta, or plump, juicy olives spiked with red pepper and oregano, it is *meze* at its simplest and best. Popular in kebab houses in Turkey, this dish makes a tasty snack or appetizer, and is good served with chunks of warm, crusty bread or toasted pitta.

Serves 4

2 large tomatoes, skinned,
   seeded and finely
   chopped
2 Turkish green peppers
   or 1 green (bell) pepper, finely
   chopped
1 onion, finely chopped
1 green chilli, seeded and finely
   chopped
1 small bunch of fresh flat leaf
   parsley, finely chopped
a few fresh mint leaves, finely
   chopped
15–30ml/1–2 tbsp olive oil
salt and ground black pepper

1 Put all the finely chopped ingredients in a bowl and mix well together.

2 Toss the mixture with the olive oil to bind the ingredients, and season to taste with salt and pepper.

3 Leave the dish to sit for a short time for the flavours to blend. Serve at room temperature, in individual bowls or one large dish.

Variations
- The salad can be turned into a paste. When you bind the chopped vegetables with the olive oil, add 15–30ml/1–2 tbsp tomato purée (paste) with a little extra chilli and 5–10ml/1–2 tsp sugar. The mixture will become a tangy paste to spread on fresh, crusty bread or toasted pitta, and it can also be used as a sauce for grilled (broiled), roasted or barbecued meats.
- Add other salad vegetables to the mixture, such as chopped cucumber and spring onions (scallions).

Carrot and Caraway Purée with Yogurt

Long, thin carrots that are orange, yellow, red and purple are a colourful feature in the vegetable markets throughout Turkey. Used mainly in salads, lentil dishes and stews, they are also married with garlic-flavoured yogurt for *meze* – sliced and deep-fried drizzled with yogurt, grated and folded in, or steamed and puréed, then served with the yogurt in the middle, as in this recipe. Try serving the carrot purée while it is still warm, with chunks of crusty bread or warm pitta to scoop it up. The caraway seeds give it an interesting, anise-like flavour, which is sharpened with lemon juice.

Serves 4

6 large carrots, thickly sliced
5ml/1 tsp caraway seeds
30–45ml/2–3 tbsp olive oil
juice of 1 lemon
225g/8oz/1 cup thick and creamy
   natural (plain) yogurt
1–2 garlic cloves, crushed
salt and ground black pepper
a few fresh mint leaves, to garnish

1 Steam the carrots for about 25 minutes, until they are very soft. While they are still warm, mash them to a smooth purée, or process them in a food processor or blender.

2 Beat the caraway seeds into the carrot purée, followed by the oil and lemon juice. Season with salt and pepper.

3 Beat the yogurt and garlic together in a separate bowl, and season with salt and pepper. Spoon the warm carrot purée around the edge of a serving dish, or pile into a mound and make a well in the middle. Spoon the yogurt into the middle, and garnish with mint.

Cook's Tip
It is always best to steam, rather than boil, vegetables, so they retain their taste, texture and goodness. This purée would not taste nearly as good if the carrots were boiled and watery.

Chilli-spiced Salad: Energy 101kcal/420kJ; Protein 2.3g; Carbohydrate 9.3g, of which sugars 8g; Fat 6.3g, of which saturates 0.9g; Cholesterol 0mg; Calcium 66mg; Fibre 2.7g, Sodium 15mg.
Carrot and Caraway Purée: Energy 157kcal/651kJ; Protein 4.2g; Carbohydrate 15.3g, of which sugars 13.6g; Fat 9.2g, of which saturates 1.6g; Cholesterol 1mg; Calcium 140mg; Fibre 3.3g; Sodium 78mg.

Turkish Eggs on Spiced Yogurt

This dish of poached eggs on a bed of garlic-flavoured yogurt is surprisingly delicious. In Turkey it is served as a hot meze dish or snack, but it works equally well as a supper dish with a green salad. Hen's eggs or duck's eggs can be used, whichever you prefer, and you can either poach or fry them. Spiked with paprika, and served with toasted flat bread or chunks of a warm, crispy loaf, this is a very simple dish, but very satisfying.

Serves 2
500g/1¼lb/2¼ cups thick
    natural (plain) yogurt
2 garlic cloves, crushed
30–45ml/2–3 tbsp white wine
    vinegar
4 large eggs
15–30ml/1–2 tbsp butter
5ml/1 tsp paprika
a few dried sage leaves,
    crumbled
salt and ground black pepper

1 Beat the yogurt with the garlic and seasoning. Spoon into a serving dish or on to individual plates, spreading it flat to create a thick bed for the eggs.

2 Fill a pan with water, add the vinegar to seal the egg whites, and bring to a rolling boil. Stir the water with a spoon to create a whirlpool and crack in the first egg. As the egg spins and the white sets around the yolk, stir the water for the next one. Poach the eggs for 2–3 minutes so the yolks are still soft.

3 Lift the eggs out of the water with a slotted spoon and place them on the yogurt bed.

4 Quickly melt the butter in a small pan. Stir in the red pepper or paprika and sage leaves, then spoon the mixture over the eggs. Eat immediately.

> **Cook's Tip**
> *Leave the yogurt at room temperature to form a contrast with the hot eggs, or heat it by placing the dish in a cool oven, or by sitting it in a covered pan of hot water.*

Baba Ganoush with Lebanese Flatbread

Baba Ganoush is a delectable aubergine dip from the Middle East. Tahini – sesame seed paste – and ground cumin are the main flavourings, giving a subtle hint of spice.

Serves 6
2 small aubergines (eggplants)
1 garlic clove, crushed
60ml/4 tbsp tahini
25g/1oz/¼ cup ground almonds
juice of ½ lemon
½ tsp ground cumin
30ml/2 tbsp fresh mint leaves
30ml/2 tbsp olive oil
salt

For the Lebanese flatbread
4 pitta breads
45ml/3 tbsp toasted sesame
    seeds
45ml/3 tbsp fresh thyme leaves
45ml/3 tbsp poppy seeds
150ml/¼ pint/⅔ cup olive oil

1 Start by making the Lebanese flatbread. Split the pitta breads horizontally through the middle and carefully open them out flat, cut-side up. Mix the sesame seeds, chopped thyme and poppy seeds in a mortar. Crush them lightly with a pestle to release their flavour.

2 Stir the olive oil into the spice mixture. Spread the mixture lightly over the cut sides of the pitta bread. Grill (broil) until golden brown and crisp. When cool enough to handle, break into rough pieces and set aside.

3 Grill the aubergines, turning them frequently, until the skin is blackened and blistered. Remove the peel, chop the flesh roughly and leave to drain in a colander.

4 Squeeze out as much liquid from the aubergine as possible. Place the flesh in a blender or food processor. Add the garlic, tahini, ground almonds, lemon juice and cumin, with salt to taste and process to a smooth paste. Roughly chop half the mint and stir into the dip.

5 Spoon into a bowl, sprinkle the remaining leaves on top and drizzle with olive oil. Serve with the Lebanese flatbread.

Baba Ganoush with Flatbread: Energy 451kcal/1878kJ; Protein 9.3g; Carbohydrate 29.5g, of which sugars 3.1g; Fat 33.8g, of which saturates 4.7g; Cholesterol 0mg; Calcium 204mg; Fibre 4.2g; Sodium 225mg.
Turkish Eggs: Energy 345kcal/1438kJ; Protein 25.4g; Carbohydrate 19.1g, of which sugars 19.1g; Fat 19.8g, of which saturates 8.3g; Cholesterol 400mg; Calcium 534mg; Fibre 0.1g; Sodium 393mg.

Spring Onions with Hot Chilli Sauce

A piquant sauce is an excellent accompaniment to deep-fried spring onions in their crisp batter.

Serves 6

18–24 plump spring onions (scallions), trimmed
sea salt and ground black pepper
lemon wedges, to serve

For the batter

225g/8oz/2 cups self-raising (self-rising) flour
150ml/¼ pint/⅔ cup lager
175–200ml/6–7fl oz/¾ water
groundnut (peanut) oil, for deep-frying

1 large egg white
2.5ml/½ tsp cream of tartar

For the sauce

2–3 large mild dried red chillies, such as Spanish ñoras or Mexican anchos or guajillos
1 large red (bell) pepper, halved
2 large tomatoes, halved and seeded
4–6 large garlic cloves, unpeeled
75–90ml/5–6 tbsp olive oil
4 slices French bread, about 2cm/¾in thick
25g/1oz/¼ cup hazelnuts, blanched and dry roasted
15ml/1 tbsp sherry vinegar
chopped fresh parsley, to garnish

1 Soak the dried chillies in hot water for about 30 minutes. Preheat the oven to 220°C/425°F/Gas 7. Place the pepper halves, tomatoes and garlic on a baking sheet and drizzle with 15ml/1 tbsp olive oil. Roast, uncovered, for about 30–40 minutes, until the pepper is blistered and blackened. Cool slightly, then peel the pepper, tomatoes and garlic.

2 Fry the bread in the olive oil until light brown on both sides, Drain the chillies, discard the seeds, then place in a food processor. Add the pepper, tomatoes, garlic, hazelnuts and bread with the oil from the pan. Add the vinegar and process to a paste. Thin the sauce with more oil, if necessary. Set aside.

3 To make the batter, sift the flour into a bowl, season, then gradually whisk in the lager, then water. Whisk the egg white with the cream of tartar until stiff, then fold it into the batter. Heat the oil for deep-frying to 180°C/350°F. Dip the spring onions in the batter and fry in batches for 4–5 minutes. Drain thoroughly on kitchen paper and sprinkle with a little sea salt. Serve hot with the sauce and lemon wedges.

Thai Curry-spiced Potato Samosas

Most samosas are deep-fried, but these are baked, making them a healthier option. They are also perfect for parties as no deep-frying is involved.

Makes 25

1 large potato, about 250g/9oz, diced
15ml/1 tbsp groundnut (peanut) oil

2 shallots, finely chopped
1 garlic clove, finely chopped
60ml/4 tbsp coconut milk
5ml/1 tsp Thai red or green curry paste
75g/3oz/¾ cup peas
juice of ½ lime
25 samosa wrappers or 10 x 5cm/4 x 2in strips of filo pastry
salt and ground black pepper
oil, for brushing

1 Preheat the oven to 220°C/425°F/Gas 7. Bring a small pan of water to the boil, add the diced potato, cover and cook for 10–15 minutes, until tender. Drain and set aside.

2 Meanwhile, heat the groundnut oil in a large frying pan and cook the shallots and garlic over a medium heat, stirring occasionally, for 4–5 minutes, until softened and golden.

3 Add the drained potato, coconut milk, red or green curry paste, peas and lime juice to the frying pan. Mash coarsely with a wooden spoon. Season to taste with salt and pepper and cook over a low heat for 2–3 minutes, then remove the pan from the heat and set aside until the mixture has cooled a little.

4 Lay a samosa wrapper or filo strip flat on the work surface. Brush with a little oil, then place a generous teaspoonful of the mixture in the middle of one end. Turn one corner diagonally over the filling to meet the long edge.

5 Continue folding over the filling, keeping the triangular shape as you work down the strip. Brush with a little more oil if necessary and place on a baking sheet. Prepare all the other samosas in the same way.

6 Bake for 15 minutes, or until the pastry is golden and crisp. Leave to cool slightly before serving.

Spring Onions with Chilli Sauce: Energy 428kcal/1791kJ; Protein 7.9g; Carbohydrate 47.9g, of which sugars 4.9g; Fat 24.1g, of which saturates 3g; Cholesterol 0mg; Calcium 103mg; Fibre 3.2g; Sodium 181mg.
Thai Curry-spiced Potato Samosas: Energy 42kcal/178kJ; Protein 1.2g; Carbohydrate 8.5g, of which sugars 0.6g; Fat 0.6g, of which saturates 0.1g; Cholesterol 0mg; Calcium 14mg; Fibre 0.5g; Sodium 4mg.

Spiced Onion Pakora

These delicious Indian onion fritters are made with chickpea flour, otherwise known as gram flour or besan. Serve with chutney or a yogurt dip.

Serves 4–5
675g/1½lb onions, halved and
 thinly sliced
5ml/1 tsp salt
5ml/1 tsp ground coriander
5ml/1 tsp ground cumin

2.5ml/½ tsp ground turmeric
1–2 green chillies, seeded and
 finely chopped
45ml/3 tbsp chopped fresh
 coriander (cilantro)
90g/3½oz/¾ cup gram flour
2.5ml/½ tsp baking powder
vegetable oil, for deep-frying

To serve
lemon wedges (optional)
fresh coriander (cilantro) sprigs
yogurt and cucumber dip

1 Place the onions in a colander, add the salt and toss. Place on a plate and leave to stand for 45 minutes, tossing once or twice. Rinse the onions, then squeeze out any excess moisture.

2 Place the onions in a bowl. Add the ground coriander, cumin, turmeric, chillies and fresh coriander. Mix well.

3 Add the gram flour and baking powder, then use your hands to mix the ingredients thoroughly. Shape the mixture by hand into 12–15 pakoras, about the size of golf balls.

4 Heat the oil for deep-frying to 180–190°C/350–375°F or until a cube of day-old bread browns in 30–45 seconds. Fry the pakoras, 4–5 at a time, until they are deep golden brown all over. Drain each batch on kitchen paper and keep warm until all the pakoras are cooked. Serve with lemon wedges, coriander sprigs and a yogurt dip.

> **Cook's Tip**
> For a cucumber dip, stir half a diced cucumber and 1 seeded and chopped fresh green chilli into 250ml/8fl oz/1 cup natural (plain) yogurt. Season with salt and cumin.

Braised Spiced Onion Salad

If you can find the small, flat Italian *cipolla* or *borettane* onions, they are excellent in this recipe – otherwise you can use pickling onions, small red onions or shallots.

Serves 6
105ml/7 tbsp olive oil
675g/1½lb small onions, peeled
150ml/¼ pint/⅔ cup dry white
 wine
2 bay leaves
2 garlic cloves, bruised

1–2 small dried red chillies
15ml/1 tbsp coriander seeds,
 toasted and lightly crushed
2.5ml/½ tsp sugar
a few fresh thyme sprigs
30ml/2 tbsp currants
10ml/2 tsp chopped fresh
 oregano
5ml/1 tsp grated lemon rind
15ml/1 tbsp chopped fresh flat
 leaf parsley
30–45ml/2–3 tbsp pine nuts,
 toasted
salt and ground black pepper

1 Place 30ml/2 tbsp olive oil in a wide pan. Add the onions and cook gently over a medium heat for about 5 minutes, or until they begin to colour. Remove the onions from the pan and set aside.

2 Add the remaining oil, the wine, bay leaves, garlic, chillies, coriander, sugar and thyme to the pan. Bring the mixture to the boil and cook briskly for 5 minutes, then return the onions to the pan.

3 Stir in the currants, then reduce the heat and cook gently for 15–20 minutes, or until the onions are completely tender but not falling apart. Use a draining spoon to transfer the onions to a serving dish.

4 Boil the liquid remaining in the pan over a high heat until it has reduced considerably. Taste it and adjust the seasoning, if necessary, then pour the reduced liquid over the onions. Sprinkle the oregano over the onions, set aside to cool and then chill them.

5 Just before serving, stir the onions to coat them in the sauce and sprinkle over the grated lemon rind, chopped parsley and toasted pine nuts.

Paprika-crusted Monkfish with Chorizo and Peppers

Monkfish is just perfect for skewering, as it is not likely to disintegrate. It can also take some fairly robust flavours, such as this smoky paprika crust and spicy chorizo, which the cool, creamy cucumber sauce complements perfectly.

Serves 4
1 monkfish tail, about 1kg/2¼lb, trimmed and filleted
10ml/2 tsp smoked paprika
2 red (bell) peppers, halved
15ml/1 tbsp extra virgin olive oil
16 thin slices of chorizo
salt and ground black pepper
4 long skewers

For the cucumber and mint sauce
150ml/¼ pint/⅔ cup natural (plain) yogurt
½ cucumber, halved lengthways and seeded
30ml/2 tbsp fresh mint, chopped

1 Place the monkfish fillets in a flat dish. Rub them all over with 5ml/1 tsp salt, then cover the dish and leave in a cool place for 20 minutes. Pour the yogurt for the sauce into a food processor. Cut the cucumber into it, season with salt and process to a pale green purée. Transfer into a bowl and stir in the mint.

2 Rinse the salt off the pieces of monkfish and lightly pat them dry with kitchen paper. Mix the smoked paprika with a pinch of salt and gently rub the mixture evenly over the fish. Slice each pepper into twelve long strips and cut each monkfish fillet into ten equal pieces. Thread six pieces of pepper and five pieces of fish on to each skewer and brush one side with a little extra virgin olive oil.

3 Grill the skewered food, oiled-side down, on a moderate-hot barbecue or a griddle for about 3½ minutes. Lightly brush the top side with oil, turn over and cook for 3–4 minutes more. Remove the skewers from the heat and keep warm. Grill the chorizo slices for a second or two until just warm.

4 Thread one piece on to the end of each skewer and serve the rest alongside. Serve with the cucumber and mint sauce.

Moroccan Grilled Fish Brochettes

Serve these delicious skewers with potatoes, aubergine (eggplant) slices and strips of red peppers, which can be cooked on the barbecue alongside the fish brochettes. Accompany them with chilli sauce and a stack of warm, soft pitta breads or flour tortillas.

Serves 4–6
5 garlic cloves, chopped
2.5ml/½ tsp paprika
2.5ml/½ tsp ground cumin
2.5–5ml/½–1 tsp salt
2–3 pinches of cayenne pepper
60ml/4 tbsp olive oil
30ml/2 tbsp lemon juice
30ml/2 tbsp chopped fresh coriander (cilantro) or parsley
675g/1½lb firm-fleshed white fish, such as haddock, halibut, sea bass, snapper or turbot, cut into 2.5–5cm/1–2in cubes
3–4 green (bell) peppers, cut into 2.5–5cm/1–2in pieces
2 lemon wedges, to serve

1 Put the garlic, paprika, cumin, salt, cayenne pepper, oil, lemon juice and coriander or parsley in a large bowl and mix together.

2 Add the fish and toss to coat. Leave to marinate for at least 30 minutes, and preferably 2 hours, at room temperature, or chill overnight.

3 About 40 minutes before you are going to cook the brochettes, light the barbecue. The barbecue is ready when the coals have turned white and grey.

4 Meanwhile, thread the fish cubes and pepper pieces alternately on to wooden or metal skewers.

5 Grill the brochettes on the barbecue for 2–3 minutes on each side, or until the fish is tender and lightly browned. Serve with lemon wedges.

Cook's Tip
If you are threading the fish on to bamboo or wooden skewers, soak the skewers in cold water for 30 minutes before use to stop them burning.

Paprika-crusted Monkfish: Energy 375kcal/1572kJ; Protein 51.7g; Carbohydrate 7.1g, of which sugars 6.8g; Fat 15.9g, of which saturates 5.6g; Cholesterol 57mg; Calcium 115mg; Fibre 2.1g; Sodium 445mg.
Moroccan Grilled Fish Brochettes: Energy 276kcal/1157kJ; Protein 33.3g; Carbohydrate 8g, of which sugars 7.6g; Fat 12.5g, of which saturates 1.9g; Cholesterol 61mg; Calcium 34mg; Fibre 2g; Sodium 118mg.

Fish Kebabs with Chilli Sauce

Robust fish such as monkfish and swordfish take well to flavouring with chilli. This recipe uses a marinade to add flavour, but don't let the fish marinate for more than an hour, as the lemon juice will start to break down the fibres of the fish after this time and it will be difficult not to overcook it.

Serves 4
120ml/4fl oz/1/2 cup olive oil
finely grated rind and juice of
  1 large lemon
5ml/1 tsp crushed chilli flakes
350g/12oz monkfish fillet, cubed
350g/12oz thick salmon fillet or
  steak, cubed

350g/12oz swordfish fillet, cubed
2 red, yellow or orange peppers,
  cut into squares
30ml/2 tbsp finely chopped fresh
  flat leaf parsley
salt and ground black pepper

**For the sweet tomato and
chilli salsa**
225g/8oz ripe tomatoes, finely
  chopped
1 garlic clove, crushed
1 fresh red chilli, seeded and
  chopped
45ml/3 tbsp extra virgin olive oil
15ml/1 tbsp lemon juice
15ml/1 tbsp finely chopped fresh
  flat leaf parsley
pinch of sugar

1 Put the oil in a shallow glass or china bowl and add the lemon rind and juice, the chilli flakes and pepper to taste. Whisk to combine the marinade ingredients, then add the fish chunks. Turn to coat evenly.

2 Add the pepper squares, stir, then cover and marinate in a cool place for 1 hour, turning occasionally.

3 Thread the fish and peppers on to eight oiled metal skewers, reserving the marinade. Barbecue or grill (broil) the skewered fish for 5–8 minutes, turning once.

4 Meanwhile, make the salsa by mixing all the ingredients in a bowl, and seasoning to taste with salt and pepper. Heat the reserved marinade in a small pan, remove from the heat and stir in the parsley, with salt and pepper to taste. Serve the kebabs hot, with the marinade spooned over, accompanied by the salsa.

Spiced Fishballs in Tomato and Paprika Sauce

Enjoy these spicy balls of minced fish and ginger, with flat bread to scoop up the delicious sauce, or with lemon-scented couscous.

Serves 6
65g/2 1/2oz bread (about 2 slices)
1kg/2 1/4lb minced (ground) fish
  such as cod, haddock or whiting
2 onions, chopped
8 garlic cloves, chopped
2.5–5ml/1/2–1 tsp ground
  turmeric
2.5ml/1/2 tsp ground ginger

2.5ml/1/2 tsp ras al hanout or
  garam masala
1 bunch fresh coriander (cilantro),
  chopped, plus extra to garnish
1 egg
cayenne pepper, to taste
150ml/1/4 pint/2/3 cup vegetable
  or olive oil or a combination
4 ripe tomatoes, diced
5ml/1 tsp paprika
1 preserved lemon, rinsed and cut
  into small strips
salt and ground black pepper
1/2 lemon, cut into wedges, to
  serve

1 Remove the crusts from the bread, put the bread in a bowl and pour over cold water. Leave to soak for about 10 minutes, then squeeze dry.

2 Add the fish to the bread with half the onions, half the garlic, half the turmeric, the ginger, half the ras al hanout or garam masala, half the coriander, the egg and cayenne pepper and seasoning. Mix together and chill while you make the sauce.

3 To make the sauce, heat the oil in a pan, add the remaining onion and garlic and fry for about 5 minutes, or until softened. Sprinkle in the remaining turmeric and ras al hanout or garam masala and warm through. Add the diced tomatoes, paprika and half the remaining coriander to the pan and cook over a medium heat until the tomatoes have formed a sauce consistency. Stir in the strips of preserved lemon.

4 With wet hands, roll walnut-size lumps of the fish mixture into balls and flatten slightly. Place in the sauce. Cook gently, for 15–20 minutes, turning twice. Garnish with coriander and serve with lemon wedges for squeezing.

Fish Kebabs with Chilli Sauce: Energy 475kcal/1975kJ; Protein 42.9g; Carbohydrate 7.7g, of which sugars 6.7g; Fat 30.4g, of which saturates 4.4g; Cholesterol 104mg; Calcium 67mg; Fibre 2.5g; Sodium 147mg.
Fishballs in Tomato and Paprika: Energy 359kcal/1496kJ; Protein 33.8g; Carbohydrate 13g, of which sugars 5.7g; Fat 19.3g, of which saturates 2.9g; Cholesterol 108mg; Calcium 55mg; Fibre 1.7g; Sodium 181mg.

Shark Steaks in Chilli-spiced Marinade

A meaty, firm-fleshed fish, shark is widely available, either fresh or frozen. It needs careful watching during cooking, as overcooking will make it dry and tough, but the flavour is excellent. The Mexican-style marinade in this recipe uses achiote seed, a vivid red spice also known as annatto, which is widely used as a natural colouring and characterizes the cooking of Yucatan.

Serves 4
grated rind and juice of 1 orange
juice of 1 small lime
45ml/3 tbsp white wine
30ml/2 tbsp olive oil
2 garlic cloves, crushed
10ml/2 tsp ground achiote seed
    (annatto powder)
2.5ml/½ tsp cayenne pepper
2.5ml/½ tsp dried marjoram
5ml/1 tsp salt
4 shark steaks
fresh oregano leaves, to garnish
4 wheat flour tortillas and any
    suitable salsa, to serve

1 Put the orange rind and juice in a shallow non-metallic dish that is large enough to hold all the shark steaks in a single layer. Add the lime juice, white wine, olive oil, garlic, ground achiote, cayenne, marjoram and salt. Mix well.

2 Add the shark steaks to the dish and spoon the marinade over them. Cover and set aside for 1 hour, turning once.

3 Heat a griddle pan until very hot and cook the marinated shark steaks for 2–3 minutes on each side. Alternatively, they are very good cooked on the barbecue, so long as they are cooked after the coals have lost their fierce initial heat.

4 Garnish the shark steaks with oregano and serve with the tortillas and salsa. A green vegetable would also go well.

> **Cook's Tip**
> Shark freezes successfully, with little or no loss of flavour on thawing, so use frozen steaks if you can't buy the fresh fish.

Grilled Stingray Wings with Chilli Sambal

Chargrilled stingray is a very popular street snack in Singapore. The stalls selling grilled chicken wings and satay often serve grilled stingray wings on a banana leaf with a generous dollop of fiery chilli sambal. The cooked fish is eaten with the fingers, or chopsticks, by tearing off pieces and dipping them in the sambal. If you can't find stingray wings, you could substitute a flat fish, such as sole or plaice. Banana leaves are available in Chinese and Asian markets, but the dish can, of course, also be served on a plate.

Serves 4
4 medium-sized stingray wings,
    about 200g/7oz, rinsed and
    patted dry
salt
4 banana leaves, about
    30cm/12in square
2 fresh limes, halved

For the chilli sambal
6–8 red chillies, seeded and
    chopped
4 garlic cloves, chopped
5ml/1 tsp shrimp paste
15ml/1 tbsp tomato purée
    (paste)
15ml/1 tbsp palm sugar (jaggery)
juice of 2 limes
30ml/2 tbsp vegetable or
    groundnut (peanut) oil

1 First make the chilli sambal. Using a mortar and pestle or food processor, grind the chillies with the garlic to form a paste. Beat in the shrimp paste, tomato purée and sugar. Add the lime juice and bind with the oil.

2 Prepare the barbecue. Rub each stingray wing with a little of the chilli sambal and place them on the grill rack. Cook the fish for 3–4 minutes on each side, until tender. Sprinkle with salt and serve on banana leaves, accompanied with the remaining chilli sambal and the limes.

> **Cook's Tip**
> The wings, cheeks and liver of the stingray are the only parts that are eaten: the rest of the fish is too rubbery.

Red Snapper with Thai Spices

Shiny, dark green banana leaves make a really good wrapping for steamed fish. Here, whole red snappers are wrapped with a fragrant mix of coconut cream, mint, coriander, kaffir lime leaves, lemon grass and chilli.

Serves 4

4 small red snapper, grouper, tilapia or red bream, cleaned
4 large squares of banana leaf (approximately 30cm/12in)
50ml/2fl oz/¼ cup coconut cream
90ml/6 tbsp chopped coriander (cilantro)
90ml/6 tbsp chopped mint
juice of 3 limes
3 spring onions (scallions), finely sliced
4 kaffir lime leaves, finely shredded
2 red chillies, seeded and finely sliced
4 lemon grass stalks, split lengthways
salt and ground black pepper
steamed rice and steamed Asian greens, to serve

1 Using a small sharp knife, score the fish diagonally on each side. Bring a wok of water to the boil and dip each square of banana leaf into it for 15–20 seconds. Rinse under cold water and dry with kitchen paper.

2 Place the coconut cream, chopped herbs, lime juice, spring onions, lime leaves and chillies in a bowl and stir well to mix. Season with salt and pepper.

3 Lay each banana leaf out flat on a work surface and place a fish and a split lemon grass stalk in the centre of each one. Spread the herb mixture over each fish. Wrap the banana leaf around each one to form four neat parcels. Secure each parcel tightly with a bamboo skewer or a cocktail stick (toothpick).

4 Place the parcels in a single layer in one or two tiers of a large bamboo steamer and place over a wok of simmering water. Cover tightly and steam for 15–20 minutes.

5 Remove the fish from the steamer and serve immediately, still in their banana-leaf wrappings, with steamed rice and steamed Asian greens.

Sweet and Sour Fish

When fish such as red mullet or snapper is quickly shallow-fried in oil in this way the skin becomes crisp, while the flesh inside remains moist and juicy. The sweet and sour sauce complements the fish beautifully.

Serves 4–6

1 large or 2 medium fish, such as snapper or mullet, heads removed
20ml/4 tsp cornflour (cornstarch)
120ml/4fl oz/½ cup vegetable oil
15ml/1 tbsp chopped garlic
15ml/1 tbsp chopped fresh root ginger
30ml/2 tbsp chopped shallots
225g/8oz cherry tomatoes
30ml/2 tbsp red wine vinegar
30ml/2 tbsp sugar
30ml/2 tbsp tomato ketchup
15ml/1 tbsp nam pla
45ml/3 tbsp water
salt and ground black pepper
coriander (cilantro) leaves and shredded spring onions (scallions), to garnish

1 Rinse and dry the fish. Score the skin diagonally on both sides, then coat the fish lightly all over with 15ml/1 tbsp of the cornflour. Shake off any excess.

2 Heat the oil in a wok or large frying pan. Add the fish and cook over a medium heat for 6–7 minutes. Turn the fish over and cook for 6–7 minutes more, until it is crisp and brown.

3 Remove the fish with a metal spatula or fish slice and place on a large platter. Pour off all but 30ml/2 tbsp of the oil from the wok or pan and reheat. Add the garlic, ginger and shallots and cook over a medium heat, stirring occasionally, for 3–4 minutes, until golden.

4 Add the cherry tomatoes and cook until they burst open. Stir in the vinegar, sugar, tomato ketchup and nam pla. Lower the heat and simmer for 1–2 minutes. Adjust the seasoning, adding more vinegar, sugar and/or nam pla, if necessary.

5 In a cup, mix the remaining 5ml/1 tsp cornflour to a paste with the water. Stir into the sauce. Heat, stirring, until it thickens. Pour the sauce over the fish, garnish with coriander and shredded spring onions and serve.

Sweet and Sour Fish: Energy 233kcal/969kJ; Protein 21.9g; Carbohydrate 6.3g, of which sugars 3g; Fat 13.5g, of which saturates 1.6g; Cholesterol 54mg; Calcium 16mg; Fibre 0.5g; Sodium 335mg.
Red Snapper with Spices: Energy 409kcal/1706kJ; Protein 31.6g; Carbohydrate 14.5g, of which sugars 12.8g; Fat 25.4g, of which saturates 3.9g; Cholesterol 56mg; Calcium 113mg; Fibre 3.6g; Sodium 973mg.

Roast Mackerel with Spicy Chermoula Paste

Chermoula is a marinade used widely in Moroccan and North African cooking. There are many variations on the flavourings used, but it is usually based on a blend of coriander (cilantro), lemon and garlic, and often includes saffron and paprika. It is especially popular with fish, but can also be used with poultry and meat. Ready-made chermoula paste is now readily available in most large supermarkets.

It can be mixed with oil and other ingredients and used as a marinade, or simply brushed on to fish and meat before cooking.

Serves 4

4 whole mackerel, cleaned and gutted
30–45ml/2–3 tbsp chermoula paste
75ml/5 tbsp olive oil
2 red onions, sliced
salt and ground black pepper

1 Preheat the oven to 190°C/375°F/Gas 5. Place each mackerel on a large sheet of baking parchment (parchment paper). Using a sharp knife, slash into the flesh of each fish several times.

2 In a small bowl, mix the chermoula with the olive oil, and spread the paste over the skin of the mackerel, rubbing the mixture into the cuts.

3 Sprinkle the red onions over the mackerel, and season with salt and pepper. Scrunch the ends of the baking parchment together to seal. Place the four parcels on a baking tray.

4 Bake for 20 minutes, until the mackerel is cooked through. Serve the fish still in their paper parcels, to be unwrapped at the table.

> **Cook's Tip**
> *Buy only very fresh mackerel: it should be firm with a bright eye.*

Stuffed Spiced Mackerel

This spectacular Turkish dish is a classic of Ottoman cuisine: the fish is emptied of flesh while keeping the skin intact, then stuffed to resemble the whole fish once more.

Serves 4

1 large, fresh mackerel, scaled and washed, but not gutted
30–45ml/2–3 tbsp olive oil
4–5 shallots, finely chopped
30ml/2 tbsp pine nuts
30ml/2 tbsp blanched almonds, finely slivered
45ml/3 tbsp walnuts, chopped
15–30ml/1–2 tbsp currants, soaked for 5–10 minutes
6–8 dried apricots, finely chopped
5–10ml/1–2 tsp ground cinnamon
5ml/1 tsp ground allspice
2.5ml/½ tsp ground cloves
2.5ml/½ tsp chilli powder
5ml/1 tsp sugar
1 small bunch each of flat leaf parsley and dill, finely chopped
juice of 1 lemon
plain (all-purpose) flour
sunflower oil, for shallow frying
salt and ground black pepper
dill, flat leaf parsley sprigs, and lemon wedges, to serve

1 Cut an opening just below the gills of the mackerel. Push your finger into the opening and remove the guts, then rinse the fish inside and out. Using a rolling pin or mallet, hit the fish gently on both sides, making sure you smash the backbone. With your hands, gently massage the skin to loosen it away from the flesh – don't pummel it too hard or the skin will tear.

2 Working from the tail end towards the head, squeeze the loosened flesh out of the opening below the gills. Remove any bits of bone from the flesh, then rinse out the skin. Set aside.

3 Heat the oil in a frying pan, stir in the shallots and cook until soft. Add the nuts and stir until they begin to colour. Add the currants, apricots, spices, chilli powder and sugar. Mix in the fish flesh and cook through for 2–3 minutes, then toss in the herbs and lemon juice and season with salt and pepper.

4 Fill the empty mackerel skin until it looks like a plump, fresh mackerel once more. Brush with a little oil and grill (broil) until the skin begins to turn brown and buckle. To serve, cut the fish into slices. Surround with dill and parsley and serve with lemon.

Red Snapper and Black Peppercorns

This Italian recipe combines red mullet with oranges and lemons, which grow in abundance there, and fragrant crushed pepper.

Serves 4

2 oranges, such as Navelina
4 red mullet or snapper, about 225g/8oz each, filleted
90ml/6 tbsp olive oil
10 black peppercorns, crushed
1 lemon
30ml/2 tbsp plain (all-purpose) flour
15g/½oz/1 tbsp butter
2 drained canned anchovies, chopped
60ml/4 tbsp shredded fresh basil
salt and ground black pepper

1 Using a sharp knife, cut the peel and pith from one of the oranges, then slice the flesh into rounds. Squeeze the juice from the other orange into a small bowl, cover and set aside.

2 Place the fish in a shallow dish in a single layer. Pour over the olive oil and sprinkle with the crushed black peppercorns. Lay the orange slices on top of the fish. Cover the dish and leave to marinate in the refrigerator for at least 4 hours.

3 Halve the lemon. Cut the skin and pith from one half using a small sharp knife and slice thinly and reserve. Squeeze the juice from the other half.

4 Carefully lift the fish out of the marinade, and pat dry with kitchen paper. Reserve the marinade and orange slices. Season the fish on both sides with salt and pepper, then dust lightly with flour. Heat 45ml/3 tbsp of the marinade in a frying pan. Add the fish and cook for 2 minutes on each side. Remove from the pan, keep warm. Discard the marinade left in the pan.

5 Melt the butter in the pan with any of the remaining original marinade. Add the anchovies and cook over a low heat until completely softened.

6 Stir in the orange and lemon juice, then check and adjust the seasoning if necessary. Simmer until the sauce has slightly reduced. Stir in the basil. Pour the sauce over the fish, garnish with the reserved orange slices and the lemon slices, and serve.

Steamed Whole Fish with Ginger and Red Chilli

In Malay and Indian cooking, fish is often steamed whole, with flavourings such as ginger and chilli rubbed into the flesh. This version is particularly popular in Penang and Singapore, where it is served with a chilli sambal.

Serves 4

3 spring onions (scallions), trimmed into 2.5cm/1in pieces and cut into strips
25g/1oz fresh root ginger, peeled and cut into 2.5cm/1in strips
4 dried shiitake mushrooms, soaked in hot water until soft and squeezed dry
1 whole fresh fish, such as pomfret or sea bass, weighing about 900g/2lb, gutted and cleaned
30ml/2 tbsp vegetable or sesame oil
30ml/2 tbsp light soy sauce
salt and ground black pepper
1 red chilli, seeded and cut into thin strips and fresh coriander (cilantro) leaves, to garnish
steamed rice and chilli sambal, to serve

1 Put the strips of spring onion and ginger in a bowl. Trim the shiitake mushrooms, discarding the hard stems, and cut them into matching thin strips. Add them to the spring onions and ginger and mix well.

2 Fill a wok one-third full with water and place a metal steaming rack in the wok (it should sit just above the level of the water). Cover with a lid and put the wok over the heat to bring the water to the boil.

3 Score the fish diagonally three or four times and season with salt and pepper. Place it on a heatproof plate and sprinkle the spring onion, ginger and shiitake strips over the top. Place the plate on the rack, cover with the lid and steam the fish for 15–20 minutes, until cooked.

4 When the fish is cooked, heat the oil in a small pan. Stir in the soy sauce and pour it over the fish. Garnish the dish with the chillies and coriander leaves and serve with steamed rice and chilli sambal.

Snapper with Peppercorns: Energy 462kcal/1929kJ; Protein 44.1g; Carbohydrate 8.5g, of which sugars 6.5g; Fat 28.6g, of which saturates 4.4g; Cholesterol 9mg; Calcium 216mg; Fibre 1.6g; Sodium 293mg.
Steamed Fish with Chilli: Energy 278Kcal/1165kJ; Protein 43.7g; Carbohydrate 0.5g, of which sugars 0.5g; Fat 11.2g, of which saturates 1.6g; Cholesterol 180mg; Calcium 296mg; Fibre 0.1g; Sodium 423mg.

Barbecued Salmon with Spices

In this Indian dish, the fish is cooked in a banana leaf parcel. The salmon really works well with the gutsy flavours of the spices.

Serves 6

50g/2oz fresh coconut, skinned and finely grated, or 65g/2¹/₂oz/scant I cup desiccated (dry unsweetened shredded) coconut, soaked in 30ml/2 tbsp water
I large lemon, skin, pith and seeds removed, chopped
4 large garlic cloves, crushed
3 large fresh mild green chillies, seeded and chopped
50g/2oz fresh coriander (cilantro), roughly chopped
25g/1oz fresh mint leaves, roughly chopped
5ml/1 tsp ground cumin
5ml/1 tsp sugar
2.5ml/¹/₂ tsp fenugreek seeds, finely ground
5ml/1 tsp salt
2 large, whole banana leaves
6 salmon fillets, total weight about 1.2kg/2¹/₂lb, skinned

1 Place all the ingredients except the banana leaves and salmon in a food processor. Pulse to a fine paste. Scrape the mixture into a bowl, cover and chill for 30 minutes.

2 To make the parcels, cut each banana leaf widthways into three and cut off the hard outer edges of each piece. Put the pieces of leaf and the edge strips in a bowl of hot water. Soak for 10 minutes. Drain, rinse, and pour over boiling water to soften. Drain, then place the leaves, smooth-side up, on a board.

3 Smear the top and bottom of each with the coconut paste. Place one fillet on each banana leaf. Bring the trimmed edge of the leaf over the salmon, then fold in the sides. Bring up the remaining edge to cover the salmon and make a neat parcel. Tie each parcel securely with a leaf strip.

4 Lay each parcel on a sheet of foil, bring up the edges and scrunch together to seal. Position a lightly oiled grill rack over a moderately-hot barbecue. Place the salmon parcels on the grill rack and cook for about 10 minutes, turning over once.

5 Place on individual plates and leave to stand for 2–3 minutes. Remove the foil, then unwrap and eat the fish out of the parcel.

Sour Carp with Tamarind, Galangal, Basil and Coriander

This dish is popular in Cambodia and Vietnam. If you want to make a simpler version, toss the cooked fish in the herbs and serve with noodles or rice and a salad.

Serves 4

500g/1¹/₂lb carp fillets, cut into 3 or 4 pieces
30ml/2 tbsp sesame oil
10ml/2 tsp ground turmeric
I small bunch each fresh coriander (cilantro) and basil, stalks removed
20 lettuce leaves or rice paper wrappers
nuoc mam or other dipping sauce, to serve

For the marinade
30ml/2 tbsp tamarind paste
15ml/1 tbsp soy sauce
juice of I lime
I green or red Thai chilli, finely chopped
2.5cm/1in galangal root, peeled and grated
a few sprigs of fresh coriander (cilantro) leaves, finely chopped

1 Mix together all the marinade ingredients in a bowl. Toss the fish pieces in the marinade, cover with clear film (plastic wrap) and chill in the refrigerator for at least 6 hours, or overnight.

2 Lift the pieces of fish out of the marinade and lay them on a plate. Heat a wok or heavy pan, add the oil and stir in the turmeric. Working quickly, so that the turmeric doesn't burn, stir-fry the fish pieces, for 2–3 minutes. Add any remaining marinade to the pan and cook for a further 2–3 minutes.

3 To serve, divide the fish among four plates, sprinkle with the coriander and basil, and add some lettuce leaves or rice paper wrappers and a small bowl of dipping sauce to each serving. To eat, tear off a bitesize piece of fish, place it on a wrapper with a few herb leaves, fold it up into a roll, then dip it into the sauce.

> **Cook's Tip**
> Any freshwater fish can be used for this recipe but, because it is stirred in a wok, you will need one with firm, thick flesh.

Whole Baked Fish in a Spiced Tomato Sauce

A whole fish, cooked in a mixture of spices, is a New Year festival treat in Sephardi Jewish communities, symbolizing the whole year to come.

Serves 6–8
1–1.5kg/2¼–3¼lb fish, such as
    snapper, cleaned, with head
    and tail left on (optional)
2.5ml/½ tsp salt
juice of 2 lemons
45–60ml/3–4 tbsp extra virgin
    olive oil
2 onions, sliced

5 garlic cloves, chopped
1 green (bell) pepper, chopped
1–2 fresh green chillies, seeded
    and finely chopped
2.5ml/½ tsp ground turmeric
2.5ml/½ tsp curry powder
2.5ml/½ tsp ground cumin
120ml/4fl oz/½ cup passata
    (bottled strained tomatoes)
5–6 fresh or canned tomatoes,
    chopped
45–60ml/3–4 tbsp chopped
    fresh coriander (cilantro) leaves
    and/or parsley
65g/2½oz pine nuts, toasted
parsley, to garnish

1 Prick the fish all over with a fork and rub with the salt. Put the fish in a roasting pan or dish and pour over the lemon juice. Leave to stand for 2 hours.

2 Preheat the oven to 180°C/350°F/Gas 4. Heat the oil in a pan, add the onions and half the garlic and fry for about 5 minutes, or until softened.

3 Add the pepper, chillies, turmeric, curry powder and cumin to the pan and cook gently for 2–3 minutes. Stir in the passata, tomatoes and herbs.

4 Sprinkle half of the pine nuts over the base of an ovenproof dish, top with half of the sauce, then add the fish and its marinade.

5 Sprinkle the remaining garlic over the fish, then add the remaining sauce and the remaining pine nuts. Cover tightly with a lid or foil and bake for 30 minutes, or until the fish is tender. Garnish with parsley.

Barbecued Red Mullet with a Hot Chilli Dressing

Red mullet are simple to cook on a barbecue, with bay leaves for flavour and a dribble of tangy dressing instead of a marinade.

Serves 4
4 red mullet, about 225–275g/
    8–10oz each, cleaned and
    descaled if cooking under a
    grill (broiler)
olive oil, for brushing

fresh herb sprigs, such as fennel,
    dill, parsley, or thyme
2–3 dozen fresh or dried bay
    leaves

For the dressing
90ml/6 tbsp olive oil
6 garlic cloves, finely chopped
½ dried chilli, seeded and
    chopped
juice of ½ lemon
15ml/1 tbsp parsley

1 Prepare the barbecue or preheat the grill (broiler) with the shelf 15cm/6in from the heat source.

2 Brush each fish with oil and stuff the cavities with the herb sprigs. Brush the grill pan with oil and lay bay leaves across the cooking rack. Place the fish on top and cook for 15–20 minutes until cooked through, turning once.

3 To make the dressing, heat the olive oil in a small pan and fry the chopped garlic with the dried chilli. Add the lemon juice and strain the dressing to remove the garlic and chilli. Add the chopped parsley and stir to combine. Serve the mullet on warmed plates, drizzled with the dressing.

> **Cook's Tips**
> - Nicknamed the woodcock of the sea, red mullet are one of the fish that are classically cooked uncleaned to give them extra flavour. In this recipe however, the fish are cleaned and herbs are used to add extra flavour.
> - If you are cooking the fish on a barbecue, light the barbecue well in advance. Before cooking, the charcoal or wood should be grey, with no flames.

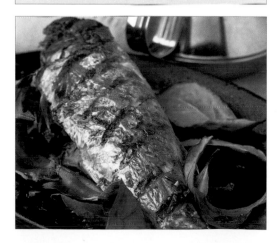

Baked Fish in Spiced Tomato: Energy 342kcal/1440kJ; Protein 35.1g; Carbohydrate 33.1g, of which sugars 11.7g; Fat 7.5g, of which saturates 1.2g; Cholesterol 78mg; Calcium 61mg; Fibre 3.8g; Sodium 127mg.
Red Mullet with Hot Chilli: Energy 290kcal/1207kJ; Protein 22.7g; Carbohydrate 2.2g, of which sugars 0.3g; Fat 21.3g, of which saturates 2.4g; Cholesterol 0mg; Calcium 91mg; Fibre 0.7g; Sodium 114mg.

Griddled Swordfish with Roasted Tomatoes and Cinnamon

When roasted with sugar and warm-flavoured spices such as cinnamon and saffron, sun-ripened tomatoes simply melt in the mouth. As an accompaniment to chargrilled fish they are sensational.

Serves 4
1kg/2¼lb large vine or plum
    tomatoes, peeled, halved
    and seeded
5–10ml/1–2 tsp ground
    cinnamon
pinch of saffron threads
15ml/1 tbsp orange flower water
60ml/4 tbsp olive oil
45–60ml/3–4 tbsp sugar
4 × 225g/8oz swordfish steaks
rind of ½ preserved lemon, finely
    chopped
small bunch of fresh coriander
    (cilantro), finely chopped
handful of blanched almonds
knob (pat) of butter
salt and ground black pepper

1 Preheat the oven to 110°C/225°F/Gas ¼. Place the tomatoes on a baking sheet. Sprinkle with the cinnamon, saffron and orange flower water. Trickle half the oil over, being sure to moisten every tomato half, and sprinkle with sugar. Place the tray in the bottom of the oven and cook the tomatoes for about 3 hours, then turn the oven off and leave them to cool.

2 Brush the remaining olive oil over the swordfish steaks and season with salt and pepper. Lightly oil a pre-heated cast-iron griddle and cook the steaks for 3–4 minutes on each side. Sprinkle the chopped preserved lemon and coriander over the steaks towards the end of the cooking time.

3 In a separate pan, fry the almonds in the butter until golden and sprinkle them over the tomatoes. Serve the fish steaks immediately with the tomatoes.

Variations
If swordfish steaks are not available, tuna or shark steaks can be cooked in the same way with excellent results.

Spicy Pan-seared Tuna with Cucumber, Garlic and Ginger

This popular Vietnamese dish is made with many types of thick-fleshed fish. Tuna is particularly suitable for pan-searing, because it is delicious served a little rare.

Serves 4
1 small cucumber
10ml/2 tsp sesame oil
2 garlic cloves, crushed
4 tuna steaks

For the dressing
4cm/1½in fresh root ginger,
    peeled and roughly
    chopped
1 garlic clove, peeled and roughly
    chopped
2 green Thai chillies, seeded and
    roughly chopped
45ml/3 tbsp raw cane sugar
45ml/3 tbsp nuoc mam
juice of 1 lime
60ml/4 tbsp water

1 To make the dressing, grind the ginger, garlic and chillies to a pulp with the sugar, using a mortar and pestle. Stir in the nuoc mam, lime juice and water, and mix well. Leave the dressing to stand for 15 minutes.

2 Cut the cucumber in half lengthways and remove the seeds. Cut the flesh into long, thin strips. Toss the cucumber in the dressing and leave to soak for at least 15 minutes.

3 Wipe a heavy pan with the oil and rub the garlic around it. Heat the pan and add the tuna steaks. Sear for a few minutes on both sides, so that the outside is slightly charred but the inside is still rare. Lift the steaks on to a warm serving dish.

4 Using tongs or chopsticks, lift the cucumber strips out of the dressing and arrange them around the steaks. Drizzle the dressing over the tuna, and serve immediately.

Cook's Tip
Tuna is easy to overcook and dries out quickly. Use a heavy pan and make sure it is really hot before you add the fish so that the outside seals and browns quickly.

Swordfish with Tomatoes: Energy 463kcal/1941kJ; Protein 47.2g; Carbohydrate 19.9g, of which sugars 19.8g; Fat 22.2g, of which saturates 4.1g; Cholesterol 103mg; Calcium 59mg; Fibre 3.1g; Sodium 352mg.
Spicy Tuna with Ginger: Energy 262Kcal/1103kJ; Protein 31g; Carbohydrate 16g, of which sugars 13g; Fat 8g, of which saturates 2g; Cholesterol 35mg; Calcium 44mg; Fibre 0.5g; Sodium 150mg

Caribbean-spiced Fish Steaks

West Indian cooks love spices and use them to good effect. This quick and easy recipe is a typical example of how the additiona of chillies, cayenne and allspice can give an exotic accent to a tomato sauce for fish.

Serves 4
45ml/3 tbsp oil
6 shallots, finely chopped
1 garlic clove, crushed

1 fresh green chilli, seeded and
finely chopped
400g/14oz can chopped
tomatoes
2 bay leaves
1.5ml/¼ tsp cayenne pepper
5ml/1 tsp crushed allspice
juice of 2 limes
4 cod steaks, each weighing
about 200g/7oz
5ml/1 tsp brown muscovado
sugar
10ml/2 tsp angostura bitters
salt

1 Heat the oil in a frying pan. Add the shallots and cook for 5 minutes until soft. Add the garlic and chilli and cook for 2 minutes, then stir in the tomatoes, bay leaves, cayenne pepper, allspice and lime juice, with a little salt to taste.

2 Cook gently for 15 minutes, then add the cod steaks and baste with the tomato sauce. Cover and cook for 10 minutes or until the steaks are cooked. Transfer the steaks to a warmed dish and keep hot.

3 Stir the sugar and angostura bitters into the sauce, simmer for 2 minutes then pour over the fish. Serve with steamed okra or green beans.

Cook's Tip
Angostura bitters give great depth of flavour to spicy sauces.

Variation
Almost any robust fish can be cooked in this way. Try haddock or swordfish. The sauce is also good over grilled pork chops.

Spiced Cod in Mustard Sauce

A firm, white-fleshed fish, cod has long been a staple ingredient of European and North American cookery. This German recipe uses flavourings typical of northern Europe, such as bay leaves and mustard, as well as more exotic spices, to make a delicious sauce.

Serves 4
900g/2lb cod fillets
1 lemon
1 small onion, sliced

15g/½oz/¼ cup chopped fresh
flat leaf parsley, whole stalks
reserved
6 allspice berries
6 whole black peppercorns
1 clove
1 bay leaf
1.2 litres/2 pints/5 cups water
30ml/2 tbsp wholegrain mustard
75g/3oz/6 tbsp butter
salt and ground black pepper
chopped parsley and bay leaves,
to garnish
boiled potatoes and carrots,
to serve

1 Place the fish on a plate. Pare two thin strips of rind from the lemon, then squeeze the juice from the lemon and sprinkle it over the fish.

2 Put the lemon rind in a large pan, together with the onion, the stalks from the parsley, the allspice, peppercorns, clove and bay leaf.

3 Pour the water into the pan. Slowly bring to the boil, cover and simmer for 20 minutes. Add the fish, cover and cook very gently for 10 minutes.

4 Remove the pan from the heat. Ladle 250ml/8fl oz/1 cup of the cooking liquid into another pan and simmer until reduced by half. Stir in the mustard.

5 Whisk the butter, a little at a time, into the reduced stock. Taste and season with salt and pepper, if needed.

6 Remove the fish from the stock and place on warmed serving dishes. Pour over a little sauce and serve the rest separately in a jug (pitcher). Garnish with chopped parsley and bay leaves and serve with boiled potatoes and carrots.

Caribbean-spiced Fish Steaks: Energy 266kcal/1114kJ; Protein 37.7g; Carbohydrate 6.5g, of which sugars 5.8g; Fat 10g, of which saturates 1.3g; Cholesterol 92mg; Calcium 33mg; Fibre 1.4g; Sodium 130mg.
Cod in Mustard Sauce: Energy 337kcal/1404kJ; Protein 42.2g; Carbohydrate 1.7g, of which sugars 1.3g; Fat 17.8g, of which saturates 10g; Cholesterol 143mg; Calcium 44mg; Fibre 0.8g; Sodium 372mg.

Fish Pie with Saffron Mash

This is the ultimate fish pie. Breaking through the golden potato crust reveals prawns and chunks of cod swathed in a creamy parsley sauce.

Serves 6

750ml/1¼ pints/3 cups milk
1 onion, chopped
1 bay leaf
2–3 peppercorns
450g/1lb each of fresh cod fillet and smoked haddock fillet
350g/12oz cooked tiger prawns (jumbo shrimp), shelled, with tails
75g/3oz/6 tbsp butter
75g/3oz/¾ cup plain (all-purpose) flour
60ml/4 tbsp chopped fresh parsley
1.3kg/3lb floury potatoes, peeled
large pinch saffron threads, soaked in 45ml/3 tbsp hot water
75g/3oz/6 tbsp butter
250ml/8fl oz/1 cup milk
45ml/3 tbsp chopped fresh dill
salt and ground black pepper

1 Put the milk, onion, bay leaf and peppercorns into a pan. Bring to the boil, simmer for about 10 minutes, and set aside. Lay the cod and haddock fillets, skin-side up, in a large pan. Strain over the milk, place over a gentle heat and simmer for 5–7 minutes until just opaque. Lift the fish out of the milk and transfer to a plate. Reserve the milk.

2 When the fish is cool enough to handle, pull off the skin and flake the flesh into large pieces, removing any bones as you go. Transfer to a large bowl and add the shelled prawns.

3 Melt the butter in a small pan. Stir in the flour and cook for a minute or so, then gradually stir in the flavoured milk from the pan until you achieve a smooth consistency. Whisk well and simmer gently for 15 minutes until thick and a little reduced, then taste and season with salt and pepper. Stir in the parsley. Pour the sauce over the fish. Carefully mix together, transfer the mixture to a pie dish and leave to cool.

4 Preheat the oven to 180°C/350°F/Gas 4. Boil the potatoes in salted water until tender, drain and mash until smooth. Using an electric whisk, beat in the saffron and its soaking water, then the butter, milk and dill to make light, fluffy mashed potato. When the fish mixture has cooled and set, pile the mash on top. Bake for 30–40 minutes, or until the potato is golden and crisp.

Cod and Bean Stew with Saffron and Paprika

In this lovely, spicy one-pot dish the chunks of fresh, flaky cod have their flavour offset by smoked paprika.

Serves 6–8

1 red (bell) pepper, halved
45ml/3 tbsp olive oil
4 rashers (strips) streaky (fatty) bacon, roughly chopped
4 garlic cloves, finely chopped
1 onion, sliced
10ml/2 tsp paprika
5ml/1 tsp smoked paprika
pinch of saffron threads soaked in 45ml/3 tbsp hot water
400g/14oz jar Spanish butter (lima) beans (judias del barco or judias blancas guisadas) or canned haricot (navy beans), drained and rinsed
about 600ml/1 pint/2½ cups fish stock or water and 60ml/4 tbsp Thai fish sauce
6 plum tomatoes, quartered
350g/12oz fresh skinned cod fillet, cut into large chunks
45ml/3 tbsp chopped fresh coriander (cilantro), plus a few sprigs to garnish
salt and ground black pepper
crusty bread, to serve

1 Preheat the grill (broiler) and line the pan with foil. De-seed the pepper halves. Place, cut-side down, in the grill pan and grill (broil) under a hot heat for about 10–15 minutes, until the skin is charred. Put into a plastic bag, seal and leave for 10 minutes. Remove from the bag, peel off the skin and discard. Chop the pepper into large pieces.

2 Heat the olive oil in a pan, then add the bacon and garlic. Fry for 2 minutes, then add the onion. Cover and cook for about 5 minutes until the onion is soft. Stir in the paprika and the saffron and its soaking water, and salt and pepper.

3 Stir the beans into the pan and add just enough stock to cover. Bring to the boil and simmer, uncovered, for about 15 minutes, stirring occasionally to prevent sticking. Stir in the chopped pepper and tomato quarters. Drop in the cubes of cod and bury them in the sauce. Cover and simmer for 5 minutes until cooked. Stir in the chopped coriander. Serve the stew in warmed soup plates or bowls, garnished with the coriander sprigs. Eat with lots of crusty bread.

Fish Curry with Coconut Milk

This curry is based on a Thai classic. The lovely green colour is imparted by chilli and fresh herbs added in the last moments of cooking.

Serves 4
225g/8oz small ready-prepared squid, rinsed and dried
225g/8oz raw tiger prawns (jumbo shrimp)
400ml/14fl oz/1²/₃ cups coconut milk
2 kaffir lime leaves, finely shredded
30ml/2 tbsp nam pla
450g/1lb firm white fish fillets, skinned, boned and cut into chunks
2 fresh green chillies, seeded and finely chopped
30ml/2 tbsp torn fresh basil or coriander (cilantro) leaves
squeeze of fresh lime juice
cooked Thai jasmine rice, to serve

For the curry paste
6 spring onions (scallions), coarsely chopped
4 fresh coriander (cilantro) stems, coarsely chopped, plus 45ml/3 tbsp chopped fresh coriander (cilantro)
4 kaffir lime leaves, shredded
8 fresh green chillies, seeded and coarsely chopped
1 lemon grass stalk, coarsely chopped
2.5cm/1in piece fresh root ginger, peeled and coarsely chopped
45ml/3 tbsp chopped fresh basil
15ml/1 tbsp vegetable oil

1 Make the curry paste by processing the ingredients, except the oil, to a paste or pound in a mortar. Stir in the oil.

2 Cut the squid bodies into rings. Heat a wok until hot, add the prawns and dry fry, without any oil, for about 4 minutes, until they turn pink. Remove the prawns from the wok, and when cool, peel off the shells, leaving a few for garnish. Make a slit along the back of each one and remove the black vein.

3 Pour the coconut milk into the wok and bring to the boil, stirring. Add 30ml/2 tbsp of curry paste, the lime leaves and fish sauce, reduce the heat and simmer for 10 minutes.

4 Add the squid, prawns and chunks of fish and cook for about 2 minutes, until the seafood is tender. Just before serving, stir in the chillies, herbs and a squeeze of lime juice. Garnish with prawns in their shells, and serve with Thai jasmine rice.

Singapore Fish Head Curry

The origins of this popular Singaporean dish have become a little blurred with time. Some say it came with immigrants from south India; others claim an Indian chef in Singapore created it as a way of using a part of the fish that was usually thrown away. It is now made in numerous versions in Singapore and Malaysia. There is a surprising amount of delicate flesh to be found on a large fish head: the succulent cheeks are particularly prized.

Serves 2
30ml/2 tbsp ghee or vegetable oil
10ml/2 tsp brown mustard seeds
5ml/1 tsp fenugreek seeds
5ml/1 tsp cumin seeds
a handful of curry leaves
15ml/1 tbsp palm sugar (jaggery)
30ml/2 tbsp tamarind pulp, soaked in 150ml/¼ pint/²/₃ cup water and strained for juice
600ml/1 pint/2½ cups coconut milk
1 large fresh fish head, such as red snapper (about 900g/2lb), cleaned
5 okra, halved diagonally
2 large tomatoes, skinned, seeded and quartered
salt and ground black pepper
steamed rice and pickles, to serve

For the spice paste
8 shallots, chopped
6 garlic cloves, chopped
4 red chillies, seeded and chopped
50g/2oz fresh root ginger, peeled and chopped
25g/1oz fresh turmeric, chopped
1 lemon grass stalk, trimmed and chopped
30ml/2 tbsp fish curry powder

1 To make the spice paste, grind all the ingredients together using a mortar and pestle or food processor.

2 Heat the ghee or oil in a wok or heavy pan. Stir in the mustard seeds, fenugreek and cumin seeds along with the curry leaves. Fry until the mustard seeds begin to pop and then stir in the spice paste. Fry until fragrant, then stir in the sugar, followed by the tamarind juice and coconut milk.

3 Bring to the boil, reduce the heat and add the fish head. Simmer gently for 10 minutes, then add the okra and tomatoes. Simmer for another 10 minutes or until the fish head is cooked. Season the sauce and serve with steamed rice and pickles.

Fish Curry with Milk: Energy 417Kcal/1760kJ; Protein 42.2g; Carbohydrate 30.4g, of which sugars 29.1g; Fat 15.2g, of which saturates 2.7g; Cholesterol 74mg; Calcium 231mg; Fibre 2.7g; Sodium 497mg.
Singapore Fish Head Curry: Energy 417kcal/1760kJ; Protein 42.2g; Carbohydrate 30.4g, of which sugars 29.1g; Fat 15.2g, of which saturates 2.7g; Cholesterol 74mg; Calcium 231mg; Fibre 2.7g; Sodium 497mg.

Mackerel with Star Anise, Garlic and Black Beans

Shiitake mushrooms, fresh ginger and pungent salted black beans are the perfect partners for robustly flavoured mackerel fillets.

Serves 4

8 x 115g/4oz mackerel fillets
20 dried shiitake mushrooms
15ml/1 tbsp finely julienned fresh root ginger
3 star anise
45ml/3 tbsp dark soy sauce
15ml/1 tbsp Chinese rice wine
15ml/1 tbsp salted black beans
6 spring onions (scallions), finely shredded
30ml/2 tbsp sunflower oil
5ml/1 tsp sesame oil
4 garlic cloves, very thinly sliced
sliced cucumber and steamed basmati rice, to serve

1 Divide the mackerel fillets between two lightly oiled heatproof plates, with the skin-side up. Using a a small, sharp knife, make 3–4 diagonal slits in each one, then set aside.

2 Soak the shiitake mushrooms in boiling water for 20–25 minutes. Drain, reserving the liquid, discard the stems and slice the caps thinly. Place a metal rack in a large wok and pour in the mushroom liquid. Add half the ginger and the star anise.

3 Push the remaining ginger strips into the slits in the fish and sprinkle over the sliced mushrooms. Bring the liquid in the wok to a boil and lower one of the prepared plates on to the rack. Cover, lower the heat and steam for 10–12 minutes, or until the mackerel is cooked through. Repeat with the second plate of fish, adding water to the liquid in the wok if necessary.

4 Transfer the fish to a serving platter. Ladle 105ml/7 tbsp of the liquid into a clean wok with the soy sauce, wine and black beans, place over a gentle heat and bring to a simmer. Spoon over the fish and sprinkle over the spring onions.

5 Wipe out the wok with kitchen paper and place the wok over a medium heat. Add the oils and garlic and stir-fry for a few minutes until lightly golden. Pour over the fish and serve immediately with cucumber and steamed rice.

Spiced Halibut and Tomato Curry

The chunky cubes of white fish contrast beautifully with the rich red spicy tomato sauce and taste just as good as they look. You can use any type of firm white fish for this recipe.

Serves 4

60ml/4 tbsp lemon juice
60ml/4 tbsp rice wine vinegar
30ml/2 tbsp cumin seeds
5ml/1 tsp turmeric
5ml/1 tsp chilli powder
5ml/1 tsp salt
750g/1lb 11oz thick halibut fillets, skinned and cubed
60ml/4 tbsp sunflower oil
1 onion, finely chopped
3 garlic cloves, finely chopped
30ml/2 tbsp finely grated fresh root ginger
10ml/2 tsp black mustard seeds
2 x 400g/14oz cans chopped tomatoes
5ml/1 tsp sugar
chopped coriander (cilantro) leaves and sliced green chilli, to garnish
basmati rice, pickles and poppadums, to serve
natural (plain) yogurt, to drizzle (optional)

1 Mix together the lemon juice, vinegar, cumin, turmeric, chilli powder and salt in a shallow non-metallic bowl. Add the cubed fish and turn to coat evenly. Cover and put in the refrigerator to marinate for 25–30 minutes.

2 Meanwhile, heat a wok over a high heat and add the oil. When hot, add the onion, garlic, ginger and mustard seeds. Reduce the heat to low and cook very gently for about 10 minutes, stirring occasionally.

3 Add the tomatoes and sugar to the wok, bring to the boil, reduce the heat, cover and cook gently for 15–20 minutes, stirring occasionally.

4 Add the fish and its marinade to the wok, stir gently to mix, then cover and simmer gently for 15–20 minutes, or until the fish is cooked through and the flesh flakes easily with a fork.

5 Serve the curry ladled into shallow bowls with basmati rice, pickles and poppadums. Garnish with fresh coriander and green chillies, and drizzle over some natural yogurt if liked.

Mackerel with Star Anise: Energy 693kcal/2872kJ; Protein 45.5g; Carbohydrate 1.9g, of which sugars 0.5g; Fat 55.9g, of which saturates 10.4g; Cholesterol 128mg; Calcium 35mg; Fibre 0.6g; Sodium 152mg.
Halibut and Tomato Curry: Energy 335kcal/1409kJ; Protein 41.9g; Carbohydrate 8.4g, of which sugars 8.1g; Fat 15.2g, of which saturates 2.1g; Cholesterol 66mg; Calcium 73mg; Fibre 2.2g; Sodium 622mg.

Baked Carp with Bay Leaves

Indigenous to Hungary, carp is a major ingredient in the cooking of the country. It is a large freshwater fish, and has a sweet, firm flesh that tastes wonderful when baked with bacon and bay leaves.

Serves 4–6

450g/1lb waxy old potatoes, scrubbed
115g/4oz rindless rashers (strips) smoked bacon
about 900g/2lb whole carp, skinned, filleted and cut into 7.5cm/3in pieces
8–12 bay leaves
15ml/1 tbsp lard
1 onion, thinly sliced
15ml/1 tbsp paprika
1 large tomato, sliced
2 green (bell) peppers, sliced
40g/1½oz/3 tbsp butter, melted
150ml/¼ pint/⅔ cup sour cream
salt
bay leaves, to garnish

1 Preheat the oven to 190°C/375°F/Gas 5. Boil the potatoes in their skins in a pan of boiling salted water for 15–20 minutes. Drain the potatoes and slice them.

2 Meanwhile, cut the bacon into strips. Make incisions in the fish fillets and push in the bacon and bay leaves.

3 Put the potatoes in a large well-buttered casserole. Add salt.

4 Melt the lard and fry the onion slices for 1–2 minutes. Stir in the paprika. Arrange the onion on the potato slices.

5 Place a layer of tomato and peppers on top of the onion then add the fish and a little more salt.

6 Pour the melted butter over the fish. Bake in the oven for 30 minutes. Pour over the sour cream and cook for a further 15 minutes. Serve garnished with bay leaves.

> **Cook's Tip**
> Pungent, salty bacon is a great partner for white fish: this is a combination found in many European cuisines.

Hungarian Paprika-spiced Fish Goulash

This wholesome meal is a cross between a stew and a soup. It is traditionally served with half a hot cherry pepper, which is placed in the centre of the plate. The goulash is then ladled over it.

Serves 6

2kg/4½lb mixed fish
4 large onions, sliced
2 garlic cloves, crushed
½ small celeriac, diced
handful of parsley stalks or cleaned parsley roots
30ml/2 tbsp paprika
1 green (bell) pepper, sliced
5–10ml/1–2 tsp tomato purée (paste)
salt
90ml/6 tbsp sour cream and 3 cherry peppers (optional), to serve

1 Skin and fillet the fish and cut the flesh into chunks. Put all the fish heads, skin and bones into a large pan, together with the onions, garlic, celeriac, parsley stalks, paprika and salt. Cover with water and bring to the boil. Reduce the heat and simmer for 1¼–1½ hours. Strain the stock.

2 Place the fish and green pepper in a large frying pan and pour over the stock. Blend the tomato purée with a little stock and pour it into the pan.

3 Heat gently but do not stir, or the fish will break up. Cook for just 10–12 minutes but do not boil. Season to taste.

4 Ladle into warmed deep plates or bowls and top with a generous spoonful of sour cream and a halved cherry pepper, if liked.

> **Cook's Tip**
> Use any firm-textured fish to make goulash, such as cod, haddock or halibut. In Hungary freshwater fish such as carp, pike or eel may be used, and it is sometimes said that the more varieties of fish go into a soup the better it will be.

Carp with Bay Leaves: Energy 410kcal/1713kJ; Protein 32.3g; Carbohydrate 18.1g, of which sugars 6.6g; Fat 23.7g, of which saturates 10.3g; Cholesterol 142mg; Calcium 109mg; Fibre 2g; Sodium 423mg.
Paprika-spiced Fish Goulash: Energy 420kcal/1761kJ; Protein 64.1g; Carbohydrate 15.2g, of which sugars 12g; Fat 5.8g, of which saturates 2.2g; Cholesterol 162mg; Calcium 104mg; Fibre 3g; Sodium 259mg.

Green Fish Curry

Any firm-fleshed fish can be used for this traditional Thai curry, which gains its rich flavour from a mixture of fresh herbs, spices and lime.

Serves 4

4 garlic cloves, coarsely chopped
5cm/2in piece fresh root ginger, peeled and coarsely chopped
2 fresh green chillies, seeded and coarsely chopped
grated rind and juice of 1 lime
5–10ml/1–2 tsp shrimp paste (optional)
5ml/1 tsp coriander seeds
5ml/1 tsp five-spice powder
75ml/6 tbsp sesame oil
2 red onions, finely chopped
900g/2lb hoki fillets, skinned
400ml/14fl oz/1²⁄₃ cups canned coconut milk
45ml/3 tbsp nam pla
50g/2oz/2 cups fresh coriander (cilantro) leaves
50g/2oz/2 cups fresh basil leaves
6 spring onions (scallions), coarsely chopped
150ml/¹⁄₄ pint/²⁄₃ cup sunflower or groundnut (peanut) oil
sliced fresh green chilli and finely chopped fresh coriander (cilantro), to garnish
cooked basmati or Thai fragrant rice and lime wedges, to serve

1 First make the curry paste. Combine the garlic, ginger, chillies, lime juice and shrimp paste, if using, in a food processor. Add the spices, with half the sesame oil. Process to a paste, then spoon into a bowl, cover and set aside.

2 Heat a wok or large, shallow pan, and pour in the remaining sesame oil. When it is hot, stir-fry the red onions over a high heat for 2 minutes. Add the fish and stir-fry for 1–2 minutes to seal the fillets on all sides.

3 Lift out the red onions and fish with a slotted spoon and put them on a plate. Add the curry paste to the wok or pan and fry for 1 minute, stirring constantly. Return the fish and onions to the pan, pour in the coconut milk and bring to the boil. Lower the heat, add the *nam pla* and simmer gently for 5–7 minutes until the fish is cooked through and tender.

4 Process the herbs, spring onions, lime rind and sunflower or groundnut oil to a coarse paste. Stir into the fish curry. Garnish with chilli and coriander and serve with rice and lime wedges.

Piquant Paprika-marinated Fish

Fresh herbs, lime and paprika are used to flavour the fish in this tasty recipe.

Serves 4

5 tomatoes
675g/1¹⁄₂lb white fish, such as cod, sea bass or monkfish
sunflower oil, for frying
500g/1¹⁄₄lb potatoes, sliced
1 onion, chopped
1–2 garlic cloves, crushed
375g/13oz fresh spinach, chopped

For the chermoula

6 spring onions (scallions), chopped
10ml/2 tsp fresh thyme
60ml/4 tbsp chopped fresh parsley
30ml/2 tbsp chopped fresh coriander (cilantro)
10ml/2 tsp paprika
generous pinch of cayenne pepper
60ml/4 tbsp olive oil
grated rind of 1 lime and 60ml/ 4 tbsp lime juice
salt

1 Plunge the tomatoes into boiling water for 30 seconds, then refresh in cold water. Peel off the skins, remove the seeds and chop the flesh. Cut the fish into pieces, discarding any skin and bones, and place in a shallow dish.

2 Blend together the ingredients for the chermoula and season well with salt. Pour over the fish, stir to mix and leave in a cool place, covered with clear film (plastic wrap), for 2–4 hours. Heat about 5mm/¹⁄₄in oil in a large, heavy pan and fry the potatoes until cooked through and golden. Drain on kitchen paper.

3 Pour off all but 15ml/1 tbsp of the oil and add the chopped onion, garlic and tomatoes. Cook over a low heat for 5–6 minutes, stirring occasionally, until the onion is soft. Place the potatoes on top and pile the chopped spinach into the pan.

4 Place the pieces of fish on top of the spinach and pour over all the marinade. Cover the pan tightly and steam for 15–18 minutes. After about 8 minutes, carefully stir the contents of the pan, so that the fish at the top is distributed throughout the dish. Cover the pan again and continue cooking, but check the contents occasionally – the dish is ready once the fish is tender and opaque and the spinach has wilted. Serve at once on individual serving plates, garnished with wedges of lime.

Green Fish Curry: Energy 575kcal/2390kJ; Protein 40g; Carbohydrate 6.2g, of which sugars 4.9g; Fat 43.5g, of which saturates 5.9g; Cholesterol 6mg; Calcium 132mg; Fibre 0g; Sodium 362mg.
Paprika-marinated Fish: Energy 433kcal/1810kJ; Protein 37.3g; Carbohydrate 28.9g, of which sugars 9.4g; Fat 19.3g, of which saturates 2.8g; Cholesterol 78mg; Calcium 206mg; Fibre 5.2g; Sodium 260mg.

Spiced Fish with Chermoula

The fish for this tagine is marinated in chermoula, which gives it an unmistakable Moroccan flavour. It is a delightful dish at any time of year, but is especially good made with new season potatoes.

Serves 4

900g/2lb monkfish tail, cut into chunks
45–60ml/3–4 tbsp olive oil
4–5 garlic cloves, thinly sliced
15–20 cherry tomatoes
2 green (bell) peppers, grilled (broiled) until charred and cut into strips
15–20 small new potatoes, scrubbed and par-boiled
large handful of kalamata or fleshy black olives
about 100ml/3½fl oz/scant ½ cup water
salt and ground black pepper
bread, to serve

For the chermoula

2 garlic cloves
5ml/1 tsp coarse salt
10ml/2 tsp ground cumin
5ml/1 tsp paprika
juice of 1 lemon
small bunch of fresh coriander (cilantro), roughly chopped
15ml/1 tbsp olive oil

1 To make the chermoula, pound the garlic with the salt using a pestle and mortar. Add the cumin, paprika, lemon juice and coriander, and gradually mix in the olive oil. Reserve a little chermoula for cooking, then rub the rest over the monkfish. Cover and leave to marinate for about 1 hour.

2 Heat the olive oil in a heavy pan and stir in the garlic. Add the tomatoes and cook until just softened. Add the peppers and the remaining chermoula, and season with salt and pepper.

3 Cut the potatoes in half lengthways and spread them over the base of a shallow pan or tagine. Spoon three-quarters of the tomato and pepper mixture over and place the fish chunks on top, with their marinade. Spoon the rest of the tomato and pepper mixture on top of the fish and add the olives.

4 Drizzle a little extra olive oil over the dish and pour in the water. Heat until simmering, cover and cook over a medium heat for about 15 minutes, or until the fish is cooked through. Serve with bread to mop up the juices.

Salt Cod in Spicy Tomato Sauce

This is a traditional Basque recipe. Look out for a loin piece of salt cod, which has very little waste; if you can't find one, buy a larger piece to ensure you have enough once any very dry bits have been removed.

Serves 4

400g/14oz salt cod loin, soaked in cold water for 24 hours
30ml/2 tbsp olive oil
1 large onion, chopped
2 garlic cloves, finely chopped
1½ green (bell) peppers, chopped
500g/1¼lb ripe tomatoes, peeled and chopped, or a 400g/14oz can tomatoes
15ml/1 tbsp tomato purée (paste)
15ml/1 tbsp clear honey
1.5ml/¼ tsp dried thyme
2.5ml/½ tsp cayenne pepper
juice of ½ lemon (optional)
2 potatoes
45ml/3 tbsp stale breadcrumbs
30ml/2 tbsp finely chopped fresh parsley
salt and ground black pepper

1 Drain the soaked salt cod and place it in a pan. Pour over enough water to cover generously and bring to the boil. Remove the pan from the heat as soon as the water boils, then set aside until cold.

2 Heat the oil in a medium pan. Fry the onion, and add the garlic after 5 minutes. Add the chopped peppers and tomatoes, and cook gently to form a sauce. Stir in the tomato purée, honey, dried thyme, cayenne, black pepper and a little salt. Taste for seasoning: a little lemon juice will make it tangier.

3 Halve the potatoes lengthways and cut into slices just thicker than a coin. Drain the fish, reserving the cooking water. Preheat the grill (broiler) to medium with a shelf 15cm/6in below it.

4 Bring the reserved fish cooking water to the boil and cook the potatoes for about 8 minutes. Do not add extra salt.

5 Remove the skin and bones from the cod, and pull it into small natural flakes. Spoon one-third of the tomato sauce into a flameproof casserole, top with the potatoes, fish and remaining sauce. Combine the breadcrumbs and parsley and sprinkle over. Heat the dish through under a grill for 10 minutes.

Spiced Fish with Chermoula: Energy 174kcal/735kJ; Protein 33.7g; Carbohydrate 6.1g, of which sugars 5.9g; Fat 1.8g, of which saturates 0.4g; Cholesterol 81mg; Calcium 32mg; Fibre 2.5g; Sodium 134mg.
Salt Cod in Tomato Sauce: Energy 292kcal/1234kJ; Protein 36g; Carbohydrate 21.8g, of which sugars 12.8g; Fat 7.4g, of which saturates 1.2g; Cholesterol 59mg; Calcium 71mg; Fibre 3.3g; Sodium 512mg.

Louisiana Seafood Gumbo

Gumbo, a chunky, spicy soup served over rice, is a staple dish in Louisiana.

Serves 6
450g/1lb mussels, cleaned
450g/1lb prawns (shrimp)
450g/1lb crab meat, half brown
  and half white
1 small bunch of parsley, leaves
  chopped and stalks reserved
150ml/5fl oz/⅔ cup oil
115g/4oz/1 cup plain (all-
  purpose) flour
1 green (bell) pepper, chopped
1 large onion, chopped
2 celery sticks, sliced
3 garlic cloves, finely chopped
75g/3oz smoked spiced sausage,
  skinned and sliced
6 spring onions (scallions),
  shredded
cayenne pepper, Tabasco sauce
  and boiled rice, to serve

1 Discard any mussels that are broken or any open ones that don't close when tapped. Bring 250ml/8fl oz/1 cup water to the boil. Add the mussels, cover tightly and cook over a high heat for 3–4 minutes to open. Strain, reserving the cooking liquid.

2 Shell the mussels, discarding any that have failed to open. Return the liquor to the pan and make up to 2 litres/3½ pints/9 cups with water. Shell the prawns and put the shells and heads into the pan. Bring to the boil, skimming off any froth. Add the parsley stalks and simmer for 15 minutes. Cool, strain and make up to 2 litres/3½ pints/9 cups with water.

3 Heat the oil in a large pan and add the flour. Stir constantly over the heat until the roux is golden brown. Add the pepper, onion, celery and garlic and continue cooking for about 5 minutes, then add the sliced sausage. Reheat the stock.

4 Stir the brown crab meat into the roux, then ladle in the stock a little at a time, stirring constantly until it is smooth. Simmer the soup for 30 minutes, partially covered. Add the prawns, mussels, white crab meat and spring onions. Return to the boil, season with salt if necessary, cayenne and a dash or two of Tabasco sauce, and simmer for a further minute.

5 Add the chopped parsley leaves and serve immediately, ladling the soup over the hot rice in soup plates.

Prawn Creole

In this famous Cajun dish, plump prawns are coated in a rich tomato sauce full of warm, spicy flavours.

Serves 6–8
75g/3oz/6 tbsp unsalted butter
1 large onion, halved and thinly
  sliced
1 large green (bell) pepper, halved
  and thinly sliced
2 celery sticks, thinly sliced
2 garlic cloves, thinly sliced
1 bay leaf
30ml/2 tbsp paprika
450g/1lb/2 cups skinned, chopped
  fresh tomatoes
250ml/8fl oz/1 cup tomato juice
20ml/4 tsp Worcestershire sauce
4–6 dashes Tabasco sauce
7.5ml/1½ tsp cornflour
  (cornstarch)
1.5kg/3lb raw prawns (shrimp),
  peeled and deveined
salt
boiled rice, to serve
chopped parsley and shreds of
  lemon peel, to garnish (optional)

1 Melt 25g/1oz/2 tbsp of the butter in a wide pan and sauté the onion, green pepper, celery, garlic and bay leaf for 1–2 minutes until all are hot and coated in butter.

2 Add the paprika, tomatoes and tomato juice, stir in the Worcestershire and Tabasco sauces, bring to the boil and simmer, uncovered, to reduce the volume by about a quarter, by which time the vegetables will have softened. Season.

3 Mix the cornflour with 75ml/5 tbsp cold water and pour it into the tomato sauce.

4 Stir the sauce continuously over the heat for a couple of minutes until it thickens, then turn off the heat.

5 Sauté the prawns in batches in the remaining butter until pink and tender – this will take 2–4 minutes, depending on the size of the prawns.

6 Meanwhile, reheat the tomato sauce. When all the prawns are cooked, add them to the sauce and stir over the heat for no more than 1 minute. Check the seasoning and serve with fluffy boiled rice, garnished, if you like, with chopped fresh parsley and shreds of lemon peel.

Seafood Gumbo: Energy 559kcal/2336kJ; Protein 31.1g; Carbohydrate 57.6g, of which sugars 3.7g; Fat 23g, of which saturates 3.4g; Cholesterol 183mg; Calcium 145mg; Fibre 1.9g; Sodium 474mg.
Prawn Creole: Energy 562kcal/2348kJ; Protein 69.3g; Carbohydrate 12.5g, of which sugars 10.1g; Fat 21.6g, of which saturates 2.6g; Cholesterol 740mg; Calcium 382mg; Fibre 3.5g; Sodium 1867mg.

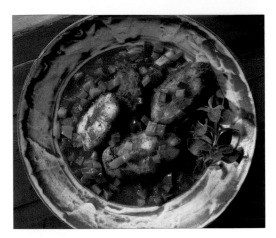

Creole Fish Stew

This delicious stew is full of the inimitable warm, spicy flavours of Mississippi cooking. It makes a simple but attractive party dish, served with rice.

Serves 4–6
2 whole red bream or large
 snapper, prepared and cut into
 2.5cm/1in pieces
30ml/2 tbsp Cajun spice
 seasoning
30ml/2 tbsp malt vinegar
flour, for dusting
oil, for frying

For the sauce
30ml/2 tbsp vegetable oil
15ml/1 tbsp butter
1 onion, finely chopped
275g/10oz fresh tomatoes,
 peeled and finely chopped
2 garlic cloves, crushed
2 thyme sprigs
600ml/1 pint/2½ cups fish stock
 or water
2.5ml/½ tsp ground cinnamon
1 red chilli, chopped
115g/4oz each red and green
 (bell) pepper, finely chopped
salt
oregano sprigs, to garnish

1 Sprinkle the fish with the Cajun spice seasoning and vinegar, turning to coat. Set aside to marinate for at least 2 hours or overnight in the refrigerator.

2 When ready to cook, place a little flour on a large plate and coat the fish pieces, shaking off any excess flour.

3 Heat a little oil in a large frying pan and fry the fish pieces for about 5 minutes until golden brown, then set aside. Don't worry if the fish is not cooked through, it will finish cooking in the sauce.

4 To make the sauce, heat the oil and butter in a large frying pan or wok and stir-fry the chopped onion for 5 minutes. Add the tomatoes, garlic and thyme, stir well and simmer for a further 5 minutes. Stir in the stock or water, cinnamon and red chilli.

5 Add the fish pieces and the chopped peppers to the pan. Simmer until the fish is cooked through, and the stock has reduced to a thick sauce. Adjust the seasoning with salt. Serve hot, garnished with oregano.

Spicy Oyster and Bacon Brochettes

Six oysters per person make a good starter, served with the seasoned oyster liquor to trickle over the skewers. Increase the oyster ration to nine and serve hot with a cool salad as a main course. You might then beat some olive oil into the sauce and use it to dress the salad.

Serves 4–6
36 oysters
18 thin-cut rashers (slices)
 rindless streaky (fatty) bacon
115g/4oz/1 cup plain (all-
 purpose) flour
30ml/1 tbsp paprika
5ml/1 tsp cayenne pepper

5ml/1 tsp salt
5ml/1 tsp garlic salt
10ml/2 tsp dried oregano
ground black pepper
oil for shallow-frying
celery leaves and red chillies,
 to garnish

For the sauce
½ red chilli pepper, seeded and
 very finely chopped
2 spring onions (scallions), very
 finely chopped
30ml/2 tbsp finely chopped fresh
 parsley
liquor from shucking oysters
juice of ¼–½ lemon
salt and ground black pepper

1 Shuck the oysters over a bowl to catch their liquor for the sauce. Wrap your left hand in a clean cloth and cup the deep shell of each oyster in your wrapped hand. Work the point of a strong short-bladed knife into the hinge and twist.

2 Push the knife in and work it to cut the muscle, holding the shell closed. Tip the liquor from the deep shell into the bowl. Cut under the flesh of the oyster to free it from the shell.

3 Halve the bacon rashers crossways and wrap each oyster in half a rasher, then thread them on to 4 or 6 skewers.

4 Mix the flour with the paprika, cayenne, salt, garlic salt, oregano and black pepper. Spread on a flat plate and roll the skewered oysters in it, shaking the surplus back on to the plate. Heat 2.5 cm/1 in depth of oil in a wide frying pan and fry the skewers, for 3–4 minutes, turning until crisp and brown. Serve with the garnish, accompanied by the bowl of sauce.

Fragrant Spanish Fish Stew

This splendid fish feast is a favourite throughout Spain.

Serves 6
60ml/4 tbsp olive oil
8 small squid, cleaned
plain (all-purpose) flour,
   for dusting
500g/1¼lb skinless, boneless
   white fish such as monkfish
   and cod, cut in large chunks
30ml/2 tbsp Ricard or Pernod
450ml/¾ pint/2 cups fish stock
250ml/8fl oz/1 cup white wine
450g/1lb mussels, cleaned
16 raw king prawns (jumbo
   shrimp), with heads, deveined

115g/4oz prawns (shrimp)
salt and ground black pepper
45ml/3 tbsp chopped fresh
   parsley, to garnish

For the broth
30ml/2 tbsp oil
1 large onion, finely chopped
2 garlic cloves, finely chopped
500g/1¼lb ripe tomatoes, peeled,
   seeded and chopped
2 bay leaves
1 dried chilli, seeded and chopped
5ml/1 tsp paprika
pinch of saffron threads
salt and ground black pepper

1 To make the broth, heat the oil in a flameproof casserole and soften the onion and garlic. Add the tomatoes, bay leaves, chilli, paprika and saffron and cook gently to make a sauce.

2 Meanwhile, heat the oil in a large pan. Put in the squid tentacles, face down, and cook for 45 seconds, to make "flowers". Reserve on a plate. Flour and fry the fish pieces for 2 minutes on each side. Cut the squid bodies into rings and fry. Pour the Ricard or Pernod into a ladle, flame it and pour over the fish remaining in the pan. Remove the fish and reserve.

3 Add the fish stock and the wine to the sauce and bring to a simmer. Add the mussels, cover for 2 minutes, then remove to a plate, discard any closed mussels, and remove the upper shells. Add the raw prawns to the casserole for 3–4 minutes, then lift out and reserve.

4 About 20 minutes before serving, add the white fish to the casserole, followed by the squid rings and then the shellfish, keeping the liquid simmering gently. Season to taste. Sprinkle over the mussels and squid flowers and garnish with parsley.

Shellfish Curry with Coconut Milk

This Vietnamese recipe is made with prawns, squid and scallops but you could use any combination of shellfish, or chunks of filleted fish. Serve with fresh bread and extra chillies.

Serves 4
4cm/1½in fresh root ginger,
   peeled and roughly chopped
3 garlic cloves, roughly chopped
45ml/3 tbsp groundnut (peanut)
   oil
1 onion, finely sliced
2 lemon grass stalks, finely sliced
2 green or red Thai chillies,
   seeded and finely sliced
15ml/1 tbsp raw cane sugar
10ml/2 tsp shrimp paste
15ml/1 tbsp nuoc mam
30ml/2 tbsp curry powder or
   garam masala
550ml/18fl oz/2½ cups coconut
   milk
grated rind and juice of 1 lime
4 medium-sized squid, cleaned
   and cut diagonally into 3 or
   4 pieces
12 king or queen scallops, shelled
20 large raw prawns (shrimp),
   shelled and deveined
1 small bunch fresh basil,
   stalks removed
salt
1 small bunch fresh coriander
   (cilantro), stalks removed, leaves
   finely chopped, to garnish

1 Using a mortar and pestle, grind the ginger with the garlic until it almost resembles a paste. Heat the oil in a flameproof clay pot, wok or heavy pan and stir in the onion. Cook until it begins to turn brown, then stir in the garlic and ginger paste.

2 Once the fragrant aromas begin to rise, add the sliced lemon grass, sliced chillies and raw cane sugar. Cook briefly before adding the shrimp paste, *nuoc mam* and curry powder or garam masala. Mix thoroughly with a wooden spoon and stir-fry gently for 1–2 minutes.

3 Add the coconut milk, lime rind and juice. Bring to the boil. Cook, stirring, for 2–3 minutes. Season to taste with salt.

4 Gently stir in the squid, scallops and prawns and bring to the boil once more. Reduce the heat and cook gently until the shellfish turns opaque. Stir in the basil leaves and sprinkle the chopped coriander over the top. Serve immediately from the pot with bread or steamed rice and fresh chillies.

Spicy Couscous with Aromatic Broth

In this Moroccan dish, the couscous absorbs all the spicy sweet flavours of the shellfish broth.

Serves 4–6
500g/1¼lb/3 cups couscous
5ml/1 tsp salt
600ml/1 pint/2½ cups warm water
45ml/3 tbsp sunflower oil
5–10ml/1–2 tsp harissa
25g/1oz/2 tbsp butter, diced

For the shellfish broth
500g/1¼lb mussels, cleaned
500g/1¼lb raw prawns (shrimp) in their shells
juice of 1 lemon
50g/2oz/2 tbsp butter
2 shallots, finely chopped
5ml/1 tsp coriander seeds, roasted and ground
5ml/1 tsp cumin seeds, roasted and ground
2.5ml/½ tsp ground turmeric
2.5ml/½ tsp cayenne pepper
5–10ml/1–2 tsp plain (all-purpose) flour
600ml/1 pint/2½ cups fish stock
120ml/4fl oz/½ cup double (heavy) cream
salt and ground black pepper
small bunch of fresh coriander (cilantro), finely chopped

1 Preheat the oven to 180°C/350°F/Gas 4. Place the couscous in a bowl. Stir the salt into the water, then pour over the couscous, stirring. Set aside for 10 minutes. Stir the sunflower oil into the harissa, then rub this paste into the couscous and break up any lumps. Tip into an ovenproof dish, arrange the butter over, cover with foil and bake for 20 minutes.

2 Put the mussels and prawns in a pan, add the lemon juice and 50ml/2fl oz/¼ cup water, cover and cook for 3–4 minutes to open the mussels. Drain, reserving the liquor, and shell about two-thirds of the shellfish. Discard any closed mussels.

3 Heat the butter in a large pan. Cook the shallots for 5 minutes, then add the spices and fry for 1 minute. Off the heat, stir in the flour, stock and shellfish liquor. Bring to the boil, stirring. Add the cream and simmer for about 10 minutes. Season, add the shellfish and most of the fresh coriander. Heat through, then sprinkle with the remaining coriander. Fluff up the couscous, working in the melted butter. Serve the couscous in bowls with the broth ladled over the top.

Spiced Scallops and Sugar Snap Peas on Crispy Noodle Cakes

Tender, juicy scallops are cooked in spices and served on a bed of crispy deep-fried noodles.

Serves 4
45ml/3 tbsp oyster sauce
10ml/2 tsp soy sauce
5ml/1 tsp sesame oil
5ml/1 tsp golden caster (superfine) sugar
30ml/2 tbsp sunflower oil
2 red chillies, finely sliced
4 garlic cloves, finely chopped
10ml/2 tsp finely chopped fresh root ginger
250g/9oz sugar snap peas
500g/1¼lb king scallops without roes, cleaned and halved
3 spring onions (scallions), finely shredded

For the noodle cakes
250g/9oz fresh thin egg noodles
10ml/2 tsp sesame oil
120ml/4fl oz/½ cup sunflower oil

1 Cook the noodles in boiling water for 1 minute, or until tender. Drain and transfer to a bowl with the sesame oil and 15ml/1 tbsp of the sunflower oil. Spread the noodles out on a large baking sheet and leave to dry in a warm place for 1 hour.

2 Heat 15ml/1 tbsp of the remaining oil in a non-stick wok over a high heat. Add one quarter of the noodle mixture to the wok and use a spatula to flatten it out and shape it into a cake. Reduce the heat slightly and cook for about 5 minutes on each side, until crisp and golden. Drain on kitchen paper and keep warm while you make three more cakes in the same way.

3 Mix the oyster sauce, soy sauce, sesame oil and sugar, stirring until the sugar has dissolved completely. Heat a wok over a medium heat and add the sunflower oil. When hot add the chillies, garlic and ginger, and stir-fry for 30 seconds. Add the sugar snap peas and stir-fry for 1–2 minutes. Add the scallops and spring onions to the wok and cook over a high heat for 1 minute. Stir in the oyster sauce mixture and cook for a further 1 minute until warmed through.

4 To serve, place a noodle cake on each of four warmed plates and top each one with the scallop mixture. Serve immediately.

Couscous with Broth: Energy 338kcal/1422kJ; Protein 33.7g; Carbohydrate 24.7g, of which sugars 12.1g; Fat 12.4g, of which saturates 1.8g; Cholesterol 23mg; Calcium 100mg; Fibre 6.6g; Sodium 517mg.
Scallops on Noodle Cakes: Energy 689kcal/2888kJ; Protein 41.4g; Carbohydrate 59.9g, of which sugars 6.2g; Fat 33.3g, of which saturates 5.4g; Cholesterol 78mg; Calcium 73mg; Fibre 5g; Sodium 700mg.

Goan Prawn Curry with Mango and Coconut Milk

This sweet, spicy, hot-and-sour curry comes from the shores of Western India. It is simple to make, and the addition of mango and tamarind produces a very full, rich flavour. If you have time, make this dish the day before to give the flavours time to develop. Simply reheat to serve.

Serves 4

5ml/1 tsp hot chilli powder
15ml/1 tbsp paprika
2.5ml/½ tsp turmeric
4 garlic cloves, crushed
10ml/2 tsp finely grated fresh root ginger
30ml/2 tbsp ground coriander
10ml/2 tsp ground cumin
15ml/1 tbsp palm sugar (jaggery)
1 green mango, sliced and stoned
400g/14oz can coconut milk
10ml/2 tsp salt
15ml/1 tbsp tamarind paste
1kg/2¼lb large prawns (shrimp), heads and tails on
chopped coriander (cilantro), to garnish
steamed white rice, to serve
chopped tomato, cucumber and onion salad, to serve

1 In a large bowl, combine the chilli powder, paprika, turmeric, garlic, ginger, ground coriander, ground cumin and palm sugar. Add 400ml/14fl oz/1⅔ cups cold water to the bowl and stir to combine.

2 Pour the spice mixture into a wok. Place the wok over a high heat and bring the mixture to the boil. Cover the wok with a lid, reduce the heat to low and leave to simmer gently for 8–10 minutes.

3 Add the mango, coconut milk, salt and tamarind paste to the wok and stir to combine. Bring to a simmer and then add the prawns. Cover the wok and cook gently for 10–12 minutes, or until the prawns have turned pink and are cooked through and the sauce is reduced.

4 Serve the curry garnished with chopped coriander, accompanied by steamed white rice and a tomato, cucumber and onion salad.

Thai Stir-fried Squid with Ginger and Garlic

The abundance of fish around the Gulf of Thailand sustains thriving markets for the restaurant and hotel trade, and every market naturally features food stalls where delicious, freshly-caught seafood is cooked in front of you and served. This quick and very tasty recipe is popular among street traders and their customers.

Serves 2

4 ready-prepared and cleaned baby squid, total weight about 250g/9oz
15ml/1 tbsp vegetable oil
2 garlic cloves, peeled and finely chopped
30ml/2 tbsp soy sauce
2.5cm/1in piece fresh root ginger, peeled and finely chopped
juice of ½ lemon
5ml/1 tsp granulated sugar
2 spring onions (scallions), chopped

1 Rinse the squid well and pat dry with kitchen paper. With a sharp knife, slice the bodies into rings and halve the tentacles lengthways, if necessary.

2 Heat the oil in a wok or frying pan and cook the garlic stirring, until golden brown, be careful not let it burn. Add the squid and stir-fry for 30 seconds over a high heat.

3 Add the soy sauce, ginger, lemon juice, sugar and spring onions. Stir-fry for a further 30 seconds, then serve.

Variations
This dish is often prepared with fresh galangal rather than ginger and works well with most kinds of seafood, including prawns (shrimp) and scallops.

Cook's Tip
Squid has an undeserved reputation for being rubbery in texture. This is always a result of overcooking it.

Prawn Curry with Mango: Energy 151kcal/648kJ; Protein 22.1g; Carbohydrate 14.1g, of which sugars 14g; Fat 1.1g, of which saturates 0.5g; Cholesterol 263mg; Calcium 143mg; Fibre 1g; Sodium 2102mg.
Stir-fried Squid with Ginger: Energy 169kcal/709kJ; Protein 20g; Carbohydrate 5.3g, of which sugars 3.6g; Fat 7.7g, of which saturates 1.2g; Cholesterol 281mg; Calcium 26mg; Fibre 0.2g; Sodium 1207mg.

Prawn and Cauliflower Curry with Fenugreek and Star Anise

This is a basic fisherman's curry from the southern coast of Vietnam. Simple to make, it would usually be eaten with noodles, rice or chunks of baguette to mop up the deliciously fragrant, creamy sauce. Fenugreek seeds, which are much used in Indian cookery, have a distinctive curry aroma, brought out by dry frying.

Serves 4
450g/1lb raw tiger prawns (jumbo shrimp), shelled and deveined
juice of 1 lime
15ml/1 tbsp sesame or vegetable oil
1 red onion, roughly chopped
2 garlic cloves, roughly chopped
2 Thai chillies, seeded and chopped
1 cauliflower, broken into florets
5ml/1 tsp sugar
2 star anise, dry fried and ground
10ml/2 tsp fenugreek, dry fried and ground
450ml/¾ pint/2 cups coconut milk
salt and ground black pepper
1 bunch fresh coriander (cilantro), stalks removed, leaves chopped, to garnish

1 In a bowl, toss the prawns in the lime juice and set aside. Heat a wok or heavy pan and add the oil. Stir in the onion, garlic and chillies. As they brown, add the cauliflower. Stir-fry for 2–3 minutes.

2 Toss in the sugar and spices. Add the coconut milk, stirring to make sure it is thoroughly combined. Reduce the heat and simmer for 10–15 minutes, or until the liquid has reduced and thickened a little.

3 Add the prawns and lime juice and cook for 1–2 minutes, or until the prawns turn opaque. Season to taste, and sprinkle with coriander. Serve immediately.

Variation
Other popular combinations include prawns with butternut squash or pumpkin.

Grilled Malaysian Prawns with Tamarind

The marinade for this Malay dish is seasoned and sweetened with a condiment called kecap manis, which is soy sauce that has been sweetened with palm sugar. You can replace this with the same quantity of dark soy sauce blended with a little muscovado sugar.

Serves 2–4
500g/1¼lb large raw prawns (jumbo shrimp)
45ml/3 tbsp tamarind pulp
30ml/2 tbsp kecap manis
15ml/1 tbsp sugar
ground black pepper
fresh coriander (cilantro) leaves and 2–4 green chillies, seeded and quartered lengthways, to garnish

1 Devein the prawns and remove the feelers and legs. Rinse well, pat dry and, using a sharp knife, make an incision along the curve of the tail.

2 Put the tamarind pulp in a bowl and add 250ml/8fl oz/1 cup warm water. Soak the pulp until soft, squeezing it with your fingers to help soften it. Strain the liquid and discard any fibre.

3 In a bowl, mix together the tamarind juice, kecap manis, sugar and black pepper. Pour it over the prawns, rubbing it over the shells and into the incisions in the tails. Cover and leave to marinate for 1 hour.

4 Prepare a barbecue, or heat a conventional grill (broiler) to a high heat, and place the prawns on the grill rack. Grill the prawns for about 3 minutes on each side until cooked through, brushing them with the marinade as they cook. Serve immediately, garnished with coriander and chillies.

Variation
This recipe works well with other shellfish, and the same marinade can be used for chicken wings and drumsticks. It makes a tangy addition to a barbecue.

Prawn Curry with Fenugreek: Energy 232Kcal/971kJ; Protein 25g; Carbohydrate 13g, of which sugars 12g; Fat 10g, of which saturates 2g; Cholesterol 219mg; Calcium 167mg; Fibre 2.2g; Sodium 500mg
Grilled Malaysian Prawns: Energy 74Kcal/309kJ; Protein 11.4g; Carbohydrate 4.9g, of which sugars 4.8g; Fat 1.1g, of which saturates 0.3g; Cholesterol 39mg; Calcium 97mg; Fibre 0.6g; Sodium 1301mg.

Baked Crab with Garlic and Ginger

The Vietnamese have made this French-inspired dish their own with a combination of bean thread noodles and cloud ear mushrooms. It is time-consuming to cook the crabs yourself, so you can use freshly cooked crab meat from your fishmonger or supermarket. Buy it in the shell, or ask the fishmonger for some shells, as you will also need four small, empty shells in which to cook the crab. Alternatively, you can bake it in individual ovenproof dishes.

Serves 4

25g/1oz dried bean thread
  (cellophane) noodles
6 dried cloud ear (wood ear)
  mushrooms
450g/1lb fresh crab meat
15ml/1 tbsp vegetable oil
10ml/2 tsp nuoc mam
2 shallots, finely chopped
2 garlic cloves, finely chopped
2.5cm/1in fresh root ginger,
  peeled and grated
1 small bunch coriander (cilantro),
  stalks removed, leaves chopped
1 egg, beaten
25g/1oz/2 tbsp butter
salt and ground black pepper
fresh dill fronds, to garnish
nuoc cham, to serve

1 Preheat the oven to 180°C/350°F/Gas 4. Soak the bean thread noodles and cloud ear mushrooms separately in bowls of lukewarm water for 15 minutes, then squeeze them dry and chop finely.

2 In a bowl, mix together the chopped noodles and mushrooms with the crab meat. Add the oil, *nuoc mam*, shallots, garlic, ginger and coriander. Season, then stir in the beaten egg.

3 Spoon the mixture into four small crab shells or use individual ovenproof dishes, packing it in tightly, and dot the top of each one with a little butter.

4 Place the shells on a baking tray and cook for about 20 minutes, or until the tops are nicely browned.

5 Garnish with dill and serve immediately with a little *nuoc cham* to drizzle over the top.

King Prawns with Ginger

Succulent steamed prawns are mixed with shredded beef and crunchy bamboo shoots then coated with a rich pine nut dressing to create a scintillating dish.

Serves 2

6 king prawns (jumbo shrimp),
  shelled and deveined
20g/³⁄₄oz fresh root ginger, peeled
  and sliced

15ml/1 tbsp mirin or rice wine
¹⁄₂ cucumber
75g/3oz bamboo shoots, sliced
90g/3¹⁄₂oz beef flank
15ml/1 tbsp vegetable oil
salt and ground white pepper

For the dressing

60ml/4 tbsp pine nuts
10ml/2 tsp sesame oil
2.5ml/¹⁄₂ tsp salt
ground black pepper

1 Prepare a steamer over a pan of boiling water, with a bowl in place under the steamer to catch any liquid. Place the prawns in the steamer with the ginger, and pour over the mirin or rice wine. Season with salt and pepper. Steam for 8 minutes. Seed the cucumber and slice it lengthways into thin strips.

2 Remove the prawns from the steamer. Remove the bowl of liquid from beneath the steamer and set it aside. Blanch the bamboo shoots in boiling water for 30 seconds. Remove, slice and sprinkle with salt. Add the beef to the boiling water and cook until tender. Drain and leave to cool.

3 Slice the prawns into 2cm/³⁄₄in pieces. Transfer to the refrigerator. Slice the beef thinly, cut into bitesize pieces and chill in the refrigerator.

4 Coat a frying pan or wok with the vegetable oil and quickly stir-fry the cucumber and bamboo shoots until they have softened. Cool then chill in the refrigerator.

5 Make the dressing, grind the pine nuts in a mortar and pestle and then transfer to a bowl. Add 45ml/3 tbsp of the prawn liquid from the bowl, add the sesame oil, season and mix well.

6 Set all the chilled ingredients on a platter and pour over the dressing before serving.

Baked Crab with Garlic: Energy 289Kcal/1206kJ; Protein 26g; Carbohydrate 8g, of which sugars 2g; Fat 17g, of which saturates 5g; Cholesterol 145mg; Calcium 39mg; Fibre 24g; Sodium 800mg
King Prawns with Ginger: Energy 416kcal/1724kJ; Protein 24.7g; Carbohydrate 3.5g, of which sugars 2.7g; Fat 33.8g, of which saturates 4.3g; Cholesterol 124mg; Calcium 62mg; Fibre 1.5g; Sodium 619mg.

Eel in a Spicy Caramel Sauce

The flesh of an eel is very rich and firm and it has a wonderful flavour. It is a fish that has become more popular in recent years. Eel needs to be eaten very fresh, and is usually sold alive or killed on the spot. This Vietnamese dish comes from the northern highlands, where eels are caught in the rivers.

Serves 4

45ml/3 tbsp raw cane sugar
30ml/2 tbsp soy sauce
45ml/3 tbsp nuoc mam

2 garlic cloves, crushed
2 dried chillies
2–3 star anise
4–5 black peppercorns
350g/12oz eel on the bone,
  skinned, cut into 2.5cm/1in
  chunks
200g/7oz butternut squash, cut
  into bitesize chunks
4 spring onions (scallions), cut into
  bitesize pieces
30ml/2 tbsp sesame oil
5cm/2in fresh root ginger, peeled
  and cut into matchsticks
salt
cooked rice or noodles, to serve

1 Put the sugar in a wok or heavy pan with 30ml/2 tbsp water, and gently heat until it turns golden. Remove from the heat. Add the soy sauce and *nuoc mam* with 120ml/4fl oz/½ cup water. Add the garlic, chillies, star anise and peppercorns.

2 Return to the heat, add the eel chunks, squash and spring onions, coating the fish in the sauce, and season with salt. Reduce the heat, cover the pan and simmer gently for about 20 minutes, until the eel and vegetables are tender.

3 Meanwhile, heat a small wok, pour in the oil and stir-fry the ginger until crisp and golden. Remove and drain on kitchen paper. Serve the eel with rice or noodles, with the crispy ginger sprinkled on top.

> **Cook's Tip**
> The fat rendered from the fish melts into the caramel sauce, making it deliciously velvety. The dish is often served with chopped fresh coriander (cilantro) on top.

Indian Prawn and Potato Curry

This delicious dish is made with a freshly prepared spice paste and roasted fennel and mustard seeds are stirred in at the end of cooking to impart all their fresh fragrance. In India this curry would generally be eaten with a yogurt dish, chutney, and flatbread to scoop it up, but it could also be served with rice.

Serves 4

30ml/2 tbsp ghee, or 15ml/1 tbsp
  vegetable oil and 15g/½oz/
  1 tbsp butter
1 onion, halved lengthways and
  sliced along the grain
a handful of curry leaves
1 cinnamon stick

2–3 medium-size waxy potatoes,
  lightly steamed, peeled and
  diced
500g/1¼lb fresh large prawns
  (shrimp), peeled and deveined
200ml/7fl oz/scant 1 cup coconut
  milk
10ml/2 tsp fennel seeds
10ml/2 tsp brown mustard seeds
salt and ground black pepper
fresh coriander (cilantro) leaves,
  roughly chopped, to garnish

For the spice paste
4 garlic cloves, chopped
25g/1oz fresh root ginger, peeled
  and chopped
2 red chillies, seeded and
  chopped
5ml/1 tsp ground turmeric
15ml/1 tbsp fish curry powder

1 To make the spice paste, grind the garlic, ginger and chillies to a coarse paste using a mortar and pestle or a food processor. Stir in the turmeric and curry powder.

2 Heat the ghee in a heavy pan or earthenware pot. Stir in the onion and fry until golden. Stir in the curry leaves, followed by the cinnamon stick and the spice paste. Fry until fragrant, then add the potatoes, coating them in the spices.

3 Toss the prawns into the pan and cook for 12 minutes. Stir in the coconut milk and bubble it up to thicken and reduce it. Season with salt and pepper to taste.

4 Roast the fennel and mustard seeds in a small heavy pan until they begin to pop and give off a nutty aroma. Stir them into the curry and serve immediately, sprinkled with a little chopped coriander.

Indian Prawn and Potato Curry: Energy 204kcal/857kJ; Protein 23.5g; Carbohydrate 13.5g, of which sugars 5.2g; Fat 6.6g, of which saturates 0.9g; Cholesterol 244mg; Calcium 126mg; Fibre 1g; Sodium 299mg.
Eel in a Spicy Caramel Sauce: Energy 204Kcal/857kJ; Protein 11g; Carbohydrate 20g, of which sugars 14g; Fat 10g, of which saturates 1g; Cholesterol 0mg; Calcium 76mg; Fibre 1g; Sodium 110mg.

Ethiopian Spiced Chicken

Long-simmered spicy stews called *wat* are a feature of Ethiopian and Eritrean food. They always start with a large amount of onion, to which meat and a spicy paste are added, and are served with a pancake-like flatbread called *injera*. The eggs are an intrinsic part of the dish, so make sure everyone receives one in their portion.

Serves 4

90ml/6 tbsp vegetable oil
6–8 onions, chopped
6 garlic cloves, chopped
10ml/2 tsp chopped fresh root ginger
250ml/8fl oz/1 cup water or chicken stock
250ml/8fl oz/1 cup passata (bottled strained tomatoes) or 400g/14oz can chopped tomatoes
1.3kg/3lb chicken, cut into 8–12 portions
seeds from 5–8 cardamom pods
2.5ml/½ tsp ground turmeric
large pinch of ground cinnamon
large pinch of ground cloves
large pinch of grated nutmeg
cayenne pepper or hot paprika, to taste
4 hard-boiled eggs
salt and ground black pepper
fresh coriander (cilantro) and onion rings, to garnish
flatbread or rice, to serve

1 Heat the oil in a pan, add the onions and cook for 10 minutes until softened but not browned. Add the garlic and ginger and cook for 1–2 minutes.

2 Add the water or chicken stock and the passata or chopped tomatoes to the pan. Bring to the boil and cook, stirring continuously, for about 10 minutes, or until the liquid has reduced and the mixture has thickened. Season.

3 Add the chicken and spices to the pan and turn the chicken in the sauce. Reduce the heat, then cover and simmer, stirring occasionally, for about 1 hour, or until the chicken is tender. Add a little more liquid if the mixture seems too thick.

4 Remove the shells from the eggs and then prick the eggs once or twice with a fork. Add the eggs to the sauce and heat gently until the eggs are warmed through. Garnish with coriander and onion rings and serve with flat bread or rice.

Moroccan Chicken Tagine with Preserved Lemons

This dish, which is particularly enjoyed in Marrakesh, celebrates two of Morocco's most famous ingredients – cracked green olives and preserved lemons – and is flavoured with saffron, ginger and cinnamon. Try it when you are looking for a new way to cook a whole chicken instead of by the usual roasting method. Serve simply with plain couscous and a salad or vegetable side dish.

Serves 4

1.3kg/3lb chicken
3 garlic cloves, crushed
small bunch of fresh coriander (cilantro), finely chopped
juice of ½ lemon
5ml/1 tsp coarse salt
45–60ml/3–4 tbsp olive oil
1 large onion, grated
pinch of saffron threads
5ml/1 tsp ground ginger
5ml/1 tsp ground black pepper
1 cinnamon stick
175g/6oz/1½ cups cracked green olives
2 preserved lemons, cut into strips

1 Place the chicken in a deep dish. Rub the garlic, coriander, lemon juice and salt into the body cavity of the chicken. Mix the olive oil with the grated onion, saffron, ginger and pepper and rub this mixture over the outside of the chicken. Cover and leave to stand for about 30 minutes.

2 Transfer the chicken to a tagine or large, heavy flameproof casserole and pour the marinating juices over. Pour in enough water to come halfway up the chicken, add the cinnamon stick and bring the water to the boil. Reduce the heat, cover with a lid and simmer for about 1 hour, turning the chicken occasionally.

3 Preheat the oven to 150°C/300°F/Gas 2. Using two slotted spoons, carefully lift the chicken out of the tagine or casserole and set aside on a plate, covered with foil. Turn up the heat and boil the cooking liquid for 5 minutes to reduce it. Replace the chicken in the liquid and baste it thoroughly. Add the olives and preserved lemon and place the tagine or casserole in the oven for about 15 minutes. Serve the chicken immediately with your chosen accompaniments.

Roast Chicken with Ginger, Garlic and Cinnamon

This dish, with its blend of spices and sweet fruit, is inspired by Moroccan flavours. Serve with couscous, mixed with a handful of cooked chickpeas.

Serves 4
1–1.6kg/2¼–3½lb chicken
115–130g/4–4½oz fresh root ginger, grated

6–8 garlic cloves, roughly chopped
juice of 1 lemon
about 30ml/2 tbsp olive oil
2–3 large pinches of ground cinnamon
500g/1¼lb seedless red and green grapes
5–7 shallots, chopped
about 250ml/8fl oz/1 cup chicken stock
salt and ground black pepper

1 Rub the chicken with half of the ginger, the garlic, half the lemon juice, the olive oil, cinnamon, salt and plenty of pepper. Leave to marinate. Cut half the grapes in half.

2 Preheat the oven to 180°C/350°F/Gas 4. Heat a heavy frying pan or flameproof casserole until hot. Remove the chicken from the marinade, add to the pan and cook until browned on all sides, add a little extra oil if necessary.

3 Put some of the shallots into the chicken cavity with the garlic and ginger from the marinade and as many of the whole grapes as will fit inside. Roast in the oven for 40–60 minutes, or until the chicken is tender.

4 Remove the chicken from the pan and cover. Pour off any oil from the pan, reserving the juices in the pan. Add the remaining shallots to the pan and cook for about 5 minutes until softened.

5 Add half of the halved grapes, the remaining ginger, the stock and any juices from the roast chicken and cook over a medium-high heat until the grapes have cooked down to a thick sauce. Season with salt, ground black pepper and the remaining lemon juice to taste. Sieve the sauce if you prefer to remove the grape skins. Serve the chicken on a warmed serving dish, surrounded by the sauce and the reserved grapes.

Thai Roast Chicken with Turmeric

In Thailand, this chicken would be spit-roasted, as ovens are seldom used. However, it works very well as a conventional roast.

Serves 4
4 garlic cloves, 2 finely chopped and 2 bruised but left whole
small bunch coriander (cilantro), with roots, coarsely chopped

5ml/1 tsp ground turmeric
5cm/2in piece fresh turmeric
1 roasting chicken, about 1.5kg/3¼lb
1 lime, cut in half
4 medium/large sweet potatoes, peeled and cut into wedges
300ml/½ pint/1¼ cups chicken or vegetable stock
30ml/2 tbsp soy sauce
salt and ground black pepper

1 Preheat the oven to 190°C/375°F/Gas 5. Calculate the cooking time for the chicken, allowing 20 minutes per 500g/1¼lb, plus 20 minutes. With a mortar and pestle, process the chopped garlic, coriander, 10ml/2 tsp salt and turmeric.

2 Place the chicken in a roasting pan and smear it with the paste. Squeeze the lime juice over and place the lime halves and garlic cloves inside. Cover with foil and roast in the oven.

3 Meanwhile, bring a pan of water to the boil and par-boil the sweet potatoes for 10–15 minutes, until just tender. Drain well and place them around the chicken in the roasting pan. Baste with the cooking juices and sprinkle with salt and pepper. Replace the foil and return the chicken to the oven.

4 About 20 minutes before the end of cooking, remove the foil and baste the chicken. Turn the sweet potatoes over. At the end of the calculated roasting time, check that the chicken is cooked. Lift it out of the roasting pan, place on a carving board, and cover with foil to rest before carving. Transfer the sweet potatoes to a dish and keep warm while you make the gravy.

5 Pour off the oil from the pan but keep the juices. Place the pan on top of the stove and heat until bubbling. Pour in the stock. Bring to the boil, scraping to incorporate the residue. Stir in the soy sauce then pour into a jug (pitcher). Carve the chicken and serve with the sweet potatoes and gravy.

Roast Chicken with Ginger: Energy 595kcal/2489kJ; Protein 32.4g; Carbohydrate 48g, of which sugars 46.8g; Fat 31.7g, of which saturates 8.3g; Cholesterol 160mg; Calcium 64mg; Fibre 2.5g; Sodium 138mg.
Thai Roast Chicken: Energy 620kcal/2581kJ; Protein 47g; Carbohydrate 21.3g, of which sugars 5.7g; Fat 38.9g, of which saturates 11.4g; Cholesterol 240mg; Calcium 43mg; Fibre 2.4g; Sodium 228mg.

Chicken with 40 Cloves of Garlic

The amount of garlic does not have to be exact: don't worry if you have 35 or 50 cloves – the important thing is that there are lots. The smell that emanates from the oven as the chicken and garlic cook is delicious.

Serves 4–5

5–6 whole heads of garlic
15g/½oz/1 tbsp butter
45ml/3 tbsp olive oil

1.8–2kg/4–4½lb chicken
150g/5oz/1¼ cups plain (all-
   purpose) flour, plus 5ml/1 tsp
75ml/5 tbsp white port, Pineau
   de Charentes or other white,
   fortified wine
2–3 fresh tarragon or rosemary
   sprigs
30ml/2 tbsp crème fraîche
   (optional)
few drops of lemon juice
   (optional)
salt and ground black pepper

1 Separate three of the heads of garlic into cloves. and peel. Leave the other three heads whole, but take off the first layer of papery skin. Preheat the oven to 180°C/350°F/Gas 4.

2 Heat the butter and 15ml/1 tbsp of the olive oil in a flameproof casserole that is just large enough to take the chicken and garlic. Add the chicken and cook over a medium heat, turning frequently, for 10–15 minutes, until it is browned.

3 Sprinkle in 5ml/1 tsp flour and cook for 1 minute. Add the port or wine. Tuck in the whole heads of garlic and the peeled cloves with the herb sprigs. Pour over the remaining oil and season to taste with salt and pepper.

4 Mix the rest of the flour with enough water to make a firm dough. Roll it into a long sausage and press it around the rim of the casserole, then press on the lid, folding the dough up and over it to create a tight seal. Cook in the oven for 1½ hours.

5 To serve, lift off the lid to break the seal and remove the chicken and whole garlic to a serving platter and keep warm. Remove and discard the herb sprigs, then place the casserole on the hob and whisk to combine the garlic cloves with the juices. Add the crème fraîche, if using, and a little lemon juice to taste. Serve the garlic sauce with the chicken.

Spanish Chicken with Paprika, Lemon and Garlic

This is one of the simplest and most delicious ways to serve chicken. Serve it as a simple supper for two, with fried potatoes and salad, or as an appetizer or tapas.

Serves 2

2 skinless chicken breast fillets
30ml/2 tbsp olive oil

1 shallot, finely chopped
4 garlic cloves, finely chopped
5ml/1 tsp paprika
juice of 1 lemon
30ml/2 tbsp chopped fresh
   parsley
salt and ground black pepper
fresh flat leaf parsley,
   to garnish
lemon wedges, to serve

1 Remove the small fillet from the back of each breast. If the breast still looks fatter than a finger, bat it with a rolling pin to make it thinner. Slice all the chicken meat into strips.

2 Heat the oil in a large frying pan. Stir-fry the chicken strips with the shallot, garlic and paprika over a high heat for about 3 minutes until cooked through.

3 Add the lemon juice and parsley and season with salt and pepper to taste. Serve hot with lemon wedges, garnished with flat leaf parsley.

> **Cook's Tip**
> Chicken breasts have a little fillet strip that easily becomes detached. Collect these, in a bag or container in the freezer, for this dish.

> **Variation**
> For a variation on this dish, try using strips of turkey breast or pork fillet. They need a slightly longer cooking time. The whites of spring onions (scallions) can replace shallots, and the chopped green tops replace the parsley.

Tandoori Chicken with Kachumbar

This classic tandoori dish, can be barbecued or baked in the oven. Kachumbar, a cool salad laced with chillies, is a perfect accompaniment. Use sweet white onions if you can't find pink ones.

Serves 6

12 small chicken drumsticks, skinned
3 garlic cloves, crushed to a paste with a pinch of salt
150ml/¼ pint/⅔ cup strained natural (plain) yogurt
10ml/2 tsp ground coriander
5ml/1 tsp ground cumin
5ml/1 tsp ground turmeric
1.5ml/¼ tsp cayenne pepper
2.5ml/½ tsp garam masala
15ml/1 tbsp curry paste
juice of ½ lemon
salt
warmed naan breads, to serve

For the kachumbar
2 pink onions, halved and thinly sliced
10ml/2 tsp salt
4cm/1½in piece of fresh root ginger, finely shredded
2 fresh long green chillies, seeded and finely chopped
20ml/4 tsp sugar, preferably palm sugar (jaggery)
juice of ½ lemon
60ml/4 tbsp chopped fresh coriander (cilantro)

1 Place the drumsticks in a non-metallic bowl. Put the garlic, yogurt, spices, curry paste and lemon juice in a food processor and whizz until smooth. Pour the mixture over the drumsticks to coat, cover and chill overnight.

2 Two hours before serving make the kachumbar. Put the onion slices in a bowl, sprinkle them with the salt, cover and leave to stand for 1 hour. Tip into a sieve (strainer), rinse well under cold running water, then drain and pat dry. Roughly chop the slices and put them in a serving bowl. Add the remaining ingredients and mix well. About 30 minutes before cooking, drain the drumsticks in a sieve set over a bowl.

3 Prepare the barbecue, if using, or preheat the oven to 190°C/375°F/Gas 5. Salt the drumsticks, wrap the tips with strips of foil to prevent them from burning, then place on the grill rack so that they are not directly over the coals. Cover with a lid or tented heavy-duty foil and grill or roast for 15–20 minutes, turning. Serve with the kachumbar and naan bread.

Israeli Spiced Barbecued Chicken

Barbecued chicken is ubiquitous in Israel and it seems that every street corner kiosk and stall sells a version of this aromatic treat. In this recipe, the Egyptian-inspired marinade is strongly scented with cumin and cinnamon, with a large amount of lemon juice to balance the sweetness of the spices. Slash the skin of the chicken to allow the flavours to penetrate.

Serves 4

5 garlic cloves, chopped
30ml/2 tbsp ground cumin
7.5ml/1½ tsp ground cinnamon
5ml/1 tsp paprika
juice of 1 lemon
30ml/2 tbsp olive oil
1.3kg/3lb chicken, cut into 8 portions
salt and ground black pepper
fresh coriander (cilantro) leaves, to garnish
warmed pitta bread, salad and lemon wedges, to serve

1 In a bowl, combine the garlic, cumin, cinnamon, paprika, lemon juice, oil, salt and pepper.

2 Add the chicken and turn to coat thoroughly. Leave to marinate for at least 1 hour or cover and place in the refrigerator overnight.

3 Light the barbecue. After about 40 minutes it will be ready for cooking.

4 Arrange the pieces of dark meat on the grill and cook for 10 minutes, turning once and basting from time to time with the marinade.

5 Place the remaining chicken pieces on the grill and cook for 7–10 minutes, turning occasionally, until golden brown and the juices run clear when pricked with a skewer. Serve immediately, with pitta breads, lemon wedges and salad.

> **Variation**
> For a Yemenite flavour, use 7.5ml/1½ tsp turmeric and a pinch of ground cardamom in place of the cinnamon.

Tandoori Chicken with Kachumbar: Energy 423kcal/1771kJ; Protein 30g; Carbohydrate 58g, of which sugars 8.5g; Fat 7.8g, of which saturates 0.7g; Cholesterol 70mg; Calcium 63mg; Fibre 1.2g; Sodium 1210mg.
Israeli Spiced Barbecued Chicken: Energy 481kcal/1997kJ; Protein 40.8g; Carbohydrate 1g, of which sugars 0.1g; Fat 34.8g, of which saturates 8.9g; Cholesterol 215mg; Calcium 14mg; Fibre 0.3g; Sodium 147mg.

Aubergine-wrapped Lemon Chicken Thighs with Allspice Berries

This elegant Ottoman dish from Turkey is usually made with chicken thighs or veal fillet, which are wrapped in strips of fried aubergine. It takes a little time to prepare, but the result is impressive. Serve it with a tomato and cucumber salad, or a salad of parsley, pepper and onion, and a buttery rice pilaff.

Serves 4

juice of 2–3 lemons
2 garlic cloves, crushed
4–6 allspice berries, crushed
8 chicken thighs, skinned and boned
3–4 aubergines (eggplants)
sunflower oil, for deep-frying
30ml/2 tbsp toasted flaked (sliced) almonds
1 lemon, cut into wedges, to serve

1 In a shallow bowl, mix together the lemon juice, garlic and allspice berries. Toss the chicken in the mixture, rolling the pieces in the juice to coat them thoroughly, then cover and leave to marinate in the refrigerator for about 2 hours.

2 Slice the aubergines thinly lengthways, discarding the outermost slices – you need 16 strips in total – then soak the slices in a bowl of salted cold water for about 30 minutes.

3 Preheat the oven to 180°C/350°F/Gas 4. Drain the aubergine slices and squeeze out the excess water. Heat enough oil for deep-frying in a wok or other deep-sided pan, and deep-fry the aubergines in batches for 2–3 minutes until golden brown. Remove with a slotted spoon and drain on kitchen paper.

4 On a board, lay two strips of aubergine over one another in a cross shape, then place a chicken thigh in the middle. Tuck the thigh into a bundle and wrap the aubergine around it. Place the parcel, seam-side down, in a greased ovenproof dish and repeat the process with the remaining aubergine strips and chicken. Pour any remaining marinade over the parcels and sprinkle with the toasted almonds. Cover with foil and bake for 35–40 minutes. Serve hot, with lemon wedges.

Chicken with Ginger and Saffron

This is one of the most famous of all Moroccan dishes. It's essential to use preserved lemon as fresh lemon simply does not have the mellow flavour that this dish requires, and which is underlined by the use of cinnamon and saffron. For a truly authentic flavour, use tan Moroccan olives.

Serves 4

30ml/2 tbsp olive oil
1 Spanish onion, chopped
3 garlic cloves
1cm/½in piece fresh root ginger, peeled and grated
2.5–5ml/½–1 tsp ground cinnamon
pinch of saffron threads
4 chicken quarters, preferably breast portions, halved if you like
750ml/1¼ pints/3 cups chicken stock
30ml/2 tbsp chopped fresh coriander (cilantro)
30ml/2 tbsp chopped fresh parsley
1 preserved lemon
115g/4oz/⅔ cup Moroccan tan olives
salt and ground black pepper
lemon slices and fresh coriander (cilantro) sprigs, to garnish

1 Heat the oil in a large flameproof casserole, add the onion and cook over a medium heat, stirring occasionally, for 6–8 minutes until lightly golden.

2 Meanwhile, crush the garlic and blend with the ginger, cinnamon, saffron and a little salt and pepper. Stir into the pan and cook for about 1 minute. Add the chicken and cook over a medium heat for 2–3 minutes, or until golden. Add the stock and herbs, and bring to the boil. Cover and simmer for about 45 minutes until the chicken is tender.

3 Rinse the preserved lemon under cold running water, discard the flesh and cut the peel into small pieces. Stir into the pan with the olives, and simmer for a further 15 minutes, or until the chicken is very tender.

4 Transfer the chicken to a plate and keep warm. Bring the sauce to the boil and cook for 3–4 minutes, or until reduced and fairly thick. Pour it over the chicken and serve, garnished with lemon slices and coriander sprigs.

Lemon Chicken Thighs: Energy 509kcal/2114kJ; Protein 34.7g; Carbohydrate 2.7g, of which sugars 2.3g; Fat 40g, of which saturates 8.4g; Cholesterol 180mg; Calcium 67mg; Fibre 2.6g; Sodium 108mg.
Chicken with Ginger: Energy 474kcal/1967kJ; Protein 36.3g; Carbohydrate 5.3g, of which sugars 3.8g; Fat 34.3g, of which saturates 8.1g; Cholesterol 209mg; Calcium 83mg; Fibre 2.6g; Sodium 807mg.

Sweet and Spicy Chicken

This Korean chicken dish has a spicy kick, mellowed by the sweetness of maple syrup and pineapple. The chilli and garlic lend real sharpness. Gochujang paste is a spicy condiment much used in Korean cookery.

Serves 3
675g/1½lb chicken breast fillets
   or boneless thighs
175g/6oz/1½ cups cornflour
   (cornstarch)
vegetable oil, for deep-frying
2 green chillies, sliced
2 dried red chillies, seeded
3 walnuts, finely chopped
salt and ground black pepper

For the marinade
15ml/1 tbsp white wine
15ml/1 tbsp dark soy sauce
3 garlic cloves, crushed
¼ onion, finely chopped

For the sauce
15ml/1 tbsp chilli oil
2.5ml/½ tsp gochujang paste
30ml/2 tbsp dark soy sauce
7.5ml/1½ tsp pineapple juice
15 garlic cloves, peeled
30ml/2 tbsp maple syrup
15ml/1 tbsp sugar

1 Slice the chicken into bitesize strips and season with the salt and pepper. Combine all the marinade ingredients in a large bowl. Mix well and add the chicken, rubbing the mixture thoroughly into the meat. Leave to marinate for 20 minutes.

2 Sprinkle the marinated chicken with a thin coating of cornflour. Fill a wok or medium heavy pan one-third full of vegetable oil and heat to 170°C/340°F, or when a cube of bread dropped into the oil browns in 15 seconds.

3 Add the chicken and deep-fry for 3–5 minutes, or until golden brown. Remove the chicken and drain on kitchen paper to remove any excess oil.

4 Blend all the sauce ingredients together in a large pan, adding the garlic cloves whole, and heat over medium heat. Once the sauce is bubbling, add the fried chicken and stir to coat the meat with the sauce. Leave to simmer until the sauce has formed a sticky glaze over the chicken, and then add the chillies. Stir well and transfer to a shallow serving dish. Garnish with the walnuts before serving.

Malaysian Fried Chicken with Turmeric and Lemon Grass

In this famous fried chicken dish, which is eaten everywhere in Malaysia and Singapore, the chicken is first cooked with spices and other flavourings to ensure that the flavours thoroughly penetrate the meat, then simply deep-fried to give the pieces an irresistibly crisp, golden skin. If you cannot find *kecap manis* substitute the same quantity of dark soy sauce and mix it with 15ml/1 tbsp soft brown or muscovado sugar.

Serves 4
2 shallots, chopped
4 garlic cloves, chopped
50g/2oz fresh root ginger or
   galangal, peeled and chopped
25g/1oz fresh turmeric, chopped
2 lemon grass stalks, chopped
12 chicken thighs or drumsticks
   or 6 whole chicken legs,
   separated into drumsticks
   and thighs
30ml/2 tbsp kecap manis
salt and ground black pepper
vegetable oil, for deep-frying
fragrant rice and a green salad
   to serve

1 Using a mortar and pestle or food processor, grind the shallots, garlic, ginger or galangal, turmeric and lemon grass to a paste. Place the chicken pieces in a heavy pan or earthenware pot and smear with the spice paste. Add the *kecap manis* and 150ml/¼ pint/⅔ cup water.

2 Bring to the boil, reduce the heat and cook the chicken for about 25 minutes, turning it from time to time, until the liquid has evaporated. The chicken should be dry, with the spices sticking to it. Season with salt and pepper.

3 Heat enough oil for deep-frying in a wok. Fry the chicken pieces in batches until golden brown and crisp. Drain them on kitchen paper and serve hot with rice and a green salad.

> **Cook's Tip**
> Watch the chicken carefully towards the end of cooking to make sure the spicy coating does not burn.

Sweet Spicy Chicken: Energy 655kcal/2749kJ; Protein 56.4g; Carbohydrate 45.3g, of which sugars 14.4g; Fat 28.8g, of which saturates 3.5g; Cholesterol 158mg; Calcium 34mg; Fibre 0.4g; Sodium 1249mg.
Malaysian Fried Chicken: Energy 396Kcal/1639kJ; Protein 27g; Carbohydrate 1.5g, of which sugars 1.1g; Fat 31.3g, of which saturates 6.8g; Cholesterol 150mg; Calcium 38mg; Fibre 0.2g; Sodium 358mg.

Mexican Chicken Fajitas

The perfect dish for casual entertaining, fajitas are a self-assembly dish: warm flour tortillas are brought to the table and everyone adds their own fillings.

Serves 6

3 skinless, chicken breast fillets
finely grated rind and juice of
  2 limes
30ml/2 tbsp caster (superfine) sugar
10ml/2 tsp dried oregano
2.5ml/½ tsp cayenne pepper
5ml/1 tsp ground cinnamon
2 onions
3 (bell) peppers (1 red, 1 yellow or
  orange and 1 green)
45ml/3 tbsp vegetable oil
12 ready-made fajitas or soft
  tortillas, guacamole, salsa and
  sour cream, to serve

1 Slice the chicken into 2cm/¾in wide strips and place them in a large bowl. Add the lime rind and juice, caster sugar, oregano, cayenne and cinnamon. Mix thoroughly. Set aside to marinate for at least 30 minutes.

2 Cut the onions in half and slice them thinly. Cut the peppers in half, remove the cores and seeds, then slice the flesh into 1cm/½in wide strips.

3 Heat a large frying pan or griddle and warm each tortilla in turn for about 30 seconds on each side, or until the surface colours and begins to blister. Keep the tortillas warm and pliable by wrapping them in a clean, dry dish towel.

4 Heat the oil in a large frying pan. Stir-fry the marinated chicken for 5–6 minutes, then add the peppers and onions and cook for 3–4 minutes more, until the chicken strips are cooked through and the vegetables are soft and tender, but still juicy. Spoon the chicken mixture into a serving bowl and take it to the table with the warm tortillas and bowls of guacamole, salsa and sour cream.

5 To eat, take a tortilla, spread, it with a little salsa, add a spoonful of guacamole and pile some of the chicken mixture in the centre. The final touch is to add a small dollop of soured cream. The tortilla is then folded and ready to eat.

Chicken with Garlic and Fennel

This is a very simple and delicious way to cook chicken. If you have time, leave the chicken to marinate for a few hours for the best flavour.

Serves 4

1.6–1.8kg/3½–4lb chicken, cut
  into 8 pieces or 8 chicken joints
250g/9oz shallots, peeled
1 head garlic, separated into
  cloves and peeled
60ml/4 tbsp extra virgin olive oil
45ml/3 tbsp tarragon vinegar
45ml/3 tbsp white wine or
  vermouth (optional)
5ml/1 tsp fennel seeds, crushed
2 bulbs fennel, cut into wedges,
  feathery tops reserved
150ml/¼ pint/⅔ cup double
  (heavy) cream
5ml/1 tsp redcurrant jelly
15ml/1 tbsp tarragon mustard
caster (superfine) sugar (optional)
30ml/2 tbsp chopped fresh flat
  leaf parsley
salt and ground black pepper

1 Place the chicken pieces, shallots and all but one of the garlic cloves in a flameproof dish or roasting pan. Add the oil, vinegar, wine or vermouth, if using, and fennel seeds. Season with pepper, then set aside to marinate for 2–3 hours.

2 Preheat the oven to 190°C/375°F/Gas 5. Add the fennel to the chicken, season with salt and stir to mix.

3 Cook the chicken in the oven for 50–60 minutes, stirring once or twice. The chicken juices should run clear, not pink, when the thickest part of the thigh meat is pierced with a sharp knife or skewer.

4 Transfer the chicken and vegetables to a serving dish and keep them warm. Skim off most of the fat and bring the cooking juices to the boil, then pour in the cream. Stir, scraping up all the delicious juices. Whisk in the redcurrant jelly followed by the mustard. Season to taste with salt and black pepper, adding a little sugar if liked.

5 Chop the remaining garlic clove with the feathery fennel tops and mix with the parsley. Pour the sauce over the chicken and scatter the chopped garlic and herb mixture over the top. Serve immediately.

Mexican Chicken Fajitas: Energy 485kcal/2044kJ; Protein 26g; Carbohydrate 67.4g, of which sugars 15.3g; Fat 14.2g, of which saturates 3.8g; Cholesterol 60mg; Calcium 118mg; Fibre 4g; Sodium 53mg.
Chicken with Garlic: Energy 568kcal/2349kJ; Protein 24.3g; Carbohydrate 6.5g, of which sugars 5.3g; Fat 49.6g, of which saturates 19.4g; Cholesterol 163mg; Calcium 76mg; Fibre 2.9g; Sodium 112mg.

Malay Chicken with Chilli Relish

This chicken curry reflects the varied population of the old region of Melaka through its use of Chinese, Malay, Portuguese and Indian spices and flavourings.

Serves 4

For the rempah spice paste
6–8 dried red chillies, soaked in warm water, seeded and squeezed dry
6–8 shallots, chopped
4–6 garlic cloves, chopped
25g/1oz fresh root ginger, grated
5ml/1 tsp shrimp paste
10ml/2 tsp ground turmeric
10ml/2 tsp Chinese five-spice powder

For the curry
15–30ml/1–2 tbsp tamarind pulp
1 fresh coconut, grated (shredded)
30–45ml/2–3 tbsp vegetable oil
1–2 cinnamon sticks
12 chicken thighs, boned and cut lengthways into bitesize strips
600ml/1 pint/2½ cups coconut milk
15ml/1 tbsp palm sugar (jaggery)
salt and ground black pepper

For the relish
1 green chilli, seeded and sliced
1 red chilli, seeded and sliced
fresh coriander (cilantro) leaves, finely chopped
2 limes
steamed rice, to serve

1 First make the rempah. Using a mortar and pestle or food processor, grind the chillies, shallots, garlic and ginger to a paste. Beat in the shrimp paste and stir in the dried spices.

2 Soak the tamarind pulp in 150ml/¼ pint/⅔ cup warm water until soft. Squeeze the pulp to soften it, then strain to extract the juice and discard the pulp. In a heavy pan, roast half the grated coconut until it is brown and smells nutty. Using a mortar and pestle or food processor, grind the roasted coconut until it resembles sugar grains.

3 Heat the oil in a wok or earthenware pot, and stir in the rempah and cinnamon sticks until fragrant. Add the chicken strips. Pour in the coconut milk and tamarind water, and stir in the sugar. Reduce the heat and cook gently for 10 minutes. Stir in half the ground roasted coconut to thicken the sauce and season. In a bowl, mix the remaining grated coconut with the chillies, coriander and juice of 1 lime to serve as a relish. Serve the chicken with rice, relish and lime wedges.

Devil's Curry

Every Eurasian household in Malaysia has its own version of this devilishly hot chicken and vegetable hotpot.
Served as a meal on its own with bread to mop up the sauce, it is often eaten at family celebration meals.

Serves 6
4–6 skinless chicken breast fillets or 12 boned chicken thighs, cut into chunks
60ml/4 tbsp vegetable oil
1 onion, halved and sliced
25g/1oz fresh root ginger, peeled and cut into julienne strips
4 garlic cloves, cut into strips
30–45ml/2–3 tbsp vinegar
10ml/2 tsp sugar
3 medium potatoes, cut into bitesize pieces
2 courgettes (zucchini), halved lengthways, seeded and sliced
8 Chinese leaves (Chinese cabbage), cut into squares
10ml/2 tsp brown mustard seeds, ground and mixed to a paste with a little water
salt
fresh crusty bread, to serve

For the spice paste
10 dried chillies, soaked in warm water, seeded and patted dry
6 fresh red chillies, seeded and chopped
8 shallots, chopped
6 garlic cloves, chopped
25g/1oz fresh root ginger, peeled and chopped
6 candlenuts or macadamia nuts
10ml/2 tsp ground turmeric

For the marinade
15ml/1 tbsp light soy sauce
15ml/1 tbsp dark soy sauce
10ml/2 tsp rice or white wine vinegar
10ml/2 tsp caster (superfine) sugar

1 Mix together the ingredients for the marinade and rub it into the chicken pieces. Leave to marinate for 30 minutes. Using a mortar and pestle or food processor, grind the chillies, shallots, garlic, ginger and nuts to a paste. Stir in the turmeric.

2 Heat the oil in a wok or heavy pan. Stir in the onion, ginger and garlic and fry until golden. Add the spice paste, stir, toss in the chicken and stir until it browns. Pour in water to cover.

3 Bring to the boil and add the vinegar, sugar and potatoes. Reduce the heat and cook until the potatoes are tender. Add the courgettes and cabbage and cook for 2 minutes. Stir in the mustard paste and season with salt. Serve hot with bread.

Circassian Chicken

This chicken and walnut dish is an Ottoman classic. Served chilled or at room temperature it is ideal for lunch or supper, or for a buffet spread.

Serves 6

1 free-range chicken, trimmed of excess fat
3 slices of day-old white bread, crusts removed
150ml/¼ pint/⅔ cup milk
175g/6oz/1½ cup shelled walnuts
4–6 garlic cloves
salt and ground black pepper

30ml/2 tbsp butter, 5ml/1 tsp paprika, and a few fresh coriander (cilantro) leaves, to garnish

For the stock

1 onion, quartered
1 carrot, chopped
2 celery sticks, chopped
4–6 cloves
4–6 allspice berries
4–6 black peppercorns
2 bay leaves
5ml/1 tsp coriander seeds
1 small bunch of fresh flat leaf parsley, stalks bruised and tied together

1 Put the chicken into a deep pan with all of the ingredients for the stock. Pour in enough water to cover the chicken. Bring to the boil. Lower the heat, cover, and simmer for about 1 hour.

2 Remove the chicken from the pan and leave until cool enough to handle. Boil the stock with the lid off for about 15 minutes until reduced, then strain and season with salt and pepper. When the chicken has cooled a little, pull off the skin and discard it. Tear the chicken flesh into thin strips and put them into a large bowl.

3 In a shallow bowl, soak the bread in the milk for a few minutes until the milk is absorbed. Using a mortar and pestle, pound the walnuts with the garlic to form a paste. Beat the soaked bread into the walnut paste, then add to the chicken mixture. Now beat in spoonfuls of the warm stock to bind the chicken and walnut mixture until it is light and creamy.

4 Spoon the mixture into mound on a serving dish. Melt the butter, stir in the paprika, and pour a cross shape over the mound. Serve garnished with coriander.

Anatolian Chicken Casserole

This classic Turkish dish is found in various forms throughout the Middle East. In the south-east of Anatolia, a generous dose of hot red pepper is added to give a fiery kick, otherwise it is usually mildly spiced.

Serves 4

30ml/2 tbsp olive oil
30ml/2 tbsp butter
1 small free-range chicken, trimmed of excess fat and cut into quarters
2 onions, cut in half lengthways and finely sliced

2–3 garlic cloves, finely chopped
5–10ml/1–2 tsp hot paprika, or 1 fresh red chilli, seeded and finely chopped
10ml/2 tsp coriander seeds
10ml/2 tsp dried oregano
5–10ml/1–2 tsp sugar
15ml/1 tbsp tomato purée (paste)
400g/14oz can chopped tomatoes
450g/1lb fresh okra, stalks removed
juice of 1 lemon
salt and ground black pepper
thick and creamy natural (plain) yogurt, to serve

1 Heat the oil with the butter in a wide, heavy pan or flameproof casserole. Add the chicken pieces and brown them on all sides. Remove from the pan and set aside.

2 Add the onions, garlic, paprika or chilli, coriander seeds and oregano to the pan. Stir in the sugar and cook until the onions begin to colour, then stir in the tomato purée and tomatoes and add 150ml/¼ pint/⅔ cup water. Bubble up the liquid for 2–3 minutes, then slip in the chicken pieces and baste them with the sauce. Cover the pan and cook gently on top of the stove, or in the oven at 180°C/350°F/Gas 4, for about 30 minutes.

3 Sprinkle the okra over the chicken and pour the lemon juice on top. Cover the pan again and cook gently for a further 20 minutes.

4 Transfer the chicken pieces to a serving dish. Toss the okra into the tomato sauce, season with salt and pepper and spoon over and around the chicken. Serve immediately, with a bowl of yogurt on the side.

Circassian Chicken: Energy 222kcal/937kJ; Protein 34.1g; Carbohydrate 7.6g, of which sugars 1.6g; Fat 6.4g, of which saturates 3.3g; Cholesterol 105mg; Calcium 53mg; Fibre 0.2g; Sodium 324mg.
Anatolian Chicken: Energy 386Kcal/1617kJ; Protein 47.3g; Carbohydrate 16g, of which sugars 13.1g; Fat 15.2g, of which saturates 5.7g; Cholesterol 139mg; Calcium 224mg; Fibre 7g; Sodium 181mg.

Fragrant Thai Chicken Curry

This dish is perfect for a party as the chicken and sauce can be prepared in advance and combined and heated at the last minute.

Serves 4

45ml/3 tbsp oil
1 onion, coarsely chopped
2 garlic cloves, crushed
15ml/1 tbsp Thai red curry paste
115g/4oz creamed coconut dissolved in 900ml/
1½ pints/3¾ cups boiling water, or 1 litre/1¾ pints/4 cups coconut milk

2 lemon grass stalks, coarsely chopped
6 kaffir lime leaves, chopped
150ml/¼ pint/⅔ cup strained natural (plain) yogurt
30ml/2 tbsp apricot jam
1 cooked chicken, about 1.5kg/3–3½lb
30ml/2 tbsp chopped fresh coriander (cilantro)
salt and ground black pepper
kaffir lime leaves, toasted coconut shreds and fresh coriander (cilantro), to garnish
boiled rice, to serve

1 Heat the oil in a large pan. Add the onion and garlic and cook over a low heat for 5–10 minutes until soft. Stir in the red curry paste. Cook, stirring constantly, for 2–3 minutes.

2 Stir in the diluted creamed coconut or coconut milk, then add the lemon grass, lime leaves, yogurt and apricot jam. Stir well. Cover and simmer for 30 minutes.

3 Remove the pan from the heat and leave to cool slightly. Transfer the sauce to a food processor or blender and process to a smooth purée, then strain it back into the rinsed-out pan, pressing as much of the puréed mixture as possible through the sieve (strainer) with the back of a wooden spoon. Set aside while you prepare the chicken.

4 Remove the skin from the chicken, slice the meat off the bones and cut it into bitesize pieces. Add to the sauce.

5 Bring the sauce back to simmering point. Stir in the fresh coriander and season to taste with salt and pepper. Garnish with extra lime leaves, shredded coconut and coriander. Serve with rice.

Spiced Coconut Chicken with Cardamom, Chilli and Ginger

You need to marinate the chicken legs overnight in an aromatic blend of yogurt and spices before gently simmering with hot green chillies in creamy coconut milk. Serve with rice or Indian breads.

Serves 4

1.6kg/3½lb large chicken drumsticks
30ml/2 tbsp sunflower oil
400ml/14fl oz/1⅔ cups coconut milk
4–6 large green chillies, halved
45ml/3 tbsp finely chopped coriander (cilantro)

salt and ground black pepper
natural (plain) yogurt, to drizzle

For the marinade

15ml/1 tbsp crushed cardamom seeds
15ml/1 tbsp grated fresh root ginger
10ml/2 tsp finely grated garlic
105ml/7 tbsp natural (plain) yogurt
2 green chillies, seeded and chopped
5ml/1 tsp ground cumin
5ml/1 tsp ground coriander
5ml/1 tsp turmeric
finely grated zest and juice of 1 lime

1 Make the marinade. Place the cardamom, ginger, garlic, half the yogurt, green chillies, cumin, coriander, turmeric and lime zest and juice in a blender. Process until smooth, season and pour into a large glass bowl.

2 Add the chicken to the marinade and toss to coat evenly. Cover the bowl and marinate in the refrigerator overnight.

3 Heat the oil in a large, non-stick wok over a low heat. Remove the chicken from the marinade, reserving the marinade. Add the chicken to the wok and brown all over, then add the coconut milk, remaining yogurt, reserved marinade and green chillies and bring to a boil.

4 Reduce the heat and simmer gently, uncovered for 30–35 minutes. Check the seasoning, adding more if needed. Stir in the coriander, ladle into warmed bowls and serve immediately. Drizzle with yogurt if liked.

Fragrant Thai Chicken Curry: Energy 237kcal/991kJ; Protein 33.8g; Carbohydrate 7.2g, of which sugars 5.9g; Fat 8.3g, of which saturates 1.6g; Cholesterol 165mg; Calcium 149mg; Fibre 3.1g; Sodium 253mg.
Spiced Coconut Chicken: Energy 706kcal/2935kJ; Protein 48.1g; Carbohydrate 15.8g, of which sugars 15.6g; Fat 50.4g, of which saturates 12.8g; Cholesterol 240mg; Calcium 91mg; Fibre 1.5g; Sodium 305mg.

Richly Spiced Cambodian Chicken Curry

There are many recipes for Cambodian chicken or seafood curries, but the one thing they all have in common is the use of Indian curry powder and coconut milk in their sauces.

Serves 4

45ml/3 tbsp Indian curry powder or garam masala
15ml/1 tbsp ground turmeric
500g/1¼lb skinless chicken thighs or chicken portions
25ml/1½ tbsp raw cane sugar
30ml/2 tbsp sesame oil

2 shallots, chopped
2 garlic cloves, chopped
4cm/1½in galangal, peeled and chopped
2 lemon grass stalks, chopped
10ml/2 tsp chilli paste or dried chilli flakes
2 medium sweet potatoes, peeled and cubed
45ml/3 tbsp nuoc mam
600ml/1 pint/2½ cups coconut milk
1 small bunch each fresh basil and coriander (cilantro), stalks removed
salt and ground black pepper

1 In a small bowl, mix together the curry powder or garam masala and the turmeric. Put the chicken in a bowl and coat with half of the spice. Set aside.

2 To make the caramel sauce, heat the sugar in a small pan with 7.5ml/1½ tsp water, until the sugar dissolves and the syrup turns golden. Remove from the heat and set aside.

3 Heat a wok or heavy pan and add the oil. Stir-fry the shallots, garlic, galangal and lemon grass. Stir in the rest of the turmeric and curry powder with the chilli paste or flakes, followed by the chicken, and stir-fry for 2–3 minutes.

4 Add the sweet potatoes, then the *nuoc mam*, caramel sauce, coconut milk and 150ml/¼ pint/⅔ cup water, mixing thoroughly to combine the flavours. Bring to the boil, reduce the heat and cook for about 15 minutes until the chicken is cooked through.

5 Season and stir in half the basil and coriander. Garnish with the remaining herbs and serve immediately.

Chicken and Pumpkin Casserole

In Cambodian homes a big pot of this casserole is made daily and placed in the middle of the table for everyone to help themselves. The flavourings include kroeung (a blend of lemon grass and galangal with fish sauce) and *tuk prahoc*, or fermented fish paste.

Serves 4–6

30ml/2 tbsp groundnut (peanut) oil
4 garlic cloves, halved and crushed
25g/1oz galangal, peeled and finely sliced
2 chillies
30ml/2 tbsp kroeung
15ml/1 tbsp palm sugar (jaggery)
12 chicken thighs

30ml/2 tbsp tuk prahoc
a handful kaffir lime leaves
600ml/1 pint/2½ cups coconut milk
350g/12oz pumpkin flesh, seeded and cut into bitesize chunks
1 long aubergine (eggplant), quartered lengthways, each quarter cut into three
115g/4oz long beans, trimmed and cut into 5cm/2in lengths
3 tomatoes, skinned, quartered, and seeded
1 handful spinach leaves, washed and trimmed
a small bunch basil leaves
sea salt and ground black pepper
1 small bunch each fresh coriander (cilantro) and mint, stalks removed, coarsely chopped, to garnish
jasmine rice, to serve

1 Heat the groundnut oil in a wok or heavy pan. Add the garlic, galangal and whole chillies and stir-fry until fragrant and golden. Add the kroeung and the palm sugar, stirring until they have dissolved.

2 Add the chicken thighs to the pan, tossing them well, and stir in the *tuk prahoc*, kaffir lime leaves and coconut milk. Reduce the heat and simmer for 10 minutes. Add the pumpkin, aubergine and beans.

3 Simmer for a further 10 minutes, until tender. If you need to add more liquid, stir in a little water. Add the tomatoes and spinach, and the basil leaves.

4 Cook for a further 2 minutes, then season to taste. Garnish with coriander and mint and serve hot with jasmine rice.

Chicken and Aubergines Braised in Sweet Spices

This is a Californian version of a traditional Persian dish. For the original recipe, lamb was often the meat of choice but in California this hearty meat dish has been transformed to a light chicken, tomato and split pea stew.

Serves 4–6
50g/2oz/¼ cup green split peas
45–60ml/3–4 tbsp olive oil
1 large or 2 small onions, finely chopped
500g/1¼lb boneless chicken thighs
500ml/17fl oz/2¼ cups chicken stock
5ml/1 tsp ground turmeric
2.5ml/½ tsp ground cinnamon
1.5ml/¼ tsp grated nutmeg
2 aubergines (eggplants), diced
8–10 ripe tomatoes, diced
2 garlic cloves, crushed
30ml/2 tbsp dried mint
salt and ground black pepper
fresh mint, to garnish
rice, to serve

1 Put the split peas in a bowl, pour over cold water to cover, then leave to soak for about 4 hours. Drain well. Heat a little of the oil in a pan, add two thirds of the onions and cook for about 5 minutes. Add the chicken and cook until golden brown.

2 Add the soaked split peas to the chicken mixture, then the stock, turmeric, cinnamon and nutmeg. Cook over a medium-low heat for about 40 minutes, until the split peas are tender.

3 Heat the remaining oil in a pan, add the aubergines and remaining onions and cook until lightly browned. Add the tomatoes, garlic and mint. Season. Just before serving, stir the aubergine mixture into the chicken and split pea stew. Garnish with fresh mint leaves and serve with rice.

> **Variation**
> To make a traditional lamb koresh, use 675g/1½lb lamb in place of the chicken. Add to the onions, add water to cover, cook for 1½ hours until tender, then proceed as above.

Spicy Chicken Casserole with Red Wine

This is a traditional chicken dish of the Greek islands. It is usually served with plain rice or orzo, the small tear-shaped pasta, which is called *kritharaki* in Greek, but it is even better with thick home-made fried potatoes.

Serves 4
75ml/5 tbsp extra virgin olive oil
1.6kg/3½lb chicken, jointed
1 large onion, peeled and roughly chopped
250ml/8fl oz/1 cup red wine
30ml/2 tbsp tomato purée (paste) diluted in 450ml/¾ pint/scant 2 cups hot water
1 cinnamon stick
3 or 4 whole allspice
2 bay leaves
salt and ground black pepper
boiled rice, orzo or fried potatoes, to serve

1 Heat the olive oil in a large pan or sauté pan and brown the chicken pieces on all sides, ensuring that the skin is cooked and lifts away from the flesh slightly. Lift the chicken pieces out with tongs and set them aside on a plate, cover with another plate or with foil and keep them warm.

2 Add the chopped onion to the hot oil in the same pan and stir it over a medium heat until it becomes translucent.

3 Return the chicken pieces to the pan, pour over the wine and cook for 2–3 minutes, until it has reduced. Add the tomato purée mixture, cinnamon, allspice and bay leaves. Season the dish well with salt and pepper.

4 Cover the pan and cook gently for 1 hour or until the chicken is tender. Serve with rice, orzo or fried potatoes.

> **Cook's Tip**
> If you have trouble finding orzo, use a different pasta, but look for a small shape. Long grained rice can also be used instead of the pasta, if you prefer.

Chicken and Aubergines in Spices: Energy 217kcal/912kJ; Protein 21.5g; Carbohydrate 14g, of which sugars 8g; Fat 8.8g, of which saturates 1.7g; Cholesterol 88mg; Calcium 39mg; Fibre 3.6g; Sodium 92mg.
Spicy Chicken Casserole: Energy 669kcal/2775kJ; Protein 48.7g; Carbohydrate 5g, of which sugars 3.8g; Fat 45.9g, of which saturates 11.1g; Cholesterol 250mg; Calcium 37mg; Fibre 0.9g; Sodium 196mg.

Sweet and Sour Chicken Curry

This quickly made curry combines a sweet and sour flavour with a creamy texture, while the inclusion of chilli powder and fresh chillies in the sauce give it some punch. It is delicious served with a pilau rice dish or warm naan.

Serves 4

45ml/3 tbsp tomato purée (paste)
30ml/2 tbsp strained natural (plain) yogurt
7.5ml/1½ tsp garam masala
5ml/1 tsp chilli powder
1 clove garlic, crushed
30ml/2 tbsp mango chutney
5ml/1 tsp salt
2.5ml/½ tsp sugar (optional)
60ml/4 tbsp corn oil
675g/1½lb/5 cups skinless chicken breast fillets, cubed
150ml/¼ pint/⅔ cup water
2 fresh green chillies, chopped
30ml/2 tbsp chopped fresh coriander (cilantro)4
30ml/2 tbsp single (light) cream

1 Blend together the tomato purée, yogurt, garam masala, chilli powder, garlic, mango chutney, salt and sugar (if using) in a medium mixing bowl.

2 Heat the oil in a deep round-bottomed pan or a large wok, Lower the heat slightly and pour in the spice mixture. Bring to the boil and cook for about 2 minutes, stirring occasionally.

3 Add the chicken pieces and stir until they are well coated in the spices.

4 Add the water to thin the sauce slightly. Continue cooking for 5–7 minutes, or until the chicken is tender.

5 Finally add the fresh chillies, coriander and cream, and cook for a further 2 minutes until the chicken is cooked through. Serve immediately.

Cook's Tip
The final addition of cream can be omitted if you prefer a slightly thinner sauce.

Balti Butter Chicken

Butter chicken is one of the most popular Balti chicken dishes. Cooked in butter, with a subtle blend of aromatic spices, cream and almonds, this mild dish will be enjoyed by everyone.

Serves 4–6

150ml/¼ pint/⅔ cup natural (plain) yogurt
50g/2oz/½ cup ground almonds
7.5ml/1½ tsp chilli powder
1.5ml/¼ tsp crushed bay leaves
1.5ml/¼ tsp ground cloves
1.5ml/¼ tsp ground cinnamon
5ml/1 tsp garam masala
4 green cardamom pods
2.5cm/1in piece fresh root ginger, grated
1 clove garlic, crushed
400g/14oz/2 cups canned tomatoes
6.5ml/1¼ tsp salt
1kg/2¼ lb/6½ cups skinless chicken breast fillets, cubed
75g/3oz/6 tbsp butter
15ml/1 tbsp corn oil
2 medium onions, sliced
30ml/2 tbsp chopped fresh coriander (cilantro)
60ml/4 tbsp single (light) cream
coriander (cilantro) sprigs, to garnish

1 Put the yogurt, ground almonds, all the dry spices, ginger, garlic, tomatoes and salt into a mixing bowl and blend together thoroughly. Put the chicken into a large mixing bowl and pour over the yogurt mixture. Set aside.

2 Melt together the butter and oil in a medium wok or deep round-bottomed frying pan. When hot, add the onions and fry for about 3 minutes.

3 Add the chicken mixture and stir-fry for 7–10 minutes. Stir in about half of the coriander and mix well.

4 Pour over the cream and stir in well. Bring to the boil. Serve garnished with the remaining chopped coriander and a few coriander sprigs.

Cook's Tip
Replace the natural yogurt with Greek (US strained plain) yogurt for an even richer and creamier flavour.

Balti Chicken

This recipe has a beautifully delicate flavour, and is another very popular Balti dish. Choose a young chicken as the result will be more flavoursome.

Serves 4–6

1–1.3kg/2¼–3lb chicken, skinned and cut into 8 pieces
45ml/3 tbsp corn oil
3 medium onions, sliced
3 medium tomatoes, halved and sliced
2.5cm/1in cinnamon stick
2 large black cardamom pods
4 black peppercorns
2.5ml/½ tsp black cumin seeds
5ml/1 tsp ginger pulp
5ml/1 tsp garlic pulp
5ml/1 tsp garam masala
5ml/1 tsp chilli powder
5ml/1 tsp salt
30ml/2 tbsp natural (plain) yogurt
60ml/4 tbsp lemon juice
30ml/2 tbsp chopped fresh coriander (cilantro)
2 fresh green chillies, chopped

1 Wash and trim the chicken pieces, and set to one side. Heat the oil in a large wok or deep round-bottomed frying pan. Throw in the onions and fry until they are golden brown. Add the tomatoes and stir well.

2 Add the cinnamon stick, cardamoms, peppercorns, black cumin seeds, ginger, garlic, garam masala, chilli powder and salt. Lower the heat and stir-fry for 3–5 minutes.

3 Add the chicken pieces two at a time, and stir-fry for at least 7 minutes until the spice mixture has penetrated the chicken. Add the yogurt to the pan and mix well.

4 Lower the heat and cover the pan with a piece of foil. Cook gently for about 15 minutes, checking to make sure the sauce is not catching. Finally, add the lemon juice, fresh coriander and green chillies, and serve at once.

> **Cook's Tip**
> Although chicken is most tender and flavoursome when cooked on the bone, you can substitute 675g/1½lb boned and cubed chicken breast fillets if you wish.

Chicken and Tomato Curry

Chicken curry is always popular when served at a family dinner or as part of a party meal. This version, which uses whole spices, is cooked covered, giving the sauce a fairly thin consistency. If you prefer a thicker sauce, remove the lid of the pan for the last 15 minutes of cooking so that it has time to reduce. Serve with rice or naan.

Serves 4–6

60ml/4 tbsp vegetable oil
4 cloves
4–6 green cardamoms
1 piece cinnamon stick, 5cm/2in long
3 whole star anise
6–8 curry leaves
1 large onion, finely chopped
5cm/2in piece fresh root ginger, finely chopped
4 cloves garlic, crushed
60ml/4 tbsp mild curry paste
5ml/1 tsp turmeric
5ml/1 tsp Chinese five-spice powder
1.3kg/3lb chicken, skinned and jointed
400g/14oz canned tomatoes, chopped
115g/4oz creamed coconut
2.5ml/½ tsp sugar
salt, to taste
50g/2oz coriander (cilantro) leaves, chopped

1 Heat the oil in a large frying pan or wok and fry the cloves, cardamoms, cinnamon stick, star anise and curry leaves over a medium heat until the cloves swell and the curry leaves are slightly charred.

2 Add the onion, ginger and garlic and fry, stirring constantly, until the onion has browned. Add the curry paste, turmeric and Chinese five-spice powder and fry until the oil separates from the spice mixture.

3 Add the chicken pieces to the pan and mix well with the spice mixture. When all the pieces are evenly sealed, cover and cook until the meat is nearly done.

4 Add the chopped tomatoes and the creamed coconut. Simmer gently until the coconut has dissolved. Mix well and add the sugar. Season with salt. Fold in the coriander leaves, reheat and serve immediately.

Balti Chicken: Energy 231kcal/971kJ; Protein 29.6g; Carbohydrate 11.1g, of which sugars 6.2g; Fat 8.1g, of which saturates 1.3g; Cholesterol 79mg; Calcium 45mg; Fibre 1.7g; Sodium 77mg.
Chicken and Tomato Curry: Energy 380kcal/1584kJ; Protein 31.7g; Carbohydrate 11.1g, of which sugars 6.2g; Fat 23.6g, of which saturates 12.7g; Cholesterol 82mg; Calcium 88mg; Fibre 3.2g; Sodium 122mg.

North African Spiced Duck with Harissa

Harissa is a fiery chilli sauce from North Africa. Mixed with cinnamon, saffron and preserved lemon, it gives this colourful casserole an unforgettable flavour.

Serves 4

15ml/1 tbsp olive oil
1.8–2kg/4–4½lb duck, quartered
1 large onion, thinly sliced
1 garlic clove, crushed
2.5ml/½ tsp ground cumin
400ml/14fl oz/1⅔ cups duck or chicken stock
juice of ½ lemon
5–10ml/1–2 tsp harissa
1 cinnamon stick
5ml/1 tsp saffron strands
50g/2oz/⅓ cup black olives
50g/2oz/⅓ cup green olives
peel of 1 preserved lemon, rinsed, drained and cut into fine strips
2–3 lemon slices
30ml/2 tbsp chopped fresh coriander (cilantro)
salt and ground black pepper
coriander sprigs, to garnish

1 Heat the oil in a flameproof casserole. Add the duck quarters and cook until browned all over. Remove with a slotted spoon and set aside. Add the onion and garlic to the oil remaining in the casserole and cook for 5 minutes until soft. Add the cumin and cook, stirring, for 2 minutes.

2 Pour in the stock and lemon juice, then add the harissa, cinnamon and saffron. Bring to the boil. Return the duck to the casserole and add the olives, preserved lemon peel and lemon slices. Season with salt and pepper.

3 Lower the heat, partially cover the casserole and simmer gently for 45 minutes until the duck is cooked through. Discard the cinnamon stick. Stir in the chopped coriander and garnish with the coriander sprigs.

> **Cook's Tip**
> Instead of jointing a whole duck, make the dish with four breast or leg portions if you prefer.

Malay Braised Duck in Aromatic Soy Sauce

The Chinese communities in Malaysia and Singapore often braise duck, goose, chicken or pork in soy sauce and warm flavourings, such as star anise and cinnamon. Malays like to add turmeric and lemon grass to these flavourings and, to achieve their desired fiery kick, chillies are always tucked into the recipe somewhere.

Serves 4–6

1 duck (about 2kg/4½lb), washed and trimmed
15–30ml/1–2 tbsp Chinese five-spice powder
25g/1oz fresh turmeric, chopped
25g/1oz galangal, chopped
4 garlic cloves, chopped
30ml/2 tbsp sesame oil
12 shallots, peeled and left whole
2–3 lemon grass stalks, halved and lightly crushed
4 cinnamon sticks
8 star anise
12 cloves
600ml/1 pint/2½ cups light soy sauce
120ml/4fl oz/½ cup dark soy sauce
30–45ml/2–3 tbsp palm sugar (jaggery)
fresh coriander (cilantro) leaves, 2 green and 2 red chillies, seeded and quartered lengthways, to garnish
steamed jasmine rice and salad, to serve

1 Rub the duck, inside and out, with the five-spice powder and place in the refrigerator, uncovered, for 6–8 hours.

2 Using a mortar and pestle or food processor, grind the turmeric, galangal and garlic to a smooth paste.

3 Heat the oil in a heavy pan and stir in the spice paste until it becomes fragrant. Stir in the shallots, lemon grass, cinnamon sticks, star anise and cloves. Pour in the soy sauces and stir in the sugar until dissolved.

4 Place the duck in the pan, baste with the sauce, and add 550ml/18fl oz/2½ cups water. Bring to the boil, reduce the heat and cover the pan. Simmer gently for 4–6 hours, basting from time to time, until the duck is very tender. Garnish with coriander and chillies, and serve with rice and salad.

Thai-style Red Duck Curry with Pea Aubergines

The rich flavour of duck is perfectly suited to this red hot curry with a spicy sauce enriched with coconut milk.

Serves 4
4 duck breast portions
400ml/14fl oz can coconut milk
200ml/7fl oz/scant 1 cup chicken
 stock
30ml/2 tbsp red Thai curry paste
8 spring onions (scallions), finely
 sliced
10ml/2 tsp grated fresh root
 ginger
30ml/2 tbsp Chinese rice wine
15ml/1 tbsp nam pla
15ml/1 tbsp dark soy sauce
2 lemon grass stalks, halved
 lengthways
3–4 kaffir lime leaves
300g/11oz pea aubergines
 (eggplants)
10ml/2 tsp caster (superfine)
 sugar
salt and ground black pepper
10–12 fresh basil and mint
 leaves, to garnish
steamed jasmine rice, to serve

1 Using a sharp knife, cut the duck breast portions into bitesize pieces.

2 Place a wok over a low heat and add the coconut milk, stock, curry paste, spring onions, ginger, rice wine, *nam pla*, soy sauce, lemon grass and lime leaves. Slowly bring to the boil.

3 Add the duck, aubergines and sugar to the wok and gently simmer for 25–30 minutes, stirring occasionally.

4 Remove the wok from the heat and leave to stand, covered, for about 15 minutes. Season to taste and serve ladled into shallow bowls with steamed jasmine rice, garnished with fresh mint and basil leaves.

> **Cook's Tip**
> Tiny pea aubergines are available in Asian stores, but if you have difficulty finding them, use larger aubergines cut into bitesize chunks.

Chinese Five-spice Sweet and Sour Duck

Mango adds natural sweetness to this colourful stir-fry. Crispy deep-fried noodles make the perfect accompaniment.

Serves 4
225–350g/8–12oz duck breast
 portions
45ml/3 tbsp dark soy sauce
15ml/1 tbsp Chinese rice wine
5ml/1 tsp sesame oil
5ml/1 tsp five-spice powder
15ml/1 tbsp soft brown sugar
10ml/2 tsp cornflour (cornstarch)
45ml/3 tbsp Chinese rice vinegar
15ml/1 tbsp tomato ketchup
1 mango, not too ripe
1 medium aubergine (eggplant)
1 red onion
1 carrot
60ml/4 tbsp groundnut (peanut) oil
1 garlic clove, sliced
2.5cm/1in piece fresh root ginger,
 cut into shreds
75g/3oz sugar snap peas

1 Thinly slice the duck breast portions and place in a bowl. Mix together 15ml/1 tbsp of the soy sauce with the rice wine, sesame oil and five-spice powder. Pour over the duck, cover and leave to marinate for 1–2 hours.

2 In a separate bowl, blend together the sugar, cornflour, rice vinegar, ketchup and remaining soy sauce. Set aside. Peel the mango, slice the flesh from the stone, then cut into thick strips. Slice the aubergine, onion and carrot into similar-sized pieces.

3 Heat a wok until hot, add 30ml/2 tbsp of the oil and swirl it around. Drain the duck, reserving the marinade. Stir-fry the duck slices over a high heat until the fat is crisp and golden. Remove and keep warm. Add 15ml/1 tbsp of the oil to the wok and stir-fry the aubergine for 3 minutes until golden.

4 Add the remaining oil and fry the onion, garlic, ginger and carrot for 2–3 minutes, then add the sugar snap peas and stir-fry for a further 2 minutes.

5 Add the mango and return the duck with the sauce and reserved marinade to the wok. Cook, stirring, until the sauce thickens slightly. Serve at once.

Braised Whole Duck Spiced with Star Anise

The Chinese are passionately fond of duck and regard it as essential at celebratory meals. Star anise is one of the most popular spices in Chinese cuisine, and goes well with duck.

Serves 4–6
60ml/4 tbsp vegetable oil
1 duck with giblets, about 2.25kg/5lb
2 garlic cloves, chopped
2.5cm/1 in piece fresh root ginger, peeled and thinly sliced
45ml/3 tbsp bean paste
30ml/2 tbsp light soy sauce
15ml/1 tbsp dark soy sauce
15ml/1 tbsp sugar
2.5ml/½ tsp five-spice powder
3 star anise
450ml/¾ pint/scant 2 cups duck stock (see Cook's Tip)
salt
shredded spring onions (scallions), to garnish

1 Heat the oil in a large pan. Fry the garlic without browning, then add the duck. Turn frequently until the outside is slightly brown. Transfer to a plate.

2 Add the ginger to the pan, then stir in the bean paste. Cook for 1 minute, then add both soy sauces, the sugar and the five-spice powder.

3 Return the duck to the pan and fry until the outside is coated. Add the star anise and stock, and season to taste. Cover tightly and simmer gently for 2–2½ hours or until tender.

4 Skim off the excess fat. Leave the duck in the sauce to cool. Cut the duck into serving portions and pour over the sauce. Garnish with spring onion curls and serve cold.

> **Cook's Tip**
> To make the stock, put the duck giblets in a pan with a small onion and a piece of bruised ginger. Cover with 600ml/1 pint/ 2½ cups water, bring to a boil and then simmer, covered, for 20 minutes. Strain into a bowl and skim off the excess fat.

Polish Roast Duck with Allspice and Orange

A sweet and sour orange sauce is the perfect foil for rich-tasting duck, and frying the orange rind intensifies its flavour. Allspice, which tastes like a combination of cinnamon, cloves and nutmeg, adds spicy warmth.

Serves 4
2.25kg/5lb oven-ready duckling
2.5ml/½ tsp ground allspice
1 orange
15ml/1 tbsp sunflower oil
30ml/2 tbsp plain (all-purpose) flour
150ml/¼ pint/⅔ cup chicken or duck stock
10ml/2 tsp red wine vinegar
15ml/1 tbsp clear honey
salt and ground black pepper
watercress and slivers of thinly pared orange rind, to serve

1 Preheat the oven to 220°C/425°F/Gas 7. Using a fork, pierce the duckling all over, except the breast, so that the fat runs out during cooking.

2 Rub all over the skin of the duckling with allspice and sprinkle with salt and pepper.

3 Put the duckling on a rack over a roasting pan and cook for about 20 minutes. Then reduce the oven temperature to 190°C/375°F/Gas 5 and cook for a further 2 hours.

4 Meanwhile, thinly pare the rind from the orange and cut into very fine strips. Heat the oil in a pan and gently fry the orange rind for 2–3 minutes. Squeeze the juice from the orange and set aside.

5 Transfer the duckling to a warmed serving dish and keep warm. Drain off all but 30ml/2 tbsp fat from the roasting pan, sprinkle in the flour and stir well.

6 Stir in the stock, vinegar, honey, orange juice and rind. Bring to the boil, stirring all the time. Simmer for 2–3 minutes. Season the sauce and serve the duckling with watercress and thinly pared orange rind.

Whole Duck with Star Anise: Energy 119kcal/498kJ; Protein 10.2g; Carbohydrate 4.6g, of which sugars 3.4g; Fat 6.9g, of which saturates 1.5g; Cholesterol 50mg; Calcium 35mg; Fibre 1.1g; Sodium 412mg.
Polish Roast Duck with Allspice: Energy 286kcal/1204kJ; Protein 32g; Carbohydrate 11.3g, of which sugars 5.5g; Fat 13g, of which saturates 3.7g; Cholesterol 169mg; Calcium 42mg; Fibre 0.8g; Sodium 177mg.

Vietnamese Roast Duck with Ginger and Lemon Grass

In a Vietnamese home, this delicious duck dish is served with pickled vegetables or a salad, several dipping sauces, and fragrant steamed rice.

Serves 4–6
1 duck, about 2.25kg/5lb
90g/3½oz fresh root ginger, peeled, and grated
4 garlic cloves, crushed
1 lemon grass stalk, halved and bruised

4 spring onions (scallions), halved and crushed
nuoc mam gung (ginger dipping sauce), pickled vegetables and salad leaves, to serve

For the marinade
80ml/3fl oz nuoc mam
30ml/2 tbsp soy sauce
30ml/2 tbsp honey
15ml/1 tbsp five-spice powder
5ml/1 tsp ground ginger

1 In a bowl, beat the ingredients for the marinade together until blended. Rub the skin of the duck lightly to loosen it, until you can get your fingers between the skin and the meat. Rub the marinade all over the duck, inside its skin and out, then place the duck on a rack over a tray and put it in the refrigerator for 24 hours.

2 Preheat the oven to 220°C/425°F/Gas 7. Stuff the ginger, garlic, lemon grass and spring onions into the duck's cavity and tie the legs with string. Using a bamboo or metal skewer, poke holes in the skin, including the legs.

3 Place the duck, breast-side down, on a rack over a roasting pan and cook it in the oven for 45 minutes, basting from time to time with the juices that have dripped into the pan. After 45 minutes, turn the duck over so that it is breast side up. Baste it generously and return it to the oven for a further 45 minutes, basting it every 15 minutes. The duck is ready once the juices run clear when the bird is pierced with a skewer.

4 Serve immediately, pulling the meat from the bones, rather than carving it. Serve with nuoc mam gung, pickled vegetables and salad leaves for wrapping.

Braised Spiced Duck

This dish of duck with orange, which comes from Vietnam and Cambodia, is inspired by the French caneton à l'orange, but the use of spices, lemon grass and chillies makes the South-east Asian version taste quite different. Serve it with steamed rice and a vegetable dish.

Serves 4
4 duck legs
4 garlic cloves, crushed

50g/2oz fresh root ginger, peeled and finely sliced
2 lemon grass stalks, trimmed, cut into 3 pieces and crushed
2 dried whole red Thai chillies
15ml/1 tbsp palm sugar (jaggery)
5ml/1 tsp Chinese five-spice powder
30ml/2 tbsp nuoc cham or tuk trey
900ml/1½ pints/3¾ cups fresh orange juice
sea salt and ground black pepper
1 lime, cut into quarters

1 Place the duck legs, skin-side down, in a large heavy pan or flameproof clay pot. Cook them on both sides over a medium heat for about 10 minutes, until browned and crispy. Transfer them to a plate and set aside.

2 Stir the garlic, ginger, lemon grass and chillies into the fat left in the pan, and cook until golden. Add the sugar, five-spice powder and nuoc cham or tuk trey.

3 Stir in the orange juice and place the duck legs back in the pan. Cover the pan and gently cook the duck for 1–2 hours, until the meat is very tender and the sauce has reduced. Season to taste and serve with lime wedges to squeeze over the duck.

> **Cook's Tip**
> Chinese five-spice powder is a blend designed to combine the five basic tastes – sweet, sour, bitter, savoury and salty balancing them in accordance with the Chinese system of yin and yang. There are various versions, one of which includes Szechuan pepper, star anise, cassia, cloves and fennel.

Roast Duck with Ginger: Energy 228Kcal/960kJ; Protein 27g; Carbohydrate 13g, of which sugars 7g; Fat 8g, of which saturates 3g; Cholesterol 131mg; Calcium 69mg; Fibre 0.3g; Sodium 140mg.
Braised Spiced Duck: Energy 280Kcal/1181kJ; Protein 31g; Carbohydrate 23.8g, of which sugars 23.8g; Fat 10g, of which saturates 2g; Cholesterol 165mg; Calcium 48mg; Fibre 0.4g; Sodium 250mg.

Moroccan Spiced Duck Legs with Cinnamon and Quince

The quince is a fruit of the ancient world, recorded in recipes from the Roman and Arab empires, both of which launched invasions on vast tracts of the Middle East and North Africa. The fruit is highly scented when cooked, and often features in dishes of lamb or rich poultry, as in this typically Moroccan recipe, in which its flavour is matched with the sweetness of cinnamon and honey.

Serves 4
4 duck legs
30ml/2 tbsp olive oil
2 lemons
600ml/1 pint/2½ cups water
2 quinces, quartered, cored
  and peeled
a little butter
25g/1oz fresh root ginger, peeled
  and grated
10ml/2 tsp ground cinnamon
30ml/2 tbsp clear honey
salt and ground black pepper
small bunch of fresh coriander
  (cilantro), chopped, to serve

1 Preheat the oven to 230°C/450°F/Gas 8. Rub the duck legs with half the olive oil, season with salt and pepper, and place on a rack in a roasting pan. Roast in the oven for about 30 minutes until the skin is crisp and golden.

2 Squeeze the juice from ½ lemon and place in a pan. Add the water and bring to the boil. Add the quince quarters and simmer for about 15 minutes until tender. Drain and refresh, then cut each quince quarter into slices. Heat the remaining olive oil and butter in a frying pan and fry the quince slices until brown. Remove from the pan, place in a dish and keep warm.

3 Take the duck out of the oven and pour 30ml/2 tbsp of the duck fat into the pan in which the fruit was cooked. Stir in the ginger and cook for 1 minute, then add the cinnamon, honey and the remaining lemon juice. Pour in 30–45ml/2–3 tbsp water and stir until it bubbles up to make a small amount of sauce; remove from the heat.

4 Arrange the duck and quince on a plate and spoon the sauce over. Sprinkle with coriander and serve immediately.

Duck with Ginger and Pineapple

This recipe takes advantage of the abundance of pineapples that grow in Vietnam and Cambodia. Allow plenty of time for the duck to marinate.

Serves 4–6
1 small duck, skinned, trimmed
  and jointed
1 pineapple, skinned, cored and
  cut in half crossways
45ml/3 tbsp sesame oil
4cm/1½in fresh root ginger,
  peeled and finely sliced
1 onion, sliced
salt and ground black pepper
1 bunch fresh coriander (cilantro),
  stalks removed, to garnish

For the marinade
3 shallots
45ml/3 tbsp soy sauce
30ml/2 tbsp nuoc mam
10ml/2 tsp Chinese five-spice
  powder
15ml/1 tbsp sugar
3 garlic cloves, crushed
1 bunch fresh basil, stalks
  removed, leaves finely chopped

1 To make the marinade, grate the shallots into a bowl, then add the remaining marinade ingredients and beat together until the sugar has dissolved. Place the duck in a wide dish and rub with the marinade. Cover and chill for 6 hours or overnight.

2 Take one of the pineapple halves and cut into 4–6 slices, and then again into half-moons, and set aside. Take the other pineapple half and chop it to a pulp. Using your hands, squeeze all the juice from the pulp into a bowl. Discard the pulp and reserve the juice.

3 Heat 30ml/2 tbsp of the oil in a wide pan. Stir in the ginger and the onion. When they begin to soften, add the duck to the pan and brown on both sides. Pour in the pineapple juice and any remaining marinade, then add water to just cover. Bring to the boil, reduce the heat and simmer for about 25 minutes.

4 Meanwhile, heat the remaining oil in a heavy pan and sear the pineapple slices on both sides – you may have to do this in two batches. Add the seared pineapple to the duck, season to taste with salt and black pepper and cook for a further 5 minutes, or until the duck is tender. Arrange on a warmed serving dish, garnish with the coriander leaves and serve.

Moroccan Spiced Duck: Energy 356Kcal/1489kJ; Protein 28g; Carbohydrate 19g, of which sugars 13g; Fat 20g, of which saturates 4g; Cholesterol 131mg; Calcium 122mg; Fibre 2g; Sodium 150mg
Duck with Ginger: Energy 253kcal/1071kJ; Protein 20.8g; Carbohydrate 33.2g, of which sugars 23.8g; Fat 6.8g, of which saturates 1.4g; Cholesterol 110mg; Calcium 31mg; Fibre 1.1g; Sodium 515mg.

Tagine of Poussins with Garlic and Cinnamon

Dates and almonds are probably the most ancient culinary combination in the cuisines of the Arab world. They are used together in sweet recipes, but also provide sweetness in meat dishes, particularly using lamb and chicken. In this case the sweetness of the dates is underlined by the addition of honey and cinnamon. Served with a Moroccan salad and couscous, this makes a lovely dinner party dish.

Serves 4
25g/1oz fresh root ginger, peeled and roughly chopped
2 garlic cloves
60ml/4 tbsp olive oil
juice of 1 lemon
30–45ml/2–3 tbsp clear honey
4 small poussins
350g/12oz/2 cups dates, pitted
5–10ml/1–2 tsp ground cinnamon
15ml/1 tbsp orange flower water
knob (pat) of butter
30–45ml/2–3 tbsp blanched almonds
salt and ground black pepper

1 Using a mortar and pestle, crush the ginger with the garlic and mix with the olive oil, lemon juice, honey and seasoning.

2 Place the poussins in a tagine or flameproof casserole and rub the ginger and garlic paste all over them. Pour in a little water to cover the base of the dish and bring to the boil.

3 Reduce the heat, cover and simmer for about 30 minutes, turning the poussins occasionally, until they are cooked through. Top up the water during cooking, if necessary.

4 Lift the poussins out of the tagine, transfer them to a plate, cover with foil and keep hot. Add the dates to the liquid in the tagine and stir in the cinnamon and orange flower water. Cook gently for about 10 minutes, or until the dates are soft and have absorbed some of the liquid.

5 Replace the poussins and cover the tagine to keep hot. Melt the butter in a separate pan and brown the almonds, then toss them over the poussins. Serve immediately.

Garlic-roasted Quails with Black Peppercorns

This is a great Indo-Chinese favourite, which may be made with either quails or poussins. Crispy, tender and juicy, the little birds are simple to prepare and delicious to eat. You can either roast them in the oven or grill them over a barbecue. Serve with fragrant steamed rice.

Serves 4
150ml/¼ pint/⅔ cup mushroom soy sauce
45ml/3 tbsp honey
15ml/1 tbsp sugar
8 garlic cloves, crushed
15ml/1 tbsp black peppercorns, crushed
30ml/2 tbsp sesame oil
8 quails or poussins
nuoc cham, to serve

1 In a bowl, beat the mushroom soy sauce with the honey and sugar until the sugar has dissolved. Stir in the garlic, crushed peppercorns and sesame oil.

2 Split the quails or poussins down the backbone, open them out flat and secure them with skewers. Put them in a dish and rub the marinade over them. Cover the dish and chill for at least 4 hours.

3 Preheat the oven to 230°C/450°F/Gas 8. Place the quails breast-side down in a roasting pan or on a wire rack set over a baking tray, then put them in the oven for 10 minutes.

4 Take them out and turn them over so they are breast-side up, baste well with the juices and return them to the oven for a further 15–20 minutes until cooked through. Serve immediately with nuoc cham for dipping or drizzling.

> **Cook's Tip**
> The quails or poussins can be roasted whole if you prefer, although opening them out and skewering them enables them to be cooked more quickly, making this dish particularly suitable for cooking on the barbecue.

Tagine of Poussins: Energy 670kcal/2810kJ; Protein 27.3g; Carbohydrate 68.9g, of which sugars 67.6g; Fat 33.7g, of which saturates 7.7g; Cholesterol 121mg; Calcium 68mg; Fibre 4.4g; Sodium 106mg.
Garlic-roasted Quails: Energy 649Kcal/2701kJ; Protein 51g; Carbohydrate 17g, of which sugars 3g; Fat 43g, of which saturates 11g; Cholesterol 250mg; Calcium 61mg; Fibre 0.2g; Sodium 200mg.

Pigeons Cooked in Spiced Vinegar

This is a Spanish dish using pigeon marinated in spiced vinegar and red wine. Cabbage is a familiar partner to pigeon, but puréed celeriac also goes very well.

Serves 4

4 pigeons (US squabs), each
  weighing about 225g/8oz,
  cleaned
30ml/2 tbsp olive oil
1 onion, roughly chopped
225g/8oz/3 cups brown cap
  (cremini) mushrooms, sliced
plain (all-purpose) flour, for dusting
300ml/½ pint/1¼ cups beef or
  game stock

30ml/2 tbsp chopped fresh
  parsley
salt and ground black pepper
fresh flat leaf parsley, to garnish

For the marinade
15ml/1 tbsp olive oil
1 onion, chopped
1 carrot, chopped
1 celery stick, chopped
3 garlic cloves, sliced
6 allspice berries, bruised
2 bay leaves
8 black peppercorns, bruised
120ml/4fl oz/½ cup red wine
  vinegar
150ml/¼ pint/⅔ cup red wine

1 Starting a day before you want to eat the dish, combine all the ingredients for the marinade in a large dish. Add the pigeons and turn them in the marinade, then cover and chill for 12 hours, turning occasionally.

2 Preheat the oven to 150°C/300°F/Gas 2. Heat the oil in a large, flameproof casserole and cook the onion and mushrooms for about 5 minutes, until the onion has softened.

3 Meanwhile, remove the pigeons to a plate using a slotted spoon and strain the marinade into a bowl, then set both aside separately.

4 Sprinkle the flour on the pigeons and add them to the casserole, breast-sides down. Pour in the marinade and stock, and add the parsley and seasoning. Cover and cook for 1½ hours or until tender.

5 Check the seasoning, then serve the pigeons on warmed plates with the sauce. Garnish with parsley.

Pigeon and Mushrooms in Rich Pepper Sauce

Use the strongest-flavoured mushrooms you can find for this Spanish dish, and serve with fried potatoes.

Serves 6

6 pigeons (US squabs), cleaned
90ml/6 tbsp olive oil
1 large onion, chopped
2 garlic cloves, finely chopped
450g/1lb/6 cups brown cap
  (cremini) or small open cap
  field (portobello) mushrooms
150g/5oz Serrano ham, diced
150ml/¼ pint/⅔ cup red wine
salt and ground black pepper

60ml/4 tbsp chopped fresh
  parsley, to garnish
fried potatoes, to serve

For the stock
1 large onion, unpeeled, roughly
  chopped
2 carrots, roughly chopped
1 celery stick, roughly chopped
6 tough parsley stalks, snapped
  or bruised
1 bay leaf
1 garlic clove, unpeeled but
  crushed
4 sprigs of fresh thyme
12 black peppercorns, crushed

1 First prepare the pigeons. Find the wishbone by pushing your forefinger and thumb in the neck end. It runs up each side; snap it out. Cut down one side of the breastbone with a large knife, then scrape along the rib cage, to get the breast meat off whole. Repeat this, and season the meat. Flatten the pigeon carcasses in a large pan. Add all the stock ingredients and just cover with water. Simmer for about 2 hours. Strain into a bowl.

2 Heat 30ml/2 tbsp of the oil in a large casserole and fry the onion and garlic gently for a few minutes. Meanwhile, remove the mushroom stalks, chop them and add to the casserole, with the ham. Fry briefly. Pour in the wine and 250ml/8fl oz/1 cup of the stock. Simmer gently to reduce a little.

3 Heat 30ml/2 tbsp oil in a large frying pan and fry the pigeon breasts for 2 minutes on each side. Remove to the casserole. Simmer for 2–3 minutes. Add the remaining oil to the pan and fry the mushroom caps. Arrange the pigeon on a plate and pile the mushrooms in the centre. Spoon the ham and sauce over, garnish with parsley and serve with fried potatoes.

Pigeons in Spiced Vinegar: Energy 361kcal/1502kJ; Protein 34.2g; Carbohydrate 4.2g, of which sugars 3.3g; Fat 20.3g, of which saturates 1.7g; Cholesterol 0mg; Calcium 57mg; Fibre 1.6g; Sodium 119mg.
Pigeon and Mushrooms: Energy 389kcal/1618kJ; Protein 39.5g; Carbohydrate 5.9g, of which sugars 4.2g; Fat 21.2g, of which saturates 1.9g; Cholesterol 15mg; Calcium 66mg; Fibre 1.9g; Sodium 412mg.

Spiced Grilled Poussins

The cumin and coriander coating on the poussins keeps them moist during grilling as well as giving them a delicious and unusual flavour. Cumin can taste bitter, and in Asian cuisines it is often used with coriander, which counteracts any bitterness.

Serves 4
2 garlic cloves, roughly chopped
5ml/1 tsp ground cumin
5ml/1 tsp ground coriander
pinch of cayenne pepper
½ small onion, chopped
60ml/4 tbsp olive oil
2.5ml/½ tsp salt
2 poussins
lemon wedges, to garnish

1 Combine the garlic, cumin, coriander, cayenne pepper, onion, olive oil and salt in a blender or food processor. Process to make a paste that will spread smoothly.

2 Cut the poussins in half lengthways. Place them skin-side up in a shallow dish and spread the skin with the spice paste. Cover the birds and leave to marinate in a cool place for at least 2 hours.

3 Grill (broil) or barbecue the poussins for 15–20 minutes, turning frequently, until cooked and lightly charred on the outside. Serve immediately, garnished with lemon wedges.

Cook's Tip
Poussins are young chickens, weighing around 500g/1¼lb and generally serving two people. The meat is tender with a delicate flavour, so it is best suited to lightly spiced marinades, sauces and coatings. They are often "spatchcocked" – split down the backbone and opened out flat to make them suitable for grilling and barbecuing.

Variation
Chicken portions and quail can also be cooked in this way, adjusting the cooking time as necessary.

Ginger-glazed Steamed Poussins with Kaffir Lime Leaves

These moist, succulent poussins coated in a spiced citrus and honey glaze make a great alternative to a roast. They need to marinate for at least 6 hours.

Serves 4
4 small poussins, weighing about 300–350g/11–12oz each
juice and finely grated rind of 2 oranges
2 garlic cloves, crushed
15ml/1 tbsp grated fresh root ginger
90ml/6 tbsp soy sauce
75ml/5 tbsp clear honey
2–3 star anise
30ml/2 tbsp Chinese rice wine
about 20 kaffir lime leaves
a large bunch of spring onions (scallions), shredded
60ml/4 tbsp butter
1 large orange, segmented

1 Place the poussins in a deep, non-metallic dish. Mix the orange rind and juice, garlic, ginger, half the soy sauce, half the honey, star anise and rice wine, and pour over the poussins. Cover, and marinate in the refrigerator for at least 6 hours.

2 To cook the poussins, line a large, heatproof plate with the kaffir lime leaves and spring onions. Place the marinated poussins on top and reserve the marinade.

3 Place a trivet or steamer rack in the base of a large wok and pour in 5cm/2in water. Bring to the boil and carefully lower the plate of poussins on to the trivet or rack. Cover, reduce the heat to low and steam for 45 minutes–1 hour, or until the poussins are cooked through and tender. (Check the water level regularly and add more when necessary.)

4 Remove the poussins from the wok and keep warm while you make the glaze. Wipe out the wok and pour in the reserved marinade, butter and the remaining soy sauce and honey. Bring to the boil, reduce the heat and cook gently for 10–15 minutes, or until thick.

5 Spoon the glaze over the poussins and serve immediately, garnished with the orange segments.

Spiced Grilled Poussins: Energy 247kcal/1029kJ; Protein 20.9g; Carbohydrate 3.5g, of which sugars 3.4g; Fat 15.2g, of which saturates 4.1g; Cholesterol 109mg; Calcium 8mg; Fibre 0g; Sodium 106mg.
Ginger Steamed Poussins: Energy 544kcal/2264kJ; Protein 36.2g; Carbohydrate 5.8g, of which sugars 5.8g; Fat 42.1g, of which saturates 14.5g; Cholesterol 215mg; Calcium 16mg; Fibre 0g; Sodium 207mg.

Roast Beef with Peppercorns and Juniper Berries

This joint looks spectacular, and served with roast potatoes and seasonal vegetables, it makes a perfect celebration meal.

Serves 8–10
45ml/3 tbsp mixed peppercorns
15ml/1 tbsp juniper berries
2.75kg/6lb rolled rib of beef
30ml/2 tbsp Dijon mustard

15ml/1 tbsp olive oil
20 shallots
5 garlic cloves, peeled
60ml/4 tbsp light olive oil
15ml/1 tbsp caster (superfine) sugar

For the gravy
150ml/¼ pint/⅔ cup red wine
600ml/1 pint/2½ cups beef stock
salt and ground black pepper
flat leaf parsley, to garnish

1 Preheat the oven to 230°C/450°F/Gas 8. Coarsely crush the peppercorns and juniper berries. Sprinkle half the spices over the meat, then transfer to a roasting pan and roast for 30 minutes.

2 Reduce the oven temperature to 180°C/350°F/Gas 4. Mix the mustard and oil into the remaining crushed spices and spread the resulting paste over the meat. Roast the meat for a further 1¼ hours for rare, 1 hour 50 minutes for medium-rare or 2 hours 25 minutes for well done. Baste frequently.

3 An hour before the beef is due to be ready, mix the shallots and garlic cloves with the light olive oil and spoon into the roasting pan around the beef. After 30 minutes, sprinkle the caster sugar over the shallots and garlic. Stir the shallots and garlic two or three times during cooking.

4 Transfer the meat to a large serving platter, cover tightly with foil and set aside to rest in a warm place for 20–30 minutes.

5 To make the gravy, simmer the wine and stock in a pan for about 5 minutes to intensify the flavour. Skim the fat from the roasting pan, then pour in the wine mixture, scraping up all the residue from the bottom. Simmer until the gravy is reduced and thickened slightly. Season to taste. Carve the beef and serve with the shallots and gravy.

East European Spicy Rolled Beef

This recipe blends Slovakian, Greek and Russian cuisines, with a spicy touch of coriander and peppercorns.

Serves 4
4 beef slices, about 10–15cm/
 4–6in thick
50ml/2fl oz/¼ cup olive oil, plus
 extra for frying
30ml/2 tbsp black peppercorns,
 roughly crushed
30ml/2 tbsp whole coriander seeds
1 onion, finely sliced
300ml/½ pint/1¼ cups red wine
1 egg, beaten

150g/5oz can chopped tomatoes
polenta and sour cream, to serve

For the filling
115g/4oz/½ cup minced
 (ground) ham
40g/1½oz/scant 1 cup
 breadcrumbs
2 spring onions (scallions), finely
 sliced
45ml/3 tbsp chopped parsley
1 egg yolk
75g/3oz green (bell) pepper,
 seeded and finely chopped
1.5ml/¼ tsp ground allspice

1 Place the slices of beef between two sheets of dampened clear film (plastic wrap). Flatten with a meat mallet or rolling pin until the meat is evenly thin. Dip the slices in the oil.

2 Lay the meat out flat and sprinkle over the crushed peppercorns, coriander seeds and onion. Roll up the meat neatly and place in a shallow glass or china dish. Pour over half of the wine, cover with clear film and chill for 2 hours.

3 Combine all the filling ingredients in a bowl and add a little water or beef stock if necessary, to moisten the stuffing.

4 Remove the beef from the bowl and shake off the spices and onion. Spoon 30–45ml/2–3 tbsp of the filling into the middle of each piece of meat. Brush the inner surface with egg and roll up. Secure with a cocktail stick (toothpick) or tie with string.

5 Heat a little oil in a frying pan and sauté the rolls until brown on all sides. Reduce the heat and pour over the remaining wine and canned tomatoes. Simmer for 25–30 minutes, or until the meat is tender. Season well and serve with polenta, sour cream and plenty of cracked pepper.

Roast Beef with Peppercorns: Energy 561kcal/2338kJ; Protein 62.9g; Carbohydrate 4.8g, of which sugars 3.8g; Fat 31.2g, of which saturates 11.2g; Cholesterol 160mg; Calcium 26mg; Fibre 0.6g; Sodium 178mg.
Spicy Rolled Beef: Energy 508kcal/2117kJ; Protein 43.7g; Carbohydrate 12g, of which sugars 4.1g; Fat 26.4g, of which saturates 8.1g; Cholesterol 202mg; Calcium 53mg; Fibre 1.3g; Sodium 547mg.

Beef Goulash

Paprika is one of the most distinctive features of Hungarian cookery. It is a spicy seasoning ground from a variety of sweet red pepper, which has been grown in this area since the end of the 16th century. Shepherds added the spice to their goulash, and fishermen used it in their stews.

Serves 4–6

30ml/2 tbsp vegetable oil or melted lard
2 onions, chopped

900g/2lb braising or stewing steak, trimmed and cubed
1 garlic clove, crushed
generous pinch of caraway seeds
30ml/2 tbsp paprika
1 firm ripe tomato, chopped
2.4 litres/4 pints/10 cups beef stock
2 green (bell) peppers, seeded and sliced
450g/1lb potatoes, diced
salt

For the dumplings
2 eggs, beaten
90ml/6 tbsp plain (all-purpose) flour, sifted

1 Heat the oil or lard in a large heavy pan. Add the onion and cook until it is soft.

2 Add the beef cubes to the pan and cook for 10 minutes, stirring frequently to prevent the meat from sticking, until it is lightly browned.

3 Add the garlic, caraway seeds and a little salt to the pan. Remove from the heat and stir in the paprika and tomato. Pour in the beef stock and cook, covered, over a gentle heat for 1–1½ hours, or until the meat is tender.

4 Add the peppers and potatoes to the pan and cook for a further 20–25 minutes stirring occasionally.

5 Meanwhile, make the dumplings by mixing the beaten eggs together with the flour and a little salt. With lightly floured hands roll out the dumplings and drop them into the simmering stew. Cook for about 2–3 minutes, or until they rise to the surface of the stew. Adjust the seasoning and serve the goulash in warm dishes.

Sweet and Sour Pot Roast

Serve this sweet and sour beef with buttered noodles.

Serves 6

1kg/2¼lb silverside of beef
30ml/2 tbsp sunflower oil
1 onion, sliced
115g/4oz smoked streaky (fatty) bacon, diced
15ml/1 tbsp cornflour (cornstarch)
50g/2oz/1 cup crushed ginger biscuits (gingersnaps)
flat leaf parsley, to garnish

For the marinade
2 onions, sliced
1 carrot, sliced
2 celery sticks, sliced
600ml/1 pint/2½ cups water
150ml/¼ pint/⅔ cup red vinegar
1 bay leaf
6 cloves
6 whole black peppercorns
15ml/1 tbsp soft dark brown sugar
10ml/2 tsp salt

1 To make the marinade, put the onions, carrot and celery into a pan with the water. Bring to the boil and simmer for 5 minutes. Add the remaining marinade ingredients and simmer for a further 5 minutes. Cover and leave to cool. Put the joint in a casserole into which it just fits. Pour over the marinade, cover and leave to marinate in the refrigerator for 3 days if possible, turning the joint daily.

2 Remove the joint from the marinade and dry thoroughly using kitchen paper. Heat the oil in a large frying pan and brown the beef over a high heat. Remove the joint and set aside. Add the onion to the pan and fry for 5 minutes. Add the bacon and cook for a further 5 minutes, until lightly browned.

3 Strain the marinade, reserving the liquid. Put the onion and bacon in a large flameproof casserole or pan, then put the beef on top. Pour over the marinade liquid. Slowly bring to the boil, cover, then simmer over a low heat for 1½–2 hours, or until the beef is very tender.

4 Remove the beef and keep warm. Blend the cornflour in a cup with a little cold water. Add to the cooking liquid with the ginger biscuit crumbs and bring to the boil, stirring. Thickly slice the beef and serve on a bed of hot buttered noodles. Garnish with sprigs of fresh flat leaf parsley and serve with the gravy.

Beef Goulash: Energy 751kcal/3136kJ; Protein 62.1g; Carbohydrate 41.1g, of which sugars 13.2g; Fat 38.9g, of which saturates 15.4g; Cholesterol 153mg; Calcium 159mg; Fibre 4.6g; Sodium 282mg.
Sweet and Sour Pot Roast: Energy 441kcal/1837kJ; Protein 42g; Carbohydrate 12.8g, of which sugars 5.8g; Fat 24.9g, of which saturates 8.9g; Cholesterol 109mg; Calcium 33mg; Fibre 0.8g; Sodium 379mg.

Green Beef Curry with Thai Aubergines

This is a very quick curry so be sure to use a good quality cut, such as sirloin. Ready-made green curry paste is widely available but for an extra authentic flavour make it yourself (see Cook's Tip).

Serves 4–6

450g/1lb beef sirloin
15ml/1 tbsp vegetable oil
45ml/3 tbsp Thai green curry paste
600ml/1 pint/2½ cups coconut milk
4 kaffir lime leaves, torn
15–30ml/1–2 tbsp nam pla
5ml/1 tsp palm sugar (jaggery) or light muscovado (brown) sugar
150g/5oz small Thai aubergines (eggplants), halved
a small handful of fresh Thai basil
2 fresh green chillies, to garnish

1 Trim off excess fat from the beef, and cut it into long, thin strips. This is easiest to do if it is well chilled. Set it aside.

2 Heat the oil in a large, heavy pan or wok. Add the curry paste and cook for 1–2 minutes, until it is fragrant. Stir in half the coconut milk, a little at a time. Cook for 5–6 minutes, stirring, until an oily sheen appears on the surface of the liquid.

3 Add the beef to the pan with the kaffir lime leaves, *nam pla*, sugar and aubergine halves. Cook for 2–3 minutes, then stir in the remaining coconut milk. Bring back to a simmer and cook until tender. Stir in the Thai basil just before serving. Finely shred the green chillies and use to garnish the curry.

Cook's Tip

To make green curry paste, put into a food processor 15 fresh green chillies, 2 lemon grass stalks, 3 shallots, 2 garlic cloves, 15ml/1 tbsp galangal, 4 kaffir lime leaves, 2.5ml/½ tsp grated kaffir lime rind, 1 tsp chopped coriander root, 6 black peppercorns, 5ml/1 tsp each roasted coriander and cumin seeds, 15ml/1 tbsp sugar, 5ml/1 tsp salt and 5ml/1 tsp shrimp paste. Process, then gradually add 30ml/2 tbsp vegetable oil.

Beef Rendang

This classic fiery Malaysian recipe dates back to the 15th century, when the Minangkabau people first came from Sumatra to settle in the country.

Serves 6

1kg/2¼lb beef topside (pot roast) or rump, cut into bitesize cubes
115g/4oz fresh coconut, grated
15ml/1 tbsp tamarind pulp, soaked in 90ml/6 tbsp water until soft
45ml/3 tbsp vegetable oil
2 onions, halved and sliced
3 lemon grass stalks, trimmed, halved and bruised
2 cinnamon sticks
1.2 litres/2 pints/5 cups coconut milk
15ml/1 tbsp sugar
salt and ground black pepper
bread and salad, to serve

For the spice paste

8–10 dried red chillies, soaked in warm water until soft, seeded and squeezed dry
8 shallots, chopped
4–6 garlic cloves, chopped
50g/2oz fresh galangal, chopped
25g/1oz fresh turmeric, chopped
15ml/1 tbsp coriander seeds
10ml/2 tsp cumin seeds
5ml/1 tsp black peppercorns

1 First make the spice paste. In a small heavy pan, dry-roast the coriander and cumin seeds with the peppercorns, until they give off a nutty aroma. Grind to a powder. Process the chillies, shallots, garlic, galangal and turmeric to a smooth paste and add the ground seed mixture. Coat the beef in the spice paste and set aside to marinate for about 1 hour.

2 Meanwhile, dry-roast the grated coconut in a heavy pan, until it is brown and emits a nutty aroma. Process until it resembles brown sugar, and set aside. Squeeze the tamarind to help soften it, then strain it to extract the juice. Discard the pulp.

3 Heat the oil in a wok or heavy pan. Add the onions, lemon grass and cinnamon sticks, and fry until the onions begin to colour. Add the beef with the paste and fry until lightly brown.

4 Pour in the coconut milk and tamarind juice and bring to the boil, stirring. Stir in the sugar and the ground coconut. Simmer gently, for 2–4 hours, stirring from time to time, until the meat is tender and the sauce is thick. Season and serve.

Beef Curry with Aubergines: Energy 264kcal/1107kJ; Protein 26.3g; Carbohydrate 9.2g, of which sugars 9.2g; Fat 13.8g, of which saturates 4.9g; Cholesterol 65mg; Calcium 54mg; Fibre 0.8g; Sodium 238mg.
Beef Rendang: Energy 289kcal/1210kJ; Protein 30.2g; Carbohydrate 15.4g, of which sugars 8.6g; Fat 12.2g, of which saturates 5g; Cholesterol 73mg; Calcium 63mg; Fibre 1.4g; Sodium 465mg.

Mussaman Curry

This dish is traditionally based on beef, but chicken, lamb or tofu can be used instead. Mussaman curry paste, available from specialist stores, imparts a rich, sweet and spicy flavour.

Serves 4–6

675g/1½lb stewing steak
600ml/1 pint/2½ cups coconut milk
250ml/8fl oz/1 cup coconut cream
45ml/3 tbsp Mussaman curry paste
30ml/2 tbsp nam pla
15ml/1 tbsp palm sugar (jaggery) or light muscovado (brown) sugar
60ml/4 tbsp tamarind juice (tamarind paste mixed with warm water)
6 green cardamom pods
1 cinnamon stick
1 large potato, about 225g/8oz, cut into even chunks
1 onion, cut into wedges
50g/2oz/½ cup roasted peanuts

1 Trim off any excess fat from the stewing steak, then, using a sharp knife, cut it into 2.5cm/1in chunks. Pour the coconut milk into a large, heavy pan and bring to the boil over a medium heat. Add the chunks of beef to the coconut milk, reduce the heat to low, partially cover the pan and simmer gently for about 40 minutes, or until tender.

2 Transfer the coconut cream to a separate pan. Cook over a medium heat, stirring constantly, for about 5 minutes, or until it separates. Stir in the Mussaman curry paste and cook rapidly for 2–3 minutes, until fragrant and thoroughly blended.

3 Return the coconut cream and curry paste mixture to the pan with the beef and stir until thoroughly blended. Simmer for a further 4–5 minutes, stirring occasionally.

4 Stir the nam pla, sugar, tamarind juice, cardamom pods, cinnamon stick, potato chunks and onion wedges into the beef curry. Continue to simmer for a further 15–20 minutes, or until the potato is cooked and tender.

5 Add the roasted peanuts to the pan and mix well to combine. Cook for about 5 minutes more, then transfer to warmed individual serving bowls and serve immediately.

Beef Stew with Star Anise

This Thai dish does not really resemble a stew in the western sense; it is really more a fragrant soup that includes thin morsels of tender beef. It is gently spiced with cinnamon and star anise, which help to bring out the sweetness of the meat. The beansprouts, spring onion and coriander are added at the end of cooking so that they stay crisp and green, for a delightful contrast in taste and texture. Serve the dish in deep bowls and eat it with spoons.

Serves 4

1 litre/1¾ pints/4 cups vegetable or chicken stock
450g/1lb beef steak, cut into slivers
3 garlic cloves, finely chopped
3 coriander (cilantro) roots, finely chopped
2 cinnamon sticks
4 star anise
30ml/2 tbsp light soy sauce
30ml/2 tbsp nam pla
5ml/1 tsp granulated sugar
115g/4oz/1½ cups beansprouts
1 spring onion (scallion), finely chopped
small bunch fresh coriander (cilantro), coarsely chopped

1 Pour the stock into a large, heavy pan. Add the beef, garlic, chopped coriander roots, cinnamon sticks, star anise, soy sauce, nam pla and sugar.

2 Bring to the boil, then reduce the heat to low and simmer for 30 minutes. Skim off any foam that rises to the surface of the liquid with a slotted spoon.

3 Meanwhile, divide the beansprouts among four individual serving bowls. Remove and discard the cinnamon sticks and star anise from the stew with a slotted spoon.

4 Ladle the stew over the beansprouts, garnish with the chopped spring onion and chopped fresh coriander and serve immediately.

Cook's Tip
Cut the beef thinly, working across the grain of the meat.

Mussaman Curry: Energy 626kcal/2610kJ; Protein 44.6g; Carbohydrate 24.8g, of which sugars 15.4g; Fat 39.3g, of which saturates 22.7g; Cholesterol 98mg; Calcium 74mg; Fibre 1.6g; Sodium 288mg.
Beef Stew with Star Anise: Energy 147kcal/615kJ; Protein 18.2g; Carbohydrate 2.8g, of which sugars 1.6g; Fat 7.1g, of which saturates 2.9g; Cholesterol 44mg; Calcium 11mg; Fibre 0.5g; Sodium 405mg.

Spicy Beef and Butternut Squash with Chilli and Herbs

Stir-fried beef and sweet, orange-fleshed butternut squash flavoured with warm spices, oyster sauce and fresh herbs make a robust main couse when served with rice or egg noodles. The addition of chilli and fresh root ginger gives the dish a wonderfully vigorous bite.

Serves 4

30ml/2 tbsp sunflower oil
2 onions, cut into thick slices
500g/1¼lb butternut squash, peeled, seeded and cut into thin strips
675g/1½lb fillet steak (beef tenderloin)
60ml/4 tbsp soy sauce
90g/3½ oz/½ cup golden caster (superfine) sugar
1 bird's eye chilli, seeded and chopped
15ml/1 tbsp finely shredded fresh root ginger
30ml/2 tbsp nam pla
5ml/1 tsp ground star anise
5ml/1 tsp Chinese five-spice powder
15ml/1 tbsp oyster sauce
4 spring onions (scallions), shredded
a small handful of basil leaves
a small handful of mint leaves

1 Heat a wok over a medium-high heat and add the oil. When hot, stir in the onions and squash. Stir-fry for 2–3 minutes, then reduce the heat, cover and cook gently for 5–6 minutes, or until just tender.

2 Place the beef between two sheets of clear film (plastic wrap) and beat, with a mallet or rolling pin, until thin. Using a sharp knife, cut into thin strips.

3 Meanwhile, in a separate wok, add the soy sauce, sugar, chilli, ginger, nam pla, star anise, five-spice powder and oyster sauce. Stir-fry over a medium heat for 3–4 minutes.

4 Add the beef strips to the wok and cook over a high heat for 3–4 minutes, or until cooked through. Remove from the heat. Add the onion and squash slices to the beef and toss with the spring onions and herbs until combined. Serve immediately.

Beef with Peppers and Black Bean Sauce

A spicy, rich dish with the distinctive flavour of black bean sauce. Made from fermented beans, it has a unique salty, spicy taste that goes particularly well with beef.

Serves 4

350g/12oz rump (round) steak, trimmed and thinly sliced
15ml/1 tbsp vegetable oil
300ml/½ pint/1¼ cups beef stock
2 garlic cloves, finely chopped
5ml/1 tsp grated fresh root ginger
1 fresh red chilli, seeded and finely chopped
15ml/1 tbsp black bean sauce
1 green (bell) pepper, cut into 2.5cm/1in squares
15ml/1 tbsp dry sherry
5ml/1 tsp cornflour (cornstarch)
5ml/1 tsp caster (superfine) sugar
45ml/3 tbsp cold water
salt
rice noodles, to serve

1 Place the sliced steak in a bowl. Add 5ml/1 tsp of the oil and stir to coat. Bring the stock to the boil in a pan.

2 Add the beef and cook for 2 minutes, stirring to prevent the slices from sticking together. Drain the beef and set aside.

3 Heat the remaining oil in a non-stick frying pan or wok. Stir-fry the garlic, ginger and chilli with the black bean sauce for a few seconds. Add the pepper squares and a little water. Cook for about 2 minutes more, then stir in the sherry. Add the beef slices to the pan and spoon the sauce over.

4 Mix the cornflour and sugar to a paste with the water. Pour the mixture into the pan. Cook, stirring, until the sauce has thickened. Season with salt. Serve at once, with rice noodles.

Cook's Tip
Use plum tomatoes or vine tomatoes from the garden, if you can. The store-bought ones are a little more expensive than standard tomatoes but have a far better flavour.

Beef and Squash with Chilli: Energy 500kcal/2093kJ; Protein 41.3g; Carbohydrate 36.9g, of which sugars 33.8g; Fat 21.7g, of which saturates 7.2g; Cholesterol 98mg; Calcium 91mg; Fibre 2.9g; Sodium 1243mg.
Beef with Peppers and Sauce: Energy 146kcal/613kJ; Protein 19.3g; Carbohydrate 2.1g, of which sugars 1.1g; Fat 6.4g, of which saturates 1.8g; Cholesterol 52mg; Calcium 5mg; Fibre 0g; Sodium 115mg.

Marinated Korean Beef

This traditional Korean recipe is made with very tender steak, flash fried on a hot griddle. The thin slivers of beef need only a few seconds to cook. It is delicious eaten with a salad of wilted spinach.

Serves 4
500g/1¼lb beef fillet (tenderloin)
15ml/1 tbsp sugar
30ml/2 tbsp light soy sauce
30ml/2 tbsp sesame oil
2 garlic cloves, mashed to a paste
 with a further 5ml/1 tsp sugar
2.5ml/½ tsp finely ground black
 pepper

For the salad
350g/12oz baby spinach leaves
10ml/2 tsp sesame oil
30ml/2 tbsp light soy sauce
15ml/1 tbsp mirin
10ml/2 tsp sesame seeds, finely
 toasted

1 Put the piece of beef in the freezer for 1 hour to make it easier to slice.

2 Remove the beef from the freezer and slice it as thinly as possible. Layer the slices in a shallow dish, sprinkling each layer with sugar. Cover and chill for 30 minutes.

3 Mix the soy sauce, sesame oil, garlic paste and pepper together in a bowl and pour over the beef, ensuring all the pieces are thoroughly coated in the mixture. Cover and chill overnight or for at least 6 hours.

4 To make the salad, blanch the spinach in boiling water for 1 minute, drain it and refresh under cold water. Drain again, pat with kitchen paper to remove any excess water and put into a serving bowl.

5 Mix the oil, soy sauce and mirin together. Fold into the spinach, together with the sesame seeds. Cover and keep in a cool place (not the refrigerator).

6 Heat a griddle on the stove over a high heat until a few drops of water sprinkled on to the surface evaporate instantly. Flash-fry the meat in batches for 15–20 seconds on each side. Serve immediately with the spinach salad.

Spicy Beef Kebabs with Hot Chickpea Purée

Try this dish for a summer barbecue. Make the kebabs as fiery as you like by adding more cayenne pepper. The smooth, soothing chickpea purée adds a sumptuous touch. You need metal skewers with wide blades.

Serves 6
500g/1¼lb minced (ground) beef
1 onion, grated
10ml/2 tsp ground cumin
10ml/2 tsp ground coriander
10ml/2 tsp paprika
4ml/¾ tsp cayenne pepper
5ml/1 tsp salt
small bunch of flat leaf parsley,
 finely chopped
small bunch of fresh coriander
 (cilantro), finely chopped

For the chickpea purée
225g/8oz/1¼ cups dried
 chickpeas, soaked overnight,
 drained and cooked
50ml/2fl oz/¼ cup olive oil
juice of 1 lemon
2 garlic cloves, crushed
5ml/1 tsp cumin seeds
30ml/2 tbsp light tahini
60ml/4 tbsp natural (plain) yogurt
40g/1½oz/3 tbsp butter,
 melted
salt and ground black pepper
salad and bread, to serve

1 Mix the minced beef with the onion, cumin, ground coriander, paprika, cayenne, salt, parsley and chopped fresh coriander. Knead the mixture well, then pound it until smooth in a mortar with a pestle or in a food processor. Place in a dish, cover and leave to stand for 1 hour.

2 Preheat the oven to 200°C/400°F/Gas 6. In a food processor, process the chickpeas with the olive oil, lemon juice, garlic, cumin seeds, tahini and yogurt. Season, tip into an ovenproof dish, cover with foil and heat through for 20 minutes.

3 Divide the meat mixture into six portions and mould each on to a metal skewer, so that the meat resembles a fat sausage. Heat the grill (broiler) on the hottest setting and cook the kebabs for 4–5 minutes on each side. Melt the butter and pour it over the hot chickpea purée. Serve the kebabs with the hot chickpea purée. Serve with salad and bread.

Marinated Korean Beef Energy 268kcal/1117kJ; Protein 32.1g; Carbohydrate 0.5g, of which sugars 0.5g; Fat 15.2g, of which saturates 5.1g; Cholesterol 92mg; Calcium 12mg; Fibre 0.2g; Sodium 186mg.
Spicy Beef Kebabs: Energy 456kcal/1898kJ; Protein 26.6g; Carbohydrate 21.8g, of which sugars 3.5g; Fat 29.8g, of which saturates 10.7g; Cholesterol 64mg; Calcium 153mg; Fibre 5.4g; Sodium 463mg.

Salt Beef Casserole

This traditional Jewish dish is baked in a very low oven for several hours. Wrapping the rice in a parcel presses it lightly and gives it a slightly chewy texture.

Serves 8

250g/9oz/1 cup chickpeas, soaked overnight
45ml/3 tbsp olive oil
1 onion, chopped
10 garlic cloves, chopped
1 parsnip, sliced
3 carrots, sliced
5–10ml/1–2 tsp ground cumin
2.5ml/½ tsp ground turmeric
15ml/1 tbsp chopped fresh ginger
2 litres/3½ pints/8 cups beef stock
1 potato, peeled and cut into chunks
½ marrow (large zucchini), sliced or cut into chunks
400g/14oz fresh or canned tomatoes, diced
45–60ml/3–4 tbsp brown or green lentils
2 bay leaves
250g/9oz salted meat such as salt beef (or double the quantity of lamb)
250g/9oz piece of lamb
½ large bunch fresh coriander (cilantro), chopped
200g/7oz/1 cup long grain rice
1 lemon, cut into wedges and a spicy sauce or fresh chillies, finely chopped, to serve

1 Preheat the oven to 120°C/250°F/Gas ½. Drain the chickpeas. Heat the oil in a large flameproof casserole, add the onion, garlic, parsnip, carrots, cumin, turmeric and ginger and cook for 2–3 minutes. Add the chickpeas, stock, potato, marrow, tomatoes, lentils, bay leaves, salted meat, lamb and coriander. Cover and cook in the oven for about 3 hours.

2 Put the rice on a double thickness of muslin (cheesecloth) and tie together at the corners, allowing enough room for the rice to expand while it is cooking. Two hours before the end of cooking, place the rice parcel in the casserole, anchoring the edge of the muslin under the lid so the parcel hangs above the soup. Continue cooking for a further 2 hours.

3 Remove the casserole from the oven. Remove the rice parcel. Skim any fat off the top of the soup and ladle the soup into bowls with a scoop of the rice and one or two pieces of meat. Serve with lemon wedges and spicy sauce or fresh chillies.

Spanish Beef with Aubergines and Chickpeas

In Spanish, this dish is called "old clothes", which sounds a good deal more romantic than leftovers. It is a dish for using up the remains of roasted meats, and the recipe has Jewish and Arab influences in its spices and flavourings.

Serves 4

2 small aubergines (eggplants)
90ml/6 tbsp olive oil
1 large onion, chopped
3 garlic cloves, finely chopped
1 red (bell) pepper, seeded and sliced
400g/14oz can tomatoes
250ml/8fl oz/1 cup meat stock
2.5ml/½ tsp ground cumin
2.5ml/½ tsp ground allspice
pinch of ground cloves
2.5ml/½ tsp cayenne pepper
400g/14oz cooked beef, cubed (or mixed turkey, ham, etc)
400g/14oz can chickpeas, drained
salt and ground black pepper
chopped fresh mint, to garnish (optional)

1 Cut the aubergines into cubes and put them into a colander. Sprinkle with 10ml/2 tsp salt, turning the cubes over with your hands. Leave to drain for about 1 hour. Rinse, then squeeze them dry using kitchen paper.

2 Meanwhile put 30ml/2 tbsp oil in a wide flameproof casserole and fry the onion and garlic until soft. Add the pepper to the casserole and stir-fry until softened.

3 Add the tomatoes and meat stock, cumin, allspice, ground cloves and cayenne pepper. Season to taste. Add the cubed meat and simmer gently.

4 Heat 45ml/3 tbsp oil over a high heat in a large frying pan. Fry the aubergine cubes, in batches if necessary, until they are brown on all sides. Add more oil if necessary.

5 Add the aubergine and chickpeas to the casserole and bring to a simmer, adding a little more stock to cover, if necessary – the dish should be almost solid. Check the seasonings, garnish with mint, if using, and serve.

Beef with Quinces and Cinnamon

This is a very exotic dish, with a combination of sweet and savoury flavours that will win everyone over, including the uninitiated. You do not need to serve anything else with this dish.

Serves 4

juice of ½ lemon
2–3 large quinces, total weight about 1kg/2¼lb
75ml/5 tbsp extra virgin olive oil
1kg/2¼lb good quality feather beef steak, or braising steak, cut in large slices
1 glass white wine, about 175ml/6fl oz/¾ cup
300ml/½ pint/1¼ cups hot water
1 cinnamon stick
45ml/3 tbsp demerara (raw) sugar mixed with 300ml/½ pint/1¼ cups hot water
1 whole nutmeg
salt

1 Add the lemon juice to a bowl of water. Quarter each quince vertically. Core and peel the pieces and drop them into the acidulated water to prevent them from discolouring.

2 Heat the olive oil in a large pan and brown the meat on both sides, turning the pieces over once. As soon as all the meat has browned, lower the heat, pour the wine over and let it bubble and reduce slightly. Pour the hot water into the pan and add the cinnamon stick. Cover and cook over a gentle heat for about 1 hour or until the meat is tender. Add salt to taste.

3 Lift the quinces out of the water, and slice each piece vertically into 2–3 pieces. Spread half the quince slices in a single layer in a large frying pan, pour half the sugared water over and cook them gently for 10 minutes, turning them over until all the liquid has been absorbed and they start caramelize.

4 Spread the caramelized quince slices over the meat in the pan and repeat the process with the remaining quince slices. Finely grate about one-quarter of a whole nutmeg over the top of the meat and fruit. If necessary, add water to cover.

5 Cover the pan and cook for 30 minutes more until both the meat and the quince slices are meltingly soft and sweet. Shake the pan occasionally to prevent the meat sticking. Serve hot.

Beef Casserole in Spicy Red Wine

This is the perfect Sunday lunch for a family, but is also an excellent choice for a dinner party. It is the kind of easy dish that can be left simmering slowly in the oven for hours without coming to any harm. Serve it with boiled rice, pasta, creamy mashed potatoes or fried potatoes.

Serves 4

75ml/5 tbsp olive oil
1kg/2¼lb good stewing or braising beef steak, cut in large cubes
3 garlic cloves, chopped
5ml/1 tsp ground cumin
5cm/2in piece of cinnamon stick
1 glass red wine, about 175ml/6fl oz/¾ cup
30ml/2 tbsp red wine vinegar
small fresh rosemary sprig
2 bay leaves, crumbled
30ml/2 tbsp tomato purée (paste) diluted in 1 litre/1¾ pints/4 cups hot water
675g/1½lb small pickling-size onions, peeled and left whole
15ml/1 tbsp demerara (raw) sugar
salt and ground black pepper

1 Heat the olive oil in a large heavy pan and brown the meat cubes, in batches if necessary, until pale golden brown all over.

2 Stir in the garlic and cumin. Add the cinnamon stick and cook for a few seconds, then pour the wine and vinegar slowly over the mixture. Let the liquid bubble for 3–4 minutes to reduce a little.

3 Add the rosemary and bay leaves, with the diluted tomato purée. Stir well, season with salt and pepper, then cover and simmer gently for about 1½ hours or until the meat is tender.

4 Dot the onions over the meat mixture and shake the pan to distribute them evenly. Sprinkle the demerara sugar over the onions, cover the pan and cook very gently for 30 minutes, until the onions are soft but have not begun to disintegrate. If necessary, add a little hot water at this stage.

5 Do not stir once the onions have been added but gently shake the pan instead to coat them in the sauce. Remove the cinnamon stick and sprig of rosemary and serve.

Tagine of Beef with Peas and Saffron

This Moroccan tagine is a popular supper dish, and can be made with lamb as an alternative to beef. Saffron imparts its own pungent taste and delicate colour to the sauce. The peas, sweet tomatoes, and tangy lemon, added towards the end of the cooking time, enliven this rich, gingery beef mixture with contrasting flavours and colours, and the brown olives provide the perfect finishing touch. This is definitely one of the dishes to look out for in Marrakesh.

Serves 6

1.2kg/2½lb chuck steak or braising steak, trimmed and cubed
30ml/2 tbsp olive oil
1 onion, chopped
25g/1oz fresh root ginger, peeled and chopped
5ml/1 tsp ground ginger
pinch of cayenne pepper
pinch of saffron threads
1.2kg/2½lb shelled fresh peas
2 tomatoes, peeled and chopped
1 preserved lemon, chopped
a handful of brown Moroccan olives
salt and ground black pepper
bread or couscous, to serve

1 Put the cubed steak in a tagine, flameproof casserole or heavy pan with the olive oil, onion, fresh and ground ginger, cayenne and saffron and season with salt and pepper.

2 Pour in enough water to cover the meat completely and bring to the boil. Then reduce the heat and cover and simmer for about 1½ hours, or until the meat is very tender. Cook for a little longer if necessary.

3 Add the peas, tomatoes, preserved lemon and olives. Stir well and cook, uncovered, for about 10 minutes, or until the peas are tender and the sauce has reduced. Check the seasoning and serve with bread or plain couscous.

> **Cook's Tip**
> Use Greek kalamata olives if Moroccan olives are not available.

Beef Stew with Star Anise and Basil

The Vietnamese prize this dish for breakfast, and on chilly mornings people queue up for a bowl of it on their way to work. Traditionally, the dish has an orange colour from the oil in which annatto seeds have been fried, but in this recipe the yellow colour comes from turmeric.

Serves 4–6

500g/1¼lb lean beef, cubed
15ml/1 tbsp ground turmeric
30ml/2 tbsp vegetable oil
3 shallots, chopped
3 garlic cloves, chopped
2 red chillies, seeded and chopped
2 lemon grass stalks, trimmed, cut into several pieces and bruised
15ml/1 tbsp curry powder
4 star anise, roasted and ground to a powder
700ml/scant 1¼ pints hot beef or chicken stock, or boiling water
45ml/3 tbsp nuoc mam
30ml/2 tbsp soy sauce
15ml/1 tbsp raw cane sugar
1 bunch fresh basil, stalks removed
salt and ground black pepper
1 onion, halved and finely sliced, and chopped fresh coriander (cilantro) leaves, to garnish
steamed fragrant or sticky rice, or chunks of baguette, to serve

1 Toss the beef in the ground turmeric and set aside. Heat a wok or heavy pan and add the oil. Add the shallots, garlic, chillies and lemon grass, and cook, stirring constantly, until they become fragrant.

2 Add the curry powder, all but 10ml/2 tsp of the roasted star anise, and the beef. Brown the beef, then pour in the stock or water, nuoc mam, soy sauce and sugar. Stir and bring to the boil. Reduce the heat and cook gently for about 40 minutes, or until the meat is tender and the liquid has reduced.

3 Season the stew to taste with salt and pepper, stir in the reserved roasted star anise, and add the basil. Transfer the stew to a serving dish and garnish with the sliced onion and coriander leaves. Serve with steamed fragrant or sticky rice, or chunks of baguette.

Tagine of Beef with Saffron: Energy 492kcal/2049kJ; Protein 57.9g; Carbohydrate 25.6g, of which sugars 7g; Fat 18.2g, of which saturates 6g; Cholesterol 126mg; Calcium 61mg; Fibre 10.1g; Sodium 134mg.
Beef Stew with Basil: Energy 314Kcal/1312kJ; Protein 33g; Carbohydrate 17g, of which sugars 11g; Fat 14g, of which saturates 4g; Cholesterol 64mg; Calcium 44mg; Fibre 1.7g; Sodium 150mg.

Paprika-spiced Italian Meatballs

These meatballs taste very good with creamed potatoes. Use a potato ricer to get them really smooth.

Serves 4
400g/14oz minced (ground) beef
115g/4oz/2 cups fresh white breadcrumbs
50g/2oz/²⁄₃ cup grated Parmesan cheese
2 eggs, beaten
pinch of paprika
pinch of grated nutmeg
5ml/1 tsp dried mixed herbs
2 slices of prosciutto, chopped

vegetable oil, for shallow frying
salt and ground black pepper
fresh basil leaves, to garnish

For the peperonata
30ml/2 tbsp olive oil
1 small onion, thinly sliced
2 yellow (bell) peppers, cut lengthways into thin strips
2 red (bell) peppers, cut lengthways into thin strips
275g/10oz/1¼ cups finely chopped tomatoes or passata
15ml/1 tbsp chopped fresh parsley

1 Put the minced beef in a bowl. Add half the breadcrumbs and all the remaining ingredients, including salt and ground black pepper to taste. Mix well with wet hands. Divide the mixture into 12 equal portions and roll each into a ball. Flatten slightly.

2 Put the remaining breadcrumbs on a plate and roll the meatballs in them until they are evenly coated. Place on a plate, cover with clear film (plastic wrap) and chill for 30 minutes.

3 Meanwhile, make the peperonata. Heat the oil in a medium pan, add the onion and cook gently for about 3 minutes, until softened. Add the pepper and cook for 3 minutes, stirring. Stir in the tomatoes or passata and parsley, with salt and pepper to taste. Bring to the boil, stirring. Cover and cook for 15 minutes, then remove the lid and continue to cook, stirring frequently, for 10 minutes more, or until reduced and thick.

4 Pour oil into a frying pan to a depth of about 2.5cm/1in. When hot but not smoking, shallow fry the meatballs for 10–12 minutes, turning them 3–4 times and pressing them flat with a fish slice or metal spatula. Remove and drain on kitchen paper. Serve hot, with the peperonata alongside. Garnish with the basil.

Seared Garlic Beef Dipped in Lime Juice

This dish is popular in both Vietnam and Cambodia, where it is sometimes made with quail instead of beef. Flavoured with lots of garlic, the tender chunks of beef are wrapped in lettuce leaves at the table and dipped in a piquant lime sauce. The beef can be seared in a pan, or chargrilled.

Serves 4
350g/12oz beef fillet (tenderloin) or sirloin, cut into bitesize chunks

15ml/1 tbsp sugar
juice of 3 limes
2 garlic cloves, crushed
7.5ml/1½ tsp ground black pepper
30ml/2 tbsp unsalted roasted peanuts, finely chopped
12 lettuce leaves

For the marinade
15ml/1 tbsp groundnut (peanut) oil
45ml/3 tbsp mushroom soy sauce
10ml/2 tsp soy sauce
15ml/1 tbsp sugar
2 garlic cloves, crushed
7.5ml/1½ tsp ground black pepper

1 To make the marinade, beat together the oil, the two soy sauces and the sugar in a bowl, until the sugar has dissolved. Add the garlic and pepper and mix well. Add the beef and coat in the marinade. Leave for 1–2 hours.

2 In a small bowl, stir the sugar into the lime juice, until it has dissolved. Add the garlic and black pepper and beat well. Stir in the peanuts and put aside.

3 Heat a wok or heavy pan and sear the meat on all sides. Serve immediately with lettuce leaves for wrapping and the lime sauce for dipping.

> **Cook's Tip**
> Small, firm-textured lettuce leaves such as Little Gem (Bibb) make perfect receptacles for wrapping meat, and are also good for scooping up dips and grains such as rice or couscous.

Paprika-spiced Meatballs: Energy 248kcal/1045kJ; Protein 28.4g; Carbohydrate 19.6g, of which sugars 7.3g; Fat 6g, of which saturates 1.7g; Cholesterol 71mg; Calcium 85mg; Fibre 2.6g; Sodium 659mg.
Seared Garlic Beef in Lime Juice: Energy 237Kcal/986kJ; Protein 22g; Carbohydrate 5.2g, of which sugars 4.7g; Fat 14g, of which saturates 4g; Cholesterol 51mg; Calcium 12mg; Fibre 0.5g; Sodium 324mg.

Charcoal-grilled Beef in a Spicy Marinade

In this Vietnamese dish, thin strips of beef are marinated, chargrilled and served with strongly flavoured shrimp sauce – a tasty combination. A spoonful of shrimp paste is also sometimes added to the marinade for the beef, but you may find the pungency of the accompanying shrimp sauce is sufficient.

Serves 4
450g/1lb beef rump, sirloin or
    fillet, cut across the grain into
    thin strips
24 bamboo or wooden skewers
lettuce leaves

1 small bunch fresh coriander
    (cilantro), to garnish
Vietnamese shrimp sauce, for
    dipping

For the marinade
2 lemon grass stalks, trimmed
    and chopped
2 shallots, chopped
2 garlic cloves, peeled and
    chopped
1 red Thai chilli, seeded and
    chopped
10ml/2 tsp sugar
30ml/2 tbsp nuoc mam
15ml/1 tbsp soy sauce
15ml/1 tbsp groundnut
    (peanut) oil

1 To make the marinade, pound the lemon grass, shallots, garlic and chilli with the sugar using a mortar and pestle, until the ingredients form a paste. Beat in the nuoc mam, soy sauce and groundnut oil.

2 Toss the beef in the marinade, cover, and marinate for 1–2 hours. Soak the bamboo or wooden skewers in water for 20 minutes so they don't burn during cooking.

3 Prepare the barbecue, or preheat a conventional grill (broiler). Thread the strips of beef on to the skewers and place them over the charcoal. Cook for not much more than 1 minute on each side.

4 Serve the beef on the skewers, garnished with fresh coriander, accompanied by lettuce leaves for wrapping and the pungent Vietnamese shrimp sauce for dipping.

Beef Ribs in Chilli Broth

This slow-cooked dish contains short ribs and cubes of mooli, or Chinese white radish, in an exquisitely rich soup, with fine dangmyun noodles just below the surface. A piquant chilli seasoning is added just before serving.

Serves 4
900g/2lb beef short ribs, cut into
    5cm/2in squares

350g/12oz mooli (daikon)
5ml/1 tsp salt
90g/3½oz dangmyun noodles

For the seasoning
45ml/3 tbsp soy sauce
15ml/1 tbsp chilli powder
50g/2oz spring onions (scallions),
    roughly chopped
5ml/1 tsp sesame oil
1 fresh green chilli, seeded and
    finely sliced
ground black pepper

1 Soak the ribs in a bowl of cold water for 10 hours to drain the blood, changing the water halfway through once it has discoloured.

2 Drain the ribs and place them in a large pan. Cover with water and place over a high heat. Once the water has boiled remove the ribs, rinse them in cold water and set aside.

3 Cut the mooli into 2cm/¾in cubes. Place the seasoning ingredients in a bowl and mix thoroughly.

4 Place the ribs in a large heavy pan and cover with 1 litre/ 1¾ pints/4 cups water. Cook over a high heat for 20 minutes, then add the mooli and season with salt. Reduce the heat and cook for 7 minutes, then add the noodles and cook for another 3 minutes.

5 Ladle the soup into bowls and add a generous spoonful of the seasoning just before serving.

> **Cook's Tip**
> Made from sweet potatoes, dangmyun noodles are readily available at Asian stores.

Charcoal Beef in Spicy Marinade: Energy 229Kcal/952kJ; Protein 26g; Carbohydrate 1.5g, of which sugars 1.1g; Fat 13g, of which saturates 5g; Cholesterol 65mg; Calcium 10mg; Fibre 0.2g; Sodium 340mg.
Beef Ribs in Chilli Broth: Energy 437kcal/1830kJ; Protein 52.1g; Carbohydrate 19.8g, of which sugars 3.1g; Fat 17g, of which saturates 6.7g; Cholesterol 126mg; Calcium 40mg; Fibre 1.6g; Sodium 1174mg.

Taquitos with Beef

In this Mexican dish, home-made corn tortillas are moulded around a tasty filling of tender steak in a spicy, flavoursome sauce.

Serves 12

500g/1½lb rump (round) steak, diced into 1cm/½in pieces
2 garlic cloves, peeled
750ml/1¼ pints/3 cups beef stock

150g/5oz/1 cup masa harina
pinch of salt
120ml/4fl oz/½ cup warm water
7.5ml/1½ tsp dried oregano
2.5ml/½ tsp ground cumin
30ml/2 tbsp tomato purée (paste)
2.5ml/½ tsp caster (superfine) sugar
salt and ground black pepper
shredded lettuce and onion relish, to serve

1 Put the beef and whole garlic cloves in a large pan and cover with the beef stock. Bring to the boil, lower the heat and simmer for 10–15 minutes, until the meat is tender. Using a slotted spoon, transfer the meat to a clean pan and set it aside. Reserve the stock.

2 Mix the *masa harina* and salt in a large bowl. Add the warm water, a little at a time, to make a dough that can be worked into a ball. Knead this on a lightly floured surface for 3–4 minutes until smooth, then wrap in clear film (plastic wrap) and leave for 1 hour.

3 Divide the dough into 12 small balls. Line the tortilla press with plastic (this can be cut from a new plastic sandwich bag). Put a ball on the press and bring the top down to flatten it into a 5–6cm/2–2½in round. Repeat with the remaining dough balls.

4 Heat a griddle or frying pan until hot. Cook each tortilla for 15–20 seconds on each side, and then for a further 15 seconds on the first side. Keep warm by folding inside a dish towel.

5 Add the oregano, cumin, tomato purée and caster sugar to the pan containing the beef, with a couple of tablespoons of the reserved beef stock. Cook gently for a few minutes to combine the flavour. To assemble, place a little of the lettuce on a warm tortilla, top with a little filling and a little onion relish, and fold in half. Serve straight away.

Mexican Spiced Beef Sopes

These small, thick corn tortillas with crimped edges resemble little tarts, filled with spicy beef.

Serves 6

250g/9oz/scant 2 cups masa harina
2.5ml/½ tsp salt
50g/2oz/¼ cup chilled lard
300ml/½ pint/1¼ cups warm water
15ml/1 tbsp vegetable oil

250g/9oz minced (ground) beef
2 garlic cloves, crushed
1 red (bell) pepper, seeded and chopped
60ml/4 tbsp dry sherry
15ml/1 tbsp tomato purée (paste)
2.5ml/½ tsp ground cumin
5ml/1 tsp ground cinnamon
1.5ml/¼ tsp ground cloves
2.5ml/½ tsp ground black pepper
25g/1oz/3 tbsp raisins
25g/1oz/¼ cup slivered almonds
fresh parsley sprigs, to garnish

1 Put the *masa harina* and salt in a large bowl. Grate the chilled lard into the bowl and rub it into the dry ingredients. Add the warm water, a little at a time, to make a dough that can be worked into a ball. Knead the dough on a lightly floured surface for 3–4 minutes until smooth. Set aside.

2 Heat the oil in a large pan. Add the beef and brown over a high heat. Stir in the garlic, continue cooking for 2–3 minutes.

3 Stir in the red pepper, sherry, tomato purée and spices. Cook for 5 minutes more, then add the raisins and the almonds. Lower the heat and simmer for 10 minutes. The meat should be cooked through and the mixture moist, not wet. Keep hot.

4 Divide the dough into six balls. Open a tortilla press and line both sides with plastic (this can be cut from a new plastic sandwich bag). Put a ball on the press and bring the top down to flatten it into a 10cm/4in round. Make five more rounds.

5 Heat a griddle or frying pan until hot. Add one of the rounds and fry until the underside is beginning to blister. Turn the round over and cook the other side briefly, until the colour is beginning to change. Slide on to a plate and crimp to form a raised edge. Fill with spicy beef and keep hot while cooking and filling the remaining tartlets. Garnish with parsley.

Taquitos with Beef: Energy 291kcal/1222kJ; Protein 31.5g; Carbohydrate 26.5g, of which sugars 1.8g; Fat 6.3g, of which saturates 2.1g; Cholesterol 74mg; Calcium 10mg; Fibre 1.1g; Sodium 97mg.
Mexican Spiced Beef Sopes: Energy 197kcal/819kJ; Protein 7g; Carbohydrate 17g, of which sugars 2.4g; Fat 11.3g, of which saturates 5.3g; Cholesterol 24mg; Calcium 82mg; Fibre 0.7g; Sodium 95mg.

Paprika-spiced Corned Beef and Egg Hash

This is real nursery, or comfort, food at its best. Whether you remember Gran's version, or prefer this American-style hash, it turns corned beef into a supper fit for any guest.

Serves 4

30ml/2 tbsp vegetable oil
25g/1oz/2 tbsp butter
1 onion, finely chopped
1 green (bell) pepper, diced
2 large firm boiled potatoes, diced
350g/12oz can corned beef, cubed
1.5ml/¼ tsp grated nutmeg
1.5ml/¼ tsp paprika
4 eggs
salt and ground black pepper
deep-fried parsley, to garnish
sweet chilli sauce or tomato sauce, to serve

1 Heat the oil and butter together in a large frying pan. Add the onion and fry for 5–6 minutes until softened.

2 In a bowl, mix together the green pepper, potatoes, corned beef, nutmeg and paprika and season well. Add to the pan and toss gently to distribute the cooked onion. Press down lightly and fry without stirring on a medium heat for about 3–4 minutes until a golden brown crust has formed on the underside.

3 Stir the mixture through to distribute the crust, then repeat the frying twice, until the mixture is well browned.

4 Make four wells in the hash and carefully crack an egg into each. Cover and cook gently for about 4–5 minutes until the egg whites are set.

5 Sprinkle with deep-fried parsley and cut into quarters. Serve hot with sweet chilli sauce or tomato sauce.

> **Cook's Tip**
> Chill the can of corned beef for about half an hour before use – it will be easier to cut it into cubes.

Korean Chilli Steak

Instead of complex flavours, this classic recipe relies on the taste of high quality sirloin steak. Kneading the meat with the marinade makes it deliciously tender, and the seasoning provides a delicate garlic flavour. The meat is briefly grilled, and the smoky aroma and taste of this dish are without equal. Serve it wrapped in lettuce leaves and accompanied by steamed rice and wilted greens.

Serves 4

450g/1lb beef sirloin
2 round (butterhead) lettuces

For the marinade
8 garlic cloves, chopped
75g/3oz oyster mushrooms, sliced
3 spring onions (scallions), finely chopped
20ml/4 tsp mirin or rice wine
10ml/2 tsp salt
ground black pepper

For the spring onion mixture
8 shredded spring onions (scallions)
20ml/4 tsp rice vinegar
20ml/4 tsp Korean chilli powder
2 tsp sugar
10ml/2 tsp sesame oil

1 Slice the beef into bitesize strips and place in a bowl. Add the garlic, mushrooms and spring onions. Pour in the mirin or rice wine and add the salt and several twists of black pepper.

2 Mix all the ingredients for the marinade together with the beef, evenly coating it, then knead the meat well to tenderize, working the marinade into it thoroughly. Chill, and leave for at least 2 hours.

3 Mix together the ingredients for the spring onion mixture. Remove the large outer leaves from the lettuces, rinse well and pat dry.

4 Place a griddle pan over medium heat, and add the marinated beef. Cook gently until the meat has darkened, and then remove.

5 To eat the meat, wrap a few of the pieces in a lettuce leaf, adding a pinch of the seasoned shredded spring onion mixture.

Paprika-spiced Corned Beef Hash (to divide by portion size): Energy 1683kcal/7030kJ; Protein 123.4g; Carbohydrate 67.9g, of which sugars 21.6g; Fat 104.6g, of which saturates 42.2g; Cholesterol 1108mg; Calcium 260mg; Fibre 6.6g; Sodium 3483mg.
Korean Chilli Steak: Energy 188kcal/786kJ; Protein 27.6g; Carbohydrate 4g, of which sugars 3.9g; Fat 6.9g, of which saturates 2.6g; Cholesterol 57mg; Calcium 26mg; Fibre 0.9g; Sodium 83mg.

Tex-Mex Baked Potatoes with Chilli

Classic chilli beef tops crisp, floury-centred baked potatoes. Easy to prepare and great for a simple yet substantial family supper.

Serves 4
2 large baking potatoes
15ml/1 tbsp vegetable oil, plus
  more for brushing
1 garlic clove, crushed
1 small onion, chopped
1/2 red (bell) pepper, chopped
225g/8oz lean minced (ground)
  beef
1/2 small fresh red chilli, seeded
  and chopped
5ml/1 tsp ground cumin
pinch of cayenne pepper
200g/7oz can chopped tomatoes
30ml/2 tbsp tomato paste
2.5ml/1/2 tsp fresh oregano
2.5ml/1/2 tsp fresh marjoram
200g/7oz can red kidney
  beans, drained
15ml/1 tbsp chopped fresh
  coriander (cilantro)
salt and ground black pepper
chopped fresh marjoram, to
  garnish
lettuce leaves, to serve
60ml/4 tbsp sour cream, to serve

1 Preheat the oven to 220°C/425°F/Gas 7. Brush or rub the potatoes with a little of the oil and then pierce them with skewers. Place the potatoes on the top shelf of the oven and bake them for 30 minutes before beginning to cook the chilli.

2 Heat the oil in a large heavy pan and add the garlic, onion and pepper. Fry gently for 4–5 minutes until softened.

3 Add the beef and fry until browned, then stir in the chilli, cumin, cayenne pepper, tomatoes, tomato paste, 60ml/4 tbsp water and the herbs. Bring to a boil then reduce the heat, cover and simmer for about 25 minutes, stirring occasionally.

4 Stir in the kidney beans and cook, uncovered, for 5 minutes. Remove from the heat and stir in the chopped coriander. Season well and set aside.

5 Cut the baked potatoes in half and place them in serving bowls. Top with the chilli mixture and a dollop of sour cream. Garnish with chopped fresh marjoram and serve hot accompanied by a few lettuce leaves.

Veal Escalopes with Grapefruit, Pink Peppercorns and Ginger

The ginger and pink peppercorns give the grapefruit sauce a subtle spiciness without being overpowering.

Serves 4
4 veal escalopes
25g/1oz/2 tbsp butter
15ml/1 tbsp olive oil
juice of 1 large ruby grapefruit
150ml/1/4 pint/2/3 cup chicken
  stock
10ml/2 tsp grated fresh root ginger
5ml/1 tsp pink peppercorns,
  drained and lightly crushed
15g/1/2oz/1 tbsp cold butter
salt

For the garnish
1 ruby grapefruit
oil, for shallow frying

1 Start by making the garnish. Wash and dry the grapefruit, then pare off thin strips of rind, using a citrus zester. Scrape off any pith that remains attached to the strips. Cut the grapefruit in half. Squeeze the juice from one half into a small bowl, add the strips of pared rind and leave to macerate for 1 hour. Cut the other half grapefruit into wedges and reserve.

2 Drain the strips of rind and pat them dry with kitchen paper. Heat oil to a depth of 1cm/1/2in in a small pan and add the strips. As soon as they are brown strain the strips through a sieve (strainer) into a bowl. Discard the oil in the bowl.

3 Place the veal escalopes between two sheets of greaseproof paper and beat with a rolling pin until about 3mm/1/8in thick. If the escalopes are very large, cut them into neat pieces.

4 Melt the butter and the oil in a heavy frying pan. Fry the veal, in batches if necessary, for 1 minute on each side. Remove the escalopes to a heated dish and keep hot.

5 Add the grapefruit juice, stock and grated ginger to the frying pan. Allow to boil until reduced by half. Strain the sauce into a clean pan, add the peppercorns and heat through. Whisk in the butter and season with salt. Pour the sauce over the veal, then garnish with fried grapefruit rind and reserved wedges.

Tex-Mex Baked Potatoes: Energy 327kcal/1369kJ; Protein 17.7g; Carbohydrate 30.6g, of which sugars 8.2g; Fat 15.7g, of which saturates 6.4g; Cholesterol 43mg; Calcium 71mg; Fibre 5.2g; Sodium 277mg.
Veal Escalopes with Grapefruit: Energy 264kcal/1107kJ; Protein 34.2g; Carbohydrate 1.6g, of which sugars 1.6g; Fat 13.5g, of which saturates 6.5g; Cholesterol 99mg; Calcium 11mg; Fibre 0g; Sodium 151mg.

Beef Rissoles with Cumin and Garlic

A delicious dish from Turkey, with a distinctive Greek influence. It is ideal for entertaining as it can be cooked in advance and reheated as needed. Serve with rice, fries or pasta.

Serves 4

2–3 medium slices of bread, crusts removed
675g/1½lb minced (ground) beef
2 garlic cloves, crushed
15ml/1 tbsp ground cumin
1 egg, lightly beaten
25g/1oz/¼ cup plain (all-purpose) flour

45ml/3 tbsp sunflower oil, for frying
salt and ground black pepper

For the sauce
45ml/3 tbsp olive oil
5ml/1 tsp cumin seeds
400g/14oz can chopped tomatoes
15ml/1 tbsp tomato purée (paste) diluted in 150ml/¼ pint/⅔ cup hot water
2.5ml/½ tsp dried oregano
12–16 green olives, preferably cracked ones, rinsed and drained

1 Soak the bread in water for 10 minutes, then drain, squeeze dry and place in a large bowl. Add the meat, garlic, cumin and egg. Season, then mix with a fork or your hands, until blended.

2 Take a small handful – the size of a large walnut – and roll it into a short, slim sausage. Set this aside. Continue until all the meat mixture has been used. Roll lightly in flour.

3 Heat the vegetable oil in a large non-stick frying pan and fry the rissoles, in batches if necessary, until golden on all sides. Lift out and place in a bowl. Discard the oil remaining in the pan.

4 Make the sauce. Heat the olive oil in a large pan. Add the cumin seeds and swirl them around for a few seconds, add the tomatoes and stir for about 2 minutes. Pour in the diluted tomato purée, mix well, then add the oregano and olives, with salt and pepper to taste. Add the rissoles, then cover and cook gently for 30 minutes, shaking the pan occasionally to prevent them from sticking. Tip into a serving dish and serve.

Greek Garlic-spiked Roast Lamb

This is the Greek equivalent of the Sunday roast, but everything is cooked in a single dish. This follows a tradition from the days when most homes did not have their own ovens. The local baker would cook all the villagers' family Sunday dinners in his huge oven as it cooled after being fired up for bread in the early morning. Each family would bring one big roasting pan containing the whole meal, so that all the flavours melded together.

Serves 6–8

1 leg of lamb, about 2kg/4½lb
3 garlic cloves, quartered lengthways, plus 6–8 whole, unpeeled garlic cloves, or 1–2 heads of garlic, halved
900g/2lb potatoes, peeled and quartered lengthways
juice of 1 lemon
45ml/3 tbsp extra virgin olive oil
450ml/¾ pint/scant 2 cups hot water
5ml/1 tsp dried Greek oregano
2.5ml/½ tsp dried Greek thyme or 5ml/1 tsp chopped fresh thyme
salt and ground black pepper

1 Preheat the oven to 220°C/425°F/Gas 7. Place the meat in a large roasting pan. Make several incisions in it and insert one or two sticks of garlic into each one.

2 Arrange the potatoes and whole garlic cloves or halved heads of garlic around the meat, pour the lemon juice and olive oil over, and add half the water to the dish. Sprinkle over half the herbs, and some seasoning.

3 Roast the lamb for 15 minutes, then reduce the oven temperature to 190°C/375°F/Gas 5. Roast for 1 hour.

4 Turn the meat over to brown the other side, sprinkle over the rest of the herbs and seasoning, and turn the potatoes over gently. Add the remaining hot water to the pan and cook for another 25–30 minutes, basting occasionally with the pan juices.

5 Cover the meat with a clean dish towel and let it rest for 10 minutes before serving. The cloves of garlic can be popped out of their skins and eaten with the meat; they will be deliciously creamy.

Beef Rissoles with Cumin: Energy 646kcal/2684kJ; Protein 38g; Carbohydrate 18g, of which sugars 4.2g; Fat 47.4g, of which saturates 14.6g; Cholesterol 149mg; Calcium 68mg; Fibre 2g; Sodium 552mg.
Greek Roast Lamb: Energy 750kcal/3132kJ; Protein 73.4g; Carbohydrate 24.3g, of which sugars 2.1g; Fat 40.4g, of which saturates 17.3g; Cholesterol 273mg; Calcium 37mg; Fibre 1.8g; Sodium 175mg.

Lamb in North African Spices

This is a wonderful way of cooking a joint of lamb. Serve it with a couscous pilaff and yogurt flavoured with garlic.

Serves 6
2kg/4¹/₂lb leg or shoulder of lamb
30ml/2 tbsp olive oil
2 large onions, halved and sliced
300ml/¹/₂ pint/1¹/₄ cups water
500g/1¹/₄lb butternut squash, peeled, and cut into chunks
2–3 green or red (bell) peppers, thickly sliced
chopped fresh coriander (cilantro), to serve

For the spice paste
15ml/1 tbsp cumin seeds
15ml/1 tbsp coriander seeds
2.5cm/1in piece cinnamon stick
7.5ml/1¹/₂ tsp paprika
good pinch of saffron strands
1 green chilli, seeded and chopped
2 garlic cloves, chopped
15g/¹/₂oz fresh coriander (cilantro), chopped
30ml/2 tbsp fresh mint, chopped
45ml/3 tbsp extra virgin olive oil
grated rind and juice of 1 lemon
250ml/8fl oz/1 cup natural (plain) yogurt
salt and ground black pepper

1 To prepare the spice paste, toast the cumin and coriander seeds in a small dry pan. Grind with the cinnamon in a spice or coffee grinder. Process with all the paste ingredients, apart from the yogurt, to make a paste. Add salt and pepper.

2 Cut deep slits all over the lamb, then rub the spice paste all over, pushing it into the slits. Place the lamb in a dish and rub the yogurt all over it. Cover and marinate for several hours.

3 Preheat the oven to 180°C/350°F/Gas 4. Scrape the marinade off the meat and reserve. Heat a large roasting pan and brown the lamb all over. Remove it, then add the oil. Cook the onions for 6–8 minutes and remove from the pan.

4 Add the marinade to the pan with the water and bring to the boil. Return the lamb to the pan, cover with the onions, cover the dish with foil and cook in the oven for 1¾–2 hours. Baste occasionally. Remove the lamb and onions, cover and keep warm. Increase the oven to 200°C/400°F/Gas 6. Add the squash and peppers and roast, uncovered, for 30–35 minutes. Transfer the lamb and vegetables to a warmed serving dish and sprinkle with the fresh coriander. Slice and serve.

Moroccan Roast Leg of Lamb

Whole roasted lamb or goat cooked outdoors over a charcoal fire in a specially prepared pit is a traditional celebration dish for feasts. The lamb is carefully tended and basted with butter and spices until it tastes quite amazing. At home, this similar, more modest version can be prepared with a marinated leg of lamb. Serve with couscous and a well-flavoured vegetable tagine.

Serves 6–8
2.25kg/5lb leg of lamb
4 garlic cloves
5ml/1 tsp coarse salt
10ml/2 tsp ground coriander
10ml/2 tsp ground cumin
10ml/2 tsp paprika
5ml/1 tsp ground black pepper
2.5ml/¹/₂ tsp cayenne pepper
175g/6oz/³/₄ cup butter
115g/4oz/1 cup moist dried pitted dates
30ml/2 tbsp blanched whole almonds
4 lemons, quartered

1 Use a small sharp knife to make small, deep incisions all over the leg of lamb. In a mortar, use a pestle to crush the garlic with the salt to a paste, then add the ground coriander, cumin, paprika, black pepper and cayenne. Pound the butter in a bowl and beat in the garlic and spice paste. Smear the spicy butter all over the leg of lamb, and into the incisions, and leave to marinate for 3–4 hours.

2 Preheat the oven to 220°C/425°F/Gas 7. Place the lamb in a roasting pan and roast for about 20 minutes. Turn the lamb and baste with the spicy cooking juices. Cook for 15 minutes, then reduce the heat to 180°C/350°F/Gas 4. Turn the lamb and baste again, and roast for a further 2 hours, basting occasionally.

3 Sprinkle the dates and almonds over and around the lamb and cook for 30 minutes, or until the meat is very tender. Serve hot with lemon quarters for squeezing over the aromatic meat.

> **Variation**
> Pound the dates and almonds to a coarse paste and smear over the lamb to give it a sticky coating.

Lamb in North African Spices: Energy 379kcal/1585kJ; Protein 35g; Carbohydrate 17.7g, of which sugars 15.4g; Fat 19.2g, of which saturates 8.8g; Cholesterol 128mg; Calcium 48mg; Fibre 3g; Sodium 151mg.
Moroccan Leg of Lamb: Energy 657kcal/2735kJ; Protein 52.7g; Carbohydrate 10.2g, of which sugars 10.1g; Fat 45.4g, of which saturates 22.6g; Cholesterol 239mg; Calcium 39mg; Fibre 0.9g; Sodium 245mg.

Malay Lamb Korma

Adapted from a traditional Indian korma, this creamy version is flavoured with coconut milk. Serve it accompanied by a fragrant rice or flatbread and a Malay-style salad of raw vegetables or a sambal.

Serves 4–6

25g/1oz fresh root ginger, peeled and chopped
4 garlic cloves, chopped
2 red chillies, seeded and chopped
10ml/2 tsp garam masala
10ml/2 tsp ground coriander
5ml/1 tsp ground cumin
5ml/1 tsp ground turmeric
675g/1½lb lamb shoulder, cut into bitesize cubes
45ml/3 tbsp ghee, or 30ml/2 tbsp vegetable oil and 15g/½ oz/ 1 tbsp butter
2 onions, halved lengthways and sliced along the grain
2.5ml/½ tsp sugar
4–6 cardamom pods, bruised
1 cinnamon stick
400ml/14fl oz/1⅔ cups coconut milk
salt and ground black pepper
30ml/2 tbsp roasted peanuts, crushed, and fresh coriander (cilantro) and mint leaves, coarsely chopped, to garnish

1 Using a mortar and pestle or food processor, grind the ginger, garlic and chillies to a paste. Stir in the garam masala, ground coriander, cumin and turmeric. Put the lamb into a shallow dish and rub the paste into it. Cover and leave to marinate for 1 hour.

2 Heat the ghee or oil and butter in a heavy pan or earthenware pot. Add the onions and sugar, and cook until brown and almost caramelized. Stir in the cardamom pods and cinnamon stick and add the lamb with all the marinade. Mix well and cook until the meat is browned all over.

3 Pour in the coconut milk, stir well and bring to the boil. Reduce the heat, cover the pan and cook the meat gently for 30–40 minutes until tender. Make sure the meat doesn't become dry – stir in a little coconut milk, or water, if necessary.

4 Season to taste with salt and pepper. Sprinkle the crushed roasted peanuts over the top and garnish with the coriander and mint. Serve immediately.

Anatolian Lamb Kebabs with Cumin

This popular Anatolian dish is traditionally made with small pieces of lamb chargrilled on flat metal kebab swords. The cooked meat is then wrapped in freshly griddled flatbread with red onion, flat leaf parsley and lemon.

Serves 4–6

2 onions
7.5ml/1½ tsp salt
2 garlic cloves, crushed
10ml/2 tsp cumin seeds, crushed
900g/2lb boneless shoulder of lamb, trimmed and cut into bitesize pieces
1 large red onion, cut in half lengthways, in half again crossways, and sliced along the grain
1 large bunch of fresh flat leaf parsley, roughly chopped
12 Turkish flatbreads (use split pitta breads if you can't find any flatbreads)
2–3 lemons, cut into wedges

1 Grate the onions on to a plate, sprinkle with the salt and leave them to weep for about 15 minutes.

2 Place a sieve (strainer) over a large bowl, tip in the onions and press down with the back of a wooden spoon to extract the juice. Discard the onions left in the sieve, then mix the garlic and cumin seeds into the onion juice and toss in the lamb. Cover and leave to marinate for 3–4 hours.

3 Prepare the sliced red onions, chopped parsley and lemon wedges ready for serving. Thread the meat on to flat kebab swords or metal skewers and cook on a hot barbecue for 2–3 minutes on each side.

4 While the meat is cooking, warm the flatbreads at the side of the barbecue, or on a hot griddle or other flat pan, flipping them over as they begin to go brown and buckle. Pile the breads up on a plate and cover with a clean dish towel to keep them warm.

5 When the kebabs are cooked, slide the meat off the skewers straight on to the flatbreads. Sprinkle sliced red onion and chopped parsley over each pile and squeeze lemon juice over the top. Wrap the breads into parcels and eat with your hands.

Malay Lamb Korma: Energy 267Kcal/1117kJ; Protein 24.3g; Carbohydrate 8.5g, of which sugars 6.8g; Fat 15.4g, of which saturates 6.4g; Cholesterol 86mg; Calcium 46mg; Fibre 1.2g; Sodium 211mg.
Anatolian Lamb Kebabs: Energy 433kcal/1821kJ; Protein 34.3g; Carbohydrate 37.1g, of which sugars 4.4g; Fat 17.5g, of which saturates 7.9g; Cholesterol 114mg; Calcium 83mg; Fibre 2.5g; Sodium 460mg.

Balti Lamb Tikka

This is a traditional tikka recipe, in which the lamb is marinated in yogurt and spices. It is then stir-fried briefly with peppers and chillies and taken sizzling to the table.

Serves 4

450g/1lb lamb, cut into strips
175ml/6fl oz/¾ cup natural
  (plain) yogurt
5ml/1 tsp ground cumin
5ml/1 tsp ground coriander
5ml/1 tsp chilli powder
5ml/1 tsp garlic pulp
5ml/1 tsp salt
5ml/1 tsp garam masala
30ml/2 tbsp chopped fresh
  coriander (cilantro)
30ml/2 tbsp lemon juice
30ml/2 tbsp corn oil
15ml/1 tbsp tomato purée
  (paste)
1 large green (bell) pepper, sliced
3 large fresh red chillies

1 Put the lamb strips, yogurt, ground cumin, ground coriander, chilli powder, garlic, salt, garam masala, fresh coriander (cilantro) and lemon juice into a large mixing bowl and stir all the ingredients together thoroughly. Set to one side for at least 1 hour to marinate.

2 Heat the corn oil in a deep round-bottomed pan or wok. Lower the heat slightly and add the tomato purée, stirring it into the oil.

3 Add the lamb strips to the pan, a few at a time, leaving any excess marinade behind in the bowl.

4 Cook the lamb, stirring frequently, for 7–10 minutes or until it is well browned.

5 Finally, add the green pepper slices and the whole red chillies. Heat through, checking that the lamb is cooked through, and serve.

Cook's Tip
The lamb for this dish is usually cut into cubes, but the cooking time can be halved by cutting it into thin strips.

Spiced Lamb with Spinach

This recipe is based on the Indian dish sag gosht – meat cooked with spinach. It is flavoured with whole spices, which are not intended to be eaten.

Serves 3–4

45ml/3 tbsp vegetable oil
500g/1¼lb lean boneless lamb,
  cut into 2.5cm/1in cubes
1 onion, chopped
3 garlic cloves, finely chopped
1cm/½in piece fresh root ginger,
  finely chopped
6 black peppercorns
4 whole cloves
1 bay leaf
3 green cardamom pods, crushed
5ml/1 tsp ground cumin
5ml/1 tsp ground coriander
generous pinch of cayenne
  pepper
150ml/¼ pint/⅔ cup water
2 tomatoes, peeled, seeded and
  chopped
5ml/1 tsp salt
400g/14oz fresh spinach,
  trimmed, washed and finely
  chopped
5ml/1 tsp garam masala
crisp-fried onions and fresh
  coriander (cilantro) sprigs, to
  garnish
naan bread or spiced basmati
  rice, to serve

1 Heat a large pan or wok until hot. Add 30ml/2 tbsp of the oil and swirl it around. When hot, stir-fry the lamb in batches until evenly browned. Remove the lamb and set aside. Heat the remaining oil in the pan, add the onion, garlic and ginger and stir-fry for 2–3 minutes.

2 Add the peppercorns, cloves, bay leaf, cardamom pods, cumin, coriander and cayenne pepper. Stir-fry for 30–45 seconds.

3 Return the lamb to the pan, add the water, tomatoes and salt and bring to the boil. Simmer, covered, over a very low heat for about 1 hour, stirring occasionally, until the meat is tender.

4 Increase the heat, then gradually add the spinach to the lamb, stirring to mix. Keep stirring and cooking until the spinach wilts completely and most, but not all, of the liquid has evaporated and you are left with a thick green sauce.

5 Stir in the garam masala. Garnish with crisp-fried onions and coriander sprigs. Serve with naan bread or spiced basmati rice.

Balti Lamb Tikka: Energy 438kcal/1827kJ; Protein 34.4g; Carbohydrate 7.8g, of which sugars 7.7g; Fat 30.3g, of which saturates 10.4g; Cholesterol 128mg; Calcium 74mg; Fibre 2.3g; Sodium 162mg.
Spiced Lamb with Spinach: Energy 359kcal/1494kJ; Protein 28.7g; Carbohydrate 7.1g, of which sugars 4.7g; Fat 24.1g, of which saturates 7.7g; Cholesterol 95mg; Calcium 237mg; Fibre 4.8g; Sodium 780mg.

Baked Lamb with Spicy Stuffing

Lamb and apricots are a classic combination in the cookery of North Africa and the Middle East. The warm flavours of cinnamon and cumin make perfect partners for the apricots in the bulgur wheat stuffing in this easy-to-carve joint.

Serves 6–8
75g/3oz/½ cup bulgur wheat
30ml/2 tbsp olive oil
1 small onion, finely chopped
1 garlic clove, crushed
5ml/1 tsp ground cinnamon
5ml/1 tsp ground cumin
175g/6oz/¾ cup ready-to-eat dried apricots, chopped
50g/2oz/⅔ cup pine nuts
1 boned shoulder of lamb, about 1.8–2kg/4–4½lb
120ml/4fl oz/½ cup red wine
120ml/4fl oz/½ cup lamb stock
salt and ground black pepper
mint sprigs, to garnish

1 Place the bulgur wheat in a bowl and add warm water to cover. Leave to soak for 1 hour, then drain thoroughly.

2 Heat the oil in a pan. Add the onion and crushed garlic and cook for 5 minutes, stirring, until the onion has softened. Stir in the bulgur wheat, then add the cinnamon, cumin, apricots and pine nuts, with salt and pepper to taste. Leave to cool. Preheat the oven to 180°C/350°F/Gas 4.

3 Open out the shoulder of lamb and spread the stuffing over the meat. Roll the joint up firmly and tie tightly with string.

4 Place the lamb in a roasting pan. Roast for 1 hour, then pour the red wine and stock into the roasting pan. Roast for 30 minutes more. Transfer the joint to a heated plate, cover with tented foil and allow the meat to rest for 15–20 minutes before carving.

5 Meanwhile, skim the surface fat from the wine-flavoured stock in the roasting pan. Place the pan over a high heat and allow the gravy to bubble for a few minutes, stirring occasionally to incorporate any sediment.

6 Carve the lamb neatly, arrange the slices on a serving platter and pour over the gravy. Serve at once, garnished with mint.

Paprika-infused Lamb Goulash

The various grades of hot or sweet paprika have been a prominent feature of Hungarian cookery for centuries, and are produced from the different varieties of pepper that grow in the region. Goulash is a dish that has travelled across Europe from Hungary and is popular in many places such as the Czech Republic and Germany. This Czech recipe is not a true goulash, because of the addition of flour to thicken the sauce – the traditional dish is really a soup not a stew – but it is a wonderful infusion of tomatoes, paprika, green peppers and marjoram.

Serves 4–6
30ml/2 tbsp vegetable oil or melted lard
900g/2lb lean lamb, trimmed and cut into cubes
1 large onion, roughly chopped
2 garlic cloves, crushed
3 green (bell) peppers, diced
30ml/2 tbsp paprika
2 × 400g/14oz cans chopped tomatoes
15ml/1 tbsp chopped fresh flat leaf parsley
5ml/1 tsp chopped fresh marjoram
30ml/2 tbsp plain (all-purpose) flour
60ml/4 tbsp cold water
salt and ground black pepper
green salad, to serve

1 Heat the oil or lard, if using, in a frying pan, and fry the pieces of lamb for 5–8 minutes, or until browned on all sides. Season well.

2 Add the onion and garlic and cook for a further 2 minutes before adding the green peppers and paprika.

3 Pour in the tomatoes and add some water, if necessary, so that the liquid just covers the meat in the pan. Stir in the herbs.

4 Bring to the boil, turn down the heat, cover and simmer very gently for 1½ hours, or until the lamb is tender.

5 Blend the flour with the cold water and pour into the stew. Bring back to the boil then reduce the heat to a simmer and cook until the sauce has thickened. Adjust the seasoning and serve with a crisp green salad.

Lamb with Spicy Stuffing: Energy 360kcal/1504kJ; Protein 26.9g; Carbohydrate 13.7g, of which sugars 8.7g; Fat 21.3g, of which saturates 7.2g; Cholesterol 95mg; Calcium 31mg; Fibre 1.6g; Sodium 112mg.
Paprika-infused Goulash: Energy 396kcal/1656kJ; Protein 32.6g; Carbohydrate 19.4g, of which sugars 13.8g; Fat 21.5g, of which saturates 8.5g; Cholesterol 114mg; Calcium 53mg; Fibre 4g; Sodium 147mg.

Spiced Lamb with Tomatoes

Select lean tender lamb from the leg for this lightly spiced curry with succulent peppers and wedges of onion. Serve with warm naan bread.

Serves 6

1.5kg/3¼lb lean boneless lamb, cubed
250ml/8fl oz/1 cup natural (plain) yogurt
30ml/2 tbsp sunflower oil
3 onions
2 red (bell) peppers, cut into chunks
3 garlic cloves, finely chopped
1 red chilli, seeded and chopped
2.5cm/1in piece fresh root ginger, peeled and chopped
30ml/2 tbsp mild curry paste
2 x 400g/14oz cans chopped tomatoes
large pinch of saffron strands, ground to powder
800g/1¾lb plum tomatoes, halved, seeded and cut into chunks
salt and ground black pepper
chopped fresh coriander (cilantro), to garnish

1 Mix the lamb with the yogurt in a bowl. Cover and chill for about 1 hour. Heat the oil in a wok or large pan. Drain the lamb and reserve the yogurt, then cook the lamb in batches until it is golden on all sides – this takes about 15 minutes in total. Remove from the pan and set aside.

2 Cut two of the onions into wedges and add to the oil remaining in the pan. Fry the onion wedges over a medium heat for about 10 minutes, or until they are beginning to colour. Add the peppers and cook for a further 5 minutes. Remove the vegetables from the pan and set aside.

3 Meanwhile, chop the remaining onion. Add it to the oil remaining in the pan with the garlic, chilli and ginger, and cook, stirring often, until softened. Stir in the curry paste and canned tomatoes with the reserved yogurt marinade. Replace the lamb, add seasoning to taste and stir well. Bring to the boil, reduce the heat and simmer for about 30 minutes.

4 Dissolve the ground saffron in a little boiling water. Add this liquid to the curry. Replace the onion and pepper mixture. Stir in the fresh tomatoes and bring back to simmering point, then cook for 15 minutes. Garnish with coriander to serve.

Spiced Lamb Kefta

Moroccan meatballs, spiced with cinnamon, are universally popular and are prepared in many ways: stuffed or plain, speared on skewers and grilled or fried. Here, eggs and tomatoes are added to the cooked kefta to make a substantial meal. This version is always eaten out of the pan and makes a great informal supper.

Serves 4

225g/8oz finely minced (ground) lamb
1 onion, finely chopped
50g/2oz fresh breadcrumbs
5 eggs
5ml/1 tsp ground cinnamon
small bunch of flat leaf parsley, finely chopped
30ml/2 tbsp olive oil
a little butter
400g/14oz can chopped tomatoes
10ml/2 tsp sugar
5ml/1 tsp ras el hanout
small bunch of fresh coriander (cilantro), roughly chopped
salt and ground black pepper
crusty bread, to serve

1 In a bowl, knead the lamb with the onion, breadcrumbs, one of the eggs, cinnamon, parsley and salt and pepper until well mixed. Lift the mixture in your hand and slap it down into the bowl several times. Take a small amount of mixture and shape it into a ball about the size of a walnut. Repeat with the remaining mixture to make about 12 balls.

2 Heat the olive oil with the butter in a large heavy frying pan. Fry the meatballs until nicely browned, turning them occasionally so they cook evenly.

3 Stir in the tomatoes, sugar, ras el hanout and most of the coriander. Bring to the boil, cook for a few minutes to reduce the liquid, and roll the balls in the sauce. Season to taste with salt and pepper.

4 Make room for the remaining four eggs in the pan and crack them into spaces between the meatballs. Cover the pan, reduce the heat and cook for about 3 minutes or until the eggs are just set. Sprinkle with the remaining coriander and serve in the pan, with chunks of bread to use as scoops.

Lamb with Tomatoes: Energy 559kcal/2343kJ; Protein 54.4g; Carbohydrate 20.5g, of which sugars 18.8g; Fat 29.6g, of which saturates 13.5g; Cholesterol 191mg; Calcium 139mg; Fibre 4.6g; Sodium 278mg.
Spiced Lamb Kefta: Energy 344kcal/1436kJ; Protein 21.6g; Carbohydrate 15.3g, of which sugars 5.3g; Fat 22.5g, of which saturates 7.5g; Cholesterol 286mg; Calcium 103mg; Fibre 1.8g; Sodium 280mg.

Lamb Couscous with Harissa

This style of couscous is often served with sour pickles throughout the Middle East. Ask your butcher to cut thin lamb cutlets for this dish.

Serves 4

45ml/3 tbsp olive oil
2 onions, quartered
4 garlic cloves, chopped
30–45ml/2–3 tbsp tomato purée (paste)
10ml/2 tsp harissa

4 fennel bulbs, stalks removed and quartered (feathery fronds reserved)
50g/2oz/¼ cup butter
8 thin lamb cutlets (US rib chops)
salt and ground black pepper

For the couscous

2.5ml/½ tsp salt
400ml/14fl oz/1⅔ cups warm water
350g/12oz/2 cups couscous
30ml/2 tbsp sunflower oil
knob (pat) of butter, diced

1 Heat the olive oil in a heavy pan, add the onions and garlic and cook for 15 minutes. Mix the tomato purée with the harissa and dilute with a little water. Pour it into the pan with 600ml/1 pint/2½ cups water. Bring to the boil and add the fennel. Reduce the heat, cover and cook for about 10 minutes.

2 To prepare the couscous, add the salt to the water, place the couscous in a bowl and stir in the water. Leave for 10 minutes. With your fingers, rub the sunflower oil into the couscous. Lift the vegetables from the cooking liquid and transfer to a dish; keep warm. Bring the liquid to the boil to reduce it.

3 Melt the butter in a heavy frying pan, add the cutlets to the pan and brown them on both sides. Add the cutlets to the reduced liquid and simmer for 15 minutes, or until tender.

4 Preheat the oven to 180°C/350°F/Gas 4. Tip the couscous into an ovenproof dish and arrange the diced butter over the top. Chop the fennel fronds and sprinkle over the couscous. Cover with foil and heat in the oven for about 20 minutes. Put the vegetables in the pan with the lamb and heat through. Fluff up the couscous then mound it on to a serving dish. Place the cutlets around the edge and spoon the vegetables over. Moisten with the cooking liquid and serve.

Lamb Tagine with Onion and Green Chilli Salad

Morocco's hearty tagines are well known for their succulent meat cooked in a combination of honey and warm spices. This delicious recipe is for one of the most traditional and popular tagines, which is best served with a crunchy salad, spiked with chilli to balance the sweetness of the main dish. Offer lots of fresh bread for mopping up the thick, syrupy sauce.

Serves 6

1kg/2¼lb boneless shoulder of lamb, trimmed and cubed
30–45ml/2–3 tbsp sunflower oil
25g/1oz fresh root ginger, peeled and chopped

pinch of saffron threads
10ml/2 tsp ground cinnamon
1 onion, finely chopped
2–3 garlic cloves, chopped
350g/12oz/1½ cups pitted prunes, soaked for 1 hour
30ml/2 tbsp clear honey
salt and ground black pepper

For the salad

2 onions, chopped
1 red (bell) pepper, chopped
1 green (bell) pepper, chopped
2–3 celery sticks, chopped
2–3 green chillies, seeded and chopped
2 garlic cloves, chopped
30ml/2 tbsp olive oil
juice of ½ lemon
small bunch of parsley, chopped
a little mint, chopped

1 Put the meat in a flameproof casserole or heavy pan. Add the oil, ginger, saffron, cinnamon, onion, garlic and seasoning, then pour in enough water to cover. Bring to the boil.

2 Cover and simmer gently for about 2 hours, topping up with water if necessary, until the meat is very tender.

3 Drain the prunes and add them to the tagine. Stir in the honey and simmer for a further 30 minutes, or until the sauce has reduced.

4 Meanwhile, to make the salad, mix the onions, peppers, celery, chillies and garlic in a bowl. Pour the olive oil and lemon juice over the vegetables and toss to coat. Season with salt and add the parsley and mint. Serve with the hot lamb tagine.

Lamb Couscous: Energy 631kcal/2643kJ; Protein 40.6g; Carbohydrate 67g, of which sugars 39.3g; Fat 24.1g, of which saturates 9.6g; Cholesterol 133mg; Calcium 160mg; Fibre 6.6g; Sodium 227mg.
Lamb Tagine with Onion: Energy 600kcal/2504kJ; Protein 42g; Carbohydrate 28.2g, of which sugars 25.8g; Fat 36.3g, of which saturates 10.9g; Cholesterol 222mg; Calcium 112mg; Fibre 4.9g; Sodium 199mg.

Warmly Spiced Lamb Pot Roast

This slow-braised dish of lamb and tomatoes, spiced with cinnamon and stewed with green beans, shows a Middle Eastern influence. Serve it with crusty bread to mop up the spicy gravy.

Serves 8
1kg/2¼lb lamb on the bone
8 garlic cloves, chopped
2.5–5ml/½–1 tsp ground cumin
45ml/3 tbsp olive oil
juice of 1 lemon
2 onions, thinly sliced
about 500ml/17fl oz/2¼ cups
    lamb, beef or vegetable stock
75–90ml/5–6 tbsp tomato purée
    (paste)
1 cinnamon stick
2–3 large pinches of ground
    allspice or ground cloves
15–30ml/1–2 tbsp sugar
400g/14oz/scant 3 cups runner
    (green) beans
salt and ground black pepper
15–30ml/1–2 tbsp chopped fresh
    parsley, to garnish

1 Preheat the oven to 160°C/325°F/Gas 3. Coat the lamb with the chopped garlic, cumin, olive oil, lemon juice, salt and pepper, rubbing the flavouring well into the meat.

2 Heat a flameproof casserole and sear the lamb on all sides. Add the onions and pour the stock over the meat to cover. Stir in the tomato purée, spices and sugar. Cover and cook in the oven for 2–3 hours, until the lamb is cooked.

3 Remove the casserole from the oven and pour off the stock into a pan. Move the onions to the side of the dish and return to the oven, uncovered, for 20 minutes to allow the meat to brown.

4 Meanwhile, add the beans to the hot stock and cook until the beans are tender and the sauce has thickened. Slice the meat and serve with the pan juices and beans. Garnish with the chopped parsley.

> **Variation**
> Make the dish with sliced courgettes (zucchini) cooked in the hot stock instead of runner beans.

Baked Lamb with Tomatoes, Garlic and Pasta

This is one of the most popular dishes in Greece, and is often made for the celebratory family lunch on 15 August, after the long fasting period of the Feast of the Assumption.

Serves 6
1 shoulder of lamb, trimmed,
    sliced into serving portions
600g/1lb 6oz ripe tomatoes,
    peeled and chopped, or
400g/14oz can chopped
    tomatoes
4–5 garlic cloves, chopped
75ml/5 tbsp extra virgin olive oil
5ml/1 tsp dried oregano
1 litre/1¾ pints/4 cups hot water
400g/14oz/3½ cups orzo pasta,
    or spaghetti, broken into short
    lengths
salt and ground black pepper
50g/2oz/½ cup freshly grated
    Kefalotyri or Parmesan cheese,
    to serve

1 Preheat the oven to 190°C/375°F/Gas 5. Wipe the meat to remove any bone splinters and place it in a large roasting pan.

2 Add the fresh or canned tomatoes, garlic, olive oil and oregano. Season with salt and pepper and stir in 300ml/½ pint/1¼ cups of the hot water.

3 Place the lamb in the oven and bake for about 1 hour, basting and turning the pieces of meat over a couple of times.

4 Reduce the oven temperature to 180°C/350°F/Gas 4. Add the remaining 700ml/scant 1¼ pints/2¾ cups hot water to the roasting pan. Stir in the pasta and add more seasoning. Mix well, return the pan to the oven and bake for 30–40 minutes more, stirring occasionally, until the meat is fully cooked and tender and the pasta feels soft. Serve immediately, accompanied by a bowl of grated cheese.

> **Variation**
> The dish can also be made with young goat (kid) or beef, but these have to be boiled first.

Braised Moroccan-spiced Lamb

This dish is traditionally eaten by Moroccan Jews at New Year, when sweet foods are served to symbolize the promise of a good year to come, and it is flavoured with warm, mellow spices such as cinnamon, ginger and nutmeg.

Serves 6

130g/4½oz/generous ½ cup pitted prunes
350ml/12fl oz/1½ cups hot tea
1kg/2¼lb lamb shoulder, cut into chunky portions
1 onion, chopped
75–90ml/5–6 tbsp chopped fresh parsley
2.5ml/½ tsp ground ginger
2.5ml/½ tsp curry powder or ras el hanout
pinch of freshly grated nutmeg
10ml/2 tsp ground cinnamon
1.5ml/¼ tsp saffron threads
30ml/2 tbsp hot water
75–120ml/5–9 tbsp honey, to taste
250ml/8fl oz/1 cup beef or lamb stock
115g/4oz/1 cup blanched almonds, toasted
30ml/2 tbsp chopped fresh coriander (cilantro) leaves
3 hard-boiled eggs, cut into wedges
salt and ground black pepper

1 Preheat the oven to 180°C/350°F/Gas 4. Put the prunes in a bowl and pour the tea over them. Cover the bowl and leave for the prunes to soak and plump up.

2 Meanwhile, put the lamb in a roasting pan and sprinkle with the chopped onion, parsley, ginger, curry powder or ras el hanout, nutmeg, cinnamon, salt and a large pinch of ground black pepper. Cover and cook in the oven for about 2 hours, or until the meat is tender.

3 Drain the prunes and add their liquid to the juices around the lamb. Combine the saffron and hot water and add to the pan with the honey and stock. Return the pan to the oven and bake, uncovered, for another 30 minutes, turning the lamb occasionally so that it browns evenly.

4 Add the prunes to the pan and stir gently to mix. Serve sprinkled with the toasted almonds and chopped coriander, and topped with the wedges of hard-boiled egg.

Spanish Paprika Lamb

Aragon and Navarre in the Pyrenees are known for their fine ingredients – and also for their simple cooking. "If the quality is there, no need to employ tricks in the kitchen", runs the Spanish proverb. For this dish the lamb is fried simply and flavoured with lemon juice and paprika: it captures the very essence of the meat.

Serves 4

800g/1¾lb very well-trimmed, tender lamb (see Cook's Tip), in cubes or strips
30ml/2 tbsp olive oil, plus extra
1 onion, chopped
2 garlic cloves, finely chopped
5ml/1 tsp paprika
juice of 2 lemons
15ml/1 tbsp finely chopped fresh parsley
salt and ground black pepper

1 Season the lamb with salt and ground black pepper. Heat the 30ml/2 tbsp olive oil in a large frying pan or casserole over a high heat and add the meat in handfuls. Add the chopped onion at the same time, and keep pushing the meat around the pan with a spatula.

2 Add more meat to the pan as each batch is sealed. Add the chopped garlic and a little more oil if necessary.

3 When all the meat is golden brown and the onion is soft, sprinkle with paprika and lemon juice. Cover the pan and simmer for 15 minutes. Check the seasonings and add a dusting of parsley, then serve.

> **Variation**
> This dish may also be made using pork in place of the lamb – its Spanish name, cochifrito, means "little pig, fried".

> **Cook's Tip**
> The sweetest lamb is cut from the shoulder. However, it also contains quite a lot of fat, often in layers through the meat, so allow extra weight, and cut it out.

Braised Spiced Lamb: Energy 618kcal/2564kJ; Protein 42.7g; Carbohydrate 0.8g, of which sugars 0.1g; Fat 49.3g, of which saturates 21.2g; Cholesterol 183mg; Calcium 16mg; Fibre 0.2g; Sodium 150mg.
Spanish Paprika Lamb: Energy 451kcal/1882kJ; Protein 41g; Carbohydrate 8.7g, of which sugars 5.9g; Fat 28.4g, of which saturates 11.2g; Cholesterol 152mg; Calcium 68mg; Fibre 2g; Sodium 180mg.

Spiced Lamb with Red Peppers and Rioja

World-famous for its red wine, Rioja also produces excellent red peppers. It even has a red pepper fair, at Lodosa every year. Together they give this lamb stew a lovely rich flavour. Boiled potatoes make a very good accompaniment.

Serves 4

15ml/1 tbsp plain (all-purpose) flour
1kg/2¼lb lean lamb, cubed
60ml/4 tbsp olive oil
2 red onions, sliced
4 garlic cloves, sliced
10ml/2 tsp paprika
1.5ml/¼ tsp ground cloves
400ml/14fl oz/1⅔ cups red Rioja
150ml/¼ pint/⅔ cup lamb stock
2 bay leaves
2 thyme sprigs
3 red (bell) peppers, halved
salt and ground black pepper
bay leaves and thyme sprigs, to garnish (optional)

1 Preheat the oven to 160°C/325°F/Gas 3. Season the flour, add the lamb and toss lightly to coat.

2 Heat the oil in a frying pan and fry the lamb until browned. Transfer to an ovenproof dish. Fry the onions and garlic until soft. Add to the meat.

3 Add the paprika, cloves, Rioja, lamb stock, bay leaves and thyme and bring the mixture to a gentle simmer.

4 Add the halved red peppers and push them into the liquid. Cover the dish with a lid or foil and cook for about 30 minutes, or until the meat is tender. Garnish with more bay leaves and thyme sprigs, if you like.

Cook's Tip
The red peppers of Lodosa are Piquillo peppers, a spicy-sweet, slightly piquant variety that is unique to the Ebro valley. They are roasted over wood fires and preserved in bottles and cans, but the fresh peppers are now also beginning to be exported.

Lamb with Ginger and Cinnamon

This Moroccan-spiced stew is gently simmered for a long time in a tagine dish or casserole. It is perfect for a large party.

Serves 6

50g/2oz/¼ cup butter
6 lamb shanks
1 onion, finely chopped
2.5ml/½ tsp ground cumin
2.5ml/½ tsp ground ginger
2.5ml/½ tsp ground cinnamon
10ml/2 tsp paprika
4 cloves
115g/4oz/1 cup ground almonds
3 large strips orange rind
225g/8oz/1 cup dried apricots
115g/4oz/1½ cup stoned (pitted) dried prunes
115g/4oz/scant 1 cup raisins

For the minted sesame couscous
375g/13oz quick-cook couscous
115g/4oz/1½ cup butter, cubed
60ml/4 tbsp chopped fresh mint
45ml/3 tbsp sesame seeds

1 Melt the butter in a large, flameproof casserole. Brown the lamb all over, then transfer to a plate. Stir the onion and spices into the pan juices and cook for 5 minutes. Add 2.5ml/½ tsp salt and plenty of pepper. Stir in the ground almonds.

2 Return the lamb to the pan with the orange rind and cover with 1.2 litres/2 pints/5 cups water. Bring to the boil, then turn the heat to low. Cover the surface of the stew with a sheet of crumpled baking parchment, then the lid. Simmer for 1 hour.

3 After this time, add the apricots, prunes and raisins, and simmer for another hour. Just before serving, prepare the minted sesame couscous. Put the couscous into a measuring jug (cup) and note the measurement. Transfer to a bowl and measure out twice its volume in water. Bring to the boil.

4 Stir the butter and mint into the boiling water, then pour over the couscous. Cover and leave to stand for 5 minutes.

5 Meanwhile, toast the sesame seeds in a frying pan until golden. Using a fork, fluff up the couscous. Fork in the sesame seeds, taste and season well. When the lamb is ready it should be falling off the bone and the sauce thickened. Taste the lamb for seasoning. Serve with the couscous.

Lamb with Red Peppers: Energy 635kcal/2646kJ; Protein 49.8g; Carbohydrate 4.1g, of which sugars 0.4g; Fat 39.4g, of which saturates 14.6g; Cholesterol 190mg; Calcium 37mg; Fibre 0.2g; Sodium 223mg.
Lamb with Ginger: Energy 565kcal/2368kJ; Protein 36.3g; Carbohydrate 60g, of which sugars 35.2g; Fat 21.6g, of which saturates 8.6g; Cholesterol 119mg; Calcium 143mg; Fibre 6g; Sodium 203mg.

Lamb and New Potato Curry

This dish makes the most of lamb shank, an economical but delicious cut of meat, by cooking it slowly until the meat is falling from the bone. Chillies and coconut cream give it lots of flavour.

Serves 4

25g/1oz/2 tbsp butter
4 garlic cloves, crushed
2 onions, sliced into rings
2.5ml/½ tsp each ground cumin, ground coriander, turmeric and cayenne pepper
2–3 red chillies, seeded and finely chopped
300ml/½ pint/1¼ cups hot chicken stock
200ml/7fl oz/scant 1 cup coconut cream
4 lamb shanks, all excess fat removed
450g/1lb new potatoes, halved
6 ripe tomatoes, quartered
salt and ground black pepper
coriander (cilantro) leaves, to garnish
spicy rice, to serve

1 Preheat the oven to 160°C/325°F/Gas 3. Melt the butter in a large flameproof casserole, add the garlic and sliced onions and cook over a low heat for 15 minutes, until the vegetables are softened and golden. Stir in the spices and chillies, then cook for a further 2 minutes.

2 Stir in the hot stock and coconut cream. Place the trimmed lamb shanks in the liquid and bring back to a simmer. Cover the casserole with foil. Cook in the oven for 2 hours, turning the shanks twice, first after about an hour or so and again about half an hour later.

3 Par-boil the potatoes for 10 minutes, drain and add to the casserole with the tomatoes, then cook uncovered in the oven for a further 35 minutes. Season to taste, garnish with coriander leaves and serve with spicy rice.

> **Cook's Tip**
> Make this dish a day in advance if possible. Cool and chill overnight, then skim off the excess fat that has risen to the surface. Reheat thoroughly before you serve it.

Barbecued Lamb with Cumin and Spiced Salt

This Moroccan speciality often consists of a whole lamb grilled slowly over a charcoal fire. This version uses a large shoulder, which is rubbed with spices and chargrilled. When cooked, the meat is hacked off and dipped in roasted salt and cumin. Use a barbecue with a lid to ensure the meat cooks slowly and evenly.

Serves 4–6

1 shoulder of lamb, about 1.8kg/4lb
4 garlic cloves, crushed
15ml/1 tbsp paprika
15ml/1 tbsp ground cumin seeds
105ml/7 tbsp extra virgin olive oil
45–60ml/3–4 tbsp finely chopped mint leaves
salt and ground black pepper
45ml/3 tbsp cumin seeds
25ml/1½ tbsp coarse sea salt

1 Open up the pockets in the flesh of the lamb and tuck the garlic cloves inside. Mix the paprika, ground cumin and seasoning and rub over the shoulder. Cover and leave the lamb for about 1 hour. Mix the oil and mint in a bowl for basting during roasting.

2 Prepare a barbecue. Once the flames have died down, rake the hot coals to one side and insert a drip tray flat beside them. Position a lightly oiled grill rack over the coals to heat.

3 When the coals are medium-hot, place the lamb shoulder on the rack, and cover with a lid or a tented sheet of heavy-duty foil. For the initial 30 minutes turn the meat frequently, basting with the mint oil. Then roast the meat for a further 2 hours, turning and basting every 15 minutes. Replenish the coals if necessary during cooking.

4 Dry-roast the cumin seeds and coarse salt for 2 minutes in a heavy frying pan. Do not let them burn. Tip them into a mortar and pound with the pestle until roughly ground.

5 When the meat is cooked, remove from the barbecue, wrap in double foil and rest it for 15 minutes. Serve sliced with the roasted cumin and salt for dipping.

Lamb and Ras el Hanout Kebabs

These little round lamb kebabs owe their exotic flavour to *ras el hanout*, a North African spice blend. Dried rose petals can be found in Moroccan and Middle Eastern stores.

Serves 4–6

30ml/2 tbsp extra virgin olive oil
1 onion, finely chopped
2 garlic cloves, crushed
35g/1¼oz/5 tbsp pine nuts
500g/1¼lb/2½ cups minced (ground) lamb
10ml/2 tsp ras el hanout
10ml/2 tsp dried pink rose petals (optional)
salt and ground black pepper
18 short wooden or metal skewers
150ml/¼ pint/⅔ cup natural (plain) yogurt and 7.5ml/ 1½ tsp rose harissa, to serve

For the fresh mint chutney

40g/1½oz/1½ cups fresh mint leaves, finely chopped
10ml/2 tsp sugar
juice of 2 lemons
2 apples, peeled and finely grated

1 If using wooden skewers, soak them in cold water for 30 minutes. Heat the oil in a frying pan on the stove. Add the onion and garlic and fry gently for 7 minutes. Stir in the pine nuts. Fry for about 5 minutes more, or until the mixture is slightly golden, then set aside to cool.

2 Make the fresh mint chutney by mixing together all of the ingredients. Set aside.

3 Prepare the barbecue. Place the minced lamb in a large bowl and add the *ras el hanout* and rose petals, if using. Tip in the cooled onion mixture and add salt and pepper. Using your hands, mix well, then form into 18 balls. Drain the skewers and mould a ball on to each one. Once the flames have died down, rake a few hot coals to one side. Position a lightly oiled grill rack over the coals to heat.

4 When the coals are cool, or with a thick coating of ash, place the kebabs on the grill over the part with the most coals. If it is easier, cover the barbecue with a lid or tented heavy-duty foil so that the heat will circulate and they will cook evenly all over. Serve with the yogurt, mixed with the rose harissa, if you like.

Shish Kebabs with Sumac

Sumac is a spice, ground from a dried purple berry with a sour, fruity flavour. In this recipe it complements the richness of the lamb.

Makes 8

675g/1½lb lamb neck fillet, trimmed and cut into 2.5cm/1in pieces
5ml/1 tsp each fennel, cumin and coriander seeds, roasted and crushed
1.5ml/¼ tsp cayenne pepper
5cm/2in piece fresh root ginger
150ml/¼ pint/⅔ cup natural (plain) yogurt
2 small red (bell) peppers
2 small yellow (bell) peppers
300g/11oz small onions
30ml/2 tbsp olive oil
15ml/1 tbsp ground sumac
salt and ground black pepper
8 long metal skewers

To serve

8 Lebanese flatbreads
150ml/¼ pint/⅔ cup natural (plain) yogurt
5ml/1 tsp ground sumac
1 bunch rocket (arugula)
50g/2oz/2 cups fresh parsley
10ml/2 tsp olive oil
juice of ½ lemon

1 Place the lamb pieces in a bowl and sprinkle over the crushed seeds and the cayenne pepper. Grate the ginger and squeeze it over the lamb. Pour over the yogurt. Mix well, cover and marinate overnight in the refrigerator.

2 Prepare the barbecue. Stand a sieve (strainer) over a bowl and pour in the lamb mixture. Leave to drain well. Cut the peppers in half, remove the cores and seeds, then cut the flesh into rough chunks. Place in a bowl. Add the onions and the olive oil. Pat the drained lamb with kitchen paper to remove excess marinade. Add the lamb to the bowl, season and toss well. Thread the lamb, peppers and onions on to the skewers.

3 On a medium hot barbecue, grill the kebabs for about 10 minutes, turning every 2 minutes. When cooked, transfer to a platter, lightly sprinkle with the sumac, and cover with foil.

4 Place the breads on the barbecue to warm. Place the yogurt in a serving bowl and sprinkle with sumac. Arrange the rocket and parsley in separate bowls and pour over the oil and lemon juice. Serve with the kebabs and the warmed flatbread.

Lamb and Ras el Hanout Kebabs: Energy 257kcal/1070kJ; Protein 17.2g; Carbohydrate 5.1g, of which sugars 4.5g; Fat 18.8g, of which saturates 6g; Cholesterol 64mg; Calcium 33mg; Fibre 0.6g; Sodium 59mg.
Shish Kebabs with Sumac: Energy 361kcal/1515kJ; Protein 22.5g; Carbohydrate 38.4g, of which sugars 8.1g; Fat 14.1g, of which saturates 5.1g; Cholesterol 64mg; Calcium 133mg; Fibre 3g; Sodium 249mg.

Turkish Kebabs with Tomato and Chilli Salsa

The mix of aromatic spices, garlic and lemon gives these kebabs a wonderful flavour – a fiery salsa makes the perfect accompaniment. If you like your salsa really hot, you can leave the seeds in the chilli.

Serves 4

2 garlic cloves, crushed
60ml/4 tbsp lemon juice
30ml/2 tbsp olive oil
1 dried red chilli, crushed
5ml/1 tsp ground cumin
5ml/1 tsp ground coriander

500g/1¼lb lean lamb, cut into 4cm/1½in cubes
8 bay leaves
salt and ground black pepper

For the tomato and olive salsa
175g/6oz/1½ cups mixed pitted green and black olives, roughly chopped
1 small red onion, finely chopped
4 plum tomatoes, peeled and finely chopped
1 fresh red chilli, seeded and finely chopped
30ml/2 tbsp olive oil

1 Mix the garlic, lemon juice, olive oil, chilli, cumin and coriander in a large shallow dish. Add the lamb cubes, with salt and pepper to taste. Mix well. Cover and marinate in a cool place for 2 hours.

2 To make the salsa, put the olives, onion, tomatoes, chilli and olive oil in a bowl. Stir in salt and pepper to taste. Mix well, cover and set aside.

3 Remove the lamb from the marinade and divide the cubes among four skewers, adding the bay leaves at intervals. Grill over a barbecue, on a ridged iron grill pan or under a hot grill (broiler), turning occasionally, for 10 minutes, until the lamb is browned and crisp on the outside and pink and juicy inside. Serve with the salsa.

Cook's Tip
Use meat from the leg for the leanest kebabs.

Cumin- and Coriander-rubbed Lamb

Spice rubs are quick and easy to prepare and can transform everyday cuts of meat such as chops and steaks into exciting and more unusual meals. Serve with a chunky tomato salad.

Serves 4
30ml/2 tbsp ground cumin
30ml/2 tbsp ground coriander
30ml/2 tbsp olive oil
8 lamb chops
salt and ground black pepper

1 Mix together the cumin, coriander and oil, and season with salt and pepper.

2 Rub the mixture all over the lamb chops, then cover and chill for 1 hour.

3 Prepare a barbecue or preheat a grill (broiler). Cook the chops for 5 minutes on each side, until the meat is lightly charred but still pink in the centre. Serve immediately.

Variation
To make ginger- and garlic-rubbed pork, use pork chops instead of lamb chops and substitute the cumin and coriander with ground ginger and garlic granules. Increase the cooking time to 7–8 minutes each side.

Cook's Tips
• If it is more convenient, spice mixtures of this kind can be rubbed into the meat well before cooking, and the meat chilled for several hours or overnight, so the flavours have plenty of time to permeate.
• If you are using ready-ground spices, buy them in small quantities and use them as fresh as possible because the aroma quickly diminishes once they are ground and once the containers are opened. For the best, most pungent flavours, it's better to buy whole spices and grind them yourself in a spice mill or coffee grinder as you need them.

Turkish Kebabs with Salsa: Energy 456kcal/1892kJ; Protein 23.9g; Carbohydrate 7g, of which sugars 6.3g; Fat 37.2g, of which saturates 9.5g; Cholesterol 86mg; Calcium 54mg; Fibre 3.2g; Sodium 1096mg.
Cumin and Coriander Lamb: Energy 494kcal/2059kJ; Protein 55.6g; Carbohydrate 0g, of which sugars 0g; Fat 30.1g, of which saturates 12.6g; Cholesterol 220mg; Calcium 18mg; Fibre 0g; Sodium 150mg.

Curried Lamb and Potato Cakes

An unusual variation on burgers or rissoles, these little lamb triangles are easy to make. They are really good served hot as part of a buffet, but they can also be eaten cold as a snack or taken on picnics.

Makes 12–15

450g/1lb new or small, firm
   potatoes
3 eggs
1 onion, grated
30ml/2 tbsp chopped fresh
   parsley
450g/1lb finely minced (ground)
   lean lamb
115g/4oz/2 cups fresh
   breadcrumbs
vegetable oil, for frying
salt and ground black pepper
sprigs of fresh mint,
   to garnish
pitta bread and herby green
   salad, to serve

1 Cook the potatoes in a large pan of boiling salted water for 20 minutes or until tender, then drain and leave to cool.

2 Beat the eggs in a large bowl. Add the onion, parsley and seasoning and beat together.

3 When the potatoes are cold, grate them coarsely and stir into the egg mixture, together with the minced lamb. Knead the mixture well for 3–4 minutes until all the ingredients are thoroughly blended.

4 Take a handful of the lamb mixture and roll it into a ball. Repeat this process until all the meat is used.

5 Roll the balls in the breadcrumbs and then mould them into fairly flat triangular shapes, about 13cm/5in long. Coat them in the breadcrumbs again.

6 Heat a 1cm/½ in layer of oil in a frying pan over a medium heat. When the oil is hot, fry the potato cakes for 8–12 minutes until golden brown on both sides, turning occasionally. Drain on kitchen paper.

7 Serve hot, garnished with mint and accompanied by pitta bread and salad.

Sumac-spiced Burgers with Relish

A sharp-sweet red onion relish works well with burgers based on Middle-Eastern style lamb. Serve with pitta bread and tabbouleh or a green salad.

Serves 4

25g/1oz/3 tbsp bulgur wheat
500g/1¼lb lean minced (ground)
   lamb
1 small red onion, finely chopped
2 garlic cloves, finely chopped
1 green chilli, seeded and finely
   chopped
5ml/1 tsp ground cumin seeds
2.5ml/½ tsp ground sumac
15g/½oz chopped fresh parsley
30ml/2 tbsp chopped fresh mint
olive oil, for frying
salt and ground black pepper

For the relish
2 red peppers, halved
2 red onions, cut into 5mm/¼in
   thick slices
75–90ml/5–6 tbsp virgin olive oil
350g/12oz cherry tomatoes,
   chopped
½–1 fresh red or green chilli,
   seeded and finely chopped
30ml/2 tbsp chopped mint
30ml/2 tbsp chopped parsley
15ml/1 tbsp chopped oregano
2.5–5ml/½–1 tsp each ground
   toasted cumin and sumac
juice of ½ lemon
caster (superfine) sugar, to taste

1 Pour 150ml/¼ pint/⅔ cup hot water over the bulgur wheat and leave to stand for 15 minutes, then drain.

2 Place the bulgur in a bowl and add the minced lamb, onion, garlic, chilli, cumin, sumac, parsley and mint. Mix together thoroughly, then season with 5ml/1 tsp salt and plenty of black pepper. Form the mixture into eight burgers and set aside while you make the relish.

3 Grill the peppers, until the skin chars and blisters. Peel off the skin, dice and place in a bowl. Brush the onions with oil and grill until browned. Chop. Add the onions, tomatoes, chilli, mint, parsley, oregano and 2.5ml/½ tsp each of the cumin and sumac to the peppers. Stir in 60ml/4 tbsp oil and 15ml/1 tbsp of the lemon juice and salt, pepper and sugar to taste. Set aside.

4 Heat a frying pan over a high heat and grease with olive oil. Cook the burgers for about 5–6 minutes on each side. Serve immediately with the relish.

Curried Lamb and Potato Cakes: Energy 181kcal/760kJ; Protein 10.0g; Carbohydrate 13.9g, of which sugars 1.1g; Fat 9.6g, of which saturates 2.8g; Cholesterol 76mg; Calcium 31mg; Fibre 0.8g; Sodium 128mg.
Sumac-spiced Burgers: Energy 537kcal/2228kJ; Protein 27.2g; Carbohydrate 19g, of which sugars 13.4g; Fat 39.6g, of which saturates 11.1g; Cholesterol 96mg; Calcium 83mg; Fibre 4.2g; Sodium 105mg.

Roast Pork with Spicy Stuffing

Pork features twice in this delicious and luxurious Mexican dish, which consists of a roast loin stuffed with a rich minced pork mixture.

Serves 6
50g/2oz/¹/₃ cup raisins
120ml/4fl oz/¹/₂ cup dry white wine
15ml/1 tbsp vegetable oil
1 onion, diced
2 garlic cloves, crushed
2.5ml/¹/₂ tsp ground cloves
5ml/1 tsp ground cinnamon
500g/1¹/₄lb minced (ground) pork
150ml/¹/₄ pint/²/₃ cup vegetable stock
2 tomatoes
50g/2oz/¹/₂ cup chopped almonds
1.3–1.6kg/3–3¹/₂lb boneless pork loin, butterflied for stuffing
2.5ml/¹/₂ tsp each salt and ground black pepper

1 To make the stuffing, put the raisins and wine in a bowl. Set aside. Heat the oil in a large pan, add the onion and garlic and cook for 5 minutes over a low heat. Add the cloves. cinnamon, and pork. Cook, stirring, until the pork has browned. Add the stock. Simmer, stirring frequently, for 20 minutes.

2 While the pork is simmering, peel the tomatoes. Cut a cross in the base of each tomato, then put them in a bowl and pour over boiling water to cover. Leave for 3 minutes, then remove the skins and chop the flesh.

3 Stir the tomatoes and almonds into the pork mixture, add the raisins and wine. Cook until reduced. Leave to cool.

4 Preheat the oven to 180°C/350°F/Gas 4. Open out the pork loin and trim. Season the stuffing with salt and pepper. Spread over the surface of the meat in an even layer.

5 Roll up the pork loin carefully and tie it at intervals with kitchen string. Weigh the pork and calculate the cooking time at 30 minutes per lb/450g, plus another 30 minutes.

6 Put the stuffed pork joint in a roasting pan, season with salt and pepper and roast for the calculated time. When cooked, transfer it to a meat platter, cover, and let it stand for 10 minutes before carving and serving.

Pork with Ginger and Cardamom

This is a traditional German recipe in which ginger biscuits are used as a thickening ingredient.

Serves 4
1.5kg/3lb cured loin of pork
about 18 prunes, chopped
45ml/3 tbsp apple juice or water
75g/3oz/1¹/₂ cups ginger biscuit (gingersnap) crumbs
3 cardamom pods
15ml/1 tbsp sunflower oil
1 onion, chopped
250ml/8fl oz/1 cup dry red wine
15ml/1 tbsp soft dark brown sugar
salt and ground black pepper
stoned prunes, apple and leek slices, fried in butter, and steamed green cabbage, to serve

1 Preheat the oven to 230°C/450°F/Gas 8. Put the pork, fat-side down, on a board. Make a cut about 3cm/1¹/₄in deep along the length to within 1cm/¹/₂in of the ends, then make two deep cuts to its left and right, to create two pockets in the meat.

2 Put the prunes in a bowl. Spoon over the apple juice or water, then add the biscuit crumbs. Remove the cardamom seeds from their pods and crush using a pestle and mortar, or on a board with the end of a rolling pin. Add to the bowl with salt and pepper. Mix the prune stuffing well and use to fill the pockets in the meat.

3 Tie the pork joint at regular intervals with string. Heat the oil in a roasting pan on the hob and brown the joint over a high heat. Remove the meat and set aside. Add the chopped onion to the pan and fry for 10 minutes, until golden. Return the pork to the pan pour in the wine and add the sugar and seasoning.

4 Roast for 10 minutes, then reduce the oven temperature to 180°C/350°F/Gas 4 and roast, uncovered, for a further 1 hour and 50 minutes, or until cooked and golden brown. Remove the joint from the pan and keep warm.

5 Strain the meat juices into a pan and simmer for 10 minutes, until slightly reduced. Carve the pork and serve with the sauce, accompanied by buttery fried prunes and apple and leek slices, and steamed green cabbage.

Pork with Spicy Stuffing: Energy 851kcal/3566kJ; Protein 83.3g; Carbohydrate 46.8g, of which sugars 30.7g; Fat 38g, of which saturates 8.6g; Cholesterol 245mg; Calcium 233mg; Fibre 6.2g; Sodium 556mg.
Pork with Ginger: Energy 867kcal/3640kJ; Protein 101g; Carbohydrate 45.6g, of which sugars 37.1g; Fat 27.6g, of which saturates 9.3g; Cholesterol 254mg; Calcium 99mg; Fibre 4.8g; Sodium 274mg.

Pork with Herbs, Spices and Rum

In the Caribbean, this spicy roast pork is usually barbecued and served on special occasions.

Serves 6–8

2 garlic cloves, crushed
45ml/3 tbsp soy sauce
15ml/1 tbsp malt vinegar
15ml/1 tbsp finely chopped celery
30ml/2 tbsp spring onion
  (scallion), chopped
7.5ml/1½ tsp dried thyme
5ml/1 tsp dried sage
2.5ml/½ tsp mixed spice
10ml/2 tsp curry powder
120ml/4fl oz/½ cup rum
15ml/1 tbsp demerara (raw) sugar
1.3–1.6kg/3–3½lb joint of pork,
  boned and scored
salt and ground black pepper
spring onion curls, to garnish
creamed sweet potato, to serve

For the sauce
25g/1oz/2 tbsp butter
15ml/1 tbsp tomato purée (paste)
300ml/½ pint/1¼ cups stock
15ml/1 tbsp chopped fresh parsley
15ml/1 tbsp demerara sugar
hot pepper sauce, to taste
salt

1 Mix together the garlic, soy sauce, vinegar, celery, spring onion, thyme, sage, mixed spice, curry powder, rum, demerara sugar and salt and pepper. Open out the pork and slash the meat, without cutting through. Spread the mixture all over the pork, pressing it well into the slashes. Rub the outside of the joint with the mixture as well. Chill overnight.

2 Preheat the oven to 190°C/375°F/Gas 5. Roll the meat up and tie tightly in several places with string. Spread a large piece of foil across a roasting pan and place the joint in the centre. Baste the pork with a few spoonfuls of the marinade and wrap the foil around the joint.

3 Bake for 1¾ hours, then remove the foil, baste with any remaining marinade and cook for a further 1 hour, basting occasionally. Transfer to a serving dish and keep warm.

4 To make the sauce, pour the pan juices into a pan. Add the butter, tomato purée, stock, parsley, sugar, hot pepper and salt to taste. Simmer until reduced. Slice the pork and serve with creamed sweet potato. Garnish with spring onion curls and serve the sauce separately.

Roast Pork with Cajun Stuffing

Onion, celery and sweet green pepper, plus a spicy rub, give a traditional Cajun flavour to this handsome roast, complete with crunchy crackling.

Serves 6

15ml/1 tbsp salt
5ml/1 tsp ground black pepper
5ml/1 tsp cayenne
5ml/1 tsp paprika
5ml/1 tsp dried oregano
30ml/2 tbsp cooking oil or
  25g/1oz/2 tbsp lard
1 small onion, finely chopped
1 celery stick, finely chopped
½ green (bell) pepper, finely
  chopped
1 garlic clove, crushed
1.6kg/3½lb boned loin of pork

1 If the pork is already tied up, untie it. Score the pork skin closely to make good crackling (you can ask your butcher to do this for you). Rub 15ml/2 tsp of the salt into the skin the night before if you can, or as far in advance of cooking as possible on the day.

2 If the meat has been refrigerated overnight, let it stand in an airy place at room temperature for a couple of hours before cooking. Preheat the oven to 220°C/425°F/Gas 7. Mix the black pepper, cayenne, paprika and oregano with the remaining 5ml/1 tsp salt and rub this mixture well into the meaty side of the meat.

3 Heat the oil or lard and gently fry the onion, celery and pepper for 5 minutes, adding the garlic for the last minute. Spread the vegetables over the inside of the meat. Roll up the meat skin-side out and tie with string in several places.

4 Roast the meat on a rack in a roasting pan. After 30 minutes reduce the heat to 180°C/350°F/Gas 4. Baste with the pan juices after 15 minutes and again every 20 minutes or so.

5 The overall roasting time should be about 2 hours. If the crackling doesn't go crisp and bubbly in the latter stages, raise the oven heat a little for the last 20–30 minutes. Allow the meat to rest in a warm place for 10–15 minutes before carving.

Roast Pork with Stuffing: Energy 436kcal/1826kJ; Protein 65.5g; Carbohydrate 1.9g, of which sugars 1.6g; Fat 18.5g, of which saturates 5.7g; Cholesterol 169mg; Calcium 30mg; Fibre 0.4g; Sodium 133mg.
Pork with Herbs and Spices: Energy 231kcal/970kJ; Protein 41.1g; Carbohydrate 3.8g, of which sugars 3.2g; Fat 4.5g, of which saturates 1.4g; Cholesterol 121mg; Calcium 16mg; Fibre 0.1g; Sodium 237mg.

Polish Bigos

Poland's deliciously spicy national casserole, *bigos*, is best made a day in advance.

Serves 8

15g/½oz/¼ cup dried
  mushrooms
225g/8oz/1 cup stoned prunes
225g/8oz lean boneless pork
225g/8oz lean boneless venison
225g/8oz chuck steak
225g/8oz kielbasa sausage (see
  Cook's Tip)

25g/1oz/¼ cup flour
2 onions, sliced
45ml/3 tbsp olive oil
60ml/4 tbsp dry Madeira
900g/2lb canned or bottled
  sauerkraut, drained and rinsed
4 tomatoes, peeled and chopped
4 cloves
5cm/2in cinnamon stick
1 bay leaf
2.5ml/½ tsp dill seeds
600ml/1 pint/2½ cups stock
salt and ground black pepper

1 Put the dried mushrooms and prunes in a bowl. Cover with boiling water and leave for 30 minutes, then drain well. Cut the pork, venison, chuck steak and *kielbasa* sausage into 2.5cm/1in cubes, then toss together in the flour. Gently fry the onions in the oil for 10 minutes. Remove.

2 Brown the meat in the pan in several batches; remove and set aside. Add the Madeira and simmer for 2–3 minutes, stirring.

3 Return the meat to the pan with the onion, sauerkraut, tomatoes, cloves, cinnamon, bay leaf, dill seeds, mushrooms and prunes. Pour in the stock and season with salt and pepper.

4 Bring to the boil, cover and simmer gently for 1¾–2 hours, or until the meat is very tender. Uncover for the last 20 minutes to let the liquid evaporate, as the stew should be thick.

5 Sprinkle with chopped parsley. Serve immediately.

> **Cook's Tip**
> Kielbasa is a garlic-flavoured pork and beef sausage, but any similar type of continental sausage can be used. Use dried porcini mushrooms, if possible.

Paprika Pork with Sauerkraut

The presence of sauerkraut and mustard in this recipe suggests a central European origin, but the addition of chillies gives it a more southern flavour.

Serves 4

450g/1lb lean pork or veal, diced
60ml/4 tbsp vegetable oil or
  melted lard
2.5ml/½ tsp paprika

400g/14oz canned or bottled
  sauerkraut, drained and
  rinsed
2 fresh red chillies
90ml/6 tbsp pork stock
salt and ground black pepper
50ml/2fl oz/¼ cup sour cream
coarse grain mustard, paprika
  and fresh sage leaves,
  to garnish
crusty bread, to serve

1 In a heavy-based frying pan cook the pork or veal in the oil until browned on all sides.

2 Add the paprika and sauerkraut. Stir well and transfer to a flameproof casserole.

3 Halve the chillies and remove the seeds before burying the chillies in the middle of the casserole.

4 Add the stock to the casserole. Cover the dish tightly and cook over a gentle heat for 1–1½ hours, stirring occasionally to prevent it sticking.

5 Remove the chillies if you wish, and season to taste with salt and pepper before serving. Spoon on the sour cream and spoonfuls of mustard, sprinkle with paprika and garnish with sage leaves. Serve with crusty bread.

> **Cook's Tip**
> Sauerkraut, or shredded fermented cabbage, is a signature ingredient in the cuisines of Germany, Poland and other central European countries. It is rich in Vitamin C and an extremely healthy food, available ready-made from supermarkets and delicatessens in jars, cans and packets.

Polish Bigos: Energy 327kcal/1367kJ; Protein 24.5g; Carbohydrate 21.7g, of which sugars 15.4g; Fat 15.6g, of which saturates 5.1g; Cholesterol 59mg; Calcium 104mg; Fibre 5.4g; Sodium 954mg.
Pork with Sauerkraut: Energy 533kcal/2248kJ; Protein 50.1g; Carbohydrate 60.2g, of which sugars 17.8g; Fat 11.9g, of which saturates 3.3g; Cholesterol 110mg; Calcium 127mg; Fibre 10.7g; Sodium 659mg.

Spicy Stuffed Onions with Harissa

This is ideal comfort food for cold winter evenings, served with buttered cabbage and rice or bread.

Serves 8
8 large onions, peeled
60ml/4 tbsp olive oil
2.5ml/½ tsp ground allspice
50g/2oz pancetta, chopped
250g/9oz minced (ground) pork
115g/4oz/2 cups breadcrumbs
45ml/3 tbsp chopped parsley
15ml/1 tbsp chopped oregano
1.5ml/¼ tsp ground cinnamon

75ml/5 tbsp water
25g/1oz/2 tbsp butter

For the tomato sauce
30ml/2 tbsp olive oil
1 garlic clove, finely chopped
2.5ml/½ tsp ground allspice
400g/14oz can chopped tomatoes
small piece of cinnamon stick
1 fresh bay leaf
30ml/2 tbsp chopped oregano
30ml/2 tbsp double (heavy) cream
1.5–2.5ml/¼–½ tsp harissa
pinch of brown sugar (optional)
salt and ground black pepper

1 Place the onions in a pan, cover with water and bring to the boil. Simmer for 10–15 minutes, drain and cool. Cut a small cap off the top of each, then hollow out, leaving 2–3 layers. Place in an ovenproof dish. Chop the flesh and set aside 15ml/3 tbsp. Heat 30ml/2 tbsp of the oil and cook the chopped onion until browned. Add the allspice and cook for 1 minute. Remove and set aside. Add the pancetta and pork and brown lightly.

2 Preheat the oven to 190°C/375°F/Gas 5. Place 75g/3oz/1½ cups of the breadcrumbs in a bowl and add the cooked onions, pork, half the parsley, oregano and cinnamon. Season and mix. Fill the onions with the stuffing. Spoon the water around them and dot with butter. Cover with foil and bake for 30 minutes.

3 To make the sauce, heat the oil and cook the reserved onion and garlic. Add the allspice, tomatoes, cinnamon stick, bay leaf and oregano. Cook, uncovered, for 15–20 minutes. Remove the cinnamon and bay leaf and process the sauce until smooth. Add the cream, seasoning, harissa and sugar to taste and pour over the onions. Cover and bake for 20–25 minutes. Sprinkle the remaining breadcrumbs and parsley over the onions, then drizzle with the remaining oil. Bake for a further 15–20 minutes, until the topping is browned and crisp. Serve immediately.

Pork Belly with Five Spices

Although five-spice powder is a Chinese blend, it has been adopted by Thai cuisine, in which a balance of the five flavours is also important. The Chinese influence on Thai cuisine stems from the early years of its history, when colonists from southern China settled in the country, bringing with them dishes like this. Thai cooks have also been influenced by Indian curries, and have provided their own unique imprint.

Serves 4
1 large bunch fresh coriander (cilantro) with roots
30ml/2 tbsp vegetable oil
1 garlic clove, crushed
30ml/2 tbsp Chinese five-spice powder
500g/1¼lb pork belly, cut into 2.5cm/1in pieces
400g/14oz can chopped tomatoes
150ml/¼ pint/⅔ cup hot water
30ml/2 tbsp dark soy sauce
45ml/3 tbsp nam pla
30ml/2 tbsp sugar
1 lime, halved

1 Cut off the coriander roots. Chop five of them finely and freeze the remainder for another occasion. Chop the coriander stalks and leaves and set them aside. Keep the roots separate from the stalks and leaves.

2 Heat the oil in a large pan and cook the garlic until golden brown. Stirring constantly, add the chopped coriander roots and then the five-spice powder.

3 Add the pork and stir-fry until the meat is thoroughly coated in spices and has browned. Stir in the tomatoes and hot water. Bring to the boil, then stir in the soy sauce, nam pla and sugar.

4 Reduce the heat, cover the pan and simmer for 30 minutes. Stir in the chopped coriander stalks and leaves, squeeze over the lime juice and serve.

> **Cook's Tip**
> Make sure that you buy Chinese five-spice powder, as the Indian variety is made up from quite different spices.

Aromatic Peppery Pork Broth

This peppery broth is a favourite at late-night hawker stalls in Singapore, where it is particularly popular with the older folk, who sip it when they gather for a chat. The pork is dipped into soy sauce infused with chillies.

Serves 4–6

500g/1¼lb meaty pork ribs, trimmed and cut into 5cm/2in lengths
225g/8oz pork loin
8 garlic cloves, bruised
2 cinnamon sticks
5 star anise
120ml/4fl oz/½ cup light soy sauce

50ml/2fl oz/¼ cup dark soy sauce
15ml/1 tbsp sugar
salt and ground black pepper
steamed rice, to serve

For the dipping sauce
120ml/4fl oz/½ cup light soy sauce
2 red chillies, seeded and finely chopped

For the spice bag
6 cloves
15ml/1 tbsp dried orange peel
5ml/1 tsp black peppercorns
5ml/1 tsp coriander seeds
5ml/1 tsp fennel seeds
a piece of muslin (cheesecloth) to hold the spices

1 To make the dipping sauce, stir the soy sauce and chillies together in a small bowl and set aside. To make the spice bag, lay the piece of muslin flat and place all the spices in the centre. Gather up the edges and tie together to form a bag.

2 Put the pork ribs and loin into a deep pan. Add the garlic, cinnamon sticks, star anise and spice bag. Pour in 2.5 litres/ 4½ pints/10 cups water and bring to the boil.

3 Skim off any fat from the surface, then stir in the soy sauces and sugar. Reduce the heat and simmer, partially covered, for about 2 hours, until the pork is almost falling off the bones. Season to taste with salt and lots of black pepper.

4 Remove the loin from the broth and cut it into bitesize pieces. Divide the meat and ribs among four to six bowls and ladle the steaming broth over the top. Serve with the soy and chilli sauce, as a dip for the pieces of pork, and steamed rice.

Singapore Spiced Pork

Traditionally made with offal, this curry represents a mix of Malay and Portuguese culinary traditions. Roasting the whole spices before grinding gives them a much fuller, richer flavour. If you are not a fan of offal, use a lean cut of pork from the hind leg.

Serves 4

1kg/2¼lb mixed pork offal (liver, lungs, intestines and heart), cleaned and trimmed
30ml/2 tbsp vegetable oil

50g/2oz fresh root ginger, peeled and shredded
15–30ml/1–2 tbsp white wine vinegar or rice vinegar
salt
bread or steamed rice, to serve

For the spice paste
8 shallots, chopped
4 garlic cloves, chopped
25g/1oz fresh root ginger, peeled and chopped
30ml/2 tbsp coriander seeds
10ml/2 tsp cumin seeds
10ml/2 tsp fennel seeds
10ml/2 tsp black peppercorns
5ml/1 tsp ground turmeric

1 First make the spice paste. Using a mortar and pestle or food processor, grind the shallots, garlic and ginger to a paste. In a heavy pan, dry-roast the coriander, cumin and fennel seeds with the peppercorns until they emit a nutty aroma. Grind the roasted spices to a powder and stir them into the spice paste with the ground turmeric.

2 Put the offal, except for the liver, into a pan and cover with water. Bring to the boil, reduce the heat and cook for 40 minutes. Add the liver and cook for a further 5 minutes, until all the offal is tender. Drain the offal but reserve the cooking broth. Cut the offal into bitesize pieces.

3 Heat the oil in a wok or earthenware pot. Stir in the ginger and fry until crisp. Lift the ginger out and set aside. Stir the spice paste into the oil and fry until fragrant.

4 Add the offal to the spice mix and toss it to brown lightly. Stir in the vinegar over a high heat and season. Stir in half the crispy, fried ginger and sprinkle the rest over the top. Serve hot with fresh, crusty bread or steamed rice.

Aromatic Peppery Pork Broth: Energy 49Kcal/206kJ; Protein 8.1g; Carbohydrate 0.8g, of which sugars 0.8g; Fat 1.5g, of which saturates 0.5g; Cholesterol 24mg; Calcium 3mg; Fibre 0g; Sodium 145mg.
Singapore Spiced Pork: Energy 444Kcal/1858kJ; Protein 53.6g; Carbohydrate 7.2g, of which sugars 1.4g; Fat 13.3g, of which saturates 5.9g; Cholesterol 650mg; Calcium 21mg; Fibre 0.4g; Sodium 218mg.

Curried Pork with Pickled Garlic

This very rich pork curry from Thailand is best accompanied by lots of plain rice and perhaps a light vegetable dish. The quantities given in this recipe are for two people, but it could serve four if eaten with a vegetable curry as well.

Serves 2
130g/4½oz lean pork steaks
30ml/2 tbsp vegetable oil
1 garlic clove, crushed
15ml/1 tbsp Thai red curry paste
130ml/4½fl oz/generous ½ cup coconut cream
2.5cm/1in piece fresh root ginger, finely chopped
30ml/2 tbsp vegetable or chicken stock
30ml/2 tbsp nam pla
5ml/1 tsp sugar
2.5ml/½ tsp ground turmeric
10ml/2 tsp lemon juice
4 pickled garlic cloves, finely chopped
strips of lemon and lime rind, to garnish

1 Place the pork steaks in the freezer for 30–40 minutes, to firm up the meat and make it easier to cut thinly. Using a very sharp knife, cut the meat into fine slivers, trimming off any excess fat.

2 Heat the oil in a wok or large, heavy frying pan and cook the garlic over a low to medium heat until golden brown. Do not let it burn. Add the curry paste and stir it in well.

3 Add the coconut cream and stir until the liquid begins to reduce and thicken. Stir in the pork. Cook for 2 minutes more, until the pork is cooked through.

4 Add the ginger, stock, nam pla, sugar and turmeric, stirring constantly, then add the lemon juice and pickled garlic. Spoon into bowls, garnish with strips of rind, and serve.

> **Cook's Tip**
> Asian stores sell pickled garlic, and it is well worth investing in a jar, as the taste is sweet and delicious. It can be used in many dishes and eaten as a relish.

Ginger- and Garlic-infused Pork Stir-fry

The combination of moist, juicy pork and mushrooms, crisp green mangetout and fragrant basil with the zestiness of ginger and garlic in this stir-fry is absolutely delicious. Served with simple steamed jasmine rice, it is a perfect, quickly made dish for supper during the week.

Serves 4
500g/1½lb pork fillet (tenderloin)
40g/1½oz cornflour (cornstarch)
15ml/1 tbsp sunflower oil
10ml/2 tsp sesame oil
15ml/1 tbsp very finely shredded fresh root ginger
3 garlic cloves, thinly sliced
200g/7oz mangetout (snow peas), halved lengthways
300g/11oz/generous 4 cups mixed mushrooms, such as shiitake, button (white) or oyster, sliced if large
120ml/4fl oz/½ cup Chinese cooking wine
45ml/3 tbsp soy sauce
a small handful of fresh basil leaves
salt and ground black pepper
steamed jasmine rice, to serve

1 Trim any fat off the pork fillet and slice it thinly. Place the cornflour in a strong plastic bag. Season well with salt and black pepper and add the sliced pork. Shake the bag to coat the pork in flour and then remove the pork and shake off any excess flour. Set aside.

2 Put the sunflower oil and sesame oil in a wok and place over a high heat. Add the ginger and garlic and cook for 30 seconds, stirring constantly so that they do not burn.

3 Add the pork and cook over a high heat for about 5 minutes, stirring often, until the pieces are sealed and lightly browned.

4 Add the mangetout and mushrooms to the wok and stir-fry for 2–3 minutes. Add the Chinese cooking wine and soy sauce, stir-fry for 2–3 minutes and remove from the heat.

5 Just before serving, stir the basil leaves into the pork. Serve with steamed jasmine rice.

Braised Pork with Spices

Pork belly becomes meltingly tender in this slow-braised dish flavoured with orange, cinnamon, star anise and ginger. Serve it simply with plain rice and some steamed Asian greens.

Serves 4

800g/1¾lb pork belly, trimmed and cut into 12 pieces
400ml/14fl oz/1⅔ cups beef stock
75ml/5 tbsp soy sauce
finely grated zest and juice of 1 large orange
15ml/1 tbsp finely shredded fresh root ginger
2 garlic cloves, sliced
15ml/1 tbsp hot chilli powder
15ml/1 tbsp dark muscovado (molasses) sugar
3 cinnamon sticks
3 cloves
10 black peppercorns
2–3 star anise
steamed greens and plain rice, to serve

1 Place the pork in a wok and pour over water to cover. Bring the water to the boil. Cover, reduce the heat and cook gently for 30 minutes. Drain the pork and return to the wok with the stock, soy sauce, orange zest and juice, ginger, garlic, chilli powder, muscovado sugar, cinnamon sticks, cloves, peppercorns and star anise.

2 Pour over water to just cover the pork belly pieces and cook over a high heat until the mixture comes to a boil.

3 Cover the wok tightly with a lid, then reduce the heat to low and cook gently for 1½ hours, stirring occasionally. (Check the pork occasionally during cooking to ensure it doesn't stick to the base of the wok.)

4 Uncover the wok and simmer for 30 minutes, stirring occasionally until the meat is very tender. Serve with steamed greens and rice.

Cook's Tip

Any type of Asian greens will go well with this dish. Try pak choi (bok choy), choi sum or Chinese broccoli.

Spicy Sausage and Bean Casserole

Bean stews made with spicy cured sausage are popular in Turkey. For this version, you can use any Turkish, Greek or Italian spicy sausage. In the Aegean region, meaty black-eyed beans are used, but any dried beans or chickpeas may be substituted. Acccompany the dish with a salad with hot green peppers and parsley, or pickled vegetables.

Serves 4–6

175g/6oz/scant 1 cup dried black-eyed beans (peas), soaked overnight in cold water
30ml/2 tbsp ghee or 15ml/1 tbsp each olive oil and butter
1 large onion, cut in half and sliced lengthways
2–3 garlic cloves, roughly chopped and bruised
5ml/1 tsp cumin seeds
5–10ml/1–2 tsp coriander seeds
5ml/1 tsp fennel seeds
5–10ml/1–2 tsp sugar or clear honey
1 spicy cured sausage, about 25cm/10in long, sliced
150ml/¼ pint/⅔ cup white wine
400g/14oz can tomatoes
1 bunch of fresh flat leaf parsley, roughly chopped
salt and ground black pepper

1 Drain the beans, tip them into a pan and fill the pan with plenty of cold water. Bring to the boil and boil for 1 minute, then lower the heat and partially cover the pan. Simmer the beans for about 25 minutes, or until they are *al dente*. Drain, rinse well under running water and remove any loose skins.

2 Preheat the oven to 180°C/350°F/Gas 4. Melt the ghee in a heavy pan or flameproof earthenware pot. Stir in the onion, garlic and spices and fry until the onion begins to colour.

3 Stir in the sugar or honey, toss in the spicy sausage and cook until it begins to brown.

4 Add the beans, followed by the wine. Cook until the wine bubbles up, then lower the heat and add the tomatoes. Stir in half the chopped parsley and season with salt and pepper.

5 Cover the dish and transfer it to the preheated oven. Bake for about 40 minutes. Before serving, taste for seasoning and sprinkle with the remaining parsley.

Braised Pork with Spices: Energy 543kcal/2260kJ; Protein 38.9g; Carbohydrate 6.6g, of which sugars 6.4g; Fat 40.4g, of which saturates 14.6g; Cholesterol 142mg; Calcium 19mg; Fibre 0g; Sodium 1475mg.
Spicy Sausage and Bean: Energy 382kcal/1594kJ; Protein 18g; Carbohydrate 20g, of which sugars 6.7g; Fat 24.4g, of which saturates 10g; Cholesterol 52mg; Calcium 55mg; Fibre 6g; Sodium 944mg.

Paprika Pork with Fennel and Caraway

Fennel seeds have a cool aniseed flavour that always tastes very good with pork, and combined with caraway seeds they add an aromatic depth to this central European dish.

Serves 4

15ml/1 tbsp olive oil
4 boneless pork steaks
1 large onion, thinly sliced
400g/14oz can chopped tomatoes
5ml/1 tsp fennel seeds, lightly crushed
2.5ml/½ tsp caraway seeds, lightly crushed
15ml/1 tbsp paprika
30ml/2 tbsp sour cream
salt and ground black pepper
paprika, to garnish
buttered noodles and poppy seeds, to serve

1 Heat the oil in a large frying pan. Add the pork steaks and cook over a high heat until the meat is sealed and brown on both sides. Lift the steaks out of the pan and reserve them on a plate.

2 Add the onion to the oil remaining in the pan. Cook for 10 minutes, until soft and golden. Stir in the tomatoes, fennel, caraway seeds and paprika.

3 Return the pork to the pan. Lower the heat, cover the pan and leave to simmer gently for 20–30 minutes until the pork steaks are tender.

4 Season the sauce to taste with salt and pepper. Lightly swirl in the sour cream and sprinkle with a little paprika.

5 Serve immediately with noodles, tossed in butter and sprinkled with poppy seeds.

> **Cook's Tip**
> *Always buy good-quality paprika and replace it regularly as it loses its distinctive flavour very quickly.*

Chinese Marinated Pork

Marinated pork, roasted and glazed with honey, is a staple of Chinese cuisine. It is irresistible on its own and can also be used as the basis for salads or stir-fries.

Serves 6

15ml/1 tbsp vegetable oil
15ml/1 tbsp hoisin sauce
15ml/1 tbsp yellow bean sauce
1.5ml/¼ tsp Chinese five-spice powder
2.5ml/½ tsp cornflour (cornstarch)
15ml/1 tbsp caster (superfine) sugar
1.5ml/¼ tsp salt
1.5ml/¼ tsp ground white pepper
450g/1lb pork fillet (tenderloin), trimmed
10ml/2 tsp clear honey
shredded spring onion (scallion), to garnish
plain boiled rice, to serve

1 Mix the oil, hoisin and yellow bean sauces, Chinese five-spice powder, cornflour, sugar and seasoning in a shallow dish. Add the pork and coat it with the mixture. Cover and chill for 4 hours or overnight.

2 Preheat the oven to 190°C/375°F/Gas 5. Drain the pork and place it on a wire rack over a deep roasting pan. Roast for 40 minutes, turning the pork over from time to time.

3 Check that the pork is cooked by inserting a skewer or fork into the centre of the meat; the juices should run clear. If they are still tinged with pink, roast the pork for 5–10 minutes more and check it again.

4 Remove the pork from the oven and brush it with the honey. Allow to cool for 10 minutes before cutting it across into thin slices. Garnish with spring onion and serve hot or cold with rice.

> **Cook's Tip**
> *In China this marinated pork is used in small amounts to add a flavoursome accent to other dishes. A few thin slices can be added to dishes such as fried rice and stir-fries.*

Casseroled Pig's Feet with Lemon Grass, Ginger and Chilli

The Vietnamese and Cambodians cook every part of the pig, including cuts such as the feet, hocks and shanks, which are now largely ignored in the West but give great richness to slow-cooked dishes. In this recipe, the pig's feet are stewed slowly to give a rich and velvety dish, best served with chunks of bread to mop up the sauce.

Serves 4
30ml/2 tbsp sugar
1 litre/1¾ pints/4 cups pork
    stock or water
30ml/2 tbsp nuoc mam *or*
    tuk trey
30ml/2 tbsp soy sauce
900g/2lb pig's feet, cleaned
4 spring onions (scallions),
    trimmed, halved and
    bruised
2 lemon grass stalks, trimmed,
    halved and bruised
50g/2oz fresh root ginger,
    peeled and sliced
2 garlic cloves, crushed
2 dried red chillies
4 star anise
4 eggs, hard-boiled and
    shelled
crusty bread or jasmine rice and
    stir-fried greens, to serve

1 In a heavy pan, melt the sugar with 15ml/1 tbsp water. When it turns golden, remove from the heat and stir in the stock, *nuoc mam* or *tuk trey* and the soy sauce.

2 Put the pan back over the heat and stir until the caramel dissolves in the other ingredients.

3 Add the pig's feet, spring onions, lemon grass, ginger, garlic, chillies and star anise. Bring to the boil, then reduce the heat and cover the pan. Simmer for 3–4 hours, until the meat is very tender and falling off the bones.

4 Skim any fat off the top and drop in the boiled eggs. Simmer uncovered for a further 10 minutes, turning the eggs over from time to time, so that they turn golden.

5 Serve the dish hot with fresh bread or jasmine rice and stir-fried greens.

Baked Cinnamon Meat Loaf

This Vietnamese meat loaf is usually served as a snack or light lunch, with a crusty baguette. Accompanied with either tart pickles or a crunchy salad, and splashed with piquant sauce, it is light and tasty.

Serves 4–6
30ml/2 tbsp nuoc mam
25ml/1½ tbsp ground cinnamon
10ml/2 tsp sugar
5ml/1 tsp ground black pepper
15ml/1 tbsp potato starch
450g/1lb lean minced (ground)
    pork
25g/1oz pork fat, very finely
    chopped
2–3 shallots, very finely chopped
oil, for greasing
chilli oil or nuoc cham,
    for drizzling
red chilli strips, to garnish
crusty bread or noodles,
    to serve

1 In a large bowl, mix together the *nuoc mam*, ground cinnamon, sugar and ground black pepper. Beat in the potato starch. Add the minced pork, the chopped pork fat, and the shallots to the bowl and mix thoroughly. Cover and put in the refrigerator for 3–4 hours.

2 Preheat the oven to 180°C/350°F/Gas 4. Lightly oil a baking tin (pan) and spread the pork mixture in it – it should feel springy from the potato starch.

3 Cover the baking tin with foil and bake for 35–40 minutes. For a brown and crunchy top, remove the foil for the last 10 minutes.

4 Turn the meat loaf out on to a board and slice it into strips. Drizzle the strips with chilli oil or *nuoc cham*, and serve them hot with bread or noodles.

Cook's Tips
• *Cut the meat loaf into wedges and take on a picnic to eat with bread and pickles or chutney.*
• *Fry slices of cold leftover meat loaf until browned and serve it with fried eggs.*

Spiced Pork Curry with Galangal, Turmeric and Fenugreek

This Thai curry can be made with butternut squash, pumpkin or winter melon. Flavoured with *kroeung*, galangal and turmeric, it is delicious served with rice and a fruit-based salad, or even just with chunks of fresh crusty bread to mop up the tasty sauce.

Serves 4–6

30ml/2 tbsp groundnut (peanut) oil
25g/1oz galangal, finely sliced
2 red Thai chillies, peeled, seeded and finely sliced
3 shallots, halved and finely sliced
30ml/2 tbsp kroeung

10ml/2 tsp ground turmeric
5ml/1 tsp ground fenugreek
10ml/2 tsp palm sugar (jaggery)
450g/1lb pork loin, cut into bitesize chunks
30ml/2 tbsp tuk prahoc
900ml/1½ pints/3¾ cups coconut milk
1 butternut squash, peeled, seeded and cut into bitesize chunks
4 kaffir lime leaves
sea salt and ground black pepper
1 small bunch fresh coriander (cilantro), coarsely chopped and 1 small bunch fresh mint, stalks removed, to garnish
plain rice or noodles and salad, to serve

1 Heat the oil in a heavy pan. Stir in the galangal, chillies and shallots and stir-fry until fragrant. Add the *kroeung* and stir-fry until it begins to colour. Add the turmeric, fenugreek and sugar.

2 Stir in the chunks of pork loin and stir-fry until golden brown on all sides. Stir in the *tuk prahoc* and pour in the coconut milk.

3 Bring to the boil, add the squash and the lime leaves, and reduce the heat. Cook gently, uncovered, for 15–20 minutes, until the squash and pork are tender and the sauce has reduced. Season to taste. Garnish the curry with the coriander and mint, and serve with rice or noodles and salad.

> **Cook's Tip**
> *Increase the number of chillies if you want a really hot curry.*

Vietnamese Caramelized Pork with Ginger and Garlic

This dish, which is cooked and served in lengths of bamboo, is inspired by the refined imperial dishes of Vietnam, in which this kind of creativity was of the essence. Serve it with plain noodles and a drizzle of *nuoc charm*.

Serves 4–6

1kg/2¼lb lean pork shoulder, cut into thin strips
2 large banana leaves

chopped fresh coriander (cilantro), to garnish

For the marinade
45ml/3 tbsp unrefined or muscovado (molasses) sugar
60ml/4 tbsp nuoc mam
3 shallots, finely chopped
6 spring onions (scallions), trimmed and finely chopped
1cm/½in fresh root ginger, peeled and finely chopped
1 green or red Thai chilli, seeded and finely chopped

1 To make the marinade, gently heat the sugar in a heavy pan with 15ml/1 tbsp water, stirring constantly until it begins to caramelize. Remove from the heat and stir in the remaining ingredients. Place the pork strips in a bowl and add the marinade. Using your fingers, toss the meat in the marinade, then cover and chill for 1–2 hours.

2 Line the bamboo halves with strips of banana leaf. Spoon in the pork, folding the edges over the top. Place the remaining bamboo halves on top to form tubes, and then tightly wrap a wide strip of banana leaf around the outside of each tube.

3 Tie the bamboo parcels with string and cook over a hot barbecue for about 20 minutes. Open up the parcels, garnish with coriander and serve with rice and *nuoc charm*.

> **Cook's Tip**
> *For this recipe, you will need two bamboo tubes, about 25cm/10in long, split in half lengthways and cleaned. You can find them in some Asian stores.*

Spiced Pork with Fenugreek: Energy 100Kcal/789kJ; Protein 18g; Carbohydrate 13.2g, of which sugars 12.2g; Fat 7g, of which saturates 2g; Cholesterol 47mg; Calcium 97mg; Fibre 1.7g; Sodium 220mg.
Caramelized Pork with Garlic: Energy 349Kcal/1469kJ; Protein 44g; Carbohydrate 17g, of which sugars 14g; Fat 12g, of which saturates 4g; Cholesterol 142mg; Calcium 71mg; Fibre 1.2g; Sodium 700mg.

Sichuan Pork with Ginger Relish

This dish works best when the pork ribs are grilled in large sections, then sliced to serve, this helps to keep the meat succulent.

Serves 4

4 pork rib slabs, each with 6 ribs, total weight about 2kg/4½lb
40g/1½oz/3 tbsp light muscovado sugar
3 garlic cloves, crushed
5cm/2in piece fresh root ginger, finely grated
10ml/2 tsp Sichuan peppercorns, finely crushed
2.5ml/½ tsp ground black pepper
5ml/1 tsp finely ground star anise
5ml/1 tsp Chinese five-spice powder

90ml/6 tbsp dark soy sauce
45ml/3 tbsp sunflower oil
15ml/1 tbsp sesame oil

For the relish
60ml/4 tbsp sunflower oil
300g/11oz shallots, chopped
9 garlic cloves, peeled and crushed
7.5cm/3in piece fresh root ginger, finely grated
60ml/4 tbsp seasoned rice wine vinegar
45ml/3 tbsp sweet chilli sauce
105ml/7 tbsp tomato ketchup
90ml/6 tbsp water
60ml/4 tbsp chopped fresh coriander (cilantro) leaves
salt

1 Lay the slabs of pork ribs in a large shallow dish. Mix the remaining ingredients in a bowl and pour the marinade over the ribs. Cover and chill overnight.

2 To make the relish, heat the oil in a heavy pan, add the shallots and cook gently for 5 minutes. Add the garlic and ginger and cook for 4 minutes. Increase the heat and add the rest of the ingredients except the coriander. Simmer for 10 minutes until thickened. Stir in the coriander. Chill until needed.

3 Remove the ribs from the refrigerator 1 hour before cooking. Remove the ribs from the marinade and pat them dry with kitchen paper. Pour the marinade into a pan. Bring it to the boil, then lower the heat and simmer for 3 minutes.

4 Grill (broil) the ribs, turning and basting occasionally with the marinade, until the meat is tender and golden brown all over. Cut into single ribs to serve, with the relish.

Sweet and Sour Pork with Ginger

Although very similar to the classic Chinese dish, this Korean version has a much subtler taste.

Serves 2

90g/3½oz/¾ cup potato starch
200g/7oz pork fillet (tenderloin)
5ml/1 tsp dark soy sauce
7.5ml/1½ tsp mirin or rice wine
15ml/1 tbsp finely grated root ginger
vegetable oil, for deep-frying
1 egg, beaten

For the sauce
1 dried shiitake mushroom, soaked in warm water for about 30 minutes until soft
½ onion
½ green (bell) pepper
¼ carrot
25g/1oz pineapple
15ml/1 tbsp vegetable oil
10ml/2 tsp dark soy sauce
60ml/4 tbsp caster (superfine) sugar
30ml/2 tbsp cider vinegar

1 Add the potato starch to 250ml/8fl oz/1 cup water and leave for 1 hour, during which the starch should sink to the bottom. Cut the pork into bitesize cubes and place in a bowl. Add the soy sauce, mirin or rice wine, and grated ginger for the marinade, and mix well. Leave to marinate for 20 minutes.

2 When the soaked shiitake mushroom for the sauce has reconstituted and become soft, drain and finely slice it, discarding the stem. Cut the onion, pepper and carrot into bitesize cubes. Finely chop the pineapple and set aside.

3 Drain the excess water from the top of the starch and water mixture. In a bowl combine the soaked starch with the beaten egg. Add the cubes of pork and coat them evenly in the batter.

4 Fill a wok one-third full of oil and heat over to 170°C/340°F. Add the battered pork and deep-fry for 1–2 minutes, or until golden brown. Remove and drain on kitchen paper.

5 To finish the sauce, coat a pan with the oil and place over high heat. Add the onion, pepper and carrot, and stir-fry to soften. Add 250ml/8fl oz/1 cup hot water, the soy sauce, sugar and vinegar, and simmer briefly. Add the mushroom and pineapple. Simmer for 1–2 minutes, then add the egg mixture to thicken. Dish the pork, pour the sauce over and serve.

Sichuan Pork with Relish: Energy 665kcal/2761kJ; Protein 46.6g; Carbohydrate 17g, of which sugars 14.8g; Fat 45.9g, of which saturates 14.2g; Cholesterol 155mg; Calcium 59mg; Fibre 1.4g; Sodium 1111mg.
Sweet and Sour Pork: Energy 727kcal/3035kJ; Protein 32.8g; Carbohydrate 76.5g, of which sugars 39.4g; Fat 32.8g, of which saturates 5.8g; Cholesterol 272mg; Calcium 85mg; Fibre 2.7g; Sodium 1048mg.

Cambodian Braised Pork with Ginger and Black Pepper

This Cambodian dish is quick, tasty and beautifully warming thanks to the ginger and black pepper in the sauce. It is sure to be a popular choice for a family meal.

Serves 4–6

1 litre/1¾ pints/4 cups pork stock or water
45ml/3 tbsp tuk trey
30ml/2 tbsp soy sauce
15ml/1 tbsp sugar
4 garlic cloves, crushed
40g/1½oz fresh root ginger, peeled and finely shredded
15ml/1 tbsp ground black pepper
675g/1½lb pork shoulder or rump, cut into bitesize cubes
steamed jasmine rice, crunchy salad and pickles or stir-fried greens, such as water spinach or yardlong beans, to serve

1 In a large heavy pan, bring the stock or water, tuk trey and soy sauce to the boil. Reduce the heat and stir in the sugar, garlic, ginger, black pepper and pork.

2 Cover the pan and simmer for about 1½ hours, until the pork is very tender and the liquid has reduced.

3 Serve the pork with steamed jasmine rice, drizzling the braising juices from the pan over it, and accompany the dish with a fresh crunchy salad, pickled vegetables or stir-fried greens, such as the delicious stir-fried water spinach with nuoc cham, or yardlong beans.

Cook's Tips
• Tuk trey is a Khmer marinade, consisting of nuoc mam (fish sauce), vinegar, lime juice, sugar and garlic. It is indispensable in Cambodian cookery.
• Yardlong beans, also known as snake or asparagus beans, are much used in stir-fries in South-east Asian cookery. They are at their best when young and tender. If they are not available, ordinary green beans are a good substitute.

Spicy Pork Stir-fry

This simple dish, called cheyuk bokum, is quick to prepare and makes thinly sliced pork fabulously spicy. The potent flavour of gochujang chilli paste predominates in the seasoning for the pork, and will set the tastebuds aflame. Serve this dish with a bowl of rice to help counterbalance its fiery chilli character.

Serves 2

400g/14oz pork shoulder
1 onion
½ carrot
2 spring onions (scallions)
15ml/1 tbsp vegetable oil
½ red chilli, finely sliced
½ green chilli, finely sliced
steamed rice and miso soup, to serve

For the seasoning
30ml/2 tbsp dark soy sauce
30ml/2 tbsp gochujang chilli paste
30ml/2 tbsp mirin or rice wine
15ml/1 tbsp Korean chilli powder
1 garlic clove, finely chopped
1 spring onion (scallion), finely chopped
15ml/1 tbsp grated fresh root ginger
15ml/1 tbsp sesame oil
30ml/2 tbsp sugar
ground black pepper

1 Freeze the pork shoulder for 30 minutes until it is firm, and then cut it with a very sharp knife into slices about 5mm/¼in thick. Cut the onion and carrot into thin strips, and roughly slice the spring onions lengthways.

2 To make the seasoning, combine the seasoning ingredients in a large bowl, mixing together thoroughly to form a paste. If the mixture is too dry, add a splash of water.

3 Heat a wok or large frying pan, and add the vegetable oil. Once the oil is smoking, add the pork, onion, carrot, spring onions and chillies. Stir-fry, keeping the ingredients moving all the time.

4 Once the pork has lightly browned add the seasoning, and thoroughly coat the meat and vegetables. Stir-fry for 2 minutes more, or until the pork is cooked through. Serve immediately with rice and a bowl of miso soup to help neutralize the spicy flavours of the dish.

Cambodian Braised Pepper Pork: Energy 147Kcal/619kJ; Protein 24g; Carbohydrate 2.7g, of which sugars 2.7g; Fat 4g, of which saturates 2g; Cholesterol 71mg; Calcium 11mg; Fibre 0.1g; Sodium 81mg.
Spicy Pork Stir-fry: Energy 430kcal/1799kJ; Protein 44.1g; Carbohydrate 21.3g, of which sugars 20.4g; Fat 19.2g, of which saturates 4.3g; Cholesterol 126mg; Calcium 44mg; Fibre 1.2g; Sodium 1216mg.

Five-spice Meatballs

In Vietnam a peanut dipping sauce is traditional with these meatballs. They are also good served with chopped coriander and lime.

Serves 4

10ml/2 tsp sesame oil
4 shallots, chopped
2 garlic cloves, finely chopped
450g/1lb/2 cups minced (ground) pork
30ml/2 tbsp nuoc mam
10ml/2 tsp five-spice powder
10ml/2 tsp sugar
115g/4oz/2 cups breadcrumbs or 30ml/2 tbsp potato starch
1 bunch fresh coriander (cilantro), stalks removed
salt and ground black pepper

For the sauce

10ml/2 tsp groundnut (peanut) oil
1 garlic clove, finely chopped
1 red chilli, seeded and chopped
30ml/2 tbsp roasted peanuts, finely chopped
15ml/1 tbsp nuoc mam
30ml/2 tbsp rice wine vinegar
30ml/2 tbsp hoisin sauce
60ml/4 tbsp coconut milk
100ml/3½fl oz/scant ½ cup water
5ml/1 tsp sugar

1 To make the sauce, heat the oil in a small wok or heavy pan, and stir in the garlic and chilli. When they begin to colour, add the peanuts. Stir-fry for a few minutes. Add the remaining ingredients, except the sugar, and boil for 1 minute. Adjust the sweetness and seasoning by adding sugar and salt, and set aside.

2 To make the meatballs, heat the oil in a wok or small pan and add the shallots and garlic. Stir-fry until golden, then leave to cool. Put the minced pork into a bowl, add the stir-fried shallots and garlic, and add the *nuoc mam*, five-spice powder and sugar. Season. Knead the mixture to combine, cover and chill for 2–3 hours or overnight.

3 Soak eight wooden skewers in water for 30 minutes. Add the breadcrumbs or potato starch to the mixture. Knead to bind. Divide the mixture into 20 and roll into balls. Thread on to the skewers. Cook either over the barbecue or under the grill (broiler), turning from time to time, until well browned.

4 Reheat the sauce. Arrange the meatballs on a serving dish with coriander leaves. Serve with the sauce.

Korean Pork with Chilli Sauce

This is a popular pork dish in Korea. Thinly sliced pork belly is griddled until crisp, leaving a smooth texture at the centre. The meat is then immersed in a salty sesame dip, before being wrapped in lettuce with a spoonful of red chilli paste to round off the combination of flavours.

Serves 3

675g/1½lb pork belly
2 round (butterhead) lettuces

For the dip

45ml/3 tbsp sesame oil
10ml/2 tsp salt
ground black pepper

For the sauce

45ml/3 tbsp gochujang chilli paste
75ml/5 tbsp doenjang soybean paste
2 garlic cloves, crushed
1 spring onion (scallion), finely chopped
5ml/1 tsp sesame oil

1 Freeze the pork belly for 30 minutes and then slice it very thinly, to about 3mm/⅛in thick.

2 To make the dip, combine the sesame oil, salt and pepper in a small bowl. To make the sauce, blend the chilli paste, *doenjang* soybean paste, garlic, spring onion and sesame oil.

3 Remove the outer leaves from the heads of lettuce, keeping them whole. Rinse and place in a serving dish.

4 Heat a griddle pan or heavy frying pan over high heat. Add the pork and cook until crisp and golden.

5 Serve the pork with the accompanying dishes of lettuce, sesame dip and chilli sauce. To eat, take a strip of pork and dip it into the sesame dip. Then place the meat in a lettuce leaf and add a small spoonful of the chilli sauce. Wrap the lettuce leaf into a parcel and eat in your hands.

> **Cook's Tip**
> You could ask the butcher to slice the pork thinly, or buy the meat pre-sliced at an Asian store.

Braised Spare Ribs with Black Pepper and Cloves

Choose really meaty ribs for this dish and trim off any excess fat before cooking, as the juices are turned into a delicious sauce.

Serves 6
25g/1oz/¼ cup plain (all-purpose) flour
5ml/1 tsp salt
5ml/1 tsp ground black pepper
1.6kg/3½lb pork spare ribs, cut into individual pieces
30ml/2 tbsp sunflower oil
1 onion, finely chopped
1 garlic clove, crushed
45ml/3 tbsp tomato purée (paste)
30ml/2 tbsp chilli sauce
30ml/2 tbsp red wine vinegar
pinch of ground cloves
600ml/1 pint/2½ cups beef stock
15ml/1 tbsp cornflour (cornstarch)
flat leaf parsley, to garnish
sauerkraut and crusty bread, to serve

1 Preheat the oven to 180°C/350°F/Gas 4. Combine the flour, salt and black pepper in a shallow dish. Add the ribs and toss to coat them in flour. Heat the oil in a large frying pan and cook the ribs, turning them until well browned. Transfer them to a roasting pan and sprinkle over the chopped onion.

2 Mix the garlic, tomato purée, chilli sauce, vinegar, cloves and stock. Pour over the ribs, then cover with foil. Roast for 1½ hours, or until tender, removing the foil for the last 30 minutes.

3 Tip the juices from the roasting pan into a small pan. Blend the cornflour with a little cold water and stir in. Bring the sauce to the boil, stirring, then simmer until thickened.

4 Arrange the ribs on a bed of sauerkraut, then pour over a little sauce. Serve the remaining sauce separately in a warmed jug. Garnish with parsley and serve with sauerkraut and bread.

> **Cook's Tip**
> If time allows, first marinate the ribs for 3–4 hours in sunflower oil mixed with red wine vinegar.

Vietnamese Stir-fried Pork Ribs

Adapted from the classic Chinese dish of sweet and sour spare ribs, the Vietnamese version includes basil leaves and *nuoc mam*, the fermented fish sauce. This is finger food, requiring finger bowls, and is perfect served with sticky rice and a salad. Look for ribs with lots of meat on them, and separate them into individual ribs if necessary.

Serves 4–6
45ml/3 tbsp hoisin sauce
45ml/3 tbsp nuoc mam
10ml/2 tsp Chinese five-spice powder
45ml/3 tbsp vegetable or sesame oil
900g/2lb pork ribs
3 garlic cloves, crushed
4cm/1½in fresh root ginger, peeled and grated
1 bunch fresh basil, stalks removed, leaves shredded

1 In a bowl, mix together the hoisin sauce, *nuoc mam* and five-spice powder with 15ml/1 tbsp of the oil.

2 Bring a large wok or pan of water to the boil, then add the pork ribs, bring back to the boil and blanch the meat for 10 minutes. Lift the pork ribs out with a slotted spoon and drain thoroughly, then set aside.

3 Heat the remaining oil in a clean wok. Add the crushed garlic and grated ginger and cook, stirring, until fragrant, then add the blanched pork ribs.

4 Stir-fry over a high heat for about 5 minutes, or until the ribs are well browned, then add the hoisin sauce mixture, turning the ribs over in the sauce so that each one is thoroughly coated.

5 Continue stir-frying for 10–15 minutes, or until there is almost no liquid in the wok and the ribs are caramelized and slightly blackened.

6 Add most of the shredded basil leaves and stir into the sauce. Sprinkle the remainder over and serve the ribs straight from the pan, offering dinner guests finger bowls and plenty of napkins to wipe sticky fingers.

Tortilla Pie with Chorizo

This is a popular Mexican breakfast dish. The fried tortilla strips stay crisp in the tomatillo, cream and cheese sauce.

Serves 6

30ml/2 tbsp vegetable oil
500g/1¼lb minced (ground) pork
3 garlic cloves, crushed
10ml/2 tsp dried oregano
5ml/1 tsp ground cinnamon
2.5ml/½ tsp ground cloves
2.5ml/½ tsp ground black pepper
30ml/2 tbsp dry sherry
5ml/1 tsp caster (superfine) sugar
5ml/1 tsp salt
12 corn tortillas

oil, for frying
350g/12oz/3 cups grated
  Monterey Jack or mild Cheddar
  cheese
300ml/½ pint/1¼ cups crème
  fraîche

For the tomatillo sauce
300g/11oz/scant 2 cups drained
  canned tomatillos
60ml/4 tbsp stock or water
2 fresh serrano chillies, seeded
  and roughly chopped
2 garlic cloves
small bunch of fresh coriander
  (cilantro)
120ml/4fl oz/½ cup sour cream

1 Preheat the oven to 180°C/350°F/Gas 4. Heat the oil in a large pan. Add the pork and garlic. Stir until the meat has browned, then stir in the oregano, cinnamon, cloves and pepper. Cook for 3–4 minutes more, stirring, then add the sherry, sugar and salt. Stir for 3–4 minutes until all the flavours are blended, then remove the pan from the heat.

2 Cut the tortillas into 2cm/¾in strips. Pour oil into a frying pan to a depth of 2cm/¾in and heat to 190°C/375°F. Fry the tortilla strips in batches until crisp and golden brown all over.

3 Spread half the pork mixture in a baking dish. Top with half the tortilla strips and grated cheese, then add dollops of crème fraîche. Repeat the layers. Bake for 20–25 minutes.

4 To make the sauce, put all the ingredients except the sour cream in a food processor. Reserve a little coriander. Process, scrape into a pan, bring to the boil, lower the heat and simmer for 5 minutes. Stir the cream into the sauce and season to taste. Pour over the bake and serve at once, sprinkled with coriander.

Pork on Lemon Grass Sticks

This simple recipe makes a substantial snack and is excellent as part of a buffet table. Using lemon grass sticks instead of skewers not only adds a subtle flavour but also makes a good talking point. Cook these appetizing pork sticks on a barbecue for the very best flavour.

Serves 4

300g/11oz minced (ground) pork
4 garlic cloves, crushed
4 fresh coriander (cilantro) roots,
  finely chopped
2.5ml/½ tsp sugar
15ml/1 tbsp soy sauce
salt and ground black pepper
8 × 10cm/4in lengths of lemon
  grass stalk
sweet chilli sauce, to serve

1 Place the minced pork, crushed garlic, chopped coriander root, sugar and soy sauce in a large bowl. Season with salt and pepper to taste and mix well.

2 Divide into eight portions and mould each one into a ball. It may help to dampen your hands before shaping the mixture to prevent it from sticking.

3 Stick a length of lemon grass halfway into each ball, then press the meat mixture around the lemon grass to make a shape like a chicken leg.

4 Prepare a barbecue or pre-heat a grill (broiler). Cook the pork sticks for 3–4 minutes on each side, until golden and cooked through. Serve with the chilli sauce for dipping.

> **Variation**
> *Slimmer versions of these pork sticks are perfect for parties. The quantities given above will be enough for 12 lemon grass sticks if you use the mixture sparingly.*

> **Cook's Tip**
> *Use the hardest part of the lemon grass stems, near the root.*

Tortilla Pie with Chorizo: Energy 874kcal/3636kJ; Protein 39.5g; Carbohydrate 40.5g, of which sugars 4.7g; Fat 60.9g, of which saturates 30.5g; Cholesterol 173mg; Calcium 565mg; Fibre 5.4g; Sodium 977mg.
Pork on Lemon Grass Sticks: Energy 132kcal/552kJ; Protein 14.7g; Carbohydrate 2g, of which sugars 1.6g; Fat 7.3g, of which saturates 2.7g; Cholesterol 50mg; Calcium 10mg; Fibre 0.2g; Sodium 317mg.

Venison in Guinness with Horseradish and Mustard Dumplings

Mustard, juniper berries and bay leaves combine with venison to create a casserole with a rich flavour and wonderful aroma.

Serves 6

15ml/1 tbsp olive oil
675g/1½lb stewing venison, cubed
3 onions, sliced
2 garlic cloves, crushed
15ml/1 tbsp plain (all-purpose) flour mixed with 5ml/1 tsp mustard powder
6 juniper berries, lightly crushed
2 bay leaves
400ml/14fl oz/1⅔ cups Guinness mixed with 10ml/2 tsp soft light brown sugar and 30ml/2 tbsp balsamic vinegar
salt and ground black pepper

For the dumplings

175g/6oz/1½ cups self-raising (self-rising) flour
5ml/1 tsp mustard powder
75g/3oz/generous ½ cup shredded beef suet (US chilled, grated shortening)
10ml/2 tsp horseradish sauce

1 Preheat the oven to 180°C/350°F/ gas 4. Heat the oil in a casserole and brown the meat in batches. Add the onions, with more oil, if necessary. Cook, stirring, for 5 minutes until soft. Add the garlic, then return the venison to the pan.

2 Sprinkle the flour and mustard over the venison and stir until the flour is absorbed. Add the juniper berries and bay leaves and gradually stir in the Guinness, sugar and vinegar. Add enough water to cover the meat. Season and bring to a simmer.

3 Cover and transfer the casserole to the oven and cook for 2–2½ hours, until the venison is tender. Stir the casserole occasionally and add a little more water, if necessary.

4 About 20 minutes before the end of the cooking time, make the dumplings. Sift the flour and mustard into a bowl. Season, and mix in the suet. Stir in the horseradish sauce and enough water to make a soft dough. With floured hands, form into six dumplings. Place these gently on top of the venison. Return the casserole to the oven and cook for 15 minutes more, until the dumplings are risen and cooked. Serve at once.

Aromatic Venison Casserole with Oranges and Allspice

Low in fat but high in flavour, venison is an excellent choice for healthy, yet rich, casseroles that make warming winter suppers. Cranberries and orange bring a festive fruitiness to this recipe, and the addition of allspice gives the sauce a complex, spicy depth of flavour. It is delicious served with small baked potatoes and steamed green vegetables.

Serves 4

30ml/2 tbsp olive oil
1 onion, chopped
2 celery sticks, sliced
10ml/2 tsp ground allspice
15ml/1 tbsp plain (all-purpose) flour
675g/1½lb stewing venison, cubed
225g/8oz cranberries
grated rind and juice of 1 orange
900ml/1½ pints/3¾ cups beef or venison stock
salt and ground black pepper

1 Heat the olive oil in a flameproof casserole. Add the onion and celery and cook for 5 minutes until softened.

2 Meanwhile, mix the ground allspice with the flour and either spread the mixture out on a large plate or place in a large plastic bag. Toss the venison in the flour mixture a few pieces at a time (to prevent them from becoming soggy) until all the meat is lightly coated.

3 When the onion and celery are softened, remove from the casserole using a slotted spoon and set aside. Add the venison pieces to the casserole in batches and cook until browned and sealed on all sides.

4 Add the cranberries, orange rind and juice to the casserole, pour in the beef or venison stock, and stir well. Return the vegetables and all the venison to the casserole and heat until simmering, then cover tightly and reduce the heat. Simmer, stirring occasionally, for 45 minutes, or until the meat is tender.

5 Season the venison casserole to taste with salt and pepper before serving.

Roast Rabbit with Three Mustards

In France rabbit and mustard are a popular combination. In this recipe each of the three different mustards adds a distinctive flavour to the dish. Rabbit, whether farmed or wild, is a lean and healthy meat, but take care not to overcook it as it dries out easily. You can either buy whole rabbits, asking the butcher to joint them for you, or buy prepared leg or loin portions in supermarkets.

Serves 4

15ml/1 tbsp Dijon mustard
15ml/1 tbsp tarragon mustard
15ml/1 tbsp wholegrain mustard
1.3–1.6kg/3–3½lb rabbit portions
1 large carrot, sliced
1 onion, sliced
30ml/2 tbsp chopped fresh tarragon
120ml/4fl oz/½ cup dry white wine
150ml/¼ pint/⅔ cup double (heavy) cream
salt and ground black pepper
fresh tarragon, to garnish

1 Preheat the oven to 200°C/400°F/Gas 6. Mix the mustards in a bowl and spread over the rabbit. Put the carrot and onion slices in a roasting pan and sprinkle the tarragon over. Pour in 120ml/4fl oz/½ cup of water, then arrange the meat on top.

2 Roast for 25–30 minutes, basting frequently with the juices, until the rabbit is tender. Remove the rabbit to a heated serving dish and keep warm. Using a slotted spoon, remove the carrot and onion slices from the roasting pan and discard.

3 Place the roasting pan on the hob and add the white wine. Boil to reduce by about two-thirds, then stir in the cream and allow to bubble up for a few minutes. Season with salt and pepper then pour over the rabbit and serve, garnished with fresh tarragon.

Variation
If the three different mustards are not available, just use one or two varieties, increasing the quantities of each accordingly. The flavour will not be quite as interesting, but the dish will still taste very good.

Spanish Venison with Chilli Sauce

Romesco is the Catalan word for the *ñora* chilli, which lends both its name and a spicy roundness to one of Spain's greatest sauces, from Tarragona. This version of fiery, garlicky romesco sauce is the ideal partner for venison chops.

Serves 4

4 venison chops, cut 2cm/¾in thick and about 175–200g/6–7oz each
30ml/2 tbsp olive oil
50g/2oz/4 tbsp butter
braised Savoy cabbage, to serve

For the romesco sauce
3 ñora chillies and 1 hot dried chilli, slit and seeds removed
25g/1oz/¼ cup almonds
150ml/¼ pint/⅔ cup olive oil
1 slice stale bread, crusts removed
3 garlic cloves, chopped
3 tomatoes, peeled, seeded and roughly chopped
60ml/4 tbsp sherry vinegar
60ml/4 tbsp red wine vinegar
salt and ground black pepper

1 Make the romesco sauce first. Soak the chillies in warm water for 30 minutes, dry on kitchen paper and chop finely.

2 Dry-fry the almonds in a frying pan over a medium heat, shaking the pan occasionally, until the nuts are toasted evenly. Transfer the nuts to a food processor or blender.

3 Add 45ml/3 tbsp oil to the frying pan and fry the bread slice until golden on both sides. Lift out and drain on kitchen paper. Tear the bread and add to the food processor or blender. Fry the chopped garlic in the oil remaining in the pan, then add with the oil into the processor. Add the soaked chillies and tomatoes. Blend the mixture to form a smooth paste.

4 With the motor running, gradually add the remaining olive oil and then the sherry and wine vinegars. When the sauce is well blended, scrape it into a bowl and season to taste. Cover with clear film (plastic wrap) and chill for 2 hours.

5 Season the chops with pepper. Heat the olive oil and butter in a heavy frying pan and fry the chops for about 5 minutes each side until cooked through. Heat the sauce gently in a pan. Serve the sauce with the chops and braised cabbage.

Roast Rabbit with Mustards: Energy 531kcal/2209kJ; Protein 31.8g; Carbohydrate 21.3g, of which sugars 8.7g; Fat 35g, of which saturates 14.6g; Cholesterol 187mg; Calcium 48mg; Fibre 0.6g; Sodium 247mg.
Spanish Venison with Chilli Sauce: Energy 415kcal/1741kJ; Protein 46.9g; Carbohydrate 6.2g, of which sugars 2.8g; Fat 24g, of which saturates 9.3g; Cholesterol 127mg; Calcium 40mg; Fibre 1.3g; Sodium 229mg.

Braised Rabbit with Paprika

This is an updated version of a classic Spanish rabbit stew. Its Spanish name, *salmorejo*, refers to the traditional ingredients – pounded garlic, bread and vinegar; the wine is a modern addition.

Serves 4
675g/1½lb rabbit, jointed
300ml/½ pint/1¼ cups dry white wine
15ml/1 tbsp sherry vinegar
several oregano sprigs
2 bay leaves
30ml/2 tbsp plain (all-purpose) flour
90ml/6 tbsp olive oil
175g/6oz baby (pearl) onions, peeled and left whole
4 garlic cloves, sliced
150ml/¼ pint/⅔ cup chicken stock
1 dried chilli, seeded and finely chopped
10ml/2 tsp paprika
salt and ground black pepper

1 Put the rabbit in a bowl. Add the wine, vinegar, oregano and bay leaves and toss together. Marinate for several hours or overnight in the refrigerator. Drain the rabbit, reserving the marinade, and pat the pieces dry with kitchen paper. Season the flour and use to dust the marinated rabbit.

2 Heat the oil in a large, wide flameproof casserole or frying pan. Fry the rabbit pieces until golden on all sides, then remove them and set aside. Fry the onions until they are beginning to colour, then reserve on a separate plate.

3 Add the garlic to the pan and fry, then add the strained marinade, with the chicken stock, chilli and paprika. Return the rabbit to the pan with the onions. Bring to a simmer, then cover and simmer gently for about 45 minutes until the rabbit is tender. Check the seasoning, adding more vinegar and paprika if necessary, and serve.

> **Cook's Tip**
> If wished, rather than cooking on the stove, transfer the stew to an ovenproof dish and bake in the oven at 180°C/350°F/Gas 4 for about 50 minutes.

Spicy Rabbit Casserole

In this Greek dish, the multi-layered sweet and savoury flavours combine with warm spices. Serve the casserole with a green salad to counterbalance its richness.

Serves 4
1 glass red wine, about 175ml/ 6fl oz/¾ cup
60ml/4 tbsp red wine vinegar
1 rabbit, jointed
2 bay leaves, crushed
45ml/3 tbsp plain (all-purpose) flour
90–105ml/6–7 tbsp olive oil
2 carrots, cut in thick batons, about 10cm/4in in length
2 celery sticks, sliced
3 garlic cloves, halved lengthways
1 cinnamon stick
3–4 whole allspice
1–2 fresh rosemary sprigs
15ml/1 tbsp tomato purée (paste) diluted in 300ml/ ½ pint/1¼ cups water
675g/1½lb shallots, peeled
15ml/1 tbsp demerara (raw) sugar
salt and ground black pepper

1 Mix the wine and vinegar in a dish large enough to hold the rabbit. Add the bay leaves and rabbit, turning to coat them in the mixture. Marinate for 4–6 hours, preferably overnight, turning the pieces over at least once. Lift the rabbit out of the marinade and pat dry with paper towels. Reserve the marinade. Coat the pieces of rabbit lightly with the flour.

2 Heat half of the oil in a large heavy frying pan and add the rabbit. Fry, turning the pieces, until they are lightly browned on both sides, then place them in a flameproof casserole. Preheat the oven to 160°C/325°F/Gas 3. Add the carrots and celery to the oil remaining in the frying pan.

3 Sauté the vegetables and garlic over a gentle heat for about 3 minutes. Add to the casserole. Pour in the marinade and bring to the boil. Add the spices, rosemary and diluted tomato purée, cover and cook in the oven for 1 hour.

4 Heat the remaining oil in the pan and fry the shallots until light golden. Sprinkle the demerara sugar over them, shake, then let them caramelize for 5–6 minutes more. Set aside. When the rabbit is cooked spread the onions on top and add hot water to almost cover. Cover and cook for 1 more hour. Serve.

Braised Rabbit with Paprika: Energy 311kcal/1294kJ; Protein 23.2g; Carbohydrate 9.5g, of which sugars 2.6g; Fat 20.4g, of which saturates 4.1g; Cholesterol 83mg; Calcium 65mg; Fibre 0.9g; Sodium 52mg.
Spicy Rabbit Casserole: Energy 456kcal/1905kJ; Protein 39.4g; Carbohydrate 28g, of which sugars 23.9g; Fat 21.5g, of which saturates 5g; Cholesterol 139mg; Calcium 200mg; Fibre 4.2g; Sodium 110mg.

Fruit and Nut Couscous with Spices

In Morocco this dish of steamed couscous with dried fruit and nuts, topped with sugar and cinnamon, is served on special celebrations. It is often presented as a course on its own, just before the dessert, but it is delicious served with spicy tagines or grilled or roasted meat.

Serves 6
500g/1¼lb medium couscous
600ml/1 pint/2½ cups warm
   water
5ml/1 tsp salt
pinch of saffron threads
45ml/3 tbsp sunflower oil
30ml/2 tbsp olive oil
a little butter
115g/4oz/½ cup dried apricots,
   cut into slivers
75g/3oz/½ cup dried dates,
   chopped
75g/3oz/generous ½ cup
   seedless raisins
115g/4oz/1 cup blanched
   almonds, cut into slivers
75g/3oz/¾ cup pistachio nuts
10ml/2 tsp ground cinnamon
45ml/3 tbsp sugar

1 Preheat the oven to 180°C/350°F/Gas 4. Put the couscous in a bowl. Mix the water, salt and saffron and pour the mixture over the couscous, stirring. Leave to stand for 10 minutes, or until the grains have plumped up and become tender. Add the sunflower oil and, using your fingers, rub it evenly through the couscous grains.

2 In a heavy pan, heat the olive oil and butter and stir in the apricots, dates, raisins, most of the almonds (reserving some to garnish the dish) and the pistachio nuts. Cook over a gentle heat until the raisins plump up, then tip the nuts and fruit into the couscous and toss together.

3 Tip the couscous into an ovenproof dish and cover with foil. Place in the oven for about 20 minutes, until heated through. Meanwhile, toast the reserved slivered almonds.

4 Pile the hot couscous in a mound on a large warmed serving dish and sprinkle with the cinnamon and sugar – these are traditionally added in vertical stripes down the mound of couscous. Sprinkle the toasted almonds over the top of the dish and serve immediately.

Aromatic Sweet Potato Tagine

The vegetables in this succulent, syrupy tagine are chosen for their sweetness and should be slightly caramelized. They are at their best when served with grilled meats, couscous or with lots of warm, crusty bread, accompanied by a leafy, herb-filled salad.

Serves 4–6
45ml/3 tbsp olive oil
a little butter
25–30 pearl or button onions,
   blanched and peeled
900g/2lb sweet potatoes, peeled
   and cut into bitesize chunks
2–3 carrots, cut into bitesize
   chunks
150g/5oz/generous ½ cup
   ready-to-eat pitted prunes
5ml/1 tsp ground cinnamon
2.5ml/½ tsp ground ginger
10ml/2 tsp clear honey
450ml/¾ pint/scant 2 cups
   vegetable stock
small bunch of fresh coriander
   (cilantro), finely chopped
small bunch of mint, finely
   chopped
salt and ground black pepper

1 Preheat the oven to 200°C/400°F/Gas 6. Heat the olive oil in a flameproof casserole with the butter and stir in the peeled onions. Cook the onions over medium heat for about 5 minutes until they are tender, then remove half the onions from the pan and set aside.

2 Add the sweet potatoes and carrots to the pan and cook until the vegetables are lightly browned. Stir in the prunes with the cinnamon, ginger and honey, then pour in the stock. Bring to the boil, season well, cover the casserole and transfer to the oven for about 45 minutes.

3 Stir in the reserved onions and bake for a further 10 minutes. Gently stir in the fresh coriander and mint, and serve the tagine immediately.

> **Cook's Tip**
> Sweet potatoes have dark red or orange skin and orange flesh with a flavour reminiscent of chestnuts. Buy fresh, firm specimens that do not "give" when pressed.

Spiced Pumpkin Gnocchi

Pumpkin adds a sweet richness to these gnocchi, which are superb on their own or served with meat.

Serves 4
450g/1lb pumpkin, peeled, seeded and chopped
450g/1lb potatoes, boiled
2 egg yolks
200g/7oz/1¾ cups plain (all-purpose) flour, plus more if necessary
pinch of ground allspice
1.5ml/¼ tsp cinnamon
pinch of freshly grated nutmeg
finely grated rind of ½ orange
salt and ground pepper

For the sauce
30ml/2 tbsp olive oil
1 shallot, finely chopped
175g/6oz/2½ cups fresh chanterelles, sliced, or 15g/½oz/¼ cup dried, soaked in warm water for 20 minutes, then drained
10ml/2 tsp almond butter
150ml/¼ pint/⅔ cup crème fraîche
a little milk or water
75ml/5 tbsp chopped fresh parsley
50g/2oz/½ cup Parmesan cheese, freshly grated

1 Wrap the pumpkin in foil and bake at 180°C/350°F/Gas 4 for 30 minutes. Pass the pumpkin and cooked potatoes through a food mill into a bowl. Add the egg yolks, flour, spices, orange rind and seasoning and mix well to make a soft dough. If the mixture is too loose add a little flour to stiffen it.

2 To make the sauce, heat the oil in a pan and fry the shallot until soft. Add the chanterelles and cook briefly, then add the almond butter. Stir to melt and stir in the crème fraîche. Simmer briefly, add the parsley and season to taste. Keep hot.

3 Flour a work surface. Spoon the gnocchi dough into a piping bag fitted with a 1cm/½in plain nozzle. Pipe on to the flour to make a 15cm/6in sausage. Roll in flour and cut crossways into 2.5cm/1in pieces. Repeat. Mark each piece lightly with a fork and drop into a pan of fast boiling salted water.

4 The gnocchi are done when they rise to the surface, after 3–4 minutes. Lift them out, drain and turn into bowls. Spoon the sauce over, sprinkle with Parmesan, and serve at once.

Spiced Vegetable Casserole

Here's a meal cooked in a single pot that's suitable for feeding large numbers of people. It's lightly spiced and includes plenty of garlic, and is popular with everyone.

Serves 4
60ml/4 tbsp olive oil
1 large onion, chopped
2 small–medium aubergines (eggplants), cut into small cubes
4 courgettes (zucchini), cut into small chunks
1 green (bell) pepper, chopped
1 red or yellow (bell) pepper, chopped
115g/4oz/1 cup fresh or frozen peas
115g/4oz French beans
450g/1lb new or salad potatoes, cubed
2.5ml/½ tsp cinnamon
2.5ml/½ tsp ground cumin
5ml/1 tsp paprika
4–5 large ripe tomatoes, skinned
400g/14oz can chopped tomatoes
30ml/2 tbsp chopped fresh parsley
3–4 garlic cloves, crushed
350ml/12fl oz/1½ cups vegetable stock
salt and ground black pepper
black olives, to garnish
fresh parsley, to garnish

1 Preheat the oven to 190°C/375°F/Gas 5. Heat 45ml/3 tbsp of the oil in a heavy pan, add the onion and fry until golden. Add the aubergines and sauté for about 3 minutes, then add the courgettes, green and red or yellow peppers, peas, beans and potatoes, together with the spices and seasoning.

2 Continue to cook for 3 minutes, stirring all the time. Transfer to a shallow ovenproof dish.

3 Halve, seed and chop the fresh tomatoes and mix with the canned tomatoes, chopped parsley, garlic and the remaining olive oil in a bowl.

4 Pour the stock over the aubergine mixture and then spoon over the prepared tomato mixture.

5 Cover and bake the dish for 30–45 minutes until the vegetables are tender. Serve hot, garnished with black olives and parsley.

Stuffed Vine Leaves with Cumin

The important ingredients in these stuffed vine leaves are the spices and fresh herbs, which give the brown rice filling its zest.

Serves 6–8

250g/9oz/1¼ cups brown rice
30–45ml/2–3 tbsp natural (plain) yogurt
3 garlic cloves, chopped
I egg, lightly beaten
5–10ml/1–2 tsp ground cumin
2.5ml/½ tsp ground cinnamon
several handfuls of raisins
3–4 spring onions (scallions), thinly sliced
½ bunch fresh mint, plus extra to garnish
about 25 preserved vine leaves, rinsed and drained
salt, if necessary

For cooking

8–10 unpeeled garlic cloves
juice of ½–1 lemon
90ml/6 tbsp olive oil

To serve

I lemon, cut into wedges or half slices
15–25 Greek black olives
150ml/¼ pint/⅔ cup natural (plain) yogurt

I Put the rice in a pan with 300ml/½ pint/1¼ cups water. Bring to the boil, reduce the heat, cover and simmer for 30 minutes, or until just tender. Drain well and leave to cool slightly.

2 Put the cooked rice in a bowl, add the yogurt, garlic, egg, cumin and cinnamon, raisins, spring onions and mint and mix.

3 Lay the vine leaves on a board, shiny side down. Place 15–30ml/1–2 tbsp of the mixture near the stalk of each leaf. Fold each one up, starting at the bottom, turning in the sides then rolling up towards the top to enclose the filling.

4 Carefully layer the rolls in a steamer and stud with the whole garlic cloves. Fill the base of the steamer with water and drizzle the lemon juice and olive oil evenly over the rolls.

5 Cover the steamer tightly and cook over a medium-high heat for about 40 minutes, adding more water if necessary. Remove from the heat and set aside to cool slightly. Arrange the vine leaves on a serving dish and serve warm. Garnish and serve with lemon, olives and a bowl of yogurt, for dipping.

Casablancan Couscous with Harissa

This dish is based on the classic Moroccan couscous recipe for a stew containing seven vegetables, which is believed to bring good luck. Serve with a dollop of thick and creamy yogurt and a spoonful of fiery harissa.

Serves 6

3 red onions, peeled and quartered
2–3 courgettes (zucchini), halved lengthways and cut across into 2–3 pieces each
2–3 red, green or yellow (bell) peppers, quartered
2 aubergines (eggplants), cut into 6–8 long segments
2–3 leeks, trimmed and cut into long strips
2–3 sweet potatoes, peeled and cut into long strips
4–6 tomatoes, quartered
6 garlic cloves, crushed
25g/1oz fresh root ginger, sliced
a few large fresh rosemary sprigs
about 150ml/¼ pint/⅔ cup olive oil
10ml/2 tsp sugar or clear honey
salt and ground black pepper
natural (plain) yogurt, harissa and bread, to serve

For the couscous

500g/1¼lb/3 cups medium couscous
5ml/1 tsp salt
600ml/1 pint/2½ cups warm water
45ml/3 tbsp sunflower oil
about 25g/1oz/2 tbsp butter

I Preheat the oven to 200°C/400°F/Gas 6. Arrange all the vegetables in a roasting pan with the garlic, ginger and rosemary. Pour olive oil over the vegetables, sprinkle with the sugar or honey, salt and pepper, and roast for about 1½ hours.

2 Meanwhile stir the salt into the water, then pour it over the couscous. Leave to stand for 10 minutes to plump up then, using your fingers, rub the sunflower oil into the grains to air them and break up any lumps. Tip the couscous into an ovenproof dish, arrange the butter over the top, cover with foil and heat in the oven for about 20 minutes.

3 Fork the melted butter into the grains of couscous and fluff it up, then pile it on a large dish and shape into a mound with a little pit at the top. Spoon some vegetables into the pit and arrange the rest around the dish. Pour the oil from the pan over the couscous. Serve with yogurt, harissa and bread.

Stuffed Vine Leaves with Cumin: Energy 220kcal/924kJ; Protein 3.5g; Carbohydrate 31.1g, of which sugars 6g; Fat 9.9g, of which saturates 1.6g; Cholesterol 24mg; Calcium 27mg; Fibre 1.2g; Sodium 18mg.
Couscous with Harissa: Energy 561kcal/2340kJ; Protein 10.4g; Carbohydrate 78.8g, of which sugars 18.7g; Fat 24.6g, of which saturates 3.5g; Cholesterol 0mg; Calcium 101mg; Fibre 7.2g; Sodium 51mg.

Vietnamese Crisp-fried Tofu in a Tangy Chilli Sauce

This is a light, tasty Vietnamese dish. Those who adhere to a vegetarian diet can enjoy it too, simply by replacing the fish sauce, *nuoc mam*, with soy sauce.

Serves 4
vegetable or groundnut (peanut) oil, for deep-frying
450g/1lb firm tofu, rinsed and cut into bitesize cubes
4 shallots, finely sliced
1 Thai chilli, seeded and chopped
25g/1oz fresh root ginger, peeled and finely chopped
4 garlic cloves, finely chopped
6 large ripe tomatoes, skinned, seeded and finely chopped
30ml/2 tbsp nuoc mam
10ml/2 tsp sugar
mint leaves and strips of red chilli, to garnish
ground black pepper

1 Heat enough oil for deep-frying in a wok or heavy pan. Fry the cubes of tofu, in batches, until crisp and golden. Remove each batch as it is done with a slotted spoon and drain on kitchen paper.

2 When the tofu is cooked, pour off most of the oil, reserving 30ml/2 tbsp in the wok. Add the shallots, chilli, ginger and garlic and stir-fry until they are fragrant. Stir in the tomatoes, *nuoc mam* and sugar.

3 Reduce the heat and simmer for 10–15 minutes until the liquid ingredients form a sauce. Stir in 105ml/7 tbsp water and bring to the boil.

4 Season the sauce with a little pepper to taste and return the tofu to the pan. Mix well and simmer gently for 2–3 minutes to heat through. Garnish with mint leaves and chilli strips and serve immediately.

Cook's Tip
This recipe is delicious as a side dish but can also be eaten as a main dish with noodles or rice.

Picnic Pie with Ginger

This is a homely version of the more elaborate and traditional Moroccan *bastilla*. It makes a delightful meal and, on a summer day, it is great to take on a picnic.

Serves 6
30ml/2 tbsp olive oil
115g/4oz/½ cup butter
8 spring onions (scallions), trimmed and chopped
2 garlic cloves, chopped
25g/1oz fresh root ginger, peeled and chopped
225g/8oz/2 cups cashew nuts, roughly chopped
5–10ml/1–2 tsp ground cinnamon, plus extra to garnish
5ml/1 tsp paprika
2.5ml/½ tsp ground coriander, plus extra for dusting
6 eggs, beaten
bunch of flat leaf parsley, finely chopped
large bunch of fresh coriander (cilantro), finely chopped
8 sheets of fresh or frozen filo pastry
salt and ground black pepper

1 Preheat the oven to 200°C/400°F/Gas 6. Heat the olive oil with a little of the butter in a heavy pan and stir in the spring onions, garlic and ginger. Add the cashew nuts and cook for a few minutes, then stir in the cinnamon, paprika and ground coriander. Season well, then add the eggs. Cook, stirring, until the eggs begin to scramble but remain moist. Remove from the heat, add the parsley and fresh coriander, and leave to cool.

2 Melt the remaining butter. Separate the sheets of filo and keep them under a slightly damp cloth. Brush an ovenproof dish with a little of the melted butter and cover with a sheet of pastry, allowing the sides to flop over the rim. Brush the pastry with a little more melted butter and place another sheet on top. Repeat with another two sheets to make four layers. Spread the nut mixture over the pastry and fold the pastry edges over the filling.

3 Cover with the remaining sheets of pastry, brushing each one with melted butter and tucking the edges under the pie, as though making a bed. Brush the top of the pie with the remaining melted butter and bake for 25 minutes, or until the pastry is crisp and golden. Dust the top of the pie with a little cinnamon before serving.

Picnic Pie with Ginger: Energy 528kcal/2190kJ; Protein 15.9g; Carbohydrate 17.6g, of which sugars 3.1g; Fat 44.5g, of which saturates 15.9g; Cholesterol 231mg; Calcium 93mg; Fibre 2.4g; Sodium 300mg.
Vietnamese Crisp-fried Tofu: Energy 423kcal/1749kJ; Protein 17.9g; Carbohydrate 7.8g, of which sugars 4.5g; Fat 35.8g, of which saturates 5.3g; Cholesterol 0mg; Calcium 607mg; Fibre 2.8g; Sodium 296mg.

Potato Rösti and Tofu

Although this dish features various different components, it is not difficult to make. Allow enough time to marinate the tofu for at least an hour before you start to cook it, to allow it to absorb the flavours of the ginger, garlic and tamari.

Serves 4
425g/15oz/3¾ cups tofu, cut into 1cm/½in cubes
4 large potatoes, about 900g/2lb total weight, peeled
sunflower oil, for frying

salt and ground black pepper
30ml/2 tbsp sesame seeds, toasted

For the marinade
30ml/2 tbsp tamari or dark soy sauce
15ml/1 tbsp clear honey
2 garlic cloves, crushed
4cm/1½in piece fresh root ginger, grated
5ml/1 tsp toasted sesame oil

For the sauce
15ml/1 tbsp olive oil
8 tomatoes, halved, seeded and chopped

1 Mix all the marinade ingredients in a bowl and add the tofu. Leave to marinate in the refrigerator for at least 1 hour, turning the tofu occasionally to allow the flavours to infuse.

2 To make the rösti, par-boil the potatoes for 10–15 minutes until almost tender. Leave to cool, then grate coarsely. Season well. Preheat the oven to 200°C/400°F/Gas 6. Drain the tofu, reserving the marinade, and spread out on a baking tray. Bake for 20 minutes, turning occasionally, until golden and crisp.

3 Meanwhile, to make the sauce, heat the oil in a pan, add the marinade and tomatoes and bring to the boil. Reduce the heat and simmer, covered, for 10 minutes. Pass through a sieve (strainer) to make smooth and keep warm.

4 Form the potato mixture into four cakes. Heat a frying pan with enough oil to cover the base. Place the cakes in the frying pan, flattening them slightly with a spatula. Cook until golden and crisp then flip over to cook the other side. To serve, place on four serving plates. Sprinkle the tofu on top, spoon over the tomato sauce and sprinkle with sesame seeds.

Spicy Stuffed Peppers

This is an unusual Thai version of this familiar dish, in that the stuffed peppers are steamed rather than baked, but the result is beautifully light and tender. The filling incorporates typical Thai ingredients such as red curry paste and mushroom ketchup, spiked with the zesty flavour of kaffir lime leaves. Choose firm, small mushrooms with a good flavour, which will be enhanced by the mushroom ketchup, for the stuffing.

Serves 4
3 garlic cloves, finely chopped
2 coriander (cilantro) roots, finely chopped
400g/14oz/3 cups mushrooms, quartered
5ml/1 tsp Thai red curry paste
1 egg, lightly beaten
15ml/1 tbsp Thai mushroom ketchup
15ml/1 tbsp light soy sauce
2.5ml/½ tsp sugar
3 kaffir lime leaves, finely chopped
4 yellow (bell) peppers, halved lengthways

1 In a mortar or spice grinder pound or blend the garlic with the coriander roots. Scrape into a bowl.

2 Put the mushrooms in a food processor and pulse briefly until they are finely chopped. Add to the garlic mixture, then stir in the curry paste, beaten egg, ketchup, soy sauce, sugar and kaffir lime leaves.

3 Place the pepper halves, cut-side up, in a single layer in a steamer basket. Spoon the mixture loosely into the pepper halves. Do not pack the mixture down tightly or the filling will dry out too much.

4 Bring the water in the steamer to the boil, then lower the heat to a simmer. Steam the peppers for 15 minutes, or until the flesh is tender. Serve hot.

> **Variation**
> Use red or orange (bell) peppers if you prefer, or a combination of the two.

Chinese Red-cooked Tofu and Mushroom Stir-fry

"Red-cooked" is a term applied to Chinese dishes that are cooked with dark soy sauce. This tasty dish can be served as either a side dish or main meal.

Serves 2–4
225g/8oz firm tofu
45ml/3 tbsp dark soy sauce
30ml/2 tbsp Chinese rice wine or medium-dry sherry
10ml/2 tsp soft dark brown sugar
1 garlic clove, crushed
15ml/1 tbsp grated fresh root ginger
2.5ml/½ tsp Chinese five-spice powder
pinch of ground roasted Szechuan peppercorns
6 dried Chinese black mushrooms
5ml/1 tsp cornflour (cornstarch)
30ml/2 tbsp groundnut (peanut) oil
5–6 spring onions (scallions), sliced into 2.5cm/1in lengths
small basil leaves, to garnish
rice noodles, to serve

1 Drain the tofu, pat dry with kitchen paper and cut into 2.5cm/1in cubes. Place in a shallow dish. In a small bowl, mix together the soy sauce, rice wine or sherry, sugar, garlic, ginger, five-spice powder and ground roasted Szechuan peppercorns. Pour the marinade over the tofu, toss well and leave to marinate for about 30 minutes. Drain, reserving the marinade.

2 Meanwhile, just cover the dried black mushrooms in warm water and soak for 20–30 minutes until softened. Drain, reserving 90ml/6 tbsp of the soaking liquid. Squeeze the mushrooms, discard the tough stalks and slice the caps. In a small bowl, blend the cornflour with the reserved marinade and the mushroom liquid.

3 Heat a wok until hot, add the oil and swirl it around. Add the tofu and fry for 2–3 minutes until evenly golden. Remove from the wok and set aside. Add the mushrooms and white parts of the spring onions to the wok and stir-fry for 2 minutes. Pour in the marinade mixture and stir for 1 minute until thickened. Return the tofu to the wok with the green parts of the onions. Simmer for 1–2 minutes. Garnish with basil leaves and serve with noodles.

Tagine of Butter Beans, Cherry Tomatoes and Olives

Serve this hearty butter bean dish with grills or roasts, particularly fish. It is substantial enough to be served on its own, with a leafy salad and fresh, crusty bread. In and around Tangier, where the Spanish influence remains quite strong, bean dishes like this often include a spicy sausage like chorizo. This would be added with the onion to lend its flavour to the whole dish.

Serves 4
115g/4oz/⅔ cup butter (lima) beans, soaked overnight
30–45ml/2–3 tbsp olive oil
1 onion, chopped
2–3 garlic cloves, crushed
25g/1oz fresh root ginger, peeled and chopped
pinch of saffron threads
16 cherry tomatoes
generous pinch of sugar
handful of fleshy black olives, pitted
5ml/1 tsp ground cinnamon
5ml/1 tsp paprika
small bunch of flat leaf parsley
salt and ground black pepper

1 Rinse the beans and place them in a large pan with plenty of water. Bring to the boil and boil for about 10 minutes, then reduce the heat and simmer gently for 1–1½ hours until tender. Drain the beans and refresh under cold water.

2 Heat the olive oil in a heavy pan. Add the onion, garlic and ginger, and cook for about 10 minutes, or until softened but not browned. Stir in the saffron threads, followed by the cherry tomatoes and a sprinkling of sugar.

3 As the tomatoes begin to soften, stir in the butter beans. When the tomatoes have heated through, stir in the olives, ground cinnamon and paprika. Season to taste and sprinkle the parsley over. Serve immediately.

> **Variation**
> If you are in a hurry, use two 400g/14oz cans butter beans for this tagine. Rinse the beans well before adding.

Tofu and Mushroom Stir-fry: Energy 118kcal/491kJ; Protein 9.3g; Carbohydrate 2.9g, of which sugars 1.1g; Fat 7.4g, of which saturates 0.9g; Cholesterol 0mg; Calcium 456mg; Fibre 1.2g; Sodium 455mg.
Tagine of Butter Beans: Energy 146kcal/615kJ; Protein 7.4g; Carbohydrate 16.2g, of which sugars 3.8g; Fat 6.3g, of which saturates 0.9g; Cholesterol 0mg; Calcium 62mg; Fibre 6g; Sodium 16mg.

Spicy Chickpeas with Fresh Ginger

Chickpeas are filling, nourishing and cheap. Here they are served with a refreshing raita made with spring onions and mint. Serve as a snack or as part of a main meal.

Serves 4–6
225g/8oz dried chickpeas
30ml/2 tbsp vegetable oil
1 small onion, chopped
4cm/1½in piece fresh root ginger, finely chopped
2 garlic cloves, finely chopped
1.5ml/¼ tsp ground turmeric

450g/1lb tomatoes, peeled, seeded and chopped
30ml/2 tbsp chopped fresh coriander (cilantro)
10ml/2 tsp garam masala
salt and pepper
fresh coriander sprigs, to garnish

For the raita
150ml/¼ pint/⅔ cup natural (plain) yogurt
2 spring onions (scallions), finely chopped
5ml/1 tsp roasted cumin seeds
30ml/2 tbsp chopped fresh mint
pinch of cayenne pepper

1 Put the chickpeas in a large bowl and pour over enough cold water to cover. Leave to soak overnight. Next day, drain the chickpeas and put them into a large pan with fresh cold water to cover them. Bring to the boil and boil hard for 10 minutes, then lower the heat and simmer gently for 1½–2 hours until tender. Drain well.

2 Heat a wok until hot, add the oil and swirl it around. Add the onion and stir-fry for 2–3 minutes, then add the ginger, garlic and turmeric. Stir-fry for a few seconds more.

3 Add the tomatoes, chickpeas and seasoning. Bring to the boil, then simmer for 10–15 minutes, until the tomatoes have reduced to a thick sauce.

4 Meanwhile, make the raita. Mix together the yogurt, spring onions, roasted cumin seeds, mint and cayenne pepper to taste. Set aside.

5 Just before the end of cooking, stir the chopped coriander and garam masala into the chickpeas. Serve at once, garnished with coriander sprigs and accompanied by the raita.

Vegetable Korma

The blending of spices is an ancient art in India. In this curry the aim is to produce subtle flavours rather than assaulting the senses.

Serves 4
50g/2oz/¼ cup butter
2 onions, sliced
2 garlic cloves, crushed
2.5cm/1in piece fresh root ginger, grated
5ml/1 tsp ground cumin
15ml/1 tbsp ground coriander
6 cardamoms
5cm/2in cinnamon stick
5ml/1 tsp ground turmeric

1 fresh red chilli, seeded and finely chopped
1 medium potato, peeled and cut into 2.5cm/1in cubes
1 small aubergine (eggplant)
115g/4oz/1½ cups mushrooms, thickly sliced
115g/4oz/1 cup French beans, cut into 2.5cm/1in lengths
60ml/4 tbsp natural (plain) yogurt
150ml/¼ pint/⅔ cup double (heavy) cream
5ml/1 tsp garam masala
salt and ground black pepper
fresh coriander (cilantro) sprigs, to garnish
poppadums, to serve

1 Melt the butter in a heavy pan. Add the onions and cook for 5 minutes until soft. Add the garlic and ginger and cook for 2 minutes. Stir in the cumin, coriander, cardamoms, cinnamon, turmeric and chilli. Cook, stirring for 30 seconds.

2 Add the potato, aubergine and mushrooms and about 175ml/6fl oz/¾ cup water. Cover the pan, bring to the boil, then lower the heat and simmer for 15 minutes. Add the beans and cook, uncovered, for 5 minutes.

3 With a slotted spoon, remove the vegetables to a warmed serving dish and keep hot. Allow the cooking liquid to bubble until it reduces a little. Season with salt and pepper, then stir in the yogurt, cream and garam masala. Pour the sauce over the vegetables and garnish with coriander. Serve with poppadums.

Variation
Any combination of vegetables can be used for this korma, including carrots, cauliflower, broccoli, peas and chickpeas.

Spicy Chickpeas with Ginger: Energy 192kcal/809kJ; Protein 10.4g; Carbohydrate 24.6g, of which sugars 5.9g; Fat 6.6g, of which saturates 0.9g; Cholesterol 0mg; Calcium 126mg; Fibre 5.1g; Sodium 44mg.
Vegetable Korma: Energy 381kcal/1577kJ; Protein 5.1g; Carbohydrate 20.9g, of which sugars 9.9g; Fat 31.4g, of which saturates 19.3g; Cholesterol 78mg; Calcium 95mg; Fibre 3.9g; Sodium 108mg.

Thai Vegetable Curry

This is a thin, soupy curry that is bursting with lots of fresh green vegetables and robust flavours. In the forested regions of Thailand, where this dish originated, it would be made using a variety of edible wild leaves and roots. Serve it with rice or noodles for a simple lunch or supper.

Serves 2
600ml/1 pint/2½ cups water
5ml/1 tsp Thai red curry paste
5cm/2in piece fresh galangal or fresh root ginger
90g/3½oz/scant 1 cup green beans
2 kaffir lime leaves, torn
8 baby corn cobs, halved widthways
2 heads Chinese broccoli, chopped
90g/3½oz/generous 3 cups beansprouts
15ml/1 tbsp drained bottled green peppercorns, crushed
10ml/2 tsp sugar
5ml/1 tsp salt

1 Heat the water in a large pan. Add the red curry paste and stir until it has dissolved completely. Bring to the boil.

2 Meanwhile, using a sharp knife, peel and finely chop the fresh galangal or root ginger.

3 Add the galangal or ginger to the pan with the green beans, lime leaves, baby corn cobs, broccoli and beansprouts. Stir in the crushed peppercorns, sugar and salt.

4 Bring back to the boil, then reduce the heat to low and simmer for 2 minutes, so that the vegetables are hot but still crisp. Serve immediately.

Cook's Tips
• The vegetables in this curry should taste fresh and retain their crispness; you can vary the ingredients depending on what is available, but choose vegetables that cook in a few minutes.
• Galangal, used in South-east Asian cookery, resembles ginger but has a more earthy aroma and a resinous flavour.

Glazed Pumpkin in Coconut Milk

Pumpkins, butternut squash and winter melons can all be cooked in this way. Throughout Vietnam and Cambodia, variations of this sweet, mellow dish are often served as an accompaniment to rice or as a side dish to offset the spicy flavours of a hot curry.

Serves 4
200ml/7fl oz/scant 1 cup coconut milk
15ml/1 tbsp mushroom ketchup
30ml/2 tbsp palm sugar (jaggery)
30ml/2 tbsp groundnut (peanut) oil
4 garlic cloves, peeled and finely chopped
25g/1oz fresh root ginger, peeled and finely shredded
675g/1½lb pumpkin, peeled, seeded and cubed
ground black pepper
handful of curry or basil leaves, to garnish
fried onion rings, to garnish
chilli oil, for drizzling
plain or coconut rice, to serve

1 In a bowl, beat the coconut milk and the mushroom ketchup with the sugar, until it has dissolved. Set aside.

2 Heat the oil in a wok or heavy pan and stir in the garlic and ginger. Stir-fry until they begin to colour, then stir in the pumpkin cubes, mixing well.

3 Pour in the coconut milk and mix well. Reduce the heat, cover and simmer for about 20 minutes, until the pumpkin is tender and the sauce has reduced.

4 Season with pepper and garnish with curry or basil leaves and fried onion rings. Serve hot with plain or coconut rice, drizzled with a little chilli oil.

Cook's Tip
Vary the squash used to make this dish according to what is in season.

Thai Vegetable Curry: Energy 328kcal/1375kJ; Protein 10g; Carbohydrate 64.9g, of which sugars 11.1g; Fat 3.3g, of which saturates 0.6g; Cholesterol 0mg; Calcium 134mg; Fibre 3.9g; Sodium 535mg.
Glazed Pumpkin in Milk: Energy 114Kcal/477kJ; Protein 1.5g; Carbohydrate 14g, of which sugars 13.4g; Fat 6g, of which saturates 1g; Cholesterol 0mg; Calcium 68mg; Fibre 1.7g; Sodium 323mg.

Luffa Squash with Mushrooms, Spring Onions and Coriander

All kinds of winter gourds, such as pumpkins, bitter melons, luffa squash and a variety of other squash that come under the kabocha umbrella, are popular ingredients in Vietnam and Cambodia for making comforting, nourishing soups and braised vegetable dishes like this one. All these vegetables have delicate, rather sweet flesh, so the spices and other flavourings used in such dishes tend to be mild and gentle.

Serves 4

750g/1lb 10oz luffa squash, peeled
30ml/2 tbsp groundnut (peanut) or sesame oil
2 shallots, halved and sliced
2 garlic cloves, finely chopped
115g/4oz/1½ cups button (white) mushrooms, quartered
15ml/1 tbsp mushroom sauce
10ml/2 tsp soy sauce
4 spring onions (scallions), cut into 2cm/¾in pieces
fresh coriander (cilantro) leaves and thin strips of spring onion (scallion), to garnish

1 Cut the luffa squash diagonally into 2cm/¾in thick pieces.

2 Heat the oil in a large wok or heavy pan. Stir in the halved shallots and garlic, stir-fry until they begin to colour and turn golden, then add the mushrooms.

3 Add the mushroom and soy sauces, and the squash. Reduce the heat, cover and cook gently for a few minutes until the squash is tender.

4 Stir in the spring onion pieces, garnish with coriander and spring onion strips, and serve.

Cook's Tip

In Cambodia, squash is sometimes sweetened and cooked with coconut milk and served as a dessert. Luffa squash or ridged gourd, available from Asian markets, resembles a long courgette (zucchini) with ridges from one end to the other.

Moroccan-spiced Aubergine Tagine

Spiced with coriander, cumin, cinnamon, turmeric and a dash of chilli sauce, this Moroccan-style stew makes a filling supper dish when served with couscous.

Serves 4

1 small aubergine (eggplant), cut into 1cm/½in dice
2 courgettes (zucchini), thickly sliced
60ml/4 tbsp olive oil
1 large onion, sliced
2 garlic cloves, chopped
150g/5oz/2 cups brown cap mushrooms, halved
15ml/1 tbsp ground coriander
10ml/2 tsp cumin seeds
15ml/1 tbsp ground cinnamon
10ml/2 tsp ground turmeric
225g/8oz new potatoes, quartered
600ml/1 pint/2½ cups passata
15ml/1 tbsp tomato purée (paste)
15ml/1 tbsp chilli sauce
75g/3oz/⅓ cup ready-to-eat unsulphured dried apricots
400g/14oz/3 cups canned chickpeas, drained and rinsed
salt and ground black pepper
15ml/1 tbsp chopped fresh coriander (cilantro), to garnish

1 Sprinkle salt over the aubergine and courgettes and leave for 30 minutes. Rinse and pat dry with a dish towel. Heat the grill to high. Arrange the courgettes and aubergine on a baking tray and toss in 30ml/2 tbsp of the olive oil. Grill for 20 minutes, turning occasionally, until tender and golden.

2 Meanwhile, heat the remaining oil in a large heavy pan and cook the onion and garlic for 5 minutes until softened, stirring occasionally. Add the mushrooms and sauté for 3 minutes until tender. Add the spices and cook for 1 minute more, stirring, to allow the flavours to mingle.

3 Add the potatoes and cook for about 3 minutes, stirring. Pour in the passata, tomato purée and 150ml/¼ pint/⅔ cup water. Cover and cook for 10 minutes to thicken the sauce.

4 Add the aubergine, courgettes, chilli sauce, apricots and chickpeas. Season and cook, partially covered, for about 15 minutes until the potatoes are tender. Add a little extra water if the tagine becomes too dry. Sprinkle with chopped fresh coriander to serve.

Luffa Squash with Coriander: Energy 194Kcal/800kJ; Protein 3g; Carbohydrate 19g, of which sugars 3g; Fat 12g, of which saturates 2g; Cholesterol 0mg; Calcium 31mg; Fibre 5.1g; Sodium 100mg.
Spiced Aubergine Tagine: Energy 359kcal/1509kJ; Protein 13.9g; Carbohydrate 45g, of which sugars 19.3g; Fat 15g, of which saturates 2.1g; Cholesterol 0mg; Calcium 123mg; Fibre 9.7g; Sodium 597mg.

Richly Spiced Dhal

Flavoured with spices, coconut milk and tomatoes, this lentil dish makes a filling supper. Warm naan bread and natural yogurt are all that are needed as accompaniments.

Serves 4

30ml/2 tbsp vegetable oil
1 large onion, finely chopped
3 garlic cloves, chopped
1 carrot, diced
10ml/2 tsp cumin seeds
10ml/2 tsp yellow mustard seeds
2.5cm/1in piece fresh root ginger, grated
10ml/2 tsp ground turmeric
5ml/1 tsp mild chilli powder
5ml/1 tsp garam masala
225g/8oz/1 cup split red lentils
400ml/14fl oz/1²⁄₃ cups water
400ml/14fl oz/1²⁄₃ cups coconut milk
5 tomatoes, peeled, seeded and chopped
juice of 2 limes
60ml/4 tbsp chopped fresh coriander (cilantro)
salt and ground black pepper
25g/1oz/¼ cup flaked almonds, toasted, to garnish

1 Heat the oil in a large heavy pan. Sauté the onion for 5 minutes until softened, stirring occasionally. Stir in the garlic, carrot, cumin and mustard seeds, and ginger. Cook for 5 minutes, stirring, until the seeds begin to pop and the carrot softens slightly.

2 Stir in the ground turmeric, chilli powder and garam masala, and cook for 1 minute or until the flavours begin to mingle, stirring to prevent the spices burning.

3 Add the lentils, water, coconut milk and tomatoes, and season well. Bring to the boil, then reduce the heat and simmer, covered, for about 45 minutes, stirring occasionally to prevent the lentils sticking.

4 Stir in the lime juice and 45ml/3 tbsp of the fresh coriander, then check the seasoning.

5 Cook for a further 15 minutes until the lentils soften and become tender. To serve, sprinkle with the remaining coriander and the flaked almonds.

Hot and Spicy Thai Vegetable Curry

This spicy curry made with coconut milk has a creamy richness that contrasts wonderfully with the heat of the chilli. Thai yellow curry paste is available in supermarkets, but you will really taste the difference when you make it yourself.

Serves 4

30ml/2 tbsp sunflower oil
200ml/7fl oz/scant 1 cup coconut cream
300ml/½ pint/1¼ cups coconut milk
150ml/¼ pint/²⁄₃ cup vegetable stock
200g/7oz green beans, cut into 2cm/¾in lengths
200g/7oz baby corn
4 baby courgettes (zucchini), sliced
1 small aubergine (eggplant), cubed or sliced
30ml/2 tbsp mushroom ketchup
10ml/2 tsp palm sugar (jaggery)
fresh coriander (cilantro) leaves, to garnish
noodles or rice, to serve

For the yellow curry paste
10ml/2 tsp hot chilli powder
10ml/2 tsp ground coriander
10ml/2 tsp ground cumin
5ml/1 tsp turmeric
15ml/1 tbsp chopped fresh galangal
10ml/2 tsp finely grated garlic
30ml/2 tbsp finely chopped lemon grass
4 red Asian shallots, finely chopped
5ml/1 tsp finely chopped lime rind

1 To make the curry paste, place all the ingredients in a food processor and blend with 30–45ml/2–3 tbsp of cold water to make a smooth paste. Add a little more water if the mixture seems too dry.

2 Heat a large wok over a medium heat and add the sunflower oil. When hot add 30–45ml/2–3 tbsp of the curry paste and stir-fry for 1–2 minutes. Add the coconut cream and cook gently for 8–10 minutes, or until the mixture starts to separate.

3 Add the coconut milk, stock and vegetables and cook gently for 8–10 minutes, until the vegetables are just tender. Stir in the mushroom ketchup and palm sugar, garnish with coriander leaves and serve with noodles or rice.

Pumpkin and Peanut Yellow Curry

This is a hearty, soothing Thai curry that is perfect for autumn or winter evenings. Its cheerful colour alone will brighten you up – and it tastes terrific.

Serves 4

30ml/2 tbsp vegetable oil
4 garlic cloves, crushed
4 shallots, finely chopped
30ml/2 tbsp Thai yellow curry paste
600ml/1 pint/2½ cups vegetable stock
2 kaffir lime leaves, torn
15ml/1 tbsp chopped galangal
450g/1lb pumpkin, peeled, seeded and diced
225g/8oz sweet potatoes, diced
90g/3½oz/scant 1 cup peanuts, roasted and chopped
300ml/½ pint/1¼ cups coconut milk
90g/3½oz/1½ cups chestnut mushrooms, sliced
15ml/1 tbsp soy sauce
30ml/2 tbsp Thai mushroom ketchup
50g/2oz/⅓ cup pumpkin seeds, toasted, and fresh green chilli flowers, to garnish

1 Heat the oil in a large pan. Add the garlic and shallots and cook over a medium heat, stirring occasionally, for 10 minutes, until softened and golden. Do not let them burn.

2 Add the yellow curry paste and stir-fry over a medium heat for 30 seconds, until the mixture is fragrant.

3 Add the stock, lime leaves, galangal, pumpkin and sweet potatoes. Bring to the boil, stirring frequently, then reduce the heat to low and simmer gently for 15 minutes.

4 Add the peanuts, coconut milk and mushrooms. Stir in the soy sauce and mushroom ketchup and simmer for 5 minutes more. Spoon into warmed individual serving bowls, garnish with the pumpkin seeds and chilli flowers and serve.

Cook's Tip
The well-drained vegetables from a curry of this kind would make a very tasty filling for a pastry or pie. This may not be a Thai tradition, but it is a good example of fusion food.

Aromatic Corn and Nut Curry

A substantial curry, this dish combines all the essential flavours of southern Thailand. It is deliciously aromatic, but the flavour is fairly mild.

Serves 4

30ml/2 tbsp vegetable oil
4 shallots, chopped
90g/3½oz/scant 1 cup cashew nuts
5ml/1 tsp Thai red curry paste
400g/14oz potatoes, peeled and cut into chunks
1 lemon grass stalk, finely chopped
200g/7oz can chopped tomatoes
600ml/1 pint/2½ cups boiling water
200g/7oz/generous 1 cup drained canned whole kernel corn
4 celery sticks, sliced
2 kaffir lime leaves, rolled into cylinders and thinly sliced into ribbons
15ml/1 tbsp tomato ketchup
15ml/1 tbsp light soy sauce
5ml/1 tsp palm sugar or light muscovado (brown) sugar
5ml/1 tsp mushroom ketchup
4 spring onions (scallions), thinly sliced
small bunch fresh basil, chopped

1 Heat the oil in a large, heavy pan or wok. Add the shallots and stir-fry over a medium heat for 2–3 minutes, until softened. Add the cashew nuts and stir-fry for a few minutes until golden.

2 Stir in the red curry paste. Stir-fry for 1 minute, then add the potatoes, lemon grass, tomatoes and boiling water. Bring back to the boil, then reduce the heat to low, cover and simmer gently for 15–20 minutes, or until the potatoes are tender.

3 Stir the corn, celery, lime leaves, tomato ketchup, soy sauce, sugar and mushroom ketchup into the pan or wok. Simmer for a further 5 minutes, until heated through, then spoon into warmed serving bowls. Sprinkle with the sliced spring onions and basil and serve.

Cook's Tip
Rolling the lime leaves into cylinders before slicing produces very fine strips – a technique known as cutting en chiffonnade. Remove the central rib from the leaves before cutting them.

Indian-spiced Parsnip Curry

The sweet flavour of parsnips goes very well with the spices in this Indian-style vegetable stew.

Serves 4

200g/7oz dried chickpeas, soaked overnight in cold water, then drained
/ garlic cloves, finely chopped
I small onion, chopped
5cm/2in piece fresh root ginger, chopped
2 green chillies, seeded and chopped
75ml/5 tbsp water
450ml/³/₄ pint/scant 2 cups water
60ml/4 tbsp groundnut oil
5ml/I tsp cumin seeds
10ml/2 tsp ground coriander
5ml/I tsp ground turmeric
2.5–5ml/¹/₂–I tsp chilli powder
50g/2oz cashew nuts, toasted and ground
250g/9oz tomatoes, peeled and chopped
900g/2lb parsnips, cut in chunks
5ml/I tsp ground cumin seeds
juice of I lime, to taste
salt and ground black pepper
fresh coriander (cilantro) leaves and toasted cashew nuts, to garnish

I Put the soaked chickpeas in a pan, cover with cold water and bring to the boil. Boil vigorously for 10 minutes, then reduce the heat so that the water boils steadily. Cook for 1–1¹/₂ hours, or until the chickpeas are tender. Drain.

2 Set 10ml/2 tsp of the garlic aside, then place the rest in a food processor or blender with the onion, ginger and half the chillies. Add the 75ml/5 tbsp water, and process until smooth.

3 Heat the oil in a large, deep, frying pan and cook the cumin seeds for 30 seconds. Stir in the coriander seeds, turmeric, chilli powder and the ground cashew nuts. Add the ginger and chilli paste and cook, stirring frequently. Add the tomatoes and stir-fry until the mixture begins to turn red-brown. Mix in the chickpeas and parsnips with the main batch of water, 5ml/I tsp salt and plenty of black pepper. Bring to the boil then simmer, uncovered, for 15–20 minutes.

4 Reduce the liquid, if necessary, by boiling fiercely. Add the ground cumin with more salt and lime juice to taste. Stir in the reserved garlic and green chilli. Sprinkle the coriander leaves and toasted cashew nuts over and serve straight away.

Tofu and Green Bean Red Curry

This Thai curry is one of those versatile recipes that should be in every cook's repertoire. This version uses green beans, but other types of vegetable work equally well. The tofu takes on the flavour of the spice paste and also boosts the nutritional value of the dish.

Serves 4–6

600ml/I pint/2¹/₂ cups canned coconut milk
15ml/I tbsp Thai red curry paste
45ml/3 tbsp mushroom ketchup
10ml/2 tsp palm sugar (jaggery) or light muscovado (brown) sugar
225g/8oz/3¹/₄ cups button (white) mushrooms
115g/4oz/scant I cup green beans, trimmed
175g/6oz firm tofu, rinsed, drained and cut into 2cm/³/₄in cubes
4 kaffir lime leaves, torn
2 fresh red chillies, seeded and sliced
fresh coriander (cilantro) leaves, to garnish

I Pour about one-third of the coconut milk into a wok or pan and cook until it starts to separate and an oily sheen appears on the surface.

2 Add the red curry paste, mushroom ketchup and sugar to the coconut milk. Mix thoroughly, then add the mushrooms. Stir and cook for I minute.

3 Stir in the remaining coconut milk. Bring back to the boil, then add the green beans and tofu cubes. Simmer gently for 4–5 minutes more.

4 Stir in the kaffir lime leaves and sliced red chillies. Spoon the curry into a serving dish, garnish with the coriander leaves and serve immediately.

> **Cook's Tip**
> The Kaffir lime is a native of Indonesia but is grown in many other parts of the world. The leaves are a popular flavouring in the cooking of Thailand, Cambodia and Laos, and are widely available fresh, frozen or dried.

Aubergine and Sweet Potato Stew

Inspired by Thai cooking, this aubergine and sweet potato stew cooked in a coconut sauce is scented with fragrant lemon grass, ginger and lots of garlic.

Serves 6

60ml/4 tbsp groundnut (peanut) oil
2 aubergines (eggplants), cut into chunks
225g/8oz Thai red shallots or other shallots
5ml/1 tsp fennel seeds, lightly crushed
4–5 garlic cloves, thinly sliced
25ml/1½ tbsp finely chopped fresh root ginger
475ml/16fl oz/2 cups vegetable stock
2 stems lemon grass, outer layers discarded, finely chopped
15g/½oz fresh coriander (cilantro), stalks and leaves chopped separately
3 kaffir lime leaves, lightly bruised
2–3 small red chillies
45–60ml/3–4 tbsp Thai green curry paste
675g/1½lb sweet potatoes, cut into thick chunks
400ml/14fl oz/1⅔ cups coconut milk
2.5–5ml/½–1 tsp light muscovado (brown) sugar
250g/9oz mushrooms, sliced
juice of 1 lime, to taste
salt and ground black pepper
18 fresh Thai basil leaves or ordinary basil, to garnish

1 Heat half the oil in a lidded frying pan. Add the aubergines and cook over a medium heat, stirring occasionally, until lightly browned on all sides. Remove from the pan and set aside.

2 Slice 4–5 of the shallots and set aside. Fry the remaining whole shallots in the pan, adding more oil if necessary, until browned. Set aside. Add the remaining oil to the pan and cook the sliced shallots, fennel, garlic and ginger until soft but not browned. Add the vegetable stock, lemon grass, coriander stalks, lime leaves and whole chillies. Cover and simmer for 5 minutes.

3 Stir in 30ml/2 tbsp of the curry paste and the sweet potatoes. Simmer for 10 minutes, return the aubergines and shallots to the pan and cook for a further 5 minutes. Stir in the coconut milk and sugar. Season to taste, then add the mushrooms and simmer for 5 minutes. Stir in more curry paste and lime juice to taste, followed by the chopped coriander leaves. Sprinkle with basil and serve.

Malay Vegetable Curry with Cumin and Turmeric

Originally from southern India, this delicious spicy dish is cooked in many Malay homes. It is substantial and flexible – choose your own assortment of vegetables, such as pumpkin, butternut squash, winter melon, yams, aubergines or beans.

Serves 4

2–3 green chillies, seeded and chopped
25g/1oz fresh root ginger, peeled and chopped
5–10ml/1–2 tsp roasted cumin seeds
10ml/2 tsp sugar
5–10ml/1–2 tsp ground turmeric
1 cinnamon stick
5ml/1 tsp salt
2 carrots, cut into bitesize sticks
2 sweet potatoes, cut into bitesize sticks
2 courgettes (zucchini), partially peeled in strips, seeded and cut into bitesize sticks
1 green plantain, peeled and cut into bitesize sticks
small coil of long (snake) beans or a handful of green beans, cut into bitesize sticks
handful fresh curry leaves
1 fresh coconut, grated
250ml/8fl oz/1 cup natural (plain) yogurt
salt and ground black pepper

1 Using a mortar and pestle or a food processor, grind the chillies, ginger, roasted cumin seeds and sugar to a paste.

2 In a heavy pan, bring 450ml/15fl oz/scant 2 cups water to the boil. Stir in the turmeric, cinnamon stick and salt. Add the carrots and cook for 1 minute. Add the sweet potatoes and cook for 2 minutes. Add the courgettes, plantain and beans and cook for a further 2 minutes. Reduce the heat, stir in the spice paste and curry leaves, and cook gently for 4–5 minutes, or until the vegetables are tender but not soft and mushy, and the liquid has greatly reduced.

3 Gently stir in half the coconut. Take the pan off the heat and fold in the yogurt. Season to taste with salt and pepper. Quickly roast the remaining coconut in a heavy pan over a high heat, until nicely browned. Sprinkle a little over the vegetables, and serve the rest separately.

Aubergine and Sweet Potato Stew: Energy 228kcal/960kJ; Protein 4.3g; Carbohydrate 34g, of which sugars 13.4g; Fat 9.3g, of which saturates 1.2g; Cholesterol 0mg; Calcium 130mg; Fibre 7.2g; Sodium 159mg.
Vegetable Curry with Turmeric: Energy 419Kcal/1753kJ; Protein 9.9g; Carbohydrate 47.7g, of which sugars 19.4g; Fat 23g, of which saturates 16.9g; Cholesterol 0mg; Calcium 176mg; Fibre 9g; Sodium 104mg.

Stir-fried Seeds and Vegetables

The contrast between the crunchy seeds and vegetables and the rich, savoury sauce is what makes this dish so delicious. Serve it alone, or with rice or noodles.

Serves 4

30ml/2 tbsp vegetable oil
30ml/2 tbsp sesame seeds
30ml/2 tbsp sunflower seeds
30ml/2 tbsp pumpkin seeds
2 garlic cloves, finely chopped
2.5cm/1in piece fresh root ginger, finely chopped
2 large carrots, cut into batons
2 large courgettes (zucchini), cut into batons
90g/3¹/₂oz/1¹/₂ cups oyster mushrooms, torn in pieces
150g/5oz watercress or spinach leaves, coarsely chopped
small bunch fresh mint or coriander (cilantro), leaves and stems chopped
60ml/4 tbsp black bean sauce
30ml/2 tbsp light soy sauce
15ml/1 tbsp palm sugar (jaggery) or light muscovado (brown) sugar
30ml/2 tbsp rice vinegar

1 Heat the oil in a wok or large frying pan. Add the seeds and toss over a medium heat for 1 minute, then add the garlic and ginger and continue to stir-fry until the ginger is aromatic and the garlic is golden. Do not let the garlic burn or the dish will taste bitter.

2 Add the carrot and courgette batons and the sliced mushrooms to the wok or pan and stir-fry over a medium heat for a further 5 minutes, or until all the vegetables are crisp-tender and are golden at the edges.

3 Add the watercress or spinach with the fresh herbs. Toss over the heat for 1 minute, then stir in the black bean sauce, soy sauce, sugar and vinegar. Stir-fry for 1–2 minutes, until combined and hot. Serve immediately.

> **Cook's Tip**
> Oyster mushrooms have acquired their name because of their texture, rather than flavour, which is quite superb. They are delicate, so it is usually better to tear them into pieces along the lines of the gills, rather than slicing them with a knife.

Leek Terrine with Red Peppers and Cumin

This pressed leek terrine looks very pretty when sliced and served on individual plates with the dressing drizzled over.

Serves 6–8

1.8kg/4lb slender leeks
4 red (bell) peppers, halved
15ml/1 tbsp extra virgin olive oil
10ml/2 tsp balsamic vinegar
5ml/1 tsp ground roasted cumin seeds
salt and ground black pepper

For the dressing

120ml/4fl oz/¹/₂ cup extra virgin olive oil
1 garlic clove, bruised and peeled
5ml/1 tsp Dijon mustard
5ml/1 tsp soy sauce
15ml/1 tbsp balsamic vinegar
pinch of caster (superfine) sugar
2.5–5ml/¹/₂–1 tsp ground roasted cumin seeds
15–30ml/1–2 tbsp chopped mixed fresh basil and flat leaf parsley

1 Line a 23cm/9in long terrine or loaf tin (pan) with clear film (plastic wrap), leaving the ends overhanging the tin. Cut the leeks to the same length as the tin. Cook in boiling salted water for 5–7 minutes, until just tender. Drain and allow to cool, then squeeze out as much water as possible and leave to drain.

2 Grill the peppers, skin-side uppermost, until the skin blisters and blackens. Place in a bowl, cover and leave for 10 minutes. Peel, cut the flesh into long strips and place in a bowl. Mix in the oil, balsamic vinegar and roasted cumin. Season.

3 Layer the leeks and strips of red pepper in the lined tin, alternating the layers. Season the leeks with a little more salt and pepper. Cover with the overhanging clear film. Top with a plate and weigh it down with heavy food cans or scale weights. Chill for several hours or overnight.

4 To make the dressing, place the oil, garlic, mustard, soy sauce and vinegar in a jar and shake. Season and add the caster sugar. Add ground cumin to taste and leave to stand for several hours. Discard the garlic, and add the fresh herbs. Unmould the terrine and cut it into slices to serve with the dressing.

Barbecued Spicy Vegetables with Chilli Salsa

Use a double layer of coals on the barbecue so they will be deep enough to make a bed for the foil-wrapped vegetables. While they are cooking, make the salsa on the grill rack above.

Serves 4–6

2 small whole heads of garlic
2 butternut squash, about
    450g/1lb each, halved
    lengthways and seeded
4–6 onions, about 115g/4oz
    each, with a cross cut in the
    top of each

4–6 baking potatoes, about
    175g/6oz each
4–6 sweet potatoes, about
    175g/6oz each
45ml/3 tbsp olive oil
fresh thyme, bay leaf and
    rosemary sprigs
salt and ground black pepper

For the chilli salsa

500g/1¼lb tomatoes, quartered
    and seeded
2.5ml/½ tsp sugar
a pinch of chilli flakes
1.5ml/¼ tsp smoked chilli powder
30ml/2 tbsp tomato chutney

1 Prepare a barbecue with plenty of coals. Sit the garlic, squash and onions separately in double layers of foil, leaving them open. Wrap the potatoes in pairs of one sweet and one ordinary potato. Drizzle a little oil over the contents of each packet, season well and add a herb sprig. Spray with a little water and scrunch up the foil to secure the parcels.

2 Once the flames have died down and the coals are hot, place the parcels on top of them. The garlic will take 20 minutes to cook, the squash 30 minutes, the onions 45 minutes and the potatoes 1 hour. As each vegetable cooks, remove the parcel and wrap in an extra layer of foil to keep warm. Set aside.

3 Meanwhile, make the salsa. Put a lightly oiled grill rack in place to heat. Sprinkle the tomatoes with sugar, chilli flakes and seasoning. Place them on the grill rack above the vegetables and cook, covered for around 15 minutes. Remove the tomatoes from the rack and spoon the flesh from the charred skins into a bowl, crush with a fork and mix in the other ingredients. Serve with the vegetables.

Summer Vegetable Kebabs with Harissa and Yogurt Dip

This simple and tasty vegetarian dish is delicious served with couscous and a fresh, crispy green salad. It also makes an excellent side dish to accompany meat-based main courses. Vegetable and fish kebabs are becoming increasingly popular in Morocco.

Serves 4

2 aubergines (eggplants), part-
    peeled and cut into chunks
2 courgettes (zucchini), cut into
    chunks
2–3 red or green (bell) peppers,
    cut into chunks
12–16 cherry tomatoes

4 small red onions, quartered
60ml/4 tbsp olive oil
juice of ½ lemon
1 garlic clove, crushed
5ml/1 tsp ground coriander
5ml/1 tsp ground cinnamon
10ml/2 tsp clear honey
5ml/1 tsp salt

For the harissa and yogurt dip

450g/1lb/2 cups natural (plain)
    yogurt
30–60ml/2–4 tbsp harissa
small bunch of fresh coriander
    (cilantro), finely chopped
small bunch of mint, finely
    chopped
salt and ground black pepper

1 Preheat the grill (broiler) on the hottest setting. Put all the vegetables in a bowl.

2 Mix the olive oil, lemon juice, garlic, ground coriander, cinnamon, honey and salt and pour the mixture over the vegetables. Turn the vegetables gently in the marinade, then thread them on to metal skewers. Cook the kebabs under the grill, turning them occasionally until the vegetables are nicely browned all over.

3 To make the dip, put the yogurt in a bowl and beat in the harissa, making it as fiery as you like by adding more harissa.

4 Add most of the coriander and mint, reserving a little to garnish, and season well with salt and pepper. While they are still hot, slide the vegetables off the skewers. Garnish with the reserved herbs and serve with the yogurt dip.

Barbecued Spicy Vegetables: Energy 244kcal/1029kJ; Protein 6.2g; Carbohydrate 42.4g, of which sugars 13g; Fat 6.7g, of which saturates 1.1g; Cholesterol 0mg; Calcium 65mg; Fibre 5.4g; Sodium 54mg.
Summer Vegetable Kebabs: Energy 274kcal/1144kJ; Protein 11.1g; Carbohydrate 28.8g, of which sugars 26.2g; Fat 13.7g, of which saturates 2.5g; Cholesterol 1mg; Calcium 303mg; Fibre 5.9g; Sodium 111mg.

Stuffed Aubergines

This Ligurian dish is spiked with paprika and allspice, a legacy from the days when spices from the East came into northern Italy via the port of Genoa.

Serves 4

2 aubergines (eggplants), about
    225g/8oz each, stalks removed
275g/10oz potatoes, peeled and
    diced
30ml/2 tbsp olive oil
1 small onion, finely chopped
1 garlic clove, finely chopped
good pinch each of ground
    allspice and paprika
1 egg, beaten
40g/1½oz/½ cup grated
    Parmesan cheese
15ml/1 tbsp fresh white
    breadcrumbs
salt and ground black pepper
fresh mint sprigs, to garnish
salad leaves, to serve

1 Bring a large pan of lightly salted water to the boil. Add the whole aubergines and cook for 5 minutes, turning frequently. Remove with a slotted spoon and set aside. Add the potatoes to the pan and cook for 20 minutes until soft.

2 Meanwhile, cut the aubergines in half lengthways and gently scoop out the flesh with a small sharp knife and a spoon, leaving a shell 5mm/¼in thick. Select a baking dish that will hold the aubergine shells snugly in a single layer. Brush it lightly with oil and arrange the shells in the dish. Chop the scooped-out aubergine flesh roughly.

3 Heat the oil in a frying pan, add the onion and cook gently, stirring frequently, until softened. Add the chopped aubergine flesh and the garlic. Cook, stirring frequently, for 6–8 minutes. Tip into a bowl. Preheat the oven to 190°C/375°F/Gas 5.

4 Drain and mash the potatoes. Add to the aubergine with the spices and egg. Set aside 15ml/1 tbsp of the Parmesan and add the rest to the aubergine mixture. Season to taste.

5 Spoon the mixture into the aubergine shells. Mix the breadcrumbs with the reserved Parmesan cheese and sprinkle over the aubergines. Bake for 40–45 minutes until the topping is crisp. Garnish with mint and serve with salad.

Bean-stuffed Mushrooms with Garlic

These bean and lemon-stuffed mushrooms are beautifully fragrant. The garlic and pine nut paste is a traditional Middle Eastern accompaniment.

Serves 4

200g/7oz/1 cup dried aduki beans
45ml/3 tbsp olive oil
1 onion, finely chopped
2 garlic cloves, crushed
30ml/2 tbsp fresh thyme leaves
8 large field (portobello)
    mushrooms, stalks chopped
50g/2oz/1 cup fresh wholemeal
    (whole-wheat) breadcrumbs
juice of 1 lemon
185g/6½oz/generous ¾ cup
    crumbled goat's cheese
salt and ground black pepper
steamed spinach leaves, to serve

For the pine nut paste
50g/2oz/½ cup pine nuts, toasted
50g/2oz/1 cup cubed white bread
2 garlic cloves, chopped
200ml/7fl oz/scant 1 cup milk
45ml/3 tbsp olive oil

1 Soak the beans overnight, then drain and rinse well. Place in a pan, add enough water to cover and bring to the boil. Boil rapidly for 10 minutes, then reduce the heat, cook for 30 minutes, or until tender, then drain.

2 Preheat the oven to 200°C/400°F/Gas 6. Heat the oil in a large, heavy frying pan, add the onion and garlic and cook over a low heat, stirring frequently, for 5 minutes, or until softened. Add the thyme and the mushroom stalks and cook for a further 3 minutes, stirring occasionally, until tender.

3 Stir in the aduki beans, breadcrumbs and lemon juice, season to taste with salt and pepper, then cook gently for 2–3 minutes. Mash about two-thirds of the beans with a fork or potato masher, leaving the remaining beans whole, then mix together.

4 Oil an ovenproof dish and the base of the mushrooms. Top each with a spoonful of the bean mixture, place in the dish, cover with foil and bake for 20 minutes. Remove the foil, top each mushroom with cheese and bake until the cheese melts.

5 To make the pine nut paste, process all the ingredients until smooth. Serve with the mushrooms, with steamed spinach.

Stuffed Aubergines: Energy 94kcal/396kJ; Protein 3.8g; Carbohydrate 12.2g, of which sugars 3.1g; Fat 3.8g, of which saturates 1.3g; Cholesterol 4mg; Calcium 73mg; Fibre 2.3g; Sodium 74mg.
Stuffed Mushrooms: Energy 350kcal/1469kJ; Protein 21.3g; Carbohydrate 30.6g, of which sugars 1.2g; Fat 16.7g, of which saturates 8.9g; Cholesterol 43mg; Calcium 115mg; Fibre 6.3g; Sodium 331mg.

Green Herb Gumbo

The variety of green ingredients is important in this Cajun dish, so choose substitutes that are also green if you can't find all of those listed.

Serves 6–8

350g/12oz piece raw smoked gammon
30ml/2 tbsp lard or cooking oil
1 large onion, roughly chopped
2–3 garlic cloves, crushed
5ml/1 tsp dried oregano
5ml/1 tsp dried thyme
2 bay leaves
2 cloves
2 celery sticks, finely sliced
1 green (bell) pepper, chopped
½ green cabbage, finely shredded
2 litres/3½ pints/9 cups light stock or water
200g/7oz spring greens or kale, finely shredded
200g/7oz Chinese mustard cabbage, finely shredded
200g/7oz spinach, shredded
1 bunch watercress, shredded
6 spring onions (scallions), finely shredded
25g/1oz/½ cup chopped fresh parsley
2.5ml/½ tsp ground allspice
¼ nutmeg, grated
salt, ground black pepper and cayenne
French bread or garlic bread, to serve

1 Dice the ham quite small, keeping the fat in one piece. Heat the lard or oil in a deep pan, add the ham and fat and cook until it sizzles. Stir in the onion, garlic, oregano and thyme and stir over a medium heat for 5 minutes.

2 Add the bay leaves, cloves, celery and green pepper and stir for another 2–3 minutes over the heat, then add the cabbage and stock or water.

3 Bring to the boil and simmer for 5 minutes. Add the spring greens or kale and mustard cabbage, boil for a further 2 minutes, then add the spinach, watercress and spring onions and lower the heat.

4 Simmer for 1 minute after it returns to the boil, then add the parsley, ground allspice and nutmeg, salt, black pepper and cayenne to taste. Remove the piece of ham fat and, if you can find them, the cloves. Serve immediately, with French bread or garlic bread.

Eggs in Remoulade Sauce

There are as many recipes for remoulade sauce as there are cooks in Louisiana. This one comes from the McIlhenny family, makers of Tabasco sauce, and naturally they splash some of the hot stuff into their remoulade.

Serves 4

45ml/3 tbsp coarse-ground mustard
10ml/2 tsp paprika
5ml/1 tsp Tabasco sauce
5ml/1 tsp salt
2.5ml/½ tsp ground black pepper
45ml/3 tbsp tarragon vinegar
250ml/8fl oz/1 cup olive oil
3 spring onions (scallions), shredded
1 celery stick, shredded
45ml/3 tbsp finely chopped fresh parsley
6 hard-boiled eggs
a handful of mustard and cress, to garnish

1 Whisk together the mustard, paprika, Tabasco sauce, salt and pepper, then beat in the vinegar.

2 Beating constantly, add the oil in a slow thin trickle, continuing to beat until the sauce is thick and smooth.

3 Stir in the spring onions, celery and parsley and mix well.

4 Cover the bowl and leave to stand for at least 2 hours to allow the flavours to blend.

5 Meanwhile, shell the hard-boiled eggs and halve them lengthways. Arrange three half eggs on each of four small plates. Spoon the remoulade sauce over the eggs, then sprinkle lightly with mustard and cress.

Cook's Tip
• Reduce the quantity of Tabasco if you want to make a less fiery sauce: it will still have plenty of flavour.
• This is an easy dish to make in a larger quantity for a buffet table. Leave the final assembly as late as you can before serving it.

Green Herb Gumbo: Energy 138kcal/573kJ; Protein 10.8g; Carbohydrate 8.8g, of which sugars 7.8g; Fat 6.8g, of which saturates 1.5g; Cholesterol 10mg; Calcium 129mg; Fibre 3.6g; Sodium 440mg.
Eggs in Remoulade Sauce: Energy 530kcal/2185kJ; Protein 10.8g; Carbohydrate 2.3g, of which sugars 1.2g; Fat 53.4g, of which saturates 8.7g; Cholesterol 285mg; Calcium 66mg; Fibre 0.3g; Sodium 444mg.

Peppers with Spiced Vegetables

Indian spices season the potato and aubergine stuffing in these colourful baked peppers.

Serves 6

6 large, evenly shaped red or
   yellow (bell) peppers
500g/1¼lb waxy potatoes
1 small onion, chopped
4–5 garlic cloves, chopped
5cm/2in piece fresh root ginger,
   chopped
2 green chillies, seeded and sliced
105ml/7 tbsp water
90–105ml/6–7 tbsp groundnut
   (peanut) oil
1 aubergine (eggplant), diced
10ml/2 tsp cumin seeds
5ml/1 tsp kalonji seeds
2.5ml/½ tsp ground turmeric
5ml/1 tsp ground coriander
5ml/1 tsp ground cumin seeds
pinch of cayenne pepper
about 30ml/2 tbsp lemon juice
salt and ground black pepper
30ml/2 tbsp chopped fresh
   coriander (cilantro), to garnish

1 Cut the tops off the peppers and discard the seeds. Cut a thin slice off the base, so they stand upright. Bring a large pan of salted water to the boil. Cook the peppers for 5–6 minutes. Drain and leave upside down in a colander.

2 Cook the potatoes in boiling salted water for 10–12 minutes. Drain, cool and peel them, then cut into 1cm/½in dice. Put the onion, garlic, ginger and green chillies in a food processor or blender with 60ml/4 tbsp of the water and process to a purée. Heat 45ml/3 tbsp of the oil in a large frying pan and stir-fry the aubergine, until browned. Remove from the pan and set aside. Add another 30ml/2 tbsp of the oil to the pan and cook the potatoes until browned. Remove and set aside.

3 Fry the cumin and kalonji seeds briefly, add the turmeric, coriander and cumin. Stir in the onion and garlic purée and fry until it begins to brown. Return the potatoes and aubergines to the pan, add salt, pepper and 2 pinches of cayenne. Add the remaining water and 15ml/1 tbsp lemon juice and cook until the liquid evaporates. Preheat the oven to 190°C/375°F/Gas 5.

4 Stuff the peppers with the potato mixture. Place on a lightly greased baking tray and bake for 30–35 minutes, until the peppers are cooked. Garnish with coriander and serve.

Fried Hard-boiled Eggs in Hot Red Sauce

A popular snack at street stalls in Malaysia and Singapore, this spicy egg dish originally comes from Indonesia. It is usually served wrapped in a banana leaf. The Malays often eat it with plain steamed rice, sliced chillies, onion and fresh coriander, and it is ideal for a quick, tasty snack.

Serves 4

vegetable oil, for deep-frying
8 eggs, hard-boiled and shelled
1 lemon grass stalk, trimmed,
   quartered and crushed
2 large tomatoes, skinned, seeded
   and chopped to a pulp
5–10ml/1–2 tsp sugar
30ml/2 tbsp dark soy sauce
juice of 1 lime
fresh coriander (cilantro) and mint
   leaves, coarsely chopped, to
   garnish

For the spice paste
4–6 red chillies, seeded and
   chopped
4 shallots, chopped
2 garlic cloves, peeled and
   chopped
2.5ml/½ tsp shrimp paste

1 Using a mortar and pestle or a food processor, grind together the ingredients for the spice paste until smooth. Set aside.

2 Heat enough oil for deep-frying in a wok or heavy pan and deep-fry the whole boiled eggs until they are golden brown. Lift them out and drain.

3 Reserve 15ml/1 tbsp of the oil in the wok or pan and discard the rest. Heat the oil in the wok or heavy pan and stir in the spice paste. Cook, stirring, until it becomes fragrant.

4 Add the lemon grass, followed by the tomatoes and sugar. Cook for 2–3 minutes, until it forms a thick paste.

5 Reduce the heat and stir in the soy sauce and lime juice. Add 30ml/2 tbsp water to thin the sauce. Toss in the eggs, making sure they are thoroughly coated, and serve hot, garnished with chopped coriander and mint leaves.

Peppers with Spiced Vegetables: Energy 234kcal/976kJ; Protein 4.2g; Carbohydrate 28.1g, of which sugars 14.8g; Fat 12.4g, of which saturates 2.4g; Cholesterol 0mg; Calcium 45mg; Fibre 5.5g; Sodium 21mg.
Fried Hard-boiled Eggs: Energy 271Kcal/1125kJ; Protein 13.3g; Carbohydrate 5.5g, of which sugars 5g; Fat 22.3g, of which saturates 4.4g; Cholesterol 381mg; Calcium 67mg; Fibre 0.7g; Sodium 679mg.

Cheese and Leek Rissoles with Tomato, Garlic and Chilli Sauce

These rissoles are based on the Welsh speciality, Glamorgan sausages. They are usually made with breadcrumbs alone, but mashed potato lightens the mix. Here they are served with a lively tomato sauce.

Serves 4

25g/1oz/2 tbsp butter
175g/6oz leeks, finely chopped
90ml/6 tbsp cold mashed potato
115g/4oz/2 cups fresh white or
  wholemeal (whole-wheat)
  breadcrumbs
150g/5oz/1¼ cups grated
  Caerphilly or Lancashire cheese
30ml/2 tbsp chopped fresh parsley
5ml/1 tsp chopped fresh sage
2 large eggs, beaten

cayenne pepper
65g/2½oz/1 cup dry white
  breadcrumbs
oil for shallow frying

For the sauce
30ml/2 tbsp olive oil
2 garlic cloves, thinly sliced
1 fresh red chilli, seeded and
  finely chopped, or a good pinch
  of dried red chilli flakes
1 small onion, finely chopped
500g/1¼lb tomatoes, peeled,
  seeded and chopped
few fresh thyme sprigs
10ml/2 tsp balsamic vinegar or
  red wine vinegar
pinch of light brown sugar
15–30ml/1–2 tbsp chopped fresh
  oregano
salt and ground black pepper

1 Melt the butter and fry the leeks for 4–5 minutes, until softened. Mix with the mashed potato, fresh breadcrumbs, cheese, parsley and sage. Add sufficient beaten egg (about two-thirds) to bind. Season well and add a good pinch of cayenne. Shape the mixture into 12 rissoles. Dip in the remaining egg, then coat with the dry breadcrumbs. Chill the coated rissoles.

2 To make the sauce, heat the oil over a low heat in a pan, add the garlic, chilli and onion and cook for 3–4 minutes. Add the tomatoes, thyme and vinegar. Add salt, pepper and sugar. Cook for 40–50 minutes, until reduced. Remove the thyme and purée in a blender. Reheat with the oregano, and adjust the seasoning.

3 Fry the rissoles in shallow oil until golden brown on all sides. Drain on kitchen paper and serve with the sauce.

Roasted Vegetables and Spicy Sauce

Served as a vegetable side dish or as a main course, a selection of roasted vegetables in a peanut sauce, enhanced by chillies and soy sauce, is a favourite throughout South-east Asia.

Serves 4

1 aubergine (eggplant), partially
  peeled and cut into long strips
2 courgettes (zucchini), partially
  peeled and cut into long strips
1 thick, long sweet potato, cut into
  long strips
2 leeks, trimmed, halved and
  sliced
2 garlic cloves, chopped
25g/1oz fresh root ginger, peeled
  and chopped

60ml/4 tbsp vegetable or oil
salt
45ml/3 tbsp roasted peanuts,
  ground, to garnish
fresh crusty bread, to serve

For the sauce
4 garlic cloves, chopped
2–3 red chillies, seeded and
  chopped
5ml/1 tsp shrimp paste
115g/4oz/1 cup roasted peanuts,
  crushed
15–30ml/1–2 tbsp dark soy sauce
juice of 1 lime
5–10ml/1–2 tsp Chinese rice
  vinegar
10ml/2 tsp palm sugar (jaggery)
  or honey
salt and ground black pepper

1 Preheat the oven to 200°C/400°F/Gas 6. Arrange the vegetables in a roasting pan. Using a mortar and pestle or food processor, grind the garlic and ginger to a paste, and smear it over the vegetables. Sprinkle with salt and pour over the oil.

2 Place the pan in the oven for about 45 minutes, until the vegetables are lightly browned, tossing halfway through cooking.

3 Meanwhile, make the sauce. Using a mortar and pestle or food processor, grind the garlic and chillies to a paste. Beat in the shrimp paste and peanuts. Stir in the soy sauce, lime juice, vinegar and sugar or honey, and blend with a little water so that the sauce is the consistency of pouring cream. Season with salt and pepper and adjust the balance of sweet and sour to taste.

4 Arrange the roasted vegetables on a plate. Drizzle the sauce over them, or serve it separately in a bowl. Sprinkle the ground peanuts over the top and serve with bread.

Cheese and Leek Rissoles: Energy 580kcal/2416kJ; Protein 19.2g; Carbohydrate 35.5g, of which sugars 6.9g; Fat 40.3g, of which saturates 15.2g; Cholesterol 164mg; Calcium 361mg; Fibre 3.6g; Sodium 604mg.
Roasted Vegetables: Energy 361Kcal/1502kJ; Protein 11.9g; Carbohydrate 22.7g, of which sugars 11.1g; Fat 25.4g, of which saturates 4.1g; Cholesterol 0mg; Calcium 76mg; Fibre 6.9g; Sodium 292mg.

Lentil Salad with Cumin and Garlic

This wonderful, earthy salad is great with barbecued food. It is best served at room temperature.

Serves 6

225g/8oz/1 cup Puy lentils
1 fresh bay leaf
1 celery stick
fresh thyme sprig
30ml/2 tbsp olive oil
1 onion or 3–4 shallots, chopped
10ml/2 tsp crushed toasted cumin
  seeds
400g/14oz young spinach
salt and ground black pepper
30–45ml/2–3 tbsp chopped fresh
  parsley, plus a few extra sprigs
French bread rounds, to serve

For the dressing
75ml/5 tbsp extra virgin olive oil
5ml/1 tsp Dijon mustard
15–25ml/1–1 ½ tbsp red wine
  vinegar
1 small garlic clove, chopped
2.5ml/½ tsp finely grated
  lemon rind

1 Rinse the lentils and place in a large pan. Add water to cover. Tie the bay leaf, celery and thyme into a bundle and add to the pan, then bring to the boil. Reduce the heat. Cook the lentils for 30 minutes, until just tender. Drain and turn into a bowl.

2 Meanwhile, to make the dressing, mix the oil, mustard, 15ml/1 tbsp vinegar, the garlic and lemon rind, and season well with salt and pepper. Add most of the dressing to the lentils and toss well, then set aside.

3 Heat the oil in a deep pan and cook the onion or shallots over a low heat for about 4–5 minutes, stirring occasionally, until they are beginning to soften. Add the cumin and cook for 1 minute. Add the spinach and season to taste, cover and cook for 2 minutes. Stir, then cook again briefly until wilted.

4 Stir the spinach into the lentils and leave the salad to cool. Bring back to room temperature if necessary. Stir in the remaining dressing and chopped parsley. Adjust the seasoning, adding extra red wine vinegar if necessary.

5 Brush the rounds of French bread with olive oil and toast under the grill (broiler). Turn the salad on to a serving platter, sprinkle over some parsley sprigs and serve with the toast.

Grilled Leek and Fennel Salad with Spicy Tomato Dressing

This is an excellent salad to make in the early autumn when young leeks are at their best. Serve with bread.

Serves 2

2 large fennel bulbs
675g/1½lb leeks, trimmed
120ml/4fl oz/½ cup olive oil
2 shallots, chopped
150ml/¼ pint/⅔ cup dry white
  wine or white vermouth
5ml/1 tsp fennel seeds, crushed
6 fresh thyme sprigs
2–3 bay leaves
pinch of dried red chilli
  flakes
350g/12oz tomatoes, peeled,
  seeded and diced
5ml/1 tsp sun-dried tomato paste
good pinch of caster (superfine)
  sugar
75g/3oz/¾ cup small black olives
salt and ground black pepper

1 Trim the fennel bulbs, reserving any feathery tops for the garnish and cut the bulbs into wedges. Cook the fennel with the leeks in boiling salted water for 4–5 minutes. Drain thoroughly and cool. Squeeze out excess water from the leeks and cut into 7.5cm/3in lengths. Toss the fennel pieces with 30ml/2 tbsp of the olive oil. Season to taste with black pepper.

2 Heat a ridged cast-iron griddle. Arrange the leeks and fennel on the griddle and cook until tinged deep brown, turning once. Remove the vegetables from the griddle, place in a large shallow dish and set aside.

3 Place the remaining olive oil, the shallots, white wine or vermouth, crushed fennel seeds, thyme, bay leaves and chilli flakes in a large pan and bring to the boil. Lower the heat and simmer for 10 minutes. Add the diced tomatoes and cook briskly for 5–8 minutes, or until reduced and thickened.

4 Add the tomato paste, and adjust the seasoning, adding a good pinch of caster sugar if you think the dressing needs it.

5 Pour the dressing over the leeks and fennel, toss to mix and leave to cool. When ready to serve, stir the salad then sprinkle the chopped fennel tops and black olives over the top.

North African Fish with Spicy Pumpkin Rice

This is a dish of contrasts – the slightly sweet flavour of pumpkin, the mildly spicy fish, and the coriander and ginger mixture that is stirred in at the end – all bound with well-flavoured rice.

Serves 4

450g/1lb sea bass or other firm fish fillets, skinned and boned
30ml/2 tbsp plain (all-purpose) flour
5ml/1 tsp ground coriander
1.5–2.5ml/¼–½ tsp ground turmeric
500g/1¼lb pumpkin flesh
30–45ml/2–3 tbsp olive oil
6 spring onions (scallions), sliced diagonally
1 garlic clove, finely chopped
275g/10oz/1½ cups basmati rice, soaked and drained
550ml/18fl oz/2½ cups fish stock
salt and ground black pepper
lime or lemon wedges and fresh coriander (cilantro) sprigs, to serve

For the flavouring mixture

45ml/3 tbsp finely chopped fresh coriander (cilantro)
10ml/2 tsp finely chopped fresh root ginger
½–1 fresh chilli, seeded and very finely chopped
45ml/3 tbsp lime or lemon juice

1 Cut the fish into 2cm/¾in chunks. Mix the flour with the coriander, turmeric and a little salt and pepper and coat the fish. Set aside. Mix all the ingredients for the flavouring mixture.

2 Cut the pumpkin into 2cm/¾in chunks. Heat 15ml/1 tbsp oil in a flameproof casserole and stir-fry the spring onions and garlic for a few minutes until softened. Add the pumpkin and cook over a fairly low heat, stirring, for 4–5 minutes. Add the rice and toss over a brisk heat for 2–3 minutes. Stir in the stock. Bring to simmering point, then lower the heat, cover and cook for 12–15 minutes.

3 Heat the remaining oil in a pan and fry the fish for about 3 minutes on each side. Stir flavouring mixture into the rice and transfer to a serving dish. Lay the fish on top. Serve with coriander, and lemon or lime wedges for squeezing.

Kedgeree

A popular Victorian breakfast dish, kedgeree has its origins in *kitchiri*, an Indian dish of rice and lentils. It can be flavoured with curry powder, but this recipe is mild.

Serves 4

500g/1¼lb smoked haddock
115g/4oz/generous ½ cup basmati rice
30ml/2 tbsp lemon juice
150ml/¼ pint/⅔ cup single (light) cream or sour cream
pinch of freshly grated nutmeg
pinch of cayenne pepper
2 hard-boiled eggs, peeled and cut into wedges
50g/2oz/4 tbsp butter, diced
30ml/2 tbsp chopped fresh parsley
salt and ground black pepper

1 Put the haddock in a shallow pan, pour in just enough water to cover and heat to simmering point. Poach the fish for about 10 minutes, until the flesh flakes easily when tested with the tip of a sharp knife. Lift the fish out of the liquid, then remove any skin and bones and flake the flesh. Reserve the cooking liquid,

2 Pour the cooking liquid into a measuring jug (cup) and make up the volume with water to 250ml/8fl oz/1 cup.

3 Pour the measured liquid into a pan and bring it to the boil. Add the rice, stir, then lower the heat, cover and simmer for about 10 minutes, until the rice is tender and the liquid has been absorbed. Meanwhile, preheat the oven to 180°C/350°F/Gas 4 and butter a baking dish.

4 When the rice is cooked, remove it from the heat and stir in the lemon juice, cream, flaked haddock, grated nutmeg and cayenne pepper. Add the egg wedges to the rice mixture and stir in gently.

5 Tip the rice mixture into the prepared baking dish. Level the surface and dot with butter. Cover the dish loosely with foil and bake for about 25 minutes.

6 Stir the chopped parsley into the baked kedgeree and add seasoning to taste. Serve immediately.

Fish with Spicy Pumpkin Rice: Energy 436kcal/1825kJ; Protein 27.9g; Carbohydrate 64.2g, of which sugars 3g; Fat 7.2g, of which saturates 1.1g; Cholesterol 52mg; Calcium 101mg; Fibre 2.3g; Sodium 73mg.
Kedgeree: Energy 320kcal/1336kJ; Protein 15.6g; Carbohydrate 46.6g, of which sugars 0g; Fat 7.6g, of which saturates 3.3g; Cholesterol 149mg; Calcium 39mg; Fibre 0g; Sodium 357mg.

Moroccan Paella

This version of paella has crossed the sea from Spain, and acquired some North African spicy touches.

Serves 6
2 large skinless chicken breast fillets about 150g/5oz squid rings
275g/10oz cod or haddock fillets, skinned and cut into chunks
8–10 raw king prawns (jumbo shrimp), peeled and deveined
8 scallops, trimmed and halved
350g/12oz mussels, cleaned
250g/9oz/1⅓ cups white long-grain rice
30ml/2 tbsp sunflower oil
5 spring onions (scallions), cut into strips

2 small courgettes (zucchini), cut into strips
1 red (bell) pepper, cut into strips
400ml/14fl oz/1⅔ cups chicken or vegetable stock
250ml/8fl oz/1 cup passata
salt and ground black pepper

For the marinade
2 fresh red chillies, seeded and roughly chopped
handful of fresh coriander (cilantro)
10–15ml/2–3 tsp ground cumin
15ml/1 tbsp paprika
2 garlic cloves
45ml/3 tbsp olive oil
60ml/4 tbsp sunflower oil
juice of 1 lemon

1 Mix the marinade ingredients with 5ml/1 tsp salt. Cut the chicken into bitesize pieces and place in a bowl. Place the fish and shellfish (apart from the mussels) in another bowl. Divide the marinade between the fish and chicken and stir. Cover with clear film (plastic wrap) and marinate for at least 2 hours.

2 Place the rice in a bowl, cover with boiling water and soak for 30 minutes. Drain the chicken and fish, and reserve the marinade. Heat the oil in a large pan and fry the chicken until lightly browned. Add the spring onions, fry for 1 minute and then add the courgettes and pepper and fry for 3–4 minutes. Remove the chicken and vegetables to plates.

3 Scrape the marinade into the pan and cook for 1 minute, then stir in the drained rice. Add the stock, passata and chicken, and season. Bring to the boil, cover and simmer for 10–15 minutes until the rice is almost tender. Add the vegetables and place the fish and mussels on top. Cover and cook for 10–12 minutes. Discard any mussels that remain closed and serve.

Fried Chilli Fish with Spicy Rice

Cooking rice in fish stock gives it a splendid flavour. Here it is served with allioli.

Serves 6
45ml/3 tbsp olive oil
6 garlic cloves, smashed
1 dried chilli, seeded and chopped
250g/9oz ripe tomatoes, peeled, seeded and chopped
pinch of saffron threads
1.6kg/3½lb mixed fish fillets such as snapper, mullet, or bass
1 litre/1¾ pints/4 cups fish stock

30ml/2 tbsp dry white wine
1 tomato, finely diced
30ml/2 tbsp chopped fresh parsley
400g/14oz/2 cups paella rice, washed
115g/4oz tiny unshelled shrimps
salt and ground black pepper

For the allioli
4 garlic cloves, finely chopped
2.5ml/½ tsp salt
5ml/1 tsp lemon juice
2 egg yolks
250ml/8fl oz/1 cup olive oil

1 To make the allioli, put the chopped garlic in a large mortar (or blender) with the salt and lemon juice and reduce to a purée. Add the egg yolks and mix thoroughly. Gradually work in the oil to make a thick, mayonnaise-like sauce.

2 Put 15ml/1 tbsp of the olive oil in a small pan and add the smashed garlic cloves and dried chilli. Fry for a few minutes then add the chopped tomato and saffron. Cook for a few minutes, then transfer to a processor and blend until smooth.

3 Heat the remaining 30ml/2 tbsp oil in a large pan or a wide flameproof casserole and fry the fish pieces until they begin to stiffen. Add the fish stock and the tomato sauce to the pan and cook gently for 3–4 minutes.

4 Remove the fish from the pan to a serving dish. Season lightly, sprinkle with the wine, diced tomato and parsley. Cover with foil and keep warm.

5 Add the rice to the stock, stir, season and bring to a simmer. Cook for 18–20 minutes. Before all the liquid is absorbed, stir in the shrimps. When the rice is tender, cover and turn off the heat. Stand until all the liquid is absorbed: about 5 minutes. Serve with the fish fillets and allioli.

Moroccan Paella: Energy 401kcal/1688kJ; Protein 46g; Carbohydrate 39.3g, of which sugars 4.4g; Fat 6.6g, of which saturates 1.1g; Cholesterol 200mg; Calcium 115mg; Fibre 1.4g; Sodium 343mg.
Chilli Fish with Spicy Rice: Energy 809kcal/3367kJ; Protein 56.9g; Carbohydrate 55.6g, of which sugars 1.9g; Fat 39g, of which saturates 5.8g; Cholesterol 198mg; Calcium 71mg; Fibre 0.7g; Sodium 412mg.

Spicy Meatballs with Red Rice

In this Moroccan dish, the nutty flavour of red rice is a perfect match for the spicy lamb meatballs.

Serves 4–6

225g/8oz/generous 1 cup Camargue red rice
675g/1½lb lamb leg steaks
2 onions
3–4 fresh parsley sprigs
3 fresh coriander (cilantro) sprigs, plus 30ml/2 tbsp chopped fresh coriander
1–2 fresh mint sprigs
2.5ml/½ tsp ground cumin
2.5ml/½ tsp ground cinnamon
2.5ml/½ tsp ground ginger
5ml/1 tsp paprika
30ml/2 tbsp sunflower oil
1 garlic clove, crushed
300ml/½ pint/1¼ cups tomato juice
450ml/¾ pint/scant 2 cups chicken or vegetable stock
salt and ground black pepper
flatbread and natural (plain) yogurt, to serve

1 Cook the rice in lightly salted water or stock for 30 minutes or according to the instructions on the packet. Drain.

2 Meanwhile, chop the lamb roughly, then place it in a food processor and process until finely chopped. Scrape the meat into a large bowl. Cut one onion into quarters and add it to the processor with the parsley, coriander and mint sprigs; process until finely chopped. Return the lamb to the processor, add the spices and seasoning and process again until smooth. Scrape the mixture into a bowl and chill for about 1 hour.

3 Shape the mixture into about 30 balls. Heat half the oil in a frying pan, add the meatballs, in batches, and brown them evenly. Transfer to a plate.

4 Chop the remaining onion finely. Drain off the excess fat from the pan, leaving around 30ml/2 tbsp, and fry the chopped onion with the garlic for a few minutes until softened. Stir in the rice. Cook, stirring for 1–2 minutes, then add the tomato juice, stock and fresh coriander. Season to taste.

5 Arrange the meatballs over the rice, cover with a lid or foil and simmer very gently for 15 minutes. Serve with flatbread and yogurt.

Spicy Lamb and Vegetable Pilaff

Tender lamb is served in this dish with basmati rice and a colourful selection of vegetables and cashew nuts. The dish is presented in cabbage leaf "bowls".

Serves 4

450g/1lb boned shoulder of lamb, cubed
2.5ml/½ tsp dried thyme
2.5ml/½ tsp paprika
5ml/1 tsp garam masala
1 garlic clove, crushed
25ml/1½ tbsp vegetable oil
900ml/1½ pints/3¾ cups stock
large Savoy cabbage leaves, to serve

For the rice

25g/1oz/2 tbsp butter
1 onion, chopped
1 medium potato, diced
1 carrot, sliced
½ red (bell) pepper, chopped
1 green chilli, seeded and chopped
115g/4oz/1 cup sliced cabbage
60ml/4 tbsp natural (plain) yogurt
2.5ml/½ tsp ground cumin
5 green cardamom pods
2 garlic cloves, crushed
225g/8oz/generous 1 cup basmati rice, soaked and drained
50g/2oz/½ cup cashew nuts
salt and ground black pepper

1 Put the lamb cubes in a large bowl and add the thyme, paprika, garam masala and garlic, with plenty of salt and pepper. Stir, cover, and leave in a cool place for 2–3 hours.

2 Heat the oil in a pan and brown the lamb, in batches, over a medium heat for 5–6 minutes. Stir in the stock, cover, and cook for 35–40 minutes. Using a slotted spoon, transfer the lamb to a bowl. Pour the liquid into a measuring jug (cup), topping it up with water if necessary to make 600ml/1 pint/2½ cups.

3 Melt the butter in a separate pan and fry the onion, potato and carrot for 5 minutes. Add the red pepper and chilli and fry for 3 minutes more, then stir in the cabbage, yogurt, spices, garlic and the reserved lamb stock. Stir well, cover, then simmer gently for 5–10 minutes, until the cabbage has wilted.

4 Stir the rice into the stew with the lamb. Cover and simmer over a low heat for 20 minutes or until the rice is cooked. Sprinkle in the cashew nuts and season to taste with salt and pepper. Serve hot, cupped in cabbage leaves.

Meatballs with Red Rice: Energy 405kcal/1694kJ; Protein 26.4g; Carbohydrate 36.1g, of which sugars 5.2g; Fat 17.3g, of which saturates 6.3g; Cholesterol 86mg; Calcium 42mg; Fibre 1.2g; Sodium 215mg.
Lamb and Vegetable Pilaff: Energy 751kcal/3135kJ; Protein 33.7g; Carbohydrate 86.3g, of which sugars 7.3g; Fat 30.1g, of which saturates 11.6g; Cholesterol 102mg; Calcium 88mg; Fibre 2.3g; Sodium 200mg.

Spiced Louisiana Rice

Aubergine and pork combine with herbs and spices to make a highly flavoursome dish that makes a meal in itself.

Serves 4

60ml/4 tbsp vegetable oil
1 onion, chopped
1 small aubergine (eggplant), diced
225g/8oz minced (ground) pork
1 green (bell) pepper, chopped
2 celery sticks, chopped
1 garlic clove, crushed

5ml/1 tsp cayenne pepper
5ml/1 tsp paprika
5ml/1 tsp ground black pepper
2.5ml/½ tsp salt
5ml/1 tsp dried thyme
2.5ml/½ tsp dried oregano
475ml/16fl oz/2 cups chicken stock
225g/8oz chicken livers, trimmed and chopped
150g/5oz/¾ cup white long grain rice
1 bay leaf
45ml/3 tbsp chopped fresh parsley

1 Heat the oil in a frying pan. When it is piping hot, add the onion and aubergine and stir-fry for about 5 minutes.

2 Add the pork and cook for 6–8 minutes until browned, using a wooden spoon to break up any lumps.

3 Stir in the green pepper, celery and garlic, and add all the spices and herbs. Cook over a high heat for 9–10 minutes, stirring frequently from the bottom of the pan to scrape up and distribute the crispy brown bits.

4 Pour in the chicken stock and stir to incorporate any sediment from the bottom of the pan. Cover and cook for 6 minutes over a moderate heat. Stir in the chicken livers and cook for 2 minutes more.

5 Stir in the rice and add the bay leaf. Lower the heat, cover the pan and simmer for 6–7 minutes. Turn off the heat and leave to stand, still covered, for 10–15 minutes more until the rice is tender.

6 Remove the bay leaf and stir in the chopped parsley. Serve the rice hot.

Brazilian Pork and Rice Casserole with Chilli and Juniper Berries

This hearty marinated pork dish with vegetables and rice is very popular in Brazil.

Serves 4–6

500g/1¼lb lean pork, such as fillet (tenderloin), cut into strips
60ml/4 tbsp corn oil
1 onion, chopped
1 garlic clove, crushed
1 green (bell) pepper, diced
about 300ml/½ pint/1¼ cups chicken stock
225g/8oz/1 cup long grain rice

150ml/¼ pint/⅔ cup double (heavy) cream
40g/1½oz/½ cup freshly grated Parmesan cheese
salt and ground black pepper

For the marinade

120ml/4fl oz/½ cup dry white wine
30ml/2 tbsp lemon juice
1 onion, chopped
4 juniper berries, lightly crushed
3 cloves
1 red chilli, seeded and sliced

1 Mix all the marinade ingredients, add the pork and set aside to marinate for 3–4 hours. Transfer the pork to a plate. Strain the marinade and set aside. Heat the oil in a heavy pan and brown the pork for a few minutes. Transfer to a plate.

2 Add the chopped onion, garlic and pepper to the pan and fry for 6–8 minutes, then return the pork to the pan. Pour in the reserved marinade and the stock. Bring to the boil and season with salt and black pepper, then lower the heat, cover and simmer for 10 minutes until the meat is nearly tender.

3 Preheat the oven to 160°C/325°F/Gas 3. Cook the rice in salted boiling water for 8 minutes or until three quarters cooked. Drain. Spread half the rice over the bottom of a buttered baking dish. Make a neat layer of meat and vegetables on top, then spread the remaining rice over the top.

4 Stir the cream and 30ml/2 tbsp of the Parmesan into the liquid in which the pork was cooked. Pour this mixture over the rice and sprinkle with the remaining Parmesan cheese. Cover with foil, bake for 20 minutes, then remove the foil and cook for 5 minutes more, to brown the top. Serve immediately.

Spiced Chicken Rice with Lemon and Mint Relish

This beautifully spiced chicken dish is quickly made with tender breast meat and makes a lovely summer meal, accompanied by a refreshing relish, sharply flavoured with lemon. The chicken and rice mixture is fragrant with cardamom, one of the most delicately aromatic of all spices.

Serves 4
250g/9oz skinless chicken breast
 fillets, diced
3 garlic cloves, chopped
5ml/1 tsp ground turmeric
30–45ml/2–3 tbsp olive oil

2 small-medium carrots, diced
 or chopped
seeds from 6–8 cardamom pods
500g/1¹/₂lb/2¹/₄ cups long grain
 rice
250g/9oz tomatoes, chopped
750ml/1¹/₄ pints/3 cups chicken
 stock

For the lemon and mint relish
3 tomatoes, diced
1 bunch or large handful of fresh
 mint, chopped
5–8 spring onions (scallions),
 thinly sliced
juice of 2 lemons
salt

1 To make the relish, put all the ingredients in a bowl and mix together. Chill until ready to serve.

2 Mix the diced chicken with half the garlic and the ground turmeric. Heat a little of the oil in a pan, add the chicken and fry briefly until the chicken has changed colour and is almost cooked. Remove the chicken from the pan with a slotted spoon and set aside.

3 Add the carrots to the pan with the remaining oil, then add the remaining garlic, cardamom seeds and the rice. Cook for 1–2 minutes, stirring thoroughly so that the grains of rice are well coated in the oil.

4 Add the tomatoes and chicken stock to the pan and bring to the boil. Cover and simmer for about 10 minutes, until the rice is tender. A few minutes before the rice is cooked, fork in the chicken. Serve with the relish.

Fragrant Rice with Chicken, Mint and Nuoc Cham

From the north of Vietnam, this refreshing dish can be served simply, drizzled with nuoc cham, or as part of a celebratory meal that might include fish or chicken, either grilled or roasted whole, accompanied by pickles and a salad.

Serves 4
350g/12oz/1¾ cups long grain
 rice, rinsed and drained
2–3 shallots, halved and finely
 sliced

1 bunch of fresh mint, stalks
 removed, leaves finely shredded
2 spring onions (scallions), finely
 sliced, to garnish
nuoc cham, to serve

For the stock
2 meaty chicken legs
1 onion, peeled and quartered
4cm/1¹/₂in fresh root ginger,
 peeled and coarsely chopped
15ml/1 tbsp nuoc mam
3 black peppercorns
1 bunch of fresh mint
sea salt

1 To make the stock, put the chicken legs into a deep pan with all the other ingredients except the salt, and add 1 litre/1¾ pints/4 cups water. Bring to the boil, skim off any foam, then reduce the heat and simmer gently with the lid on for 1 hour.

2 Remove the lid, increase the heat and simmer for a further 30 minutes to reduce. Skim off any fat, strain the stock and season with salt. Measure 750ml/1¼ pints/3 cups stock. Remove the chicken meat from the bone and shred it.

3 Put the rice in a heavy pan and stir in the stock. When the rice settles, check that the stock sits roughly 2.5cm/1in above the rice; if not, top it up. Bring the liquid to the boil, cover the pan and cook for about 25 minutes, or until all the water has been absorbed.

4 Remove the pan from the heat and, using a fork, add the shredded chicken, shallots and most of the mint. Cover the pan again and leave for 10 minutes for the flavours to mingle. Tip the rice into bowls, or on to a serving dish, garnish with the mint and spring onions, and serve with nuoc cham.

Chicken Rice with Relish: Energy 629kcal/2630kJ; Protein 26g; Carbohydrate 106.7g, of which sugars 6.8g; Fat 10.3g, of which saturates 1.6g; Cholesterol 44mg; Calcium 73mg; Fibre 2.8g; Sodium 61mg.
Fragrant Rice with Nuoc Cham: Energy 370Kcal/1569kJ; Protein 12g; Carbohydrate 79g, of which sugars 1g; Fat 3g, of which saturates 0g; Cholesterol 26mg; Calcium 41mg; Fibre 0.8g; Sodium 200mg.

Chicken and Vegetable Tagine

Moroccan tagines are usually served with couscous, but rice makes an equally delicious accompaniment.

Serves 4
30ml/2 tbsp groundnut (peanut) oil
4 skinless chicken breast fillets, cut into large pieces
1 large onion, chopped
2 garlic cloves, crushed
1 parsnip, diced
1 small turnip, diced
3 carrots, diced
4 tomatoes, chopped
4 cloves
1 cinnamon stick
5ml/1 tsp ground ginger
1 bay leaf
2.5ml/½ tsp cayenne pepper
350ml/12fl oz/1½ cups chicken stock
400g/14oz can chickpeas, drained
1 red pepper, sliced
150g/5oz green beans, halved
1 piece of preserved lemon peel, thinly sliced
20–30 brown or green olives
salt
45ml/3 tbsp chopped fresh coriander (cilantro)

For the rice and couscous
750ml/1¼ pints/3 cups chicken stock
225g/8oz/1 cup long grain rice
115g/4oz/⅔ cup couscous

1 Heat half the oil in a large casserole and fry the chicken until evenly browned. Transfer to a plate. Heat the remaining oil and fry the onion, garlic, parsnip, turnip and carrots for 4–5 minutes until browned. Lower the heat, cover and sweat for 5 minutes.

2 Add the tomatoes, cook for a few minutes, then add the cloves, cinnamon, ginger, bay leaf and cayenne. Cook for 1–2 minutes. Pour in the stock and add the chickpeas and chicken. Season with salt, cover and simmer for 25 minutes.

3 Meanwhile, to cook the rice and couscous mixture, bring the chicken stock to the boil, add the rice and simmer for about 5 minutes until almost tender. Remove the pan from the heat, stir in the couscous, cover tightly and leave for about 5 minutes.

4 When the vegetables are almost tender, stir in the pepper and green beans and simmer for 10 minutes. Add the lemon and olives, stir well and cook for 5 minutes more. Stir in the coriander and serve with the rice and couscous.

Chinese Clay Pot Rice with Chicken

This Cantonese dish is a great family one-pot meal. It is traditionally cooked in a clay pot, which ensures that the ingredients remain moist while allowing the flavours to mingle. Any earthenware pot that can be used on the hob will work well. This recipe is also delicious when made with prawns or strips of pork fillet.

Serves 4
500g/1¼lb skinless chicken breast fillets, cut into thin strips
5 dried shiitake mushrooms, soaked in hot water for 30 minutes, until soft
1 Chinese sausage, sliced
750ml/1¼ pints/3 cups chicken stock
225g/8oz/generous 1 cup long grain rice, thoroughly washed and drained
fresh coriander (cilantro) leaves, finely chopped, to garnish

For the marinade
30ml/2 tbsp sesame oil
45ml/3 tbsp oyster sauce
30ml/2 tbsp soy sauce
25g/1oz fresh root ginger, finely grated
2 spring onions (scallions), trimmed and finely sliced
1 red chilli, seeded and finely sliced
5ml/1 tsp sugar
ground black pepper

1 In a bowl, mix together the ingredients for the marinade. Toss in the chicken, making sure it is well coated and set aside.

2 Make sure the shiitake mushrooms are soft (leave them to soak for longer, if necessary). Squeeze them to get rid of any excess water. Using a sharp knife, remove any hard stems and halve the caps. Add the mushroom caps and the Chinese sausage to the chicken.

3 Bring the stock to the boil in the clay pot. Stir in the rice and bring it back to the boil. Reduce the heat, cover the pot, and simmer on a low heat for 15–20 minutes, until almost all the liquid has been absorbed.

4 Spread the marinated chicken and mushroom mixture over the top of the rice and cover the pot. Leave to steam for about 10–15 minutes, until all the liquid is absorbed. Garnish with coriander and serve.

Chicken Tagine: Energy 450kcal/1891kJ; Protein 46.9g; Carbohydrate 36.2g, of which sugars 16.4g; Fat 14g, of which saturates 2.3g; Cholesterol 105mg; Calcium 131mg; Fibre 10.8g; Sodium 901mg.
Chinese Rice with Chicken: Energy 371Kcal/1560kJ; Protein 36.2g; Carbohydrate 46.8g, of which sugars 1g; Fat 4g, of which saturates 1.2g; Cholesterol 93mg; Calcium 54mg; Fibre 0.7g; Sodium 721mg.

Curried Chicken and Rice

This simple meal is made in a single pot, so it is perfect for casual entertaining. It can be made using virtually any meat or vegetables that you have to hand, but chicken is quick and easy to cook and takes extremely well to Indian spicing.

Serves 4

60ml/4 tbsp vegetable oil
4 garlic cloves, finely chopped
1 medium-sized chicken or 1.3kg/3lb chicken portions, skin and bones removed and meat cut into bitesize pieces
5ml/1 tsp garam masala
450g/1lb/2⅔ cups jasmine rice, rinsed and drained
10ml/2 tsp salt
1 litre/1¾ pints/4 cups chicken stock
small bunch fresh coriander (cilantro), chopped, to garnish

1 Heat the oil in a wok or flameproof casserole that has a lid. Add the garlic and cook over a low to medium heat until golden brown. Add the chicken, increase the heat and brown the pieces on all sides.

2 Add the garam masala, stir well to coat the chicken pieces all over in the spice, then tip in the drained rice. Add the salt and stir to mix.

3 Pour in the stock, stir well, then cover the wok or casserole and bring to the boil. Reduce the heat to low and simmer gently for 10 minutes, until the rice is tender.

4 Lift the wok or casserole off the heat, leaving the lid on, and leave for 10 minutes for the flavours to mingle. Fluff up the rice grains with a fork and spoon on to a platter. Sprinkle with the coriander and serve.

> **Cook's Tip**
> You will probably need to brown the chicken in batches. Don't be tempted to add too much chicken to the pan at once, as this will lower the temperature of the oil and the chicken will stew rather than frying.

Paprika Chicken with Rice

This Spanish rice dish with chicken is a casserole, intended to be more liquid than a paella. You can vary the recipe by adding seasonal vegetables, and peas and corn can also be included if you wish. The paprika and the slices of chorizo give the rice a warm spicy flavour.

Serves 4

60ml/4 tbsp olive oil
6 chicken thighs, halved along the bone
5ml/1 tsp paprika
1 large Spanish onion, roughly chopped
2 garlic cloves, finely chopped
1 chorizo sausage, sliced
115g/4oz Serrano or cooked ham or gammon, diced
1 red (bell) pepper, roughly chopped
1 yellow (bell) pepper, roughly chopped
225g/8oz/1 generous cup paella rice, washed and drained
2 large tomatoes, chopped or 200g/7oz can chopped tomatoes
120ml/4fl oz/½ cup amontillado sherry
750ml/1¼ pints/3 cups chicken stock
5ml/1 tsp dried oregano or thyme
1 bay leaf
salt and ground black pepper
15 green olives and chopped fresh flat leaf parsley, to garnish

1 Heat the oil in a wide flameproof casserole. Season the chicken pieces with salt and paprika. Fry until nicely brown all over, then reserve on a plate.

2 Add the onion and garlic to the pan and fry gently until beginning to soften. Add the sliced chorizo and ham or gammon and stir-fry. Add the chopped peppers and cook until they begin to soften.

3 Sprinkle in the drained rice and cook, stirring, for 1–2 minutes. Add the tomatoes, sherry, chicken stock and dried herbs and season well. Arrange the chicken pieces deep in the mixture, and tuck in the bay leaf.

4 Cover and cook over a very low heat for 30–40 minutes, until the chicken and rice are done. Stir, then garnish with olives and chopped parsley and serve.

Curried Chicken and Rice: Energy 715kcal/2994kJ; Protein 56.3g; Carbohydrate 89.8g, of which sugars 0g; Fat 13.8g, of which saturates 1.9g; Cholesterol 140mg; Calcium 32mg; Fibre 0g; Sodium 120mg.
Paprika Chicken with Rice: Energy 194kcal/813kJ; Protein 26g; Carbohydrate 2.1g, of which sugars 1.6g; Fat 9.1g, of which saturates 1.4g; Cholesterol 74mg; Calcium 42mg; Fibre 1.1g; Sodium 69mg.

Spiced Caribbean Chicken Rice

Golden caramelized chicken tops a rich vegetable rice in this delicious supper dish. Use borlotti beans if pigeon peas are not available.

Serves 4

5ml/1 tsp allspice
2.5ml/½ tsp ground cinnamon
5ml/1 tsp dried thyme
pinch of ground cloves
1.5ml/¼ tsp grated nutmeg
4 skinless chicken breast fillets
45ml/3 tbsp groundnut (peanut) or sunflower oil
15g/½oz/1 tbsp butter
1 onion, chopped
2 garlic cloves, crushed
1 carrot, diced
1 celery stick, chopped
3 spring onions (scallions), chopped
1 fresh red chilli, seeded and thinly sliced
400g/14oz can pigeon peas
225g/8oz/generous 1 cup long grain rice
120ml/4fl oz/½ cup coconut milk
550ml/18fl oz/2½ cups chicken stock
30ml/2 tbsp demerara (raw) sugar
salt and cayenne pepper

1 Mix together the allspice, cinnamon, thyme, cloves and nutmeg. Rub the mixture all over the pieces of chicken. Set aside for 30 minutes.

2 Heat 15ml/1 tbsp of the oil with the butter in a pan. Fry the onion and garlic over a medium heat until soft and beginning to brown. Add the carrot, celery, spring onions and chilli. Sauté for a few minutes, then stir in the pigeon peas, rice, coconut milk and chicken stock. Season with salt and cayenne pepper. Bring to simmering point, cover and cook over a low heat for about 25 minutes.

3 About 10 minutes before the rice mixture is cooked, heat the remaining oil in a heavy frying pan, add the sugar and cook, without stirring, until it begins to caramelize.

4 Carefully add the chicken to the pan. Cook for 8–10 minutes until the chicken has a browned, glazed appearance and is cooked through. Transfer the chicken to a board and slice it thickly. Serve the pigeon pea rice in individual bowls, with the chicken on top.

Thai Fried Rice

This substantial and tasty dish is based on jasmine rice. Diced chicken, red pepper and corn add colour and extra flavour.

Serves 4

475ml/16fl oz/2 cups water
50g/2oz/½ cup coconut milk powder
350g/12oz/1¾cups jasmine rice, rinsed
30ml/2 tbsp groundnut (peanut) oil
2 garlic cloves, chopped
1 small onion, finely chopped
2.5cm/1in piece fresh root ginger, peeled and grated
225g/8oz skinless chicken breast fillets, cut into 1cm/½in dice
1 red (bell) pepper, sliced
115g/4oz/1 cup drained canned whole kernel corn
5ml/1 tsp chilli oil
5ml/1 tsp hot curry powder
2 eggs, beaten
salt
spring onion (scallion) shreds, to garnish

1 Pour the water into a pan and whisk in the coconut milk powder. Add the rice and bring to the boil. Reduce the heat, cover and cook for 12 minutes, or until the rice is tender and the liquid has been absorbed. Spread the rice on a baking sheet and leave to get completely cold.

2 Heat the oil in a wok, add the garlic, onion and ginger and stir-fry over a medium heat for 2 minutes. Push to the sides of the wok, add the chicken to the centre and stir-fry for 2 minutes. Add the rice and toss well. Stir fry over a high heat for about 3 minutes more, until the chicken is cooked through.

3 Stir in the sliced red pepper, corn, chilli oil and curry powder, with salt to taste. Toss over the heat for 1 minute.

4 Pour in the beaten eggs and cook for 1 minute more, stirring constantly. Garnish with the spring onion shreds and serve.

> **Cook's Tip**
> It is important that the rice is cooked in advance and allowed to get completely cold before being fried.

Caribbean Chicken Rice: Energy 559kcal/2349kJ; Protein 41.7g; Carbohydrate 75g, of which sugars 15.4g; Fat 10.7g, of which saturates 1.5g; Cholesterol 88mg; Calcium 115mg; Fibre 7.1g; Sodium 509mg.
Thai Fried Rice: Energy 508kcal/2127kJ; Protein 24.7g; Carbohydrate 83.9g, of which sugars 8.7g; Fat 8g, of which saturates 1.6g; Cholesterol 135mg; Calcium 57mg; Fibre 1.3g; Sodium 204mg.

Pumpkin and Pistachio Risotto

Vegetarians will love this elegant combination of creamy, golden saffron rice and orange pumpkin, and so will everyone else. It would look impressive served in the hollowed-out pumpkin shell.

Serves 4

1.2 litres/2 pints/5 cups vegetable stock or water
generous pinch of saffron strands
30ml/2 tbsp olive oil
1 onion, chopped
2 garlic cloves, crushed

900g/2lb pumpkin, peeled, seeded and cut into 2cm/³⁄₄in cubes (about 7 cups)
400g/14oz/2 cups risotto rice
200ml/7fl oz/scant 1 cup dry white wine
30ml/2 tbsp freshly grated Parmesan cheese
50g/2oz/¹⁄₂ cup pistachios, coarsely chopped
45ml/3 tbsp chopped fresh marjoram or oregano, plus leaves to garnish
salt, freshly grated nutmeg and ground black pepper

1 Bring the stock or water to the boil and reduce to a low simmer. Ladle a little of it into a small bowl. Add the saffron strands and leave to infuse.

2 Heat the oil in a large, heavy pan or deep frying pan. Add the onion and garlic and cook gently for 5 minutes until softened. Add the pumpkin and rice and stir to coat everything in oil. Cook for a few more minutes until the rice looks transparent.

3 Pour in the wine and allow it to bubble hard. When it has been absorbed, add a quarter of the hot stock or water and the saffron liquid. Stir until all the liquid has been absorbed. Gradually add the remaining stock or water, a little at a time, allowing the rice to absorb the liquid before adding more, and stirring constantly.

4 After 20–30 minutes the rice should be golden yellow, creamy and al dente. Stir in the Parmesan cheese, cover the pan and leave to stand for 5 minutes. To finish, stir in the pistachios and marjoram or oregano. Season to taste with a little salt, nutmeg and pepper; sprinkle over a few marjoram or oregano leaves and serve.

Cuban-style Rice

Arroz a la cubana, garnished with fried eggs and bananas, is a Spanish dish popular in the Canary Islands and Catalonia. Fried bacon is sometimes served with it as well as eggs.

Serves 4

3 garlic cloves
120ml/4fl oz/¹⁄₂ cup olive oil
300g/11oz/1¹⁄₂ cups long grain rice

15g/¹⁄₂oz/1 tbsp butter
4 small bananas or 2 large bananas
4 eggs
salt and paprika

For the tomato sauce
30ml/2 tbsp olive oil
1 onion, chopped
2 garlic cloves, finely chopped
800g/1lb 12oz can tomatoes
4 thyme or oregano sprigs
salt and ground black pepper

1 To make the tomato sauce, heat the oil in a pan, add the onion and garlic and fry gently, stirring, until soft. Stir in the tomatoes and thyme or oregano sprigs and simmer gently for 5 minutes. Add seasoning to taste. Remove the herb sprigs and keep the sauce warm.

2 Put 850ml/1 pint 8fl oz/3¹⁄₂ cups water in a pan with two whole garlic cloves and 15ml/1 tbsp oil. Bring to the boil, add the rice and cook for 18 minutes until it is tender and the liquid has been absorbed.

3 Heat a pan with 30ml/2 tbsp oil and gently fry one chopped garlic clove. Tip in the rice, stir, season well, then turn off the heat and cover the pan.

4 Heat the butter in a frying pan with 15ml/1 tbsp oil. Halve the bananas lengthways and fry briefly on both sides. Remove from the pan and keep warm.

5 Add 60ml/4 tbsp oil to the pan and fry the eggs over a medium-high heat, so that the edges turn golden. Season with salt and paprika.

6 Serve the rice surrounded by tomato sauce and the fried bananas and eggs.

Pumpkin and Pistachio Risotto: Energy 585kcal/2441kJ; Protein 14.4g; Carbohydrate 87.3g, of which sugars 5.7g; Fat 15.9g, of which saturates 3.5g; Cholesterol 8mg; Calcium 196mg; Fibre 3.2g; Sodium 151mg.
Cuban-style Rice: Energy 668kcal/2781kJ; Protein 13.9g; Carbohydrate 76.5g, of which sugars 15.4g; Fat 34g, of which saturates 7.3g; Cholesterol 198mg; Calcium 64mg; Fibre 2.7g; Sodium 112mg.

Chilli-spiced Courgette Pilaff

This is a recipe from the Balkans, but it bears testimony to the influence of Italy, just on the other side of the Adriatic Sea, on the region's cuisine.

Serves 4

1kg/2¼lb small or medium courgettes (zucchini)
60ml/4 tbsp olive oil
3 onions, finely chopped
3 garlic cloves, crushed
5ml/1 tsp chilli powder
400g/14oz can chopped tomatoes
200g/7oz/1 cup risotto or round grain rice
600–750ml/1–1¼ pints/ 2½–3 cups vegetable or chicken stock
30ml/2 tbsp chopped fresh parsley
30ml/2 tbsp chopped fresh dill
salt and ground white pepper
sprigs of dill and olives, to garnish
thick natural (plain) yogurt, to serve

1 Preheat the oven to 190°C/375°F/Gas 5. Top and tail the courgettes and slice into large chunks.

2 Heat half the olive oil in a large pan and gently fry the onions and garlic until just soft. Stir in the chilli powder and tomatoes and simmer for about 5–8 minutes before adding the courgettes and salt to taste.

3 Cook over a gentle to medium heat for 10–15 minutes, before stirring the rice into the pan. Add the stock to the pan, cover and simmer for about 45 minutes or until the rice is tender. Stir the mixture occasionally.

4 Remove from the heat and stir in pepper to taste, parsley and dill. Spoon into an ovenproof dish and bake for about 45 minutes. Halfway through cooking, brush the remaining oil over the courgette mixture. Garnish with the dill and olives. Serve with the yogurt.

Cook's Tip
Add extra liquid if necessary, during baking, to prevent the mixture from sticking.

Pumpkin Stuffed with Saffron Pilaff

A pumpkin makes an ideal cooking vessel, whether filled with an aromatic pilaff as in this recipe, or with meat and rice, vegetables or soup.

Serves 4–6

1 medium-sized pumpkin, weighing about 1.2kg/2½lb
225g/8oz/generous 1 cup long grain rice, well rinsed
30–45ml/2–3 tbsp olive oil
15ml/1 tbsp butter
pinch of saffron threads
5ml/1 tsp coriander seeds
2–3 strips of orange peel, sliced
45–60ml/3–4 tbsp shelled pistachio nuts
30–45ml/2–3 tbsp dried cranberries, soaked in boiling water for 5 minutes and drained
175g/6oz/¾ cup dried apricots, sliced or chopped
1 bunch of fresh basil, leaves
1 bunch each of fresh coriander (cilantro), mint and flat leaf parsley, coarsely chopped
salt and ground black pepper
lemon wedges and thick natural (plain) yogurt, to serve

1 Preheat the oven to 200°C/400°F/Gas 6. Wash the pumpkin and cut off the top to use as a lid. Scoop the seeds out of the middle with a metal spoon, and pull out the stringy bits. Replace the lid, put the pumpkin on a baking tray and bake for 1 hour.

2 Meanwhile, tip the rice into a pan and pour in just enough water to cover. Add a pinch of salt and bring to the boil, then lower the heat and partially cover the pan. Simmer for 10–12 minutes, until all the water has been absorbed and the grains of rice are cooked but still have a bite.

3 Heat the oil and butter in a wide, heavy pan. Stir in the saffron, coriander seeds, orange peel, pistachios, cranberries, apricots, and rice, season with salt and pepper, and mix. Turn off the heat, cover the pan with a dish towel and press the lid on top. Leave to steam for 10 minutes, then toss in the herbs.

4 Take the pumpkin out of the oven. Lift off the lid and spoon the pilaff inside. Replace the lid and cook for 20 minutes. To serve, remove the lid, slice off the top of the pumpkin, place on a plate and spoon pilaff in the middle. Continue until everyone is served. Serve with lemon wedges and a bowl of yogurt.

Chilli-spiced Courgette Pilaff: Energy 199kcal/826kJ; Protein 5.5g; Carbohydrate 29.8g, of which sugars 8g; Fat 6.5g, of which saturates 1g; Cholesterol 0mg; Calcium 66mg; Fibre 2.9g; Sodium 9mg.
Pumpkin with Saffron Pilaff: Energy 345kcal/1443kJ; Protein 9.9g; Carbohydrate 50.1g, of which sugars 18.6g; Fat 12g, of which saturates 2.6g; Cholesterol 5mg; Calcium 299mg; Fibre 9.6g; Sodium 93mg.

Sweet Rice with Sour Chickpeas

Lemon is the sour note in this spicy dish perfumed with cloves and cardamom.

Serves 6

225g/8oz tomatoes, skinned
350g/12oz/2 cups dried
   chickpeas, soaked overnight
60ml/4 tbsp vegetable oil
1 large onion, very finely chopped
15ml/1 tbsp ground coriander
15ml/1 tbsp ground cumin
5ml/1 tsp ground fenugreek
5ml/1 tsp ground cinnamon
1–2 fresh green chillies, seeded
   and thinly sliced
2.5cm/1in piece fresh root ginger,
   peeled and grated

60ml/4 tbsp lemon juice
15ml/1 tbsp chopped fresh
   coriander (cilantro)
salt and ground black pepper

For the rice

40g/1½oz/3 tbsp butter
4 green cardamom pods
4 cloves
650ml/22fl oz/2¾ cups boiling
   water
350g/12oz/1¾ cups basmati
   rice, soaked for 30 minutes
   and drained
5–10ml/1–2 tsp granulated
   sugar
5–6 saffron threads, soaked in
   warm water

1 Chop the skinned tomatoes. Set aside. Drain the chickpeas into a large pan. Cover with water, bring to the boil, cover and simmer, for 1–1¼ hours. Drain, reserving the cooking liquid.

2 Heat the oil in a pan. Reserve 30ml/2 tbsp of the onion and add the remainder to the pan. Cook over a medium heat for 4–5 minutes, stirring. Add the tomatoes. Cook over a low heat for about 5 minutes, stirring, until soft. Stir in the ground coriander, cumin, fenugreek and cinnamon. Cook for 30 seconds, then add the chickpeas and 350ml/12fl oz/1½ cups of the reserved cooking liquid. Season with salt, then cover and simmer gently for 15–20 minutes. Add more liquid if needed.

3 Melt the butter in a saucepan and fry the cardamom pods and cloves for 30 seconds. Add the rice, stir well, then pour in the boiling water. Cover tightly and simmer for 10 minutes, then turn off the heat and stir in the sugar and saffron liquid. Cover.

4 Add the reserved chopped onion, chillies, ginger, lemon juice, and coriander to the chickpeas. Serve with the rice.

Cardamom-infused Lentils and Rice with Spiced Onions

This dish of rice and lentils is a classic Middle Eastern meal, popular from Egypt and Libya to Galilee and Greece. It is often eaten with a bowl of vegetables, accompanied by yogurt and a plate of crisp salad.

Serves 6–8

400g/14oz/1¾ cups large brown
   or green lentils

45ml/3 tbsp olive oil
3–4 onions, 1 chopped and
   2–3 thinly sliced
5ml/1 tsp ground cumin
2.5ml/½ tsp ground cinnamon
6 cardamom pods
300g/11oz/1½ cups long grain
   rice, rinsed
about 250ml/8fl oz/1 cup
   vegetable stock
salt and ground black pepper
natural (plain) yogurt, to serve

1 Put the lentils in a saucepan with enough water to cover generously. Bring to the boil, then simmer for about 30 minutes, or until tender. Skim off any scum that forms on top.

2 Meanwhile, heat half the oil in a pan, add the chopped onion and fry for 10 minutes, or until softened and golden brown. Stir in half the cumin and half the cinnamon.

3 When the lentils are cooked, add the spicy fried onions to the pan, together with the cardamom pods, rice and stock. Stir well and bring to the boil, then reduce the heat, cover the pan and simmer gently until the rice is tender and all the liquid has been absorbed. If the mixture appears to be getting a little too dry, add some extra water or stock. Season with salt and pepper to taste.

4 Meanwhile, heat the remaining oil in a pan, add the sliced onions and fry for about 10 minutes, until dark brown, caramelized and crisp. Sprinkle in the remaining cumin and cinnamon just before the end of cooking.

5 To serve, pile the rice and lentil mixture on to a serving dish, then top with the browned, caramelized onions. Serve immediately, with yogurt.

Rice with Sour Chickpeas: Energy 556kcal/2327kJ; Protein 18.2g; Carbohydrate 84.6g, of which sugars 8.2g; Fat 16.8g, of which saturates 4.7g; Cholesterol 14mg; Calcium 130mg; Fibre 7.6g; Sodium 70mg.
Cardamom-infused Lentils and Rice: Energy 394kcal/1656kJ; Protein 17.5g; Carbohydrate 68g, of which sugars 5.1g; Fat 6.6g, of which saturates 0.9g; Cholesterol 0mg; Calcium 54mg; Fibre 3.8g; Sodium 23mg.

Jewelled Vegetable Rice with Crispy Deep-fried Eggs

Inspired by the traditional Indonesian dish *nasi goreng*, this vibrant, colourful stir-fry makes a tasty light meal. Alternatively, serve it as an accompaniment to simply grilled meat or fish. For an extra healthy version, use brown basmati rice in place of the white rice.

Serves 4
30ml/2 tbsp sunflower oil
2 garlic cloves, finely chopped
4 red Asian shallots, thinly sliced
1 small red chilli, finely sliced
90g/3½oz carrots, cut into thin matchsticks
90g/3½oz fine green beans, cut into 2cm/¾in lengths
90g/3½oz fresh sweetcorn kernels
1 red (bell) pepper, diced
90g/3½oz baby button (white) mushrooms
500g/1¼lb cooked, cooled long grain rice
45ml/3 tbsp light soy sauce
10ml/2 tsp green Thai curry paste
4 crispy fried eggs, to serve
crisp green salad leaves and lime wedges, to garnish

1 Heat the sunflower oil in a wok over a high heat. When hot, add the garlic, shallots and chilli. Stir-fry for about 2 minutes.

2 Add the carrots, green beans, sweetcorn, red pepper and mushrooms to the wok and stir-fry for 3–4 minutes. Add the cooked, cooled rice and stir-fry for a further 4–5 minutes.

3 Mix together the light soy sauce and curry paste and add to the wok. Toss to mix well and stir-fry for 2–3 minutes until piping hot. Ladle the rice into four bowls or plates and top each portion with a crispy fried egg. Serve with crisp green salad leaves and wedges of lime to squeeze over.

> **Cook's Tip**
> For this dish, it is important to use cold cooked rice rather than hot, freshly cooked rice. Hot boiled rice tends to clump together when it is stir-fried, whereas the grains of cooled rice will remain separate.

Moroccan Aubergine Pilaff with Cinnamon and Mint

This North African rice dish varies from region to region, but all recipes include meaty chunks of aubergine.

Serves 4–6
2 large aubergines (eggplants)
30–45ml/2–3 tbsp olive oil
30–45ml/2–3 tbsp pine nuts
1 large onion, finely chopped
5ml/1 tsp coriander seeds
30ml/2 tbsp currants, soaked for 5–10 minutes and drained
10–15ml/2–3 tsp sugar
15–30ml/1–2 tbsp ground cinnamon
15–30ml/1–2 tbsp dried mint
1 small bunch of fresh dill, finely chopped
3 tomatoes, skinned, seeded and finely chopped
350g/12oz/generous 1¾ cups long or short grain rice, well rinsed and drained
sunflower oil, for deep-frying
juice of ½ lemon
salt and ground black pepper
fresh mint and lemon, to serve

1 Quarter the aubergines lengthways, then slice each quarter into chunks and place in a bowl of salted water. Leave to soak for at least 30 minutes.

2 Meanwhile, heat the olive oil in a heavy pan, stir in the pine nuts and cook until they turn golden. Add the onion and cook until soft, then stir in the coriander seeds and currants. Add the sugar, cinnamon, mint and dill and stir in the tomatoes.

3 Toss in the rice, stirring until well coated, then pour in 900ml/1½ pints/3¾ cups water, season with salt and pepper and bring to the boil. Lower the heat, partially cover the pan, and simmer for 10–12 minutes, until almost all the liquid has been absorbed. Turn off the heat, cover with a dish towel and the lid and leave the rice to steam for about 15 minutes.

4 Heat enough sunflower oil for deep-frying in a wok. Drain the aubergines and squeeze them dry, then fry them in batches. When they are golden brown, lift out and drain on paper towels. Tip the rice into a serving bowl and toss the aubergine chunks through it with the lemon juice. Garnish with fresh mint and serve warm or cold, with lemon wedges for squeezing.

Cambodian Wheat Noodles with Stir-fried Pork

Wheat noodles are popular in Cambodia, where bunches of noodles drying in the open air, hanging from bamboo poles, are a common sight in the markets. This simple recipe using traditional Cambodian spice blends comes from a noodle stall in Phnom Penh.

Serves 4

225g/8oz pork loin, cut into thin strips
225g/8oz dried wheat noodles, soaked in lukewarm water for 20 minutes

15ml/1 tbsp groundnut (peanut) oil
2 garlic cloves, finely chopped
2–3 spring onions (scallions), trimmed and cut into bitesize pieces
45ml/3 tbsp kroeung
15ml/1 tbsp tuk trey
30ml/2 tbsp unsalted roasted peanuts, finely chopped
chilli oil, for drizzling

For the marinade

30ml/2 tbsp tuk trey
30ml/2 tbsp soy sauce
15ml/1 tbsp groundnut oil
10ml/2 tsp sugar

1 In a bowl, combine the ingredients for the marinade, stirring constantly until all the sugar has dissolved. Toss in the strips of pork, making sure the meat is well coated in the marinade, and set aside for 30 minutes.

2 Drain the wheat noodles. Bring a large pan of water to the boil and drop in the noodles, untangling them with chopsticks, if necessary. Cook for 4–5 minutes, until tender.

3 Drain the noodles thoroughly, then divide them among individual serving bowls. Keep the noodles warm until the dish is ready to serve.

4 Heat a wok, add the oil and stir-fry the garlic and spring onions, until fragrant. Add the pork, tossing it around the wok for 2 minutes. Stir in the kroeung and tuk trey and cook for another 2 minutes – add a splash of water if the wok gets too dry – then tip the pork on top of the noodles. Sprinkle the peanuts over the top and drizzle with chilli oil to serve.

Fried Noodles with Spicy Peanut Sauce, Beef and Fragrant Herbs

If you like chillies and peanuts, this delicious dish makes the perfect choice. The stringy rice sticks can be fiddly to stir-fry as they have a tendency to cling together, so work quickly. In Vietnam this dish is usually served with a salad or pickled vegetables.

Serves 4

300g/11oz beef sirloin
15–30ml/1–2 tbsp vegetable oil
225g/8oz dried rice sticks (vermicelli), soaked in warm water for 20 minutes
225g/8oz/1 cup beansprouts
5–10ml/1–2 tsp nuoc mam
1 small bunch each of fresh basil and mint, stalks removed, leaves shredded, to garnish
Vietnamese pickles, to serve

For the peanut sauce

4 dried Serrano chillies, seeded
60ml/4 tbsp groundnut (peanut) oil
4–5 garlic cloves, crushed
5–10ml/1–2 tsp medium curry powder
40g/1½oz/⅓ cup roasted peanuts, finely ground

1 To make the peanut sauce, grind the chillies in a mortar with a pestle. Heat the oil in a heavy pan and stir in the garlic until it begins to colour. Add the chillies, curry powder and ground peanuts and stir over a low heat, until the mixture forms a paste. Remove the pan from the heat and leave to cool.

2 Slice the beef thinly, cutting across the grain. Heat a wok or heavy pan, and pour in 15ml/1 tbsp of the oil. Add the sliced beef and cook for 1–2 minutes, then stir in 7.5ml/1½ tsp of the spicy peanut sauce. Tip the beef on to a clean plate and set aside. Drain the rice sticks.

3 Add 7.5ml/1½ tsp oil to the wok and add the rice sticks and 15ml/1 tbsp peanut sauce. Toss the noodles until coated in the sauce and cook for 4–5 minutes, or until tender. Toss in the beef for 1 minute, then add the beansprouts with the nuoc mam.

4 Tip the noodles on to a serving dish and sprinkle with the basil and mint. Serve with pickles.

Cambodian Noodles with Pork: Energy 357Kcal/1494kJ; Protein 17g; Carbohydrate 51g, of which sugars 4.8g; Fat 9g, of which saturates 2g; Cholesterol 35mg; Calcium 21mg; Fibre 0.7g; Sodium 495mg.
Fried Noodles and Herbs: Energy 603Kcal/2507kJ; Protein 26g; Carbohydrate 52g, of which sugars 2g; Fat 32g, of which saturates 6g; Cholesterol 38mg; Calcium 73mg; Fibre 2.2g; Sodium 200mg.

Thai Curried Noodles

Chicken or pork can be used to make this tasty dish from southern Thailand. It is very quick and easy to prepare and cook.

Serves 2

30ml/2 tbsp vegetable oil
10ml/2 tsp Thai magic paste
1 lemon grass stalk, finely
   chopped
5ml/1 tsp Thai red curry paste
90g/3½oz skinless chicken breast
   fillets or pork fillet (tenderloin),
   sliced into slivers

30ml/2 tbsp light soy sauce
400ml/14fl oz/1⅔ cups coconut
   milk
2 kaffir lime leaves, rolled into
   cylinders and thinly sliced
250g/9oz dried medium egg
   noodles
90g/3½oz Chinese leaves
   (Chinese cabbage), finely
   shredded
90g/3½oz spinach or watercress,
   stalks removed, shredded
juice of 1 lime
small bunch fresh coriander
   (cilantro), chopped

1 Heat the oil in a wok or large, heavy frying pan. Add the Thai magic paste and lemon grass and stir-fry over a low to medium heat for 4–5 seconds, until they give off their aroma.

2 Stir in the curry paste, then add the chicken or pork. Stir-fry over a medium to high heat for 2 minutes, until the meat is coated in the paste and seared on all sides.

3 Add the soy sauce, coconut milk and sliced lime leaves. Bring to a simmer, then add the noodles. Simmer gently for 4 minutes, tossing the mixture occasionally to make sure that the noodles cook evenly.

4 Add the Chinese leaves and the spinach or watercress. Stir well, then add the lime juice. Spoon into a warmed bowl, sprinkle with the coriander and serve.

Cook's Tip
Magic paste, available from Asian markets and supermarkets, is a spice blend that includes garlic, coriander and pepper.

Sweet and Hot Vegetable Noodles

This noodle dish has the colour of fire, but only the mildest suggestion of heat. Ginger and plum sauce give it its fruity flavour.

Serves 4

130g/4½oz dried rice noodles
30ml/2 tbsp groundnut (peanut)
   oil
2.5cm/1in piece fresh root ginger,
   sliced into thin batons
1 garlic clove, crushed
130g/4½oz drained canned
   bamboo shoots, sliced in batons
2 medium carrots, sliced in batons

130g/4½oz/1½ cups beansprouts
1 small white cabbage, shredded
30ml/2 tbsp nam pla
30ml/2 tbsp soy sauce
30ml/2 tbsp plum sauce
10ml/2 tsp sesame oil
15ml/1 tbsp palm sugar (jaggery)
   or light muscovado (brown)
   sugar
juice of ½ lime
90g/3½oz mooli (daikon), sliced
   into thin batons
small bunch fresh coriander
   (cilantro), chopped
60ml/4 tbsp sesame seeds,
   toasted

1 Cook the noodles in a large pan of boiling water, following the instructions on the packet. Meanwhile, heat the oil in a wok or large frying pan and stir-fry the ginger and garlic together for 2–3 minutes over a medium heat, until golden.

2 Drain the noodles and keep warm. Add the bamboo shoots to the wok, increase the heat to high and stir-fry for 5 minutes. Add the carrots, beansprouts and cabbage and stir-fry for a further 5 minutes, until they are beginning to char at the edges.

3 Stir in the sauces, sesame oil, sugar and lime juice. Add the mooli and coriander, toss to mix, and serve with the noodles in warmed bowls, sprinkled with toasted sesame seeds.

Cook's Tip
Use a large, sharp knife for shredding cabbage. Remove any tough outer leaves, if necessary, then cut the cabbage into quarters. Cut off and discard the hard core from each quarter, place flat side down, then slice the cabbage very thinly to make fine shreds.

Potato Skins with Cajun Dip

These crisp potato skins are served with a chilli dip.

Serves 2
2 large potatoes, baked
vegetable oil for deep-frying

120ml/4fl oz/½ natural (plain) yogurt
1 garlic clove, crushed
½ fresh green chilli, seeded and chopped
salt and ground black pepper

1 Cut the baked potatoes in half, scoop out the flesh, leaving a thin layer on the skins. Cut in half again. Mix together the yoghurt, garlic, chilli and salt and pepper in a small bowl.

2 Deep-fry the potato skins until crisp and golden. Drain and serve immediately with the yogurt and chilli dip.

Spicy Spanish Potatoes

There are many variations on this popular potato and chilli dish, but the most important thing is the spice mix, sharpened with vinegar.

Serves 4
675g/1½lb small new potatoes
75ml/5 tbsp olive oil
2 garlic cloves, sliced

3 dried red chillies, seeded and chopped
2.5ml/½ tsp ground cumin
10ml/2 tsp paprika
30ml/2 tbsp red or white wine vinegar
1 red or green (bell) pepper, sliced
coarse sea salt, for sprinkling (optional)

1 Scrub the potatoes and put them into a pan of salted water. Bring to the boil and cook for 10 minutes, or until almost tender. Drain and leave to cool slightly. Cut into chunks. Heat the oil in a large pan and fry the potatoes, turning, until golden.

2 Meanwhile, crush together the garlic, chillies and cumin using a mortar and pestle. Mix the paste with the paprika and wine vinegar, then add to the potatoes with the sliced pepper and cook, stirring, for 2 minutes. Sprinkle with salt, if using, and serve hot as a tapas dish or cold as a side dish.

Spicy Potato Wedges with Chilli Dip

For a healthy snack with a superb flavour, try these dry-roasted potato wedges. The crisp spice crust makes them taste irresistible, especially when they are served with a vibrant chilli dip.

Serves 2
2 baking potatoes, about 225g/ 8oz each
30ml/2 tbsp olive oil
2 garlic cloves, crushed
5ml/1 tsp ground allspice

5ml/1 tsp ground coriander
15ml/1 tbsp paprika
salt and ground black pepper

For the chilli dip
15ml/1 tbsp olive oil
1 small onion, finely chopped
1 garlic clove, crushed
200g/7oz can chopped tomatoes
1 fresh red chilli, seeded and finely chopped
15ml/1 tbsp balsamic vinegar
15ml/1 tbsp chopped fresh coriander (cilantro), plus extra to garnish

1 Preheat the oven to 200°C/400°F/Gas 6. Cut the potatoes in half, then cut each half lengthways into eight wedges.

2 Place the wedges in a pan of cold water. Bring to the boil, then lower the heat and simmer gently for 10 minutes or until the potatoes have softened slightly. Drain well and pat dry on kitchen paper.

3 Mix the oil, garlic, allspice, coriander and paprika in a roasting pan and add salt and pepper to taste. Add the potatoes to the pan and shake to coat them thoroughly in the spicy oil. Roast for 20 minutes, turning the potato wedges occasionally, or until they are browned, crisp and fully cooked.

4 Meanwhile, to make the chilli dip, heat the oil in a pan and add the onion and garlic. Cook over a medium heat for 5–10 minutes until softened. Add the tomatoes, with their juice. Stir in the chilli and vinegar.

5 Cook gently for 10 minutes until the mixture has reduced and thickened, then check the seasoning. Stir in the fresh coriander and serve hot, with the potato wedges, garnished with salt and fresh coriander.

Potato Skins with Cajun Dip: Energy 211kcal/873kJ; Protein 2.7g; Carbohydrate 12.5g, of which sugars 3.3g; Fat 17g, of which saturates 2.2g; Cholesterol 0mg; Calcium 62mg; Fibre 0.7g; Sodium 35mg.
Spicy Spanish Potatoes: Energy 273kcal/1148kJ; Protein 4.6g; Carbohydrate 39.5g, of which sugars 5.9g; Fat 11.9g, of which saturates 1.9g; Cholesterol 0mg; Calcium 22mg; Fibre 3.1g; Sodium 39mg.
Spicy Potato Wedges with Chilli Dip: Energy 239kcal/1001kJ; Protein 4g; Carbohydrate 30.8g, of which sugars 4.9g; Fat 11.9g, of which saturates 1.9g; Cholesterol 0mg; Calcium 23mg; Fibre 2.6g; Sodium 28mg.

Cumin and Fennel Spiced Potatoes

If you like chillies, you'll love these potatoes. However, if you're not a fan of very fiery flavours, simply leave out the chilli seeds, from both the dried and fresh chillies, and use the flesh by itself.

Serves 4
12–14 small new or salad potatoes, halved
30ml/2 tbsp vegetable oil

2.5ml/¹/₂ tsp dried red chillies, crushed
2.5ml/¹/₂ tsp white cumin seeds
2.5ml/¹/₂ tsp fennel seeds
2.5ml/¹/₂ tsp crushed coriander seeds
5ml/1 tsp salt
1 onion, sliced
1–4 fresh red chillies, chopped
15ml/1 tbsp chopped fresh coriander (cilantro), plus extra to garnish

1 Cook the potatoes in boiling salted water until tender but still firm. Remove from the heat and drain off the water. Set aside until needed.

2 In a deep frying pan, heat the oil over a medium-high heat, then reduce the heat to medium. Add the crushed chillies, cumin, fennel and coriander seeds and salt and fry, stirring, for 30–40 seconds.

3 Add the sliced onion and fry until softened and golden brown. Then add the potatoes, red chillies and chopped fresh coriander and stir well.

4 Reduce the heat to very low, then cover and cook for 5–7 minutes. Serve the potatoes hot, garnished with more fresh coriander.

> **Cook's Tips**
> • To prepare fresh chillies, trim the stalk end, slit down one side and scrape out the seeds, unless you want a really hot dish. Finely slice or chop the flesh.
> • Wear rubber gloves if you have very sensitive skin and wash your hands thoroughly after handling chillies. Avoid touching your eyes if you have any trace of chilli on your fingers.

Aloo Saag

Traditional Indian spices – mustard seed, ginger and chilli – give a really good kick to potatoes and spinach in this delicious and authentic curry.

Serves 4
450g/1lb spinach
30ml/2 tbsp vegetable oil

5ml/1 tsp black mustard seeds
1 onion, thinly sliced
2 garlic cloves, crushed
2.5cm/1in piece root ginger, finely chopped
675g/1¹/₂lb firm potatoes, cut into 2.5cm/1in chunks
5ml/1 tsp chilli powder
5ml/1 tsp salt
120ml/4fl oz/¹/₂ cup water

1 Wash the spinach in several changes of water then blanch it in a little boiling water for 3–4 minutes.

2 Drain the spinach thoroughly and leave to cool. When it is cool enough to handle, use your hands to squeeze out any remaining liquid.

3 Heat the oil in a large pan and fry the mustard seeds for 2 minutes, stirring, until they begin to splutter.

4 Add the onion, garlic and ginger to the pan and fry for 5 minutes, stirring.

5 Stir in the potatoes, chilli powder, salt and water and cook for about 8 minutes, stirring occasionally.

6 Finally, add the spinach to the pan. Cover and simmer for 10–15 minutes until the spinach is very soft and the potatoes are tender. Serve hot.

> **Cook's Tip**
> To make certain that the spinach is dry before adding it to the potatoes, put it in a clean dish towel, roll up tightly and squeeze gently to remove any excess liquid. Choose a firm waxy variety of potato or a salad potato so the pieces do not break up during cooking.

Aloo Saag: Energy 201kcal/845kJ; Protein 6.2g; Carbohydrate 30.2g, of which sugars 4.7g; Fat 6.9g, of which saturates 0.9g; Cholesterol 0mg; Calcium 205mg; Fibre 4.3g; Sodium 668mg.
Cumin and Fennel Potatoes: Energy 260kcal/1091kJ; Protein 4.8g; Carbohydrate 35.2g, of which sugars 2.8g; Fat 12.1g, of which saturates 1.5g; Cholesterol 0mg; Calcium 39mg; Fibre 3.4g; Sodium 40mg.

Potatoes in Spicy Yogurt Sauce

Tiny potatoes cooked with their skins on are delicious in this fairly spicy yet tangy yogurt sauce. Serve with any meat or fish dish or just with hot chapatis.

Serves 4

12 small new or salad potatoes, halved
275g/10oz/1¼ cups natural (plain) low-fat yogurt
300ml/½ pint/1¼ cups water
1.5ml/¼ tsp turmeric
5ml/1 tsp chilli powder
5ml/1 tsp ground coriander
2.5ml/½ tsp ground cumin
5ml/1 tsp salt
5ml/1 tsp soft brown sugar
30ml/2 tbsp vegetable oil
5ml/1 tsp white cumin seeds
15ml/1 tbsp chopped fresh coriander (cilantro)
2 fresh green chillies, sliced
1 coriander sprig, to garnish (optional)

1 Cook the potatoes in their skins in boiling salted water until just tender, then drain and set aside.

2 Mix together the yogurt, water, turmeric, chilli powder, ground coriander, ground cumin, salt and sugar in a bowl. Set aside.

3 Heat the oil in a medium pan over a medium-high heat and stir in the white cumin seeds.

4 Reduce the heat to medium, and stir in the prepared yogurt mixture. Cook the sauce, stirring continuously, for about 3 minutes.

5 Add the fresh coriander, green chillies and potatoes to the sauce. Mix well and cook for 5–7 minutes, stirring occasionally.

6 Transfer to a serving dish, garnish with the coriander sprig, if wished and serve hot.

Cook's Tip

If new or salad potatoes are unavailable, use 450g/1lb large potatoes instead, but choose a waxy not a floury variety. Peel them and cut into large chunks, then cook as described above.

Masala Mashed Potatoes

These well-spiced potatoes are delicious served alongside rich meats such as duck, lamb or pork.

Serves 4

3 medium floury potatoes
15ml/1 tbsp mixed chopped fresh mint and coriander (cilantro)
5ml/1 tsp mango powder or mango chutney
5ml/1 tsp salt
5ml/1 tsp crushed black peppercorns
1 fresh red chilli, finely chopped
1 fresh green chilli, finely chopped
50g/2oz/4 tbsp butter, softened

1 Cook the potatoes in a large pan of lightly salted boiling water until tender. Drain thoroughly and mash them well with a potato masher.

2 Blend together the remaining ingredients in a small bowl. Stir the mixture into the mashed potatoes reserving a little for a garnish, and mix together with a fork. Serve hot in a pile, with the remaining mixture on the top.

Garlic Mashed Potatoes

This wonderful creamy mash is ideal with fried fish.

Serves 6–8

3 whole garlic bulbs, separated into cloves, unpeeled
115g/4oz/8 tbsp butter
1.3kg/3lb floury potatoes, boiled until soft and drained
175ml/6fl oz/½ cup milk
salt and black pepper

1 Preheat the oven to 190°C/375°F/Gas 5. Blanch two-thirds of the garlic cloves in a pan of water for 2 minutes. Drain and then peel. Place the remaining cloves in a roasting pan and bake in the oven for 30–40 minutes. Gently fry the blanched garlic cloves in half the butter until golden and tender.

2 Warm the milk in a pan with the remaining butter. Put all the garlic into a food processor, purée, add the potatoes and milk and process until smooth. Reheat gently before serving.

Potatoes in Spicy Yogurt Sauce: Energy 161kcal/677kJ; Protein 5.9g; Carbohydrate 24.7g, of which sugars 7g; Fat 5.1g, of which saturates 1g; Cholesterol 1mg; Calcium 154mg; Fibre 1.1g; Sodium 73mg.
Masala Mashed Potatoes: Energy 219kcal/919kJ; Protein 3.1g; Carbohydrate 28.9g, of which sugars 3g; Fat 10.9g, of which saturates 6.7g; Cholesterol 27mg; Calcium 13mg; Fibre 1.8g; Sodium 600mg.
Garlic Mashed Potatoes: Energy 261kcal/1093kJ; Protein 5g; Carbohydrate 33.3g, of which sugars 3.8g; Fat 12.8g, of which saturates 7.9g; Cholesterol 32mg; Calcium 43mg; Fibre 2.4g; Sodium 118mg.

Bombay Potatoes

This is a classic Indian vegetarian dish of potatoes slowly cooked in a richly flavoured curry sauce, with fresh chillies for an added kick. It is one of the most popular side dishes in Indian cuisine.

Serves 4–6

450g/1lb new or small salad
  potatoes
5ml/1 tsp turmeric
60ml/4 tbsp vegetable oil

2 dried red chillies
6–8 curry leaves
2 onions, finely chopped
2 fresh green chillies, finely
  chopped
50g/2oz coriander leaves,
  coarsely chopped
1.5ml/¼ tsp asafoetida
2.5ml/½ tsp each cumin,
  mustard, onion, fennel and
  nigella seeds
lemon juice
salt
fresh fried curry leaves, to garnish

1 Chop the potatoes into small chunks and cook in boiling lightly salted water with ½ tsp of the turmeric until tender. Drain, then coarsely mash. Set aside.

2 Heat the oil in a large heavy pan and fry the red chillies and curry leaves until the chillies are nearly burnt.

3 Add the onions, green chillies, coriander, remaining turmeric, asafoetida and spice seeds and cook until the onions are tender.

4 Fold in the potatoes and add a few drops of water. Cook on a low heat for about 10 minutes, mixing well to ensure the even distribution of the spices. Remove the dried chillies and curry leaves.

5 Serve the potatoes hot, with lemon juice squeezed or poured over, and garnish with the fresh fried curry leaves.

> **Cook's Tip**
> Asafoetida is the ground dried sap of a plant native to Iran. It is very pungent raw, but when cooked it becomes much milder and develops an onion-like aroma with a hint of truffle.

Glazed Sweet Potatoes with Ginger and Allspice

Fried sweet potatoes acquire a candied coating when cooked with ginger, syrup and allspice. The addition of cayenne pepper cuts through the sweetness and prevents the dish from becoming cloying.

Serves 4

900g/2lb sweet potatoes
50g/2oz/¼ cup butter

45ml/3 tbsp vegetable oil
2 garlic cloves, crushed
2 pieces preserved stem ginger,
  drained and finely chopped
10ml/2 tsp ground allspice
15ml/1 tbsp syrup from the
  preserved ginger jar
salt and cayenne pepper
10ml/2 tsp chopped fresh thyme,
  plus a few thyme sprigs,
  to garnish

1 Peel the sweet potatoes and cut them into 1cm/½in cubes. Melt the butter with the oil in a large frying pan. Add the sweet potato cubes and fry, stirring frequently, for about 10 minutes, until they are just soft.

2 Stir in the garlic, chopped ginger and allspice. Cook, stirring constantly, for 5 minutes more. Stir in the ginger syrup. Season with salt and a generous pinch of cayenne pepper and add the chopped thyme. Stir for 1–2 minutes more, then serve, sprinkled with thyme sprigs.

> **Variation**
> For a less sweet, unglazed version of this dish, use a 2.5cm/1in piece of fresh ginger, finely chopped, instead of the preserved ginger and omit the syrup.

> **Cook's Tip**
> Some sweet potatoes have white flesh and some have yellow. Although they taste similar, the yellow-fleshed variety look particularly colourful and attractive.

Roasted Root Vegetables with Whole Spice Seeds

These spiced vegetables can be roasted alongside a joint of meat or a whole chicken. They will virtually look after themselves and make a delicious side dish.

Serves 4

3 parsnips, peeled
3 potatoes, peeled
3 carrots, peeled
3 sweet potatoes, peeled
60ml/4 tbsp olive oil
8 shallots, peeled
2 garlic cloves, sliced
10ml/2 tsp white mustard seeds
10ml/2 tsp coriander seeds, lightly crushed
5ml/1 tsp cumin seeds
2 bay leaves
salt and ground black pepper

1 Preheat the oven to 190°C/375°F/Gas 5. Bring a saucepan of lightly salted water to the boil. Cut the parsnips, potatoes, carrots and sweet potatoes into chunks. Add them to the pan and bring the water back to the boil. Boil for 2 minutes, then drain the vegetables thoroughly.

2 Pour the olive oil into a large, heavy roasting pan and place over a moderate heat. When the oil is hot add the drained vegetables together with the whole shallots and garlic. Fry, tossing the vegetables over the heat, until they are pale golden at the edges.

3 Add the mustard, coriander and cumin seeds and the bay leaves. Cook for 1 minute, then season with salt and pepper.

4 Transfer the roasting pan to the oven and roast for about 45 minutes, turning the vegetables occasionally, until they are crisp and golden and cooked through.

Variation
Vary the selection of vegetables according to what is available. Try using swede (rutabaga) or pumpkin instead of, or as well as, the vegetables suggested.

Mexican-spiced Beans

These "cowboy beans" taste rather like Boston baked beans, but with considerably more punch. The flavour improves on keeping, so make the dish the day before you want to serve it.

Serves 6

2 x 400g/14oz cans pinto beans
120ml/4fl oz/½ cup Mexican beer
115g/4oz/⅔ cups drained pickled jalapeño chilli slices
2 tomatoes, peeled and chopped
5ml/1 tsp ground cinnamon
175g/6oz bacon fat
1 onion, chopped
2 garlic cloves, crushed
175g/6oz rindless smoked lean bacon, diced
45ml/3 tbsp soft dark brown sugar
wheat flour tortillas, to serve

1 Put the drained pinto beans in a pan. Stir in the beer and cook over a high heat for 5 minutes, until some of the beer has been absorbed.

2 Lower the heat slightly and stir in the jalapeño chilli slices, then add the tomatoes and cinnamon. Continue to cook, stirring occasionally, for about 10 minutes.

3 Meanwhile, heat the fat bacon in a frying pan until the fat runs. The quantity suggested should yield about 45ml/3 tbsp bacon fat.

4 Lift out the bacon and set aside, then add the onion and garlic to the pan and fry for about 5 minutes, until browned. Using a slotted spoon, lift out the garlic and onions and stir them into the beans.

5 Return the diced smoked bacon to the fat remaining in the frying pan and fry until crisp. Add the bacon and any remaining fat to the beans and mix well.

6 Stir the sugar into the bean and bacon mixture and cook over a low heat, stirring constantly, until the sugar has dissolved. Serve immediately or spoon into a bowl, leave to cool, cover, then chill for reheating next day. Serve with warmed wheat flour tortillas.

Roasted Root Vegetables: Energy 290kcal/1213kJ; Protein 11.5g; Carbohydrate 32.5g, of which sugars 13.3g; Fat 13.6g, of which saturates 1.6g; Cholesterol 0mg; Calcium 175mg; Fibre 9.1g; Sodium 271mg.
Mexican-spiced Beans: Energy 235kcal/997kJ; Protein 19.2g; Carbohydrate 37.4g, of which sugars 13g; Fat 2g, of which saturates 0.5g; Cholesterol 18mg; Calcium 92mg; Fibre 9.5g; Sodium 221mg.

Grilled Polenta with Chilli Salsa

This creamy polenta dish served with a tangy salsa is from Chile, where it is served for Sunday brunch teamed with crisp bacon.

Serves 6–12
10ml/2 tsp dried chilli flakes
1.3 litres/2¼ pints/5²/₃ cups water
250g/9oz/1¼ cups quick cook polenta
50g/2oz/¼ cup butter
75g/3oz Parmesan cheese, grated
30ml/2 tbsp chopped fresh dill
30ml/2 tbsp chopped fresh coriander (cilantro)
30ml/2 tbsp olive oil
salt

For the salsa
½ pink onion, finely chopped
4 drained bottled sweet cherry peppers, finely chopped
1 fresh medium hot red chilli, seeded and finely chopped
1 small red (bell) pepper, quartered
10ml/2 tsp raspberry vinegar
30ml/2 tbsp olive oil
4 tomatoes, halved, cored, seeded and roughly chopped
45ml/3 tbsp chopped fresh coriander (cilantro)

1 Put the dried chilli flakes in a pan with the water. Bring to the boil and add a pinch of salt. Pour the polenta into the water in a continuous stream, whisking. Reduce the heat and continue to whisk for a few minutes.

2 When the polenta is thick and bubbling like a volcano, whisk in the butter, Parmesan and herbs. Season with salt. Pour into a greased 33 × 23cm/13 × 9in baking tray and leave to cool. Chill overnight.

3 About an hour before you plan to serve the meal, make the salsa. Place the onion, sweet cherry peppers and chilli in a mortar. Slice the skin from the red pepper quarters. Dice the flesh finely and place in a food processor, with the raspberry vinegar and olive oil. Process until smooth, then tip into a serving dish. Stir in the tomatoes and coriander. Cover.

4 Cut the polenta into 12 even triangles and brush the top with oil. Heat a griddle and grill in batches, oiled-side down, for about 2 minutes, then turn through 180 degrees and cook for 1 minute more, to get a chequered effect. Serve with the salsa.

Broad Beans with Bacon and Paprika

This dish is associated with Ronda, in southern Spain, the home of bull fighting, where broad beans are fed to fighting bulls to build them up. It is also found elsewhere in Spain where it is known as *habas españolas*. The salty, smoky bacon and paprika are the perfect foil for the earthy flavour of broad beans.

Serves 4
30ml/2 tbsp olive oil
1 small onion, finely chopped
1 garlic clove, finely chopped
50g/2oz rindless smoked streaky (fatty) bacon, roughly chopped
225g/8oz broad (fava) beans, thawed if frozen
5ml/1 tsp paprika
15ml/1 tbsp sweet sherry
salt and ground black pepper

1 Heat the olive oil in a large frying pan or sauté pan. Add the chopped onion, garlic and bacon and fry over a high heat for about 5 minutes, stirring frequently, until the onion is softened and the bacon browned.

2 Add the beans and paprika to the pan and stir-fry for 1 minute. Add the sherry, lower the heat, cover and cook for 5–10 minutes until the beans are tender. Season with salt and pepper to taste and serve hot or warm.

Variations
• Replace the bacon with the same quantity of chorizo sausage, thickly sliced.
• For a vegetarian version of the dish, replace the bacon with sun-dried tomatoes, cut into slivers.

Cook's Tip
Unless you are using very young, tender broad beans, which are delicious as they are, it is worth taking time to remove their grey skins to reveal the soft bright green beans beneath.

Beans with Bacon and Paprika: Energy 139kcal/577kJ; Protein 6.8g; Carbohydrate 8.7g, of which sugars 1.6g; Fat 9g, of which saturates 1.9g; Cholesterol 8mg; Calcium 38mg; Fibre 3.9g; Sodium 163mg.
Grilled Polenta with Chilli Salsa: Energy 154kcal/639kJ; Protein 4.6g; Carbohydrate 15.4g, of which sugars 0.1g; Fat 8g, of which saturates 3.7g; Cholesterol 15mg; Calcium 85mg; Fibre 0.7g; Sodium 95mg.

Sweet and Sour Rice

This popular Middle Eastern rice dish is flavoured with fruit and spices. Zereshk are small dried berries – use cranberries as a substitute.

Serves 4

50g/2oz/1/2 cup zereshk or fresh cranberries
45g/11/2oz/3 tbsp butter
50g/2oz/1/3 cup raisins
50g/2oz/11/4 cup sugar
5ml/1 tsp ground cinnamon
5ml/1 tsp ground cumin
350g/12oz/13/4 cups basmati rice, soaked
2–3 saffron strands, soaked in 15ml/1 tbsp boiling water
pinch of salt

1 Thoroughly wash the zereshk in cold water at least four or five times to rinse off any bits of grit. Drain well. Melt 15g/1/2oz/1 tbsp of the butter in a frying pan and fry the raisins for 1–2 minutes.

2 Add the zereshk, fry for a few seconds, and then add the sugar, with half of the cinnamon and cumin. Cook briefly and then set aside.

3 Drain the rice, then put it in a pan with plenty of boiling, lightly salted water. Bring back to the boil, reduce the heat and simmer for 4 minutes. Drain and rinse once again.

4 Melt half the remaining butter in the cleaned pan, add 15ml/1 tbsp water and stir in half the rice. Sprinkle with half the raisin and zereshk mixture and top with all but 45ml/3 tbsp of the rice. Sprinkle over the remaining raisin and zereshk mixture.

5 Mix the remaining cinnamon and cumin with the reserved rice, and sprinkle this mixture evenly over the layered mixture. Melt the remaining butter, drizzle it over the surface, then cover the pan with a clean dish towel. Cover with a tight-fitting lid, lifting the corners of the cloth back over the lid. Steam the rice over a very low heat for 20–30 minutes.

6 Just before serving, mix 45ml/3 tbsp of the rice with the saffron water. Spoon the sweet and sour rice on to a large, flat serving dish and sprinkle the saffron rice over the top, to garnish.

Garlic and Ginger Rice with Coriander

In Vietnam and Cambodia, when rice is served as a side dish it may be either plain or fragrant with the flavours of ginger and herbs. The combination of garlic and ginger is popular in both countries and complements almost any vegetable, fish or meat dish.

Serves 4–6

15ml/1 tbsp vegetable or groundnut (peanut) oil
2–3 garlic cloves, finely chopped
25g/1oz fresh root ginger, finely chopped
225g/8oz/generous 1 cup long grain rice, rinsed in several changes of water and drained
900ml/11/2 pints/33/4 cups chicken stock
bunch of fresh coriander (cilantro), stalks removed, leaves finely chopped
bunch of fresh basil and mint, stalks removed, leaves finely chopped (optional)

1 Heat the oil in a clay pot or heavy pan. Stir in the garlic and ginger and fry until golden. Stir in the rice and allow it to absorb the flavours for 1–2 minutes. Pour in the stock and stir to make sure the rice doesn't stick. Bring the stock to the boil, then reduce the heat.

2 Sprinkle the coriander, and other herbs if using, over the surface of the stock, cover the pan, and leave to cook gently for 20–25 minutes, until the rice has absorbed all the liquid. Turn off the heat and gently fluff up the rice to mix in the herbs. Cover and leave to infuse for 10 minutes before serving.

> **Variations**
> *Rice cooked this way can be spiced up with many different combinations of flavourings. Take inspiration from the dish you are serving with the rice, and add warm Indian spices such as turmeric and cinnamon, or cardamom and cloves, or add Thai flavours with lemon grass and kaffir lime leaves. Simply adding a couple of cardamom pods will give rice a lovely mild fragrance, and stirring in fresh herbs adds colour and flavour.*

Persian Rice with Fried Onions

Persian cuisine is exotic and delicious, with intense flavours. This dish forms a lovely crust on the bottom.

Serves 6–8

450g/1lb/2⅓ cups basmati rice, soaked and drained
150ml/¼ pint/⅔ cup sunflower oil
2 garlic cloves, crushed
2 onions, 1 chopped, 1 sliced
150g/5oz/⅔ cup green lentils, soaked
600ml/1 pint/2½ cups stock
50g/2oz/⅓ cup raisins
10ml/2 tsp ground coriander
45ml/3 tbsp tomato purée (paste)
1 egg yolk, beaten
10ml/2 tsp natural (plain) yogurt
75g/3oz/6 tbsp melted butter
a few saffron strands, soaked in a little hot water
salt and ground black pepper

1 Cook the rice in boiling salted water for 10–12 minutes. Drain. Heat 30ml/2 tbsp of the oil in a large pan and fry the garlic and chopped onion for 5 minutes. Stir in the lentils, stock, raisins, coriander and tomato purée. Bring to the boil, lower the heat, cover and simmer for 20 minutes.

2 Mix the egg yolk and yogurt in a bowl. Spoon in about 120ml/4 fl oz/½ cup of the cooked rice and mix thoroughly. Season. Heat about two-thirds of the remaining oil in a large pan and sprinkle the egg and yogurt rice over the bottom.

3 Place a layer of rice in the pan, then a layer of lentils. Build up the layers in a pyramid shape away from the sides. Finish with a layer of plain rice. With a wooden spoon handle, make three holes down to the bottom of the pan; drizzle over the melted butter. Bring to a high heat, then wrap the pan lid in a wet dish towel and place on top. When the rice is steaming well, lower the heat and cook slowly for about 30 minutes.

4 Fry the onion slices in the remaining oil until browned and crisp. Drain. Remove the rice pan from the heat, and dip the base into cold water to loosen the crust. Strain the saffron water into a bowl and stir in a few spoons of cooked rice. Toss the rice and lentils together in the pan and spoon on to a serving dish. Sprinkle the saffron rice on top. Break up the crust and place around the mound. Top with the onions and serve.

Sour Cherry and Caraway Pilaff

Turkey is famous for its succulent cherries, and this is a popular summer pilaff, made with small, sour cherries rather than the plump, sweet ones. With its refreshing fruity bursts of intense cherry flavour, it goes with most vegetable, meat and fish dishes.

Serves 3–4

30ml/2 tbsp butter
225g/8oz fresh sour cherries, such as morello, pitted
5–10ml/1–2 tsp sugar
5ml/1 tsp caraway seeds
225g/8oz/generous 1 cup long grain rice, well rinsed and drained
salt and ground black pepper

1 Melt the butter in a heavy pan. Set a handful of the cherries aside to garnish the finished dish, and toss the rest in the butter with the sugar and caraway seeds. Cook for a few minutes.

2 Add the rice and 600ml/1 pint/2½ cups water and season with salt and pepper. Bring to the boil, lower the heat and partially cover the pan. Simmer for 10–12 minutes, until most of the water has been absorbed.

3 Turn off the heat, cover the pan with a clean dish towel and put the lid tightly on top. Leave for 20 minutes.

4 Fluff up the rice with a fork, tip on to a serving dish and garnish with the reserved cherries.

> **Variation**
> Use dried cranberries as a sweeter alternative to the sour cherries in this dish.

> **Cook's Tip**
> Due to their acidity, sour cherries are usually consumed cooked. They are delicious in savoury dishes like this one, but can also be poached with sugar and used in sorbets, jam, cakes or tangy compôtes to spoon over rice or yogurt.

Brown Rice with Lime, Spices and Lemon Grass

It is unusual to find brown rice used in a Thai recipe, but the nutty flavour of the grains is enhanced by the fragrance of limes and lemon grass in this delicious dish.

Serves 4

2 limes
1 lemon grass stalk
225g/8oz/generous 1 cup brown
   long grain rice
15ml/1 tbsp olive oil
1 onion, chopped
2.5cm/1in piece fresh root ginger,
   peeled and finely chopped
7.5ml/1½ tsp coriander seeds
7.5ml/1½ tsp cumin seeds
750ml/1¼ pints/3 cups vegetable
   stock
60ml/4 tbsp chopped fresh
   coriander (cilantro)
spring onions (scallions) and
   toasted coconut strips,
   to garnish
lime wedges, to serve

1 Pare the limes, using a cannelle knife (zester) or fine grater, taking care to avoid cutting into the bitter white pith. Set the rind aside. Finely chop the lower portion of the lemon grass stalk and set it aside.

2 Rinse the rice in plenty of cold water until the water runs clear. Tip it into a sieve (strainer) and drain thoroughly.

3 Heat the oil in a large pan. Add the onion, ginger, coriander and cumin seeds, lemon grass and lime rind and cook over a low heat for 2–3 minutes.

4 Add the rice to the pan and cook, stirring constantly, for 1 minute, then pour in the stock and bring to the boil. Reduce the heat to very low and cover the pan. Cook gently for 30 minutes, then check the rice. If it is still crunchy, cover the pan and cook for 3–5 minutes more until the rice is tender. Remove from the heat.

5 Stir in the fresh coriander, fluff up the rice grains with a fork, cover the pan and leave to stand for 10 minutes. Transfer to a warmed dish, garnish with the green part of spring onions and toasted coconut strips, and serve with lime wedges.

Rice with Cinnamon and Star Anise

Originating from China, this thick rice porridge or "congee", known as *bubur* in Malaysia and Indonesia, has become popular all over South-east Asia. The basic recipe is nourishing but rather bland, and the joy of the dish is derived from the ingredients that are added.

Serves 4–6

25g/1oz fresh root ginger, peeled
   and sliced
1 cinnamon stick
2 star anise
2.5ml/½ tsp salt
115g/4oz/½ cup short grain
   rice, thoroughly washed
   and drained

1 Bring 1.2 litres/2 pints/5 cups water to the boil in a heavy pan. Stir in the spices, the salt and the rice.

2 Reduce the heat, cover the pan, and simmer gently for 1 hour, or longer if you prefer a thicker, smoother consistency. Serve piping hot.

Variations
The Teochew version of bubur *is called* muay. *With its addition of pickles, strips of omelette and braised dishes, it is popular for supper in Singapore. In Malaysia, bubur is enjoyed for breakfast with fried or grilled fish, chicken and beef, as well as with pickles. Often flavoured with ginger, cinnamon and star anise, it is usually cooked until it is thick but the grains are still visible, whereas some of the Chinese versions are cooked for longer, so that the rice breaks down completely and the texture is quite smooth. The consistency varies from family to family: some people like it soupy and eat it with a spoon.*

Cook's Tip
This dish is often eaten for breakfast, in Malaysia, and some domestic rice cookers have a "congee" setting, which allows the dish to be prepared the night before and slowly cooked overnight, in order to be ready in the morning.

Rice with Spices and Lemon Grass: Energy 235kcal/996kJ; Protein 4.3g; Carbohydrate 47.3g, of which sugars 1.9g; Fat 4.5g, of which saturates 0.8g; Cholesterol 0mg; Calcium 35mg; Fibre 1.9g; Sodium 6mg.
Rice with Cinnamon and Star Anise: Energy 69Kcal/288kJ; Protein 1.4g; Carbohydrate 15.3g, of which sugars 0g; Fat 0.1g, of which saturates 0g; Cholesterol 0mg; Calcium 4mg; Fibre 0g; Sodium 164mg.

Aromatic Indian Rice with Peas

This fragrant, versatile rice dish is often served as part of an elaborate meal at Indian festivals and celebratory feasts, which might include several meat and vegetable curries, a yogurt dish, and chutneys. Ground turmeric or grated carrot is sometimes added for an extra splash of colour. Sprinkle the pilaff with chopped fresh mint and coriander (cilantro), if you like, or with roasted chilli and coconut.

Serves 4
350g/12oz/1¾ cups basmati rice
45ml/3 tbsp ghee or 30ml/2 tbsp
  vegetable oil and a small
  amount of butter
1 cinnamon stick
6–8 cardamom pods, crushed
4 cloves
1 onion, halved lengthways and
  sliced
25g/1oz fresh root ginger, peeled
  and grated
5ml/1 tsp sugar
130g/4½oz fresh peas, shelled, or
  frozen peas
5ml/1 tsp salt

1 Rinse the rice and put it in a bowl. Cover with plenty of water and leave to soak for 30 minutes. Drain thoroughly.

2 Heat the ghee, or oil and butter, in a heavy pan. Stir in the cinnamon stick, cardamom and cloves. Add the onion, ginger and sugar, and fry until golden. Add the peas, followed by the rice, and stir for 1 minute to coat the rice in ghee.

3 Pour in 600ml/1 pint/2½ cups water. Add the salt, stir once and bring the liquid to the boil. Reduce the heat and allow to simmer for 15–20 minutes, until the liquid has been absorbed.

4 Turn off the heat, cover the pan with a clean dish towel and the lid, and leave the rice to steam for a further 10 minutes. Spoon the rice on to a serving dish.

> **Variation**
> This Indian pilaff also works with diced carrot or beetroot (beet), or chickpeas. Instead of turmeric, you can add a little tomato paste to give the rice a red tinge.

Malay Yellow Rice

Coloured yellow by vibrant turmeric powder, nasi kuning is a delicately flavoured rice often served at Malay festivals. It is also one of the popular dishes at the Malay nasi campur and Indonesian nasi padang stalls, where it is served with a variety of meat and vegetable dishes. This simple rice dish is cooked in the same way as plain steamed rice, using the absorption method.

Serves 4
30ml/2 tbsp vegetable or
  sesame oil
3 shallots, finely chopped
2 garlic cloves, peeled and finely
  chopped
450g/1lb/generous 2 cups long
  grain rice, thoroughly washed
  and drained
400ml/14fl oz/1⅔ cups coconut
  milk
10ml/2 tsp ground turmeric
4 fresh curry leaves
2.5ml/½ tsp salt
ground black pepper
2 red chillies, seeded and finely
  sliced, to garnish

1 Heat the oil in a heavy pan and stir in the shallots and garlic. Just as they begin to colour, stir in the rice until the grains are coated in the oil.

2 Add the coconut milk, 450ml/¾ pint/scant 2 cups water, turmeric, curry leaves, salt and pepper.

3 Bring to the boil, then turn down the heat and cover. Cook gently for 15–20 minutes, until all the liquid has been absorbed.

4 Turn off the heat and leave the rice to steam in the pan for 10 minutes. Fluff up the rice with a fork and serve garnished with red chillies.

> **Cook's Tip**
> Regular long grain rice, or other types such as jasmine rice, short grain or sticky rice, can all be used for this recipe.

Malay Yellow Rice: Energy 481Kcal/2011kJ; Protein 8.8g; Carbohydrate 95.9g, of which sugars 5.8g; Fat 6.4g, of which saturates 0.9g; Cholesterol 0mg; Calcium 54mg; Fibre 0.2g; Sodium 356mg.
Aromatic Indian Rice: Energy 451Kcal/1880kJ; Protein 8.9g; Carbohydrate 75.7g, of which sugars 2.6g; Fat 12.2g, of which saturates 5.4g; Cholesterol 0mg; Calcium 28mg; Fibre 1.8g; Sodium 328mg.

Spiced Pumpkin Wedges and Sautéed Spinach

Warmly spiced roasted pumpkin, combined with creamy spinach and the fire of chilli, makes a lovely accompaniment for grills and roasts.

Serves 4–6
10ml/2 tsp coriander seeds
5ml/1 tsp cumin seeds
5ml/1 tsp fennel seeds
5–10ml/1–2 tsp cinnamon
2 dried red chillies, chopped
coarse salt
2 garlic cloves
30ml/2 tbsp olive oil
1 medium pumpkin, halved, seeded, cut into 6–8 wedges

For the sautéed spinach
30–45ml/2–3 tbsp pine nuts
30–45ml/2–3 tbsp olive oil
1 red onion, halved and sliced
1–2 dried red chillies, finely sliced
1 apple, peeled, cored and sliced
2 garlic cloves, crushed
5–10ml/1–2 tsp ground roasted cumin
10ml/2 tsp clear honey
450g/1lb spinach, steamed and roughly chopped
60–75ml/4–5 tbsp double (heavy) cream
salt and ground black pepper
a handful of fresh coriander (cilantro) leaves, chopped, to garnish

1 Preheat the oven to 200°C/400°F/Gas 6. Grind the coriander, cumin and fennel seeds, cinnamon and chillies with a little coarse salt in a mortar with a pestle. Add the garlic and a little of the olive oil and pound to form a paste. Rub the spice mixture over the pumpkin segments and place them, skin-side down, in an ovenproof dish or roasting pan. Bake the spiced pumpkin for 35–40 minutes, or until tender.

2 To make the sautéed spinach, roast the pine nuts in a dry frying pan until golden, then tip on to a plate. Add the olive oil to the pan. Sauté the onion with the chilli until soft, then stir in the apple and garlic. Once the apple begins to colour, stir in most of the pine nuts, most of the cumin and the honey.

3 Toss in the spinach and, once it has heated through, stir in most of the cream. Season to taste and remove from the heat. Swirl the last of the cream on top, sprinkle with the reserved pine nuts and roasted cumin, and a little coriander. Serve.

Braised Baby Leeks in Red Wine with Aromatics

Coriander seeds and oregano lend a Greek flavour to this dish of braised leeks. Serve it as part of a mixed hors d'oeuvre or as a partner for baked white fish.

Serves 6
12 baby leeks or 6 thick leeks
15ml/1 tbsp coriander seeds, lightly crushed
5cm/2in cinnamon stick
120ml/4fl oz/½ cup olive oil
3 fresh bay leaves
2 strips pared orange rind
5–6 fresh or dried oregano sprigs
5ml/1 tsp sugar
150ml/¼ pint/⅔ cup fruity red wine
10ml/2 tsp balsamic or sherry vinegar
30ml/2 tbsp coarsely chopped fresh oregano or marjoram
salt and ground black pepper

1 Wash and trim the leeks. Leave baby leeks whole, but if you are using thick ones cut them into 5–7.5cm/2–3in lengths.

2 Place the coriander seeds and cinnamon stick in a pan wide enough to take all the leeks in a single layer. Dry-fry the whole spices over a medium heat for 2–3 minutes, until they are fragrant, then stir in the oil, bay leaves, orange rind, oregano, sugar, wine and vinegar. Bring the mixture to the boil and simmer for 5 minutes.

3 Add the leeks. Bring back to the boil, reduce the heat and cover the pan. Cook gently for 5 minutes. Uncover and simmer gently for another 5–8 minutes, until the leeks are just tender when tested with the tip of a sharp knife.

4 Use a draining spoon to transfer the leeks to a serving dish. Boil the juices rapidly until reduced to about 75–90ml/5–6 tbsp. Add salt and pepper to taste and pour the liquid over the leeks. Leave to cool.

5 The leeks can be left to stand for several hours. If you chill them, bring them back to room temperature again before serving. Sprinkle chopped oregano or marjoram over the leeks just before serving them.

Braised Baby Leeks in Red Wine: Energy 151kcal/621kJ; Protein 1.1g; Carbohydrate 1.7g, of which sugars 1.3g; Fat 13.7g, of which saturates 2g; Cholesterol 0mg; Calcium 29mg; Fibre 1.5g; Sodium 5mg.
Pumpkin and Spinach: Energy 456kcal/1897kJ; Protein 18.9g; Carbohydrate 22.1g, of which sugars 17.1g; Fat 31.9g, of which saturates 13.2g; Cholesterol 45mg; Calcium 635mg; Fibre 10g; Sodium 337mg.

Southern Thai Curried Vegetables

Rich curry flavours are found in the food of southern Thailand, where many dishes are made with coconut milk and spiced with turmeric.

Serves 4

90g/3½oz Chinese leaves
  (Chinese cabbage), shredded
90g/3½oz/generous 1 cup
  beansprouts
90g/3½oz/scant 1 cup green
  beans, trimmed
100g/3½oz broccoli florets
15ml/1 tbsp sesame seeds,
  toasted

For the sauce

60ml/4 tbsp coconut cream
  (see Cook's Tip)
5ml/1 tsp Thai red curry paste
90g/3½oz/1¼ cups oyster
  mushrooms or field (portobello)
  mushrooms, sliced
60ml/4 tbsp coconut milk
5ml/1 tsp ground turmeric
5ml/1 tsp thick tamarind juice,
  made by mixing tamarind
  paste with a little warm water
juice of ½ lemon
60ml/4 tbsp light soy sauce
5ml/1 tsp palm sugar (jaggery)
  or light muscovado (brown)
  sugar

1 Blanch the shredded Chinese leaves, beansprouts, green beans and broccoli in boiling water for 1 minute per batch. Drain, place in a bowl and leave to cool.

2 To make the sauce, pour the coconut cream into a wok or frying pan and heat gently for 2–3 minutes, until it separates. Stir in the red curry paste. Cook over a low heat for 30 seconds. Increase the heat, add the mushrooms and cook for a further 2–3 minutes. Pour in the coconut milk and stir in the turmeric, tamarind juice, lemon juice, soy sauce and sugar.

3 Pour the mixture over the prepared vegetables and toss well to combine. Sprinkle with the toasted sesame seeds and serve.

Cook's Tips
To make coconut cream use a carton or can of coconut milk. Skim the cream off the top and cook 60ml/4 tbsp of it before adding the curry paste. Add the measured coconut milk later, as described in the recipe.

Malay Pak Choi in Spiced Coconut Milk

Among the rich and varied food traditions of Melaka, Penang and Singapore, the cooking that evolved among early immigrants from China is a unique blend of Chinese, Malay and Portuguese influences. The style is sweet and rich, with plentiful use of pungent shrimp paste, which is a key ingredient, and Malaysia's abundant vegetables are often cooked in coconut milk. For this dish, you could use green beans, curly kale, or any type of cabbage, all of which are delicious served with steamed, braised or grilled fish dishes.

Serves 4

4 shallots, chopped
2 garlic cloves, peeled and finely
  chopped
1 lemon grass stalk, trimmed and
  chopped
25g/1oz fresh root ginger, peeled
  and chopped
2 red chillies, seeded and
  chopped
5ml/1 tsp shrimp paste
5ml/1 tsp ground turmeric
5ml/1 tsp palm sugar (jaggery)
15ml/1 tbsp sesame or groundnut
  (peanut) oil
400ml/14fl oz/1⅔ cups coconut
  milk
450g/1lb pak choi (bok choy),
  separated into leaves
salt and ground black pepper

1 Using a mortar and pestle or food processor, grind the shallots, garlic, lemon grass, ginger and chillies to a paste. Beat in the shrimp paste, turmeric and sugar.

2 Heat the oil in a wok or heavy pan, and stir in the spice paste. Cook until it is fragrant and beginning to colour. Pour in the coconut milk, mix well, and bubble it up until it thickens. Drop in the cabbage leaves, coating them in the coconut milk, and cook for a minute or two until wilted. Season to taste and serve immediately.

Variation
Make the dish using Chinese leaves (Chinese cabbage) or kale, cut into thick ribbons, or a mixture of the two.

Spicy Chickpeas with Spinach

This richly flavoured dish makes a great main meal for vegetarians, but it will be equally popular with meat-eaters. It is particularly good served drizzled with a little lightly beaten natural yogurt – the sharp, creamy flavour complements the complex spices perfectly.

Serves 4

200g/7oz dried chickpeas
30ml/2 tbsp sunflower oil
2 onions, halved and thinly sliced
　along the grain
10ml/2 tsp ground coriander
10ml/2 tsp ground cumin
5ml/1 tsp hot chilli powder
2.5ml/½ tsp turmeric
15ml/1 tbsp medium curry
　powder
400g/14oz can chopped
　tomatoes
5ml/1 tsp caster (superfine)
　sugar
30ml/2 tbsp chopped fresh mint
　leaves
115g/4oz baby leaf spinach
salt and ground black pepper
plain steamed rice or bread and
　natural (plain) yogurt, to serve

1 Soak the chickpeas in cold water overnight. Drain, rinse and place in a large pan. Cover with water and bring to the boil. Reduce the heat and simmer for 45 minutes, or until just tender. Drain and set aside.

2 Heat the oil in a wok or large frying pan, add the sliced onions and cook over a low heat for 15 minutes, stirring occasionally, until soft and lightly golden.

3 Add the ground coriander and cumin, chilli powder, turmeric and curry powder and stir-fry for 1–2 minutes.

4 Add the tomatoes, sugar and 105ml/7 tbsp water to the wok and bring to the boil. Cover, reduce the heat and simmer gently for 15 minutes.

5 Add the chickpeas to the wok, season well and cook gently for 8–10 minutes. Stir in the chopped mint.

6 Divide the spinach leaves between shallow bowls, top with the chickpea mixture and serve with some steamed rice or bread and natural yogurt.

Stir-fried Spinach with Garlic, Pine Nuts and Yogurt

There are endless versions of traditional spinach and yogurt *meze* dishes in Turkish cookery, ranging from plain steamed spinach served with yogurt, to this sweet and tangy creation tamed with garlic-flavoured yogurt. Serve warm, with flatbread or chunks of a crusty loaf to accompany it.

Serves 3–4

350g/12oz fresh spinach leaves,
　thoroughly washed and drained
about 200g/7oz/scant 1 cup thick
　natural (plain) yogurt
2 garlic cloves, crushed
30–45ml/2–3 tbsp olive oil
1 red onion, cut in half
　lengthways, in half again
　crossways, and sliced along
　the grain
5ml/1 tsp sugar
15–30ml/1–2 tbsp currants,
　soaked in warm water for
　5–10 minutes and drained
30ml/2 tbsp pine nuts
5–10ml/1–2 tsp hot paprika, or
　1 fresh red chilli, seeded and
　finely chopped
juice of 1 lemon
salt and ground black pepper
a pinch of paprika, to garnish

1 Steam the spinach for 3–4 minutes, until wilted and soft. Drain off any excess water and chop the spinach.

2 In a bowl, beat the yogurt with the garlic. Season to taste and set aside.

3 Heat the oil in a heavy pan and fry the onion and sugar, stirring constantly to prevent the sugar burning, until the onion begins to colour. Add the currants, pine nuts and paprika or chilli and fry until the nuts begin to colour.

4 Add the spinach, tossing it around the pan until well mixed with the other ingredients, then pour in the lemon juice and season with salt and pepper.

5 Serve the spinach straight from the pan with the yogurt spooned on top, or tip into a serving dish and make a well in the middle, then spoon the yogurt into the well, drizzling some of it over the spinach. Serve hot, sprinkled with a little paprika.

Spicy Chickpeas with Spinach: Energy 267kcal/1122kJ; Protein 13.3g; Carbohydrate 35.5g, of which sugars 10.2g; Fat 9g, of which saturates 1.1g; Cholesterol 0mg; Calcium 170mg; Fibre 8.2g; Sodium 83mg.
Stir-fried Spinach with Garlic: Energy 145kcal/603kJ; Protein 5.8g; Carbohydrate 10.2g, of which sugars 9.8g; Fat 9.3g, of which saturates 1.3g; Cholesterol 1mg; Calcium 252mg; Fibre 2.2g; Sodium 165mg.

Fiery Dhal with Spicy Topping

Boost your pulse rate with this delectable dish of red lentils with a spicy topping.

Serves 4
50g/2oz/¼ cup butter
10ml/2 tsp black mustard seeds
1 onion, finely chopped
2 garlic cloves, finely chopped
5ml/1 tsp ground turmeric
5ml/1 tsp ground cumin
2 fresh green chillies, seeded and
  finely chopped

225g/8oz/1 cup red lentils
300ml/½ pint/1¼ cups canned
  coconut milk
crisply fried sliced onion and
  sprigs of fresh coriander
  (cilantro), to garnish
warm naan, to serve

For the spicy topping
30ml/2 tbsp ghee
10ml/2 tsp black mustard seeds
2.5ml/½ tsp asafoetida
8 dried curry leaves

1 Melt the butter in a large heavy pan. Add the mustard seeds. When they start to pop, add the onion and garlic and cook for 5–10 minutes until soft.

2 Stir in the turmeric, cumin and chillies and cook for about 2 minutes. Stir in the lentils, 1 litre/1¾ pints/4 cups water and coconut milk. Bring to the boil, then cover and simmer for 40 minutes, adding water if needed. The lentils should be soft and should have absorbed most of the liquid.

3 To prepare the topping, melt the ghee in a frying pan. When it is hot add the black mustard seeds and cover the pan until they start to pop. Remove from the heat and add the asafoetida and curry leaves. Stir into the hot ghee, then pour immediately over the dhal.

4 Garnish the dish with onion rings, fried until deep brown and crisp, and coriander leaves and serve at once, with warm naan to mop up the sauce.

> **Variation**
> This dish is excellent made with moong dhal, the yellow split mung bean that is widely used in Indian cookery.

Garlic-flavoured Lentils with Coriander and Sage

Adapted from a traditional Ottoman Turkish dish, which is flavoured with mint and dill, this simple recipe uses sage instead. Dried sage leaves have a really strong herby aroma, and are ideal for this dish, though you could also make it using fresh sage. Serve these lentils with grilled, broiled or barbecued meats, or on their own with a dollop of yogurt seasoned with garlic, salt and pepper.

Serves 4–6
175g/6oz/¾ cup green lentils
45–60ml/3–4 tbsp fruity olive oil
1 onion, sliced
3–4 plump garlic cloves, roughly
  chopped and bruised
5ml/1 tsp coriander seeds
a handful of dried sage leaves
5–10ml/1–2 tsp sugar
4 carrots, sliced
15–30ml/1–2 tbsp tomato purée
  (paste)
salt and ground black pepper
1 bunch of fresh sage or flat leaf
  parsley, to garnish

1 Pick over the lentils, rinse them in cold water and drain. Bring a pan of water to the boil and tip in the lentils. Lower the heat, partially cover the pan and simmer for 10 minutes. Drain and rinse well under cold running water.

2 Heat the oil in a heavy pan, stir in the onion, garlic, coriander, sage and sugar, and cook until the onion begins to colour. Toss in the carrots and cook for 2–3 minutes.

3 Add the drained lentils to the carrots in the pan and pour in 250ml/8fl oz/1 cup water, making sure the lentils and carrots are covered.

4 Stir in the tomato purée and cover the pan, then cook the lentils and carrots gently for about 20 minutes, until most of the liquid has been absorbed. The lentils and carrots should both be tender, but still have some bite.

5 Season the dish with salt and pepper to taste. Transfer to a serving dish and garnish with the fresh sage or flat leaf parsley. Serve hot or at room temperature.

Fiery Dhal with Spicy Topping: Energy 381kcal/1599kJ; Protein 14.9g; Carbohydrate 39.1g, of which sugars 6g; Fat 19.7g, of which saturates 10.4g; Cholesterol 27mg; Calcium 69mg; Fibre 3g; Sodium 182mg.
Garlic-flavoured Lentils with Sage: Energy 166kcal/696kJ; Protein 7.6g; Carbohydrate 21.1g, of which sugars 6.7g; Fat 6.2g, of which saturates 0.9g; Cholesterol 0mg; Calcium 38mg; Fibre 4g; Sodium 22mg.

Root Vegetable Gratin with Indian Spices

Subtly spiced with curry powder, turmeric, coriander and mild chilli powder, this rich gratin is substantial enough to serve on its own for lunch or supper. It also makes a good accompaniment to a vegetable or bean curry.

Serves 4

2 large potatoes, total weight about 450g/1lb
2 sweet potatoes, total weight about 275g/10oz
175g/6oz celeriac
15ml/1 tbsp unsalted butter
5ml/1 tsp medium curry powder
5ml/1 tsp ground turmeric
2.5ml/½ tsp ground coriander
5ml/1 tsp mild chilli powder
3 shallots, chopped
salt and ground black pepper
150ml/¼ pint/⅔ cup single (light) cream
150ml/¼ pint/⅔ cup semi-skimmed (low-fat) milk
chopped fresh flat leaf parsley, to garnish

1 Thinly slice the potatoes, sweet potatoes and celeriac, using a sharp knife or the slicing attachment on a food processor. Immediately place the vegetables in a bowl of cold water to prevent them discolouring.

2 Preheat the oven to 180°C/350°F/Gas 4. Heat half the butter in a heavy pan and add the curry powder, turmeric and coriander and half the chilli powder. Cook for 2 minutes, then leave to cool slightly.

3 Drain the vegetables, then pat dry with kitchen paper. Place in a bowl, add the spice mixture and the shallots and mix well.

4 Arrange the vegetables in layers in a gratin dish, seasoning each layer. Mix together the cream and milk, pour over the vegetables, then sprinkle the remaining chilli powder on top.

5 Cover with greaseproof (waxed) paper and bake for about 45 minutes. Remove the greaseproof paper, dot with the remaining butter and bake for a further 50 minutes until the top is golden. Serve garnished with chopped fresh parsley.

Paprika-spiced Pepper Stew

Many Hungarian vegetable recipes are substantial, flavoursome dishes, which are usually intended to be eaten by themselves, as with this recipe, and not just as an accompaniment to meat, poultry or fish dishes. In its most basic form of a thick tomato and onion purée, this warming dish is also used as the basis for stews and other dishes.

Serves 6–8

30ml/2 tbsp vegetable oil or melted lard
1 onion, sliced
5 green or yellow (bell) peppers, cut into strips
450g/1lb plum tomatoes, peeled and chopped
15ml/1 tbsp paprika
sugar and salt, to taste
grilled (broiled) bacon rashers (strips), to garnish
crusty bread, to serve

1 Heat the oil or lard in a large frying pan. Add the sliced onion and cook over a low heat for 5 minutes, stirring occasionally, until just softened.

2 Add the strips of pepper to the pan and cook the mixture gently for 10 minutes.

3 Add the chopped tomatoes and paprika and season with a little sugar and salt.

4 Simmer the mixture over a low heat for 20–25 minutes, until the vegetables are very soft and the tomatoes have collapsed into a thick sauce.

5 Taste and correct the seasoning, and serve immediately, topped with crisply grilled bacon and accompanied by plenty of crusty bread.

> **Variations**
> • To eat the stew as a main course, serve it with steamed rice or dumplings.
> • Add 115g/4oz/1 cup sliced salami, or some lightly scrambled eggs to the vegetables.

Vegetable Gratin with Spices: Energy 268kcal/1129kJ; Protein 5.8g; Carbohydrate 37.7g, of which sugars 9.8g; Fat 11.6g, of which saturates 7.1g; Cholesterol 31mg; Calcium 127mg; Fibre 3.6g; Sodium 117mg.
Paprika-spiced Pepper Stew: Energy 118kcal/492kJ; Protein 3.2g; Carbohydrate 18.4g, of which sugars 16g; Fat 4g, of which saturates 0.6g; Cholesterol 0mg; Calcium 35mg; Fibre 4.3g; Sodium 15mg.

Greek-style Aromatic Mushrooms

There are many variations
of this classic dish of
mushrooms stewed in olive
oil, but they all contain
coriander seeds.

Serves 4
60ml/4 tbsp olive oil
2 carrots, peeled and diced
375g/12oz baby onions
120ml/4fl oz/½ cup dry
    white wine

5ml/1 tsp coriander seeds, lightly
    crushed
2 bay leaves
pinch of cayenne pepper
1 garlic clove, crushed
375g/12oz button mushrooms
3 tomatoes, peeled, seeded and
    quartered
salt and ground black pepper
45ml/3 tbsp chopped fresh
    parsley, to garnish
crusty bread, to serve

1 Heat 45ml/3 tbsp of the olive oil in a deep frying pan. Add
the carrots and onions and cook, stirring occasionally, for about
20 minutes until the vegetables have browned lightly and are
beginning to soften.

2 Add the white wine, coriander seeds, bay leaves, cayenne,
garlic, button mushrooms and tomatoes, with salt and pepper
to taste. Cook gently, uncovered, for 20–30 minutes until the
vegetables are soft and the sauce has thickened.

3 Transfer to a serving dish and leave to cool. Cover
and chill until needed. Before serving, pour over the
remaining olive oil and sprinkle with the parsley. Serve
with crusty bread.

Variation
*This treatment is ideal for other vegetables. Try leeks, fennel or
artichokes, with or without baby onions.*

Cook's Tip
*Don't trim too much from either the top or root end of the
onions: if you do, the centres will pop out during cooking.*

Japanese Fried Chilli Aubergine with Miso Sauce

Stir-fried aubergine is coated
in a rich miso sauce. Make
sure the oil is very hot
when adding the aubergine,
so that it does not absorb
too much oil.

Serves 4
2 large aubergines (eggplants)
1–2 dried red chillies

45ml/3 tbsp sake
45ml/3 tbsp mirin
45ml/3 tbsp caster (superfine)
    sugar
30ml/2 tbsp shoyu
45ml/3 tbsp red miso (use either
    dark red aka miso or even
    darker hatcho miso)
90ml/6 tbsp sesame oil
salt

1 Cut the aubergines into bitesize pieces and place in a large
colander, sprinkle with some salt and leave for 30 minutes to
remove the bitter juices. Squeeze the aubergine pieces with
your hands to extract the moisture. Remove the seeds from
the chillies and chop the chillies into thin rings.

2 Mix the sake, mirin, sugar and shoyu in a cup. In a separate
bowl, mix the red miso with 45ml/3 tbsp water to make a
loose paste.

3 Heat the oil in a large pan and add the chilli. When you see
pale smoke rising from the oil, add the aubergine, and stir-fry
for about 8 minutes, or until browned and tender. Lower the
heat to medium.

4 Add the sake mixture to the pan, and stir for 2–3 minutes. If
the sauce starts to burn, lower the heat. Add the miso paste to
the pan and cook, stirring, for another 2 minutes. Serve hot.

Variation
*Sweet (bell) peppers could be used for this dish instead of
aubergine. Take 1 red, 1 yellow and 2 green peppers. Remove
the seeds and chop them into 1cm/½in strips, then follow the
rest of the recipe.*

Stir-fried Carrots with Mango and Ginger

Ripe mango adds its unique fruity sweetness to carrots and ginger in this spicy vegetable dish from Morocco. Cooked in this way, humble carrots are turned into an excellent and exciting dish. It can be served as an accompaniment for grilled meat or couscous, but the dish is also very good on its own with yogurt and a salad. The mango must be ripe, otherwise you will need to add a little honey to balance the flavours.

Serves 4–6
15–30ml/1–2 tbsp olive oil
1 onion, chopped
25g/1oz fresh root ginger, peeled and chopped
2–3 garlic cloves, chopped
5–6 carrots, sliced
30–45ml/2–3 tbsp shelled pistachio nuts, roasted
5ml/1 tsp ground cinnamon
5–10ml/1–2 tsp ras el hanout
1 small firm but ripe mango, peeled and coarsely diced
small bunch of fresh coriander (cilantro), finely chopped
juice of ½ lemon
salt

1 Heat the olive oil in a heavy frying pan or wok. Stir in the onion, ginger and garlic and fry for 1 minute.

2 Add the carrots, tossing them in the pan to make sure that they are thoroughly mixed with the flavouring ingredients, and cook until they begin to brown.

3 Add the pistachio nuts, cinnamon and ras el hanout, then mix in the pieces of mango, stirring gently to avoid breaking them up. Sprinkle with coriander; season with salt and pour over the lemon juice. Serve immediately.

> **Cook's Tip**
> To prepare a mango, use a sharp knife to cut down either side of the large stone. Score a lattice into the flesh of each half without cutting the skin, then run the knife between the flesh and the skin to release the cubes of mango.

Stir-fried Brussels Sprouts with Bacon and Caraway Seeds

Brussels sprouts are not usually associated with stir-frying, but this style of cooking helps to retain their crunchy texture. Shredding the sprouts and cooking them briefly guarantees that there will not be a single soggy sprout in sight.

Serves 4
450g/1lb Brussels sprouts, trimmed and washed
30ml/2 tbsp sunflower oil
2 streaky (fatty) bacon rashers (strips), finely chopped
10ml/2 tsp caraway seeds, lightly crushed
salt and ground black pepper

1 Using a sharp knife, cut the Brussels sprouts into fine shreds and set aside. Heat the oil in a wok or large frying pan and add the bacon. Cook for 1–2 minutes, or until the bacon is beginning to turn golden.

2 Add the shredded sprouts to the wok or pan and stir-fry for 1–2 minutes, or until lightly cooked.

3 Season the sprouts with salt and ground black pepper to taste and stir in the caraway seeds. Cook for a further 30 seconds, then serve immediately.

> **Variation**
> Add a few sliced water chestnuts to the stir-fry to introduce an extra crunchy texture. Cook fresh chestnuts for about 5 minutes, canned for 2 minutes to retain their crispness.

> **Cook's Tip**
> • The sulphurous flavour that many people dislike in Brussels sprouts is produced when they are overcooked. Briefly stir-frying them avoids this problem.
> • Caraway seeds have a flavour rather like aniseed and are much used in Central and Eastern European cookery.

Herbed Potato Salad

Mixing the potatoes with the dressing when hot means they absorb it better.

Serves 4–6
675g/1½lb new potatoes
4 spring onions (scallions)

45ml/3 tbsp white wine
   vinegar
45ml/3 tbsp olive oil
175ml/6fl oz/¾ cup mayonnaise
a handful of fresh chives,
   snipped
salt and ground black pepper

1 Boil the potatoes in their skins until tender. Slice the spring onions into thin rounds. Whisk the vinegar and oil together. Drain the potatoes and immediately toss in the oil and vinegar.

2 Stir the mayonnaise and chives together, season, then mix in with the dressed potatoes. Leave to cool a little, then serve.

Hot Hot Cajun Potato Salad

In Cajun country in Louisiana, where Tabasco sauce originates, hot means really hot, so you can go to town with this salad if you think you can take it.

Serves 6–8
8 waxy potatoes
1 green (bell) pepper, diced
1 large gherkin, chopped

4 spring onions (scallions),
   shredded
3 hard-boiled eggs, shelled and
   chopped
250ml/8fl oz/1 cup mayonnaise
15ml/1 tbsp Dijon mustard
salt and ground black pepper
Tabasco sauce, to taste
pinch or two of cayenne
sliced gherkin, to garnish
mayonnaise, to serve

1 Cook the potatoes in their skins in boiling salted water until tender. Drain and leave to cool.

2 When the potatoes are cool enough to handle, but while they are still warm, peel them and cut into coarse chunks. Place them in a large bowl.

3 Add the green pepper, gherkin, spring onions and hard-boiled eggs to the potatoes and toss gently to combine.

4 In a separate bowl, mix the mayonnaise with the mustard and season with salt, black pepper and Tabasco sauce to taste.

5 Pour the dressing over the potato mixture and toss gently so that the potatoes are well coated. Sprinkle with a pinch or two of cayenne and garnish with a few slices of gherkin. Serve with extra mayonnaise.

Cook's Tips
• The salad is good to eat immediately, when the potatoes are just cool. If you make it in advance and chill it, let it come back to room temperature before serving.
• Tabasco is one of thousands of commercial hot pepper sauces on the market, of varying intensity: use your favourite brand to make this salad.

Potato Salad with Mango Dressing

This sweet and spicy salad is a wonderful accompaniment to roasted meats.

Serves 4–6
15ml/1 tbsp olive oil
1 onion, sliced into rings
1 garlic clove, crushed
5ml/1 tsp ground cumin
5ml/1 tsp ground coriander

1 mango, diced
30ml/2 tbsp demerara (raw)
   sugar
30ml/2 tbsp lime juice
900g/2lb new potatoes, cut in
   half and boiled
15ml/1 tbsp sesame seeds
salt and ground black pepper
deep-fried coriander (cilantro)
   leaves, to garnish

1 Heat the oil in a frying pan and fry the onion and garlic over a low heat for 10 minutes until they start to brown. Stir in the cumin and coriander and fry for a few seconds. Stir in the mango and sugar and fry for 5 minutes, until soft. Remove the pan from the heat and squeeze in the lime juice. Season.

2 Place the potatoes in a large bowl and spoon the mango dressing over. Sprinkle with sesame seeds and garnish with the coriander leaves. Serve while the dressing is still warm.

Hot Hot Cajun Potato Salad: Energy 289kcal/1197kJ; Protein 4g; Carbohydrate 10.3g, of which sugars 2.7g; Fat 26.1g, of which saturates 4.2g; Cholesterol 95mg; Calcium 21mg; Fibre 0.9g; Sodium 229mg.
Herbed Potato Salad: Energy 218kcal/913kJ; Protein 3g; Carbohydrate 27g, of which sugars 2.3g; Fat 11.6g, of which saturates 1.7g; Cholesterol 0mg; Calcium 23mg; Fibre 2g; Sodium 21mg.
Potato Salad with Mango Dressing: Energy 174kcal/737kJ; Protein 3.3g; Carbohydrate 33.7g, of which sugars 11.2g; Fat 3.8g, of which saturates 0.7g; Cholesterol 0mg; Calcium 34mg; Fibre 2.5g; Sodium 18mg.

Lentil Salad with Red Onion and Garlic

This delicious, garlicky Moroccan lentil salad is frequently served as an accompaniment to kebabs, as part of a meze or by itself as an appetizer. It is equally good eaten warm or cooled. Try it together with a generous spoonful of natural yogurt.

Serves 4

45ml/3 tbsp olive oil
2 red onions, chopped
2 tomatoes, peeled, seeded and
  chopped
10ml/2 tsp ground turmeric
10ml/2 tsp ground cumin
175g/6oz/³⁄₄ cup brown or green
  lentils, picked over, rinsed
  and drained
900ml/1¹⁄₂ pints/3³⁄₄ cups
  vegetable stock or water
4 garlic cloves, crushed
small bunch of fresh coriander
  (cilantro), finely chopped
salt and ground black pepper
1 lemon, cut into wedges, to serve

1 Heat 30ml/2 tbsp of the oil in a large pan or flameproof casserole and fry the onions until soft. Add the tomatoes, turmeric and cumin, then stir in the lentils.

2 Pour in the stock or water and bring to the boil, then reduce the heat and simmer until the lentils are tender and almost all the liquid has been absorbed.

3 In a separate pan, fry the garlic in the remaining oil until brown and frizzled. Toss the garlic into the lentils with the fresh coriander and season to taste.

4 Serve warm or at room temperature, with wedges of lemon for squeezing over.

> **Cook's Tips**
> • If you prefer, you can replace the lentils with mung beans – they work just as well.
> • When including this dish in a meze, serve it with a creamy dip and a fruity salad to balance the different textures.

Sautéed Herb Salad with Chilli and Preserved Lemon

Firm-leafed fresh herbs, such as flat leaf parsley, mint and coriander (cilantro), can be used as tasty ingredients in their own right rather than just as flavourings. Tossed in a little olive oil and seasoned with salt, they make a fabulous salad to serve as part of a meze spread, and they also go wonderfully with spicy kebabs or tagines. Lightly sautéed with garlic and served warm with yogurt, this dish is delightful even on its own.

Serves 4

large bunch of flat leaf parsley
large bunch of mint
large bunch of fresh coriander
  (cilantro)
bunch of rocket (arugula)
large bunch of spinach leaves
  (about 115g/4oz)
60–75ml/4–5 tbsp olive oil
2 garlic cloves, finely chopped
1 green or red chilli, seeded and
  finely chopped
¹⁄₂ preserved lemon, finely
  chopped
salt and ground black pepper
45–60ml/3–4 tbsp strained
  natural (plain) yogurt, to serve

1 Roughly chop the parsley, mint, coriander, rocket and spinach leaves.

2 Heat the olive oil in a wide, heavy pan. Stir in the garlic and chilli, and fry until they begin to colour.

3 Toss in the chopped herbs, rocket and spinach and cook over a low heat, stirring gently, until they begin to soften and wilt. Add the preserved lemon and season to taste.

4 Turn the salad into a serving dish and serve while still warm with a dollop of yogurt.

> **Variation**
> Garlic-flavoured yogurt makes a good accompaniment: crush a clove of garlic and stir it into the yogurt with salt and ground pepper to taste.

Indian-spiced Winter Melon Relish

Cooks in southern India make a variety of side dishes like this one, Known as *pachadi* or raita, they are all designed to cool the palate and aid digestion when eating the hot, spicy food for which the region is renowned. The dishes are yogurt-based and are made with a variety of cooling vegetables and herbs, such as winter melon, okra, courgette, spinach, pumpkin and cucumber with mint. They also often include small amounts of spicier ingredients such as chilli.

Serves 4

225g/8oz winter melon, peeled, seeded and diced
5ml/1 tsp ground turmeric
5ml/1 tsp red chilli powder
300ml/½ pint/1¼ cups strained natural (plain) yogurt
2.5ml/½ tsp salt
2.5ml/½ tsp sugar
15g/½oz fresh root ginger, peeled and grated
1 green chilli, seeded and finely chopped
15ml/1 tbsp vegetable oil
1.5ml/¼ tsp ground asafoetida
5ml/1 tsp brown mustard seeds
8–10 dried curry leaves
1 dried red chilli, seeded and roughly chopped

1 Put the winter melon in a heavy pan with the turmeric and chilli powder and pour in enough water to just cover. Bring to the boil and cook gently, uncovered, until the winter melon is tender and all the water has evaporated.

2 In a bowl, beat the yogurt with the salt and sugar until smooth and creamy. Add the ginger and green chilli, and fold in the warm winter melon.

3 Heat the oil in small pan. Stir in the asafoetida and mustard seeds. As soon as the seeds begin to pop, stir in the curry leaves and dried chilli. When the chilli darkens, add the spices to the yogurt and mix thoroughly. Serve at room temperature.

Cook's Tip
This dish can made a day or two in advance, so that the flavours have time to mingle and blend.

Malay Beansprout Salad

Kelantan in the north of Malaysia is well known for its rich Malay cuisine, particularly *nasi kerabu*, the famous dish of blue rice, and this beansprout salad, *kerabu*, which is served with it. In the Kota Bharu markets up near the Thai border, blue rice is wrapped in a banana leaf with *kerabu* and eaten as a snack. This beansprout salad is also served as a refreshing side dish to accompany other highly spiced Malay dishes.

Serves 4

115g/4oz fresh coconut, grated
30ml/2 tbsp dried prawns (shrimp), soaked in warm water until soft
225g/8oz beansprouts, rinsed and drained
1 small cucumber, peeled, seeded and cut into julienne strips
2–3 spring onions (scallions), trimmed, cut into 2.5cm/1in pieces and halved lengthways
handful of young, tender mangetouts (snow peas), halved diagonally
handful of green beans, halved lengthways
handful of fresh chives, chopped into 2.5cm/1in pieces
handful of fresh mint leaves, finely chopped
2–3 red chillies, seeded and sliced finely lengthways
juice of 2 limes
10ml/2 tsp sugar
salt and ground black pepper

1 Dry-roast the coconut in a heavy frying pan until it starts to emit a nutty aroma and is lightly browned. Using a mortar and pestle or a food processor, grind the coconut to a coarse powder. Drain the soaked dried prawns and grind them coarsely too.

2 Put the vegetables, herbs and chillies into a bowl. Mix the lime juice with the sugar and pour it over the salad. Season with salt and pepper. Scatter the ground coconut and dried prawns over the salad, and toss well until thoroughly mixed.

Cook's Tip
Aim to cut all the vegetables into thin strips that are about the same size and shape as the beansprouts.

Indian-spiced Melon Relish: Energy 127Kcal/527kJ; Protein 5.1g; Carbohydrate 5.3g, of which sugars 5.3g; Fat 10.5g, of which saturates 4.2g; Cholesterol 0mg; Calcium 120mg; Fibre 0.2g; Sodium 316mg.
Malay Beansprout Salad: Energy 230Kcal/947kJ; Protein 12.6g; Carbohydrate 15.9g, of which sugars 13.9g; Fat 12.9g, of which saturates 10.2g; Cholesterol 0mg; Calcium 151mg; Fibre 7.8g; Sodium 24mg.

Cooling Coriander, Coconut and Tamarind Chutney

Cooling fragrant chutneys are very popular with the Jewish community in India, and this delicious blend of coriander, mint and coconut, with a hint of chilli, a tang of tamarind and the sweet flavour of dates, is a traditional condiment.

Makes about 450g/1lb/ 2 cups
30ml/2 tbsp tamarind paste
30ml/2 tbsp boiling water
I large bunch fresh coriander (cilantro), roughly chopped
I bunch fresh mint, roughly chopped
8–10 pitted dates, roughly chopped
75g/3oz dried coconut or 50g/2oz creamed coconut, coarsely grated
2.5cm/1 in piece fresh root ginger, chopped
3–5 garlic cloves, chopped
2–3 fresh chillies, chopped
juice of 2 limes or lemons
about 5ml/1 tsp sugar
salt
30–45ml/2–3 tbsp natural (plain) yogurt to serve

1 Place the tamarind paste in a bowl and pour over the boiling water. Stir thoroughly until the paste is completely dissolved and set aside.

2 Place the fresh coriander, mint leaves and pitted dates in a food processor and process briefly until finely chopped. Alternatively, chop the ingredients finely by hand using a sharp knife. Place in a bowl.

3 Add the coconut, ginger, garlic and chillies to the chopped herbs and dates and stir in the tamarind. Season with citrus juice, sugar and salt. Spoon into sterilized jars, seal and chill. To serve, thin the chutney with the yogurt.

Cook's Tips
• This chutney can be stored in the refrigerator for up to 2 weeks, adding the yogurt just before serving.
• Adjust the amount of ginger, garlic and chillies to taste.

Cucumber and Shallot Salad with Cumin

In Malaysia and Singapore, this light, refreshing salad is served with Indian food almost as often as the cooling and familiar mint-flavoured cucumber raita. The Malays also enjoy this salad with many of their spicy fish and grilled meat dishes. It can be made ahead of time and kept in the refrigerator. Serve it as a salad, or a relish.

Serves 4
5–10ml/1–2 tsp whole cumin seeds
I cucumber, peeled, halved lengthways and seeded
4 shallots, halved lengthways and sliced finely along the grain
1–2 green chillies, seeded and sliced finely lengthways
60ml/4 tbsp coconut milk
salt
I lime, quartered, to serve

1 Dry-roast the cumin seeds in a heavy frying pan until they emit their aroma. Put them in a mortar and grind to a fine power using a pestle, or grind them in a spice mill. Set aside.

2 Slice the cucumber halves finely. Put them on a plate and sprinkle with salt. Set aside for about 15 minutes then rinse well and leave in a colander to drain off any excess water.

3 Put the cucumber in a bowl with the sliced shallots and chillies. Pour in the coconut milk and toss well. Sprinkle most of the roasted cumin over the top.

4 Just before serving, toss the salad again, season with salt, and sprinkle the rest of the roasted cumin over the top. Serve with lime wedges to squeeze over the salad.

Cook's Tip
Cumin seeds are a key flavouring in Indian food, and therefore appear in Malay dishes with Indian influences, but they are equally popular in Central America. Their bitter flavour, enhanced by roasting, brings out the sweetness of other ingredients.

Coriander Chutney: Energy 536kcal/2232kJ; Protein 10.1g; Carbohydrate 47g, of which sugars 39.5g; Fat 35.5g, of which saturates 29.8g; Cholesterol 0mg; Calcium 144mg; Fibre 6.6g; Sodium 39mg.
Cucumber and Shallot Salad with Cumin: Energy 17Kcal/68kJ; Protein 0.7g; Carbohydrate 3.3g, of which sugars 2.7g; Fat 0.1g, of which saturates 0g; Cholesterol 0mg; Calcium 19mg; Fibre 0.7g; Sodium 15mg.

Pineapple Pickle

This spicy sweet and sour pickle is ideal to serve with hot grilled foods or as an accompaniment to curries or vegetable dishes.

Serves 6–8
15ml/1 tbsp brown mustard seeds
2 dried chillies, soaked in water until soft, seeded, and squeezed dry
15g/½oz fresh root ginger, peeled and chopped
1 garlic clove, chopped
5ml/1 tsp ground turmeric
200ml/7fl oz/scant 1 cup white wine vinegar or rice vinegar
15ml/1 tbsp palm sugar (jaggery)
1 ripe pineapple, peeled, cored and diced
salt

1 Put the mustard seeds a small, heavy pan over a medium heat. Cover the pan and dry-roast the seeds until they pop. Remove from the heat.

2 Using a mortar and pestle or food processor, grind the chillies, ginger and garlic to a paste. Stir in the mustard seeds and ground turmeric. Add the vinegar and sugar, stirring until the sugar has completely dissolved.

3 Put the pineapple pieces in a bowl and pour over the pickling sauce. Add salt to taste.

> **Variation**
> Try adding spices such as cloves, cinnamon and allspice to the spice paste for a sweeter flavour.

> **Cook's Tips**
> • Malays and Indians often serve a selection of condiments with every meal. Sambals, pickles and chutneys can all be interchanged with the spicy food of these cultures.
> • This pickle will keep for 2–3 days in the refrigerator, and in fact is better made in advance as it will improve as the flavours mingle.

Fragrant Persian Halek

Charoset, the sweet mixture of apples, nuts, honey and cinnamon, is made by Jews at Passover in remembrance of the mortar used by the Israelites to bond bricks while in slavery in Egypt. Persian Jews make this more elaborate version, which is fragrant with rose water and the sweet flavours of many different dried fruits and nuts, which are so important a part of the Persian culinary tradition.

Serves 10
60ml/4 tbsp blanched almonds
60ml/4 tbsp unsalted pistachio nuts
60ml/4 tbsp walnuts
15–30ml/1–2 tbsp skinned hazelnuts
30ml/2 tbsp unsalted shelled pumpkin seeds
90ml/6 tbsp raisins, chopped
90ml/6 tbsp pitted prunes, diced
90ml/6 tbsp dried apricots, diced
60ml/4 tbsp dried cherries
sugar or honey, to taste
juice of ½ lemon
30ml/2 tbsp rose water
seeds from 4–5 cardamom pods
pinch of ground cloves
pinch of freshly grated nutmeg
1.5ml/¼ tsp ground cinnamon
fruit juice of choice, if necessary

1 Roughly chop the almonds, pistachio nuts, walnuts, hazelnuts and pumpkin seeds and put in a bowl. Add the chopped raisins, prunes, apricots and cherries to the nuts and seeds and toss to combine. Stir in sugar or honey to taste and mix well until thoroughly combined.

2 Add the lemon juice, rose water, cardamom seeds, cloves, nutmeg and cinnamon to the fruit and nut mixture and mix until thoroughly combined.

3 If the halek is too thick, add a little fruit juice to thin the mixture. Pour into a serving bowl, cover and chill in the refrigerator until ready to serve.

> **Cook's Tip**
> Some cooks observe a tradition of using 40 ingredients to make halek, echoing 40 years of wandering in the desert.

Fragrant Persian Halek: Energy 207kcal/863kJ; Protein 5.1g; Carbohydrate 14.9g, of which sugars 14.5g; Fat 14.6g, of which saturates 1.4g; Cholesterol 0mg; Calcium 66mg; Fibre 2.8g; Sodium 42mg.
Pineapple Pickle: Energy 56Kcal/238kJ; Protein 0.7g; Carbohydrate 12.5g, of which sugars 12.2g; Fat 0.2g, of which saturates 0g; Cholesterol 0mg; Calcium 20mg; Fibre 1.3g; Sodium 4mg.

Red Onion, Garlic and Lemon Relish

This powerful relish is flavoured with North African spices and punchy preserved lemons, which are available from delicatessens and larger supermarkets or from specialist Middle Eastern food stores.

Serves 6

45ml/3 tbsp olive oil

3 large red onions, sliced

2 heads of garlic, separated into
   cloves and peeled

10ml/2 tsp coriander seeds,
   crushed but not finely ground

10ml/2 tsp light muscovado
   (brown) sugar, plus a little extra

pinch of saffron strands

5cm/2in piece cinnamon stick

2–3 small whole dried red chillies
   (optional)

2 fresh bay leaves

30–45ml/2–3 tbsp sherry vinegar

juice of ½ small orange

30ml/2 tbsp chopped preserved
   lemon

salt and ground black pepper

1 Heat the oil in a heavy pan. Add the onions and stir, then cover and reduce the heat to the lowest setting. Cook for 10–15 minutes, stirring occasionally, until the onions are soft.

2 Add the garlic cloves and coriander seeds. Cover and cook for 5–8 minutes until they are soft. Add a pinch of salt, lots of pepper and the sugar, and cook, uncovered, for 5 minutes.

3 Soak the saffron in about 45ml/3 tbsp warm water for 5 minutes, then add to the onions, with the soaking water. Add the cinnamon stick, dried chillies, if using, and bay leaves. Stir in 30ml/2 tbsp of the sherry vinegar and the orange juice.

4 Cook over a low heat, uncovered, until the onions are very soft and most of the liquid has evaporated. Stir in the preserved lemon and cook gently for a further 5 minutes, then taste and adjust the seasoning, adding more salt, sugar and/or vinegar to taste.

5 Serve warm or cold, but not hot or chilled. The relish tastes best if it is allowed to stand for 24 hours before serving for the flavours to blend and mellow.

Lime Pickle

This classic Indian pickle is popular everywhere, and various commercial brands are widely available in supermarkets and Asian stores, but the homemade version is far finer, and you can tailor its heat exactly to your family's preferences. In India the pickle is eaten mainly as an accompaniment to fiery curries.

Serves 8–10

8–10 limes

30ml/2 tbsp salt

150ml/5fl oz/⅔ cup sesame or
   groundnut (peanut) oil

10–15ml/2–3 tsp brown mustard
   seeds

3–4 garlic cloves, cut into thin
   sticks

25g/1oz fresh root ginger, peeled
   and cut into thin sticks

5ml/1 tsp coriander seeds

5ml/1 tsp cumin seeds

5ml/1 tsp fennel seeds

10ml/2 tsp ground turmeric

10ml/2 tsp hot chilli powder
   or paste

handful of fresh or dried curry
   leaves

1 Put the whole limes in a bowl. Cover them with boiling water and leave to stand for 30 minutes. Drain the limes and cut each into quarters. Rub the lime pieces with salt and put them into a sealed sterilized jar. Leave the limes to cure in the salt for 1 week.

2 Heat the oil in a wok and stir in the mustard seeds. When they begin to pop, stir in the garlic, ginger, spices and curry leaves. Cook gently for a few minutes to flavour the oil, then stir in the lime pieces and the juices from the jar. Reduce the heat and simmer for about 45 minutes, stirring from time to time.

3 Store the pickle in sterilized jars and keep in a cool place for 1–2 months.

Cook's Tips
- Lime pickle is delicious served with grilled or fried fish, and spicy stir-fried noodles.
- You can make the pickle as fiery as you like by adding more chilli powder.

Red Onion, Garlic and Lemon Relish: Energy 79kcal/326kJ; Protein 1.3g; Carbohydrate 10.4g, of which sugars 8.1g; Fat 3.9g, of which saturates 0.5g; Cholesterol 0mg; Calcium 27mg; Fibre 1.4g; Sodium 4mg.
Lime Pickle: Energy 96Kcal/395kJ; Protein 0.3g; Carbohydrate 0.9g, of which sugars 0.6g; Fat 10.1g, of which saturates 1.5g; Cholesterol 0mg; Calcium 25mg; Fibre 0.2g; Sodium 1185mg.

Harissa

This hot sauce features strongly in North African cooking. It can be used as a condiment, served with food according to individual tastes; it can be added to dishes to give them a fiery kick; or it can be served as a dip for warm bread, either on its own or blended with a little yogurt. Traditionally, the ingredients are pounded to a paste using a pestle and mortar, but whizzing them in a blender is far simpler and quicker. This recipe makes a small amount for a dip, or enough for several dishes.

Makes I small jar
6–8 dried red chillies (preferably New Mexico variety), seeded
2 garlic cloves, crushed
2.5ml/¹/₂ tsp sea salt
5ml/1 tsp ground cumin
2.5ml/¹/₂ tsp ground coriander
120ml/4fl oz/1¹/₂ cup olive oil

1 Soak the chillies in warm water for about 40 minutes, until soft. Drain and squeeze out the excess water. Place them in a blender with the other ingredients and process the mixture to form a paste.

2 Spoon the harissa into a small jar, cover with a thin layer of olive oil and seal tightly. Store in the refrigerator for up to 1 month.

> **Cook's Tip**
> *Though harissa is perhaps the most famous of the spice mixes of the Middle East and North Africa, the most complex and refined is probably ras el hanout, which originates in Morocco. Its name means "top of the shop" in Arabic – referring to the fact that it is made from the shopkeeper's best spices – and its composition reflects the centuries of trade, war and cross-cultural exchange of Morocco's history. It includes cardamoms, nutmeg, mace, galangal, cinnamon, ginger and curcuma from India and the Far East and guinea pepper, cloves and cyparacee from Africa, plus orris root, ash berries, monk's pepper, belladonna berries, fennel flowers, lavender, black pepper and rose buds.*

Tahini Sauce

Made of ground sesame seeds and spiced with garlic and lemon juice, this is a versatile and popular Middle Eastern sauce. It makes a delicious dip, served with pitta bread, and can also be thinned with water to a pouring consistency.

Serves 4–6
150–175g/5–6oz/²/₃–³/₄ cup tahini
3 garlic cloves, finely chopped
juice of 1 lemon
1.5ml/¹/₄ tsp ground cumin
small pinch of ground coriander
small pinch of curry powder
50–120ml/2–4fl oz/¹/₄–¹/₂ cup water
cayenne pepper
salt

For the garnish
15–30ml/1–2 tbsp extra virgin olive oil
chopped fresh coriander (cilantro) leaves or parsley
handful of olives and/or pickled vegetables
a few chillies or a hot pepper sauce

1 Put the tahini and garlic in a food processor or bowl and mix together well. Stir in the lemon juice, cumin, ground coriander and curry powder.

2 Slowly add the water to the tahini, beating all the time. The mixture will thicken, then become thin. Season with cayenne pepper and salt.

3 To serve, spread the mixture on to a serving plate, individual plates or into a shallow bowl. Drizzle over the oil and sprinkle with the other garnishes.

> **Cook's Tip**
> *Tahini sauce forms the basis of many salads and dips made throughout the Middle East. It is most often poured over falafel, the spicy fried balls made from chickpeas, typically eaten in a pitta as street food. But tahini sauce can also be used as a sauce for grilled meat or vegetables such as potatoes or cauliflower. By adding a little more olive oil it can be turned into a salad dressing.*

Tahini Sauce: Energy 175kcal/725kJ; Protein 5.2g; Carbohydrate 12g, of which sugars 0.3g; Fat 16.7g, of which saturates 2.4g; Cholesterol 0mg; Calcium 184mg; Fibre 2.5g; Sodium 7mg.
Harissa: Energy 306kcal/1280kJ; Protein 15.6g; Carbohydrate 37.2g, of which sugars 0.6g; Fat 13.7g, of which saturates 2g; Cholesterol 0mg; Calcium 191mg; Fibre 0g; Sodium 36mg.

Spiced Apple Pie

If you use eating apples bursting with flavour, loads of butter and sugar, and make your own shortcrust pastry, then you can't go wrong. However, adding a buttery caramel to the apples takes it one step further and, coupled with the mixed spice, gives a rich flavour to the juices in the pie.

Serves 6
900g/2lb eating apples
75g/3oz/6 tbsp unsalted (sweet) butter
45–60ml/3–4 tbsp demerara (raw) sugar
3 cloves
2.5ml/½ tsp mixed (apple pie) spice

For the pastry
250g/9oz/2¼ cups plain (all-purpose) flour
pinch of salt
50g/2oz/¼ cup lard or white cooking fat, chilled and diced
75g/3oz/6 tbsp unsalted (sweet) butter, chilled and diced
30–45ml/2–3 tbsp chilled water
a little milk, for brushing
caster (superfine) sugar, for dredging
clotted cream, ice cream or double (heavy) cream, to serve

1 Preheat the oven to 200°C/400°F/Gas 6. Sift the flour and salt into a bowl. Rub in the lard or fat and butter until the mixture resembles fine breadcrumbs. Stir in enough chilled water to bring the pastry together. Knead lightly then wrap in cling film (plastic wrap) and chill for 30 minutes.

2 To make the filling, peel, core and thickly slice the apples. Melt the butter in a frying pan, add the sugar and cook for 3–4 minutes allowing it to melt and caramelize. Add the apples and stir around to coat. Cook over a brisk heat until the apples take on a little colour, add the spices and tip out into a bowl.

3 Divide the pastry in two and, on a lightly floured surface, roll out into two rounds to fit a deep 23cm/9in pie plate. Line the plate with one round. Spoon in the cooled apple. Cover with the remaining pastry, sealing and crimping the edges. Make a 5cm/2in long slit through the top of the pastry to allow the steam to escape. Brush the pie with milk and dredge with caster sugar. Place the pie on a baking sheet and bake in the oven for 25–35 minutes until golden and firm. Serve warm.

Almond-stuffed Baked Apples

The first spoonful of this baked apple dessert is always a delightful surprise. The pastry wrapping the apple acts as an oven, which bakes the apple and keeps in its flavour, and this mingles perfectly with the almonds.

Serves 8
8 eating apples
1 egg yolk
30ml/2 tbsp water
double (heavy) cream, whipped with 5ml/1 tsp vanilla sugar, to serve

For the pastry
575g/1¼lb/5 cups plain (all-purpose) flour
225g/8oz/1 cup unsalted (sweet) butter
100g/4oz/½ cup caster (superfine) sugar
1 egg, beaten

For the almond stuffing
25g/1oz/2 tbsp unsalted (sweet) butter
100g/4oz/1 cup ground almonds
50g/2oz/4 tbsp caster (superfine) sugar
10ml/2 tsp ground cinnamon

1 To make the pastry, put the flour in a food processor. Cut the butter into small pieces, add to the flour and then, using a pulsating action, mix together until the mixture resembles fine breadcrumbs. Add the sugar and egg and mix to form a dough. Wrap in greaseproof (waxed) paper and place in the refrigerator for 1 hour.

2 Preheat the oven to 200°C/400°F/Gas 6. To make the almond stuffing, melt the butter and leave to cool but not set. Put the ground almonds, caster sugar and cinnamon in a bowl. Add the melted butter and mix together. Remove the cores from the apples and then use the stuffing to fill their centres.

3 Divide the pastry into eight pieces. On a floured surface, roll each piece out to a thickness of about 5mm/¼in and, using a 20–23cm/8–9in plate, cut into a round. Put a round over the top of each apple and wrap the pastry around, pinching it in at the bottom. Place on a baking sheet.

4 Beat the egg yolk and water together and brush over the pastry to glaze. Bake in the oven for about 30 minutes until golden brown. Serve hot, with the vanilla-flavoured cream.

Spiced Apple Pie: Energy 610kcal/2566kJ; Protein 8.1g; Carbohydrate 86.1g, of which sugars 40.2g; Fat 28.5g, of which saturates 8.8g; Cholesterol 14mg; Calcium 168mg; Fibre 8.1g; Sodium 413mg.
Almond-stuffed Apples: Energy 735kcal/3080kJ; Protein 11.2g; Carbohydrate 87.7g, of which sugars 32.6g; Fat 40.2g, of which saturates 20.6g; Cholesterol 129mg; Calcium 159mg; Fibre 5.2g; Sodium 245mg.

Ginger-spiced Black Rice Pudding

This very unusual rice pudding from Indonesia, which uses black glutinous rice flavoured with bruised fresh root ginger, is quite delicious. Serve it with a little coconut cream poured over each helping.

Serves 6
115g/4oz black glutinous rice
475ml/16fl oz/2 cups water
1cm/½in fresh root ginger
50g/2oz dark brown sugar
50g/2oz caster (superfine) sugar
300ml/½ pint/1¼ cups coconut
    milk or cream, to serve

1 Rinse the rice in a sieve (strainer) under cold running water. Drain and put in a large pan, with the water. Bring to the boil and stir to prevent the rice settling on the bottom. Cover and cook for about 30 minutes. Peel and bruise the ginger.

2 Add the ginger and both the brown and caster sugar. Cook for a further 15 minutes, adding a little more water if necessary, until the rice is cooked and porridge-like. Remove the ginger and serve warm, in bowls, topped with coconut milk.

English Rice Pudding

A proper English rice pudding is smooth and creamy with a hint of spice.

Serves 4
600ml/1 pint/2½ cups milk
1 vanilla pod (bean)

50g/2oz/generous ¼ cup short
    grain pudding rice
45ml/3 tbsp caster (superfine)
    sugar
25g/1oz/2 tbsp butter
freshly grated nutmeg
jam, to serve

1 Bring the milk to simmering point in a pan, together with the vanilla pod, and leave for 1 hour to infuse. Preheat the oven to 150°C/300°F/Gas 2. Put the rice and sugar in an ovenproof dish. Add the milk to the rice, discarding the vanilla pod. Stir, then dot the surface with butter.

2 Bake uncovered for 2 hours. After 40 minutes stir to break up the skin, and grate nutmeg over the top. Serve hot with jam.

Caribbean Spiced Rice Pudding

Allspice, otherwise known as Jamaica pepper, flavours this exotic pudding. Caribbean recipes can be extremely sweet, and you may find you can reduce the quantity of sugar in this pudding because of the natural sweetness of the fruit. Don't try to reduce it too much, however, as the toffeeish sweetness is part of the special character of this indulgent dish.

Serves 4–6
25g/1oz/2 tbsp butter
1 cinnamon stick
115g/4oz/½ cup soft brown sugar
115g/4oz/⅔ cup ground rice
1.2 litres/2 pints/5 cups full-cream
    (whole) milk
2.5ml/½ tsp allspice
50g/2oz/⅓ cup sultanas (golden
    raisins)
75g/3oz mandarin orange, pith
    removed, chopped
75g/3oz fresh pineapple,
    chopped

1 Melt the butter in a non-stick pan and then add the cinnamon stick and sugar. Heat over a medium heat until the sugar begins to caramelize: watch the pan carefully and remove it from the heat as soon as this happens.

2 Carefully stir in the rice and three-quarters of the milk. Bring to the boil, stirring all the time, without letting the milk burn. Reduce the heat and simmer for 10 minutes until the rice is cooked, stirring constantly.

3 Add the remaining milk, the allspice and the sultanas. Leave to simmer for 5 minutes, stirring occasionally.

4 When the rice is thick and creamy, allow to cool slightly, then stir in the pieces of mandarin orange and pineapple. Serve straight away or leave to cool and serve at room temperature or chilled.

> **Variation**
> Instead of stirring the fresh fruit into the rice pudding, serve it separately, either as a cool contrast with the hot rice, or after the rice has cooled.

Caribbean Rice Pudding: Energy 341kcal/1428kJ; Protein 8.3g; Carbohydrate 52.4g, of which sugars 37.1g; Fat 11.4g, of which saturates 7.2g; Cholesterol 37mg; Calcium 261mg; Fibre 0.7g; Sodium 116mg.
Ginger-spiced Black Rice Pudding: Energy 249kcal/1044kJ; Protein 4g; Carbohydrate 42.5g, of which sugars 14.4g; Fat 7g, of which saturates 5.5g; Cholesterol 0mg; Calcium 33mg; Fibre 1.4g; Sodium 78mg.
English Rice Pudding: Energy 433kcal/1829kJ; Protein 5.8g; Carbohydrate 85.6g, of which sugars 65.7g; Fat 6.9g, of which saturates 3.3g; Cholesterol 112mg; Calcium 113mg; Fibre 0.5g; Sodium 68mg.

Indian-spiced Rice Pudding

This sweet rice pudding, known as *kheer*, is popular throughout India.

Serves 4–6
15ml/1 tbsp ghee
5cm/2in cinnamon stick
175g/6oz soft brown sugar
115g/4oz coarsely ground rice
1.2 litres/2 pints/5 cups full-cream (whole) milk
5ml/1 tsp ground cardamom
50g/2oz sultanas (golden raisins)
25g/1oz almond flakes
2.5ml/½ tsp freshly grated nutmeg, to serve

1 Melt the ghee in a heavy pan and add the cinnamon and sugar. Cook until the sugar begins to caramelize. Reduce the heat immediately when this happens. Add the rice and half the milk. Bring to the boil, stirring. Reduce the heat and simmer until the rice is cooked, stirring regularly.

2 Add the remaining milk, cardamom, sultanas and almonds and leave to simmer, but keep stirring to prevent the pudding from sticking to the base of the pan. When the mixture has thickened it is ready to serve, sprinkled with nutmeg.

Portuguese Rice Pudding

This rice pudding is traditionally served chilled, perfect for summer weather.

Serves 4–6
175g/6oz short grain rice
600ml/1pint/2½ cups whole milk
2–3 strips pared lemon rind
65g/2½oz/5 tbsp butter
115g/4 oz/½ cup caster (superfine) sugar
4 egg yolks
salt
ground cinnamon and lemon wedges, to serve

1 Partially cook the rice in boiling water for 5 minutes. Drain then return to the pan. Add the milk, lemon rind and butter. Bring to the boil, cover, reduce the heat and simmer for 20 minutes.

2 Remove from the heat, discard the lemon rind, stir in the sugar and egg yolks, mix and cool, then chill. Serve dusted with cinnamon and with lemon wedges for squeezing.

Sweet Rice Vermicelli

The combination of sweetened rice vermicelli, dried fruit, nuts and spices may sound a little unusual, but it makes a deliciously moist, aromatic dessert that tastes divine drizzled with cream or served with big scoops of ice cream.

Serves 4
60g/2½oz/5 tbsp unsalted (sweet) butter
60ml/4 tbsp vegetable oil
185g/6½oz thin rice vermicelli, broken into 3cm/1¼in lengths
1.5ml/¼ tsp ground allspice
30ml/2 tbsp roasted unsalted cashew nuts
15ml/1 tbsp chopped almonds
30ml/2 tbsp sultanas (golden raisins)
50g/2oz/⅓ cup ready-to-eat dried apricots, roughly chopped
90g/3½oz/½ cup caster (superfine) sugar
175ml/6fl oz/¾ cup warm water
15ml/1 tbsp rose water
pistachio nuts, to garnish
single (light) cream or vanilla ice cream, to serve (optional)

1 Put the butter and oil in a wok or a large, deep frying pan and place over a low heat. When the butter has melted, add the rice vermicelli and stir-fry for 3–4 minutes, or until the vermicelli starts to turn a light golden brown.

2 Add the allspice, cashew nuts, almonds, sultanas and apricots to the wok and stir-fry for 1–2 minutes.

3 Sprinkle the sugar over the vermicelli mixture and stir to combine, then add the warm water. Cover the pan and bring to the boil. Reduce the heat and simmer gently for 8–10 minutes until the liquid has been absorbed and the vermicelli is tender.

4 Stir the rose water into the vermicelli mixture until well mixed, then ladle into individual warmed bowls, sprinkle the nuts over and serve with single cream or ice cream if liked.

> **Cook's Tip**
> Also known as thin rice noodles or rice sticks, rice vermicelli is available in Asian stores and large supermarkets.

Indian-spiced Rice Pudding: Energy 228kcal/961kJ; Protein 7.3g; Carbohydrate 44.7g, of which sugars 21.8g; Fat 2.7g, of which saturates 1.6g; Cholesterol 9mg; Calcium 188mg; Fibre 0g; Sodium 105mg.
Portuguese Rice Pudding: Energy 368kcal/1534kJ; Protein 7.6g; Carbohydrate 47.9g, of which sugars 24.6g; Fat 16.6g, of which saturates 9.2g; Cholesterol 172mg; Calcium 151mg; Fibre 0g; Sodium 116mg.
Sweet Rice Vermicelli: Energy 589kcal/2455kJ; Protein 8.6g; Carbohydrate 71.1g, of which sugars 29.4g; Fat 31.1g, of which saturates 10.3g; Cholesterol 32mg; Calcium 64mg; Fibre 0.7g; Sodium 124mg.

Cardamom-spiced Pear Tarte Tatin

Cardamom is a spice that is
equally at home in sweet
and savoury dishes and is
delicious with pears. It has
an exquisite but evanescent
fragrance, so it is best to
buy whole pods and extract
the seeds as you need them.

Serves 2–4
50g/2oz/¼ cup butter, softened
50g/2oz/¼ cup caster (superfine)
   sugar
10 cardamom pods
225g/8oz puff pastry, thawed
   if frozen
3 ripe pears

1 Preheat the oven to 220°C/425°F/Gas 7. Spread the butter over the base of a 18cm/7in heavy cake tin or an omelette pan with an ovenproof handle. Spread the sugar evenly over the bottom of the tin or pan. Extract the seeds from the cardamom pods and sprinkle them evenly over the butter and sugar.

2 On a floured surface, roll out the pastry to a circle slightly larger than the cake tin or omelette pan. Prick the pastry lightly, support it on a baking sheet and chill.

3 Peel the pears, cut out the cores and slice them lengthways into halves. Arrange the pear halves, rounded-side down, on top of the butter and sugar. Set the cake tin or omelette pan over a medium heat until the sugar melts and begins to bubble with the butter and juice from the pears. If any areas appear to be browning more than others, move the pan around, but do not stir the contents.

4 As soon as the sugar has caramelized, remove the pan carefully from the heat. Place the circle of pastry on top of the pears, tucking the edges down the side of the pan. Transfer to the oven and bake for 25 minutes until the pastry is well risen and golden.

5 Leave the tart in the tin or pan for 2–3 minutes until the juices have stopped bubbling. Invert the tin over a plate and shake to release the tart. It may be necessary to slide a spatula underneath the pears to loosen them. Serve the tart warm with cream.

Sweet Couscous with Fruit Compôte

Aside from its essential
savoury role, couscous is
also eaten in Morocco as a
dessert or a nourishing
breakfast. This sweet, filling
and nutritious dish is lovely
served with a dried fruit
compôte and it is
particularly popular in the
mountainous regions of the
country, where the winters
can be long and cold.

Serves 6
300ml/½ pint/1¼ cups water
225g/8oz/1⅓ cups medium
   couscous
50g/2oz/scant ⅓ cup raisins

50g/2oz/¼ cup butter
50g/2oz/¼ cup caster (superfine)
   sugar
120ml/4fl oz/½ cup milk
120ml/4fl oz/½ cup double
   (heavy) cream

For the fruit compôte
225g/8oz/2 cups dried apricots
225g/8oz/1 cup pitted prunes
115/4oz/¾ cup sultanas
   (golden raisins)
115g/4oz/1 cup blanched
   almonds
175g/6oz/generous ¾ cup caster
   (superfine) sugar
30ml/2 tbsp rose water
1 cinnamon stick

1 Prepare the fruit compôte a couple of days in advance. Put the dried fruit and almonds in a bowl and pour in just enough water to cover. Gently stir in the sugar and rose water, and add the cinnamon. Cover and leave to soak for 48 hours – the water and sugar will form a lovely golden-coloured syrup.

2 To make the couscous, bring the water to the boil in a pan. Stir in the couscous and raisins, and cook for 1–2 minutes over a low heat, until the water has been absorbed. Remove the pan from the heat, cover tightly and leave the couscous to steam for 10–15 minutes. Meanwhile, heat the compôte.

3 Tip the couscous into a bowl and separate the grains with your fingertips. Melt the butter and pour it over the couscous. Sprinkle on the sugar then, using your fingertips, rub the butter and sugar into the couscous. Divide among six bowls.

4 Heat the milk and cream together in a small, heavy pan until just about to boil, then pour the mixture over the couscous. Serve immediately, with the dried fruit compôte.

Cardamom Pear Tarte Tatin: Energy 265kcal/1107kJ; Protein 2.5g; Carbohydrate 30.2g, of which sugars 16.8g; Fat 16.1g, of which saturates 4.4g; Cholesterol 18mg; Calcium 36mg; Fibre 1.7g; Sodium 170mg.
Couscous with Fruit: Energy 708kcal/2974kJ; Protein 10.6g; Carbohydrate 106.6g, of which sugars 86.8g; Fat 29.5g, of which saturates 12.1g; Cholesterol 46mg; Calcium 165mg; Fibre 6.5g; Sodium 87mg.

Sweet and Spicy Rice Fritters

These delicious little golden balls of rice are scented with sweet, warm spices and will fill the kitchen with wonderful aromas while cooking. To enjoy them at their best, serve them piping hot. They are great at any time of day – as a mid-morning or late afternoon snack, a simple dessert, or even as a late night treat.

Serves 4
175g/6oz cooked basmati rice
2 eggs, lightly beaten

60ml/4 tbsp caster (superfine)
    sugar
a pinch of nutmeg
2.5ml/½ tsp ground cinnamon
a pinch of ground cloves
10ml/2 tsp vanilla extract
50g/2oz/½ cup plain
    (all-purpose) flour
10ml/2 tsp baking powder
a pinch of salt
25g/1oz desiccated (dry
    unsweetened shredded)
    coconut
sunflower oil, for frying
icing (confectioners') sugar,
    to dust

1 Place the cooked rice, eggs, sugar, nutmeg, cinnamon, cloves and vanilla extract in a large bowl and whisk to combine. Sift in the flour, baking powder and salt and add the coconut. Mix well.

2 Fill a wok or deep pan one-third full of oil and heat to 180°C/350°F (or until a cube of bread, dropped into the oil, browns in 30 seconds).

3 Very gently, drop tablespoonfuls of the mixture into the oil, one at a time, and fry for 2–3 minutes, or until golden. Carefully remove the fritters from the wok using a slotted spoon and drain well on kitchen paper.

4 Divide the fritters into four portions, or simply pile them up on a single large platter. Dust them with icing sugar and serve immediately.

> **Cook's Tip**
> Unlike many cookies, these little fritters are gluten-free, so make a perfect snack for anyone with a gluten intolerance.

Greek Cheesecake with Cinnamon

This is a kind of Aegean cheesecake, made with fragrant Greek honey and the fresh, unsalted local cheese, called *myzithra*. It is similar to Italian ricotta, which makes a good substitute if necessary.

Serves 6–8
225g/8oz/2 cups plain
    (all-purpose) flour sifted with
    a pinch of salt
30ml/2 tbsp caster (superfine)
    sugar

115g/4oz/½ cup unsalted
    (sweet) butter, cubed
45–60ml/3–4 tbsp cold water

For the filling
4 eggs
50g/2oz/¼ cup caster (superfine)
    sugar
15ml/1 tbsp plain (all-purpose)
    flour
500g/1¼lb/2½ cups fresh
    myzithra or ricotta cheese
60ml/4 tbsp Greek thyme-scented
    honey
2.5ml/½ tsp ground cinnamon

1 Mix the flour and sugar in a bowl, then rub in the butter until the mixture resembles breadcrumbs. Add the water, a little at a time, until the mixture clings together and forms a dough. It should not be too wet. Draw it into a ball, wrap it in clear film (plastic wrap) and chill for 30 minutes.

2 Preheat the oven to 180°C/350°F/Gas 4. Put a baking sheet in the oven to heat. Roll out the pastry thinly on a lightly floured surface and use to line a 25cm/10in round springform tin (pan). Carefully trim off any excess pastry.

3 To make the filling, beat the eggs in a bowl, add the sugar and flour and beat until fluffy. Add the cheese, honey and half the cinnamon and beat until well mixed. Pour into the pastry case and level the surface. Place the tart on the hot baking sheet and cook for 50–60 minutes, until light golden. Sprinkle with the remaining cinnamon while still hot.

> **Cook's Tip**
> Save time by using a 500g/1¼lb packet of ready-made shortcrust pastry instead of making your own.

Steamed Ginger Custards

Delicate and warming, this ginger custard is a favourite among the Chinese inhabitants of Singapore. Often served warm, straight from the steamer, the individual custards are enjoyed as a sweet mid-afternoon snack or even late at night. They are equally delightful served cold as a dessert.

Serves 4

115g/4oz fresh root ginger, chopped
400ml/14fl oz/1²⁄₃ cups coconut milk
60ml/4 tbsp sugar
2 egg whites

1 Using a mortar and pestle or food processor, grind the ginger to a fine paste. Press the ginger paste through a fine sieve (strainer) set over a bowl, or twist it in a piece of muslin (cheesecloth), to extract the juice.

2 Fill a wok one-third full with water. Place a bamboo steamer in the wok, bring the water to the boil and then reduce the heat to low.

3 In a bowl, whisk the coconut milk, sugar and egg whites with the ginger juice until the mixture is smooth and the sugar has dissolved.

4 Pour the mixture into four individual heatproof bowls and place them in the steamer. Cover with a lid and steam for 15–20 minutes, until the mixture sets.

5 Remove the bowls from the steamer and leave to cool. Eat the custards while still slightly warm, or cover the bowls with clear film (plastic wrap) and place in the refrigerator overnight. Serve the custards chilled or at room temperature.

> **Cook's Tip**
> To check that the custards are cooked, lift the lid of the steamer and shake one of the bowls gently: the custard should wobble only slightly in the centre.

Lemon, Ginger and Pistachio Steamed Puddings

These moist little desserts, served with a luscious cardamom-spiced syrup, make a good winter dessert.

Serves 4

150g/5oz/10 tbsp butter
150g/5oz/³⁄₄ cup golden caster (superfine) sugar
10ml/2 tsp ground ginger
finely grated rind of 2 lemons
2 eggs
150g/5oz/1¹⁄₄ cups self-raising (self-rising) flour
a pinch of salt

115g/4oz/1 cup finely chopped pistachio nuts
shredded lemon rind, pistachio nuts and chopped preserved stem ginger, to garnish

For the syrup

150g/5oz/³⁄₄ cup golden caster (superfine) sugar
1.5ml/¹⁄₄ tsp crushed cardamom seeds
5ml/1 tsp ground ginger
10ml/2 tsp finely grated lemon rind and juice of 2 lemons
5ml/1 tsp arrowroot powder

1 To make the syrup, place the sugar, cardamom seeds and ginger in a non-stick pan and add 150ml/¹⁄₄ pint/²⁄₃ cup water. Heat gently until the sugar has dissolved, then add the lemon rind and juice. Bring to the boil and cook for 3–4 minutes.

2 Mix the arrowroot with 30ml/2 tbsp cold water and whisk into the syrup. Simmer gently for 2 minutes, or until the syrup has thickened slightly. Transfer to a bowl and set aside. Grease 4 × 200ml/7fl oz/scant 1 cup heatproof bowls and set aside.

3 Whisk together the butter and sugar until pale and fluffy. Add the ginger and beat in the eggs, one at a time. Sift in the flour and salt and add the chopped nuts, mixing to combine.

4 Spoon 20ml/4 tsp of the syrup into the base of each greased bowl and swirl to coat the sides. Spoon in the pudding mixture. Cover tightly with foil and secure with string. Steam for 1¹⁄₄ hours, until risen and firm to the touch. Reheat the remaining syrup, unmould the puddings on to individual plates and spoon over the syrup. Garnish with the lemon rind, pistachio nuts and preserved stem ginger and serve.

Lemon and Ginger Puddings: Energy 868kcal/3630kJ; Protein 12.4g; Carbohydrate 98.4g, of which sugars 69.1g; Fat 50g, of which saturates 22.5g; Cholesterol 175mg; Calcium 139mg; Fibre 7.9g; Sodium 420mg.
Steamed Ginger Custards: Energy 89Kcal/380kJ; Protein 2g; Carbohydrate 20.8g, of which sugars 20.8g; Fat 0.4g, of which saturates 0.2g; Cholesterol 0mg; Calcium 50mg; Fibre 0.3g; Sodium 159mg.

Spiced Spanish Leche Frita

The name of this dessert means "fried milk". It has a melting, creamy centre and crunchy, golden coating.

Serves 6–8
550ml/18fl oz/2½ cups milk
3 finely pared strips of lemon rind
½ cinnamon stick
90g/3½oz/½ cup caster (superfine) sugar
60ml/4 tbsp cornflour (cornstarch)

30ml/2 tbsp plain (all-purpose) flour
3 egg yolks and 2 whole eggs
90–120ml/6–8 tbsp breadcrumbs
sunflower oil, for frying
ground cinnamon, for dusting

For the sauce
450g/1lb blackberries or blackcurrants
90g/3½oz/½ cup caster (superfine) sugar

1 Put the milk, lemon rind, cinnamon stick and sugar in a pan and bring to the boil. Cover and leave to infuse for 20 minutes. Mix the cornflour and flour in a bowl and beat in the egg yolks. Add a little of the milk and beat to make a smooth batter.

2 Strain the remaining hot milk into the batter, then pour back into the pan. Cook over a low heat, stirring constantly until it thickens. Beat the mixture hard for a smooth consistency. Pour into an 18–20cm/7–8in, 1cm/½in deep rectangular dish, and smooth the top. Cool, then chill until firm.

3 To make the sauce, cook the fruit with the sugar and a little water for about 10 minutes until soft. Reserving 30–45ml/2–3 tbsp whole fruit, put the rest in a processor and blend to make a smooth purée. Return to the pan and keep warm.

4 Cut the chilled custard into eight or twelve squares. Beat the eggs in a shallow dish and spread the breadcrumbs on a plate. Coat each square in egg, then in crumbs.

5 Heat about 1cm/½in oil in a frying pan until very hot. Fry the squares in batches for a couple of minutes, shaking or spooning the oil over the top, until golden. Drain on kitchen paper while frying the other batches. Arrange on plates and sprinkle with sugar and cinnamon. Pour a circle of warm sauce round the squares, distributing the whole berries evenly.

Rich Cinnamon-spiced Pumpkin

Rich, sticky and sweet, this Mexican way of cooking pumpkin in brown sugar creates a warming and indulgent dessert that looks very attractive and is not at all difficult to prepare. The mildly flavoured flesh of the pumpkin, equally suited to sweet and savoury dishes, responds particularly well to cooking with sweet spices.

Serves 6
1 small pumpkin, about 800g/1¾lb
350g/12oz/1½ cups soft dark brown sugar
120ml/4fl oz/½ cup water
5ml/1 tsp ground cloves
12 cinnamon sticks, each about 10cm/4in long
fresh mint sprigs, to decorate
thick yogurt or crème fraîche, to serve

1 Halve the pumpkin, remove the seeds and fibres and cut into wedges. Arrange in a single layer in a shallow, flameproof casserole or heavy pan. Fill the hollows with the sugar.

2 Pour the water carefully into the pan, taking care not to wash all the sugar to the bottom. Make sure that some of the water trickles down to the bottom to prevent the pumpkin from burning. Sprinkle on the ground cloves and add two of the cinnamon sticks.

3 Cover the pan tightly and cook over a low heat for about 30 minutes, or until the pumpkin is tender and the sugar and water have formed a syrup. Check the casserole or pan occasionally to make sure that the pumpkin does not dry out or catch on the bottom.

4 Transfer the pumpkin to a platter and pour the hot syrup over. Decorate each portion with mint and cinnamon sticks and serve with thick yogurt or crème fraîche.

Cook's Tip
Pumpkin cooked in this way makes an ideal filling for sweet empanadas, so it's worth cooking the whole pumpkin and using the leftovers in this way for another meal.

Rich Cinnamon-spiced Pumpkin: Energy 247kcal/1054kJ; Protein 1.2g; Carbohydrate 63.9g, of which sugars 63.2g; Fat 0.3g, of which saturates 0.1g; Cholesterol 0mg; Calcium 70mg; Fibre 1.3g; Sodium 4mg.
Spiced Spanish Leche Frita: Energy 257kcal/1089kJ; Protein 6.9g; Carbohydrate 45.9g, of which sugars 30.6g; Fat 6.4g, of which saturates 2.7g; Cholesterol 133mg; Calcium 159mg; Fibre 2.3g; Sodium 143mg.

Vanilla, Honey and Saffron Pears

These sweet juicy pears, poached in a honey syrup fragrant with vanilla, saffron and lime, make a truly elegant dessert. They are lovely eaten just as they are, but for a really luxurious, indulgent treat, serve them with thin pouring cream or ice cream.

Serves 4
150g/5oz/¾ cup caster (superfine) sugar
105ml/7 tbsp clear honey
5ml/1 tsp finely grated lime rind
a large pinch of saffron
2 vanilla pods (beans)
4 large, firm ripe dessert pears
single (light) cream or ice cream, to serve

1 Place the caster sugar and honey in a medium, non-stick wok or large pan, then add the lime rind and the saffron strands. Using a small, sharp knife, split the vanilla pods in half and scrape the seeds into the wok, then add the pods as well.

2 Pour 500ml/17fl oz/scant 2¼ cups water into the wok and bring the mixture to the boil. Reduce the heat to low and simmer, stirring occasionally, while you prepare the pears.

3 Peel the pears, then add to the wok and gently turn in the syrup to coat evenly. Cover the wok and simmer gently for 12–15 minutes, turning the pears halfway through cooking, until they are just tender.

4 Lift the pears from the syrup using a slotted spoon and transfer to four serving bowls. Set aside.

5 Bring the syrup back to the boil and cook gently for about 10 minutes, or until thickened. Spoon the syrup over the pears and serve warm or chilled with single cream or ice cream.

> **Variations**
> Try using different flavourings in the syrup: add 10ml/2 tsp chopped fresh root ginger and 1–2 star anise, or 1 cinnamon stick and 3 cloves. The honey can be replaced with the same quantity of maple syrup.

Rich Spiced Carrot and Raisin Halwa

Halwa is a classic Indian sweet, and there are many variations on the basic recipe. In this version, which comes from the Udupi cuisine of south-west India, grated carrots are cooked in milk with ghee, sugar, spices and raisins until meltingly tender and sweet. You will only need a small bowl because it is very rich.

Serves 4
90g/3½oz ghee
300g/11oz carrots, coarsely grated
250ml/8fl oz/1 cup milk
150g/5oz/¾ cup golden caster (superfine) sugar
5–6 lightly crushed cardamom pods
1 clove
1 cinnamon stick
50g/2oz/scant ½ cup raisins

1 Place a wok or a large deep frying pan over a low heat and add half the ghee. When the ghee has melted, add the grated carrot and stir-fry for 6–8 minutes.

2 Pour the milk into the wok, stir into the carrots and raise the heat to bring the mixture to the boil. Once it is bubbling reduce the heat to low again and leave to simmer gently for 10–12 minutes.

3 Stir the remaining ghee into the carrot mixture, then stir in the caster sugar, crushed cardamom pods, clove, cinnamon stick and raisins.

4 Gently simmer the carrot mixture for 6–7 minutes, stirring occasionally, until it is thickened and glossy. Fish out the whole spices if you wish, and serve scoops of the halwa immediately in small serving bowls.

> **Cook's Tip**
> Ghee is clarified butter, widely used in Indian cooking. It is an essential ingredient in halwa and is available in cans from Asian stores and many supermarkets.

Pears in Mulled Wine

This classic, mellow dish is perfect for autumn days when the finest dessert pears are at their best and most abundant. Poaching in red wine gives the pears a beautiful deep ruby colour, and the spices contribute a lovely flavour to the finished syrup, with a hint of heat from the ginger and the aromatic peppercorns.

Serves 4
1 bottle full-bodied red wine
1 cinnamon stick
4 cloves
2.5ml/½ tsp grated nutmeg
2.5ml/½ tsp ground ginger
8 peppercorns
175g/6oz/¾ cup caster
  (superfine) sugar
thinly pared rind of ½ orange
thinly pared rind of ½ lemon
8 firm ripe pears

1 Pour the wine into a large, heavy pan into which all the pears will fit snugly together in a single layer when standing upright. Add the cinnamon stick, cloves, nutmeg, ginger, peppercorns, caster sugar and citrus rinds and stir into the wine to dissolve the sugar.

2 Peel the pears, leaving the stalks intact, and stand them in the pan. The wine should only just cover the pears.

3 Bring the liquid to the boil, lower the heat, cover and simmer very gently for 30 minutes or until the pears are tender. Using a slotted spoon, transfer the pears to a bowl.

4 Boil the poaching liquid until it has reduced by half and is syrupy. Strain the syrup over and around the pears and spoon it over them again as it cools and thickens.

Cook's Tips
- *Serve the pears with a mascarpone cream, made by combining equal quantities of mascarpone cheese and double (heavy) cream, adding a little vanilla extract for extra flavour if you like.*
- *The dish can be served warm or cold, but is probably at its best when just cool.*

Caribbean Bananas with Ground Allspice and Ginger

Tender baked bananas in a rich and spicy sauce make an irresistible dessert for those with a sweet tooth. The lime juice and ginger give it a sharp edge.

Serves 4
25g/1oz/2 tbsp butter
8 firm ripe bananas
juice of 1 lime
75g/3oz/scant ½ cup soft dark
  brown sugar
5ml/1 tsp ground allspice
2.5ml/½ tsp ground ginger
seeds from 6 cardamom pods,
  crushed
30ml/2 tbsp rum
pared lime rind, to decorate
crème fraîche, to serve

1 Preheat the oven to 200°C/400°F/Gas 6. Use a little of the butter to grease a shallow baking dish large enough to hold the bananas snugly in a single layer.

2 Peel the bananas and cut them in half lengthways. Arrange the bananas in the dish and pour over the lime juice.

3 Put the sugar in a bowl and mix in the allspice, ginger and crushed cardamom seeds. Sprinkle this mixture over the bananas. Dot with the remaining butter. Bake in the preheated oven, basting once, for about 15 minutes, or until the bananas are soft.

4 Remove the dish from the oven. Warm the rum in a small pan or metal soup ladle, then set it alight as you pour it over the bananas. As soon as the flames have died down, spoon the syrup from the bottom of the dish over the bananas. Decorate the dessert with the pared lime rind and serve each portion with a dollop of crème fraîche.

Variation
For a version that will appeal more to children and anyone who doesn't like alcohol, use orange juice instead of lime juice and omit the rum.

Fresh Figs Baked with Honey, Vanilla and Cinnamon

Baking fruit with honey is an ancient cooking method, devised perhaps when local fruit harvests were so abundant there was too much to eat fresh. This recipe from Greece is a dish most often made with apricots or figs. Spices and herbs, such as aniseed, cinnamon, rosemary and lavender, are often used for flavouring. If you choose ripe figs with a sweet, pink interior, and an aromatic honey, you can't go wrong.

Serves 3–4

12 ripe figs
30ml/2 tbsp vanilla sugar
 (see Cook's Tip)
3–4 cinnamon sticks
45–60ml/3–4 tbsp clear honey
225g/8oz/1 cup chilled thick
 natural (plain) yogurt or
 clotted cream

1 Preheat the oven to 200°C/400°F/Gas 6. Wash the figs and pat them dry. Using a sharp knife, cut a deep cross from the top of each fig to the base, keeping the skin at the bottom intact. Fan the quarters of each fig out, so that it looks like a flower, then place them upright in a baking dish, preferably an earthenware one.

2 Sprinkle the vanilla sugar over each fig flower, tuck in the cinnamon sticks and drizzle with honey. Bake the dish for 15–20 minutes, until the sugar is slightly caramelized but the honey and figs are still moist.

3 Eat the figs straight away. Spoon a dollop of yogurt or cream into the middle of each one and scoop them up with your fingers, or serve them in bowls and let everyone help themselves to the yogurt or cream.

> **Cook's Tip**
> To make the vanilla sugar for this recipe, split a vanilla pod (bean) lengthways in half, scrape out the seeds and mix them with 30ml/2 tbsp caster (superfine) sugar.

Clementines with Star Anise and Cinnamon

Although they are now available for several months of the year, clementines are still evocative of winter festivities, particularly when they are partnered with warm spicy fragrances. This fresh dessert, delicately flavoured with mulling spices, makes the perfect ending for a party meal.

Serves 6

350ml/12fl oz/1½ cups sweet
 dessert wine
75g/3oz/6 tbsp caster (superfine)
 sugar
6 star anise
1 cinnamon stick
1 vanilla pod (bean)
30ml/2 tbsp Cointreau
1 strip of thinly pared lime rind
12 clementines

1 Put the wine, sugar, star anise and cinnamon in a pan. Split the vanilla pod and add it to the pan with the strip of lime rind. Bring to the boil, lower the heat and simmer for about 10 minutes to form a syrup. Leave for 10 minutes to cool, then stir in the Cointreau.

2 Peel the clementines, removing all the pith and white membranes from the outside of the fruit. Cut some clementines in half and arrange them all in a glass dish. Pour over the spiced wine and chill overnight.

> **Cook's Tip**
> Leave the whole spices in the syrup as they will continue to add their flavour to the dish, and add greatly to its appearance, particularly the star anise, which have a festive look – try to use whole stars rather than broken pieces.

> **Variation**
> Tangerines or oranges can be used instead of clementines. If you use large fruits, slice them horizontally or split into segments instead of leaving them whole.

Clementines with Star Anise: Energy 149kcal/632kJ; Protein 0.9g; Carbohydrate 24.7g, of which sugars 24.7g; Fat 0.1g, of which saturates 0g; Cholesterol 0mg; Calcium 40mg; Fibre 1g; Sodium 12mg.
Fresh Figs Baked with Cinnamon: Energy 198kcal/845kJ; Protein 2.3g; Carbohydrate 48.2g, of which sugars 48.2g; Fat 1g, of which saturates 0g; Cholesterol 0mg; Calcium 155mg; Fibre 4.5g; Sodium 39mg.

Baklava

This famous Turkish confection is one of the greatest creations of the Ottoman pastry chefs. It is traditionally made with eight layers of pastry and seven layers of chopped walnuts, but fillings vary from a mixture of chopped nuts to a moist, creamy almond paste or a delicately flavoured pumpkin purée.

Serves 12
175g/6oz/³⁄₄ cup butter
100ml/3¹⁄₂fl oz/scant ¹⁄₂ cup
*   sunflower oil*
450g/1lb filo pastry
450g/1lb walnuts, or a mixture of
*   walnuts and almonds, chopped*
5ml/1 tsp ground cinnamon

For the syrup
450g/1lb sugar
30ml/2 tbsp rose water

1 Preheat the oven to 160°C/325°F/Gas 3. Melt the butter and oil in a small pan, then brush a little over the bottom and sides of a 30cm/12in round or square cake tin (pan).

2 Place a sheet of filo in the bottom of the tin and brush it with melted butter and oil. Continue until you have used half the filo sheets, brushing each one with butter and oil. Ease the sheets into the corners and trim the edges if they flop over the rim.

3 Spread the nuts over the last buttered sheet and sprinkle with the cinnamon, then continue as before with the remaining filo sheets. Brush the top one as well, then, using a sharp knife, cut diagonal parallel lines right through all the layers to the bottom to form small diamond shapes.

4 Bake for about 1 hour, until the top is golden. Meanwhile make the syrup. Put the sugar into a heavy pan, pour in 250ml/8fl oz/1 cup water and bring to the boil, stirring all the time. When the sugar has dissolved, lower the heat and stir in the rose water, then simmer for about 15 minutes, until the syrup thickens. Leave to cool in the pan.

5 When the baklava is ready, remove it from the oven and slowly pour the cooled syrup over the hot pastry. Return to the oven for 2–3 minutes to soak up the syrup, then take it out and leave to cool before lifting the pieces out of the tin.

Little Nutmeg Custard Tarts

These luxurious little tarts are a real treat to eat with afternoon tea or as a classic dessert at a supper party.

Serves 8
600ml/1 pint/2¹⁄₂ cups full-cream
*   (whole) milk*
6 egg yolks
75g/3oz/6 tbsp caster (superfine)
*   sugar*
a whole nutmeg

For the rich butter pastry
175g/6oz/1¹⁄₂ cups plain (all-
*   purpose) flour*
a good pinch of salt
75g/3oz/6 tbsp unsalted
*   (sweet) butter, at room*
*   temperature*
75g/3oz/6 tbsp caster (superfine)
*   sugar*
3 egg yolks, at room temperature
2.5ml/¹⁄₂ tsp vanilla extract

1 Make the pastry first. Sift the flour and salt on to a sheet of baking parchment. Put the butter, sugar, egg yolks and vanilla extract in a food processor and process until the mixture resembles scrambled eggs. Tip in the flour and combine. Transfer the dough to a floured surface and knead gently until smooth. Form into a ball, flatten and wrap in cling film (plastic wrap). Chill for at least 30 minutes.

2 Roll out the pastry thinly and use to line eight individual 10cm/4in loose-based tart pans. (You can use smaller, deeper pans, but remember they will need slightly longer cooking.) Place the pans on a baking sheet and chill for 30 minutes.

3 Preheat the oven to 200°C/400°F/Gas 6. To make the filling, heat the milk in a pan until just warmed but not boiling. Beat the egg yolks and sugar together in a bowl until pale and creamy. Pour the milk on to the yolks and stir well to mix. Do not whisk as this will produce too many bubbles. Strain the milk mixture into a jug (pitcher) and pour into the tart cases.

4 Liberally grate fresh nutmeg over the surface of the tartlets. Bake for about 10 minutes, then lower the heat to 180°C/350°F/Gas 4 and bake for another 10 minutes, or until the filling has set and is just turning golden. Don't overbake as the filling should be a bit wobbly when the tartlets come out of the oven. Remove from the pans to cool slightly but serve warm.

Baklava: Energy 973kcal/4059kJ; Protein 12.2g; Carbohydrate 89.9g, of which sugars 60.9g; Fat 65.2g, of which saturates 15.6g; Cholesterol 47mg; Calcium 139mg; Fibre 3.1g; Sodium 141mg.
Little Nutmeg Custard Tarts: Energy 336kcal/1409kJ; Protein 7.9g; Carbohydrate 40g, of which sugars 23.4g; Fat 17.1g, of which saturates 8.6g; Cholesterol 257mg; Calcium 157mg; Fibre 0.7g; Sodium 101mg.

Aromatic Stuffed Pastries

These aromatic sweet pastry crescents from Greece are packed with candied citrus peel and walnuts, which have been soaked in a coffee syrup.

milk, to glaze
caster (superfine) sugar, for sprinkling

Makes 16
60ml/4 tbsp clear honey
60ml/4 tbsp strong brewed coffee
75g/3oz/1/2 cup mixed candied citrus peel, finely chopped
175g/6oz/11/2 cups walnuts, chopped
1.5ml/1/4 tsp freshly grated nutmeg

For the pastry
450g/1lb/4 cups plain (all-purpose) flour
2.5ml/1/2 tsp ground cinnamon
2.5ml/1/2 tsp baking powder
pinch of salt
150g/5oz/10 tbsp butter
30ml/2 tbsp caster (superfine) sugar
1 egg
120ml/4fl oz/1/2 cup milk, chilled

1 Preheat the oven to 180°C/350°F/Gas 4. To make the pastry, sift the flour, cinnamon, baking powder and salt into a bowl. Rub or cut in the butter until the mixture resembles breadcrumbs. Stir in the sugar and make a well in the mixture.

2 Beat the egg and milk together and pour into the well in the dry ingredients. Mix to a soft dough. Divide the dough into two and chill for 30 minutes. Meanwhile, mix the honey and coffee in a mixing bowl. Add the candied peel, walnuts and nutmeg. Stir well, cover and leave for 20 minutes.

3 Roll out one portion of the dough on a lightly floured surface to a thickness of 3mm/1/8in. Stamp out rounds, using a 10cm/4in plain pastry cutter. Place a heaped teaspoonful of filling on one side of each round. Brush the edges with a little milk, then fold over and press together to seal. Repeat with the second piece of pastry until all the filling has been used.

4 Place the pastries on lightly greased baking sheets, brush lightly with a little milk, and then sprinkle with a little caster sugar. Make a steam hole in the centre of each. Bake for 35 minutes, until golden. Cool on a wire rack before serving.

Moroccan Cinnamon Swirl

This pastry, whose Arabic name means "the snake", is the most famous, traditional sweet dish in Morocco. The coiled pastry looks impressive and tastes divine when freshly made.

Serves 8–10
115g/4oz/1 cup blanched almonds
300g/11oz/23/4 cups ground almonds
50g/2oz/1/2 cup icing (confectioners') sugar
115g/4oz/2/3 cup caster (superfine) sugar
115g/4oz/1/2 cup butter, softened, plus 20g/3/4oz for cooking nuts
5–10ml/1–2 tsp ground cinnamon
15ml/1 tbsp orange flower water
3–4 sheets filo pastry
1 egg yolk
icing (confectioners') sugar and ground cinnamon, to dust

1 Fry the blanched almonds in a little butter until golden brown, then pound them using a pestle and mortar. Place the nuts in a bowl and add the ground almonds, icing sugar, caster sugar, butter, cinnamon and orange flower water. Form the mixture into a smooth paste. Cover and chill.

2 Preheat the oven to 180°C/350°F/Gas 4. Open out the sheets of filo pastry, keeping them in a pile so they do not dry out, and brush the top one with a little melted butter. Take lumps of the almond paste and roll them into fingers. Place them end to end along the long edge of the top sheet of filo, then roll the filo up into a roll the thickness of your thumb, tucking in the ends to stop the filling oozing out. Repeat with the other sheets of filo, until all the filling is used up.

3 Grease a large baking sheet. Lift one of the filo rolls in both hands and gently push it together from both ends, like an accordion, to relax the pastry before coiling it in the centre of the pan or baking sheet. Do the same with the other rolls, placing them end to end to form a tight coil like a snake.

4 Mix the egg yolk with a little water and brush the pastry, then bake for 30–35 minutes, until crisp. Top the freshly cooked pastry with a liberal sprinkling of icing sugar, and add lines of cinnamon. Serve at room temperature.

Moroccan Cinnamon Swirl: Energy 261kcal/1091kJ; Protein 3.8g; Carbohydrate 25.9g, of which sugars 17.9g; Fat 16.6g, of which saturates 6.7g; Cholesterol 45mg; Calcium 55mg; Fibre 1.2g; Sodium 74mg.
Aromatic Stuffed Pastries: Energy 278kcal/1162kJ; Protein 5g; Carbohydrate 30.2g, of which sugars 8.7g; Fat 16.1g, of which saturates 5.7g; Cholesterol 32mg; Calcium 69mg; Fibre 1.5g; Sodium 80mg.

Spicy Pumpkin and Orange Bombe

Pumpkin has a subtle flavour that is truly transformed with the addition of citrus fruits and spices.

Serves 8

For the sponge
115g/4oz/½ cup unsalted butter
115g/4oz/½ cup caster (superfine) sugar
115g/4oz/1 cup self-raising (self-rising) flour
2.5ml/½ tsp baking powder
2 eggs

For the ice cream
Juice and pared rind of 1 orange
300g/11oz/scant 1½ cups golden granulated sugar
300ml/½ pint/1¼ cups water
2 cinnamon sticks, halved
10ml/2 tsp whole cloves
30ml/2 tbsp orange flower water
400g/14oz can unsweetened pumpkin purée
300ml/½ pint/1¼ cups extra thick double cream
2 pieces stem ginger, grated
icing (confectioners') sugar, to dust

1 Preheat the oven to 180°C/350°F/Gas 4. Grease and line a 450g/1lb loaf tin (pan). Beat the butter, caster sugar, flour, baking powder and eggs until creamy. Turn into the tin, level the surface and bake for 30 minutes, until firm in the centre. Leave to cool.

2 Make the ice cream. Cut the pared orange rind into very fine shreds. Heat the sugar and water in a heavy pan until the sugar dissolves, then boil rapidly for 3 minutes. Stir in the orange shreds, juice, cinnamon and cloves and heat gently for 5 minutes. Strain, reserving the rind and spices. Measure 300ml/½ pint/1½ cups of the syrup and reserve. Return the spices to the remaining syrup with the orange flower water.

3 Beat the pumpkin purée with 175ml/6fl oz/¾ cup of the measured syrup, the cream and ginger. Pour the mixture into a shallow container and freeze until firm.

4 Line a 1.5 litre/2½ pint/6¼ cup basin with clear film (plastic wrap). Cut the cake into 1cm/½in slices. Dip them briefly in the remaining strained syrup and use to line the basin, trimming the pieces to fit. Chill, then fill with the ice cream, level the surface and freeze until firm, preferably overnight. To serve, invert the ice cream on to a serving plate and peel away the film. Dust with icing sugar and serve in wedges with the spiced syrup.

Saffron and Cardamom Crème Caramel with Butter Cookies

This Moroccan version of a simple but much-loved dessert adds the subtle colour and flavour of saffron and the fragrance of delicate cardamom. Crisp orange-flower-scented cookies are a lovely accompaniment.

Serves 4–6
600ml/1 pint/2½ cups milk
115g/4oz/⅔ cup sugar, plus 60ml/4 tbsp for caramel
pinch of saffron threads
2.5ml/½ tsp cardamom seeds
15–30ml/1–2 tbsp rose water
4 eggs, lightly beaten
60ml/4 tbsp boiling water

For the cookies
200g/7oz/scant 1 cup butter
130g/4½oz/generous 1 cup icing (confectioners') sugar, sifted
5–10ml/1–2 tsp orange flower water
250g/9oz/2¼ cups plain (all-purpose) flour, sifted
handful of blanched almonds

1 Preheat the oven to 180°C/350°F/Gas 4. Heat the milk, sugar, saffron and cardamom in a pan until the milk is just about to boil. Set aside to cool. Add the rose water, then gradually pour the mixture into the eggs, beating all the time. Set aside.

2 To make the caramel, heat the 60ml/4 tbsp sugar in a small heavy pan until melted and dark brown. Stir in the boiling water and let it bubble before tipping it into individual dishes. Swirl the dishes to coat evenly. Leave to cool. Pour the custard into the dishes and stand them in a roasting pan. Add water to two-thirds of the way up the dishes. Bake for about 1 hour, until set. Cool, then chill for several hours or overnight.

3 To make the cookies, melt the butter in a pan and leave to cool. Stir in the icing sugar and orange flower water, then gradually beat in the flour to form a smooth, stiff dough. Chill.

4 Preheat the oven to 180°C/350°F/Gas 4. Grease a baking sheet. Break off walnut-size pieces of dough and roll into balls. Place on the baking sheet and flatten slightly. Press a nut into the centre of each. Bake for 20 minutes, or until golden. Invert the crème caramel on to plates. Serve with the butter cookies.

Pumpkin and Orange Bombe: Energy 571kcal/2387kJ; Protein 4.2g; Carbohydrate 67g, of which sugars 56.1g; Fat 33.6g, of which saturates 20.5g; Cholesterol 130mg; Calcium 122mg; Fibre 1g; Sodium 168mg.
Saffron Crème Caramel: Energy 969kcal/4065kJ; Protein 17.8g; Carbohydrate 120g, of which sugars 72.3g; Fat 50g, of which saturates 29.3g; Cholesterol 306mg; Calcium 338mg; Fibre 1.9g; Sodium 443mg.

Cinnamon and Coffee Parfait

This French-style ice cream is flecked with cinnamon and mixed with a hint of coffee. As it is made with a boiling sugar syrup it doesn't require beating during freezing, so can be poured straight into freezerproof serving dishes.

Serves 6

15ml/1 tbsp instant coffee granules
30ml/2 tbsp boiling water
7.5ml/1½ tsp ground cinnamon
4 egg yolks
115g/4oz/generous ½ cup sugar
120ml/4fl oz/½ cup cold water
300ml/½ pint/1¼ cups double (heavy) cream, lightly whipped
200g/7oz/scant 1 cup crème fraîche
extra ground cinnamon, to decorate

1 Spoon the coffee into a heatproof bowl, stir in the boiling water until dissolved, then stir in the cinnamon. Put the egg yolks in a large heatproof bowl and whisk them lightly until frothy. Bring a medium pan of water to the boil and lower the heat so that it simmers gently.

2 Put the sugar in a small pan, add the cold water and heat gently, stirring occasionally, until the sugar has dissolved.

3 Increase the heat and boil for 4–5 minutes without stirring until the syrup registers 115°C/239°F on a sugar thermometer. Alternatively, test by dropping a little of the syrup into a cup of cold water, then pour off the water. If the syrup can be moulded to a soft ball, it is ready.

4 Put the bowl of egg yolks over the pan of simmering water and whisk in the sugar syrup. Keep whisking until the mixture is very thick and then remove from the heat. Continue whisking until it is cool.

5 Whisk the coffee and cinnamon into the egg yolk mixture, then fold in the cream. Pour into a tub or individual freezerproof glass dishes. Freeze for 4 hours or until firm. If you froze the ice cream in a tub, scoop into bowls to serve and decorate with a dusting of cinnamon.

Lemon and Cardamom Ice Cream

The classic partnership of lemon and cardamom gives this rich ice cream a lovely clean tang. It is the perfect choice for serving after a spicy main course.

Serves 6

15ml/1 tbsp cardamom pods
4 egg yolks
115g/4oz/generous ½ cup caster (superfine) sugar
10ml/2 tsp cornflour (cornstarch)
grated rind and juice of 3 lemons
300ml/½ pint/1¼ cups milk
300ml/½ pint/1¼ cups whipping cream
fresh lemon balm sprigs and icing (confectioners') sugar, to decorate

1 Put the cardamom pods in a mortar and crush to release the seeds. Pick out and discard the shells, then grind the seeds.

2 Put the egg yolks, sugar, cornflour, lemon rind and juice in a bowl. Add the cardamom seeds and whisk well. Bring the milk to the boil in a pan, then pour over the egg yolk mixture, stirring well. Return the mixture to the pan and cook over a very low heat, stirring constantly until thickened.

3 Pour the custard into a bowl, cover the surface with baking parchment and leave to cool, then chill.

4 When the custard is very cold and firm, whip the cream lightly and fold it in. Pour into a container and freeze for 3–4 hours, beating twice to break up the ice crystals. If you are using an ice cream maker, whisk the cream lightly into the custard and churn the mixture until it holds its shape.

5 Scoop into glasses and decorate with the lemon balm and icing sugar.

> **Cook's Tips**
> • Transfer the ice cream from the freezer to the refrigerator about 30 minutes before serving so that it softens slightly.
> • Buy cardamom whole, in the pod, and grind the seeds as you require them. Once ground, they quickly lose their flavour.

Cinnamon and Coffee Parfait: Energy 490kcal/2030kJ; Protein 3.6g; Carbohydrate 21.7g, of which sugars 21.6g; Fat 43.9g, of which saturates 26.8g; Cholesterol 241mg; Calcium 70mg; Fibre 0g; Sodium 26mg.
Lemon Ice Cream: Energy 338kcal/1406kJ; Protein 4.9g; Carbohydrate 25.3g, of which sugars 23.7g; Fat 24.9g, of which saturates 14.3g; Cholesterol 197mg; Calcium 116mg; Fibre 0g; Sodium 42mg.

Chilli Sorbet

Served to refresh the palate between courses, or at the end of a meal, this unusual sorbet is sure to become a talking point. It has all the zing and refreshing citrus flavour of a conventional lemon sorbet, but after the first taste the surprising kick of chilli will delight your guests.

Serves 6
1 fresh red chilli
finely grated rind and juice of 2 lemons
finely grated rind and juice of 2 limes
225g/8oz/1 cup caster (superfine) sugar
750ml/1¼ pints/3 cups water
pared lemon or lime rind, to decorate

1 Cut the chilli in half, removing all the seeds and any pith with a small sharp knife, and then chop the flesh very finely.

2 Put the chilli, lemon and lime rind, sugar and water in a heavy pan. Heat gently and stir while the sugar dissolves. Bring to the boil, then simmer for 2 minutes without stirring. Let cool.

3 Add lemon and lime juice to the chilli syrup and chill until very cold.

4 If you are making the sorbet by hand, pour the mixture into a container and freeze for 3–4 hours, beating twice as it thickens. Return to the freezer until ready to serve.

5 If you are using an ice cream maker, churn the mixture until it holds its shape. Scrape into a container and freeze until ready to serve. Spoon into glasses and decorate with the thinly pared lemon or lime rind.

Cook's Tips
• Use a medium-hot chilli rather than any of the really fiery varieties.
• For an added kick, drizzle the sorbet with tequila or vodka before serving.

Mulled Wine Sorbet

This dramatic-looking sorbet has a festive flavour, but is also very refreshing and provides a brief and welcome respite from the general overindulgence that takes place during the party season. It is spicy and flavoursome, with quite a powerful kick to revive you.

Serves 6
1 bottle medium red wine
2 clementines or 1 large orange
16 whole cloves
2 cinnamon sticks, halved
1 eating apple, roughly chopped
5ml/1 tsp ground mixed spice
75g/3oz/scant ½ cup light muscovado (brown) sugar
150ml/¼ pint/⅔ cup water
200ml/7fl oz/scant 1 cup freshly squeezed orange juice
45ml/3 tbsp brandy
strips of pared orange rind, to decorate

1 Pour the wine into a pan. Stud the clementines or orange with the cloves, then cut them in half. Add to the wine, with the cinnamon sticks, apple, mixed spice, sugar and water. Heat gently, stirring occasionally, until the sugar has dissolved.

2 Cover the pan and cook the mixture gently for 15 minutes. Remove from the heat and leave to cool.

3 Strain the mixture into a large bowl, then stir in the orange juice and brandy. Chill until very cold.

4 If you are making the sorbet by hand, pour the mixture into a container and freeze for 3–4 hours, beating twice as it thickens. Return to the freezer until ready to serve.

5 If you are using an ice cream maker, churn the mixture until it holds its shape. Scrape into a container and freeze until ready to serve. To serve, spoon or scoop into small glasses and decorate with the strips of pared orange rind.

Variation
Replace the brandy with lemon juice for a fresher flavour.

Chilli Sorbet: Energy 150kcal/640kJ; Protein 0.5g; Carbohydrate 39.4g, of which sugars 39.4g; Fat 0.1g, of which saturates 0g; Cholesterol 0mg; Calcium 23mg; Fibre 0g; Sodium 3mg.
Mulled Wine Sorbet: Energy 163kcal/684kJ; Protein 0.4g; Carbohydrate 16.3g, of which sugars 16.3g; Fat 0g, of which saturates 0g; Cholesterol 0mg; Calcium 19mg; Fibre 0g; Sodium 1.3mg.

Watermelon and Spiced Orange Granitas

These refreshing granitas make a glorious dessert for a summer meal.

Serves 6–8
1 pineapple, peeled and sliced
1 mango, peeled and sliced
2 bananas, peeled and halved
45–60ml/3–4 tbsp icing (confectioners') sugar

For the watermelon granita
1kg/2¼lb watermelon, deseeded
250g/9oz/1¼ cups caster (superfine) sugar
150ml/¼ pint/⅔ cup water
juice of ½ lemon
15ml/1 tbsp orange flower water
2.5ml/½ tsp ground cinnamon

For the orange granita
900ml/1½ pints/3¾ cups water
350g/12oz/1¾ cups sugar
5–6 cloves
5ml/1 tsp ground ginger
2.5ml/½ tsp ground cinnamon
600ml/1 pint/2½ cups fresh orange juice
15ml/1 tbsp orange flower water

1 To make the watermelon granita, purée the watermelon flesh in a blender. Put the sugar and water in a pan and stir until dissolved. Bring to the boil, simmer for 5 minutes, then cool.

2 Stir in the lemon juice, orange flower water and cinnamon, then beat in the watermelon purée. Pour the mixture into a bowl; place in the freezer. Stir every 15 minutes for 2 hours then at intervals for 1 hour, so the mixture freezes but is slushy.

3 To make the spiced orange granita, heat the water and sugar together in a pan with the cloves, stirring until the sugar has dissolved, then boil for about 5 minutes. Leave to cool and stir in the ginger, cinnamon, orange juice and orange flower water. Remove the cloves, then pour the mixture into a bowl, cover and place in the freezer. Freeze as for the watermelon granita.

4 Preheat the grill (broiler) on the hottest setting. Arrange the pineapple, mango and banana on a baking sheet. Sprinkle with icing sugar and grill for 3–4 minutes until slightly softened and lightly browned. Arrange the fruit on a serving platter and scoop the granitas into dishes. Serve immediately.

Lekach

This classic Jewish honey cake is richly spiced, redolent of ginger, cinnamon and other sweet, aromatic scents. It is a favourite at Rosh Hashanah, when sweet foods, particularly honey, are eaten in the hope of a sweet New Year.

Serves 8
175g/6oz/1½ cups plain (all-purpose) flour
75g/3oz/⅓ cup caster (superfine) sugar
2.5ml/½ tsp ground ginger
2.5–5ml/½–1 tsp ground cinnamon
5ml/1 tsp mixed spice (apple pie spice)
5ml/1 tsp bicarbonate of soda (baking soda)
225g/8oz/1 cup clear honey
60ml/4 tbsp vegetable or light olive oil
grated rind of 1 orange
2 eggs
75ml/5 tbsp orange juice
10ml/2 tsp chopped fresh root ginger, or to taste

1 Preheat the oven to 180°C/350°F/Gas 4. Line a rectangular baking tin (pan), measuring 25 × 20 × 5cm/10 × 8 × 2in, with baking parchment. In a large bowl, mix together the flour, sugar, ginger, cinnamon, mixed spice and bicarbonate of soda.

2 Make a well in the centre of the dry ingredients and pour in the clear honey, vegetable or olive oil, orange rind and eggs. Using a wooden spoon or electric whisk, beat until smooth, then add the orange juice. Stir in the chopped ginger.

3 Pour the cake mixture into the prepared tin and bake for about 50 minutes, or until firm to the touch. Leave the cake to cool in the tin, then turn out and wrap in foil. Store at room temperature for 2–3 days before eating so the flavours mature.

> **Cook's Tip**
> This honey cake keeps very well. It can be made in two loaf tins (pans), so that one cake can be eaten, while the other is wrapped in clear film (plastic wrap) and stored or frozen for a later date.

Granitas: Energy 605kcal/2585kJ; Protein 2.9g; Carbohydrate 156.1g, of which sugars 155.5g; Fat 1g, of which saturates 0.2g; Cholesterol 0mg; Calcium 107mg; Fibre 2.8g; Sodium 23mg.
Lekach: Energy 264kcal/1115kJ; Protein 3.8g; Carbohydrate 49.1g, of which sugars 32.4g; Fat 7.2g, of which saturates 1.1g; Cholesterol 48mg; Calcium 45mg; Fibre 0.7g; Sodium 23mg.

Ginger Cake

Three forms of ginger make this the ultimate indulgence for all lovers of this versatile and warming spice.

Makes 12 squares

225g/8oz/2 cups self-raising (self-rising) flour
15ml/1 tbsp ground ginger
5ml/1 tsp ground cinnamon
2.5ml/½ tsp bicarbonate of soda (baking soda)
115g/4oz/½ cup butter
115g/4oz/½ cup soft light brown sugar
2 eggs
25ml/1½ tbsp golden syrup (corn syrup)
25ml/1½ tbsp milk

For the topping

6 pieces stem ginger, plus 20ml/4 tsp syrup, from the jar
115g/4oz/1 cup icing (confectioners') sugar
lemon juice

1 Preheat the oven to 160°C/325°F/Gas 3. Grease a shallow 18cm/7in square cake tin (pan) and line the base and sides with baking parchment.

2 Sift the flour, ginger, cinnamon and bicarbonate of soda into a bowl. Rub in the butter, then stir in the sugar. Make a well in the centre. In a bowl, whisk together the eggs, syrup and milk. Pour into the dry ingredients and beat until smooth and glossy.

3 Spoon into the prepared tin and bake for 45–50 minutes until well risen and firm to the touch. Leave in the tin for 30 minutes, then remove to a wire rack to cool completely. Cut each piece of stem ginger into quarters and arrange the pieces on top of the cake.

4 Sift the icing sugar into a bowl and stir in the ginger syrup and enough lemon juice to make a smooth icing. Put the icing into a baking parchment icing bag and drizzle over the top of the cake. Leave to set, then cut the cake into squares.

Cook's Tip
This cake benefits from being kept in an airtight tin for a day before eating.

Semolina and Cinnamon Cake

This Greek cake is a universal family treat, loved by everyone, and every Greek housewife would be able to recite the recipe for it. It takes very little time to make – about 20 minutes – and makes a perfect accompaniment to coffee. Extra virgin olive oil is traditionally used, but a lighter oil gives a less obvious flavour.

Serves 6–8

500g/1¼lb/2½ cups caster (superfine) sugar
1 litre/1¾ pints/4 cups cold water
1 cinnamon stick
250ml/8fl oz/1 cup olive oil
350g/12oz/2 cups coarse semolina
50g/2oz/½ cup blanched almonds
30ml/2 tbsp pine nuts
5ml/1 tsp ground cinnamon

1 Put the sugar in a heavy pan, pour in the water and add the cinnamon stick. Bring to the boil, stirring until the sugar has dissolved, then boil without stirring for about 4 minutes.

2 Meanwhile, heat the oil in a separate, heavy pan. When it is almost smoking, add the semolina gradually and stir until it turns light brown. Lower the heat, add the almonds and pine nuts and brown together for 2–3 minutes, stirring. Take the semolina mixture off the heat and set aside. Remove the cinnamon stick from the hot syrup using a slotted spoon and discard it.

3 Protecting your hand with an oven glove or dish towel, carefully add the hot syrup to the semolina mixture, stirring all the time. The mixture will hiss and spit at this point, so stir it at arm's length.

4 Return the pan to a gentle heat and stir until all the syrup has been absorbed by the semolina and the mixture looks smooth. Remove the pan from the heat, cover it with a clean dish towel and leave it to stand for 10 minutes so that any remaining moisture is absorbed.

5 Turn the mixture into a 20–23cm/8–9in round cake tin (pan), preferably fluted, and set it aside. When it is cold, unmould it on to a platter and dust it all over with the ground cinnamon.

Ginger Cake: Energy 235kcal/989kJ; Protein 3.3g; Carbohydrate 37g, of which sugars 22.1g; Fat 9.3g, of which saturates 5.3g; Cholesterol 52mg; Calcium 49mg; Fibre 0.6g; Sodium 79mg.
Semolina and Cinnamon Cake: Energy 660kcal/2776kJ; Protein 6.8g; Carbohydrate 99.8g, of which sugars 65.7g; Fat 28.7g, of which saturates 3.6g; Cholesterol 0mg; Calcium 56mg; Fibre 1.5g; Sodium 10mg.

Date and Walnut Spice Cake

This deliciously moist and richly spiced cake is topped with a sticky honey and orange glaze. Serve it as a dessert with a generous spoonful of crème fraîche.

Serves 8

115g/4oz/1/2 cup unsalted butter, plus extra for greasing
175g/6oz/3/4 cup soft dark brown sugar
2 eggs
175g/6oz/1 1/2 cups unbleached self-raising (self-rising) flour
5ml/1 tsp bicarbonate of soda (baking soda)
2.5ml/1/2 tsp grated nutmeg
5ml/1 tsp mixed (apple pie) spice
pinch of salt
175ml/6fl oz/3/4 cup buttermilk
50g/2oz/1/3 cup ready-to-eat stoned dates, chopped
25g/1oz/1/4 cup walnuts, chopped

For the topping
60ml/4 tbsp clear honey
45ml/3 tbsp fresh orange juice
15ml/1 tbsp grated orange rind, plus extra to decorate

1 Grease and lightly flour a 23cm/9in spring-form cake tin (pan). Preheat the oven to 180°C/350°F/Gas 4. Cream together the butter and sugar until fluffy and creamy. Add the eggs, one at a time, and beat well to combine. Sift together the flour, bicarbonate of soda, spices and salt. Gradually add this to the creamed mixture, alternating with the buttermilk. Stir in the dates and walnuts.

2 Spoon the mixture into the prepared tin and level the top. Bake for 50 minutes or until a skewer inserted into the centre of the cake comes out clean. Leave to cool for 5 minutes, then turn out on to a wire rack to cool completely.

3 To make the topping, heat the honey, orange juice and rind in a small pan. Boil rapidly for 3 minutes, without stirring, until syrupy. Make holes in the cake with a skewer, and pour over the syrup. Decorate with orange rind.

> **Cook's Tip**
> To make your own buttermilk substitute, mix 15ml/1 tbsp lemon juice with 250ml/8fl oz/1 cup semi-skimmed milk.

Spicy Overnight Cake

Many old recipes for cakes contained lists of ingredients with weights and proportions that were easy to remember – ideal for passing down from generation to generation. This one has no added sugar; all its sweetness comes from the dried fruit it contains. It is at its most delicious if eaten when just cooled, on the day it is baked. Its crust is crisp and flaky while the inside is soft and moist.

Makes a thin 23cm/9in round cake

225g/8oz/2 cups plain (all-purpose) flour
5ml/1 tsp ground cinnamon
5ml/1 tsp ground ginger
115g/4oz/1/2 cup butter, cut into cubes
115g/4oz/2/3 cup mixed dried fruit
2.5ml/1/2 tsp bicarbonate of soda (baking soda)
15ml/1 tbsp vinegar
300ml/1/2 pint/1 1/4 cups full-cream (whole) milk

1 Sift the flour and spices. Add the butter and rub in until the mixture resembles fine breadcrumbs. Stir in the dried fruit and enough milk to make a soft mix.

2 Mix the bicarbonate of soda with the vinegar and, as the combination begins to froth, quickly stir it into the cake mixture. Cover the bowl and leave at room temperature for about 8 hours, or overnight.

3 Preheat the oven to 180°C/360°F/Gas 4. Grease a shallow 23cm/9 in round cake tin (pan) and line its base with baking parchment.

4 Spoon the cake mixture into the prepared tin and level the top. Put into the hot oven and cook for about 1 hour or until the cake is firm to the touch and cooked through – a skewer inserted in the centre should come out free of sticky mixture. If the top starts to get too brown during cooking, cover it with baking parchment.

5 Leave the cake in the tin to cool for 15–20 minutes, then turn out and cool completely on a wire rack.

Date Spice Cake: Energy 2666kcal/11243kJ; Protein 61.2g; Carbohydrate 429.6g, of which sugars 243.9g; Fat 90.2g, of which saturates 12.3g; Cholesterol 18mg; Calcium 650mg; Fibre 34.0g; Sodium 163mg.
Spicy Overnight Cake: Energy 2069kcal/8681kJ; Protein 34.7g; Carbohydrate 267.9g, of which sugars 96.5g; Fat 103g, of which saturates 63.6g; Cholesterol 263mg; Calcium 780mg; Fibre 9.5g; Sodium 888mg.

Spiced Walnut Cake

This luscious cake is the finest Greek dessert of all. Its soft texture, with the sweetness of the walnuts, makes it irresistible. The cake tastes even better the day after it is made.

Serves 10–12
150g/5oz/²⁄₃ cup butter
115g/4oz/¹⁄₂ cup caster
  (superfine) sugar
4 eggs, separated
60ml/4 tbsp brandy

2.5ml/¹⁄₂ tsp ground cinnamon
300g/11oz/2³⁄₄ cups shelled
  walnuts, coarsely chopped
150g/5oz/1¹⁄₄ cups self-raising
  (self-rising) flour
5ml/1 tsp baking powder
salt

For the syrup
250g/9oz/generous 1 cup caster
  (superfine) sugar
30ml/2 tbsp brandy
2–3 strips of pared orange rind
2 cinnamon sticks

1 Preheat the oven to 190°C/375°F/Gas 5. Grease a 35 × 23cm/14 × 9in baking dish that is at least 5cm/2in deep. Cream the butter in a large mixing bowl until soft, then add the sugar and beat well until the mixture is light and fluffy.

2 Add the egg yolks one by one, beating after each addition. Stir in the brandy and cinnamon. Mix the chopped walnuts in to the mixture. Sift the flour with the baking powder and set aside.

3 Whisk the egg whites with a pinch of salt until they are stiff. Fold them into the creamed mixture, alternating with tablespoons of flour until both have all been incorporated. Spread the mixture evenly in the prepared pan or dish. It should be about 4cm/1¹⁄₂in deep. Bake for about 40 minutes, until the top is golden and a skewer inserted in the cake comes out clean. Take the cake out of the oven and let it rest in the pan or dish while you make the syrup.

4 Mix the sugar and 300ml/¹⁄₂ pint/1¹⁄₄ cups water in a small pan. Heat gently, stirring, until the sugar dissolves. Bring to the boil, lower the heat, add the brandy, orange rind and cinnamon sticks. Simmer for 10 minutes. Slice the cake into diamond shapes and strain the syrup slowly over it. Let it stand for 10–20 minutes until the syrup is absorbed.

Spicy Apple Cake

Hundreds of German cakes and desserts include apples. This moist and spicy *apfelkuchen* is perfect with a cup of coffee or tea.

Serves 12
115g/4oz/1 cup plain (all-
  purpose) flour
115g/4oz/1 cup wholemeal
  (whole-wheat) flour
10ml/2 tsp baking powder
5ml/1 tsp cinnamon
2.5ml/¹⁄₂ tsp mixed spice (apple
  pie spice)
225g/8oz cooking apple, cored,
  peeled and chopped

75g/3oz/6 tbsp butter
175g/6oz/generous ³⁄₄ cup soft
  light brown sugar
finely grated rind of 1 small
  orange
2 eggs, beaten
30ml/2 tbsp milk
whipped cream dusted with
  cinnamon, to serve

For the topping
4 eating apples, cored and thinly
  sliced
juice of ¹⁄₂ orange
10ml/2 tsp caster (superfine) sugar
45ml/3 tbsp apricot jam, warmed
  and sieved (strained)

1 Preheat the oven to 180°C/350°F/Gas 4. Grease and line a 23cm/9in round loose-bottomed cake tin (pan). Sift the flours, baking powder and spices together into a bowl. Toss the chopped cooking apple in 30ml/2 tbsp of the flour mixture.

2 Cream the butter, brown sugar and orange rind together until light and fluffy. Gradually beat in the eggs, then fold in the flour mixture, the chopped apple and the milk. Spoon the mixture into the cake tin and level the surface.

3 For the topping, toss the apple slices in the orange juice and set them in overlapping circles on top of the cake mixture, pressing down lightly.

4 Sprinkle the caster sugar over the top of the cake and bake for 1–1¹⁄₄ hours, or until risen and firm. Cover with foil if the apples start to brown too much.

5 Cool in the tin for 10 minutes, then remove to a wire rack. Glaze the apples with the sieved jam. Cut into wedges and serve with whipped cream, sprinkled with cinnamon.

Spicy Apple Cake: Energy 587kcal/2471kJ; Protein 5.5g; Carbohydrate 92g, of which sugars 69.7g; Fat 24.5g, of which saturates 10.6g; Cholesterol 40mg; Calcium 95mg; Fibre 2.5g; Sodium 129mg.
Spiced Walnut Cake: Energy 563kcal/2349kJ; Protein 8.5g; Carbohydrate 50.6g, of which sugars 39.2g; Fat 35.3g, of which saturates 10.1g; Cholesterol 108mg; Calcium 114mg; Fibre 1.5g; Sodium 177mg.

Swedish Spice Bread

Cardamom and caraway seeds are widely used in Scandinavian cooking. Serve this interesting bread sliced with butter.

Makes a 23cm/9in round loaf

25g/1oz/2 tbsp butter
45ml/3 tbsp clear honey
275g/8oz/2 cups strong white bread flour
225g/8oz/2 cups rye flour
2.5ml/½ tsp salt
7g/¼oz sachet easy-blend (rapid-rise) dried yeast
5ml/1 tsp ground cardamom
5ml/1 tsp ground caraway seeds
2.5ml/½ tsp ground star anise
30ml/2 tbsp caster (superfine) sugar
grated rind and juice of 1 orange
175ml/6fl oz/¾ cup lager
1 egg, beaten

For the glaze
4 tbsp boiling water
1 tbsp clear honey

1 Melt the butter with the honey in a small pan, then leave to cool. Sift the flours and salt into a bowl and stir in the yeast, cardamom, caraway, star anise, caster sugar and orange rind.

2 Mix the lager with the boiling water. Stir the orange juice and beaten egg into the melted butter and honey, then stir this mixture into the flour. Add enough of the warm lager and water to make a soft and slightly sticky, but manageable dough. Place the dough on a lightly floured surface and knead for 5 minutes until smooth and elastic. Place in an oiled bowl, cover and leave to rise until doubled in bulk. Knead briefly, then divide the dough in two. Roll out each piece into a long snake.

3 Grease a 23cm/9in round cake tin (pan). Starting at the edge of the tin, coil the dough round and round to the centre, joining the second piece to the first with a little water. Cover with oiled clear film (plastic wrap) and leave until doubled in size. Preheat the oven to 190°C/375°F/Gas 5. Bake the bread for 10 minutes, then turn the oven down to 160°C/325°F/Gas 3 and bake for 40–50 minutes more, until the bread is lightly browned and sounds hollow when rapped underneath.

4 To make the glaze, mix the honey with 15ml/1 tbsp hot water, then brush it over the loaf. Leave on a wire rack to cool.

Orange and Coriander Brioches

The warm spicy flavour of coriander seeds combines really well with orange.

Makes 12

225g/8oz/2 cups strong white bread flour
10ml/2 tsp easy-blend (rapid rise) dried yeast
2.5ml/½ tsp salt
15ml/1 tbsp caster (superfine) sugar
10ml/2 tsp coriander seeds, coarsely ground
grated rind of 1 orange
2 eggs, beaten
50g/2oz/¼ cup butter, melted
1 small egg, beaten, to glaze

1 Grease 12 individual brioche tins (pans). Sift the flour into a bowl and stir in the yeast, salt, sugar, coriander seeds and orange rind. Make a well in the centre, pour in 30ml/2 tbsp hand-hot water, the eggs and the melted butter and beat to make a soft dough. Turn on to a lightly floured surface and knead for 5 minutes until smooth and elastic. Return to the clean, lightly oiled bowl, cover with clear film (plastic wrap) and leave in a warm place for 1 hour until doubled in bulk.

2 Turn on to a floured surface, knead again briefly and roll into a sausage. Cut into 12 pieces. Break off a quarter of each piece and set aside. Shape the larger pieces of dough into balls and place in the prepared tins.

3 With a floured wooden spoon, press a hole in each dough ball. Shape each small piece of dough into a little plug and press into the holes. Place the brioche tins on a baking sheet. Cover with lightly oiled clear film and leave in a warm place until the dough rises almost to the top of the tins.

4 Preheat the oven to 220°C/425°F/Gas 7. Brush the brioches with beaten egg and bake for 15 minutes until golden brown. Sprinkle over shreds of orange rind, and serve warm with butter.

Cook's Tip
These brioches look particularly attractive if they are made in special brioche tins, but they can also be made in muffin tins.

Cinnamon Doughnuts

These doughnuts are made to an Eastern European recipe and are, of course, best eaten on the day they are made. They are dusted with sugar and cinnamon, and are also an ideal showcase for your finest homemade jam: in the Balkans they are usually filled with a thick fruity jam such as cherry, plum or apricot.

Makes 10–12
225g/8oz/2 cups strong flour
2.5ml/½ tsp salt
7g/¼oz sachet easy-blend (rapid-rise) dried yeast
1 egg, beaten
60–90ml/4–6 tbsp milk
15ml/1 tbsp sugar
about 60ml/4 tbsp cherry jam
oil, for deep-fat frying
50g/2oz/¼ cup caster (superfine) sugar
2.5ml/½ tsp cinnamon

1 Sift the flour into a bowl with the salt. Stir in the yeast. Make a well in the dry ingredients and add the egg, milk and sugar.

2 Mix together thoroughly, adding a little more milk if necessary, to make a smooth, but not sticky, dough. Beat well, then cover with clear film (plastic wrap) and leave for 1–1½ hours in a warm place until the dough has doubled in size.

3 Grease a baking sheet. Knead the dough on a lightly floured surface and divide it into 10–12 pieces. Shape each into a round and put 5ml/1 tsp of jam in the centre.

4 Dampen the edges of the dough with water, then draw up to form a ball, closing firmly so the jam will not escape during cooking. Place on the baking sheet and leave for 15 minutes.

5 Heat the oil in a large saucepan or deep fryer to 180°C/350°F, or until a 2.5cm/1in cube of bread dropped into the oil turns golden in about 60 seconds. Fry the doughnuts fairly gently for 5–10 minutes, until golden brown. Drain well on kitchen paper.

6 Mix the caster sugar and ground cinnamon together on a plate or in a large plastic bag and use to liberally coat the doughnuts while still warm.

Cornish Saffron Bread

This loaf is traditionally made at Easter, and is served sliced and buttered. Saffron, the precious spice from western Asia, may have been introduced to Cornwall by Phoenician traders 3,000 years ago.

Makes 1 loaf
good pinch of saffron threads
450g/1lb/4 cups plain (all-purpose) flour
2.5ml/½ tsp salt
50g/2oz/4 tbsp butter, diced
50g/2oz/4 tbsp lard, diced
10ml/2 tsp fast-action yeast granules
50g/2oz caster (superfine) sugar
115g/4oz/½ cup currants, raisins or sultanas (golden raisins), or a mixture
50g/2oz chopped mixed candied peel
150ml/¼ pint/⅔ cup milk
beaten egg, to glaze

1 Put the saffron in a bowl and add 150ml/¼ pint/⅔ cup boiling water. Cover and leave for several hours to allow the colour and flavour to develop.

2 Sift the flour and salt into a large bowl. Add the butter and lard and rub them into the flour until the mixture resembles fine breadcrumbs. Stir in the yeast granules, sugar, dried fruit and chopped mixed peel. Make a well in the centre.

3 Add the milk to the saffron water and warm to body heat. Tip the liquid into the flour and stir until it can be gathered into a ball. Cover with oiled clear film (plastic wrap) and leave in a warm place for about 1 hour, until doubled in size.

4 Grease and line a 900g/2lb loaf tin (pan) with baking parchment. Turn the dough on to a lightly floured surface and knead gently and briefly. Put the dough in the prepared tin, cover and leave in a warm place for 30 minutes until nearly doubled in size.

5 Preheat the oven to 200°C/400°F/Gas 6. Brush the top of the loaf with beaten egg and cook for 40 minutes or until risen and cooked through; cover with foil if it starts to brown too much. Leave in the tin for about 15 minutes before turning out on to a wire rack to cool.

Cinnamon Doughnuts: Energy 192kcal/803kJ; Protein 2.5g; Carbohydrate 22.6g, of which sugars 8.3g; Fat 10.8g, of which saturates 1.4g; Cholesterol 16mg; Calcium 37mg; Fibre 0.6g; Sodium 11mg.
Cornish Bread: Energy 3041kcal/12821kJ; Protein 50.7g; Carbohydrate 516.8g, of which sugars 173.9g; Fat 99.9g, of which saturates 48.7g; Cholesterol 162mg; Calcium 1018mg; Fibre 18.5g; Sodium 541mg.

Ginger-topped Shortbread Fingers

Topping a ginger shortbread base with a sticky ginger topping may be gilding the lily, but it tastes delicious!

Makes about 40
225g/8oz/2 cups plain (all purpose) flour
5ml/1 tsp ground ginger
75g/3oz/6 tbsp caster (superfine) sugar

3 pieces preserved stem ginger, finely chopped
175g/6oz/3/4 cup butter

For the topping
15ml/1 tbsp golden (corn) syrup
50g/2oz/1/4 cup butter
60ml/4 tbsp icing (confectioners') sugar, sifted
5ml/1 tsp ground ginger

1 Preheat the oven to 180°C/350°F/Gas 4. Grease a shallow rectangular 28 × 18cm/11 × 7in baking tin (pan). Sift the flour and ground ginger into a bowl and stir in the sugar and chopped stem ginger. Rub in the butter until the mixture begins to stick together.

2 Press the mixture into the prepared tin and smooth over the top with a palette knife. Bake for 40 minutes until the ginger shortbread base is very lightly browned.

3 Make the topping while the shortbread is baking. Put the syrup and butter in a small pan. Heat gently until both have melted. Stir in the icing sugar and ground ginger and beat until smooth.

4 Remove the cake tin from the oven and pour the topping over the shortbread base while both are still hot. Allow to cool slightly, then cut into fingers. Remove the pieces to a wire rack to cool completely.

Cook's Tips
• Don't overwork the dough or the shortbread will be tough: press it lightly into the tin.
• Use some of the syrup from the jar of stem ginger instead of golden syrup in the topping, if you prefer.

Apple and Cinnamon Muffins

Cinnamon is the perfect partner for apples, and these spicy muffins are quick and easy to make. They are ideal for serving for breakfast or afternoon tea, preferably while still warm.

Makes 6 large muffins
1 egg, beaten
40g/1½oz/3 tbsp caster (superfine) sugar
120ml/4fl oz/½ cup milk

50g/2oz/¼ cup butter, melted
150g/5oz/1¼ cups plain (all-purpose) flour
7.5ml/1½ tsp baking powder
1.5ml/¼ tsp salt
2.5ml/½ tsp ground cinnamon
2 small eating apples, peeled, cored and finely chopped

For the topping
12 brown sugar cubes, roughly crushed
1 tsp ground cinnamon

1 Preheat the oven to 200°C/400°F/Gas 6. Line six large muffin tins with paper cases.

2 Mix the egg, sugar, milk and melted butter in a large bowl. Sift in the flour, baking powder, salt and cinnamon. Add the chopped apple and mix roughly, without breaking up the apple.

3 Spoon the mixture into the prepared muffin cases. Make the topping by mixing the crushed sugar cubes with the cinnamon. Sprinkle over the muffins. Bake the muffins for 30–35 minutes until they are well risen and golden. Cool on a wire rack.

Variations
Experiment with other combinations of fruit and spice. Add grated nutmeg to the recipe, or replace the ground cinnamon with mixed (apple pie) spice. Or replace the chopped apple with 115g/4oz/½ cup dried blueberries.

Cook's Tip
Do not overmix the muffin mixture – it should be lumpy.

Golden Ginger Macaroons

With their warm, spicy, ginger flavour, these slightly chewy little biscuits are good served with vanilla ice cream and will go very well with mid-morning or after-dinner coffee.

Makes about 20
1 egg white
75g/3oz/scant ½ cup soft light brown sugar
115g/4oz/1 cup ground almonds
5ml/1 tsp ground ginger

1 Preheat the oven to 180°C/350°F/Gas 4. Line two baking sheets with baking parchment.

2 In a large, grease-free bowl, whisk the egg white until it is stiff and standing in peaks, but not crumbly, then whisk in the brown sugar.

3 Sprinkle the ground almonds and ginger over the whisked egg white, and gently fold them together.

4 Using two teaspoons, place spoonfuls of the mixture on the baking sheets, leaving plenty of space between each for the biscuits to spread. Bake for about 20 minutes until pale golden brown and just turning crisp.

5 Leave the macaroons to cool slightly on the baking sheets before transferring them to a wire rack to cool completely.

Cook's Tip
For the best flavour, buy whole unblanched almonds and grind them yourself in a food processor.

Variation
You can substitute other ground nuts, such as hazelnuts or walnuts, for the almonds in this recipe. Ground cinnamon or mixed spice could be added to the mixture instead of ginger for another variation.

Lebkuchen

These sweet and spicy Bavarian cakes are traditionally baked at Christmas. In German, their name means "cake of life".

Makes 20
115g/4oz/1 cup blanched almonds, finely chopped
50g/2oz/⅓ cup candied orange rind, finely chopped
finely grated rind of ½ lemon
3 cardamom pods
5ml/1 tsp cinnamon

1.5ml/¼ tsp nutmeg
1.5ml/¼ tsp ground cloves
2 eggs
115g/4oz/scant ¾ cup caster (superfine) sugar
150g/5oz/1¼ cups plain (all-purpose) flour
2.5ml/½ tsp baking powder

For the icing
½ egg white
75g/3oz/¾ cup icing (confectioners') sugar, sifted
5ml/1 tsp white rum

1 Preheat the oven to 180°C/350°F/Gas 4. Set aside some of the almonds for sprinkling and put the remainder in a bowl with the candied orange and lemon rind.

2 Remove the seeds from the cardamom pods and crush using a pestle and mortar. Add to the bowl with the cinnamon, nutmeg and cloves and mix well.

3 Whisk the eggs and sugar in a mixing bowl until thick and foamy. Sift in the flour and baking powder, then gently fold into the eggs before adding to the nut and spice mixture.

4 Line two baking sheets with baking parchment and spoon the mixture on to them, allowing room for it to spread. Sprinkle over the reserved almonds.

5 Bake for 20 minutes, until golden. Leave the biscuits (cookies) to cool on the baking sheets for a few minutes, then remove them to a wire rack to cool completely.

6 Put the egg white for the icing in a bowl and lightly whisk with a fork. Stir in the icing sugar a little at a time, then add the rum. Drizzle the icing over the biscuits and leave to set. Store the *lebkuchen* in a tin for 2 weeks before serving.

Golden Ginger Macaroons: Energy 5kcal/21kJ; Protein 0.1g; Carbohydrate 0.4g, of which sugars 0.4g; Fat 0.3g, of which saturates 0g; Cholesterol 1mg; Calcium 2mg; Fibre 0g; Sodium 0mg.
Lebkuchen: Energy 105kcal/444kJ; Protein 2.4g; Carbohydrate 16.3g, of which sugars 11.7g; Fat 3.9g, of which saturates 0.4g; Cholesterol 19mg; Calcium 33mg; Fibre 0.7g; Sodium 16mg.

Spicy Hearts and Stars

These soft, sweet cookies have a wonderfully chewy texture and a deliciously warm, fragrant flavour. Serve with coffee at the end of a festive meal, or pack a batch in a pretty box as a gift for a special occasion.

1 egg
50g/2oz/1½ tbsp golden (corn) syrup
50g/2oz/1½ tbsp black treacle (molasses)
400g/14oz/3½ cups self-raising (self-rising) flour
10ml/2 tsp ground ginger

Makes about 25
115g/4oz/½ cup unsalted (sweet) butter, softened
115g/4oz/generous ½ cup light muscovado (brown) sugar

For the toppings
200g/7oz plain (semisweet) or milk chocolate
150g/5oz/1¼ cups icing (confectioners') sugar, sifted

1 Put the softened butter and sugar in a large bowl and beat together until creamy. Add the egg, syrup and treacle to the creamed mixture and beat together.

2 Sift the flour and ginger over the batter and mix gently to form a firm dough. Chill for 20 minutes. Meanwhile, preheat the oven to 180°C/350°F/Gas 4 and line two large baking sheets with sheets of baking parchment.

3 Roll out the dough on a lightly floured surface to just under 1cm/½in thick and use biscuit (cookie) cutters to stamp out heart and star shapes. Place the cookies, spaced slightly apart, on the prepared baking sheets and bake for about 10 minutes, or until risen and lightly coloured. Remove from the oven and leave to cool on the baking sheets for 10 minutes, then remove to a wire rack to cool completely.

4 Melt the chocolate in a microwave or in a heatproof bowl set over a pan of barely simmering water. Use the melted chocolate to coat the heart-shaped cookies.

5 Put the icing sugar into a bowl and mix with enough warm water to make a coating consistency, then use this to glaze the star-shaped cookies.

Spiced Crescent Biscuits

Lightly spiced and delicately flavoured with orange flower water and almonds, these crisp little crescents are perfect for parties and festive occasions such as christenings and weddings.

pinch of ground nutmeg
10ml/2 tsp orange flower water
50g/2oz/½ cup icing (confectioners') sugar, plus extra for dusting
90g/3½oz/¾ cup plain (all-purpose) flour
115g/4oz/1 cup ground almonds
25g/1oz/¼ cup whole almonds, toasted and chopped

Makes about 20
115g/4oz/½ cup unsalted (sweet) butter, softened

1 Preheat the oven to 160°C/325°F/Gas 3. Line two large baking sheets with baking parchment.

2 Beat the butter in a large bowl until soft and creamy. Beat in the nutmeg and the orange flower water. Add the icing sugar and beat until fluffy.

3 Add the flour, ground and chopped almonds and mix well, then use your hands to bring the mixture together to form a dough, being careful not to overwork it.

4 Shape small pieces of the dough into sausages about 7.5cm/3in long. Curve each one into a crescent shape and place, spaced well apart, on the prepared baking sheets.

5 Bake for about 15 minutes, or until the biscuits (cookies) are firm but still pale in colour. Leave on the baking sheets for about 5 minutes to cool, then dust with a little icing sugar and remove to a wire rack to cool completely.

> **Variation**
> Replace the nutmeg with another spice if you like, such as ground cinnamon or allspice, or omit the spice from the mixture altogether and add 5ml/1 tsp ground cinnamon to the icing (confectioners') sugar used to dust the biscuits.

Spicy Hearts and Stars: Energy 185kcal/781kJ; Protein 2.3g; Carbohydrate 31.5g, of which sugars 19.3g; Fat 6.5g, of which saturates 3.8g; Cholesterol 18mg; Calcium 44mg; Fibre 0.7g; Sodium 41mg.
Spiced Crescent Biscuits: Energy 111kcal/461kJ; Protein 1.9g; Carbohydrate 6.6g, of which sugars 3g; Fat 8.7g, of which saturates 3.3g; Cholesterol 12mg; Calcium 25mg; Fibre 0.7g; Sodium 36mg.

Easter Biscuits

These sweet, lightly spiced English cookies are dusted with sugar and flecked with currants. They were traditionally baked at Easter, particularly in Devon and Cornwall, where they are sometimes known as Easter cakes rather than biscuits. However, they are too good to make only once a year, and are delicious at any time. They are always cut out with fluted edges.

Makes 16–18
115g/4oz/½ cup soft butter
85g/3oz/6 tbsp caster (superfine)
   sugar, plus extra for sprinkling
I egg
200g/7oz/1¾ cups plain
   (all-purpose) flour
2.5ml/½ tsp mixed (apple pie)
   spice
2.5ml/½ tsp ground cinnamon
55g/2oz/scant ½ cup currants
15ml/1 tbsp chopped mixed
   candied peel
15–30ml/1–2 tbsp milk

I Preheat the oven to 200°C/400°F/Gas 6. Lightly grease two baking sheets or line with baking parchment.

2 Beat together the butter and sugar until light and fluffy. Separate the egg, reserving the white, and beat the yolk into the mixture.

3 Sift the flour and spices over the mixture, then fold in the currants and candied peel, adding sufficient milk to make a fairly soft dough.

4 Knead the dough lightly on a floured surface then roll out to 5mm/¼in thick. Cut out circles using a 5cm/2in fluted biscuit (cookie) cutter. Arrange on the prepared baking sheets and bake for 10 minutes.

5 Beat the egg white and brush gently over the biscuits. Sprinkle with caster sugar and return to the oven for a further 10 minutes until golden. Transfer to a wire rack to cool.

> **Variation**
> *The milk used in the dough can be replaced with brandy.*

Chocolate Cinnamon Tuiles

Because of their curved shape, these crisp, delicate cookies, are named after traditional curved French roof tiles. Though they look impressive they are not really difficult to make, and are the perfect foil for creamy desserts and ice creams, or just to eat with after-dinner coffee.

Makes 12
I egg white
50g/2oz/¼ cup caster (superfine)
   sugar
30ml/2 tbsp plain (all-purpose)
   flour
40g/1½oz/3 tbsp unsalted
   (sweet) butter, melted
15ml/1 tbsp cocoa powder
2.5ml/½ tsp ground cinnamon

I Preheat the oven to 200°C/400°F/Gas 6. Lightly grease two large baking sheets. Whisk the egg white in a clean, grease-free bowl until it forms soft peaks. Gradually whisk in the sugar to make a smooth, glossy mixture.

2 Sift the flour over the meringue mixture and fold in evenly and gently: try not to deflate the mixture. Stir in the butter. Transfer about 45ml/3 tbsp of the mixture to a small bowl and set it aside.

3 In a separate bowl, mix together the cocoa and cinnamon. Stir this into the larger quantity of mixture until well combined.

4 Leaving plenty of room for the biscuits (cookies) to spread while cooking, drop spoonfuls of the chocolate-flavoured mixture on to the prepared baking sheets, then spread each gently with a palette knife to make a neat round.

5 Using a small spoon, drizzle the reserved plain mixture over the chocolate rounds. Swirl each one lightly with the spoon to give a marbled effect.

6 Bake for 4–6 minutes, until just set. Using a palette knife, lift each biscuit while still soft and drape it over a rolling pin, to give a curved shape as it hardens. Allow the tuiles to set, then remove them to a wire rack to finish cooling. Serve them on the same day they are made.

Chocolate Cinnamon Tuiles: Energy 125kcal/523kJ; Protein 1.2g; Carbohydrate 12.3g, of which sugars 9.7g; Fat 8.3g, of which saturates 5.2g; Cholesterol 18mg; Calcium 17mg; Fibre 0.2g; Sodium 42mg.
Easter Biscuits: Energy 116kcal/485kJ; Protein 1.5g; Carbohydrate 15.4g, of which sugars 7g; Fat 5.7g, of which saturates 3.4g; Cholesterol 24mg; Calcium 25mg; Fibre 0.4g; Sodium 46mg.

Cinnamon and Vanilla Biscuits

These melt-in-the-mouth cinnamon and vanilla biscuits are traditionally served at Mexican weddings. They are perfect for serving with coffee.

Makes about 40
225g/8oz/1 cup butter, softened
50g/2oz/¼ cup caster (superfine) sugar

225g/8oz/2 cups plain (all-purpose) flour
115g/4oz/1 cup cornflour (cornstarch)
5ml/1 tsp vanilla extract

For dusting
50g/2oz/½ cup icing (confectioners') sugar
5ml/1 tsp ground cinnamon

1 Preheat the oven to 160°C/325°F/Gas 3. Lightly grease two or three baking sheets.

2 In a bowl, cream the butter with the caster sugar until light and fluffy. Sift the flour and cornflour together and gradually work into the creamed butter and sugar mixture with the vanilla extract.

3 Roll heaped teaspoons of the mixture into balls and place on the prepared baking sheets. Bake for 30 minutes or until the biscuits (cookies) are pale golden.

4 Sift the icing sugar and ground cinnamon together into a bowl. While the biscuits are still warm, toss them in the icing sugar mixture. Leave on a wire rack to cool, then store in an airtight tin for up to 2 weeks.

Cook's Tips
• The biscuit mixture can be prepared in a food processor.
• Vanilla is one of the most complex of spices, and is available in various forms. Pure vanilla extract is made by soaking chopped vanilla pods (beans) in alcohol and water. The best quality extracts are expensive, but keep indefinitely. Don't be tempted to buy cheaper products that use imitation vanilla flavouring, as the taste is synthetic and inferior.

Dutch Marzipan Cookies

These Dutch cookies, made from a spicy dough wrapped around a rich marzipan filling, are eaten on the feast of St Nicholas, 6 December.

Makes about 35
175g/6oz/1½ cups ground hazelnuts
175g/6oz/1½ cups ground almonds
175g/6oz/scant 1 cup caster (superfine) sugar
175g/6oz/1½ cups icing (confectioners') sugar

1 egg, beaten
10–15ml/2–3 tsp lemon juice
250g/9oz/2¼ cups self-raising (self-rising) flour
5ml/1 tsp mixed (apple pie) spice
75g/3oz/⅓ cup light muscovado (brown) sugar
115g/4oz/½ cup unsalted (sweet) butter, diced
2 eggs
15ml/1 tbsp milk
15ml/1 tbsp caster (superfine) sugar
about 35 blanched almond halves

1 To make the filling, put the ground hazelnuts, almonds, caster sugar, icing sugar, beaten egg and 10ml/2 tsp lemon juice in a bowl and mix to a firm paste, adding more lemon juice if needed. Divide the mixture in half and roll each piece into a sausage shape about 25cm/10in long. Wrap in foil and chill.

2 To make the dough, sift the flour and mixed spice into a large mixing bowl then stir in the muscovado sugar. Add the butter and rub in well with your fingertips. Beat one of the eggs, add to the mixture and mix together to form a dough. Knead lightly, then wrap in clear film (plastic wrap) and chill for 15 minutes. Preheat the oven to 180°C/350°F/Gas 4 and line a baking sheet with baking parchment.

3 Roll out the pastry on a lightly floured surface to a 30cm/12in square and cut in half to make two rectangles. Beat the remaining egg and brush some all over the pastry rectangles.

4 Place a roll of filling on each piece of pastry and roll to enclose the filling. Place, join-side down, on the baking sheet. Beat the remains of the egg with the milk and sugar and brush over the rolls. Press almond halves along the top, bake for 35 minutes, and leave to cool before cutting diagonally into slices.

Cinnamon and Vanilla Biscuits: Energy 65kcal/273kJ; Protein 0.9g; Carbohydrate 7.8g, of which sugars 3.1g; Fat 3.6g, of which saturates 2.2g; Cholesterol 14mg; Calcium 15mg; Fibre 0.2g; Sodium 28mg.
Dutch Marzipan Cookies: Energy 181kcal/757kJ; Protein 3.5g; Carbohydrate 19.5g, of which sugars 13.8g; Fat 10.4g, of which saturates 2.4g; Cholesterol 23mg; Calcium 44mg; Fibre 1.1g; Sodium 28mg.

Chilli Cornbread

This golden yellow cornbread spiked with chilli makes an excellent accompaniment to soups and salads.

Makes 9 slices
2 eggs
450ml/¾ pint/1⅞ cups buttermilk
50g/2oz/¼ cup butter, melted
65g/2½oz/½ cup plain (all-purpose) flour
2.5ml/½ tsp ground mace
5ml/1 tsp bicarbonate of soda (baking soda)
10ml/2 tsp salt
250g/9oz/2¼ cups fine cornmeal
2 fresh red chillies, seeded and finely chopped
shredded red chillies and sea salt, to serve

1 Preheat the oven to 200°C/400°F/Gas 6. Grease and line a 23 × 7.5 cm/9 × 3 in loaf tin (pan). In a large bowl, whisk the eggs until frothy, then whisk in the buttermilk and melted butter.

2 Sift the flour, mace, bicarbonate of soda and salt together and gradually stir into the egg mixture. Fold in the cornmeal a little at a time, then stir in the fresh chillies.

3 Pour the mixture into the prepared tin and bake for 25–30 minutes until the top is firm to the touch.

4 Leave the loaf to cool in the tin for a few minutes before turning out. Scatter over the red chillies and sea salt, then cut into slices and serve warm.

Variation
For a loaf with a more rustic appearance, use medium or coarse cornmeal.

Cook's Tip
This cornbread is flavoured with ground mace, a spice that comes from the same plant as nutmeg. It has a similar but more delicate flavour and also adds a bright orange colour.

Chilli Cheese Muffins

These muffins are flavoured with chilli purée, which is widely available in tubes or jars and is a really instant way to add spicy heat to recipes of all kinds.

Makes 12
115 g/4 oz/1 cup self-raising (self-rising) flour
15ml/1 tbsp baking powder
5ml/1 tsp salt
225g/8oz/2 cups fine cornmeal
150g/5oz/1¼ cups grated mature Cheddar cheese
50g/2oz/4 tbsp butter, melted
2 eggs, beaten
5ml/1 tsp chilli purée
1 garlic clove, crushed
300ml/½ pint/1¼ cups milk

1 Preheat the oven to 200°C/400°F/Gas 6. Thoroughly grease 12 deep muffin tins (pans) or line the tins with paper muffin cases.

2 Sift the flour, baking powder and salt into a bowl, then stir in the cornmeal and 115g/4oz/1 cup of the grated cheese.

3 Pour the melted butter into a bowl and stir in the eggs, chilli purée, crushed garlic and milk. Pour on to the dry ingredients and mix quickly until just combined.

4 Spoon the batter into the prepared muffin tins, sprinkle the remaining cheese on top and bake for 20 minutes until risen and golden brown.

5 Leave to cool for a few minutes before turning the muffins out on to a wire rack to cool completely.

Cook's Tips
- *Take care not to over-mix the mixture or the finished muffins will be heavy. Stir the mixture just enough to combine the ingredients roughly.*
- *The muffins are best eaten on the same day they are made, preferably while still slightly warm.*
- *Other strongly flavoured cheeses, such as Parmesan or Gruyère, can also be used.*

Chilli Cornbread: Energy 229kcal/959kJ; Protein 6.9g; Carbohydrate 32.8g, of which sugars 4.9g; Fat 8.2g, of which saturates 1.4g; Cholesterol 48mg; Calcium 98mg; Fibre 1g; Sodium 514mg.
Chilli Cheese Muffins: Energy 166kcal/698kJ; Protein 5.1g; Carbohydrate 19.3g, of which sugars 4.4g; Fat 8.1g, of which saturates 4.6g; Cholesterol 60mg; Calcium 93mg; Fibre 0.6g; Sodium 96mg.

Spiced Cocktail Biscuits

These savoury biscuits are ideal for serving with pre-dinner drinks. Each of the spice seeds in the mixture contributes its own distinct character to the flavour. For bitesize cocktail snacks use a tiny round cookie cutter, or you could cut out fancy shapes such as stars and crescents.

Makes 20–30

150g/5oz/1¼ cups plain (all-purpose) flour
10ml/2 tsp curry powder
115g/4oz/½ cup butter
75g/3oz/¾ cup grated mature Cheddar cheese
10ml/2 tsp poppy seeds
5ml/1 tsp black onion seeds
1 egg yolk
cumin seeds, to decorate

1 Grease two baking sheets or line them with sheets of baking parchment. Sift the flour and curry powder into a bowl.

2 Rub in the butter until the mixture resembles breadcrumbs, then stir in the grated cheese, poppy seeds and black onion seeds.

3 Stir in the egg yolk and mix to a firm dough. Wrap the dough in clear film (plastic wrap) and chill for 30 minutes.

4 Roll out the dough on a floured surface to a thickness of about 3mm/⅛in. Cut into shapes with a cookie cutter. Arrange on the prepared baking sheets and sprinkle with the cumin seeds. Chill for 15 minutes.

5 Preheat the oven to 190°C/375°F/Gas 5. Bake the biscuits (cookies) for about 20 minutes until crisp and golden. Transfer to a wire rack to cool, and serve soon after baking.

Cook's Tip
These biscuits are at their best when they are freshly baked. The dough can be made in advance and chilled until required, so that all you need to do is cut out the shapes and put the biscuits in the oven.

Fennel and Chilli Ring Cookies

Based on an Italian recipe, these cookies are made with yeast and are appetizingly savoury and crumbly. Try them as nibbles with drinks, to go with dips or with antipasti. Fennel seeds have an anise-like taste similar to that of the herb, and they add a rounded flavour that goes well with the heat added by the chillis.

Makes about 30

500g/1lb 2oz/4½ cups type 00 flour
115g/4oz/½ cup white vegetable fat
5ml/1 tsp easy-blend (rapid-rise) dried yeast
15ml/1 tbsp fennel seeds
10ml/2 tsp crushed chilli flakes
15ml/1 tbsp olive oil
400–550ml/14–18fl oz/1⅔–2½ cups lukewarm water
olive oil, for brushing

1 Put the flour in a bowl and rub in the fat until the mixture resembles fine breadcrumbs. Add the yeast, fennel and chilli and mix well. Add the oil and enough water to make a soft but not sticky dough. Turn out on to a floured surface and knead lightly.

2 Take small pieces of dough and shape into sausages about 15cm/6in long. Shape into rings and pinch the ends together.

3 Place the rings on a non-stick baking sheet and brush lightly with olive oil. Cover with a dish towel and set aside at room temperature for 1 hour to rise slightly.

4 Meanwhile, preheat the oven to 150°C/300°F/Gas 2. Bake the cookies for 1 hour until they are dry and very slightly browned. Leave on the baking sheet to cool completely.

Cook's Tip
Type 00 is an Italian grade of flour, principally used for pasta. It is milled from the centre part of the endosperm so that the resulting flour is much whiter than plain (all-purpose) flour. It contains 70 per cent of the wheat grain. It is available from Italian delicatessens and some large supermarkets. If you cannot find it, try using strong white bread flour instead.

Spiced Cocktail Biscuits: Energy 67kcal/278kJ; Protein 1.5g; Carbohydrate 4g, of which sugars 0.1g; Fat 5g, of which saturates 2.7g; Cholesterol 17mg; Calcium 38mg; Fibre 0.3g; Sodium 44mg.
Fennel and Chilli Ring Cookies: Energy 94kcal/396kJ; Protein 1.8g; Carbohydrate 13g, of which sugars 0.3g; Fat 4.3g, of which saturates 1.5g; Cholesterol 1mg; Calcium 30mg; Fibre 0.6g; Sodium 31mg.

Spiced Normandy Coffee

Normandy is known for its apple orchards, and gives its name to many dishes made with apple juice or apple sauce. This recipe blends apples with spices for a delicious, tangy coffee drink.

Serves 4

475ml/16fl oz/2 cups strong black coffee (espresso strength, or filter/plunger brewed at 75g/13 tbsp/scant 1 cup coffee per 1 litre/33fl oz/4 cups of water)
475ml/16fl oz/2 cups apple juice
30ml/2 tbsp brown sugar, to taste
3 oranges, thinly sliced
2 small cinnamon sticks
pinch of ground allspice
pinch of ground cloves
cinnamon stick, to serve

1 Bring all the ingredients to the boil over a moderate heat, then reduce the heat and simmer for 10 minutes. Strain the liquid into a preheated flask or serving jug. Pour into cups, adding a cinnamon stick to each, if you wish.

Café de Olla

This is one of the most popular drinks in Mexico. Its name means "out of the pot", referring to the container in which the coffee is made. This richly spiced coffee is always drunk without milk.

Serves 4

1 litre/1¾ pints/4 cups water
115g/4oz/½ cup soft dark brown sugar
4 cinnamon sticks
4 star anise
50g/2oz/⅔ cup freshly ground coffee, from dark-roast beans

1 Place the water, sugar, star anise and cinnamon sticks in a pan. Heat gently, stirring occasionally to make sure that the sugar dissolves, then bring to the boil. Boil rapidly for about 20 minutes until the syrup has reduced by a quarter.

2 Add the ground coffee to the syrup and stir well, then bring the liquid back to the boil. Remove from the heat, cover the pan and leave to stand for around 5 minutes. Strain the coffee, pour into cups and serve immediately.

Mexican Coffee with Cinnamon

Many Mexicans start the day with this spiced milky coffee, and those who have enjoyed a hearty midday meal will often opt for a cup of it with a pastry as their afternoon snack.

Serves 4

50g/2oz/⅔ cup ground coffee
475ml/16fl oz/2 cups boiling water
475ml/16fl oz/2 cups milk
4 cinnamon sticks
sugar, to taste

1 Put the ground coffee in a cafetière or jug, pour on the boiling water and leave for a few minutes until the coffee grounds settle at the bottom. Push down the plunger of the cafetière or strain the jug of coffee to separate the liquid from the grounds. Pour the strained coffee into a clean jug.

2 Pour the milk into a heavy pan, add the cinnamon sticks and bring to the boil, stirring occasionally. Using a slotted spoon, lift out the cinnamon sticks and use a smaller spoon to press down on them to release any liquid they have absorbed. Set the cinnamon sticks aside for serving.

3 Add the coffee to the hot milk, then pour into cups. Add a cinnamon stick. Add sugar to taste as required.

Chocolate and Vanilla Latte

A straight latte is a cappucino with extra milk. This vanilla-spiced version, with real chocolate pieces melted through it, is perfect for a special treat.

Serves 2

750ml/1¾ pints/3 cups water
1 vanilla pod (bean)
2 shots of espresso coffee
10ml/2 tsp sugar
115g/4oz plain dark chocolate

1 Heat the milk in a pan with the vanilla pod and set aside to infuse for about 10 minutes. Add the coffee to the milk.

2 Return to the heat, add the sugar and simmer, stir in the chocolate and stir while it melts. Serve in tall mugs.

Spiced Normandy Coffee: Energy 77kcal/330kJ; Protein 0.4g; Carbohydrate 20g, of which sugars 19.6g; Fat 0.1g, of which saturates 0g; Cholesterol 0mg; Calcium 16mg; Fibre 0g; Sodium 3mg.
Café de Olla: Energy 118kcal/503kJ; Protein 1.1g; Carbohydrate 30.3g, of which sugars 30.1g; Fat 0g, of which saturates 0g; Cholesterol 0mg; Calcium 24mg; Fibre 0g; Sodium 7mg.
Mexican Coffee with Cinnamon: Energy 66kcal/277kJ; Protein 4.6g; Carbohydrate 6.9g, of which sugars 5.6g; Fat 2.5g, of which saturates 1.4g; Cholesterol 7mg; Calcium 149mg; Fibre 0g; Sodium 52mg.
Chocolate and Vanilla Latte: Energy 313kcal/1313kJ; Protein 2.9g; Carbohydrate 41.8g, of which sugars 41.2g; Fat 16.1g, of which saturates 9.7g; Cholesterol 3mg; Calcium 22mg; Fibre 1.5g; Sodium 4mg.

Spiced Coffee Lassi

This is a coffee variation on traditional lassi, the refreshing Indian yogurt drink, which may be sweet or savoury. The sweet version is traditionally flavoured with sugar and ground cinnamon, while the salty one often contains a little cumin and may be garnished with mint.

Serves 2
350ml/12fl oz/1½ cups cold black coffee (filter/plunger brewed using about 65g/11½ tbsp/¾ cups coffee per 475ml/16fl oz/2 cups of water)
350ml/12fl oz/1½ cups natural (plain) yogurt
20ml/4 tsp sugar
a pinch of ground cinnamon, to taste

1 Combine all the ingredients in a blender. Mix until creamy. Serve sprinkled with cinnamon.

Mexican Hot Chocolate

This is hot chocolate as it should be, made with best quality real dark chocolate and warming spices: it is a far superior drink to the instant powders sold commercially.

Serves 4
1 litre/1¾ pints/4 cups milk
1 cinnamon stick
2 whole cloves
115g/4oz plain dark chocolate, chopped into small pieces
2–3 drops of almond essence

1 Heat the milk gently with the spices in a pan until almost boiling, then stir in the plain chocolate over a moderate heat until melted.

2 Strain into a blender, add the almond essence and whizz on high speed for about 30 seconds until frothy. Alternatively, whisk the mixture with a hand-held electric mixer or wire whisk. Pour into warmed heatproof glasses and serve immediately.

Iced Mint and Chocolate Cooler

Try this delicious minty chilled chocolate milk on a hot summer's day. It makes the perfect cooling drink.

Serves 4
60ml/4 tbsp drinking chocolate

400ml/14fl oz/1⅔ cups cold milk
150ml/¼ pint/⅔ cup natural (plain) yogurt
2.5ml/½ tsp peppermint essence
4 scoops chocolate ice cream
mint leaves and chocolate shapes, to decorate

1 Place the drinking chocolate in a small pan and stir in about 120ml/4fl oz/½ of the milk. Heat gently, stirring, until almost boiling, then remove the pan from the heat.

2 Pour the hot chocolate milk into a heatproof bowl or large jug and whisk in the remaining cold milk. Add the natural yogurt and peppermint essence and whisk again. Pour into four tall glasses, filling them no more than three quarters full. Top each with a scoop of ice cream, decorate with mint leaves and chocolate shapes. Serve immediately.

Spiced Mexican Rice Milk

This aromatic rice drink tastes creamy, yet does not contain a drop of milk.

Serves 4
150g/1lb/2¼ cups long grain rice
750ml/1¼ pints/3 cups water

150g/5oz/1¼ cups blanched whole almonds
10ml/2 tsp ground cinnamon
finely grated rind of 1 lime, plus strips of rind, to decorate
50g/2oz/¼ cup sugar
ice cubes, to serve

1 Rinse the rice under cold running water then soak for at least 2 hours. Drain, reserving 600ml/1 pint/2½ cups of the soaking liquid. Spoon the rice into a food processor or blender and grind as finely as possible.

2 Add the almonds and continue to process until finely ground. Add the cinnamon, grated lime rind and sugar to the ground rice and almonds. Add the reserved soaking water from the rice and mix until all the sugar has dissolved.

3 Serve in tall glasses with ice cubes. Decorate with strips of lime rind.

Mexican Hot Chocolate: Energy 220kcal/924kJ; Protein 8.1g; Carbohydrate 25.3g, of which sugars 25.1g; Fat 10.4g, of which saturates 6.4g; Cholesterol 13mg; Calcium 248mg; Fibre 0.6g; Sodium 88mg.
Iced Mint and Chocolate Cooler: Energy 231kcal/968kJ; Protein 8.1g; Carbohydrate 27.9g, of which sugars 27.5g; Fat 10.5g, of which saturates 6.3g; Cholesterol 6mg; Calcium 247mg; Fibre 0g; Sodium 138mg.
Spiced Coffee Lassi: Energy 155kcal/657kJ; Protein 9g; Carbohydrate 28.3g, of which sugars 28.3g; Fat 1.8g, of which saturates 0.9g; Cholesterol 2mg; Calcium 340mg; Fibre 0g; Sodium 146mg.
Spiced Mexican Rice Milk: Energy 683kcal/2850kJ; Protein 16.3g; Carbohydrate 105.4g, of which sugars 14.6g; Fat 21.5g, of which saturates 1.7g; Cholesterol 0mg; Calcium 118mg; Fibre 2.8g; Sodium 6mg.

Warm and Creamy Egg Nog

Just the words "egg nog" suggest something rich and creamy. Popular in North America, it is associated with Christmas and other winter celebrations. It is thought to have Scandinavian origins and is usually served cold, but in this version it is warmed to bring out the flavour of the brandy and rum, and is served with cinnamon sticks for stirring.

Serves 4
475ml/16fl oz/2 cups double (heavy) cream
3 long strips orange rind
2.5ml/½ tsp freshly grated nutmeg
1 cinnamon stick
4 eggs, separated
30ml/2 tbsp caster (superfine) sugar
175ml/6fl oz/¾ cup golden rum
250ml/8fl oz/1 cup brandy
extra grated nutmeg and 4 cinnamon sticks, to serve

1 Pour the cream into a small pan, add the orange rind, nutmeg and the cinnamon stick and bring slowly to the boil. In a mixing bowl, beat the egg yolks with the sugar until really pale and creamy. When the cream is boiling, pour on to the egg mixture and whisk well.

2 Pour the mixture back into the pan and cook over a very gentle heat, stirring all the time, until it forms a custard as thick as pouring cream.

3 Pour the rum and brandy into a pan and warm through. Stir into the egg custard. Whisk the egg whites until they form soft peaks and carefully fold into the warm custard.

4 Pour into a warmed punch bowl. Sprinkle the surface of the egg nog with extra nutmeg to serve at the table or just ladle straight into warmed glasses or mugs. Put a cinnamon stick stirrer into each mug or glass before filling with egg nog.

> **Cook's Tip**
> Do not overheat the cream and egg mixture or it will curdle: it should thicken just enough to coat the back of the spoon.

Hot Toddy

Bed suggests warmth and comfort – a place where you can be safe and warm. Hot drinks are sheer luxury in bed, especially if you are feeling a little down or under the weather. A hot toddy is warming, soothing and has a lovely, almost fresh taste – the lemon, honey and whisky combine to take care of the most miserable cold.

Serves 2
2 strips of pared lemon rind
4 slices of fresh root ginger
5ml/1 tsp honey
175ml/6fl oz/¾ cup water
175ml/6fl oz/¾ cup Scotch whisky, Irish whiskey or American bourbon

1 Put the lemon rind, ginger, honey and water in a small pan and bring to the boil.

2 Remove the pan from the heat and leave for 5 minutes for the flavours to infuse. Stir the alcohol into the pan and allow time for it to warm through before serving, but don't heat it further or the alcohol will be driven off.

Hot Buttered Rum

Hot rum is luxurious and pampering, especially when sipped through a layer of melted butter.

Serves 2
475ml/16fl oz/2 cups milk

15ml/1 tbsp caster (superfine) sugar
1 cinnamon stick
175ml/6fl oz/¾ cup dark rum
25g/1oz/2 tbsp salted butter, diced
freshly grated nutmeg

1 Heat the milk in a pan with the sugar and cinnamon stick. Pour in the rum and heat gently for 1–2 minutes.

2 Pour the mixture into warmed mugs and dot the surface with the butter. Grate nutmeg over the top. To drink, sip the rum through the thin layer of melted butter, to mix the saltiness of the butter and the spicy sweetness of the drink.

Warm and Creamy Egg Nog: Energy 928kcal/3832kJ; Protein 8.2g; Carbohydrate 9.9g, of which sugars 9.9g; Fat 69.3g, of which saturates 41.2g; Cholesterol 353mg; Calcium 91mg; Fibre 0g; Sodium 97mg.
Hot Toddy: Energy 206kcal/854kJ; Protein 0g; Carbohydrate 3.1g, of which sugars 3.1g; Fat 0g, of which saturates 0g; Cholesterol 0mg; Calcium 0mg; Fibre 0g; Sodium 1mg.
Hot Buttered Rum: Energy 426kcal/1776kJ; Protein 8.2g; Carbohydrate 19.1g, of which sugars 19.1g; Fat 14.3g, of which saturates 9.1g; Cholesterol 41mg; Calcium 291mg; Fibre 0g; Sodium 179mg.

Mulled Red Wine and Ruby Port with Spicy Oven-roasted Nuts

This great drink and nibble combination is good at Christmas or Thanksgiving. This recipe makes 1 litre/ 1³⁄₄ pints/4 cups wine and 450g/1lb nuts.

For the mulled wine
15g/1½oz fresh root ginger
1 cinnamon stick
4 whole cloves

1 star anise
6 allspice berries, crushed
600ml/1 pint/2½ cups red wine
150ml/¼ pint/²⁄₃ cup ruby port

For the spicy nuts
40g/1½oz/3 tbsp butter
15ml/1 tbsp garam masala
450g/1lb nuts, such as almonds, cashew nuts and hazelnuts

1 To make the spiced nuts, preheat the oven to 150°C/300°F/ Gas 2. Melt the butter in a roasting pan and stir in the garam masala, then add the nuts and stir until well coated. Roast for 30 minutes to 1 hour until the nuts are golden, stirring from time to time.

2 Remove the nuts from the oven and toss them lightly with the salt. Allow to cool completely, then store for at least a day before eating. They will keep in an airtight container for two weeks, and it is worth making a double quantity.

3 To prepare the mulled wine, bruise the ginger, then place, along with the spices, in a stainless steel pan and cover with 600ml/1 pint/2½ cups water. Bring slowly to the boil, then boil rapidly for 10 minutes until it is reduced by half and all the flavours are infused. Remove the pan from the heat.

4 Mix the wine and port together. Line a sieve (strainer) with paper towels, then strain the spiced reduction into the wine and port mixture. Rinse out the pan well.

5 Return the wine and port mixture to the pan and reheat. Put a silver spoon into each warmed glass – this will diffuse the heat and stop the glass cracking – pour in the mulled wine and serve with the spiced nuts.

Mulled Cider

This hot cider cup is easy to make and traditionally served at Hallowe'en, but it makes a good warming brew for any winter gathering. Depending on the type of apple juice and cider you use, you may want to add a little sugar to taste.

Makes about 20 glasses
2 lemons
1 litre/1³⁄₄ pints/4 cups apple juice
2 litres/3½ pints/9 cups medium sweet cider
3 small cinnamon sticks
4–6 whole cloves
slices of lemon, to serve (optional)

1 Wash the lemons and pare the rinds with a vegetable peeler. Blend all the ingredients together in a large stainless steel pan.

2 Set over a low heat and heat the mixture through to infuse (steep) for 15 minutes; do not allow it to boil. Strain the liquid and serve with extra slices of lemon, if you like.

Scottish Het Pint

This drink, whose name means "hot pint" is traditionally served in Scotland at Hogmanay.

Makes about 3 litres/5 pints
1.2 litres/2 pints/5 cups lemonade

1.2 litres/2 pints/5 cups dark beer
5ml/1 tsp ground nutmeg
75g/3oz/⅓ cup caster (superfine) sugar
3 eggs
300ml/½ pint/1¼ cups Scotch whisky

1 Put the lemonade and beer into a large heavy pan over a low heat. Add the nutmeg and heat gently to just below boiling point. Add the sugar and stir to dissolve.

2 Whisk the eggs in a bowl and very slowly, while still beating, pour in a couple of ladlefuls of the hot mixture. Return the egg mixture to the pan, whisking to make sure it does not curdle.

3 Add the whisky slowly, stirring, and heat through to just below boiling point. Serve immediately.

Wine and Port: Energy 3754kcal/15554kJ; Protein 98.2g; Carbohydrate 56.9g, of which sugars 39.5g; Fat 285.9g, of which saturates 41.1g; Cholesterol 85mg; Calcium 1163mg; Fibre 33.3g; Sodium 359mg.
Mulled Cider: Energy 61kcal/258kJ; Protein 0.1g; Carbohydrate 9.3g, of which sugars 9.3g; Fat 0.1g, of which saturates 0g; Cholesterol 0mg; Calcium 12mg; Fibre 0g; Sodium 8mg.
Scottish Het Pint: Energy 1806kcal/7552kJ; Protein 22.7g; Carbohydrate 174.4g, of which sugars 174.4g; Fat 16.6g, of which saturates 4.7g; Cholesterol 571mg; Calcium 281mg; Fibre 0g; Sodium 371mg.

Index

chickpea purée with paprika
and pine nuts 65
chickpea rissoles coated with
sesame seeds 53
falafel 52
spicy chickpeas with fresh
ginger 168
spicy chickpeas with spinach
208
sweet rice with sour
chickpeas 192
chilli
baked potatoes with chilli 129
beef and squash with chilli 120
beef ribs in chilli broth 126
beef, chilli and soy broth 12
Brazilian pork and rice
casserole with chilli 185
butternut, prawn and chilli
soup 9
Caribbean chilli crab cakes 37
chicken with chilli relish 101
chilli and dill dressing 20
chilli aubergine with miso 211
chilli cheese muffins 246
chilli cornbread 246
chilli dip 196
chilli dressing 77
chilli salsa 19, 142, 176, 201
chilli sauce 68, 71, 156, 160,
165
chilli sorbet 234
chilli-spiced courgette pilaff
191
chilli-spiced fried plaice 29
chilli-spiced marinade 72
chilli-spiced rouille 11
chilli-spiced Turkish salad 66
chilli-stuffed grilled squid 36
coconut chicken with chilli
103
fennel and chilli cookies 247
feta pepper dip with chillies
63
fish with ginger and chilli 75
garlic and chilli cured beef 42
green chilli stuffed tofu 56
griddled corn on the cob with
chipotle chillies 57

herb salad with chilli 214
lamb with chilli salad 136
pig's feet with chilli 152
stingray with chilli sambal 72
Turkish chilli prawns 41
vegetable quesadillas with
green chillies 57
chocolate
chocolate and vanilla latte 248
chocolate cinnamon tuiles 244
Mexican hot chocolate 249
mint and chocolate cooler
249
spicy hearts and stars 243
chorizo 70
tortilla pie with chorizo 158
cider, mulled 251
cinnamon 16, 21, 33, 78, 95, 123
apple and cinnamon muffins
241
aubergine pilaff with cinnamon
and mint 193
baked cinnamon meat loaf 152
cheesecake with cinnamon
224
chocolate cinnamon tuiles 244
cinnamon and coffee parfait
233
cinnamon and vanilla biscuits
245
cinnamon doughnuts 240
cinnamon fish cakes with
currants, pine nuts and herbs
26
cinnamon lamb kebabs 46
cinnamon-scented chickpea
and lentil soup 21
cinnamon-spiced pumpkin 226
cinnamon-spiced Turkish
wedding soup 14
clementines with star anise
and cinnamon 229
duck legs with cinnamon 112
figs with honey, vanilla and
cinnamon 229
lamb with cinnamon 139
meatballs with cinnamon 45
Mexican coffee with cinnamon
248
Moroccan cinnamon swirl 231
mussels with cinnamon pilaff
39
rice with cinnamon 204
saffron fish cakes with
cucumber and cinnamon 26
semolina cinnamon cake 236
tagine of poussins with garlic
and cinnamon 113
clams, spiced 38
clementines with star anise and
cinnamon 229

cloves 157
coconut 90, 103, 216
coconut and seafood soup
with Thai spices 9
coconut milk 81, 88, 169, 207
coffee and cinnamon parfait 233
coffee lassi 249
coffee, Normandy 248
coffee with cinnamon 248
coriander 76, 142, 170, 202, 209
cooling coriander, coconut and
tamarind chutney 216
orange and coriander
brioches 239
corn and nut curry 172
corn on the cob with chipotle
chillies 57
courgettes 59
Asian courgette tempura 61
chilli courgette pilaff 191
couscous 22
couscous with harissa 162
fruit and nut couscous 162
lamb couscous with harissa
136
spicy couscous with broth 89
sweet couscous with fruit
compôte 223
crab
Caribbean chilli crab cakes 37
crab with garlic and ginger 92
Japanese-style crab cakes with
ginger and wasabi 37
cucumber 26, 78
cucumber and shallot salad
with cumin 216
cumin 25, 32, 130, 132, 140, 216
artichoke and cumin dip 65
cumin spiced potatoes 197
cumin-rubbed lamb 142
cumin-spiced hummus 63
lamb with cumin 44
leek terrine with cumin 175
lentil salad with cumin 181
lentil soup with cumin 18
Malay vegetable curry with
cumin and turmeric 174
vine leaves with cumin 164

date and walnut spice cake 237
dill 28
braised spiced duck 111
braised whole duck spiced
with star anise 110
duck with ginger and
pineapple 112
five-spice duck broth 18
lime and ginger-infused duck
soup 17
Malay duck in soy sauce 108
Moroccan spiced duck with
cinnamon and quince 112
North African spiced duck
with harissa 108
Polish roast duck with allspice
and orange 110
sweet and sour duck 109
Thai-style red duck curry with
pea aubergines 109
Vietnamese roast duck with
ginger and lemon grass 111

Easter biscuits 244
eel in a spicy caramel sauce 93
eel wrapped in bacon with lemon
grass and ginger 32
eggs 32
corned beef and egg hash 128
creamy egg nog 250
eggs in remoulade sauce 178
fried hard-boiled eggs in hot
red sauce 179
rice with deep-fried eggs 193
spiced Spanish leche frita 226
Turkish eggs on spiced yogurt
67

fennel 16, 100, 151
fennel and chilli cookies 247
fennel spiced potatoes 197
leek and fennel salad 181
sardines with fennel salad 28
fenugreek 18, 91, 153
figs baked with honey, vanilla and
cinnamon 229
fish
baked carp with bay leaves 83
barbecued red mullet with a
hot chilli dressing 77
barbecued salmon 76
Caribbean-spiced fish steaks
79
chargrilled sardines with chilli
and dill dressing 28
chilli-spiced fried plaice 29
cinnamon fish cakes 26
cod and bean stew with
saffron and paprika 80
cod in mustard sauce 79
Creole fish stew 87